W9-BLS-238

New York, New Jersey & Pennsylvania

Jeff Campbell

Sarah Chandler, Bridget Gleeson, David Ozanich

ELEVATION

3000ft
2000ft
1000ft
0

Georgian Bay

Lake Huron

CANADA

Kingston

◦ Belleville

ONTARIO

◦ Toronto

Lake Ontario

104 Seaway Trail
Erie Canal

Niagara
Falls 490 ◦ Rochester

Niagara Falls

◦ London

◦ Hamilton

104

90 Newark Seneca Aub
Falls

◦ **Buffalo** 20

390 *Canandaigua Lake* Seneca Lake Cayuga Lake

New York State Thruway (Toll)

219 Penn Yan *Finger Lakes* Taughan Falls

Robert H
Treman
State Park

Hammondsport ◦ Watkins Butterm
Glen Falls
State Pa
Elmira

Presque Isle
State Park

◦ **Erie**

17 Corning ◦

◦ Jamestown Allegheny
State Park ◦ Olean 417

◦ Cleveland

90 6 ◦ Edinboro

79

62 6 59

Oil Creek
State Park ◦ Titusville Allegheny
National 6 Wellsboro

◦ Oil City Forest

322 Ridgway ◦ **PENNSYLVANIA** 15 14

287

255 Williamsport

◦ Akron

◦ Youngstown

180

80

80

Pittsburgh (p354)
Warhol's hometown, amazing
art museums and galleries,
delightful riverfront

Ohio River

422 119 219 220

**State
College** 322 522 15

28

OHIO

22 ◦ **Pittsburgh**

76 ◦ Altoona *Appalachian Mountains* 22

40 79 22 Johnstown ◦

Harrisburg ◦ Hersh

522 **Pennsylvania Turnpike (Toll)** Manheim

◦ Wheeling *Ohio River* 76 Lancas

70 81

119 Mill Run 70 *Allegheny Mountains* York ◦
Fallingwater & Gettysburg ◦
Kentuck Knob Hanover ◦
Ohiopyle
79 Farmington State Park 70

◦ Morgantown Cumberland ◦

MARYLAND

Ohiopyle State Park (p374)
Whitewater rafting,
epic Laurel Highlands Trail,
cross-country skiing,
mountain biking

Gettysburg (p337)
The Civil War's most
famous and sobering
battlefield

◦ Baltimore

Appalachian Trail

WEST VIRGINIA

Annapol

VIRGINIA ◦ Washington DC

Lake Erie

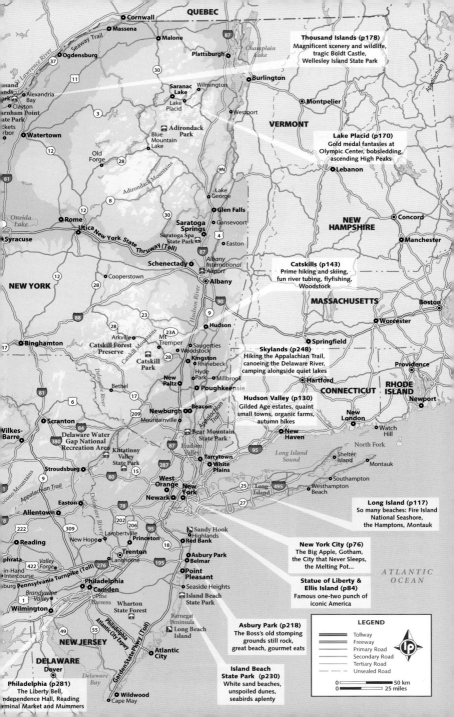

QUEBEC

Cornwall
Massena
Malone
Ogdensburg
Seaway Trail
Plattsburgh
Champlain Lake

Thousand Islands (p178)
Magnificent scenery and wildlife,
tragic Boldt Castle,
Wellesley Island State Park

Alexandria Bay
Clayton
Farnham Point State Park
Watertown

Saranac Lake
Wilmington
Lake Placid
Burlington
Westport
Montpelier
VERMONT

Adirondack Park
Blue Mountain Lake

Lake Placid (p170)
Gold medal fantasies at
Olympic Center, bobsledding,
ascending High Peaks

Old Forge

Adirondack Mountains

9N

Lebanon

Oneida Lake
Rome
Utica
New York State Thruway (Toll)
Syracuse
Cooperstown

Lake George
Glen Falls
Gansevoort
Saratoga Springs
Saratoga Spa State Park
Easton
Schenectady
Albany International Airport
Albany

NEW HAMPSHIRE

Concord
Manchester

NEW YORK

Binghamton
Arkville
Catskill Forest Preserve
Mt Tremper
Woodstock
Catskill Park
Bethel
New Paltz

Hudson

Saugerties
Kingston
Rhinebeck
Hyde Park
Millbrook
Poughkeepsie

Newburgh
Mountainville

Catskills (p143)
Prime hiking and skiing,
fun river tubing, flyfishing,
Woodstock

MASSACHUSETTS

Worcester
Springfield

Boston

Skylands (p248)
Hiking the Appalachian Trail,
canoeing the Delaware River,
camping alongside quiet lakes

Hartford

CONNECTICUT

RHODE ISLAND

Providence
Newport

Hudson Valley (p130)
Gilded Age estates, quaint
small towns, organic farms,
autumn hikes

Scranton
Wilkes-Barre
Delaware Water Gap National Recreation Area
Stroudsburg
Kittatinny Valley State Park
Easton
Allentown
Reading
Ephrata
Valley Forge
Pennsylvania Turnpike (Toll)

Bear Mountain State Park
Tarrytown
White Plains
West Orange
Newark
NEW YORK
Princeton
Trenton
Langhorne
Philadelphia
Camden

New London
New Haven
Watch Hill
North Fork
Long Island Sound
Shelter Island
Montauk
Southampton
Westhampton Beach
Long Island

Long Island (p117)
So many beaches: Fire Island
National Seashore,
the Hamptons, Montauk

New York City (p76)
The Big Apple, Gotham,
the City that Never Sleeps,
the Melting Pot...

Statue of Liberty &
Ellis Island (p84)
Famous one-two punch of
iconic America

ATLANTIC OCEAN

Sandy Hook
Highlands
Red Bank
Asbury Park
Belmar
Point Pleasant
Seaside Heights
Island Beach State Park

Asbury Park (p218)
The Boss's old stomping
grounds still rock,
great beach, gourmet eats

New Hope
Lambertville
Pine Barrens
Wharton State Forest
Barnegat Peninsula
Long Beach Island
Atlantic City

Island Beach State Park (p230)
White sand beaches,
unspoiled dunes,
seabirds aplenty

Brandywine Valley
Wilmington
NEW JERSEY
DELAWARE
Dover

Delaware Bay

Wildwood
Cape May

Philadelphia (p281)
The Liberty Bell,
Independence Hall, Reading
Terminal Market and Mummers

LEGEND
Tollway
Freeway
Primary Road
Secondary Road
Tertiary Road
Unsealed Road

0   50 km
0   25 miles

On the Road

JEFF CAMPBELL Coordinating Author
Never canoe alone on the Delaware River (p71) – not because it's dangerous, but just because you can't have a water fight all by yourself. I'm on the right as we head out to spend a day on the lazy river. We pulled over at sandy banks and islands, and shouted our way through every tiny riffle we encountered. The nephews had the water guns, but the uncles had the paddles, which work exceedingly well when broadsided across the surface.

SARAH CHANDLER
How could I miss a tête-à-tête with one of America's greatest presidents? After hanging out with the venerable Franklin D (Roosevelt, that is) at his gorgeous old Hyde Park (p136) stomping grounds, I cruised down to the Culinary Institute of America (p137). Inspired by FDR's words 'The only thing we have to fear is fear itself,' I feasted fearlessly.

BRIDGET GLEESON
Every Pennsylvania girl knows the value of freshly pressed apple cider. At the Bird-in-Hand farmers' market (p329), I was delighted to discover that you can still buy a cup for 25 cents. Five minutes later, a Mennonite woman lent a pair of scooters to my sister and me, and we took a short ride down a country road – it was a thoroughly wholesome day.

DAVID OZANICH
Here I am in the sculpture garden at the Nassau County Museum of Art (p121) on Long Island's Gold Coast. I was touring with Karen, a native, and we spent the day exploring Gatsby-esque manors and ornamental gardens. Between attempts to find 'F Scott Fitzgerald realness,' we searched for the perfect place to relax with a cocktail.

For full author biographies see p427

New York, New Jersey & Pennsylvania Highlights

As this selection of places and experiences makes clear, there is no single highlight that encapsulates this region. In fact, we have to be a bit careful. When New York City is your centerpiece, it's easy to collapse into a descriptive spasm of superlatives and overstatements. But then you visit, and it's still undersold: the architecture and history, the neighborhoods and museums, the streets teeming with humanity – all conspire to blow your mind, and that's without crossing the Hudson River. Make sure you do, though, because from Jersey beaches to Adirondack peaks, from Philly cheesesteaks to Finger Lakes wineries, this region is so much more than the Big Apple.

MICHELLE BENNETT

❶ METROPOLITAN MUSEUM OF ART

New York's most famous museum (p95) holds over two million works of art divided into 19 curatorial departments. Utterly massive, it can't be seen in just one visit. In fact, it would probably take a lifetime to see even a portion of the holdings. Highlights of the collection include the arms and armor of medieval knights, works of art from Ancient Egypt, Asian art, decorative art, the Costume Institute and more Old Masters than you can shake a stick at. Truly marvelous to behold, it has something for everyone, and its location on the eastern edge of Central Park makes it even more majestic. Check out the rooftop garden for spectacular views of the city.

David Ozanich

HISTORIC DOWNTOWN PHILADELPHIA

When I was a kid, I thought Philadelphia (p281) was just a big bell and a bunch of men in white powdered wigs. But walking down crazy, colorful South St, it's clear we're not in field trip territory anymore.

Bridget Gleeson

2

ANDY WARHOL MUSEUM

3

Making my way through the film wing of the Andy Warhol Museum (p358), I feel like I'm lost in an eerie funhouse of larger-than-life moving screens: Edie Sedgwick popping bubble gum, a haggard old man staring directly into the lens, young lovers in an extended moment of passion, and the pop-art icon himself, fragile and elegant, talking quietly about the importance of fashion.

Bridget Gleeson

CAPE MAY

People who only know Jersey as 'Joisey' should come to Cape May (p274), which almost doesn't seem like it exists in the same state, which it almost doesn't. Rife with meticulously cared for Victorian architecture, Cape May evokes what you imagine those old seaside resorts were like a century ago – social and friendly, quiet and relaxed, but not staid. It has a little bit of everything: a real sense of community, ridiculously beautiful beaches and parks, wonderful restaurants, fun history. In September, after school starts, it's nearly perfect.

Jeff Campbell

4

FINGER LAKES

The beauty and wine of Tuscany and Provence, wrapped up in the low-key pace and eco-awareness of the Finger Lakes region? Yes, please. Pick up coffee and bagels in Ithaca, blast the music, and cruise this region (p186) along winding roads all afternoon from vineyard to friendly vineyard, tasting rieslings and chardonnays until you beg for mercy in the form of dinner (locally grown and organic, naturally). Head back to your B&B at sunset, when the hills grow cinematic: glittering blue lakes and undulating green as far as you can see. Is it just the wine, or is this place heavenly? Yes.

Sarah Chandler

5

6 PRINCETON UNIVERSITY

In the fall, when the leaves turn and the students arrive, the expansive, historic Princeton campus (p252) epitomizes everything 'Ivy League': Nobel laureates thoughtfully pace the quads, undergraduates sprawl on the lawns, organ concerts fill the chapel with melody, rowing teams practice on the river. It's enough to make you want to buy a PU muffler and have an earnest conversation about Kant, or Philip Roth, or the socio-economic dynamics of international aid in emerging nations. Here, it's okay to be that dirty word: intellectual.

Jeff Campbell

CANOEING THE DELAWARE RIVER

There are lots of ways in which you can enjoy canoeing the Delaware River (p398). You can tube, raft, kayak, canoe and even swim. You can camp and picnic on forested islands. But the most important thing to remember is: bring water guns.

Jeff Campbell

BILL BACHMANN

8 PENNSYLVANIA DUTCH COUNTRY

Little boys in straw hats steer horse-drawn buggies down country roads, primly dressed ladies carry their shoofly pies to the market, freshly laundered clothes flutter in the breeze beside a red barn: this is Amish country (p319), a quiet and fascinating place.

Bridget Gleeson

RICHARD CUMMINS

9 ATLANTIC CITY

The casino nightclub and restaurant scene in Atlantic City (p262) has changed so much in recent years it's hard to believe. 'Gourmet' and 'trendy' have not historically got much use here. Then again, until recently, there wasn't anything like the pools at Harrah's and the Water Club, which really take all the sting out of losing at the blackjack tables. Indeed, there's more fun to be had off the casino floor than on it.

Jeff Campbell

10 BROOKLYN FLEA MARKET

Antiquers and gourmands will thrill at the vast assortment of wares available at this staple of Brooklyn life. On Saturday the market (p113) is outdoors in Fort Greene while on Sunday it moves indoors to the Williamsburg Savings Bank, the tallest building in Brooklyn. Everything from table linens to vintage clothing to artisan jams and pickles are available in this vast marketplace. A great place for strolling and browsing, it makes New York feel like a small town.

David Ozanich

VALLEY FORGE

Here at the Revolutionary War–era winter encampment (p313) of the Continental Army, the guide's explanation of 'fire cake' – a bland flour and water mixture that men survived on during those bitterly cold months – is enough to make me want to head back to South Philly for a proper 2000-calorie cheesesteak.

Bridget Gleeson

MCLAIN WARD AND SAPPHIRE, WINNERS OF THE $250,000 FTI GRAND PRIX AT THE 2009 HAMPTON CLASSIC HORSE SHOW ©ESI PHOTOGRAPHY

INVASION OF THE PINES

Anyone with a passing interest in drag queens will not want to miss their wildly loony and hysterical 'invasion' of the Fire Island Pines (p129). Every July 4th, transvestites descend upon the resort via boat and parade about the boardwalks causing general havoc and mayhem. Though it marks an infamous event long ago in which a drag queen was denied entrance to a Pines bar, today those summering on this popular Long Island sandbar crowd the harbor to cheer on their festive 'invaders.' Grab a cocktail and wear your best stilettos.

David Ozanich

KATHARINE ANDRIOTIS PHOTOGRAPHY, LLC / EDITORIAL / ALAMY

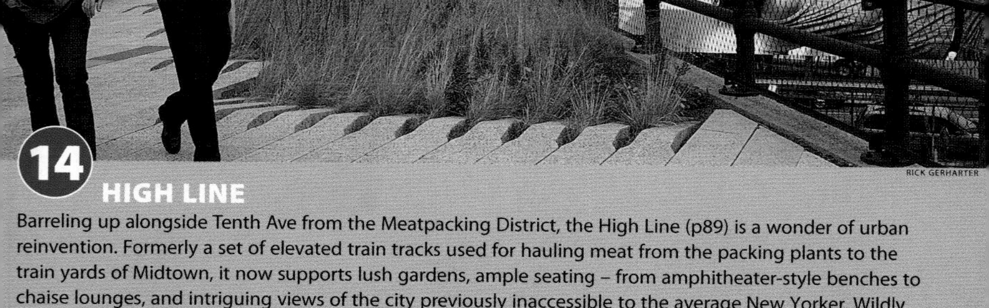

12

HAMPTON CLASSIC HORSE SHOW

The big finale of the summer season in the Hamptons, the Hampton Classic (p127) is a Grand Prix show-jumping event held annually on Labor Day weekend in Bridgehampton on Long Island's south fork. Ladies festooned in large hats drink champagne while tuxedoed waiters pass hors d'oeuvres to the gentry in the VIP tent. A fundraiser for Southampton Hospital, this is a mustattend event for anyone seeking to climb the social ladder. But don't worry, even if you're not a Real Housewife of New York, you can still get a ticket.

David Ozanich

13

RICK GERHARTER

14

HIGH LINE

Barreling up alongside Tenth Ave from the Meatpacking District, the High Line (p89) is a wonder of urban reinvention. Formerly a set of elevated train tracks used for hauling meat from the packing plants to the train yards of Midtown, it now supports lush gardens, ample seating – from amphitheater-style benches to chaise lounges, and intriguing views of the city previously inaccessible to the average New Yorker. Wildly popular, it's a great destination for watching visitors strut their stuff down the imaginary catwalk.

David Ozanich

GLENN VAN DER

15 HIGH PEAKS OF THE ADIRONDACKS

It's hard not to catch Olympic fever here, no matter what time of the year it is. Hike all day in the pristine High Peaks (p172), crash out in rustic splendor in a 1920s lodge, and live out your gold-medal fantasies as you cruise down the bobsled run at what seems like 100 miles an hour and – surprise! – come out in one piece. Now you've earned a sunset drink on the enchanting shores of Mirror Lake (p170). So what if it's too late to learn that triple axel? The High Peaks themselves are reward enough.

Sarah Chandler

SHANNON RACE

16 THE CATSKILLS

I'm flying down the rapids on the Esopus Creek (p151) with nothing but a bikini and an inner tube to protect me from the rocks, but it's a gorgeous day in the mountains, so who cares? Later, we'll hit some waterfalls and wind up eating dinner in Woodstock (p149). We'll stroll the village green, dine on organic vegies that will keep us young forever, keep an eye out for aging rock stars going incognito, and pretend it's still the Summer of Love. Here, in the lush green heart of the Catskills, it almost feels like it is.

Sarah Chandler

Contents

Regional Map Contents

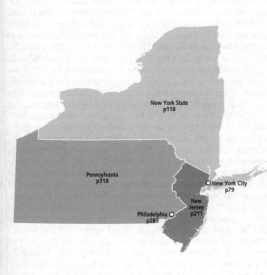

New York State
p118

Pennsylvania
p318

New York City
p79

New Jersey
p211

Philadelphia
p283

16

Destination New York, New Jersey & Pennsylvania

In this region, all things connect to New York City. It is the heart pumping blood down arterial highways to the limbs and vital organs in upstate New York, New Jersey and Pennsylvania. It is the brain sending electrical impulses along every potholed street to the very tips of the region's toes. There are many wonderful sights in each of these three states, but it is impossible to start anywhere else, or to long escape the city's magnetic pull. And it should be said that this arrangement doesn't please everyone, in part because New Yorkers – from the West Village to the West Side, from Brooklyn to the Bronx – have perfected the annoying habit of assuming that everything (by which they mean anything worth noticing) revolves around them.

Make no mistake: Manhattan is 'the city,' despite the presence of nearby Philadelphia and Pittsburgh. Indeed, as much as (or more than) Paris or London, Tokyo or Hong Kong, New York is *the city* – the poetic, intoxicating distillation, the ultimate expression, of what we understand an international city to be. New York overwhelms – stifling and crowded, belching hoards from below, looming above, pedestrians and taxis straining at each red light, everyone hustling amid the grit and bodegas and skyscrapers – to the point that it defies logic and comprehension. New York should not be able to function. Yet it does, its sea of humanity spreading out daily to do its job, and later returning to sweltering apartments lifted five, 10, 15 stories above restless streets.

With pride, New Yorkers will list all of the iconic places they have never been: the Statue of Liberty, the Empire State Building, the Metropolitan Museum of Art, Times Square, the Museum of Natural History, Broadway. They wait for out-of-town friends and family to drag them to these famous sights, and even then may feign a sudden weakness to avoid going. For residents, the city is not about attractions or museums. It is the ineffable magic of living in the rough-knuckled, lofty center of the modern world, which is, ironically, most often experienced in those small, serendipitous, incongruous moments of connection and beauty that could only happen in New York – a place where the meadows of Central Park and the molded seats of the subway hold everyone equally.

To a lesser degree, this sense of entitled exceptionalism pervades the entire region. America was conceived in Philadelphia, where the nation's raw, wrinkled babyhood remains lovingly swaddled in the city's historic district – in Independence Hall, the National Constitution Center and the Liberty Bell Center. The birth pangs of the Revolutionary War still resound at nearby Valley Forge, and at New Jersey's Morristown, Trenton and Princeton. The region was, and largely remains, the engine of American industry and commerce, from the former steel mills of Pittsburgh to the canyons of Wall Street. In fact, from Gettysburg to Ellis Island, from Ground Zero to Seneca Falls, these states have witnessed and survived epochal events that helped shape the country's most cherished ideals, its proudest profile. Whatever hard times hit, locals know they're too tough to ever be knocked down long.

This East Coast braggadocio is most amusingly expressed by New Jersey, the put-upon middle sibling. Benjamin Franklin famously dubbed the state 'a barrel tapped at both ends,' succinctly capturing Jersey's geographical curse. Despite its gorgeous coastline and seaside resorts, it has forever been dismissed by big-city snobs. Residents live with a permanent chip on their shoulders, which breeds an I'll-do-it-my-way scrappiness, embodied by Frank Sinatra, Bruce Springsteen, and suffragette Alice Paul. Thomas Edison invented the phonograph and the movies in Menlo Park, and Princeton University has been home to Albert Einstein and Toni Morrison, yet respect never comes. New Jersey will always be 'Joisey,' the home of *The Sopranos* and *Jersey Shore,* but travelers might be surprised to learn that the Garden State is as much wilderness as suburb, with as many farms as interstates.

For sure, the New York–Philly–North Jersey monstropolis is the nation's most urbanized, densely populated slab of concrete and asphalt, but this fun fact is misleading. If you've come to visit the states, not just the cities, prepare for vast stretches of wilderness and bucolic, wooded Appalachian Mountains. The Adirondacks are America's largest protected landscape outside Alaska, preserved by state constitution to be 'forever wild.' Most of Pennsylvania is farmland and forest, and all three states are threaded by major river systems, such as the Delaware, the Allegheny, the Susquehanna and the Hudson. You could, in fact, spend all your time hiking, biking, canoeing, sailing, swimming, fishing and climbing and never once hear a car honk.

Further, while New Yorkers would have you believe there is no culture but their culture – none so refined and ethnically diverse, so important, so avant-garde – there is sophistication even in the hinterlands: in Newark and New Brunswick, in Andy Warhol's Pittsburgh and Hyde Park, in Ithaca and Saratoga Springs. In contrast, Pennsylvania's Amish have preserved their spiritual, rural lifestyle, maintaining anti-modern customs that are a humble, quiet rebuke to all that Manhattan stands for.

Did we mention hard times? When the stock market collapsed in 2008, due to falling home prices, Wall Street nearly went belly up, and its captains of finance were largely blamed for gaming the system for their own good (a twice-told tale if there ever was one). The result has been a national Great Recession that has crippled state budgets in New York, New Jersey and Pennsylvania. All three states have laid off workers and slashed funds for schools and essential services, and seen unemployment skyrocket, with no lasting relief on the horizon.

Political scandals have also made headlines. In 2008, New York Governor Elliot Spitzer was caught with a New Jersey call girl and promptly resigned; his replacement, Governor David Paterson, later confessed to adultery and to snorting cocaine; as these happened before he was governor, Paterson stayed in office. In 2004, New Jersey Governor James McGreevey, an ostensibly happily married man, was seen with a male aide, came out as gay and promptly resigned. Then in 2009, the largest federal sting operation in New Jersey history (and that's saying something) led to the arrest of 44 people – including three mayors, two state legislators and five rabbis – on charges of political corruption, money laundering and trying to sell a human kidney.

More troubling, however, was the September 2009 arrest of three al Qaeda terrorists who pleaded guilty to planning a trio of suicide bombings in the Manhattan subway. For New Yorkers particularly, the events of 9/11 (see p42) remain fresh memories, even though 2011 marks the 10-year anniversary of the attacks. The pulsating life of the city hardly stops, for anything, but these are sobering reminders of tragedy.

In the end, everything revolves around New York City, a resilient, multifaceted, soaring metropolis on a narrow island at the mouth of the Hudson River. In a region that offers so much – a veritable cornucopia of American life, history and culture – it stands supreme, lending any visit the impression that one has also seen the world.

'In a region that offers so much – a veritable cornucopia of American life, history and culture – New York City stands supreme, lending any visit the impression that one has also seen the world'

Getting Started

WHEN TO GO

New York, New Jersey and Pennsylvania are four-season destinations, with climate and weather patterns common to the US Northeast. As a rule, spring and fall are mild and pleasant, with warm days and cool nights, while summer and winter hold the extremes: July and August can become unbearably muggy with highs over 90°F (32°C), and January and February can get buried by snowstorms and see days of below-freezing temperatures. Precipitation is fairly consistent year-round, with slightly more summer rain on the coast and more winter snow in the mountains.

Locals will tell you the 'best' seasons are spring and fall, but that has nothing to do with your agenda. Deciding the best time to visit depends entirely on what you want to do.

If cities are your main focus, then the worst time is summer, which is usually considered to be from Memorial Day to Labor Day. That's when most tourists arrive, clogging up the queues, and it's no fun sightseeing the concrete jungle when you could fry eggs on the pavement. If Manhattan, Philadelphia and Pittsburgh are your destinations, choose spring, fall or early winter (through December). City cultural institutions are very lively through Christmas, which is a magical time.

See Climate Charts (p406) for more information.

If you want to frolic on Atlantic coast beaches, then arrive from June through September, or forget it. Only a few Jersey and Long Island towns are year-round tourist destinations (like Cape May); otherwise, you swim while it's hot or not at all.

If you're looking to explore the outdoors – hiking, canoeing, fishing and so on – then summer and fall are the prime seasons. Autumn foliage is spectacular, and the season encourages hiking and camping with low humidity and fewer bugs, particularly the farther north you go, such as the Adirondacks (June is blackfly season). Spring can be good too, but rain and melting snow can make for muddy, buggy trails.

If you want to ski, of course, then arrive December through March. If you don't mind the weather, winter can be a quiet, fun time in the cities.

Then there are the wildcards: major events and festivals (p23) happen year-round, many worth planning trips around. Plus, if you want to fit in pro sports, then your ideal season isn't weather-related.

COSTS & MONEY

Just so you know: you can see this region successfully on the equivalent of a collegiate's stipend or a CEO's expense account. Naturally, most people fall somewhere in the middle, and what constitutes a reasonable budget depends on the when, where and how of your trip.

Let's start at the top: Manhattan will bleed you dry. Finding hotel rooms for less than $200 a night is tough, and then meals, transportation and sightseeing are all more expensive. For a couple, a moderate budget might be $500 a day, not including show tickets; spending less takes willpower. Philadelphia is not as expensive; budget $400 per day. You knew this, though. So here are a few things to keep in mind: avoid having a rental car in either city. Only rent one when, or if, you leave town. If you only want to visit Manhattan for a day or two, consider sleeping outside the city and day-tripping in.

Also, generally speaking, accommodations in cities are more expensive during the week, less expensive on weekends. Conversely, beach towns and vaca

---

DON'T LEAVE HOME WITHOUT...

- Street smarts, a credit card, and a money belt or pouch.
- Quitting smoking. Seriously, it's bad for you. It's expensive (over $12 a pack in NYC!). And all three states ban smoking in most public buildings, except for bars in Pennsylvania and casinos in Atlantic City.
- A Manhattan street and subway map (oh right, you're holding one).
- Getting a visa or registering online under the Visa Waiver Program (p408).
- Hotel reservations in Manhattan (p103) or the Jersey shore (p213).
- Seeing what festivals are happening while you're here (p23).

---

tion resorts are cheaper midweek, raising rates on the weekend; on the Jersey shore, summer weekend hotel rates can be equivalent to Manhattan. You're money ahead seeing cities on the weekend and parks and beaches midweek.

Outside of the major cities and high seasons, good hotels for $100 to $150 are typical. The region is not well-served by hostels, but it has a wealth of good camping (usually $20 per night).

Your food budget can vary wildly. The region is legendary for its inexpensive comfort foods – hot dogs, pizza, cheesesteaks. Stick to NYC's rolling carts – a veritable smorgasbord – and your per person per day meal budget might not top $30. Visit one of the region's many gourmet restaurants, and $30 doesn't cover the tip.

Within and between major cities, public transportation is a viable option: buses are cheapest; trains more pleasant and expensive. While commuter trains and buses serve the wider metropolitan region, they are less useful for sightseeing. Instead, a car is the most flexible option; for visits to the rural countryside, it's really the only choice. Rates vary depending on where you rent, but minimum daily/weekly rentals usually start from $35/140, plus gas and insurance.

Since small savings add up, remember to check museums for 'free' days (most have one monthly) and see Discounts (p407).

TRAVELING RESPONSIBLY

Lonely Planet encourages readers to tread lightly and travel responsibly, which means considering the impact of our choices on the environment and local communities. Of course, 'green travel' is just as important in the New York metropolitan area – America's most urbanized region – as it is in the wilderness of the Alleghenies and the Adirondacks; indeed, New York, Philadelphia and Pittsburgh are all making concerted efforts to turn themselves into models for 'sustainable cities.' For more information on environmental issues, and for a list of environmental organizations, see the Environment chapter (p60).

'Sustainable tourism' really involves two things: it's about making 'green' choices, and it's a way of interacting with people and the environment. The list on p21, Top Ways to Go Green, highlights a few specific ways to practice low-impact tourism; generally, these include choosing nonmotorized recreation, taking public transportation instead of driving, and buying local products, such as at farmers markets. In addition, there is a growing number of ecofriendly hotels; some are highlighted in this book. For more, see the following organizations:

Green Hotels Association (www.greenhotels.com) A membership organization promoting green hotels and travel nationwide.

HOW MUCH?

Push-cart hot dog: $2

Manhattan subway ride: $2.50

New Jersey beach tag: $5-10

Yankees bleacher seats: $14

Broadway show: $100-300

Greenopia (www.greenopia.com) Ecoguides for city living in New York, Philadelphia, Pittsburgh.
offManhattan (www.offmanhattan.com) Promotes car-free, green travel around Manhattan.
Sierra Club (www.sierraclub.org) Has local chapters in all three states, with news and outings.

When renting a car, consider getting an ecofriendly model, such as a hybrid or electric car; these are increasingly available from national rental companies (p419), or instead of renting, consider a Zipcar. The auto association Better World Club (p419) supports environmental legislation and offers ecofriendly services. For more information and advice, and the fun of calculating your personal carbon footprint, visit **Climatecrisis.net** (www.climatecrisis.net).

TRAVEL LITERATURE

So many excellent books have been written about NYC and the region. This short, eclectic list is focused on travel writing and memoirs that evoke a sense of place. For regional literature, see the Culture chapter (p44); for regional histories, see the History chapter (p32).

Let's start by getting weird – *Weird NJ*, that is. What started as an occasional newsprint magazine highlighting New Jersey's creepy legends, haunted sights and murder mysteries has grown into a series of books, including editions of *Weird New York* and *Weird Pennsylvania*. Writers and paranormal aficionados Mark Moran and Mark Sceurman keep things loose, lively and funny.

One hot summer, EB White sat in his sweltering Manhattan apartment and penned a shimmering sketch of the city, boldly titled *Here Is New York* (1949). Yet here it is, Gotham reduced to its purest essence and readable in the time it takes to get from Wall St to Harlem on the 3.

New York Times book critic Anatole Broyard arrived in Manhattan in the mid-1940s, and fell in love in so many ways it's hard to count. He had a bawdy, bohemian good time in an era when New York vibrated with joy and intellectual excitement, vividly captured in graceful, crisp prose in *Kafka Was the Rage: A Greenwich Village Memoir* (1993).

Few places in the world have as much going on underground as above ground. In *Subwayland* (2004), Randy Kennedy takes us on a tour of New York's subway culture through this collection of his *NY Times* 'Tunnel Vision' columns.

Little Chapel on the River (2005) by Gwendolyn Bounds documents how one New Yorker coped after 9/11 and found a renewed sense of hope and community in a rural town in the Hudson Valley, which, as such towns often do, revolved around the local watering hole, Guinan's.

Make fun if you want, but New Jersey is truly an odd place filled with unforgettable characters and more muffler men (giant fiberglass characters) per capita than any state. Okay, so we made that last bit up, but you can track them all down with the help of Pete Genovese's *New Jersey Curiosities* (2007). Genovese is the guy who drives the *Star-Ledger's* Munchmobile, so he knows the backroads.

One of America's finest writers, John McPhee, wrote *The Pine Barrens* (1967), which was such a revelation about this vast New Jersey wilderness that it was the fulcrum leading to their conservation. He brought piney culture to life as well in this Jersey classic.

Photojournalist Harry Dorer captured New Jersey as it transitioned from the rural Garden State to the nation's most urban state from the 1920s to the 1950s. His photos – of FDR and the Pulaski Skyway, of glassmakers and fox hunts, of workers constructing the George Washington Bridge – are a portrait of America, even if the title humbly promises *This Was New Jersey* (2007); it's edited by historian John Cunningham.

'an era when New York vibrated with joy and intellectual excitement is vividly captured in *Kafka Was the Rage: A Greenwich Village Memoir*'

TOP PICKS

WAYS TO GO GREEN

Going green needn't be complicated. It's simple: slow down, avoid motors, enjoy and protect nature, eat local produce and patronize ecofriendly businesses.

- Use the subway: New York (p113) and Philadelphia (p312) both have great city subways and rail lines.
- Ride a bike: Manhattan, Pittsburgh and Philadelphia have easy, bike-friendly cycling routes. See p69.
- Get into nature. For a list of top natural areas, see p63.

- Buy local farm produce: Jersey is the Garden State, so partake (p246). Philadelphia has two great food markets, Reading Terminal (p294) and the Italian Market (p296), plus Amish Country (p319).
- Get informed (p60)
- Volunteer (p412)

PLACES TO POP A CHILL PILL

Manhattanites are known to be a little *tense*. Here are some of their favorite places to relax. They're nice even when you aren't wound tighter than a midtown cabbie.

- The Cloisters (p99)
- The beach: try Robert Moses State Park (p186) or Island Beach State Park (p230), or get naked on Sandy Hook (p213).
- Sheep Meadow, Central Park (p91)
- Delaware River: take a lazy float along the Delaware & Raritan canal (p258) or on the lakes in the Delaware Water Gap NRA (p398).

- The Catskills (p143) for fall leaf-peeping.
- Atlantic City spas, like at the Chelsea (p268), the Water Club (p268), and Harrah's (p264).
- Pennsylvania Dutch country (p319), the definition of unplugged.
- Lady Mendl's Tea Salon (p108) in Manhattan.
- Tivoli (p141) in the Hudson River Valley.

IDIOSYNCRATIC ART EXPERIENCES

Fine art is a highlight of this region, but it needn't be ponderous. Here are some don't-miss highlights, ranging from art glass to fluorescent lights, from mindblowing sculpture parks to loopy homemade environments.

- New York Earth Room, NYC (p87)
- Philadelphia's Magic Gardens, Philadelphia (p296)
- Dan Flavin Art Institute, Bridgehampton, Long Island (p124)
- Longhouse Reserve, East Hampton, Long Island (p124)
- Grounds for Sculpture, Hamilton, NJ (p256)

- Andy Warhol Museum, Pittsburgh (p358)
- Dia:Beacon, Hudson River Valley (p132)
- International Museum of Photography and Film, Rochester, NY (p198)
- WheatonArts, Millville, NJ (p278)
- Whitney Museum of American Art, NYC (p95)

INTERNET RESOURCES

Lonely Planet (www.lonelyplanet.com) Travel news and summaries, the Thorn Tree bulletin board and links to more web resources.

New Jersey Division of Tourism (www.visitnj.org) The Garden State's official visitor portal; full trip planning and calendar, and you can order brochures.

New York Division of Tourism (www.iloveny.com) Same as New Jersey's, with comprehensive information.
New York Times Travel (http://travel.nytimes.com) It covers the region and its home turf as well as the world.
Pennsylvania Division of Tourism (www.visitpa.com) Ditto, for Pennsylvania.
Weird NJ (www.weirdnj.com) A local legend for local legends and roadside attractions, with links to more weirdness in New York and Pennsylvania.

Events Calendar

Many more festivals are listed in Festivals & Events sections throughout this guide. For a list of major sporting events, see 'Root & Race' (p73), and for more food festivals, see p57.

JANUARY

MUMMERS' PARADE   Jan 1
Unique Italian-American parade (www.mummers. com) in Philly, with over 25,000 strutting in fancy handmade costumes; see p305.

APRIL-MAY

TRIBECA FILM FESTIVAL   late Apr
Major New York film festival (www.tribecafilm. com) started by Robert DeNiro in the wake of 9/11.

GETTYSBURG BLUEGRASS FESTIVAL   May
This close to the Mason-Dixon Line, expect top-flight, kickin' bluegrass (www.gettysburgbluegrass.com). All the top names show up, such as Alison Krauss in 2010.

THE BAMBOOZLE   early May
A huge two-day music festival (www.thebamboozle.com) in the New Jersey Meadowlands. Features over 100 bands, focusing on new groups, from R&B to punk to hip hop to Ke$ha. Draws 60,000.

WILDWOOD KITE FESTIVAL   Memorial Day weekend
A four-day extravaganza on the Jersey shore, drawing kitemakers from around the world, with stunt kite and indoor kite competitions.

HARRISBURG ARTSFEST   Memorial Day weekend
One of the nation's biggest arts festivals (www. harrisburgarts.org/artsfest), with three days of music, film and kids' art.

JUNE

ITHACA FESTIVAL   early Jun
Enjoy crunchy-granola fun in Ithaca, New York (www.ithacafestival.org), with three days of art, activism, folk music and cultural awareness, plus a funky parade.

THREE RIVERS ARTS FESTIVAL   early Jun
Ten days of funky visual and performing arts (www.artsfestival.net), with a strong focus on sustainable Pittsburgh and lots of family entertainment.

CRAWFISH FEST   early Jun
For three days in Augusta, NJ, Michael Arnone dishes up the best New Orleans festival (www. crawfishfest.com) north of the Mason-Dixon Line. Louisiana music, dancing, camping and tons of tasty Creole and Cajun cooking.

THE TONY AWARDS   mid-Jun
Didn't bring a tux? Rent one and get tickets for Broadway's star-studded awards ceremony (www. tonyawards.com).

GAY PRIDE   late Jun
On Gay Pride weekend, New York City hosts a slew of raucous events and a huge parade, but everyone also comes out in Philadelphia and Asbury Park for equally colorful shenanigans.

CLEARWATER'S GREAT HUDSON RIVER REVIVAL   late Jun
Started by Pete Seeger to highlight Hudson River cleanup efforts, and now a major two-day celebration (www.clearwater.org/festival) of folk music and environmental awareness.

MERMAID PARADE   late Jun
Cross Carnivale, Mardi Gras and Coney Island (www.coneyisland.com/mermaid.shtml) and you get this bohemian saunter of spangles, mermaids, drag queens and other fantabulously costumed sea creatures.

JERSEY SHORE JAZZ & BLUES FESTIVAL   early Jun
Jersey's oldest and largest jazz and blues event (www.jerseyshorefestival.org) usually takes over hip Red Bank for a June weekend, but it has moved around in recent years.

JULY-AUGUST

INDEPENDENCE DAY   Jul 4
Fireworks in New York Harbor, Philadelphia and Wildwood are the biggest of the region-wide celebrations, plus historic parks in Philly and Morristown have public readings of the Declaration of Independence.

NEW JERSEY SANDCASTLE CONTEST mid-Jul
Belmar is the setting for the most amazing and ephemeral engineering feats known to sand (www.njsandcastle.com).

NEW JERSEY STATE BARBECUE CHAMPIONSHIP mid-Jul
Got pig? There's serious prize money at stake for this Kansas City–sanctioned statewide competition in Wildwood (www.njbbq.com). There's serious blues music, too.

CAPE VINCENT FRENCH FESTIVAL mid-Jul
In New York State's Thousand Islands, once home to French colonies, this two-day festival (www.capevincent.org/frenchfestival.asp) features French food, folks in period dress, drum and bugle corps, and a float parade led by Napoleon.

ALL POINTS WEST FESTIVAL mid-Aug
In Jersey's Liberty State Park, this newcomer in the rock-festival circuit draws major headliners like Jay-Z and Coldplay for three loud, crowded days in the shadow of Lady Liberty (www.apwfestival.com).

MISS CRUSTACEAN HERMIT CRAB BEAUTY PAGEANT early Aug
Think hermit crabs in elegant frippery on miniature floats, and crab races (www.ocnj.us) in Ocean City, New Jersey. Silly? You bet. But Miss America isn't so seriously judged.

PHILADELPHIA FOLK FESTIVAL late Aug
This three-day festival (www.pfs.org) features music by the best, such as Taj Mahal. Camping is big, and there's tons of kid fun.

DUTCHESS COUNTY FAIR late Aug
In the Hudson Valley's Rhinebeck, expect six days of classic county-fair fun (www.dutchessfair.com): rides, music, horse shows, racing pigs, pony rides, corn dogs and more. Draws a half million folks.

PENNSYLVANIA RENAISSANCE FAIRE Aug-Oct
Find fair wenches and jousting knights, fire-eaters and sword fights at this quintessential and popular medieval blast from the past (www.parenfaire.com) on weekends at Mount Hope Winery.

SEPTEMBER-OCTOBER

CLOWNFEST mid-Sep
Seaside Heights has an image problem, and hundreds of rainbow-wigged clowns pratfalling on the boardwalk for four days probably doesn't help (www.clownfest.com). Not to be missed.

SAN GENNARO FESTIVAL mid-Sep
For a fortnight in NYC's Little Italy, a million people celebrate the patron saint of Naples (www.sangennaro.org). This 80-year-old religious festival includes a famous procession, a celebratory mass, and lots of food and music.

CAPE MAY FOOD & WINE FESTIVAL late Sep
Cape May is known for its gourmet restaurants, and everybody shows up for this delicious weeklong festival (www.capemaymac.org), with seminars, classes, tastings, a chowder contest and restaurant-server relay races.

CHOWDERFEST early Oct
The definitive chowder contest is held at Beach Haven (www.chowderfest.com), where every one of the 15,000 attendees gets to participate in the judging. Bring an appetite.

HALLOWEEN Oct 31
Check out New York's Village Halloween Parade (www.halloween-nyc.com), the nation's largest costumed revelry. Or enter the haunted house at Philadelphia's Eastern State Penitentiary (www.easternstate.org/halloween).

NOVEMBER-DECEMBER

LIGHT UP NIGHT mid-Nov
Pittsburgh kicks off its holiday season with this tree-lighting festival (www.downtownpittsburgh.com), a pre-Thanksgiving weekend that includes a bridge party, carriage parade and fireworks.

THANKSGIVING 4th Thu in Nov
NYC's famous Macy's Parade, with its helium character balloons, includes Santa's arrival. Visit the Museum of Natural History the night before to see the balloons blown up. Philadelphia also holds a major float parade.

NEW YEAR'S EVE Dec 31
A million people cram Times Square (www.timessquarenyc.org) to watch the crystal ball drop to ring in the New Year.

Itineraries
CLASSIC TRIPS

CITY MOUSE, COUNTRY MOUSE
one week/NYC to Lake Placid

With only a week, the best thing is to take your first three or four days and give them to the **Big Apple** (p76). Of course, you can't see everything, but if this is your first time, use your feet and indulge in iconic Manhattan: stroll **Central Park** (p91), walk the canyons of **Wall Street** (p80), trip your way through **Greenwich Village** (p87). Join the locals on the **High Line** (p89), and book a ferry for the **Statue of Liberty** (p84). And wander **Times Square** (p90) on your way to a **Broadway show** (p111).

Now pick up that rental car and go north on Rte 9. In the **Hudson Valley** (p130), visit **Hyde Park** (p136) and the **Catskills** (p143). Either rest your legs in **Woodstock** (p149) or hike **Minnewaska State Park** (p144). Next stop: **Saratoga Springs** (p159) – where the spas will soothe your bones. With your last day or two, get a taste of the **Adirondacks** (p166), either in **Lake George** (p167) or **Lake Placid** (p170), where Olympians still train and High Peaks await.

The first few days, you won't drive at all as you bite into the Big Apple. Then it's just 300 miles from New York City to Lake Placid. There are so many reasons to stop, it'll hardly feel like a driving trip at all.

URBAN CULTURAL ODYSSEY   two weeks/NYC to Pittsburgh

Love art and history? You've come to the right place. Naturally, start in New York City: visit the **Met** (p95) and **MoMA** (p91) if you've never been, and fit in the **Whitney** (p95), the **Cloisters** (p99), the **Chelsea galleries** (p89) and the **Morgan Library** (p91). Each evening, New York is a smorgasbord of **music and theater** (p109), but check the schedule at Newark's **NJ Performing Arts Center** (p241), too.

After three to four days, take I-95 west to **Princeton** (p252), soak up the campus and make a trip to **Grounds for Sculpture** (p256) in Trenton. Then keep going to **Philadelphia** (p281). Spend a day in **Independence National Historic Park** (p285) – where America was conceived – make like Rocky up the **Museum of Art** (p299) steps, and visit the funky **Philadelphia Magic Gardens** (p296). Philadelphia's **nightlife** (p309) is no slouch either.

Valley Forge (p313) is a worthwhile Revolutionary side trip; then head east on I-76. The first stop is **Lancaster** (p319) and a day relaxing in **Amish Country** (p319). Then visit the national park at **Gettysburg** (p337) for a sobering dose of the Civil War. True buffs will want to detour to Harrisburg's **National Civil War Museum** (p346).

Keep going west on I-76. You'll need reservations and nearly a day to detour to Frank Lloyd Wright's masterpiece **Fallingwater** (p371), but it's an architectural treasure; don't miss it. Then end your journey with two to three days in **Pittsburgh** (p354). Between the wonderful **Andy Warhol Museum** (p358), the massive **Carnegie** (p361) and the wild **Mattress Factory** (p360), you'll stay busy. Simply walking the yellow bridges over the Allegheny River is a stylish way to end.

Stringing together the region's three big cities – Manhattan, Philly and Pittsburgh – is an ideal trip, allowing for tons of improvisations and detours in between. This route is nearly 500 miles, but it's all about the destinations.

BEACH-STOPPING

two weeks/Montauk to Cape May

Yes, locals tend to pick one beach for two weeks and not move. This trip, though, is much more interesting and allows plenty of time for sunning and swimming.

The first few days, take day trips from **New York City** (p76) to **Coney Island** (p101), especially if you have kids, as well as to crowded **Jones Beach** (p128) and gorgeous **Robert Moses State Park** (p186). Or spend a few days in a town on **Fire Island National Seashore** (p128). Your main chance for celebrity-spotting will be on **Hamptons beaches** (p123), and those seeking more quiet and less swimming can go all the way to **Montauk** (p125).

After five days or so, go 'down the shore' in Jersey. **Sandy Hook** (p213) is a perfect place to start, especially if you prefer sunbathing nude. Then bunk down for a couple of days in resurgent, funky **Asbury Park** (p218) for its nightlife and restaurants, with a visit to pretty **Ocean Grove** (p221) next door.

Next, stay in raucous **Seaside Heights** (p226) for a few days. One day rattle your spine on the amusement pier, and recover the next in beautiful **Island Beach State Park** (p230). After that, take another two days in **Atlantic City** (p262). Indulge in a little casino gambling and trendy nightclub hopping (bring tailored clothes). If you have kids, consider a few days of amusement-pier fun and soporific beaches in either **Ocean City** (p270) or **Wildwood** (p271).

Finally, go past Garden State Parkway exit 0 to **Cape May** (p274), the most relaxed Jersey shore resort. A few more days of gourmet food, Victorian-era ambience and white-sand beaches, and all your troubles will be forgotten.

Call this, at most, 400 miles, depending on how far out on Long Island you go. More important than distance, though, is timing: hit the highway with everyone else, and 2 miles could take two hours. Strategize your beach assaults like MacArthur.

ROADS LESS TRAVELED

MOUNTAINS & RIVERS   Three weeks/Montreal to NYC

Outdoors types have a lot of options in New York and Pennsylvania. But you'll need to pick and choose activities to keep this to three weeks.

It's easiest to fly into Montreal, take I-15 south to New York's I-87, and stop first in the Adirondack's **Lake Placid** (p170). With hiking the High Peaks, visiting the Olympic sites and canoeing the Fulton Chain of Lakes, you can easily spend three to four days.

Take picturesque Rte 3 west to I-81 and go north to **Alexandria Bay** (p178) and the **Thousand Islands** (p178) for several days of wildlife-watching, canoeing and fishing, such as on **Wellesley Island** (p180).

Head southwest (along I-81 and I-90) to the **Finger Lakes** (p186); bunk in **Skaneateles** (p196) and enjoy winery tours and lake fun. Detour into Rochester for the **photography museum** (p198), and then gape at mighty **Niagara Falls** (p204).

Continue on I-90 west to Pennsylvania's **Presque Isle State Park** (p381), then pick up Rte 6: where the elk herds, river floats and wooded hikes of the **Allegheny National Forest** (p391) deserve several days. Follow Rte 6 to **Pine Creek Gorge** (p395), the 'Grand Canyon of Pennsylvania.'

Past Scranton, await the **Poconos** (p397) and the **Delaware Water Gap** (p398). You'll find canoeing and rafting on the Delaware and Lehigh Rivers, and plenty of biking and hiking, including the Appalachian Trail, and on the Jersey side of the **Gap** (p247), you can hike more of the AT. When you've had enough, cruise into **NYC** (p76).

Easily 1100 miles, with long stretches on 40mph mountain roads behind lumbering RVs. So, keep two things in mind: this is amazing, gorgeous scenery, especially in fall. The road is your destination. And keep your schedule loose. You'll be coming back, anyway.

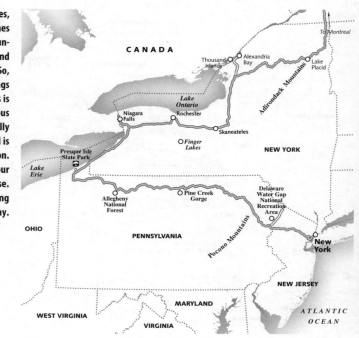

TAILORED TRIPS

ELEPHANTS & OTHER ROADSIDE ATTRACTIONS

The bible of regional weirdness is Weird NJ (www.weirdnj.com), and indeed, New Jersey has a wealth of roadside oddities. The most iconic is **Lucy the Elephant** (p270), near Atlantic City, while the best place to find the Jersey Devil is **Asbury Park** (p220). Marvel over confiscated anti-tank guns and the Lindbergh baby kidnapping at the **NJ State Police Museum** (p256) in Trenton. Ocean City's overwhelming **Discovery Seashell Museum** (p271) seems to have emptied the ocean, and the doo-wop nostalgia of **Wildwood** (p271) is classic roadside Americana.

Pennsylvania has its own elephants, at **Mr Ed's Elephant Museum** (p345). Bigger is always better, and several 'world's largest' claims – shoes, Christmas, candy, flags – cluster near **Hermitage** (p390). In Philadelphia, don't miss the flamboyant **Mummers' Museum** (p297), the **Mütter Museum** (p293) and **Eastern State Penitentiary** (p298) – this creepy prison once held Al Capone!

Like goosebumps? Visit Ossining's **Sing Sing Museum** (p134) and stop by 112 Ocean Ave in 'Oh the Horror' **Amityville** (p124). Smaller is funner: the world's smallest church is in **Oneida** (p197). In NYC, visit the haunted **Chelsea Hotel** (p104), funhouse **Coney Island** (p101) and don't leave without tipping the Naked Cowboy in **Times Square** (p90).

DAMN YANKEES

In sports-mad America, few places can match this region. The world-champion Yankees tend to tower over everyone else, but **NYC** (p109) also has baseball's Mets, and Madison Sq Garden hosts the Knicks (basketball) and the Rangers (hockey). Upstate, there are Cooperstown's **Baseball Hall of Fame** (p165), **Saratoga Springs Racetrack** (p164) and Lake Placid's **Olympic Museum** (p172). Plus, **Buffalo** (p203) has the Bills (football), Sabres (hockey) and the minor-league-baseball Bisons.

Jersey only has **minor-league baseball teams** (p257), but there are plenty to choose from, plus there's the overlooked **Yogi Berra Museum** (p245) in Montclair. In Newark's **Prudential Center** (p243), the Devils (hockey) and the Nets (basketball) play. While **Meadowlands** (p243) has the biggest, baddest new NFL stadium, hosting the Giants and the Jets, two 'New York' teams who actually play in Jersey.

Philadelphia's (p311) often long-suffering fans enjoy pro baseball, football, basketball and hockey in the Phillies, Eagles, 76ers and Flyers, respectively. On Pennsylvania's west end, fans in **Pittsburgh** (p369) root for their hometown Pirates (baseball), Steelers (football) and Penguins (hockey). And let's not forget the kids: in August, **Williamsport** (p397) hosts the Little League World Series, and has a Little League Museum. Now, play ball!

VILLAGE PEOPLE

With the exception of San Francisco and maybe LA, it doesn't get much gayer than **NYC** (p109), where 1969's Stonewall riot sparked the gay rights movement. Today, five neighborhoods have notable GLBT scenes: the West Village, East Village, Chelsea, Hell's Kitchen and Brooklyn's Williamsburg. For city fun, **Philadelphia** (p281) also has a notable gay scene, though it's far more low-key.

When it's time to hit the beach, perhaps the nation's leading gay resort is **Fire Island** (p129), especially the villages of the Pines and Cherry Grove. Here,

the highlight of the year is July 4's Invasion of the Pines drag-queen celebration. However, don't forget **Asbury Park** (p218) in New Jersey, which is out and proud, while the shore towns of **Atlantic City** (p262) and **Cape May** (p274) also have (much smaller) gay scenes. Another mellow but visible scene exists in the sister cities of **New Hope** (p314) and **Lambertville** (p258), which hold hands over the Delaware River.

In June, Gay Pride inspires one of the nation's biggest celebrations in New York, along with major parades in Philadelphia and Asbury Park. Plus, you can belt out 'YMCA' along with 40,000 others at **Yankee Stadium** (p110), where it's the ground crew's seventh-inning theme song.

EAST COAST EATS

The East Coast has a deep, proprietary love of its comfort foods. Don't even try to talk someone out of their favorite pizza, bagel, hoagie, hot dog, cheesesteak, cheesecake, ice cream, cannoli or diner joint. It's not gonna happen. So just enjoy and don't question it.

Gourmands make for themselves an endless buffet of the pushcart cuisine in **Manhattan** (p76); walk and you will find. Upstate, **Buffalo** (p199) is the home of Buffalo wings, naturally, and **Saratoga Springs** (p159) invented the potato chip. In Western New York, try the horrible-sounding sandwich 'Beef on Weck' (p206).

Down the **Jersey shore** (p272), the pizza wars are fierce and the hot-dog places legendary. Saltwater taffy was invented in **Atlantic City** (p262), which also boasts **White House Subs** (p268). For cannolis, two choices: Hoboken's **Carlo's**

Bakery (p237), home of TLC's *Cake Boss*, and Newark's **Calandra's Bakery** (p242). With over 600 diners, Jersey could be the Diner State; New Brunswick's **Skylark** (p251) is deliciously upscale.

Philadelphia has two don't-miss food markets: **Reading Terminal Market** (p294) and the **Italian Market** (p296). They have cheesesteaks, which have grown into an epic **Pat's vs Geno's vs Jim's cheesesteak rivalry** (p309). Dutch Country is famous for scrapple, shoofly pie and Amish sausage; simply peruse the **Bird-in-Hand Farmer's Market** (p329). In Pittsburgh, **Primanti Brothers** (p366) sandwiches have stopped hearts.

HISTORY BUFFS

America's roots run deep here: Henry Hudson's discovery of New York Harbor in 1609 predated the Pilgrims' arrival in Massachusetts by a decade. However, America was conceived in Philadelphia, where the superlative **Independence National Historic Park** (p285) vividly brings these events, people and ideas to life. Significant Revolutionary War sights include nearby **Valley Forge** (p313) and New Jersey's **Washington Crossing** (p258), Washington's headquarters in **Morristown** (p245), and **Trenton** (p255) and **Princeton** (p252).

Ellis Island and the Statue of Liberty (p84) also symbolize national ideals and America's immigrant heritage. In addition, **Federal Hall** (p85) focuses on Washington and Alexander Hamilton, and the **Tenement Museum** (p87) re-creates late-19th-century immigrant life.
Though it is still mostly a construction zone, Manhattan's **Ground Zero** (p85) is one of modern history's most significant memorials.

It's a historical footnote, but memories of the War of 1812 are preserved in New York's **Sackets Harbor** (p185) and towns along the **St Lawrence Seaway** (p185). **Seneca Falls** (p196) is famous as the birthplace of the women's rights movement.

In Pennsylvania, **Gettysburg** (p337) commemorates the most important battle of the Civil War, while **Harrisburg** (p346) has a major Civil War museum. For a look at the beginnings of oil barons like Rockefeller, detour to **Oil City** (p388), near where the first oil well was dug.

BY THE TIME WE GOT TO WOODSTOCK

Music is another highlight. The region features legendary venues and history in just about every major style: rock, jazz, folk, hip hop, opera, the symphony and more. You're spoiled for choice just in **NYC** (p110) what with Lincoln Center and Birdland, Carnegie Hall and Harlem's **Apollo Theater** (p98) – not to mention its plethora of punk-rock nightclubs. **Philadelphia** (p309) also offers the full buffet: from top-flight opera and classical to funky rock, blues and jazz spots.

Surprisingly or not, New Jersey as a state keeps pace with both cities. Newark's **NJPAC** (p241) is a world-class cultural center, and **New Brunswick's theaters** (p251) are renowned statewide. Hoboken has the indie club **Maxwell's** (p238), and **Red Bank** (p216) has a thriving music scene. Tops for independent rock, though, is **Asbury Park** (p220), where the Stony Pony launched Bruce Springsteen and leads a vibrant scene. Looking for Dire Straits and Lady Gaga? Try **Atlantic City** (p269), whose casinos pull the top names.

Upstate New York has, first of all, **Woodstock** (p149), which tends the Summer of Love flame, and folk music is a regional favorite. In Chautauqua, the **Chautauqua Institution** (p207) has classical music in summer, and the **Saratoga Performing Arts Center** (p163) is upstate's primary music venue for big acts.

Plus, check the Calendar (p23) for music festivals year-round.

History

TURTLE ISLAND & NATIVE AMERICANS

Two major groups of Native Americans lived in this region when Europeans first arrived – the Algonquians and the Iroquois. Algonquian is a linguistic term denoting tribes that spoke dialects of the same language family. Algonquian-speaking tribes occupied the Hudson Valley, Long Island, Manhattan Island, New Jersey, the Delaware River Valley and central Pennsylvania. They were made up of the Lenni Lenape (called the Delaware by the British), Shawnee, Mohegan (or Mohican) and Munsee.

The Lenape – whose name means the 'Real People' or 'Ancient Ones' – were regarded by other tribes as the oldest northeastern Algonquian culture. Like all Algonquian peoples, they lived in small groups or bands and moved with the seasons; they mixed hunting-and-gathering and agriculture; and they lived in temporary shelters. From shell mounds, it's clear they relied on the abundance of the sea, and they grew the 'three sisters': corn, beans, and squash. The Lenape had no written language, but they gave us the creation myth of North America as 'Turtle Island.' As the story goes, at first there was only water, and then the turtle raised its back and the earth dried. A tree grew in the middle; from the roots sprouted the first man, and the first woman sprouted from the tip of the tree as it bent over and touched the earth.

The Iroquois were a military and political confederacy of different Native American tribes that occupied most of upstate New York and parts of northern Pennsylvania. They included the Cayuga, Mohawk, Oneida, Onondaga and Seneca peoples, who together formed the powerful Iroquois League (or Iroquois Confederacy) in the 1500s, either just before or soon after first contact with Europeans. The Susquehannock people were also Iroquois and were named after the Susquehanna River where they lived. The Iroquois were strong-willed, empire-minded, expansionist tribes who had more highly developed agriculture and made war on their southern Algonquian neighbors.

It's impossible to know how many Native Americans lived in the region prior to European contact. Some estimate that New Jersey had no more than 20,000 people, and Manhattan may have been home to 1000. Nearly all initial European encounter stories describe tribes as agreeable and peaceful and willing to trade. Native American tribes, but particularly the Iroquois, developed complex trading partnerships with Europeans, and they got caught up in the European feuds for New World dominance. But inevitably, whether Native Americans were treated with disdain or respect, whether it was done through treaty or war, the end result never varied: native tribes were displaced and disenfranchised and forced to leave or be killed.

Journey into Mohawk Country by George O'Connor (2006) turns the translated journal of a 23-year-old Dutch trader in New York in 1634 into a graphic novel, slyly bringing to colorful life the world between the lines.

TIMELINE

1500s	1524	1609
Iroquois League is formed, eventually comprised of six nations in upstate New York. The Iroquois call themselves Haudenosaunee (People of the Longhouse), having lived around the Finger Lakes at least since 1000 AD.	Italian navigator Giovanni da Verrazano sails into New York Bay, the first European to do so. He anchors at Sandy Hook, and today the Verrazano-Narrows Bridge, connecting Brooklyn and Staten Island, honors his feat.	In September, English explorer Henry Hudson arrives in New York Bay in the *Half Moon* and sails as far up the Hudson River as he can. He exchanges knives for tobacco with the natives, who are, he says, 'very civil.'

The displacement of Native American tribes was a slow, torturous process. It occurred incrementally throughout the late 1600s and 1700s, as European settlements grew into colonies and cities, and then into a new nation. By the early 1800s, every single remaining organized tribe had been relocated west, many to Oklahoma.

NO CHINA, JUST BEAVER PELTS

In 1524, about 32 years after Christopher Columbus ran headlong into the North American continent, Italian navigator Giovanni da Verrazano, representing France, was the first European to sail the Atlantic coast and enter New York Bay. There wasn't much follow-up, so this event has largely taken a backseat to the arrival of English explorer Henry Hudson, who sailed into New York Bay in 1609 and claimed the area for the Dutch.

Hudson was looking for the fabled 'Northwest Passage' – a western sea route to the bejeweled Orient that would revolutionize European trade and the balance of power. No luck, but Hudson did report on the excellent harbor, the abundance of fur animals and the enterprising nature of the locals. The Dutch were ecstatic, and by 1624, the Dutch West India Company had established several settlements to exploit the fur trade, at Fort Orange (present-day Albany, NY) and at places in New Jersey like modern-day Jersey City and Camden. In 1626, the Dutch purchased Manhattan Island from the Algonquians and named it New Amsterdam.

Manhattan Island was clearly the most strategic location on the best harbor. New Amsterdam was a company town whose sole purpose was commerce, attracting traders from all over the known world and resulting in an extremely diverse, libertine society whose only unbreakable law was free trade (see p34). The influence of this Dutch settlement has since been largely overwritten by the English, who followed, but at least initially, the British made few changes to the settlement's essential character.

Other nations also arrived, such as Swedish and Finnish traders who established New Sweden along the Delaware River in 1638 (near present-day Philadelphia), though the Dutch annexed this colony in 1655. The English also expanded into the region, and in 1664, they strong-armed the Dutch into turning over New Amsterdam to them. They renamed the island New York after the Duke of York, brother of King Charles II.

The English also acquired New Jersey, and in 1681, King Charles II gave English Quaker William Penn a charter to own land west of the Delaware River (to pay off a debt). William Penn founded his Pennsylvania colony as a 'holy experiment' in religious freedom and liberal government. Rather optimistically, he named his capital Philadelphia (Greek for 'Brotherly Love'). He established a fairly progressive code of laws that guaranteed religious tolerance, trial by jury and protection of property.

A masterful piece of narrative history, The Island at the Center of the World (2004) by Russell Shorto evokes the cantankerous, unruly 17th-century Dutch colony of New Amsterdam, without which America wouldn't have been the same.

Don't lug this tome to the beach, but for the definitive story of Manhattan, read Gotham (2000) by Edwin Burrows and Mike Wallace. New York City's story is indeed a 'saga of the nation.'

1626	1664	1682
A famous real estate swindle involves the Dutch 'buying' Manhattan Island from Algonquian tribes for 60 guilder's worth of household goods. Though a symbol of Native American disenfranchisement, the Algonquians don't actually leave.	A British naval fleet parks off New Amsterdam, threatening war with the Dutch settlement. Peg-legged Dutch director Peter Stuyvesant, without any defenses, is forced to surrender the Manhattan colony to England.	Quaker William Penn visits his Pennsylvania colony, befriends the Lenape and institutes freedom of religion, trial by jury and free elections. He successfully markets his 'holy experiment' to other persecuted religious minorities.

These were superseded by the 1701 Charter of Privilege, a constitution giving the Pennsylvania colonial assembly more power than any legislative body in Britain. Even more than New York, Pennsylvania would become the richest, most populous and most influential of Britain's colonies in 18th-

NEW AMSTERDAM: SEED OF THE BIG APPLE

The story of America's founding is typically one of Pilgrims and Plymouth Rock, taxes and representative assemblies, religious freedoms and… w-what? Were we snoring?

What we want to know is – *where were the pirates and the prostitutes?*

Apparently, they were in New Amsterdam, the Dutch settlement on the tip of Manhattan Island. And even more: they might have had as much to do with the eventual character of the new republic as those uptight Puritans and Jamestown noblemen.

Amsterdam itself was the most tolerant city in Europe, a progressive, diverse capital where many of those high-minded Enlightenment ideals first got kicked around. Indeed, when they left England to escape religious persecution, the Pilgrims first sought shelter in Holland before making the big leap across the pond.

The Dutch interest in the New World was strictly commercial, and by luck and good judgment, they set up shop on an island in the coast's best harbor, along a river leading deep into the continent's natural wealth. This was something many people wanted, and beginning in 1626, the Dutch welcomed them all.

In its early years, New Amsterdam was a Hollywood-perfect, rough-and-ready port town: a rogue's gallery of scalawags and sailors, smugglers and pirates, who used New Amsterdam as a base of operations. Prostitutes openly flaunted their wares – taking payment in money or pelts – and the town supported dozens of breweries. Slaves brought in chains sometimes found themselves freed, or purchased their freedom, to become carpenters and blacksmiths. Mohawks, Jews, Norwegians, Italians: everyone mixed and mingled – even if they didn't get along – so that in a settlement of 1000 people you could hear a Babel of 18 tongues. Orthodox governor Peter Stuyvesant punished but could never stop the wenching and carousing.

Without question, the settlement was badly managed. The Dutch West India Company struggled to make a profit, and eventually turned it into a free-trade port, meaning that anyone was free to trade, so long as the company got a cut. Then New Amsterdam, modeling a Dutch tradition, offered 'burgher status' to residents. This granted residents a say and stake in their community, and nearly everyone applied for and achieved it. What happened next is quite interesting: a robust merchant class developed, one that everyone could aspire to. Everyone became a trader, and everyone benefited as the town actually tidied itself up – a little.

From around 1640 until the English kicked the Dutch out in 1664, New Amsterdam was truly unique: an egalitarian, entrepreneurial melting pot of races, cultures and classes. Tolerance was, for the Dutch, simply good business; it was pragmatic, not idealistic nor universally practiced. Likewise, egalitarian didn't necessarily mean equal.

Still, is this not modern-day Manhattan? The Dutch showed how it was done, that it could be done: that free enterprise and the democratic impulse could make a new world.

1758	1774	1776
During the French and Indian War, the Battle of Fort Carillon (now Fort Ticonderoga) is the war's bloodiest: 4000 French hold off 16,000 British soldiers, causing 3000 casualties. The incompetent English commander is later called a 'blockhead.'	During Philadelphia's First Continental Congress, the New Jersey governor, William Franklin (Ben's son), supports the British, as do wealthy New York merchants, while the pacifist Pennsylvania Quakers and Amish argue against going to war.	The Declaration of Independence is approved by all 13 colonies and signed by 56 delegates in Independence Hall, Philadelphia. John Hancock, as Congress president, signs first, and the signatories officially become traitors of England.

century North America. As Enlightenment ideas percolated worldwide – concerning individualism, equality and freedom – they found the raw materials and room for expression in New World colonies.

FRANCE, INDIAN ALLIANCES & EMPIRE

European nations brought their rivalries to the New World as they jockeyed for supremacy. No one knew the full measure of the continent, but its impressive natural wealth rang dollar signs in everyone's eyes. Fur traders pierced the wilderness, making deals with Native Americans, and they increasingly bumped into each other.

By the 1750s, England lay claim to most of the Atlantic seaboard, from Georgia to Maine. France was its main competitor: they controlled territory from Canada down through the continent's interior to Louisiana, including portions of northwest New York and Pennsylvania. France was particularly protective of the Ohio River Valley – which was an essential link between their colonies – and they became unhappy as English merchants from Pennsylvania and Virginia encroached inland. Neither nation maintained a standing army in the New World, but in the 1750s, France built a line of forts through western Pennsylvania to protect their interests, such as Fort Duquesne (present-day Pittsburgh) at the confluence of the Ohio, Allegheny and Monongahela Rivers.

In fact, territorial claims were fairly loose. Large areas remained dominated by Native American tribes, and European trading fortunes depended largely on developing alliances with them. As the French-English conflicts escalated into fighting, northern tribes in Canada and the western Great Lakes region supported France, while the British developed alliances with the Cherokee and most significantly the Iroquois, who became a significant factor in Britain's eventual success.

In 1753, the British sent George Washington to tell the French to leave the Ohio country. France dismissed the warning, and in July 1754 they defeated Washington at the Battle of Fort Necessity in southwestern Pennsylvania (see p376). With this, the French and Indian War (called the Seven Years' War in Europe) was underway.

The French and Indian War became a true world war, with fighting in North America, Europe and the West Indies. Fighting in the New World – which ranged from Pennsylvania through New York and into Canada – ended around 1760, but the war did not end until 1763. The French got the upper hand in 1756–57, but the British turned the tide in 1758, when they were able to secure the St Lawrence River. Then, in 1759, the English captured Fort Carillon (today Fort Ticonderoga) at their second attempt, along with Fort Niagara and Quebec, and the following year France negotiated a surrender of their North American territories, though the war continued in other theaters.

An excellent, well-written compilation, *Pennsylvania: History of the Commonwealth* (2002) by Randall Miller & William Pencak is a wide-ranging look at the Keystone State by a range of expert scholars.

1777	1791	1803
In November, the Articles of Confederation establishes a weak federal Congress with no power to tax states or compel them to supply the Continental Army. As such, Congress wages war with a nearly bankrupt national treasury.	The Bill of Rights amends the Constitution to guard against the abuse of centralized power. It declares citizens' rights to freedom of speech, assembly, religion, the press and the right to bear arms and a fair trial.	With the Louisiana Purchase, France's Napoleon (preparing for war with England) sells the Louisiana territory to the US for $15 million, thereby extending US territory from the Mississippi River to the Rocky Mountains.

Despite Britain's ultimate victory, the French and Indian War proved extremely costly. Britain's national debt had almost doubled, and it now had more land than it knew what to do with. Up till now, the American colonies had been pretty much left alone to manage themselves, but that changed. England permanently stationed an army in North America, they passed laws forbidding settlement west of the Appalachian Mountains and north of the Ohio River (to avoid more wars), and they passed a series of taxes to pay off the war debt and support the Crown.

These weren't, from England's perspective, unreasonable requests; they had just won a war for the colonists, after all. Still, colonists became incensed. They resented British taxation and limits on their expansion, imposed without their say. Heated debates arose over the merits of representative government versus monarchy. Colonists argued with and boycotted the British – Philadelphians even turned away a British tea ship in 1773, though they didn't burn it as Bostonians did. England responded by enforcing its imperial authority with military might.

In 1774, representatives from 12 colonies convened the First Continental Congress in Philadelphia's Congress Hall to decide what to do. Consensus eluded them, but few found the situation acceptable, and both sides readied for a fight.

THE FIGHT FOR INDEPENDENCE

In April 1775, British troops engaged patriot militias in Massachusetts, and the Revolutionary War began. Very quickly, in May 1775, the Second Continental Congress convened in Philadelphia, establishing the Continental Army with George Washington as commander-in-chief. Trouble was, Washington lacked gunpowder and money, and his troops were a motley collection of poorly armed farmers and merchants. Plus, colonial leaders had yet to articulate what they were fighting for.

The 'father of New Jersey history,' John Cunningham, examines the long winters Washington and his soldiers endured in between battles, and how they nearly undid the patriots' cause, in *The Uncertain Revolution* (2010).

In January 1776, Thomas Paine published the wildly popular *Common Sense*, making a passionate case for independence from England. Soon independence came to seem not just logical but noble and necessary. On July 4, 1776, Philadelphia's Continental Congress adopted the Declaration of Independence, largely written by Thomas Jefferson, and all 13 colonies established their own state governments.

This impressed the British – who could muster the largest professional army in the world – not a bit. They took the fight from New England to New York, routing Washington's troops through the fall – the English kicked the patriots off Long Island, Manhattan and Staten Island (so they could control the vital Hudson River) and sent the colonial army retreating all the way across New Jersey into Pennsylvania. From this point on, most of the early war took place within these three states, with the British headquartered on Manhattan, the colonists strategizing in Philadelphia and their armies often meeting in New Jersey.

1804	1812-15	1825
Alexander Hamilton – founding father and the first US Secretary of the Treasury – is shot and killed by his political rival Aaron Burr in a famous duel fought in Weehawken Heights, New Jersey.	The War of 1812, which involves fighting in New York and Canada, ends inconclusively. The British abandon their Ohio River valley forts, and the US renews its vow to avoid Europe's 'entangling alliances.'	The Erie Canal is completed, connecting the Hudson River with Lake Erie (via Albany and Buffalo) and allowing easy ship access to the ports of the western Great Lakes.

With winter approaching, Washington was desperate for a victory to stave off mass desertions among his demoralized troops. On December 25, 1776, he took a high-stakes gamble: after recrossing the ice-choked Delaware River at night back into New Jersey, he orchestrated a successful sneak attack on Hessian mercenaries guarding Trenton. This led to a series of advances and victories that saved the nascent revolution from a quick demise.

Nevertheless, the patriots were outmanned and underfunded. In September 1777, British troops marched into Pennsylvania, defeating Washington's forces at the Battle of Brandywine, and then capturing and occupying Philadelphia. Unable to take it back, the colonists managed to win a key battle at Saratoga, New York, in October. Afterward, they spent a critical, disease-plagued winter in Valley Forge, Pennsylvania: here, Washington trained and reconstituted his short-term militia into a long-term regular army (see Winter, Wages & Mutiny, p38).

Meanwhile, Philadelphian Benjamin Franklin (see American Legend, p295) was wooing France – never reluctant to trouble England – who in early 1778 agreed to enter the war on the side of the revolutionaries. To a large degree, French ships, soldiers and supplies proved the critical difference.

Ahead of France's arrival, the British voluntarily withdrew from Philadelphia in June 1778 to regroup. Then, over the next three years, fighting spread to the South and involved a seesaw of victories and setbacks. Eventually, America and its allies wore down the British Army, which surrendered in Yorktown, Virginia, in October 1781. Despite the start of peace talks, sporadic fighting continued until 1783, when the 'Treaty of Paris' formally recognized the United States of America.

Washington's Crossing (2004) focuses on the Revolutionary War's most iconic moment, which, seen closely, reveals much about why Washington and his unprofessional army overcame the British. At least, in David Hackett Fischer's capable hands it does.

MAKING A NATION

Having thrown off the yolk of monarchy, the revolutionaries now came to the hard part: creating a nation. Many colonial leaders were opposed to forming a national government, but there was so much squabbling that it became clear the country's 1777 Articles of Confederation was inadequate. In 1787, a federal constitutional convention was held in Philadelphia, where Federalists – led by John Jay, James Madison and Alexander Hamilton – made the case that to be united, the states needed a strong federal center. After much debate and tinkering, state delegates finally approved the US Constitution, which balanced power between an elected president, a representative Congress and the judiciary.

In 1789, George Washington was inaugurated as the first US president in New York City, and from 1790 to 1800, the nation's capital was in Philadelphia, after which it moved to Washington, DC.

With a federal government, though, came federal taxes, leading to some familiar results. During the 1794 Whiskey Rebellion, western Pennsylvania farmers rebelled against taxes on homemade whiskey. To

1848	**1863**	**1877**
The first women's rights convention is held in Seneca Falls, New York, where suffragette Elizabeth Cady Stanton drafts a 'Declaration of Sentiments' that proposes 'all men and women are created equal.'	In November, President Abraham Lincoln delivers his famous 'Gettysburg Address' while dedicating the Gettysburg national cemetery. Lasting two minutes, and calling for a 'new birth of freedom,' it remains America's most famous speech.	Thomas Edison invents the phonograph in Menlo Park, New Jersey. It's the first machine to record and play back sound. He tests it by reciting 'Mary had a little lamb' and having the machine record it on tinfoil.

suppress the farmers, President George Washington had to call out an army larger than the one he commanded during the Revolutionary War. Five years later, eastern Pennsylvanians – taxed according to the number of windows in their houses – engaged in the Hot Water Rebellion, so-called because homeowners threw hot water on assessors. When Thomas Jefferson was elected president in 1800, he reduced taxes and the revolts subsided.

WINTER, WAGES & MUTINY

Washington waged two battles during the Revolutionary War: one with the British, the other with his own troops. Particularly early on, desertions and mutiny were as dangerous to the cause of liberty as the redcoats.

The most famous winter encampment was in 1777–78 in Valley Forge, Pennsylvania, where Washington's 'ragtag militia' was transformed into a trained army. In addition to the drills, however, Washington changed recruitment strategies: he knew a short-term militia would never prevail, so he offered land and more money to those who'd enlist for three years or the war's duration. Soldiers were also promised an annual suit of new clothes, new blankets, occasional rum and around $6 a month. People responded from across the colonies, and in a real way, the army came to reflect the society it was fighting for: English, Dutch, French, Swedes, Germans, Irish, Spaniards, enslaved Africans seeking freedom and even Native Americans served together in integrated regiments.

Yet over 2000 men died at Valley Forge – less from the cold winter than from the disease that flourished in the warmth of spring. Washington learned how to manage camps to avoid disease, but he never could conjure food, rum, clothing and money out of empty colonial coffers.

Two years later, the winter of 1779–80 was the worst in a century, far worse than at Valley Forge. The Continental Army – nearly 13,000 soldiers – built a hut city in New Jersey's Jockey Hollow. Then they did nothing but starve as 28 snowstorms lashed the Watchung Mountains. Though less than a hundred men died, an untold number deserted – simply ran away – while Washington continually petitioned the congress in Philadelphia for money and supplies, to no avail. By spring, the troops were bitter and demoralized. Tempers flared, and three Connecticut regiments defied officers and nearly paraded themselves into the countryside before being convinced to stay.

The biggest mutiny, though, occurred the following winter of 1780–81. About 2500 'bad clothed men of Pennsylvania,' to quote Washington, encamped, again, in the Watchung Mountains. As the men starved, rancor spread over the army's broken promises and inability to feed and clothe its own soldiers. Besides, for many, their three-year term was up, so on January 1 they decided to leave.

Around 1500 Pennsylvania soldiers marched to Princeton, took over the town, and over the course of several days of tense negotiations, demanded their discharges along with the pay and clothing owed them. Nearly all were granted their request.

That this didn't happen more often is perhaps more surprising than that it did. Mutinies aside, Washington voiced nothing but profound respect for his rough-hewn troops: 'Naked and starving as they are, we cannot enough admire the incomparable patience and fidelity of the soldiery.'

1885	1892	1904
A gift from France, the Statue of Liberty arrives in New York Harbor in 350 pieces. It's assembled and dedicated in 1886, 10 years late, to celebrate the centennial anniversary of American Independence.	Ellis Island Immigration Station opens; nearly 450,000 immigrants come through in the first year. At its peak in 1907, over a million immigrants arrive. Immigration only slows after the 1924 Immigration Act establishes quotas.	The New York Subway opens its first line in October, called the IRT (Interborough Rapid Transit). Due to electrical problems, service fails twice on the first day; within the first year, there's a transit strike.

Trade between Britain and the US resumed relatively quickly, but relations remained tense. When the British began harassing US ships (as part of its blockade of Napoleonic Europe), the US declared war on Britain again. This time, though, the three-year War of 1812 (which included several battles in New York) ended without a clear winner and without much gained by either side.

Yet America emerged with a stronger sense of national identity and economic self-sufficiency. Led by Philadelphia and New York – the nation's centers of politics, commerce and finance – the Mid-Atlantic states spurred the nation's growth. The 1790s discovery of anthracite coal in northeastern Pennsylvania provided the fuel, and the building of canals – especially New York's Erie Canal in 1825 and New Jersey's Morris and Delaware & Raritan Canals in the 1830s – provided the transportation links that facilitated America's expansion into the Midwest and beyond.

In the 1840s, this expansionist fever grew into a widespread belief in Manifest Destiny, in American exceptionalism – that the United States was divinely fated to hold the entire continent, sea to shining sea.

SLAVERY & CIVIL WAR
When it was ratified, the US Constitution left undecided the issue of slavery. More specifically, whether to allow slavery in new states as they were added to the union. Initially, Thomas Jefferson had proposed that new states be free of slaves. That this didn't become law is partly New Jersey's fault: apparently, in 1784, a vote on the issue was deadlocked 6-6, but the NJ congressman fell ill and couldn't attend the vote, so Jefferson's measure failed to pass.

Slavery was never entrenched in Northern states, whose economies relied more on manufacturing and commerce – in contrast to the slave-dependent cotton plantations in the South. In addition, large Quaker communities in Pennsylvania and New Jersey actively opposed it. In 1780, the Pennsylvania legislature passed the Gradual Emancipation Act, which said that henceforth no child born in Pennsylvania could be enslaved. By 1850, all black people living in Pennsylvania were free.

When it was ratified, the US Constitution left undecided the issue of slavery.

Further, Pennsylvania, New Jersey and New York played key roles in the Underground Railroad – a network of homes and people that helped shelter and guide escaped slaves as they sought freedom in Canada. Abolitionist Harriet Tubman used Cape May as a base for 'conducting' slaves north; one route flowed in and around Philadelphia, through southern Jersey, and then through Brooklyn and upstate New York.

Nevertheless, New Jersey was ambivalent about slavery. When Abraham Lincoln was elected president in 1860, he won in New York and Pennsylvania, but New Jersey split its vote with Douglas. Lincoln ran on a platform of limiting slavery in new states, and his election victory alone was threatening enough that 11 Southern states decided to secede from the Union.

1908	1916-17	1927
The Melting Pot, a play written by Jewish immigrant Israel Zangwill, debuts on Broadway and runs for 136 weeks. Its hopeful message about New York's multiethnic society introduces the term into our cultural lexicon.	German saboteurs blow up munitions depots in Jersey City and the Meadowlands. In part, these incidents spur President Woodrow Wilson to declare war on Germany in 1917, and the United States enters WWI.	The $48-million, 1.5-mile Holland Tunnel is completed, allowing cars to cross the Hudson River into New Jersey for the first time under their own power. Each auto is charged 50 cents for the privilege.

Fighting broke out between the northern Union and the southern Confederacy in April 1861, and the ensuing Civil War became one of history's bloodiest conflicts. The men, manufactured goods and resources from New York and Pennsylvania, and to a lesser degree New Jersey, were crucial to the Union's eventual victory. New York furnished the most Union troops, about 450,000, and Pennsylvania was second, with 338,000; these two states were among those with the highest casualties as well, losing over 80,000 men between them.

Southern forces tried to invade the North through Maryland in 1862, and they tried again in June 1863 along Pennsylvania's Cumberland Valley. This invasion – a force of 75,000 Confederates led by General Robert E Lee – was halted in early July by 97,000 Union soldiers under General Meade during the bloody three-day Battle of Gettysburg (see p337). More soldiers fought and died at Gettysburg than at any other battle in US history, and it is regarded as the Civil War's deciding conflict, causing horrific losses from which the South never recovered. However, it was two more years before the war ended, in April 1865.

ROBBER BARONS & IMMIGRANTS

After the war, America's westward expansion resumed, as did the laying of rail lines, and Pennsylvania was the locomotive. Pittsburgh was then producing 50% of America's iron and steel, and western Pennsylvania was the center for coal mining, crude oil and oil refining; by the 1880s, Pennsylvania wells were producing 85% of US crude oil.

In the 1870s, Scottish-born immigrant Andrew Carnegie founded Carnegie Steel in Pittsburgh, modernizing and expanding steel production, while Pittsburgh coal magnate Henry Clay Frick bought up the state's coal reserves and expanded the coke industry (for more on Carnegie, see p361; Frick, p365). Meanwhile, New York–born John D Rockefeller got his start in oil in Pennsylvania's Titusville, where the first oil well was drilled in 1859, and he founded Standard Oil in 1870.

These industrialists attempted to monopolize every aspect of their businesses horizontally and vertically while swallowing their competitors – and in the process becoming the world's richest men. In the 1880s, Frick merged his coal company with Carnegie Steel, which expanded into US Steel in 1901 with the help of New York financier JP Morgan, who created General Electric in 1892. Through century's end, Rockefeller's Standard Oil controlled 80% of the *world's* oil refining, making Rockefeller earth's first billionaire.

Manufacturing and innovation also exploded across New York and New Jersey (home of Thomas Edison), yet to a large degree, the region's growth and industrial prowess depended on the sweat and hard labor of newcomers. The first waves of immigrants arrived in the 1840s and 1850s, but after the war, immigrants flooded in from Western and Eastern Europe. From 1880

Steeped in firsthand sources, *Stand Firm, Ye Boys from Maine* (2009) by Thomas DesJardin vividly re-creates the battle for Little Round Top at Gettysburg, while humanizing its mythic Union general, Joshua Chamberlain.

Herbert Asbury turned his newspaperman's jaundiced eye on late-19th-century New York's brutal underworld, penning the unforgettable *Gangs of New York* (1928) while the bloodstains were fresh. It's worth reading for the names alone.

1929

In October, after a six-year run of fivefold profits, Wall Street investors panic over gloomy economic predictions. Everyone pulls their money out at once, causing a stock-market crash that leads to the Great Depression.

1932

The Winter Olympics are held in Lake Placid, New York (where they will return in 1980). New York Governor Franklin Roosevelt presides over the games; later that year, Roosevelt is elected US president.

1937

In Lakehurst, New Jersey, the *Hindenburg* zeppelin explodes into a fireball; of the 97 people aboard, 36 die. The 804ft German ship – the largest aircraft ever flown – is Hitler's pride and joy; some believe it was sabotaged.

to 1930, 27 million foreigners came to America, and 20 million funneled through the brick archways of Ellis Island.

Manhattan grew exponentially, quickly eclipsing Philadelphia in stature. New York City became the nation's undisputed capital of finance and commerce, an incubator of culture, a 'melting pot' forging a new, multiethnic national identity. This wasn't, of course, an easy process. There were cultural and racial tensions, but also, unchecked oligarchal corporate power led to an unrelenting abuse of workers, newly arrived or not.

Labor unions and a reformist Progressive movement arose to combat and curb the robber barons, and Pennsylvania was at the forefront. The three largest nationwide labor unions were founded in the Keystone State – the Knights of Labor (in 1869), the American Federation of Labor (in 1888) and the Congress of Industrial Organizations (in 1938). Pittsburgh witnessed several major labor strikes: the Great Railroad Strike of 1877, the violent Homestead Strike in 1892 (aimed at Carnegie Steel) and the widespread 1919 steel strike.

One of the leaders of the reform movement was New Jersey Governor Woodrow Wilson, who served as US president from 1913 to 1921. President Wilson helped break up the monopolies and pass labor reforms that eased the worst industry abuses.

Despite the upheavals of WWI, the Great Depression in the 1930s, and WWII, the region's character and prominence held steady: New York City reigned, euphorically so immediately after WWII, while the multiethnic cities of New Jersey and Pennsylvania remained major manufacturing powerhouses.

SUBURBAN SWING, EAST COAST BLUES

Then, the social changes of the 1950s led to hard times for the Mid-Atlantic states, particularly its cities. Roads and automobiles, jet travel, middle-class prosperity: increased mobility and income fed the American Dream to own your own home, to create a better life. In the 1950s and 1960s, suburbs spread like mushrooms after a rain, and in ever-increasing numbers, people left the smudged, cramped cities and their back-breaking factory jobs.

The decline of manufacturing and the 'white flight' to the suburbs spelled trouble for the East Coast. African Americans, still suffering the racial inequalities of segregation, largely remained in the cities, and unemployment transformed many once-vibrant downtowns and neighborhoods into impoverished, crime-ridden ghettos. In July 1964, allegations of police brutality ignited a race riot in Harlem, which touched off a wave of race rioting across all three states. In 1967, more race riots scarred Newark and Buffalo. While the 1960s Civil Rights Movement eventually swept away most of America's racist laws, it didn't change the dynamics of inner-city poverty.

DID YOU KNOW?

In the 1920s and 1930s, New York's Harlem Renaissance was an African-American cultural movement led by some of the 20th century's greatest artists: Billie Holiday, Ella Fitzgerald, Paul Robeson, Langston Hughes, Duke Ellington and Count Basie.

Boardwalk Memories (2006) by Emil Salvini traces the varied fates of Jersey's shore resorts, from the experimental religious communities to the 'showplace of the nation,' Atlantic City. A wealth of historic photos.

1938	1939-45	1964
Orson Welles, adding injury to insult, has Martians invade Grovers Mill, New Jersey, in his famous *War of the Worlds* radio broadcast, setting off region-wide panic. The aliens trample the Pulasky Skyway and invade Newark.	During WWII, New York shipyards play a major role, and New York harbor is harassed by German U-boats. However, alone among major world cities, New York City emerges from the war unscathed.	The July 18 shooting of a black teen by a white police officer sparks six days of rioting in Harlem. Over the next six weeks, violent race riots occur in Rochester, Jersey City, Elizabeth, Paterson and Philadelphia.

Meanwhile, immigration reforms in the 1960s opened America's doors to Asian and Latin American countries like never before. A new wave of immigrants from Puerto Rico, the Philippines, Vietnam, Cuba, Mexico, India and more flooded into Manhattan, Newark, Jersey City and Philadelphia. Social and cultural conflicts simmered and boiled over seemingly everywhere. The 1969 Stonewall riots in Greenwich Village started the gay rights movement, while the women's movement and the Vietnam War led to more protests. The nadir occurred in July 1977, when a two-day blackout in New York City degenerated into uncontrolled looting, arson and chaos.

Plus, the region's longstanding urban and industrial pollution had resulted in ecological carnage. The Hudson River was a sewer, the Adirondacks were pockmarked with dead lakes, chemical pollution at New York's Love Canal led to a federal health emergency, and in 1979, a nuclear reactor at Pennsylvania's Three-Mile Island partially melted down (for more, see p64).

Suffice it to say, the East Coast had lost its mojo. People left in droves. In fact, the region now almost seemed like the nation's shadow, a place broken and in decline, and possibly unfixable.

BOOMS, BUSTS & THE NEW MILLENNIUM

Through the 1980s and 1990s, like fictional boxer Rocky Balboa, the region valiantly picked itself up off the mat. As the nation's economy shifted toward white-collar telecommunications and services, the region was poised to take

---

REVIEWING *THE SOPRANOS*

La Cosa Nostra, the Italian mafia. In modern-day New York, there are, tradition has it, Five Families, such as the Gambino crime family, once run by John Gotti. In addition, Philadelphia has a family, and – stuck in the middle, smaller and overlooked – New Jersey has an organization, the DeCavalcante family.

The New York mafia has always been the big fish. In popular culture, they have been romanticized and glorified many times over, in *The Godfather* and *Goodfellas*, in *Donnie Brasco* and *Once Upon a Time in America*. They epitomize in many ways the immigrant experience itself: the urban gangster as the ultimate outsider, making his way but never assimilating.

The Sopranos offered a Jersey version, a new metaphor – the domesticated gangster, working his day job almost like any other schmuck and coming home to his wife and kids in the suburbs. Where did they get that idea? Maybe from 'Vinny Ocean' Palermo, acting boss of the New Jersey DeCavalcante family in the 1990s, since that's pretty much how he lived – though ironically, after taking care of mob business in Jersey, he returned to his home on Long Island.

Not long before the FBI took down Palermo and most of the DeCavalcante family in 1999, several DeCavalcante wiseguys were recorded talking about the show.

'Yeah, I caught it one night,' one said. 'I didn't think it was really that bad.'

To which another barked, 'What characters. Great acting.'

1969	1976-77	1979
On August 15-17, a half million people attend the Woodstock Festival in the New York's Catskills. Living up to its billing as 'three days of peace and music,' this hippie highpoint is never again matched.	For two years, New York City is terrorized by David Berkowitz, aka the 'Son of Sam,' who taunts police over the course of eight shootings that kill six people and wound seven more. Berkowitz is still in jail.	On March 28, the Three-Mile Island nuclear reactor, near Harrisburg, Pennsylvania, experiences a partial meltdown and releases radioactive gas; exactly how much is disputed. The cleanup costs $1 billion and galvanizes anti-nuclear groups.

advantage. New York City – home of Wall St, Fifth Ave and Madison Ave – remained the epicenter of finance, cultural trends and business, and New Jersey led the early telecommunications revolution. As this morphed into the 1990s internet revolution, the region prospered, even though the lead in innovation shifted to California.

Through these decades, New York City steadily became financially solvent and brought crime under control, largely due to Mayors Ed Koch and Rudolph Giuliani, who did something no one thought possible: cleaned up Times Square. Philadelphia struggled with drug-fueled gang warfare in the 1980s, but things turned around in the 1990s under Mayor Ed Rendell, and the city spruced up its historic center. The implosion of the steel industry meant cleaner air but hard times for Pittsburgh through the 1980s. However, by the end of the 1990s it was again drawing residents, not simply watching them go.

The high-tech stock bubble burst in 2000, and this augured tough times again. Then, on September 11, 2001, Islamic terrorists shocked the nation with an act of war. Al-Qaeda extremists hijacked four commercial airplanes: two were flown into New York's World Trade Center towers, which collapsed. A third was flown into the Pentagon in Washington, DC. The fourth, United flight 93, never reached its intended target; instead, the 37 passengers, 17 from New Jersey, overwhelmed the terrorists and the plane crashed near Shanksville, Pennsylvania.

Many of the nearly 3000 who died on 9/11 were from New York, New Jersey and Pennsylvania, and their loss seemed to match the hole in the skyline where Manhattan's Twin Towers used to be. In the following years, Ground Zero slowly evolved from a pit of rubble into a construction site, with the planned 9/11 memorial a work in progress. This was fitting. Psychologically and emotionally, 9/11 remained an unhealed wound for many residents, even as life went on.

As a nation, as is well-known, America responded by waging war in Afghanistan, and then in Iraq. And economically, flush times returned a few years later, as rising housing prices sent the stock market on another impossibly good run. Of course, the financial good times didn't last. They never do. In 2008, the housing market collapsed like a proverbial house of cards, and Wall Street's reputation collapsed with it (for more on current events, see p16). Yet despite all these troubles, the East Coast had grabbed its mojo back. No longer in decline, it had found strength and hope in its resilience.

A collection of short essays, delicious nuggets, and odd personalities, *There's More to New Jersey than the Sopranos* (2009) by Marc Mappen is an amusing, accessible introduction to the enigma that is the Garden State.

25th Hour (2003) by Spike Lee is a provocative meditation on lost chances that resonates with elegiac images of Ground Zero and post-September 11 NYC.

1993	**2001**	**2008**
Islamic terrorists from Jersey City detonate a truck bomb in the basement garage of the World Trade Center in February. Despite a three-story crater, the tower doesn't fall. Eventually, all the jihadists are arrested.	Of the estimated 17,000 people in the World Trade Center when the 9/11 attacks occur, 2,605 cannot get out and die when the buildings collapse, including 411 emergency workers. In all, the dead include people from over 70 countries.	The housing market bubble collapses, throwing America into the Great Recession. Over 100 mortgage lenders fold, including Wall Street titans Bear Stearns, Lehman Brothers, Merrill Lynch, Washington Mutual, Wachovia and AIG.

The Culture

REGIONAL IDENTITY

Being among the thirteen original colonies that revolted against the British, New York, New Jersey, and Pennsylvania are very much a piece of core America, hard to define though that may be. New York was the first capital of the country, and Philadelphia is the cradle of liberty. The diversity of the region is vast. Ethnic enclaves retain a toe-hold in this region in ways they haven't in other areas of the United States, harking back to an age when this area served as the major point of entry for immigrants. It's also a part of what is known colloquially as the 'Northeast Corridor,' a stretch of urban and suburban areas that reach from Washington DC in the south to Boston in the north. Primarily, the corridor is known as a bastion of liberal politics and financial and cultural interests often at odds with more conservative regions of the US.

New York State is, of course, the big man on campus in the region with its hulking New York City. Residents of NYC often get the reputation of being a bit short-tempered and mean. This isn't generally the case. Most city dwellers are exceedingly friendly and willing to offer assistance or advice to visitors. However, most still believe the world revolves around them and their city. Which, in many ways, it does!

The rest of the state, which comprises most of New York, tends to be more conservative and a bit more industrial, especially up towards the Rust Belt cities of Rochester and Buffalo. Eight hours away by car, Buffalo can seem like another planet compared to the urban intensity of New York City.

New Jersey gets a bad rap. It's not nearly as bad as you think. In fact, it can be quite lovely, especially around Princeton and the Jersey Shore. Often it's assumed that only Italian-Americans (or 'guidos,' in local parlance) live there. While many do, they are by no means the only people calling New Jersey home.

Pennsylvania is probably the most diverse. Its urban centers, Philadelphia and Pittsburgh, are very much a part of the Northeast's general demeanor of liberal politics and commitment to the arts. But get outside those areas and you'll find communities – such as the Pennsylvania Dutch in Amish country – that seem worlds away .

The 'New York 400' is a famous term for the crème de la crème of New York society. The list originated because Mrs Astor, one of the city's top socialites, could only fit 400 people in her ballroom on any given evening.

LIFESTYLE

There's something for everyone in this area of the country. 'Old money' mixes with the nouveau riche, from Park Ave and the Hamptons to Philadelphia and Pittsburgh. With New York City as the country's (if not the globe's) financial capital, massive amounts of money are made and spent in the elite enclaves of the region.

At the other end of the scale, severe poverty has led to urban blight in many of the area's regions, from Camden and Newark in New Jersey to the Bronx in New York City and the cities of the aforementioned Rust Belt, which have struggled as manufacturing and industrialization have waned.

Like most of America, though, the area is primarily home to vast swaths of the middle class who make their homes all over the region. America's first suburb, Levittown, was built on Long Island.

ECONOMY

With the financial collapse of 2008, New York City received unwelcome attention for the role Wall Street financiers played in the economic misfortune.

That said, the area continues to be one of the wealthiest in America. This does not always extend to the outer reaches of the states, but residents tend to earn more per household than anywhere else in America. Not everyone's driving luxury cars, though, as the cost of living is dramatically higher in this region than in most parts of the United States.

SPORTS

All major league sports that are played in the United States have teams in the region – and so do most of the B- and C-List sports as well.

Baseball, played in the summer into the early autumn, is probably the most iconic in the region thanks to the Yankees. A team that divides sports fans, you either love 'em or you hate 'em. Mostly people hate them because they have so much money that they can buy all the best players, which means winning more World Series championships than any other team. That said, the Yankees are the pride and joy of New York and have received many a ticker-tape parade through downtown Manhattan's 'Canyon of Heroes.' Superstars of the game, like Babe Ruth and Mickey Mantle, have all worn the pinstripes.

Just as much love is given to the New York Mets, the perennial also-rans of New York sports teams. Having won just two World Series (with the last one being in 1986) the true New Yorker with a passion for baseball tends to prefer the Mets to the Yankees. A highlight of the baseball season is the 'Subway Series,' when the Mets face off against their hometown rivals, the Yankees.

One thing all New Yorkers can agree on is that they hate the Boston Red Sox.

Pennsylvania also has two baseball teams. The Philadelphia Phillies won one of their two World Series titles as recently as 2008 and can trace their history back to 1883 when they were founded as the 'Quakers.' The Pittsburgh Pirates play out of eastern Pennsylvania. They've managed to snag an impressive five championship titles, but not since 1979. Sigh.

Philadelphia is doing a bit better with one of its National Football League teams, the Pittsburgh Steelers. The Steelers won the Superbowl in 2008, their sixth win at the ultimate American sporting event.

Also playing out of Pennsylvania are the Philadelphia Eagles. Sadly, they haven't won the Superbowl since 1960.

New York State and New Jersey are serviced by both the New York Giants and the New York Jets. Strangely, despite the fact that these teams are identified as New York teams, they both play out of the New Meadowlands Stadium in East Rutherford, New Jersey. The only NFL team to play in New York State is the Buffalo Bills.

Finally, in terms of the 'big three' sports in American culture (sorry, Europeans, soccer doesn't count as one over here) there's basketball. The New York Knicks haven't been particularly noteworthy with regards to winning their games during recent years. More interestingly, they are one of only two teams in the NBA that are still in their original cities (the other is rival Boston Celtics). Begun in 1946, they were originally called the 'Knickerbockers.' Also in the area are the Philadelphia 76ers, a team that crossed the state border in 1963 from Syracuse, NY where they had been known as the Nationals.

In similar state-switching antics, the long-lamented New Jersey Nets are planning a switch back to New York, where they'll land in a brand-new Brooklyn arena. (At least that's the plan as of this writing – it's cross-state politics so anything can happen.)

New York also hosts a Grand Slam tennis event every August, the US Open, and even horse fans have things to enjoy at the Hamptons Classic.

The Yankees have won 27 World Series titles. The first was in 1923 and the most recent was 2009.

Baseball fans should make a pilgrimage to Montclair, NJ to see the Yogi Berra Museum (p245).

Baseball might be the national pastime, but the Superbowl is the most-watched event (sporting or otherwise) in the United States. Viewership can exceed over 100 million people.

THE MYSTERIES OF MICHAEL CHABON

One of the most appealing novelists writing today is Michael Chabon, who spent much of his youth in and around eastern Pennsylvania and attended both Carnegie-Mellon University and the University of Pittsburgh. His first novel, *The Mysteries of Pittsburgh,* was published when he was just 25 and was an immediate success. It follows a young man as he drifts through his summer alternately falling in love with a man and a woman.

His second major novel, the superb and moving *Wonder Boys,* paints a portrait of literary students and professors yearning to make human connections while struggling to write great books. Wickedly funny, we can't recommend this book enough.

Chabon shifted his focus to Jewish immigrants in New York and the comic-book industry with his Pulitzer Prize-winning *The Amazing Adventures of Kavalier & Clay.*

MULTICULTURALISM & RELIGION

This area of the United States supports a proud and long heritage of hosting and welcoming peoples from all over the world. Strong and prevalent faith-based communities leave their mark all over the place with churches, synagogues and temples as well as traditional cuisines, arts, performance and rituals. Though Christianity is the most prominent religion there are large congregations of Jews, Muslims and Buddhists, as well as everything else.

Many immigrant communities are still vibrantly intact, especially in the big cities, but proud heritages are represented everywhere by African-Americans, Latinos, Asians, and even the Irish.

ARTS

The story of art in the region is immense – and all three states have contributed in big ways. For instance, what would the world of soap operas be without New Jersey's own Kelly Ripa? Kidding aside, Pennsylvania can boast such luminaries as author James Michener and pop artist Andy Warhol. New Jersey has musical legends like rockers Bruce Springsteen and Bon Jovi. The fact of the matter, though, is that art is writ large across the sidewalks of New York. No history of art, movies, fashion, TV, architecture or theater would be complete without acknowledging the role of New York City. Its place as a laboratory for new ideas cannot be overstated.

Literature

Some of the great American literature has been written in and around the region. Gothic horror master Edgar Allen Poe lived for a time in Philadelphia before settling in New York City while working on such pieces as 'The Raven,' and 'The Pit and the Pendulum.' Speaking of gothic writers, Washington Irving turned the area around his Tarrytown estate on the Hudson River in upstate New York into the famed short story 'The Legend of Sleepy Hollow.'

New York natives Henry James and Edith Wharton wrote frequently about their hometown. Despite the fact that he lived most of his adult life in England, James penned *Washington Square* about an heiress who is possibly being taken advantage of by her better-looking suitor. Wharton's best known work is probably her examination of star-crossed lovers tossed amidst the waves of turn-of-the-century New York society in *The Age of Innocence.*

Arguably amongst the most famous poets to ever live, Walt Whitman was born on Long Island and spent the twilight years of his career writing in New Jersey. His *Leaves of Grass* is the most renowned collection of American poetry ever published.

As New York City became the center of the publishing industry, more and more writers and authors made there home there. An iconic group of

Irish author Colm Toibin meditates on the life of Henry James in his critically acclaimed novel *The Master.* Fans of his should also read his novel about mid-century New York titled *Brooklyn.*

poets, essayists and playwrights gathered around the Algonquin Round Table during the 1920s. Most recognized among them today is Dorothy Parker, whose humorous poems still resonate. She was joined by the likes of Robert Benchley, Edna Ferber, James Thurber and *New Yorker* founder Harold Ross.

Many authors, following in the traditions of Wharton and James, focused their prose on the city itself. Notable works include the JD Salinger masterpiece *The Catcher in the Rye;* Truman Capote's ode to prostitution and consumerism *Breakfast at Tiffany's;* Jay McInerney's cocaine-fueled second-person trip *Bright Lights, Big City;* Tamara Jankowitz's *Slaves of New York* about the 1980s art scene; and Jonathan Lethem's *Chronic City* which paints a portrait of a Manhattan that has gone slightly off the rails.

Cinema & Television

The movies began in New York. It is here that the first impresarios of the silver screen turned on their cameras to record the human condition. Early in the 20th century, most film production was shot in the east, before the industry packed up and left for sunny southern California. Despite this change of location, no city has been filmed more than New York. In particular, early Hollywood cinema was fascinated with the world of showgirls and making it on Broadway.

Film noir became big in the 1930s and '40s with such classics as *The Naked City* (1948) and *The Sweet Smell of Success* (1957). The 1950s saw Hitchcock turn his lens to the city, famously filming the Plaza Hotel's bars for *North by Northwest* (1959) and setting *Rear Window* (1954) in Greenwich Village. But it isn't until the 1970s that two of the filmmakers most associated with the

---

FILMS ABOUT NEW YORK YOU SHOULD SEE

There are more films about New York than just about anywhere in the world (save maybe Los Angeles). Even London and Paris pale in comparison. Maybe Bollywood has more about Mumbai, but we're not experts in Indian cinema, so who can say? Here are six really interesting films about the city that should not be missed:

- **The Sweet Smell of Success** (1957) Gossip columnists vie for power, love and the ultimate 'get. A film noir delight.

- **The Warriors** (1979) A campy, comic book spin on Homer's *Odyssey,* featuring a gang from Coney Island fighting their way back home after a disastrous turn of events in the Bronx. Myriad costumed gangs stalk them on the street as wild scenes are played out in the Union Square subway station, Central Park and, of course, the beach of Coney Island.

- **Working Girl** (1988) Melanie Griffith battles Sigourney Weaver for a place at the conference table in the canyons of Lower Manhattan. Along the way she falls in love with Harrison Ford and rides the Staten Island Ferry, all to the music of Carly Simon.

- **When Harry Met Sally** (1989) Woody Allen's style of urban romantic comedy gets an update from Nora Ephron and Rob Reiner in this film starring Billy Crystal and Meg Ryan. It gets bonus points for having the delectable Carrie Fisher in a supporting role. Ephron is a classic Upper West Sider. If you've seen this one, try *Heartburn,* in which Meryl Streep plays Ephron during her marriage to Carl Bernstein, one of the journalists who uncovered the Watergate scandal.

- **Arthur** (1981) Dudley Moore and the indefatigable Liza Minnelli play lovers caught between the moon and New York City. It's the best that they can do to fall in love. This class-based comedy comes with an Oscar-winning song by Christopher Cross.

- **The French Connection** (1971) Heroin and Gene Hackman prove a lethal mix in this action movie that sets a new standard for the genre in terms of gritty, abrasive realness.

Thomas Edison, inventor
of the motion picture,
developed it in his New
Jersey laboratory.

city began the work that would make them *auteurs* of the first order: Martin
Scorsese and Woody Allen.

Martin Scorsese is known primarily as a chronicler of the city's mean
streets. In fact, he named his first major film just that: *Mean Streets* (1973).
Coming out of NYU's young film school, Scorsese turned his back on the
overblown and fusty Hollywood narrative and instead took a close look at
the down-and-out residents of the city, those wallowing in or near the gut-
ters. But perhaps his most famous film about the city is *Taxi Driver* (1976),
which follows a loose-cannon cabbie (Robert De Niro) as he romances a girl
(the lovely Cybill Shepherd) and slowly loses his grasp on reality. The hal-
lucinatory scenes of a 1970s Times Square, matched with grim narration and
a moody, bluesy score probably captures the feeling of President Ford–era
New York City better than any other film.

Scorsese's also brought us the intriguing *New York, New York* (1977),
about the Jazz Age and starring De Niro and a nubile Liza Minnelli. (With
that film came the title song 'New York, New York' that is now the standard
city anthem about how if you can make it there you can make it anywhere.)
From there he has continued to move back in time, examining turn-of-the-
century New York society in *The Age of Innocence* (1993) and further back
even still with his portrait of the Lower East Side's dog days in *The Gangs of
New York* (2002). The splendid *Goodfellas* (1990), with its festive, party-like
view of a life in crime, is perhaps Scorsese's most famous film to deal with
the New York and New Jersey mob.

New York Stories
(1989) consists of three
vignettes directed by
Woody Allen, Martin
Scorsese, and Francis Ford
Coppola, who himself
made a rather famous
New York movie with *The
Godfather*.

On the other side of the tracks is Woody Allen. Born and raised in a
middle-class home in Brooklyn, the comic cut his teeth in the comedy clubs
of Greenwich Village, but made a name for himself documenting on screen
the romantic and intellectual ennui of a certain brand of Manhattanite.
Allen won an Oscar for *Annie Hall* (1977), a love letter to a lost lover. His
then-muse, Diane Keaton, won an Oscar for the role of Annie, in one of the
great comic performances in film history.

But any fan of Allen (attention French readers!) will no doubt thrill to
his other masterpieces like *Manhattan* (1979) and *Hannah and Her Sisters*
(1986). *Manhattan* again examines love among the bourgeoisie, this time with
haunting, delicate black and white cinematography and a stirring Gershwin
score. It should make any city-lover cry. *Hannah and Her Sisters* teases
out the hopes and dreams of its lovelorn characters, lost amid bookstores,
Thanksgivings and *Cats* auditions.

Seen all the super well-
known Allen and Scorsese
films? Then try Scorsese's
farce *The King of Comedy*
(1982) with De Niro,
Jerry Lewis and a young
Sandra Bernhard, or Al-
len's darkly comic *Crimes
and Misdemeanors* (1989)
with Sam Waterston
and Jerry Orbach in their
pre-*Law & Order* days.
Anjelica Huston ain't half
bad in that one either.

In the 1990s New York was home to several independent film studios
like Miramax. These heady days of money and cinema led to extraordinary
filmmaking. Its perhaps most relevantly on display in the work of Spike Lee,
whose *Do the Right Thing* (1989) is a rousing, technicolor ode to life on the
streets of Brooklyn. Kevin Smith, to a lesser extent, has mined the fields of
New Jersey in some indie gems like *Clerks* (1994). We'll let his *Jersey Girl*
(2004) speak for itself. (No we won't – it's terrible! Avoid.)

TV also began in New York City, with earliest broadcasts emanating from
towers atop its skyscrapers. Early shows that still carry historical weight like
Playhouse 90 and *The Tonight Show* were taped live from the studios of Midtown
Manhattan. Like the movies that came before, though, eventually much production headed west to California despite the fact that many shows of the golden
age of TV like *I Love Lucy* took place there. Several other iconic New York
shows were also taped in Los Angeles, including *Rhoda*, *Seinfeld* and *Friends*.

Law & Order was an important show for New York in that it was not only
shot in New York exclusively but it also helped rebuild the infrastructure to
support more TV production in New York. This trend perhaps reached its
zenith with six seasons of *Sex and the City* that completed the trend started

---

A FEW FILMS YOU SHOULD SEE ABOUT OTHER PLACES

Tired of all this talk about New York City? Yeah, so is everyone else who doesn't live there. With those Pennsylvania and New Jersey fans in mind, here are a handful of movies not about New York:

■ *Witness* (1985) Harrison Ford. Elijah Wood. Kelly McGillis. Need we go on? OK, fine. Han Solo plays a grizzled cop who can't seem to find the right woman. That is, he can't until a young Amish woman shows up in his precinct with her adorable son seeking refuge from nasty bad guys. He learns to love while raising barns and learning the simple life of Pennsylvania Mennonites. Great stuff, and there's action scenes with guns in between the scenes of crop harvesting and carriage rides!

■ *Atlantic City* (1980) French maestro Louis Malle (fun fact: he was married to Candice Bergen!) observes the lives of a New Jersey bar wench played by Susan Sarandon and her gambler paramour, played by an aging Burt Lancaster.

■ *Flashdance* (1983) Duh. Jennifer Beals is awesome as a 'steel town girl on Saturday night' who dances as good as she welds. Great music makes this wacky '80s movie a must.

■ *Rocky* (1976) Double duh! Sylvester Stallone's triumphant run up the stairs of the Philadelphia Museum of Art is the stuff of cinematic legend. This boxer with the whole lot of moxie did more for Philly's image than 'anyone since Ben Franklin,' said a local official.

■ *Wonder Boys* (2000) Based on the novel by Michael Chabon, this comedy of literary manners takes place at a Pennsylvania university and stars Michael Douglas, Frances McDormand, Tobey Maguire and Robert Downey Jr as a tranny-loving agent.

---

with *Law & Order* by presenting the city as a fantasy playground for in-the-know dames and their lovers.

Unlike movies, TV is much more likely to cast its sights on New Jersey and Pennsylvania. Long running daytime soap operas *All My Children* and *One Life to Live* both take place in fictional towns outside of Philadelphia. Cable has also turned its eye to the Keystone State with *It's Always Sunny in Philadelphia,* and *Queer as Folk,* that takes place in Pittsburgh (though admittedly it was filmed in Toronto).

New Jersey was most recently the locale for the critical success *The Sopranos* about a New Jersey mafia family. And out of due diligence, we'll mention the uproarious *Jersey Shore* reality show on MTV that follows the drinking lives of several young adults bent on making asses of themselves. This show no doubt makes the New Jersey tourist board cringe.

Fashion

Alongside Paris and Milan, New York is one of the most important fashion capitals in the world. Since its inception, New York was a primary marketplace for fashion in the United States due to its status as a port city. In the 1890s, the 'Gibson Girl' look became popular and began distinguishing the loose-fitting styles popular on these shores (especially in New York) from the stodgier, more formal, European designs.

During the mid-20th century, the 'Garment District' in Midtown Manhattan was a major source for textile manufacturing, and thriving businesses produced ready-to-wear clothing for the American consumer. Today, as more and more of that work heads to China or beyond, the district has become mostly a collection of button and fabric shops along with a few small operations still dedicated to producing high-quality clothes. A giant button, by the sculptor Claus Oldenburg, pays homage to the garment district on Seventh Ave and 39th St in Manhattan.

It wasn't until the 1970s that American designers began to play prominently on the international fashion scene. These included such names as

Halston, Perry Ellis, Bill Blass, Geoffrey Beene and Donna Karan. Later, as the decades wore on, designers such as Calvin Klein, Ralph Lauren, Tommy Hilfiger, and Marc Jacobs came to be the *enfants terribles* of the New York fashion world. Jacobs, still at the top of his game, is known for his classic American looks that have been worn by celebrities to the Oscars and to court (ahem, Winona Ryder).

Music

Halston, a king of 70s discotheque wear, was just as famous for hanging out at Studio 54 with his glamorous patrons as he was for his slinky designs.

The music of the region is as varied as the citizens within it. No one musical form can pegged as the ultimate local form, in the way that, say, jazz can be identified with New Orleans or country music with Nashville.

Classical music has long been a favorite, and New York City established itself as its national capital in the mid-19th century. The music of primarily European composers was played in the city's famous music halls, such as Carnegie Hall. However, in 1924, George Gershwin changed things forever with his classical/ragtime blend 'Rhapsody in Blue.'

Jazz and ragtime are the musical genres where local musicians began to play a large role not just in the performance, but in the conception. Ragtime is thought to trace its roots to the minstrel shows of the 1880s, but it didn't reach the masses until around 1896 when it was introduced in the vaudeville stages of the day. The form reached the zenith with Irving Berlin's 1911 hit *Alexander's Ragtime Band*, the most popular song of its day (and still darn catchy).

Jazz, on the other hand, has never left. Though not as central to the development of the form as Chicago or New Orleans, New York has long been integral to this style of music. Most early recordings were produced in

---

GREAT SONGS ABOUT NEW YORK, NEW JERSEY AND PENNSYLVANIA

Balladeers have spent many a refrain extolling the virtues of this region. Some of them are so famous (like 'New York, New York' by Frank Sinatra or 'New York State of Mind' by Billy Joel) that it seems silly to list them here. Here's a few we think you'll like that are a little bit more off-the-beaten-path:

- **Manhattan** Blossom Dearie
- **The Only Living Boy in New York** Simon & Garfunkel
- **Allentown** Billy Joel
- **Philadelphia Freedom** Elton John
- **Atlantic City** Bruce Springsteen
- **My Hometown** Bruce Springsteen
- **The Best That You Can Do (When You Get Caught Between the Moon and New York City)** Christopher Cross
- **Maniac** Hall & Oates
- **Brooklyn Owes the Charmer Under Me** Steely Dan
- **Back in the New York Groove** Ace Frehley
- **NYC** Interpol
- **America** Simon & Garfunkel
- **Autumn in New York** Billie Holiday
- **New York City Boy** The Pet Shop Boys
- **Chelsea Morning** Joni Mitchell
- **Chelsea Hotel £2** Leonard Cohen

the city, while legends of the form like Duke Ellington composed music for elaborate pseudo-African revues at the Cotton Club in Harlem. The Apollo Theater also has a role in this story, having 'discovered' Ella Fitzgerald at its famed amateur night in the 1930s. Billie Holiday was a leading proponent of the 'torch song,' a sad and melancholy ballad, during her engagement at Café Society in Sheridan Square in 1939.

Jazz clubs still abound in New York City, with sites like Arthur's Tavern (p110), Birdland (p110), the Village Vanguard (p110) and the Lincoln Center (p110) offering it up almost nightly.

Tin Pan Alley was a district in New York City that had a high concentration of composers and music publishers from the 1880s to the 1930s. Their work primarily played in Broadway theaters, which provided the main artery for popular music of the day to be introduced. Among the famed maestros working the alley were Irving Berlin, Jerome Kern, Fats Waller, George Gershwin, Cole Porter, Richard Rogers, Lorenz Hart and Oscar Hammerstein II. Most hit songs from the early 20th century (commonly referred to as the 'American Songbook') were written here, including 'Ain't Misbehavin'' and 'Give My Regards to Broadway.'

Rock 'n' Roll music also spent many of its early days in the wilds of New York. Rather than being located on Tin Pan Alley, these writers were mostly located in the Brill Building at 1619 Broadway in Manhattan. It was here that famed songwriters like Carole King, Neil Sedaka, Bobby Darin, Neil Diamond and Burt Bacharach got their starts. But as the Beatles and the British Invasion left a path of destruction across the pop charts, the music scene shifted to smaller clubs like Max's Kansas City and Electric Circus, where Lou Reed and the Velvet Underground sang about drug addiction and all tomorrow's parties. At the venerable CBGB-OMFUG (the abbreviation standing for Country, Bluegrass and Blues, and Other Music for Uplifting Gourmandizers) punk bands made names for themselves in one of New York's unique contributions to the rock scene. Acts like the New York Dolls, the Ramones, Patti Smith, Blondie and the Talking Heads all performed in the shady, seedy club.

It's not all New York when it comes to rock 'n' roll, though. New Jersey has made more than a few major contributions to the pantheon. Best known, perhaps, is Bruce Springsteen, son of Asbury Park. His yearning, plaintive songs evoke a hard-scrabble lifestyle common in a certain strain of 1970s and 1980s rock. One of his most famous albums is named *Greetings from Asbury Park, NJ*, after the town where he got his start. That scene (p220) still hums with emerging rockers to this day. Another major New Jersey act is Bon Jovi.

Rap and hip-hop are also important music scenes with roots in New York. Beginning in the 1970s at Harlem parties, DJs began using several turntables to mix and scratch recordings by the likes of James Brown and George Clinton. Though this mostly happened live, the music started drifting towards recorded tracks like Sugar Hill Gang's 'Rapper's Delight' and 'The Message' by Grandmaster Flash and the Furious Five. As the genre was embraced by white audiences along with its traditional African-American audience, major performers like LL Cool J, Big Daddy Kane, Run-DMC and Public Enemy became associated with New York City or 'East Coast rap.'

Architecture

Within the region is a grand collection of world-class architectural masterpieces, with special focus on practitioners of the modern. There is likely no better classroom than New York City, with its ever-evolving portrait of architectural style in which examples from the 1700s press their noses against the 21st century's latest conceits. Any student or admirer of architecture will thrill to see the examples of Federalist, Greek revival, Gothic, Beaux Arts,

The film *Manhattan* opens with majestic shots of the New York City skyline with 'Rhapsody in Blue' playing over the top.

Other famed practitioners of jazz who made New York their home base include Dizzy Gillespie, Benny Goodman, Miles Davis, and Charlie Parker.

Check out Lou Reed's complete album *New York* on which all the tracks are reflections on the city he calls home.

ARCHITECTURAL GEMS

Here are some top places (mostly in New York) to see if you like the building arts:

- **Grace Church** (p88) James Renwick Jr's gothic church on Broadway that predates his efforts on St Patrick's Cathedral
- **Whitney Museum of American Art** (p95) Marcel Breuer's brutalist cube sitting ominously over Madison Ave
- **Snug Harbor Cultural Center** (p102) This former home for 'aged and decrepit soldiers' is a playground of Greek Revival on Staten Island
- **Woolworth Building** (p85) Cass Gilbert's skyscraper masterpiece that presides over Lower Manhattan
- **Morgan Library** (p91) A Stanford White mansion topped with a Renzo Piano glass cube
- **Cooper Union** (p88) Boasts a brand-new Morphosis academic building in the East Village
- **Central Park** (p91) Let's not forget landscape architecture, with this bucolic Olmstead & Vaux classic

---

art deco, modernism, brutalism, postmodernism and just about any other architectural style you can think of. The city continues to evolve, with modern works by Renzo Piano, Frank Gehry and Morphosis erecting buildings at an impressive clip.

Several important architects of international renown have constructed their visions in New York City. However, most take a back seat to the enormous influence of the firm McKim, Mead & White, who built more churches, apartment buildings, mansions and museums than any other firm in the city, around the turn of the 20th century as part of the 'City Beautiful' movement. Its work remains prized among aesthetes and scores of public and private buildings are still visible in the city. McKim, Mead & White helped transform the city from brownstone to marble with their often Italian palazzi inspirations. Among some of its works still standing are the Morgan Library, the Brooklyn Museum of Art and the Metropolitan Museum of Art.

Many fans of architecture will also be familiar with Frank Lloyd Wright, whose graceful forms were revolutionary in his time. While he built the curvy, seductive Guggenheim Museum on Manhattan's Upper East Side, his more famous work is the serene and fantastic Fallingwater house in Eastern Pennsylvania.

Stanford White, the resident star of McKim, Mead & White, was shot dead by Harry K Thaw in 1905. Thaw suspected the architect of having an affair with his wife Evelyn Nesbit on the roof of the original Madison Square Garden, a building White designed. The movie *The Girl in the Red Velvet Swing* (1955) dramatizes the events.

Painting & Sculpture

You'd be hard pressed to find a region with more art on tap than there is here. The history of art is rich. Most major artists show in the major museums of the area, from Princeton, NJ to Philadelphia, PA.

Much of American art history takes place in the galleries of New York and the patronage of the New York social elite was vital to the evolution. The first major American art movement to be recognized and grouped in an academic fashion was the Hudson River School, which focused on romantic, idyllic still-lifes of the majestic, unvarnished countryside found in the Adirondacks, Catskills, and White Mountains. These painters included Thomas Cole, Asher B Durand, Jasper F Cropsey and Thomas Worthington Whittredge. However, this naturalist genre fell out of favor after the Civil War, as art students flocked to the more avant-garde styles of the European impressionists.

In the early 20th century, artists such as Georgia O'Keeffe, Edward Hopper and Alfred Steiglitz stormed onto the scene, all using New York City as their subject matter.

HUNGRY FOR SOME SOUP?

Of all the contemporary artists, perhaps none is better recognized for his flagrant disregard for the traditions of art than the mercurial Andy Warhol. Born in Pittsburgh, PA, he moved to New York and began working as a commercial illustrator. Gaining regard in this industry, he switched focus to the world of high art and started producing silkscreen prints of everyday objects such as dollar bills and Campbell's Soup cans. These began his prolific artistic journey that brought him through the 1980s, during which he painted hundreds of pictures of celebrities (Marilyn, Liz and Elvis come to mind) all the while promoting bands (the Velvet Underground), founding magazines (*Interview*) and attending discos (Studio 54).

The ultimate shrine to Andy Warhol (though he can be found in just about every museum of note) is the Andy Warhol Museum in Pittsburgh (p358), which boasts five floors crammed with his work, including his intriguing *Time Capsules*, which bring to mind the visceral life of the great artist.

In the aftermath of WWII, many artists from around the world made their way to the East Coast to settle. Here they created the form of Abstract Expressionism, which was often exhibited by members of the influential New York School in the 1940s and '50s. This movement was led by Jackson Pollock and Willem de Kooning, and included such notorious artists as Barnett Newman, Mark Rothko, Franz Kline, Lee Krasner and Adolph Gottleib.

Important work continues to be created in the area and there are several museums dedicated to it. American work is dealt with exclusively at the Whitney Museum of American Art (p95), that has an impressive collection of Edward Hopper among other things. You can also root out important local artists at the Museum of Modern Art (p91), the Philadelphia Museum of Art (p299), the Mattress Factory (p360) in Pittsburgh, Dia:Beacon (p132) in Beacon, NY, the Princeton Museum of Art (p252) in New Jersey and, of course, on Manhattan's Museum Mile (p95), which includes places like the Metropolitan Museum of Art and the Museum of the City of New York.

Theater

No performance art is more identified with New York than the theater, especially Broadway. It is here on the Great White Way that careers have been made and destroyed. Generally there are two major categories of theater: musicals and straight plays. Both have an illustrious history.

The golden age of the musical is linked to the era of Rodgers and Hammerstein (*South Pacific, Oklahoma, The King and I, Carousel, The Sound of Music*), though major shows from this era still play frequently in repertory include *Guys and Dolls, West Side Story, How to Succeed in Business Without Really Trying* and *Gypsy*. The major American composer of the late 20th century is Stephen Sondheim, whose musicals include *Follies, Company, A Little Night Music, Sweeney Todd: The Demon Barber of Fleet Street* and *Into the Woods*. In the 1980s, the British invaded, with shows like *The Phantom of the Opera* and *Les Miserables*. The success of these shows eventually led to blockbuster American shows, written by New York composers like Jonathan Larson's *Rent* and Stephen Schwartz's *Wicked*.

It is also in New York that great voices of the American theater found their voices. Among them are Edward Albee (*Who's Afraid of Virginia Woolf*), Tennessee Williams (*A Streetcar Named Desire*), Arthur Miller (*Death of a Salesman*), David Mamet (*Glengarry Glen Ross*), and John Guare (*Six Degrees of Separation*). Broadway and Off-Broadway continue to be fertile grounds for new playwrights. Go check them out!

You can visit the house that Pollock built, or cottage rather, in East Hampton, NY where his studio is kept intact, including paint splatters all over the floor, mimicking his drippy style.

See *Gold Diggers of 1933* (1933) or *42nd Street* (1933) for Hollywood's take on Broadway.

Food & Drink

Eating and drinking are taken very seriously here. In the taverns of Philadelphia the early dreams of America were mapped. Fortunes have been made and lost over a three-martini lunch at the chic Four Seasons. Careers have been launched and legendary reputations destroyed in seedy bars on the wrong side of town. If life in the region is a three-ring circus, dining and boozing occupy the center.

For the curious gastronomic traveler, this diverse section of the Northeast offers almost every possible variation on the word 'food' and 'drink'. The local culinary diet draws richly on the traditions inherited from the multitudes of immigrants who have traveled here over the past few centuries. New York Harbor has long been a gateway to America and the hordes of adventurers who have passed through have left their mark on the regional cuisine. While there are certain hometown favorites, no doubt, practically any ethnic cuisine – from first to third world – can be found lurking somewhere in New York, New Jersey and Pennsylvania.

Unsurprisingly, New York City (with apologies to *Rocky*-centric Philadelphia) is the heavyweight in the region. You can trace that back to **Delmonico's** (☎ 212-509-1144; www.delmonicosny.com; 56 Beaver St; mains $28-49; ☽ lunch & dinner), perhaps the first modern 'restaurant' (ie not a pub or tavern) to introduce the type of refined dining we take for granted now. Opened in Lower Manhattan in 1827, it went on to become the most famous eatery of the 19th Century. It was here that such famed dishes as the Lobster Newburg and baked Alaska were invented.

To this day, many of the world's greatest chefs sling hash in New York at some of the most highly acclaimed and exclusive eateries in existence. Recently the vaunted Michelin Guide began rating its restaurants and you'll be as delighted by the food at these top haunts as you are shocked by the high prices. But haute cuisine, while marvelous, is not the only option for the discerning eater. Just as New York is not the be all and end all of sophisticated dining (though it probably thinks it is), there are fine pleasures to be had at the Italian trattorias of New Jersey, the lobster shacks of Long Island, and the sizzling cheesesteak stands of Philadelphia.

STAPLES AND SPECIALTIES

New York would come to a stand still if its supply of bagels should ever be cut off. Truly a staple of the native diet, the bagel can be found in nearly every bodega, deli, supermarket, and sidewalk breakfast cart. Its provenance is a bit murky, but it's most certainly associated with the large Jewish population that calls the area home. Traditionally served with cream cheese and lox, there are literally hundreds of variations on the schmear, with everything from scallions to raisins to peppers mixed in. For our money we recommend heading uptown to the bagel's spiritual homeland on the city's Upper West Side.

Another staple of the New Yorker's diet is pizza. Originally a mainstay of Italy's poorer people, the doughy, cheesy slice can be found all over the region. Deciding who exactly has the best pizza in New York is often a contentious issue and every person you ask will have a different opinion; we recommend checking out the pies at the marvelous World Pie (p126) in Bridgehampton, NY.

Before we wrap up New York City, we must also mention the ubiquitous hot dog. Yes, lots of people eat their dogs right on the street bought from vendors with those iconic carts, but we frankly prefer the non-boiled kind

Delmonico's still exists in downtown Manhattan, but for our money, we'd prefer to go to Peter Luger Steakhouse (p122), another relic of an earlier era.

To dine at a Michelin-starred restaurant, try Blue Hill (p107) and the Spotted Pig (p107) in NYC.

of dog. Connoisseurs will not want to miss Coney Island Lunch (p380), a hot dog cafe in, yes, Coney Island; ask about the annual hot dog–eating contest on the Fourth of July. We also recommend the marvelously gourmet Bark (p107) in Park Slope, Brooklyn.

There's also, of course, New York strip steak and Manhattan clam chowder. But do these really count? Sure, why not? So does New York cheesecake. More specifically, the buffalo wing – spicy chicken wings covered in a chili sauce and served with ranch dressing and celery – is in fact native to Buffalo, NY.

There is quite a bit of farming on the eastern part of Long Island, as is the case in upstate New York where several farms provide the fresh produce that arrives in the city where the 'slow food' movement has taken hold. You can't beat the selection that arrives almost daily at New York's farmers markets. There's tons of them, from Montauk to Rochester, but the most famous might be the Union Square Greenmarket (p90) in downtown Manhattan.

Those interested in visiting an actual farm should not miss the tony Blue Hill at Stone Barns (p107) in Westchester. Here super chef Dan Barber grows and raises just about everything that goes into his legendary farm-fresh meals. Take a quick look around the farm and then settle in for the night's tasting menu at the precious restaurant. Reservations go quickly, so make sure to book in advance. If you're stuck in New York and can't make the train to go upstate, you should get a table at Blue Hill (p107), his Greenwich Village outpost that also serves the bounty of the Westchester farm.

Out on Long Island things get a bit fishy. And by fishy, we mean they serve great seafood. The lobster shacks along the highway to Montauk (p125) serve up your classic Northeastern fare.

PENNSYLVANIA DUTCH SHOOFLY PIE RECIPE

A staple of tables around Intercourse, PA, shoofly pie is a delicious treat. Here's a recipe adapted from the divine Martha Stewart whom we trust in all matters of baking.

- Pie dough
- 1 cup all purpose flour
- ½ cup packed brown sugar
- 1 teaspoon ground cinnamon
- ½ teaspoon freshly grated nutmeg
- salt
- 6 tablespoons cold unsalted butter, cut into ½-inch pieces
- 1 cup boiling water
- ½ cup unsulfered molasses
- ½ cup light corn syrup
- 1 teaspoon baking soda
- 1 large egg, lightly beaten

Directions
1. Roll out the dough on a lightly floured surface until its about 1/8 inch thick. Fit the dough into a 9-inch pie plate and let it rest for at least half an hour.
2. Preheat the oven to 325°F. Whisk together flour, brown sugar, cinnamon, nutmeg, and ¼ teaspoon salt in a medium bowl. Add butter, and work mixture through your fingers until it forms fine crumbs. Set crumb topping aside.
3. Stir together boiling water, molasses, and corn syrup in a medium bowl. Whisk in baking soda, egg, and a pinch of salt. Pour molasses mixture into the pie shell and scatter the crumb topping over the filling. Place the pie on a rimmed baking sheet. Bake about 50 minutes until filling is set and the topping is a deep golden brown. Let cool for at least 30 minutes before serving.

But it's not all New York, right? Heading into Pennsylvania should give you a few other opportunities to sample the local cuisine. In Philadelphia, you really can't say you've had a complete trip if you haven't wolfed down a delicious Philadelphia Cheesesteak. Roast beef is smothered in onions, peppers, and cheez whiz. Yes, you read that correctly. Gourmands may want to switch out for some provolone, but an authentic cheesesteak is always – ALWAYS – topped with that delicious yellowy-orange goop known as cheez whiz. Hey, we didn't make the rules – we're just reporting fact.

Over in Pittsburgh you should probably make sure to try something on which you can smear delicious Heinz ketchup, the hometown condiment.

Pennsylvania is also known for its pretzels and legend has it the best can be found in Pennsylvania Dutch Country. While you're there, try some of their apple dumplings or, even better, their shoofly pie, a tart filled with molasses and brown sugar.

Any serious resident of New Jersey will no doubt be a proud eater of hoagies and visitors will want to get their hands around a hefty submarine sandwich piled high with Italian meats and cheeses.

DRINKING

Drinking is everyone's favorite pastime be it St Patrick's Day, Gay Pride, Cinco de Mayo, Easter, Christmas, a Tuesday evening, a Thursday afternoon, or a Sunday morning.

It has a long history in the area, dating back to at least 1641 and the Stadt Herbergh of New Amsterdam. So popular was this drinking hall that it became the actual Town Hall of the fledgling colony. At one point in fact in the mid-17th century, 25% of all the city's establishments sold alcohol. The percentage has gone down in the intervening centuries, but not by much.

Like everything else in this part of America, the story of drinking is a story of immigrants. The English, when they took control of the colony and renamed it New York, brought with them the notion of the tavern. Usually centered around a large hearth, food was prepared along with generous servings of ale (often safer to drink than the water).

The Bloody Mary was introduced to Americans in New York at the King Cole Bar (p109) where its called the Red Snapper.

As immigrants poured in and the Germans brought their beer halls and the Irish their saloons, these remained the central meeting places just as they had been in the early Dutch days. For most of this time, women were not allowed in any of these establishments, though this began to erode during the egalitarian days of prohibition. By 1960, most bars were co-ed, but McSorley's Old Ale House (p108) in Manhattan's Lower East Side remained resolutely men only until 1970, proudly advertising their bar with the slogan 'good ale, raw onions, and no ladies.' If only the barkeeps at McSorley's knew that just a few years later gay bars would pop up nearby and reinstate their own unofficial 'no ladies' policies.

TV OPTIONS FOR THE FOODIE

Several famous chefs broadcast TV shows out of the region. Options include:

- **The Martha Stewart Show** The domestic doyenne tapes her daily talk show in Chelsea. You can request free tickets at http://www.marthastewart.com/get-tickets. We had a great time when we went and can say with confidence 'It's a good thing.'

- **The Barefoot Contessa** Ina Garten cooks rustic meals in her gracious East Hampton home. Airs frequently on the Food Network.

- **Simply Homemade** Say what you will about Sandra Lee, but she likes to drink and is coupled with Andrew Cuomo, scion of one of New York's most prestigious political families. So check her out. She also airs on the Food Network.

- **Cake Boss** This popular show follows the extreme cake making of a New Jersey baker boss.

The Long Island iced tea has a dubious reputation and is more likely to be found in the beach bars of New Jersey than in any reputable Long Island establishment. Basically it combines every liquor you can think of along with a splash of cola. Guaranteed to turn you green, it's a quick and cheap way to a big buzz, but don't blame us if you end up worshipping the porcelain goddess after downing a couple.

Though Californian and European wines take up the most room on local wine lists, the wineries of the Finger Lakes (p192) in Upstate New York make great whites especially. There are also several microbreweries throughout the region, one of the most popular being the Brooklyn Brewery. You can find their beers in most bars in the New York City metro area as well as beyond.

Coffee, not tea, is the primary caffeinated beverage of choice. There are several places to get a good cup of joe, and most of these places will also sell tea. Try Joe (p108) or Grounded Organic Coffee & Tea House (p108) in Greenwich Village. High tea can be found in several places, usually fancy hotels. One choice is the gracious drawing room of Lady Mendl's Tea Salon (p108).

CULINARY CALENDAR & FOOD FESTIVALS

MARCH
Pennsylvania Maple Festival (www.pamaplefestival.com) The last couple of weekends of March are time for Meyersdale, PA to celebrate all things maple and crown the Maple Queen. The promise of a real, live Maple Queen alone should be reason enough to check this out.

MAY
James Beard Foundation Awards (www.jbfawards.com) The Oscars for chefs, this is the event to catch culinary masters and rising stars of the food trade. The public can attend both the awards and a variety of events held around it in early May. It all comes at a price, though. This is Manhattan after all.

Pittsburgh Wine Festival (www.pittsburghwinefestival.com) Scores of vineyards are represented at this serious wine fest with VIP Grand Tasting events and even private dinners. Look for it in May.

NJ State Chili & Salsa Cook Off (www.downtowntomsriver.com) Tom's River, NJ offers up lots of chili in May. Yes, there is a competition for best chili. Enter if you think you can hack it.

Greek Festival (www.stathanasiosnj.org) St Athanasios Greek Orthodox Church has been celebrating souvlaki, baklava, and more for over 35 years in Paramus, NJ. The dancing and music are usually mid-May.

Rhubarb Festival (www.kitchenkettle.com) The third Friday and Saturday of May brings rhubarb mania to Intercourse, PA. There's a rhubarb derby, a rhubarb dessert contest, and a million different ways to consume ... RHUBARB!

JUNE
Big Apple Barbecue Block Party (www.bigapplebbq.com) Madison Square in Manhattan turns itself over to the country's greatest pitmasters for this weekend-long party that has music, booze, and is usually VERY well-attended. The party usually rages in mid-June.

JULY
Blueberry Festival (www.historicbethlehem.org) Mid-July is the time to get that blueberry craving taken care of in Bethlehem, PA. A horse-drawn carousel and colonial games make this especially fun for kids who probably weren't going to be very impressed by that wine festival you were eyeing anyway.

Finger Lakes Wine Festival (www.flwinefest.com) Wine and gourmet food in Watkins Glen in upstate New York. In July.

Italian Heritage Festival (www.buffaloitalianfestival.com) In July, Buffalo, NY hosts what it calls the 'second largest Italian Street Festival in the country.' No word on what the largest

Those with a taste for old-timey drinking haunts should try two of New York's oldest bars, Julius (p88) and the Ear Inn (p108).

Sometimes a person just wants a civilized cocktail. Try the Manhattan, made with bourbon and sweet vermouth. It usually comes adorned with a cherry.

is – but we'll hazard a guess and suggest it's the San Gennaro festival (p86) in New York's Little Italy.

Atlantic City Food & Wine Festival (www.gourmetshows.com) Take a break from the slots and check out this gourmet show with everything for your kitchen. Late July.

SEPTEMBER
Pocono Garlic Festival (www.poconogarlic.com) Shawnee, PA hosts this ode to the stinking rose in early September.

Hudson Valley Wine & Food Fest (www.hudsonvalleywinefest.com) Each September, on the weekend after Labor Day, the Dutchess County Fairgrounds in Rhinebeck, NY gets all artisan about their food. As if they weren't already.

WHERE TO EAT & DRINK
Due to the region's population density, there will never be a shortage of places to grab a bite or a cocktail so long as you aren't camping in the middle of nowhere.

Almost every town will have a diner that likely serves breakfast all day along with an assortment of hamburgers, salads, and sandwiches. These tend to be the most cost-effective options. Towns that cater to a tourist industry will invariably also offer at least one upscale restaurant with a more adventurous menu.

Urban areas, obviously, have a much wider selection of eateries. Most cities are packed with fancy restaurants, cozy coffee shops, simple sandwich joints and eclectic ethnic eateries. New York, the Hamptons, Philadelphia and Pittsburgh are all known for their vibrant culinary scenes.

Try reading Nora Ephron's autobiographical *Heartburn* about the love life of a New York foodie. Comes with recipes!

Most restaurants are open for lunch from about 11:30am until 2:30pm, and for dinner from 5pm until 9pm or 10pm (later on weekends, especially in urban areas). Some places might serve breakfast from about 7am until 10am. On weekends, most restaurants serve brunch, while there is lots of variation, this guide will list specific opening hours only when they deviate drastically from the norm.

As for costs, breakfast will run $5 to $15 depending on whether you are at a diner or a culinary hot spot. Lunch tends to be in the same range. A satisfying dinner in a pleasant, not-too-fancy restaurant costs $15 to $25 per person, not including tax, tip, or drinks. In large cities and upscale resorts, it is not unusual to see a bill of $50 to $75 per person, especially if cocktails or wine are consumed.

VEGETARIANS & VEGANS
Many restaurants offer vegetarian options and do so with panache. Of course, it is easier to find vegetarian entrees in cosmopolitan areas than in tiny towns, but, usually, even at the local diner you can find something healthy and meat-free. Natural food markets are popping up all over. Special effort has been made in this guide to highlight restaurants with exceptional vegetarian options.

Connoisseurs of the raw food movement should make a special effort to dine at the fanciest vegetarian place we've ever seen – Pure Food & Wine (p107) near Manhattan's Gramercy Park.

EATING WITH KIDS
Everyone gets cranky when they are hungry, especially children. They are welcome in most midrange establishments, but we'd think twice before bringing them along to the upper echelon of dining options. Each section of this book includes specific advice for traveling with children in the area and offers places that are particularly kid-friendly. If you are traveling through New York City, we can't recommend Serendipity 3 (p102) on the Upper East Side enough. Your offspring will thank you forever after you order them the frozen hot chocolate.

HABITS & CUSTOMS

The duration of meals, table manners, and etiquette change with different dining situations but here are a few tips. In fast-food restaurants you are expected to clear your own tray. Meals at midrange to top end eateries require a 15% to 20% tip for your server. Do not forget to tip! A visit to a fine restaurant will take about 1½ to two hours from start to finish, depending on the number of courses you order. Smoking is forbidden in most restaurants. If you are having dinner with an American family at their home, it is polite to bring a bottle of wine or something to share.

EAT YOUR WORDS

A guide to some of the local parlance when it comes to dining.

heroes	submarine sandwich in New York
grinders	submarine sandwich in New Jersey
hoagies	submarine sandwich in Pennsylvania
scrapple	Pennsylvania dish of cornmeal and meat fried together
pie	a complete pizza
slice	a portion of pizza
half & half	a very light cream, typically used in coffee
brunch	a meal, often served on weekends, that is breakfast-oriented but served in the afternoon.
mimosa	a classic brunch cocktail of champagne and orange juice
bellini	a variation on the mimosa, this time champagne and peach puree
joe	coffee

When ordering coffee:

black	no sugar, no cream
light	cream only
regular	cream and sugar
sweet	sugar only

Don't forget to tip your waiter. This happens more often than you would think and is considered terribly gauche. Don't be that person whom all the servers talk bad about once you leave.

Environment

THE LAND

Geographically, this three-state region is an interplay of mountain ranges, plateaus and plains. Broadly defined, all the mountains form part of the ancient Appalachians, a tremendous complex of ranges paralleling the eastern seaboard.

Once they reached the Rocky Mountains, America's pioneers must have looked back with amusement at these modest ridges, once considered a barrier to westward expansion. The region's highest peak – Mt Marcy, at 5344ft – is in upstate New York's Adirondacks – mountains so far north they are also considered part of the Canadian Shield. Meanwhile, Pennsylvania's highest point is 3213ft Mt Davis, in its southwest corner, and New Jersey tops out at 1803ft, at High Point in the Kittatinny Mountains along the Delaware River. Filed down by Ice Age glaciers, this region is as gently wrinkled as an old washboard.

Between the ranges are wide fertile plateaus, where original deciduous forests were felled for timber and agriculture. The enormous Appalachian Plateau extends southwest of the Adirondacks to include the Catskills, the Allegheny Mountains in Pennsylvania and the shores of Lake Erie and Lake Ontario.

Next, and parallel, is the Appalachian Ridge and Valley Province, a long narrow strip running from Canada to Alabama. This lies across the northwestern edge of New Jersey and southeastern Pennsylvania (and includes Pennsylvania's anthracite coal region); this is where the region's section of the Appalachian Trail passes. The northern end of the Blue Ridge Mountains also poke into the southern portion of Pennsylvania (and include Gettysburg).

South and still parallel, the Piedmont Plateau constitutes rich lowlands that are responsible for northern Jersey's famous 'gardens' and Pennsylvania Dutch Country farms, and includes that once-bucolic isle, Manhattan.

Finally, the rolling hills subside and give way to the unrelentingly flat Atlantic Coastal Plain, another epic geographical region that covers the bottom half of New Jersey (plus Long Island and a small portion of Pennsylvania) and continues to Texas. This is epitomized by New Jersey's coastal wetlands and the sandy, soggy interior forests of the Pine Barrens, creating an ecological transition zone that supports great biodiversity.

Yet for all this complex topography, water is perhaps the region's most dramatic and defining element. First, the region's major cities all lie along important rivers, which were the nation's highways before it had highways (and before it was a nation): Manhattan at the mouth of the Hudson River, Philadelphia on the Delaware River, and Pittsburgh in the Ohio River Valley, at the confluence of the Ohio, Allegheny and Monongahela Rivers.

New York State abuts two of the Great Lakes – Erie and Ontario – which are linked by the region's most iconic natural wonder, Niagara Falls. New Jersey and Long Island, meanwhile, face the Atlantic Ocean, and draw much of their wealth and personality from the sea.

Further, thanks to the scouring paws of those continental ice sheets 10,000 years ago, the region's irregular washboard cups thousands of lakes and is threaded by countless rivers and rivulets. New York's Finger Lakes and Lake Champlain are the biggest, and the Adirondacks are the source for five river systems. Pennsylvania also dips its toe into Lake Erie and its center is drained by the mighty Susquehanna River system. New Jersey, a peninsula surrounded by water, is so covered in lakes and humid wetlands (about 20% of the state) it could pass for the Northeast's answer to Florida.

Imagine reverse-engineering Manhattan to see it like Henry Hudson did in 1609. Now flash-forward: what will the city be like in 2409? Amazingly, Eric Sanderson presents both in *Mannahatta* (2009), a stunning feat of natural history.

In the documentary *Swim for the River* (2006), Tom Weidlinger does something no one should do: swims the 315-mile length of the Hudson River. It's his personal crusade to raise ecological awareness, but – yuck!

WILDLIFE

This region's forests and animals provided much of the food, fuel and wealth that drove the continent's original settlement, and eventually the founding of America. It is now one of the most altered landscapes in the US. Long before America figured out that it's natural wealth had limits, it had already spent its down payment in the Northeast.

Animals

Before the arrival of Europeans, the region boasted many of the continent's legendary species: black bear, herds of bison and elk, packs of wolves, bald eagles and stealthy panthers. And, of course, too many beaver to count.

All were hunted and driven from the region, with minor exceptions, by the end of the 19th century, but with the return of second-growth forests, elk have been successfully reintroduced in Pennsylvania, and black bears have returned in enough numbers to cause occasional conflicts in area suburbs. In the Adirondacks, moose are wandering down from Canada again. Smaller mammals remain the most common: raccoon, beaver, skunks, bobcats, fox and coyotes. White-tailed deer are everywhere and so numerous they are considered a pest.

The region's rivers and lakes support a huge variety of fish, such as black bass, catfish, walleyed pike, pickerel, salmon, trout, muskellunge, shad and whitefish. The ocean still supports major commercial fisheries, as well as sportfishing, with bluefish, marlin, tuna and flounder, as well as crabs, clams, scallops and oysters.

However, migratory birds are the region's wildlife highlight. Migrating raptors use the updrafts and topography of the Appalachian Ridge and Valley terrain as an interstate, and waterfowl flock to the coast's wetlands and barrier islands. After the low point of the 1970s, when hunting and environmental pollution threatened many birds of prey with extinction, raptors like bald eagles, osprey, peregrine falcons, turkey vultures and hawks again fill skies in fall and nest in the region.

Migrating herons, egrets, geese, ducks and other waterfowl make New Jersey a birding mecca, particularly for such strange, seasonal events as flocks of shorebirds feasting on horseshoe crab eggs along the Delaware Bay shoreline. For more, see Wildlife-Watching (p72).

Meanwhile, year-round avian residents include numerous songbirds, such as orioles, bluebirds, cardinals, goldfinches and eastern meadowlarks, plus owls and woodpeckers. Also more abundant recently is the wild turkey, once so ubiquitous that Ben Franklin wanted it to be the national bird. Thankfully, he lost that vote.

Plants

The Northeast was originally one endless, complex deciduous forest that mixed with evergreens in the mountains and other places. The five main eastern forest types – spruce, fir, hemlock, pine-oak, and northern and cove

DID YOU KNOW?
A third of the public transportation trips in the US each year are made in NYC, which is a leader in urban planning and green buildings.

The Audubon Society (www.audubon.org), a national birding and habitat conservation organization, has very active chapters in all three states, with birding guides and events calendars.

WORLD HERITAGE SITES & BIOSPHERE RESERVES

In this region, Unesco has recognized two World Heritage Sites for their international cultural significance: Philadelphia's Independence Hall (p285) and New York's Statue of Liberty (p84).

These states also contain two Unesco-designated Biosphere Reserves: the Champlain-Adirondack region in New York, and New Jersey's Pinelands (p261). Biosphere Reserves recognize significant conservation efforts and sustainable development.

For more information on these designations and sites, visit www.unesco.org and whs.unesco.org.

hardwood – included over 130 species of trees. Through the 18th and 19th centuries, virtually all these 'old-growth' forests were cleared for farmland and used for lumber and charcoal. Large patches of old-growth forest remain in Pennsylvania's Cook Forest State Park (p392) and in New York's Adirondack Park (p166), which shelters the largest intact deciduous forest in the world (and is the largest US park outside of Alaska).

In the 20th century, preservation and reforestation have successfully increased the amount of second-growth forest, so much so that over half of New York and Pennsylvania and over 40% of New Jersey are again covered in shaggy woods, whose autumn colors inspire leaf-peeping pilgrimages. Northern broad-leaved hardwoods dominate, particularly beech and sugar maple, but there are also ash, birch, cherry, hickory, red maple, walnut and oak. Some forests, especially along the Atlantic coast, are made up chiefly of softwood conifers such as cedar, fir, hemlock, spruce and white and yellow pine.

Spring wildflowers also put on a show, and include the azalea, black-eyed Susan, daisy, buttercup, honeysuckle, mountain laurel, orchid and violet; dogwood trees are also common.

New Jersey's Pine Barrens, a Unesco-designated Biosphere Reserve, is a unique environment of wetlands and sand, where pitch pines rely on fire to reproduce and pygmy pines struggle to reach 8ft. This rich ecosystem has perhaps 800 plant species, including over 30 types of wild orchids and a number of carnivorous plants, plus blood-red cranberry bogs in fall.

Also notable, the Sunken Forest on Fire Island is a rare maritime holly forest. Stands of holly, sassafras and serviceberry – with some vine-draped specimens over 300 years old – are misshapen by constant sea spray and unable to grow taller than 25ft, or the height of the protecting dunes.

DID YOU KNOW?

The aquifer beneath Jersey's Pine Barrens is the largest in the northeast. It holds 17 trillion gallons of water, which is enough to cover the state in a lake 10ft deep.

NATIONAL & STATE PARKS

Though they contain several of America's blockbuster national historical parks and national monuments, New York, New Jersey and Pennsylvania contain no national parks. However, they do contain a range of other mixed-use federal lands. For camping and recreation information on all federal lands, visit **Recreation.gov** (www.recreation.gov).

The region has two national recreation areas (NRA), which are managed by the **National Park Service** (NPS; www.nps.org). Gateway NRA includes three units in the New York/New Jersey Estuary: in Brooklyn's Jamaica Bay, on Staten Island, and on Sandy Hook in New Jersey. On the Pennsylvania/New Jersey border, the Delaware Water Gap NRA covers the Delaware River as it winds through the Kittatinny Ridge.

Also managed by the NPS are Fire Island National Seashore (on Long Island's barrier islands), and in New Jersey, the Pinelands National Reserve (Pine Barrens), though NJ state parks provide the main public access.

About 390 of the 2175 miles of the Appalachian National Scenic Trail wander through these three states. The Appalachian Trail, or AT, is a unit of the National Park Service, but management is a complex enterprise; for details, see the Outdoors chapter (p66).

Between them, the three states contain 17 national wildlife refuges (NWR), which are managed by the **US Fish & Wildlife Service** (USFWS; www.fws.gov/refuges) to preserve wildlife habitat and ecosystems. As the mandate implies, these are often excellent places for bird- and wildlife-watching (see p72).

There are two national forests, which are administered by the **US Forest Service** (USFS; www.fs.fed.us). The large, 797-sq-mile Allegheny National Forest, which borders New York's Allegheny State Forest, and the much smaller Finger Lakes National Forest in central New York.

NEW YORK, NEW JERSEY & PENNSYLVANIA'S TOP 15 NATURAL AREAS

Natural area	Features	Activities	Visit	Page
New York				
Adirondack Park, High Peaks	towering forested mountains, lakes, rivers, Olympic Center	hiking, skiing, canoeing, biking, rock climbing	year-round	p166
Catskills Park	forested mountains, trout-filled rivers, Kaaterskill Falls	hiking, skiing, fishing	year-round	p143
Finger Lakes	gorges, waterfalls, 11 long lakes, wineries	hiking, biking, canoeing, cross-country skiing	year-round	p186
Fire Island National Seashore	sandy beaches, Sunken Forest, protected barrier island ecology	swimming, hiking, bird-watching	May-Oct	p128
Hudson River Valley	historic, beautiful river, myriad parks	hiking, biking, rock climbing, cross-country skiing	year-round	p130
Niagara Falls	two waterfalls stretch a combined 3600ft wide	gaping wonderment, boat tours	year-round	p204
New Jersey				
Cape May Point State Park	white sand beaches, nature trails, dolphins offshore, migratory seabirds	wildlife-watching, hiking, sunbathing	Apr-Nov	p275
Island Beach State Park	white sand beaches, preserved barrier island ecosystem	swimming, hiking, fishing, wildlife-watching	May-Oct	p230
Pinelands National Preserve (Pine Barrens)	preserved wetlands, pygmy pine forests, swimming lakes	hiking, camping, canoeing, swimming	May-Oct	p261
Sandy Hook	miles of sand, nude beach, historic fort	swimming, biking, hiking, wildlife-watching	May-Oct	p213
Pennsylvania				
Allegheny National Forest	old-growth forests, preserved wilderness, lakes & rivers	hiking, canoeing, fishing, camping	Apr-Oct	p391
Delaware Water Gap	lazy wide river, Appalachian Trail, sandy beaches	canoeing, rafting, hiking, swimming, fishing	May-Oct	p398
Ohiopyle State Park	Youghiogheny River Gorge, forested mountains	whitewater rafting, hiking, cross-country skiing	May-Sep	p374
The Poconos	forested mountains, lakes, ski resorts	skiing, hiking, mountain biking, canoeing	year-round	p397
Presque Isle State Park	peninsula in Lake Erie, bird sanctuary	bird-watching, hiking, swimming, sailing	May-Oct	p381

Of the nation's 756 federally designated wilderness areas, this region has five. All are within other national forests or national wildlife refuges, such as New Jersey's Great Swamp NWR and Pennsylvania's Allegheny National Forest. For more information, visit **Wilderness.net** (www.wilderness.net).

While these federal lands have much to recommend them, many of the region's natural highlights and most exciting recreational excursions are contained within state parks and forests, of which the region boasts over 325. These include Niagara Falls, the Catskills and the Adirondacks in New York, New Jersey's Island Beach State Park and its portion of the Appalachian Trail, and Pennsylvania's Pocono Mountains and Ohiopyle and Presque Isle State Parks.

The Nature Conservancy helps to preserve habitat. Its website (www.nature.org) has overviews of landscapes and wildlife where it works.

However, a note of caution: due to tough fiscal times and budget cuts, the state park systems in both New York and New Jersey have been threatened with widespread closures in recent years. None of these have yet come to pass, but be aware that unexpected closures remain a possibility.

For information, see the following state agencies:

New Jersey Division of Parks and Forestry (☎ 609-984-0370, 800-843-6420; www.njparksandforests.org)

New York Department of Environmental Conservation (☎ 518-402-8000; www.dec.ny.gov) For the Catskills and Adirondacks.

New York State Office of Parks, Recreation & Historic Preservation (☎ 518-474-0456; http://nysparks.state.ny.us/parks)

Pennsylvania Department of Conservation and Natural Resources (☎ 888-727-2757; www.dcnr.state.pa.us/stateparks)

Wondering about those 'No Fracking Way!' signs in upstate New York? The Shaleshock Action Alliance (www.shaleshock.org) is seeking to limit gas drilling (known as 'fracking') in the Finger Lakes region.

For a list of the region's best parks, see p63.

ENVIRONMENTAL ISSUES

Where do you start in a region with by far the highest number of Superfund hazardous waste sites in the country? One whose dubious legacy includes landscapes so toxic they inspired the USA's modern environmental movement? The short story: there is an ecological price to pay for being one of the coal-black manufacturing hearts of the Industrial Revolution and then growing into the most populated, urbanized region in America.

Given this, it's notable that forest preservation in New York began as early as 1894, when the state added the 'forever wild' clause to its constitution to protect the Adirondacks and Catskills from rampant logging. This preceded the founding of the National Park Service by over a decade.

However, for the majority of the 20th century, it's been a very different tale. Pennsylvania coal mining and oil drilling, and manufacturing in Pittsburgh, Philadelphia, New York City and New Jersey, polluted waterways, fouled the air and created toxic industrial landfills. Things only got worse by midcentury as the region's manufacturing died, leaving behind abandoned factories and poisoned environments.

Pittsburgh is now a leader in green building. The Pittsburgh Greenstory (www.pittsburghgreenstory.org) tells the city's surreal story of pollution and rehabilitation.

As America's environmental awareness and attempts at preservation rose in the 1960s and 1970s – spurred in large part by Pennsylvania-native Rachel Carson's book *Silent Spring* (see the boxed text) – the region began to take stock and repair the damage. Skip forward to today, and the progress and restoration of nature is remarkable, at times stunning, though as everyone is quick to add, much more needs to be done.

For instance, what about those Superfund sites? In fact, the creation of the federal Superfund agency itself was a response to New York's infamous 1978 Love Canal disaster – when a Niagara Falls neighborhood, built over a chemical waste dump, caused such high rates of cancer and birth defects it led to the first federal health emergency. The Superfund is designed to clean up the nation's worst pollution sites that endanger human health. In 1981, 114 'national priority' sites were identified: 12 in New Jersey, and eight each in New York and Pennsylvania. In 2010, New Jersey could boast of having 111 Superfund sites, the most in the nation. Pennsylvania was second with 95, and New York fourth with 86 (California had 94). That's bad. Yet between them, the three states have also cleaned up and had delisted over 80 sites, equal to two-thirds of the original national list. So there's progress.

By the 1960s, the Hudson River was described as an 'open sewer,' a flowing dump for raw sewage and untreated chemical waste, and this helped spur the national environmental movement. A 1970s fight over a proposed new utility plant along the river led to the requirement that major projects using

CANARY IN A COAL MINE

In the 1950s, birds were dying, and not just a few. In some towns all the birds would, seemingly overnight, be gone. People were falling sick in unexplained ways; bees would disappear, and unpollinated fruit trees withered. As Rachel Carson wrote, 'Everywhere was a shadow of death.'

A marine biologist, Carson was not the first to notice the effects of chemicals on nature, but she was the first to focus on the problem and get everyone's attention. Carson came from the small town of Springdale, just northeast of Pittsburgh, a steel-and-coal city once called 'hell with the lid taken off.' After four years of work, Carson published *Silent Spring* in 1962.

In its particulars, *Silent Spring* examined how the indiscriminate and unexamined use of poisons and insecticides (like DDT) to control 'pests' was creating an environmental Armageddon. But Carson was also self-consciously ringing an alarm about our entire modern industrialized world. At root, she questioned the 'distorted sense of proportion' that allowed humans seeking 'to control a few unwanted species' to choose 'a method that contaminated the entire environment and brought the threat of disease and death even to their own kind.'

Carson showed how poisons remained in the soil, how these toxins entered and were stored in the bodies of animals and humans, and how these chemicals transformed, causing sickness and cancer. She traced these connections meticulously, rigorously, as a trained scientist, and it was well that she did: upon publication, *Silent Spring* was relentlessly attacked by the chemical industry as the rantings of a hysterical insect-loving woman with no basis in fact.

Carson's research and conclusions withstood these challenges, and her book became a rallying cry for the 1960s environmental movement. Her work led directly to the 1970 creation of the Environment Protection Agency and the 1972 ban on DDT. The era also included the landmark passage of the 1963 Clean Air Act, the 1973 Endangered Species Act and the 1977 Clean Water Act.

Carson herself did not live to see the impact of her work. She died in April 1964 from breast cancer. In 2006, Pittsburgh named the Rachel Carson Bridge over the Allegheny River in her honor.

federal funds must conduct environmental-impact studies. Cleanup efforts also inspired the first Riverkeeper organization in 1983, now an international movement. Today, the majority of the river meets EPA standards for acceptable water quality.

Similar stories of renewal are unfolding at two of the region's infamous landfills: at 2200 acres, Staten Island's Fresh Kills was once the world's largest landfill – its peak was higher than the Statue of Liberty. Closed in 2001 (at a cost of $1 billion), it is now reclaiming wetlands and being remade into a nature park three times the size of Central Park (tentatively to open in 2016). New Jersey's 30-sq-mile Meadowlands, formerly an unregulated dump (and legendary mob burial ground) with 51 different landfills, is today restoring its wetlands and trying to become a model for renewable energy and green building. Today, Jersey City's Liberty State Park (p239) is convincing evidence of what can be done.

The Adirondacks are another emblem of environmental action: by the 1970s, a rash of dead, fishless lakes caused by acid rain (here and across the Northeast) led to efforts to curb manufacturing, power plant and auto emissions. In 1990, this inspired revisions to the Clean Air Act that today have cut acid rain by 50%. However, while water quality has improved significantly, soils still contain high levels of mercury (a byproduct of acid rain) – so fish live, but can be too contaminated to eat.

Cities have also been cleaning themselves up, none more dramatically than Pittsburgh. Through the mid-20th century, it was arguably America's dirtiest city, so smoky it led the country in respiratory and lung disease, and streetlights burned 24 hours a day. Cleanup efforts were greatly assisted by the collapse of the steel and iron industry in the 1980s, and today Pittsburgh enjoys blue skies and is a leader in green building.

The environmental organization Scenic Hudson (www.scenichudson.org) works to restore the Hudson River Valley.

DID YOU KNOW?

Living in Manhattan is good for the environment: the average New Yorker emits 7.1 tons of CO_2 a year; the country average is 24.5 tons a year.

Outdoor Activities

As everyone will tell you, this is the most urbanized region in the country. From New York City through northern New Jersey to Philadelphia run more highways, air lanes and concrete sidewalks than anywhere else across America. Outside of this, however, is preserved wilderness of surprising vastness: New York's Adirondacks are the largest protected area in the lower 48 – bigger than Grand Canyon, Yellowstone, Everglades and Glacier National Parks combined. New Jersey's Pine Barrens are about equal in size to Grand Canyon National Park, and it's the Mid-Atlantic's largest preserved coastal wilderness. Meanwhile, Pennsylvania's Allegheny National Forest is 800 sq miles, a skootch smaller than Great Smoky Mountains National Park.

Does this mean these natural areas also match those famous landmarks for heart-stopping majesty and adrenaline-pumping adventure? Not quite. The mountains here aren't the tallest, the rivers aren't the fastest and the waves aren't the biggest, though some of the lakes are the greatest – Lakes Erie and Ontario being two of the Great Lakes. Yet what the region may lack in iconic splendor it more than makes up for in its abundance of forested beauty and opportunity. All three states are four-season destinations where you can pretty much do it all, and every activity has at least a few choices that rate high on most national best lists. Even better, the most popular and rewarding activities are also the easiest: hiking, biking and lazy river and lake canoeing.

In other words, in this region, go to the big cities to get your thrills, and come outdoors to breathe deep and relax.

For complete lists of resources, organizations and websites for these activities, turn to the Directory (p403).

An Appalachian Trail classic, *A Walk in the Woods* by Bill Bryson finds our cantankerous, ill-prepared traveler ruminating on long-distance hiking, nature preservation, friendship and sore feet.

HIKING

Bill Bryson got it mostly right: you don't need to be in shape to take a walk in the woods, though if you're going to tackle the entirety of the East Coast's most epic route – the Appalachian Trail – it doesn't hurt. What's great about regional hiking is just this: with so many trails so easily accessed, the full panorama of the region's bucolic, rolling landscape is within reach of all levels of fitness and exuberance.

Take, for instance, the **Appalachian Trail**: it extends some 2170 miles from Georgia to Maine and meanders through all three states. AT through-hikers typically go south to north, starting in early spring, and reach this region in June-July. They are recognized by their flowing gaits, large packs and beards (on the men); bribe them with chocolate, and they'll often sit to tell

---

TOP FIVE ADVENTURES

If you need your palms to sweat and your heart to race, try these:

- Whitewater rafting Pennsylvania's Youghiogheny River (p376)
- Rock climbing Hudson Valley's Shawangunks (p144)
- Hiking the Adirondacks' Mt Marcy (p172)
- Bobsledding at Lake Placid's Olympic Center (p172)
- Mountain biking in the Finger Lakes' Letchworth State Park (p68)

their tale. Day hikers, though, can sample this route easily: in New York's
Harriman State Park (p130) and Bear Mountain (p131); New Jersey's state
parks at High Point (p249), Stokes (p248) and Worthington (p248); and
near the Poconos' Hawk Mountain (p336).

Interestingly, despite the AT's fame, it is rarely the most interesting trail
in the parks it passes through. Following level ridges, it circumnavigates the
most memorably scenic peaks (and valleys), such as the highly recommended
tops of Bear Mountain and High Point.

In New York, the Catskills (p143) are wonderful: the adjacent Shawungunk
Mountains and Minnewaska State Park (p144) have awesome ledge hikes
(hunt for Gertrude's Nose), and other highlights are Slide Mountain, Hunter
Mountain, Mt Tremper and the Red Hill Fire Tower Trail. The massive,
560-mile **Finger Lakes Trail** connects to the Catskills but here, too, the epic
trails are overshadowed by Finger Lakes waterfall hikes: Watkins Glen State
Park (p191) has supremely gorgeous routes leading behind waterfalls, and
Taughannock Falls (p190), Buttermilk Falls (p188) and Ithaca (p186) itself
are superior.

Mountaineers and serious backpackers need to focus on the Adirondacks
(p166), with over 2000 miles of wilderness trails and 42 peaks over 4000ft
high (see p68). Lake Placid (p170) is in the heart of the High Peaks region,
and perhaps the greatest, most beautiful hike is up Mt Marcy, the tallest at
5344ft. Lake George (p167), at the park's southern end, also has a wealth
of great hiking.

On Long Island's Fire Island (p128), the Sunken Forest is a moody, rare
maritime forest of misshapen, 300-year-old trees, and don't forget New York
City's Central Park (p91), along with all the other excellent urban hikes (p69).

In New Jersey, the best hiking along the shore usually coincides with prime
bird-watching territory in protected wetlands and estuaries; see Wildlife-
Watching (p72). The main destinations are Sandy Hook (p213) and Island
Beach State Park (p230) and Cape May (p274). Meanwhile, the most popular
trails are in the Skylands (p248) region, such as the state parks mentioned
for the AT earlier.

Nearly everyone overlooks the Pine Barrens (p261), which is hard to do,
considering its size. Don't miss this unique landscape, however: aim for
Batsto (p261) and do a portion of the 50-mile Batona Trail. The firetower at
Apple Pie Hill reveals pine forest to the horizon. For more marshy delights,
just north are the wilderness trails in the Great Swamp (p246).

In Pennsylvania, a good base for exploring the Poconos (p397) is the
incredibly scenic town Jim Thorpe (p397), set deep in the Lehigh River
valley; you should also check out the Pennsylvania side of the Delaware
Water Gap (p398).

Without question, the Allegheny National Forest (p391) shelters some of
PA's most unforgettable backcountry trails in a patchwork of public lands.
Drive Route 6 to reach the dramatic, deep Pine Creek Gorge (p395) and the
extensive Susquehannock Trail System (p395). Also in northern PA, Presque
Isle State Park (p381) has pretty trails along Lake Erie.

Southwestern Pennsylvania has more excellent hiking, beginning with
Ohiopyle State Park (p374) along the Youghiogheny River. From here, the
70-mile Laurel Highlands Trail (p374) connects with Laurel Mountain
State Park.

Finally, we have yet to mention the wealth of converted rail and canal
trails: all three states have hundreds of miles of flat, sometimes paved paths
along these abandoned transportation corridors. See Cycling & Mountain
Biking (p68) for recommendations.

The excellent Menasha Ridge Press series *The Best in Tent Camping* has editions for all three states. It has selective listings and good recreation advice as well.

The Rails-to-Trails Conservancy (www.railstotrails.org) produces various New York and compilation guides for canal towpaths and rail-trails, and they list and review trails at www.traillink.com.

ADIRONDACK 46ERS VS THE QUARTER-MILE-HIGH CLUB

You may have heard of peakbagging, which refers to climbing all of the peaks over a certain elevation within a defined geographic region. Most famous are the Seven Summits, the highest mountains on each continent. In New York from 1918–25, three mountaineers – Robert and George Marshall and Herbert Clark – were the first to ascend all 46 peaks in the Adirondacks above 4000ft, setting the challenge thereafter for all **Adirondack 46ers** (www.adk46r.org). While geological surveys later showed that four of the peaks are slightly lower than 4000ft, you still have to climb them all to join the club and get your patch.

The Catskills have their own peakbagging club, the **3500 Club** (http://catskill-3500-club.org), which as the name implies requires hiking all 35 of the Catskill peaks over 3500ft. The highest is 4180ft Slide Mountain.

Not to be left out, vertically challenged New Jersey now has its own peakbagging challenge: 'climbing' all 52 of the state's undeveloped mountains over 1000ft. On your map, five of those peaks will be labeled 'hills' (the highest peak is 1803ft High Point), and the tongue-in-cheek hikers who created the list call themselves the 'quarter-mile-high club,' or **1Kers** (www.nj1k.org). See how many you can knock out in a day! There is as yet no patch to honor 1Ker membership, just the warm fuzzy feeling that comes from saying you did it.

BICYCLING & MOUNTAIN BIKING

Cycling is huge in this region. If anything, cyclists have more, and more varied, opportunities than hikers. Nearly every park mentioned under Hiking is also recommended for cycling and mountain biking, as most contain a good selection of multiuse trails. The largest exception is the Appalachian Trail, which is hiking only.

Nearly every ski resort (see Skiing) gives over its hillsides to mountain bikers in summer; many country and coastal roads provide popular cycling routes, as do the paved roads through state forests and parks; and canal towpaths and rail-to-trail conversions are ideal for both leisure and long-range cyclists. Finally, Manhattan, Philadelphia and Pittsburgh offer bike routes and expansive parks (see p69) to cyclists.

> Beginners and experts will find great choices among the 25 routes in *Mountain Biking in the Adirondacks* by Gary Thomann. Good topo maps and general mountain-biking advice.

More specifically: on Long Island, Montauk (p125) provides great biking along quiet roads around the lighthouse, and Shelter Island (p127) is also a good ride; both are ideal in quiet fall. In the Catskills (p143), the Catskill Scenic Trail is a flat 26-mile trail on the former railbed of the Ulster & Delaware Railroad.

About two-thirds complete, the Erie Canalway Trail will ultimately connect 524 miles of trails from Lake Champlain to Lake Erie, essentially following upstate New York's old canal system, including the famous Erie Canal. Near the Hudson River, routes run from Troy and from Albany, whose 35-mile Mohawk-Hudson Bikeway Trail goes to Schenectady. Egregiously bucolic portions can also be found near Utica, Syracuse, Rochester and Buffalo.

Mountain bikers will find a little-known treasure at **Letchworth State Park**, with some 20 miles of single track along the rim of the 'Grand Canyon of the East.' This is on the western fringe of the Finger Lakes (p186), whose parks contain many other options.

In the Adirondacks, the routes around Lake Placid (p170) are very popular, such as the cross-country ski trails at Mt Van Hoevenberg (p172). Two other epic cycling routes are the Seaway Trail, a well-marked series of trails 450 miles long paralleling the St Lawrence Seaway (p186) and Lakes Erie and Ontario. Another 363 miles of trails and paved bike paths encircle Lake Champlain.

In New Jersey, most shore towns are popular with cyclists, though Sandy Hook (p213), Island Beach State Park (p230) and Cape May (p274) are standouts for beauty. Also, near Atlantic Highlands (p215), the 22-mile Henry Hudson Trail is a popular paved route. The extremely popular 70 miles of towpaths along the Delaware & Raritan Canal (p258) reach from Frenchtown on the Delaware River to Trenton, and then inland to New Brunswick. Mountain bikers should check out the state parks and ski resorts in the Skylands (p248), but Jersey's most challenging single track rings Round Valley Reservoir, near Lebanon.

In the Poconos, mountain bikers head to Jim Thorpe (p397), a great base for exploring the 25 miles of trails in Lehigh Gorge State Park (p398) and, beginning in town, the rugged 15-mile Switchback Gravity Railroad Trail.

The Pocono ski resorts are also summertime destinations, as are the mountain-bike trails in Denton Hill State Park (p395) along Route 6. A gentler ride on the shores of Lake Erie can be had at Presque Isle State Park (p381).

In southwestern Pennsylvania, Ohiopyle State Park (p374) has an immensely popular 25-mile cycling route along the river, and north of Pittsburgh, Moraine State Park (p375) has more pretty bike trails around Lake Arthur.

For biking and rail-trail organizations, see the Directory (p403).

American Trails (www.americantrails.org) is a national advocacy group. It links to tons of state resources, including hiking, biking, horse riding, and waterways; it partners with www.trails.com for trail guides and maps.

SKIING

Out of the four times the Winter Olympics have been held in the US, New York's Lake Placid has hosted them twice – in 1932 and 1980 – and between them, New York and Pennsylvania have nearly 60 ski resorts. Locals love to ski, and they flock to snow-clad hills as soon as winter cooperates.

However, despite this love and long history, truth be told, the mountains here are a bit too modest to provide Olympic-sized thrills. There are plenty of great opportunities to ski, but except for Lake Placid, the slopes don't compare to the Rockies or even Vermont.

Ski season is generally mid-December to mid-April, but resorts will remain open as long as they can maintain a snowpack.

Combine adventure and activism with the Sierra Club (www.sierraclub.org), which has local chapters in all three states and organizes outings.

Downhill Skiing

Reflecting the height of their peaks, the Adirondacks, Catskills and Poconos have the region's best skiing, in that order. Bigger resorts are typically self-contained, all-inclusive experiences, with lodges, restaurants, lessons and so

---

URBAN JUNGLE EXPEDITIONS

Don your pith helmet, lace your boots or mount your two-wheeled steed: here are the best places to hike and bike without leaving the city.

New York

- Central Park (p91)
- The High Line (p89)
- Hudson River Park (p98), from Battery Park to the George Washington Bridge
- New York Botanical Garden (p101)
- Brooklyn Botanic Garden (p100)

Elsewhere

- Liberty State Park, NJ (p239)
- Fairmount Park, Philadelphia (p299)

on, while many smaller resorts are day-only. Snowboarding is easily as, or more, popular than downhill.

In terms of ski resorts, Lake Placid (p170) is one of America's best, and Whiteface Mountain (p172), with over 80 trails and a 3400ft vertical drop, is lauded for downhill, snowboarding and backcountry skiing. Part of what makes Lake Placid so great is the Mt Van Hoevenberg Olympic Sports Complex (p172): athletes still train on the ski jump, bobsled tracks and ice rinks. Not only can you watch, but you can brave the luge yourself. Other Adirondack ski resorts are at Gore Mountain, West Mountain and Snow Ridge Ski Area.

In the Catskills, Hunter Mountain (p152) is the most diverse and popular ski resort, with three mountains, over 50 trails, a 1600ft drop and enormous snowmaking capabilities. Indeed, proximity to NYC means most Catskills resorts get crowded. Windham Mountain (p152) is a great destination for beginners, as is Belleayre Mountain (p152).

Pennsylvania's Poconos (p397) have dozens of ski areas, but vertical drops are all under 1000ft. The most popular are Camelback, Shawnee Mountain and the Jack Frost & Big Boulder Ski Areas. West along Route 6, the Denton Hill Ski Area (p395) is another good spot. Southeast of Pittsburgh, in the Laurel Highlands region (p376) are Seven Springs Mountain Resort and Hidden Valley Resort.

New Jersey has one main ski resort – Mountain Creek (p249) – which has above-average snowboarding and is the closest resort to New York City.

Cross-Country Skiing

Cross-country skiing (or Nordic skiing) is extremely popular and more widespread. Most of the ski resorts already mentioned offer it, and some have full Nordic centers – the best is at Whiteface Mountain in Lake Placid. Overall, the Adirondacks (p166) and the Finger Lakes (p186) provide great experiences and wonderful scenery; get information through the state parks mentioned under Hiking (p66). Hudson Valley parks maintain excellent groomed trails, particularly Minnewaska State Park (p144) and Bear Mountain (p131).

In Pennsylvania, Poconos resorts support cross-country skiing, while the Allegheny National Forest (p391) has several extensive trails, like the Laurel Mill Trail and those in Moshannon State Forest. In southwestern PA, the 70-mile Laurel Highlands Trail (p374) becomes another major cross-country destination in winter.

In New Jersey, the parks in the Skylands region (p248) enjoy cross-country skiing, and High Point (p249) has a Nordic center.

FISHING

Look at a map, and wherever you see water – the Atlantic Ocean, the Great Lakes, the Delaware River, any of the thousands of ponds and streams – you'll find avid anglers. Freshwater fish include varieties of trout, salmon, bass and pike, as well as giant muskellunge (muskie), shad and walleyed pike; in the Atlantic you'll find bluefish, flounder, tuna, shark and even marlin.

The Catskills (p143) are legendary for trout fishing, and Adirondack lakes (p173) are home to bass, pike and salmon (though mercury levels can make eatin' an issue). Fishing for largemouth bass, northern pike and muskie is a prime draw in the Thousand Islands (p178); indeed, Clayton (p182) is home to the Muskie Hall of Fame! While Sackets Harbor (p185) in Lake Ontario is famed for trophy-sized salmon and trout.

The lakes and rivers of Allegheny National Forest (p391) have some of the best fishing in the country's northeast, and as mentioned, the Delaware River is rich with a wide variety of fish, including eel.

Transportation Alternatives (www.transalt.org) is firstly an advocacy group promoting alternate modes of Manhattan locomotion. It also organizes regular bike tours and has city cycling resources.

Need gear? No sweat. You're never far from one of the region's main sports retailers: REI (rei.com), Sports Authority (www.sportsauthority.com) and Eastern Mountain Sports (www.ems.com).

CANOEING, KAYAKING & RAFTING

In our humble opinion, the region's outdoor highlight is out there on the water: canoeing the region's splendid collection of rivers and lakes. Canoeing is simply the most fun and relaxed way to explore – floating, gliding, paddling, splashing, getting wet and negotiating riffles that get your heart racing.

First off, what's not to love when you can kayak for free in the Hudson River off Manhattan's West Side? Really! The nonprofit **Downtown Boathouse** (www.downtownboathouse.org) has walk-up paddling at Pier 40, Pier 96 and 72nd St, mostly weekends. Somehow, the city towers even more majestically when you're bobbing alongside it.

Whitewater Rafting

Let's get this out of the way: as true river rats will tell you, the epic whitewater rivers are just south of Pennsylvania in West Virginia, and all of this region's whitewater is what they'd call 'crowded,' as in clogged with commercial operators. That's not necessarily bad. What it means is that every good river is easily accessed. Also, spring is whitewater season, and some rivers have regular dam releases that pump up the excitement.

Perhaps the most popular whitewater is on Pennsylvania's **Youghiogheny River**, accessed at Ohiopyle State Park (p374). Called the 'Yough,' it has three sections, with the most exciting being the 'Upper Yough,' technically in northern Maryland. This is over 10 miles of Class IV–V rapids (on a scale where Class VI rapids are essentially unnavigable). In the Poconos, check out the **Lehigh River** near Jim Thorpe (p397), which is mainly a Class II/III river.

The other destination for whitewater is the Adirondacks. The **Black River**, accessed through Clayton (p182) is primarily a Class III/IV adventure, and the **Moose River**, near Old Forge (p177), has intermediate sections as well as advanced Class V. Meanwhile, the further north you go in the **Hudson River Gorge**, near Lake George (p177), the more exciting it gets, with stretches of Class III/IV.

River & Lake Canoeing

On the lazy rivers, tubing, rafting, canoeing and kayaking – basically, anything that floats while you're on or in it – are all popular, and there are so many canoeing lakes and reservoirs we couldn't name them all.

A designated Wild & Scenic River, the **Delaware River** runs 330 miles from Hancock, New York, to the Atlantic Ocean in Delaware Bay. While the tidal surge extends inland 130 miles to Trenton, past which you can't canoe, that still leaves 200 dam-free miles for scenic, lazy paddles through easy Class I/II ripples (and a few Class III). See the Delaware Water Gap (p247) and the Delaware & Raritan Canal (p258).

In Pennsylvania's Allegheny National Forest (p391), the **Clarion River** is a similar 60 miles of relaxation, and the **Allegheny Reservoir** and **Allegheny River** are popular too. Within **Lake Erie**, Presque Isle (p381) offers pretty paddles among the waterbirds.

In New York's Catskills (p151), **Esopus Creek** is a wildly popular tubing river, but it's cold! In the Finger Lakes, Letchworth State Park has canoeing beneath a 600ft gorge along the **Genesee River.**

The Adirondacks are the mecca for canoe-camping adventures: the lauded St Regis Canoe Area (p175) is a network of 58 motorboat-free lakes and ponds, and the **Adirondack Canoe Route** runs 90 miles through the **Fulton Chain of Lakes**, including **Saranac Lake**. What's a little portage for true wilderness?

Then there are the endless possibilities of the St Lawrence Seaway (p178), and its thousand or so islands.

For more wilderness canoeing, try the **Mullica River** in New Jersey's scruffy Pine Barrens (p261), which has other waterways. The barrier islands of the Jersey shore offer canoeing as well as sea kayaking, as at Island Beach State Park (p230). Long Island's Montauk (p125) is also popular for sea kayaking.

There's much, much more, but this *should* get you started…

Along the Atlantic Ocean, beaches draw surfcasters, and charter boats get to deeper water. On Long Island, top spots are Fire Island (p128), Sag Harbor (p124) and Montauk (p125). Along the Jersey shore, the most active harbors are found in Belmar (p222), Point Pleasant (p225), Long Beach Island (p232), the Wildwoods (p273) and Cape May (p277). The last two are also good for bayside crabbing, and Island Beach State Park (p230) has such good surf fishing that anglers do it all night.

To fish, you need the appropriate state license and to abide by seasonal and regional regulations. These are complicated, and ever-changing; saltwater fishermen also may need to register with national agencies. See the Directory (p404) for state permit resources.

SURFING & WINDSURFING

When it comes to surfing, the East Coast, as everyone knows, isn't California or Hawaii. But the waves still break, and occasionally curl, and there's not a local surfer who doesn't hit the water when they do. As a rule, fall is best, particularly August and September; spring is unpredictable and summer suffers long flat spells and crowds.

Down the Jersey shore, highlights include Seaside Heights (p227), where Casino Pier sees long tube rides. Asbury Park (p219) and Long Beach Island (p232) have dedicated surfer scenes. Manasquan (p224) has a particularly good break, and Wildwood (p273) is a destination for beginners.

New York's Long Island is similarly sprinkled with excellent breaks, and with lessons, rentals and shops. Heading west, notable scenes and waves can be found at Long Beach, Fire Island (p128), Southampton (p124) and Montauk (p125).

Windsurfers and kitesurfers will not be disappointed by the winds at Sandy Hook (p213); Long Beach Island (p230) and Atlantic City (p262) also have recommended sights. Long Island (p117), particularly on Long Island Sound, is good, and local windsurfers have a great deal of fun on New York lakes, particularly as you go further to the north. See the Directory (p405) for resources.

WILDLIFE-WATCHING

When peregrine falcons nest on Manhattan skyscrapers, and black bears wander through New Jersey towns, you know there is wildlife to witness even in the nation's urbanized heart. Get out into the countryside, and you'll find some true wildlife spectacles.

The wetlands, bogs, marshes and estuaries of coastal and southern New Jersey are part of a major migratory flyway – the bird-watching here is so superior that the state is home to the World Series of Birding, a 24-hour

---

BEST SOPORIFIC SUNNING

Doing nothing (ie napping) was never more satisfying than at these gorgeous getaways lapped by the Atlantic Ocean.

- Fire Island (p128), especially Robert Moses State Park (p186)
- The Hamptons (p123)
- Sandy Hook (p213)
- Spring Lake (p224)
- Island Beach State Park (p230)
- Higbee Beach, Cape May (p277)

ROOT & RACE

Whether participating or spectating, the following sporting events and competitions are highlights of the outdoor sports calendar:

- **World Series of Birding** (www.birdcapemay.org) A 24-hour birding competition in Cape May; mid-May.

- **Five Boro Bike Tour** (www.bikenewyork.org) This 42-mile, traffic-free ride in NYC draws 30,000 cyclists; May.

- **Hamptons Polo Classic** (www.thehamptons.com/polo) Celebrities descend on Bridgehampton for polo season; late July to August.

- **Saratoga Springs Racing Season** (www.nyra.com/saratoga) Upstate New York's historic racecourse draws top horses; late July to early September.

- **US Open Tennis Tournament** (www.usopen.org) Grand Slam tennis in Queens; August.

- **New York Marathon** (www.ingnycmarathon.org) One of the world's largest marathons, this draws two-million spectators in NYC; early November.

- **Philadelphia Marathon** (www.philadelphiamarathon.com) Major national marathon through historic Philly; mid-November.

---

competition to spot the most species (winners' totals: around 230). The finish line for competitors, Cape May Point State Park (p275), is bird central, with other notable destinations at Edwin B Forsythe NWR (p262), the Pine Barrens (p261), the Great Swamp (p246) and Sandy Hook (p213).

Shorebirds and raptors are a highlight at many other places as well: on Long Island's Fire Island (p128), and in Pennsylvania at Presque Isle State Park (p381), at Erie NWR (p387), and at Hawk Mountain (p336), where 20,000 raptors pass by each fall.

Meanwhile, just offshore, the Atlantic Ocean provides glimpses of dolphins and migrating whales. Get a boat at New York's Montauk (p125) and New Jersey's Cape May (p277) and Wildwood (p273), among others.

If you yearn to see North America's larger mammals, a herd of some 800 elk wander Pennsylvania's Allegheny National Forest (p392), while moose, black bear, coyote, bobcats, beaver and more frequent the wilds of New York's Adirondacks, as well as Robert Moses State Park (p186) in the St Lawrence Seaway and Wellesley Island (p180) in the Thousand Islands. The Catskills (p143) and the Finger Lakes (p186) are also popular wildlife-watching destinations.

Can't find the animals you want to see? Visit Watchable Wildlife (www.watchablewildlife.org), a nonprofit that promotes wildlife viewing and lists the best local spots at www.wildlifeviewingareas.com.

ROCK CLIMBING

One of the better rock-climbing destinations in the nation is the Shawangunk Mountains in the Catskills. The ridge stretches some 50 miles, and Minnewaska State Park (p144) and the Mohonk Preserve (p144) provide the best access spots. Near to the action, the town of New Paltz (p143) is climbing headquarters, with plenty of climbing shops, outfitters and tour groups.

The Adirondacks have plenty of good climbs near Lake George (p167) and Lake Placid (p172), and lots of schools, and you can practice your ice climbing in winter.

In Pennsylvania, beginners and experts can find routes in McConnell's Mill State Park (p375), north of Pittsburgh. Other popular rock-climbing spots are Wissahickon Creek in Philadelphia's Fairmount Park (p299), Delaware Water Gap (p247), and Lehigh Gorge State Park in the Poconos (p398).

SAILING

Naturally, with such vast lakes and glorious coastal waters, sailing is a big draw, and excellent training programs can be found at several large sailing schools, such as the Nelson Sailing Center (p229) near Seaside Heights, and the New Jersey Sailing School in Point Pleasant (p225). Other Jersey shore destinations for nautical types are Long Beach Island (p232) and Cape May (p277).

Inland, Pennsylvania's best sailing is in Lake Arthur in Moraine State Park (p375) and in Lake Erie from Presque Isle State Park (p381). In New York, the usual suspects are the Finger Lakes (p186), Oneida Lake near Syracuse (p194), and Lake George (p168) in the Adirondacks.

Covering the entire route, *Canoeing the Delaware River* by Gary Letcher is a perfect resource for day trips and longer river camping excursions, with good info on access points.

SCUBA DIVING

Where there are ships, there are bound to be shipwrecks, and coastal waters off New Jersey and Long Island are littered with the barnacle-encrusted hulks of ill-fated sailing vessels. Point Pleasant (p225) is a popular diving destination, as is Long Beach Island (p230), where the Museum of NJ Maritime History is a veritable catalog of storm-tossed bad luck and bad judgment. The most comprehensive information is available from **Scuba Diving – New Jersey & Long Island** (http://njscuba.net), which lists dive sites and operators and has lots of scuba advice. To hook into the local scuba-diver network, visit **NJ Dive** (www.njdive.com).

If you don't mind cold water, then consider a lake dive to 18th-century wooden warships in Lake George (p167). More wrecks await in the Thousand Islands (p178), and in Lakes Ontario and Erie.

HORSEBACK RIDING

Hundreds of miles of multiuse trails traverse the region's public lands, and there are scores of horseback-riding ranches, stables and clubs offering guided trips and lessons. Undoubtedly, one of the coolest rides is in New York City's Central Park (p91), which has a 6-mile bridle path around the reservoir and

---

ARRIVE PREPARED, LEAVE NO TRACE

It's amazing that so much wilderness exists so close to New York City's greater megalopolis. Indeed, enormous conservation efforts are required to preserve it, and we do our part when we tread lightly during those outdoor adventures these wildlands provide.

First, be prepared, particularly when camping. Most advice is common sense. Know what you are getting into: get maps and firsthand advice from rangers. Pack for changeable weather (it can rain anytime) and for the unexpected: bring a first-aid kit, flashlight, and something for water treatment. June is blackfly season in the Adirondacks, and insect repellent is helpful year-round. For more preparedness and first-aid advice, see the comprehensive website **Survive Outdoors** (www.surviveoutdoors.com).

Once in the wild, do everything possible to minimize your impact. As they say, take only pictures, leave only footprints. Stick to established trails and campsites. Be particularly sensitive to riparian areas; don't wash yourself or your dishes in streams or rivers, and camp at least 200ft away from them. Use a stove for cooking and make fires only in established fire rings (using only downed wood). When you leave, take out everything you brought in and clean up every trace of your visit.

Conduct yourself as if you were a guest in someone's home – which you are. Observe wildlife, but don't approach or feed it. In fact, bears are again common in the mountains, so if you don't secure your food, they (or the raccoons) will find you.

For more useful advice, visit the websites of the **Leave No Trace Center** (www.lnt.org) and the **American Hiking Society** (www.americanhiking.org), as well as the list of hiking organizations in the Directory (p401).

North Meadow. For guided horse rides here, contact **Riverdale Equestrian Center** (☎ 914-633-0303; www.riverdaleriding.com). Sadly, New York's legendary Claremont Riding Academy closed in 2007.

Upstate New York has popular bridle trails in most of the state parks and lands mentioned above, as in the Catskills and the Adirondacks, around the Finger Lakes, and so on. For a good list of trails, contact the **New York State Horse Council** (www.nyshc.org), an advocacy group with statewide resources and trail information.

The same is true in New Jersey and Pennsylvania: you can find stables and trails around the Delaware Water Gap; in the Pine Barrens, along the shore; in Allegheny National Forest; in the Poconos; and much more. A useful website for finding local stables is **Horse and Travel** (www.horseandtravel. com), which lists them by state.

CAVING

Pennsylvania has vast expanses of limestone, which as experienced spelunkers know is easily gouged by water into tremendous cave networks. As a result, the state has over half a dozen popular caverns where guided tours are offered. These include Indian Echo Caverns (p350), near Hershey, and Pennsylvania's biggest cavern, Laurel Caverns (p376), south of Pittsburgh. Upstate New York also has a few underground explorations. For more information, visit the **Pennsylvania Caves Association** (www.pacaves.com) and the **National Caves Association** (http://cavern.com).

Plan to explore a lot of federal lands? Considering getting an annual America the Beautiful pass (www.nps.gov/ fee_passes.htm). For $80, you get unlimited access to all NPS parks and federal lands. Buy online at http://store. usgs.gov/pass.

New York City

It's a helluva town. The crown jewel of North America, if not the western hemisphere, New York, New York is everything you imagine it to be: big, fancy, scary, sexy, gilded, seedy, magical, monumental and, not least of all, friendly. The adventurous traveler is welcome here so long as you keep moving swiftly down the sidewalks. If you want to take a picture, please do! Just move to the side and out of the flow of traffic.

What's there to say about New York City that hasn't already been said? Walt Whitman to Woody Allen have all weighed in on the topic. There's the history, the architecture, the cuisine, the fashion, the nightlife, the art, the underbelly, the skyboxes and, most importantly, the myths – the eight million stories in the Naked City. And they are all true. Yet with so many things to do and see and try, how can the curious visitor attack it with the verve and vigor required? Get ready to walk, to ride the subway, to hail a cab, and see this city for all the spectacular glory that makes it a world-class destination of legend.

Nearly everything that is interesting about this endlessly fascinating metropolis is located outside of Midtown Manhattan. There are notable exceptions that prove the rule, of course, but it is a guarantee that you will find a more memorable dinner in Tribeca, a better bar in Williamsburg, and superior shopping in the West Village. Anything you want to do can be done here – so kick ass and take names and go exploring!

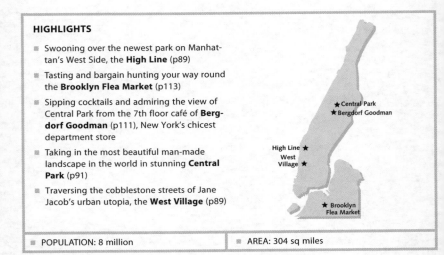

HIGHLIGHTS

- Swooning over the newest park on Manhattan's West Side, the **High Line** (p89)
- Tasting and bargain hunting your way round the **Brooklyn Flea Market** (p113)
- Sipping cocktails and admiring the view of Central Park from the 7th floor café of **Bergdorf Goodman** (p111), New York's chicest department store
- Taking in the most beautiful man-made landscape in the world in stunning **Central Park** (p91)
- Traversing the cobblestone streets of Jane Jacob's urban utopia, the **West Village** (p89)

★ Central Park
★ Bergdorf Goodman

High Line ★
West
Village ★

★ Brooklyn
Flea Market

- POPULATION: 8 million
- AREA: 304 sq miles

HISTORY

Henry Hudson gets all the credit for discovering what we now call New York. Actually, it was first explored by a Florentine named Giovanni da Verrazano in 1524. And, of course, before Giovanni showed up there were the Lenape, the tribe of Native Americans who occupied the islands before the New World became the New World.

But the story of modern New York starts with good ol' Henry Hudson on his mission to explore the New World for the Dutch West India Company and with the founding of New Amsterdam on the southern tip of Manahatta Island. Flash forward a few decades and we get the English coming in and usurping the power, at which point the settlement gets re-christened New York.

After that came the American Revolution (though New York was 'occupied' territory for much of that time) and for a brief spell New York was the capitol of the United States. That designation didn't last long, but the harbor and the Hudson River continued to guarantee New York its status as a financial capitol of trade, and with that came its eventual transformation into the cultural capitol it is known as today.

In the intervening centuries the city has seen its fair share of ups-and-downs – industrialization during the Gilded Age, unionization of the working class, Prohibition, the building of the UN, President Gerald Ford famously telling the city to 'drop dead' during the fiscal crisis of the 1970s, the booming financial and art markets of the 1980s and '90s and perhaps the most recent down in 2001 when hijacked airplanes scarred the city in such a deeply terrifying event that the city has yet to heal completely.

Gotham is a resilient place and no matter how gnarly each situation seems, the city has always picked itself up and dusted itself off in its inexorable march towards the future.

For more history, see p32.

ORIENTATION

New York City consists of five 'boroughs' that bound themselves together in 1898 to form Greater New York City. The traditional visitor looking to trip the light fantastic on the sidewalks of New York will be primarily interested in exploring the borough of Manhattan. Fortunately, thanks to some early city planners the island of Manhattan is generally divided up into 'the Grid.' Numbered Avenues and their brethren like the Park and Amsterdam run north and south with First Ave on the East Side and Twelfth Ave on the West. (Let it be known that Sixth Ave is alternately known as Avenue of the Americas.) Anything labeled a 'Street', on the other hand, runs east and west with the lower numbers in the Village rising ever upwards towards Harlem and the Bronx. It is commonly used local shorthand that 20 blocks uptown or downtown equals a mile, with three or four cross-town blocks (the Avenues) equaling roughly the same distance.

Manhattan is primarily separated into three sections: Downtown (anything south of 14th Street), Midtown (south of 59th St) and Uptown (north of 59th St). Places are also commonly classified as on the East Side or the West Side with Fifth Ave providing the dividing line. These designations can all be further deconstructed into the various neighborhoods like Tribeca, Chelsea, and Hell's Kitchen along Manhattan's West Side (along with the slightly more obvious ones like the West Village and the Upper West Side) and Chinatown, Gramercy Park, and Murray Hill running up the east side.

On Manhattan, things get a bit screwy south of Houston St that divides Greenwich Village from Soho and the Lower East Side. Most of downtown Manhattan's streets are named not numbered and it can get a bit wonky. We'd recommend keeping a map handy when venturing downtown.

Across the East River from Manhattan are the boroughs of Brooklyn and Queens. These actually sit on the landmass more commonly known as Long Island, but its western edge is incorporated by New York City (with Brooklyn to the south and Queens to the north). Both of these boroughs are brimming with activities and are exceedingly navigable by subway. The farther east one gets into both boroughs, the harder it is to use public transportation, but most truly interesting sites will be within easy walking distance of a subway stop.

Buses are just about the only public way to navigate Staten Island, which is southwest of Manhattan. Travel here is difficult without a car (and, frankly, a GPS system). The easiest way for the car-less traveler to reach Staten Island is by the ferry.

The Bronx, to the north of Manhattan and Queens, is the only borough actually connected to the US mainland. All the others, you may have noticed, are surrounded by water, making bridges and tunnels vital. Like Brooklyn and Queens, most destinations of interest in the Bronx are accessible by subway.

INFORMATION
Bookstores

Barnes & Noble (www.barnesandnoble.com) Union Square (Map p92; ☎ 212-253-0810; 33 E 17th St; 10am-10pm); Lincoln Triangle (Map p96; ☎ 212-595-6859; 1972 Broadway at 66th St; 9am-midnight) This corporate giant has locations all over the city; these are the two biggest stores.

Flight 001 (Map p82; ☎ 212-989-0001; www.flight001.com; 96 Greenwich Ave; 11am-8pm Mon-Sat, 12-6pm Sun) This trendy little store in the West Village specializes in travel and is a great place to pick up maps and travel books along with just about everything else you could need.

Shakespeare & Co. (www.shakespeareandco.com) Downtown (Map p82; ☎ 212-529-1330; 716 Broadway at Washington Place; 10am-11pm Mon-Fri, 12-9pm Sat & Sun); Upper East Side branch (Map p96; ☎ 212-570-0201; 939 Lexington Ave at 69th St; 9am-8pm Mon-Fri, 10am-7pm Sat, 11am-6pm Sun) This venerable New York independent bookseller has a few locations and is a favorite with college kids for its impressive drama and theater sections along with well curated literary fiction and obscure magazines.

Strand (Map p82; ☎ 212-473-1452; www.strandbooks.com; 828 Broadway at 12th St; 9:30am-10:30pm Mon-Sat, 11am-10:30pm Sun) This is THE iconic used bookstore in New York. Boasting 18 miles of books, it's the place for finding the rare and out-of-print.

Emergency

Ambulance, Police, Fire (☎ 911)

Internet Access

This is one wired city and just about every coffee retailer and library branch will offer you a connection. If you're without a computer, try:

Apple Store (Map p96; ☎ 212-336-1440; 767 Fifth Ave at 59th St; 24hr)

New York Public Library (Map p92; ☎ 917-275-6975; www.nypl.org; Fifth Ave at 42nd St; 10am-6pm Mon-Sat)

Libraries

New York Public Library (Map p92; ☎ 917-275-6975; www.nypl.org; Fifth Ave at 42nd St; 10am-6pm Mon-Sat, closed Sun) The big and super famous main branch is guarded by stone lions and has beautiful Bryant Park as its backyard. There are branches throughout the city.

Jefferson Market Library (Map p82; ☎ 212-243-4334; 425 Sixth Ave at 10th Street; 12-8pm Mon & Wed, 12-6pm Tue, Thu & Fri, 10am-5pm Sat) A branch of the New York Public Library. Situated in a grand Calvert Vaux–designed high-Victorian gothic building with a marvelous tower and garden.

Media

New York Post (www.nypost.com) Tabloid trash from the right and home of the Page Six gossip column – possibly the greatest, most hysterical paper in the world.

New York Times (www.nytimes.com) The Grey Lady, its nickname, is the paper of record and the big kahuna in town.

The New Yorker (www.newyorker.com) This highbrow weekly magazine offers comprehensive cultural listings and withering, arch criticism.

New York Magazine (www.nymag.com) A more gossipy and city-centric magazine than the New Yorker, NY Mag also has comprehensive listings, including dining options.

Next Magazine (www.nextmagazine.com) The place to go for all your gay and lesbian entertainment options.

Time Out New York (www.newyork.timeout.com) Will point you to every club, band, play, movie, and whatever else is happening during the week.

Medical Services

If you don't want to be overly hassled for medical insurance, try the following:

Bellevue Medical Center (Map p92; ☎ 212-562-1000; 462 First Ave at 28th St) Bellvue's a city hospital and its psych ward is the stuff of scary legend, but it rates high on service and satisfaction generally.

New York Presbyterian Hospital – Columbia Campus (off Map p96; ☎ 212-927-0112; 1051 Riverside Dr at 168th St) An uptown hospital where Bill Clinton gets his cardiac surgery so that's probably a good sign.

Money

ATMs are plentiful in New York City and can be found in most delis, bodegas and drug stores along with traditional banks. Most large banks will exchange foreign currency.

Omnex (Map p92; ☎ 212-279-6150; www.nyforeignexchange.com; 43 W 33rd St; 9am-6pm Mon-Fri, 10am-5pm Sat) Near the Empire State Building.

Post

James A Farley Post Office (Map p92; ☎ 212-330-3296; www.usps.com; 421 Eighth Ave; 7am-10pm Mon-Fri, 9am-9pm Sat, 11am-7pm Sun) This is the city's

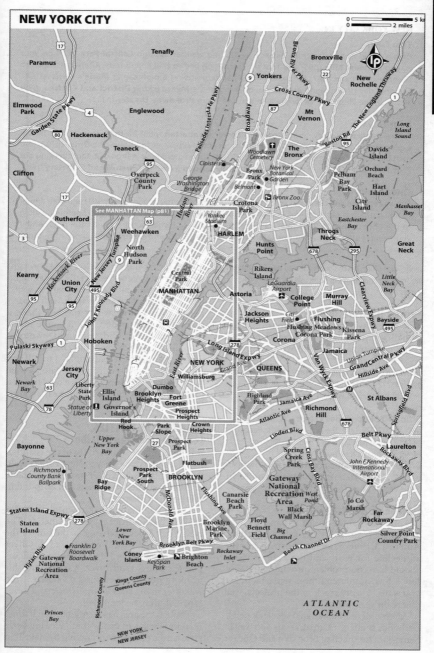

NEW YORK CITY

0 — 5 km
0 — 2 miles

Paramus
17
Elmwood Park
Garden State Pkwy
80
Hackensack
Teaneck
Clifton
95
17
Overpeck County Park
Rutherford
3
Kearny
Union City
95
495
John F Kennedy Blvd
Hoboken
Pulaski Skyway
1
Newark
Newark Bay
63
78
Jersey City
Liberty State Park
Statue of Liberty
Ellis Island
Governor's Island
Red Hook
Bayonne
Richmond County Bank Ballpark
Staten Island Expwy
278
Staten Island
Rylan Blvd
Gateway National Recreation Area
Franklin D Roosevelt Boardwalk
Princes Bay

Tenafly
Englewood
Palisades Interstate Pkwy
Broadway
Hudson River
Cloisters
George Washington Bridge
63
Weehawken
North Hudson Park
New Jersey Turnpike
9
Central Park
MANHATTAN
East River
NEW YORK
Williamsburg
Dumbo
Brooklyn Heights
Fort Greene
Prospect Heights
Park Slope
Crown Heights
Prospect Park
27
Prospect Park South
Flatbush
BROOKLYN
Bay Ridge
McDonald Ave
Flushing Ave
Upper New York Bay
Lower New York Bay
Bay Ridge
Coney Island
KeySpan Park
Brighton Beach
Kings County
Queens County
NEW YORK
NEW JERSEY

See MANHATTAN Map (p81)

9
Yonkers
Cross County Pkwy
Bronx River Pkwy
87
Mt Vernon
Woodlawn Cemetery
The Bronx
Boston Rd
95
Bronx Park
New York Botanical Garden
Belmont
Bronx Zoo
Crotona Park
HARLEM
Yankee Stadium
Hunts Point
Rikers Island
LaGuardia Airport
Astoria
College Point
Jackson Heights
Citi Field
Long Island Expwy
278
Grand Ave
QUEENS
Highland Park
Jamaica Ave
Atlantic Ave
Linden Blvd
Spring Creek Park
Cross Bay Blvd
Gateway National Recreation Area
West Pond
Black Wall Marsh
Floyd Bennett Field
Big Channel
Brooklyn Marine Park
Canarsie Beach Park
Brooklyn Belt Pkwy
Rockaway Inlet
Beach Channel Dr

Bronxville
22
New Rochelle
1
Mt Vernon
Long Island Sound
Davids Island
Pelham Bay Park
Orchard Beach
Hart Island
City Island
Eastchester Bay
Throgs Neck
678
295
Manhasset Bay
Great Neck
Little Neck Bay
Clearview Expwy
Murray Hill
Flushing
Flushing Meadows Corona Park
Corona
Kissena Park
Bayside
495
Jamaica
Union Turnpike
Grand Central Pkwy
Hillside Ave
St Albans
Van Wyck Expwy
Richmond Hill
678
Belt Pkwy
Laurelton
Springfield Blvd
Rockaway Blvd
John F Kennedy International Airport
Jo Co Marsh
Far Rockaway
Silver Point Country Park

ATLANTIC OCEAN

NEW YORK CITY IN....

Two Days
Grab a bagel and coffee from **Zabar's** (p113) and wander through **Central Park** (p91) on your way to **Museum Mile** (p95) and tour the institution or two that sound best. Afterwards, head to **Greenwich Village** (p87) for some dinner before grabbing a nightcap at **Marie's Crisis** (p108). The next day go shopping and gallery-hopping in the **Meatpacking District and Chelsea** (p89) and walk the High Line before heading to see some **Broadway theater** (p111).

Four Days
Follow the first itinerary, then venture to **Lower Manhattan** (p80) for the historical sites before exploring **Soho** (p86). Head to Williamsburg for some supper at the boho-chic **Diner** (p108) and then bar hop while communing with the hipsters. Spend more time in Brooklyn, too, checking out **Prospect Park** (p100) and the **Brooklyn Botanic Garden** (p100) or **Green-Wood Cemetery** (p99).

One Week
Subway uptown and check out some sights in the Bronx like the famous **zoo** (p101) and grab dinner in the 'authentic' Little Italy of **Arthur Ave** (p101). Explore the **East Village** (p87) before heading to the **Christopher St Pier** (p98) for some dining al fresco while you hang with the boys. And if you haven't already been to **Rockefeller Center** (p91) or **Grand Central** (p91), now's the time.

central post office, besides being adorned by a breathtaking series of columns, it's miraculously open seven days a week

Tourist Information
New York City has a great local tourism office, with different sites scattered over Manhattan. It has an extremely helpful website as well: www.nycgo.com.

Official NYC Information Center – Midtown (Map p92; ☎ 212-484-1222; 810 Seventh Ave at 52nd St; ☽ 8:30am-6pm Mon-Fri, 9am-5pm Sat & Sun, to 3pm holidays)

Official NYC Information Center – Harlem (Map p96; ☎ 212-222-1014; The Studio Museum in Harlem, 144 W 125th St near Malcolm X Blvd; ☽ 9am-7pm, except Christmas & New Year's Day)

Official NYC Information Center – Chinatown (Map p82; ☎ 212-484-1222; ☽ 10am-6pm, to 3pm holidays) At the triangle where Canal, Walker & Baxter Sts meet.

DANGERS & ANNOYANCES
Despite its reputation for urban grit, New York City is probably the safest big city in America. Crimes rates have been on an overall decline for years and the average visitor should have no problem providing they follow a few simple common-sense tactics. If you want to score crack in the projects, well, you're on your own.

Almost all of Manhattan, especially neighborhoods south of 125th St, is safe and well lit. Same goes for much of Brooklyn and Queens,

though the far-flung reaches of these boroughs can get a bit rougher, especially late at night. The Bronx can a bit dicey after dark as well.

Women might want to walk with a partner as the evening wears on, but that's a precaution you needn't take if you're in the busier sections of Midtown and Downtown Manhattan. When in doubt, hail a cab or ask a bartender or restaurant host to call you car service. Subways are pretty safe as well, though like everything else, we'd advise you to keep your wits about you in the early morning hours.

SIGHTS & ACTIVITIES
Lower Manhattan & Tribeca
It is here, on the southern tip of the island of Manhattan that the story of New York is built. Several of the New York's most recognizable buildings, statues and streets can be found in this bustling district.

Lower Manhattan is known globally for Wall St, the financial center of America. The New York Stock Exchange is the hub of the 'greed is good' world epitomized in Oliver Stone's memorable 1980s take-down of corporate culture, *Wall Street*. A walk along this iconic thoroughfare, starting at Church Street, will offer many sites, both historic and modern, including Federal Hall.

Though the area has seen some tough times it still manages to exude that *Working Girl*–style magic of dreamers craving to make it in

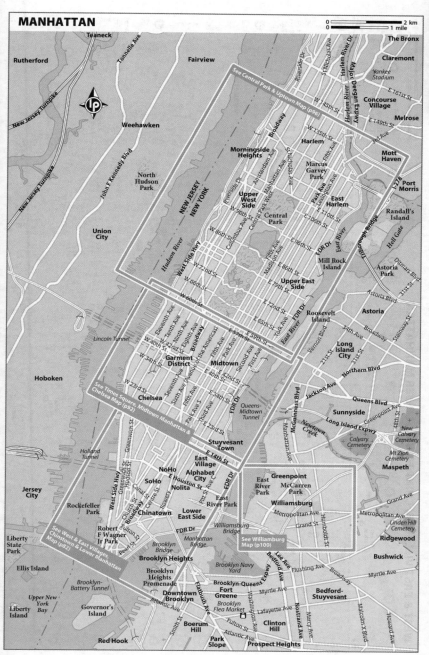

MANHATTAN

0 ———— 2 km
0 ———— 1 mile

Teaneck

Rutherford

Fairview

The Bronx

Claremont

Yankee Stadium

E 161st St

Concourse Village

Weehawken

New Jersey Turnpike

John F Kennedy Blvd

Tonnelle Ave

E 149th St

Melrose

3rd Ave

W 145th St

W 135th St

Broadway

Harlem

North Hudson Park

Morningside Heights

Amsterdam Ave

Marcus Garvey Park

Park Ave

Lexington Ave

East Harlem

Mott Haven

Port Morris

NEW JERSEY
NEW YORK

See Central Park & Uptown Map (p96)

St Nicholas Ave

Harlem River

Major Deegan Expwy

Union City

Hudson River

Riverside Dr

Upper West Side

W 96th St

W 86th St

Columbus Ave

Central Park West

Manhattan Ave

Central Park North

Central Park

E 106th St

Fifth Ave

Madison Ave

E 96th St

E 86th St

Mill Rock Island

Randall's Island

Hell Gate

Astoria Park

Triborough Bridge

Otrmar's Blvd

W 72nd St

West Side Hwy

W 66th St

W 60th St

Upper East Side

E 79th St

E 72nd St

E 65th St

Roosevelt Island

Astoria Blvd

Astoria

Broadway

Steinway St

FDR Dr

East River

East End Ave

York Ave

Vernon Blvd

Long Island City

31st St

21st St

34th Ave

Lincoln Tunnel

Eleventh Ave

Tenth Ave

Ninth Ave

W 42nd St

W 40th St

W 34th St

Eighth Ave

Broadway

Seventh Ave

Avenue of the Americas

Fifth Ave

Park Ave

Garment District

Midtown

E 57th St

E 42nd St

E 40th St

E 34th St

Northern Blvd

Jackson Ave

Queens Blvd

Sunnyside

Long Island Expwy

Hoboken

W 23rd St

Chelsea

Sixth Ave

Third Ave

Second Ave

First Ave

E 23rd St

FDR Dr

Queens-Midtown Tunnel

McGuinness Blvd

Manhattan Ave

Newtown Creek

Calvary Cemetery

New Calvary Cemetery

Mt Zion Cemetery

Maspeth

Holland Tunnel

Greenwich St

Hudson St

West Side Hwy

Bleecker St

W Houston St

E 14th St

Stuyvesant Town

East Village

NoHo

SoHo

Nolita

E Houston St

Alphabet City

FDR Dr

East River Park

Greenpoint

East River Park

McCarren Park

Williamsburg

Metropolitan Ave

Grand St

Humboldt St

Metropolitan Ave

Linden Hill Cemetery

Grand Ave

Ridgewood

Bushwick

Jersey City

Rockefeller Park

Canal St

Centre St

Bowery

Broadway

Church St

Pitt St

Chinatown

Lower East Side

Williamsburg Bridge

See Williamsburg Map (p100)

Bedford Ave

Lee Ave

Flushing Ave

Broadway

Myrtle Ave

Liberty State Park

See West & East Villages, Chinatown & Lower Manhattan Map (p82)

Robert F Wagner Jr Park

Fulton St

Pearl St

FDR Dr

Manhattan Bridge

Brooklyn Bridge

Brooklyn Heights

Brooklyn-Queens Expwy

Bedford-Stuyvesant

Myrtle Ave

Ellis Island

Brooklyn-Battery Tunnel

Brooklyn Heights Promenade

Downtown Brooklyn

Flatbush Ave

Brooklyn Navy Yard

Fort Greene

Washington Ave

Lafayette Ave

Clinton Hill

Nostrand Ave

Marcy Ave

Malcolm X Blvd

Howard Ave

Liberty Island

Upper New York Bay

Governor's Island

Red Hook

Boerum Hill

Smith St

Atlantic Ave

Fulton St

Park Slope

Atlantic Ave

Brooklyn Flea Market

Prospect Heights

See Times Square, Midtown Manhattan & Chelsea Map (p92)

East River

Long Island City

NEW YORK CITY

WEST & EAST VILLAGES, CHINATOWN & LOWER MANHATTAN

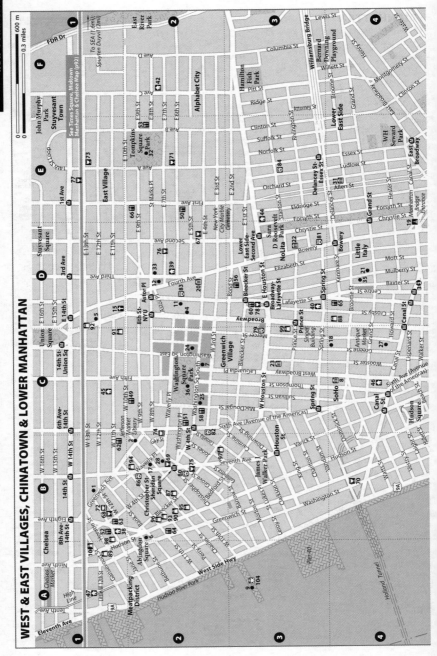

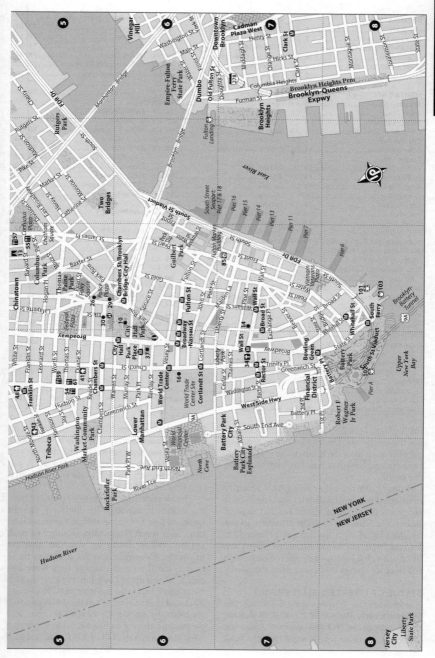

NEW YORK CITY

the big city. Though several high-end condos dot the landscape, Lower Manhattan tends to get a bit quiet after dark, when the investment bankers and businessmen have left work for the night.

Tribeca, on the other hand, is a recently revitalized residential district that has carved gorgeous lofts out of old industrial spaces. Robert De Niro has brought attention to the neighborhood with his annual Tribeca film festival (p103). Old cobblestone streets are lined with chic eateries and marvelous shops full of fancy things that every urbanist needs.

STATUE OF LIBERTY & ELLIS ISLAND
Along with the Empire State Building, the **Statue of Liberty** (Map p81; ☎ 212-363-3200; www.nps. gov/stli; admission free; 🕑 9:30am-3pm winter, 8:30am-6pm summer) is the most iconic sight in New York City. In Upper New York Bay, the statue, on Liberty Island, is reachable only by **ferry** (www. statuecruises.com; depart Battery Park; adult/child/senior incl Ellis Island $12/5/10; 🕑 ferries every 15-30 mins). A gift from the French, Lady Liberty was dedicated on October 28th, 1886.

The clever visitor will make a point of buying tickets in advance for the ferry as wait times in line for those without reservations can easily reach 90 minutes or more in peak season. When doing so, you can also get in on the Crown action for an extra three bucks. Until recently, statue fans were unable to climb up to Lady Liberty's headpiece. Now you can, *if* you have a ticket. It was announced that the statue would undergo some renovations during its 125th year that will necessitate closing public access to the statue itself starting in the fall of 2011. Call ahead if getting inside Lady Liberty herself is your sole reason for visiting.

Ferry rides to Liberty Island include a stop at **Ellis Island** (Map p81), the house that immigration built. Around 12,000 people a day were processed through here between 1892 and 1954. The Immigration museum occupies the beautifully detailed red brick building. Guided tours, as well as audio tours, are available. To be completely honest, though, Ellis Island is a bit dull and dry. But it's famous so, you know, it has that going for it.

If you want to see both Ellis Island and the Statue of Liberty, get on a boat before 1pm, otherwise you may not have enough time.

FEDERAL HALL

Completed in 1842, **Federal Hall** (Map p82; ☎ 212-825-6888; www.nps.org/feha; 26 Wall St; admission free; ☺ 9am-5pm Mon-Fri) is a stunning Greek revival structure built on the site of the original City Hall. It is also the site where George Washington took the oath of office as America's first president in 1789. Today it is a very appealing museum dedicated to postcolonial life in the freshly-minted United States and features a massive statue of Washington. There is quite a bit of space devoted to the fascinating statesman Alexander Hamilton, who was infamously shot down by Aaron Burr in a duel on the western shore of the Hudson River in Weekhawken, NJ.

TRINITY CHURCH

If you're feeling like seeing where former statesman Alexander Hamilton is now, walk west to Broadway and check out **Trinity Church** (Map p82; ☎ 212-602-0800; www.trinitywallstreet.org; Broadway at Wall St; ☺ 7am-6pm Mon-Fri, 8am-4pm Sat, 7am-4pm Sun), once the tallest building in New York with its 280ft high bell tower. It is in the Trinity Cemetery that he is buried. Though founded in 1697 by King William III, the current building is the third incarnation of the church on this site. Designed by Richard Upjohn, this 1846 building helped usher in the neo-Gothic fad of architecture that dominated church construction for much of the rest of the century. Even if you aren't a big churchgoer, Trinity is one worth visiting.

GROUND ZERO

This is a tough one. Everyone seems to want to visit, but as of this writing, **Ground Zero** (Map p82; 79 Leonard St btwn Broadway & Church St) is still just a hole in the ground. One World Trade Center is currently being built on the site and a memorial is supposed to be completed by 2011 for the 10th Anniversary of the tragic terrorist attacks of September 11th, 2001. Currently there's not much to see – it's just a construction site, though One World Trade Center (formerly called the Freedom Tower) is rising at a rapid clip.

WOOLWORTH BUILDING

An underappreciated architectural masterpiece, the **Woolworth Building** (Map p82; 233 Broadway at Park Pl) rises for 60 magnificent stories above City Hall Park. Designed by Cass Gilbert in 1913 for FW Woolworth, this 'cathedral of

---

DUNK DUNK. THESE ARE THEIR STORIES

Anyone who's been stuck home sick has surely spent a day watching back-to-back *Law & Order* episodes on cable TV. For those super-fans out there (you know who you are), you won't want to miss **City Hall Park** (Map p82; Broadway at Chambers St) and its surrounding buildings which have served as the backdrop for literally hundreds of episodes of this quintessential New York show.

Charge up the steps of the **Supreme Court of New York State** (60 Centre St) like DA Jack McCoy and rail against injustice and criminality. Better yet, bring a sexy lady Assistant DA to go with your stern demeanor. Beside that is the imposing monolith of **One Police Plaza**, headquarters of New York's Finest. Across the park is, unsurprisingly, **City Hall** with its cupola-topped limestone and marble façade. Its beautiful restoration in the mid-1950s prompted the noted architecture critic Ada-Louise Huxtable to call it a 'symbol of taste, excellence and quality not always matched by the policies inside.'

The grand marmalade-colored Siena marble interior of the Hall of Records aka **Surrogate's Court Building** (31 Chambers Street) houses the Municipal Archives. It has served as the location of interior shoots on *L&O* and dozens of other programs. The court's landmark French Renaissance edifice is topped by a tony mansard roof.

NEW YORK CITY

commerce' boasts a soaring neo-Gothic style of masonry and terracotta. It was the tallest building in the world until 1929.

Chinatown & Little Italy

Of these two ethnic enclaves, only Chinatown is still populated by the folks from whom it gets its name. Little Italy has long ago been passed over to the hipster kids of downtown Manhattan. While there are still remnants of Martin Scorcese and *Goodfellas* in the bars and restaurants, if you are truly interested in seeing some guidos, we recommend heading up to Arthur Ave in the Bronx (p101) for a more authentic Italian-American scene.

CANAL STREET

The main commercial artery of Chinatown, **Canal Street** is as well known for its packed sidewalks as it is for the knockoff designer goods and pungent restaurants decorated with whole ducks strung up by their necks. Have we tempted you into stopping by yet? The shopper looking for quality knockoffs though will be hard-pressed as there has been a recent crackdown on the trade.

BUDDHIST TEMPLES

Chinatown is home to Buddhist temples large and small, public and obscure. They are easily stumbled upon during a stroll of the 'hood, but two are of particular note. The **Eastern States Buddhist Temple** (Map p82; 64 Mott St btwn Bayard & Canal Sts) is filled with hundreds of Buddhas, while the **Mahayana Buddhist Temple** (Map p82; 133 Canal St at Manhattan Bridge Plaza) holds one golden, 16ft-high Buddha, sitting on a lotus.

MULBERRY STREET

This central stretch of Little Italy is the heart of the old neighborhood. It's here that a million and one myths about the Mob came to life. There are still vestiges of the Italian lifestyle on Mulberry Street, mostly on the handful of blocks between Broome and Canal Sts. You can stop into **Umberto's Clam House** (Map p82; ☎ 212-431-7545; 386 Broome St at Mulberry St), outside of which mobster Joey Gallo was gunned down in the 1970s. Just a little way down is the **Mulberry Street Bar** (Map p82; ☎ 212-226-9345; 176½ Mulberry St) formerly known as Mare Chiaro. The social club decor hasn't changed much in the century since it's been slinging drinks, and its been featured in such mob classics as *Donnie Brasco* and *The Sopranos*.

The best time to visit this area is during the lively **San Gennaro Festival** (www.sangennaro.org) that takes place annually during late September. The streets are packed with games and vendors and all the Italian restaurants offer street seating.

Soho, Noho & Nolita

This area of town is probably best known for its world class shopping options. Soho (short for South of Houston St) is really the only legit neighborhood, with Noho (North of Houston) and Nolita (North of Little Italy) being more realtors' terms than actual designations, though admittedly they have seeped into the local lexicon.

Soho's highlights, other than the aforementioned fabulous shopping, are the marvelous cast iron buildings that are the predominant architectural style of the neighborhood. Two examples are the most noteworthy. The first is known colloquially as the **King of Greene Street** (Map p82; 72 Greene St) and is a beautiful example of French Renaissance and Second Empire styles. **Queen of Greene Street** (Map p82; 28-30 Greene St) has fantastic Corinthian columns and is topped by a mansard roof with protruding dormer windows.

MERCHANT'S HOUSE MUSEUM

If you're the kind of person who loves Edith Wharton and Henry James, you should definitely step back in time at the little visited, but massively appealing, **Merchant's House Museum** (Map p82; ☎ 212-777-1089; www.merchantshouse.com; 29 E 4th St at the Bowery; adult/senior/student $10/5/5; ☽ noon-5pm Thu-Mon). The elegant late-Federal/Greek revival row house was built in 1832 and was owned by the same family until 1933. It remains remarkably preserved, both inside and out.

Lower East Side

If any neighborhood in Manhattan was a poster-child for gentrification, it's this one. Bursting at the seams with hipsters, trendy bars, groovy music joints and edgy boutiques, this section of the city used to be about as sleazy and sketchy as you could possibly imagine. Today, however, it's a great place to see some art and grab some brewskis.

Rising high above the Bowery, long ago home of New York's theater district before becoming known for its fleabag hotels, is the **New Museum of Contemporary Art** (Map p82; ☎ 212-219-

1222; www.newmuseum.org; 235 Bowery at Prince St; adult/
senior/student $12/10/8; ☺ 12-6pm Wed, 12-9pm Thu & Fri,
12-6pm Sat & Sun). A series of stacked white boxes,
rising seven stories and featuring a rainbow
sign that reads 'Hell Yes!', this art space offers
decidedly contemporary shows that vary from
the sublime to flat-out weird. The real star is
the architecture. On weekends you can hang
out in the Sky Box on the top floor with soaring views of downtown Manhattan.

Those who want a taste of what it was like
for the hundreds-of-thousands of immigrants
who lived on the Lower East Side should check
out the **Tenement Museum** (Map p92; ☎ 212-431-
0233; www.tenement.org; 97 Orchard St at Delancey St; adult/
senior/student $20/15/15; ☺ first tour at 10:30am, last tour at
5pm). This fine destination is highlighted by re-
creations of the cramped railroad apartments
that were ubiquitous of lower-class life in New
York between 1873 and 1929.

East Village

Formerly known as the Lower East Side, the
area north of Houston, south of 14th St, and
east of the Bowery was rechristened the East
Village a couple of decades ago.

East of First Ave is Alphabet City, where
the avenues become lettered. This particular
neighborhood gained a degree of fame when
it became the setting for the long-running
musical *Rent*.

If you like punk, rock and roll, and the latest in hipster fashions, you will find yourself
quite pleased by the main drag, **St. Mark's Place**
which is essentially East 8th St east of Third
Ave. Tons of junky stores and cheap eats can
be found. If you're looking for a little fetish
wear or something tight with lots of chains
and studs, you should definitely check out
Trash and Vaudeville (Map p82; ☎ 212-982-3590; 4 St
Mark's Pl), perhaps the most iconic store recall-
ing the era when the Ramones and Blondie
were gallivanting about the area.

TOMPKINS SQUARE PARK
The 'town square' of the East Village is
Tompkins Square Park (Map p82; btwn 7th & 10th
Streets & Aves A & B). Hipsters picnic on the grassy
knolls, canines cavort in the dog run, and locals shoot hoops on the courts. In the late 80s
and early 90s, Tompkins had become a needle
park and there was a tent city of homeless
living here until the cops notoriously swept
them out. This is referenced and musicalized
in the aforementioned *Rent*. Once that was

taken care of, it was time for gentrification
and a batch of yuppies and NYU students
started moving into the area. Still, this park
is lovely to use and is much safer than it was
20 years ago.

Greenwich Village & the West Village
It is the professional opinion of your authors
that this is the loveliest part of all New York
City. Cobblestone streets meander off towards
the water as the rigid grid plan breaks down
and the streets go all haywire, allowing you to
end up at seemingly incongruous corners like
W 4th St and W 11th St.

The spiritual center of Greenwich Village is
Washington Square Park (Map p82; at the southern terminus of Fifth Ave) and its famous Arch. The park has
had a major renovation in the past couple of
years and it seems to actually sparkle as dusk
approaches and the lights begin to flicker on.
Popular with skateboarders, bohemians, and
guitarists, this is a great place to get a taste of
the communal life of New Yorkers.

Washington Square also serves as the central campus for **New York University** (Map p82)
that has gobbled up much of the property
around the park. Those interested in taking a
brief walking tour should take note of a couple
of interesting buildings in the area. The first is
Bobst Library (Washington Sq S & LaGuardia Pl), NYU's
imposing Brutalist cube designed by Phillip

> **REMNANTS OF THE SOHO ART SCENE**
>
> The Dia Art Foundation has maintained
> Walter De Maria's conceptual 'interior earth
> sculpture' since 1980. The **New York Earth
> Room** (Map p82; www.diaart.org; 141 Wooster St
> btwn Prince & Houston Sts; admission free; ☺ 12-
> 6pm Wed-Sun, closed 3-3:30pm & mid-Jun–mid-
> Sep) is basically 250 cubic yards of dirt in
> a Soho loft space. It requires docents to
> de-mushroom and rake it out frequently.
> Really funky, it's a neat throwback to the
> Soho days of yore when the area was known
> for its dynamic art scene. Those with a
> taste for this sort of thing can check out
> De Maria's other long-term installation, also
> in Soho. The **Broken Kilometer** (393 West
> Broadway; ☺ 12-6pm Wed-Sun, closed 3-3:30pm
> & mid-Jun–mid-Sep) is 500 highly polished two
> meter poles laid out in five parallel rows.
> You know you want to see it.

NEW YORK CITY

COOPER UNION & THE PUBLIC THEATER

This tuition-free university was founded in 1849 and continues to be an elite institution. The spectacular **Great Hall** (Map p82; 41 Cooper Sq btwn Third & Fourth Aves) has hosted such illustrious orators as Abraham Lincoln (1860) and Barack Obama (2009). Also take note of Cooper Union's nifty, shiny, brand new nine-story environmentally friendly Morphosis-designed academic building. Just to the north of this area you'll find Astor Place and its iconic sculpture 'Alamo' known locally as the Astor Place cube.

On Lafayette St you will find the old Astor Library which is now home to the famed **Public Theater** (Map p82; ☎ 212-539-8500; www.publictheater.org; 425 Lafayette St). This New York institution, responsible for the annual Shakespeare in the Park, is where such mega-hits as *A Chorus Line* and *Hair* debuted. It continues to serve up edgy, contemporary performances in its collection of theaters and their sexy lounge, **Joe's Pub** (Map p82; ☎ 212-539-8778; www.joespub.com).

Across the street admire **Colonnade Row** (429–434 Lafayette) and the four Greek revival residences that remain of the original nine.

Johnson. Also on Washington Square South at the western edge of the park is the **NYU School of Law** with its charming courtyard. One of the country's top law schools, it's where a young John F Kennedy, Jr studied.

A walk up Fifth Ave will take you to the handful of blocks of **West 9th–West 12th Streets**, among the most elegant and pristine streets in the Village and the city. Scores of celebs from Uma Thurman to Barbara Bush (the younger) to Meryl Streep live or have lived in apartments and townhouses on these tree-lined streets. Radical activists might be interested in strolling past 18 W 11th St. In 1970, this was a safe house for the Weather Underground, a left-wing political activist (terrorist?) group fighting to end the Vietnam War. On March 6th of that year, three members of the group died when a nail bomb they were constructing exploded and blew up the building. Today you'll notice the townhouse has a strange angular façade at odds with the rest of the block.

Continue heading west into what is known as the **West Village** and wind your way to **Bleecker Street**. This shop-lined gift to the consumer is one of the best spots for shopping in downtown. Decidedly more low-impact than Soho or Madison Ave, this charming street and the surrounding ones like West 4th and Hudson are dotted with scores of superb stores and restaurants that make this feel like a true village. It's particularly good between Seventh and Eighth Aves – the eastern stretch is pocked with NYU student bars and falafel joints.

Christopher Street is quite lovely with the most famous site on the block being the **Stonewall Inn** (Map p82; 53 Christopher St). It was

here that assorted homosexuals rioted against police mistreatment in 1969, launching the modern gay movement. The West Village is still very much the spiritual 'gayborhood' of New York even as Chelsea, Hell's Kitchen and the East Village have all become more hip and trendy. One popular watering hole is **Julius** (Map p82; ☎ 212-243-1928; 159 W 10th St at Waverly Pl), which has been slinging drinks since 1864 making it the oldest bar in the Village. It began attracting a gay clientele in the 1950s and is considered to be the oldest gay bar as well.

ABINGDON SQUARE

One of the most delightful jewel parks in the city, this small but extraordinary garden bursts with color in the spring and summer and has a lovely assortment of perennials year-round. Benches abound in the **square** (Map p82; btwn Eighth Ave & Hudson St at 12th St), which is dominated by the statue of a WWI doughboy honoring neighborhood soldiers lost in battle. Practically perfect in every way, this is an ideal place to sip on a latte or scarf down a sandwich while watching the world go by after a long afternoon wandering the Village.

GRACE CHURCH

This is our favorite church in the city. It's not the biggest, but its easily one of the most beautiful. Episcopalian **Grace Church** (Map p82; ☎ 212-254-2000; www.gracechurchnyc.org; 802 Broadway at 10th St) is a stunning Gothic revival with a towering spire, bucolic yard, and elaborate carvings in marble and stone. It was designed by James Renwick, Jr whose work on this project was so admired that the Catholics hired him to design the much larger (but in our opinion less thrilling) St Patrick's Cathedral in Midtown.

Chelsea & the Meatpacking District

This is a very curious area of the city and we are extremely fond of it. Originally a privately-owned farm, Chelsea was a working class community for much of the following centuries. In the last couple of decades two distinct forces have shaped the historic neighborhood: the gallerists and the gays.

Eighth Ave between 14th and 23rd Sts, known in certain circles as 'Queens Boulevard,' is the main drag (bad pun intended). Lined with restaurants and stores of variable quality, Chelsea is usually teeming with 'Chelsea Boys' – a stereotype of buff, chiseled gay gym rats. Unsurprisingly, the blocks are now packed with some great stores selling men's fashion and expensive home furnishings.

The other primary force in the neighborhood is the art scene. After Soho got too expensive, the art dealers started setting up shop in the large warehouses and industrial spaces of West Chelsea.

Just south of Chelsea is the Meatpacking District. Only about a decade ago this cobblestone corner of Manhattan was just that: a place for packing meat. Littered with cow carcasses and a couple of shady bars like Hogs 'n' Heffers and the Lure, the Meatpacking District has been aggressively gentrified. Now it is a bastion of trendy hotels, luxury boutiques, and fine dining. It's hard to hate it because there's a lot of great stuff to buy and eat and the area has a fine urban elegance, but it can get overwhelming with the crowds playing Carrie Bradshaw and company on weekends.

HIGH LINE

The neighborhood's best place to visit by a long shot is the fantastic and wondrous **High Line** (Map p92; www.thehighline.org; west of Tenth Ave, south entrance at Gansevoort St, north entrance at 20th St, elevator access at 14th & 16th Sts; ⏱ 7am-10pm), formerly elevated train tracks for transporting meat and now a marvel of urban reinvention. Long abandoned, the High Line had become a natural landscape with grass and even trees having taken root on its forgotten tracks. In danger of being torn down, residents rallied to turn it into a much-needed public space and for once, the public won. Now this is one of the most treasured new jewels in town. The area currently renovated, from Gansevoort to 20th Sts is an oasis of trees, chaise lounges, prairie plants, and disarming views of the city and river. The second phase, stretching from 20th to 30th Sts, is scheduled to open in the spring of 2011.

CHELSEA GALLERIES

Art lovers should not miss strolling along the gallery-covered blocks (mostly between 21st and 26th Sts and west of Tenth Ave) that make up the Chelsea art scene. Check out www.ChelseaGalleryMap.com for the latest

---

LET US NOW PRAISE FAMOUS WOMEN

Enjoying the West Village, are you? Then you might want to snap a picture in front of **555 Hudson** which is where local activist and preservationist Jane Jacobs wrote *The Death and Life of American Cities*, quite possibly the most influential book on urban planning published in the 20th century.

Railing against the powers that be, Jacobs despised the modernist planning prevalent in the 1950s and 60s that sought to tear down much of what she felt was the fabric of the city and replace it with massive urban developments. She preferred a mixed-use approach that had an assortment of business, manufacturing and living spaces in order to create a vibrant urban environment, much like Greenwich Village, which she used extensively as an example in the book.

Notably she battled Robert Moses, the ridiculously powerful 'master builder' of New York in the mid-20th century, when he sought to tear down most of Soho, the Lower East Side and the lower Village in favor of erecting the Lower Manhattan Expressway. He lost (thank God) and it was a spectacular defeat for Moses as he'd rarely been opposed in the past (he'd already destroyed large swaths of the Bronx with his Cross-Bronx Expressway).

Death and Life is considered a text of monumental importance and continues to influence urban planners to this day, especially as we witness the rebirth of the city as the suburbs lose their luster.

See also Robert Caro's lacerating *The Power Broker* about the enormous impact of Robert Moses on NYC.

information on what's showing. But three stalwarts of the area are: big man on campus **Gagosian** (Map p92; ☎ 212-741-1111; www.gagosian.com; 555 W 24th St; ☺ 10am-6pm Tue-Sat), the slightly edgier **Andrea Rosen Gallery** (Map p92; ☎ 212-627-6000; www.andrearosengallery.com; 525 W 24th St; ☺ hours vary), and **Jim Kempner Fine Art** (Map p92; ☎ 212-206-6872; www.jimkempnerfineart.com; 501 W 23rd at 10th Ave; ☺ 10am-6pm Tue-Sat) inside a modernist cube of metal and glass.

Union Square, the Flatiron District & Gramercy Park

This large swath of middle Manhattan covers a variety of cityscapes from the skater and student infested park to the old-world civility of Irving Place. The main feature of this area is **Union Square** (Map p92; 14th St at Broadway & Park Ave), a throbbing and dynamic hub in the city. It's prominence comes chiefly from its position as a major subway station with several lines converging here. Above ground, the large park is both historic and notorious. It became yet another needle park until its rebirth concurrent with NYU's expansion north and the general economic revival of New York.

Fountains, statues and lawns abound, but Union Square's most appealing attraction is the **Union Square Greenmarket** (Map p92; ☺ 8am-6pm Mon, Wed, Fri & Sat) in which scores of farmers hock their produce and wares. A staple of New York's epicurean scene, you shouldn't be surprised to see many of the city's top chefs browsing for inspiration on early mornings. Two other sites of interest are **Andy Warhol's Factory** (Map p92; 33 Union Sq West) – this was the second location, the first being a loft on 47th St – and **Metronome** (Map p92; 1 Union Sq S), a public art piece on the façade of 1 Union Square South that boasts a digital clock that simultaneously counts the hours of the day up and down. It even occasionally blows smoke.

If you wander up Broadway into the **Flatiron District** you'll enter what was once known as Ladies' Mile, a long stretch of fashionable department stores in the latter part of the 19th century. The old **Lord & Taylor building** (cnr of Broadway & 20th St) is a particularly majestic relic of the past, having opened in 1870. The building's ornate and columned façade is crowned by an appealing mansard roof dotted by dormers. Those looking to do a little shopping themselves should step into the nearby ABC Carpet & Home (p112) to pick a few essentials for that new apartment you're thinking of getting.

The gems of the neighborhood are **Madison Square Park** (Map p92; Madison Sq) and the **Flatiron Building** (Map p92; 23rd St at Broadway & Fifth Ave). It is our opinion that this edifice ranks only behind the Empire State and Chrysler Buildings in terms of New York architectural iconography. This 1902 triangular building has been photographed more times than you can imagine with its graceful form and pride of place perhaps most famously captured by the photographer Alfred Steiglitz. The park, often brimming with highbrow public art installations, is one of the city's loveliest. Foodies will want to check out the Shake Shack, upscale restaurateur Danny Meyer's take on the burger stand.

Eastwards is **Gramercy Park** (Map p92; Lexington & Irving Pl btwn 20th & 21st Sts), the city's only remaining private, gated park. Only residents who pay to maintain the park are given a key and access remains one of the city's most exclusive gets. You can enjoy it from the outside, though, and the area is marvelous and serene. The **National Arts Club** (Map p92; 15 Gramercy Park South) is a Calvert Vaux–designed façade decorated by small busts of famous writers and other ornate carvings. Take a walk down Irving Place towards 14th St and you'll pass several appealing eateries along with refined architecture. We'd recommend stopping in Lady Mendl's Tea Salon (p108) or Pete's Tavern (p108) where O Henry penned his prose.

Midtown & Times Square

Oy. Midtown can be great, but let's be honest – Times Square is generally awful. There's a lot of words we could use, one of which rhymes with cluster-schmuck. **Times Square** (Map p92; Seventh Ave & Broadway btwn 42nd & 50th Sts) is the 'Crossroads of the World' and is ridiculously famous worldwide. So run in, get your picture taken, and then get the heck out of here. The only reason any New Yorker goes to Times Square is to see theater. This is a very good reason to go. Visiting the Hershey Store or Sbarro Pizza is not.

Yet Midtown, however infuriating with its traffic and crowds, has many of New York's most famed buildings and illustrious institutions. There is much to see but we urge you to not spend your entire vacation in this vicinity.

EMPIRE STATE BUILDING

It's famous! It's tall! It's deco! Go stand on top of it! *King Kong, Sleepless in Seattle, Love Affair*! Built in an amazingly speedy 410 days, the **Empire State Building** (Map p92; www.esbnyc.com; 34th St at Fifth Ave; adult/child/senior $20/14/18; 8am-2am) debuted its limestone façade in 1931 at the height of the Depression. The best time to check out the view is after dark, when the crowds have waned and the building is floodlit in a variety of colors, usually marking something famous.

GRAND CENTRAL

Popularly known around the world as Grand Central Station, **Grand Central Terminal** (Map p92; 42nd St at Park Ave S) is a Beaux Arts masterpiece worthy of its acclaim. Even if you aren't catching a train, it's worth wandering through the massive main hall and its adjacent environs, despite its oddities. For instance, the constellations that splay across the vaulted ceiling of Grand Central are actually backwards, presenting a God's eye view rather than an earthbound one. Yet you'll be hard pressed to find a more elegiac ode to travel. There's something rather magical about this place and if you're just passing through, try having some raw fish at the oyster bar or grab a margarita to go on the underground dining concourse.

ROCKEFELLER CENTER

This tremendous ode to all things art deco features epic plazas and massive sculptures of Prometheus and Atlas among other highlights. Comprised of 14 original buildings (five are newer), the complex was a marvel in the 1930s when it was built despite the Depression and continues to wow visitors. **Rockefeller Center** (Map p92; 212-632-3975; www.rockefellercenter.com; from Fifth to Seventh Aves btwn 48th & 51st Sts) is full of shops, both touristy (the NBC Store) and fancy (Thomas Pink) as well as a few high-end restaurants (the Sea Grill adjacent to the rink is a nice one). To the western end is **Radio City Music Hall** (Map p92; 212-247-4777; www.radiocity.com; 1260 Ave of the Americas) and all its attendant concerts and events. Visitors with a taste for the sky should amble up to the **Top of the Rock** (212-698-2000; www.topoftherocknyc.com; 30 Rockefeller Plaza at 49th St; adult/child/senior $21/14/19; 8am-midnight) at the top of the GE Building that houses the NBC studios.

MUSEUM OF MODERN ART

One of NYC's big guns on the world art scene, **MoMA** (Map p92; 212-708-9400; 11 W 53rd St; adult/child/student/senior $20/free/12/16; 10:30am-5:30pm Wed-Mon, to 8pm Fri) is rife with cultural treasures. Matisse, Picasso, Van Gogh, Monet, Warhol, Lichtenstein, Rothko, Pollock, Flavin, Kahlo, Duchamp, Miro, Chagal – and that's just on the top two floors. The rest of the museum teems with new shows that often inspire. Massive, splashy, crowded and thrilling – MoMA should be seen at least once by every visitor to the city.

MORGAN LIBRARY & MUSEUM

A shrine for scholars of the arts and letters, the **Morgan Library** (Map p92; 212-685-0008; www.themorgan.org; 225 Madison Ave at 36th St; adult/child/senior/student $12/8/8/8; 10:30am-5pm Tue-Thu, 10:30am-9pm Fri, 10am-6pm Sat, 11am-6pm Sun) is one of the best museums in the city, made even better thanks to the Renzo Piano overhaul in 2006 that created a glass atrium in which to sip tea and spirits. The museum is mostly comprised of robber baron JP Morgan's Stanford White–designed former mansion with all its ornate turn-of-the-century flourishes. The library is but one of many breathtaking rooms and houses not one but three Gutenberg Bibles. The rest of the museum dedicates itself to rare literary works and thoughtfully curated shows of illustration and more. This is a real treat for folks who are looking for alternatives to the Met or MoMA as it offers not only fine art but also a peek into New York's past.

FIFTH AVENUE

When shopaholics talk about Fifth Ave, they mean the midtown blocks between 50th and 59th Sts. Here is where you'll find Prada, Gucci, and most of the other superstars of blockbuster fashion lined up and ready to swipe your card. Three of the best stores are Bergdorf Goodman (p111) and it's notoriously overdressed windows, the iconic Tiffany & Co (p112) where Audrey dreamed of diamonds, and the kid-friendly palace of toys that is FAO Schwartz (p112).

Central Park

No visit to New York is complete without the requisite stroll through **Central Park** (www.centralpark.com; btwn Fifth & Eighth Aves & 59th & 110th Sts), the city's public backyard. First opened in the winter of 1859, the Frederick Law Olmstead

TIMES SQUARE, MIDTOWN MANHATTAN & CHELSEA

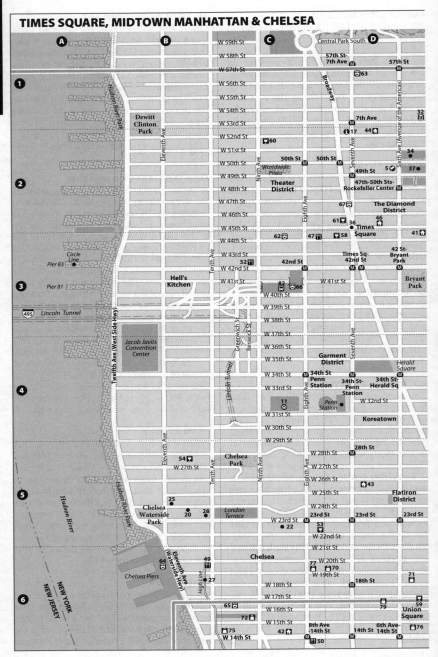

NEW YORK CITY

and Calvert Vaux design led to the first land-scaped park in America. Yes, that means that absolutely none of Central Park is natural – the pastoral, picturesque and formal elements were constructed.

Lots of people like the Great Lawn with its playing fields and huge expanse, but for our money, we prefer the more petit, but still grand, **Sheep Meadow** (Map p96; near Central Park West & 67th St) where the trees are crowned by the spires and towers of Midtown Manhattan in the distance.

The most popular site in the park is a little ways north – **Strawberry Fields** (Map p96; near Central Park W & 72nd St). This memorial to John Lennon is within sight of the Dakota apartment building where the Beatle was assassinated. Yoko Ono still lives there and donated $1 million towards the upkeep of the tear-shaped garden which has a simple tile mosaic that reads 'Imagine' as its central element.

Those too young to have heard of the Beatles will be more interested in the south-eastern corner of the park where more kid-friendly activities abound. The classics include ice-skating at **Wollman Rink** (Map p96; ☎ 212-439-6900; adult/child/senior $14/5.50/8.50; East

Side btwn 62nd & 63rd Sts; 🕑 Nov-March; ♿) or amusement park rides in the summer when it becomes the **Victorian Gardens** (🕑 late-May–mid-Sep). Young kids will also be thrilled by the vintage **Carousel** (Map p96; mid-park near 64th St; 🕑 year-round, weather permitting) that has long been a favorite of city kids.

Lots of playgrounds can be found all over Central Park. Our favorite is the **Diana Ross Playground** (Map p96; Central Park W & 81st St) for the simple reason that it's named after our favorite Supreme. Another thing we like just for its name is the **Jacqueline Kennedy Onassis Reservoir** (Map p96; betw 86th & 96th Sts), which stretches for several blocks. This is what everyone jogs around.

Perhaps the most iconic locale within the park are the **Bethesda Fountain** and the **Rowboat Lake** (Map p96; at 72nd St & Terrace Dr). This has been seen in numerous films, perhaps most memorably in *Hair* when dancers career up and down the stairs while doing intricate Twyla Tharp choreography. Nearby is the **Boathouse** (Map p96; near 72nd St & Park Drive N; 🕑 lunch & dinner) that sports a great patio for cocktails and a high-end restaurant. There are few things lovelier than watching the rowboats drift lazily in the rippling water as the sun sets over the Upper West Side.

The **Conservatory Garden** (Map p96; Fifth Ave at 105th St; 🕑 8am-dusk) will appeal to those with a taste for formal gardens. Here the elaborate gardens are divided into three distinct styles: French, Italian and English. This garden is often too far north to attract much attention save for wedding photographers who seem to adore posing brides in front of the fountains and flowers. It's worth the trek up to explore.

Upper East Side

Gossip Girl here with your guide to the gilded, diamond-encrusted world of Manhattan's elite. The Upper East Side is where the really rich Manhattanites live like billionaire Mayor Bloomberg, Woody Allen, and most of the people who attend thousand-dollar-a-plate charity galas.

Built over the train tracks heading north from Grand Central, Park Ave is lined with grand apartments and penthouses. **Madison Avenue** is lined with tony boutiques like Tom Ford (p112) and luxury department stores like Barneys New York (p111). Down south it's the land of Mad Men, but up here its ladies who lunch and their walkers. All in all, it's a sparkling section of NYC, though it lacks that certain 'oomph' that wilder parts of the city exude.

MUSEUM MILE

Fifth Ave, on the Upper East Side, is commonly referred to as Museum Mile for its plethora of art institutions. The big man on campus is, of course, the **Metropolitan Museum of Art** (The Met; Map p96; ☎ 212-535-7710; www.metmuseum.org; 1000 Fifth Ave at 82nd St; adult/child under 12/student/senior $20/free/10/15; 🕑 9:30am-5:30pm Tue-Thu & Sun, 9:30am-9pm Fri & Sat, open holiday Mondays). Arguably the most famous museum in the United States, the Met is considered the most comprehensive in the western hemisphere. It has particularly deep collections of Egyptian, Medieval, Asian and Decorative art. The roof often hosts exciting sculpture during the summer months along with its views of Central Park. This place is so massive you can't possibly see it all in one visit. Don't try. Just relax and wander.

To the south is the **Frick Collection** (Map p96; ☎ 212-288-0700; www.frick.org; 1 E 70th St; adult/student/senior $18/5/12, no children under 10; 🕑 10am-6pm Tue-Sat, 11am-5pm Sun) in the industrialist Henry

Clay Frick's former Fifth Ave mansion. The impressive collection focuses mainly on European painting in addition to bronzes, furniture, Limoges enamels, and Chinese porcelains. Really exquisite, this is probably the most elegant of the choices.

The **Whitney Museum of American Art** (Map p96; ☎ 212-570-3600; www.whitney.org; 945 Madison Ave at 75th St; adult/child/student/senior $18/free/12/12; 🕑 11am-6pm Wed, Thu, Sat & Sun, 1-9pm Fri) is one of the most adventurous museums along Museum Mile and is located in a fabulous brutalist building by Marcel Breuer. Most famous for their 'Biennial' that surveys the contemporary art world, the Whitney has an extensive Edward Hopper collection on permanent view among others. Mostly it stages thoughtful exhibitions on contemporary American artists like Nan Goldin or Ed Ruscha. This is our favorite pick on the strip.

Another iconic museum, perhaps more famous for its architecture than its art, is the **Solomon R Guggenheim Museum** (Map p96; www.guggenheim.org; 1071 Fifth Ave at 89th St; adult/child under 12/student/senior $18/free/15/15; 🕑 10am-5:45pm Sun-Wed & Fri, 10am-7:45pm Sat) designed by Frank Lloyd Wright. The cylindrical swoops of this tour-de-force are what draw in the crowds. Yet the art inside, especially when it's Kandinsky (in whom they specialize), can be splendid. They don't tend to show a whole lot of their permanent collection, so knowing what show is on is important to those who are interested in more than the building.

The **Museum of the City of New York** (Map p96; ☎ 212-534-1672; www.mcny.org; 1220 Fifth Ave at 103rd St; adult/child under 12/senior/student $10/free/6/6; 🕑 10am-5pm Tue-Sun) is a groovy art and historical museum that offers intriguing shows focusing on...wait for it...New York City. The **Neue Galerie** (Map p96; ☎ 212-628-6200; www.neuegalerie.org; 1048 Fifth Ave at 86th St; adult/student/senior $15/10/10; 🕑 11am-6pm Thu-Mon) points its academic eye on Austrian and German art and recently acquired a handful of Gustav Klimpts that is the main attraction.

Upper West Side

Ah, the intellectual capitol of the city – or so they'd like to think. The Upper West Side has become a sort of pseudo-suburban enclave for the chattering class who work in media and education. Of course it's more than that, but if the Upper East Side is home to investment bankers and trust funders, the Upper West

NEW YORK CITY

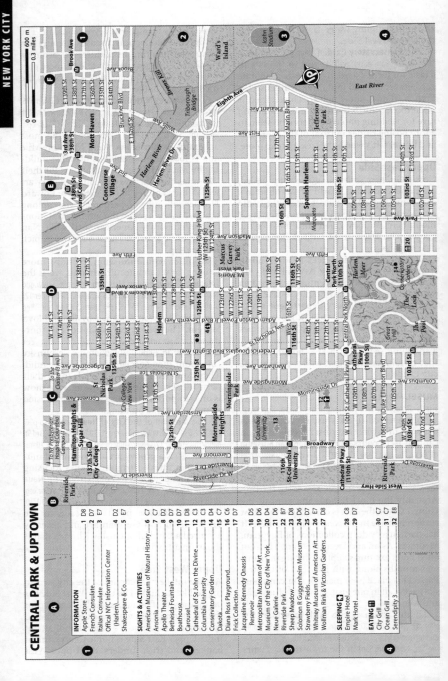

CENTRAL PARK & UPTOWN

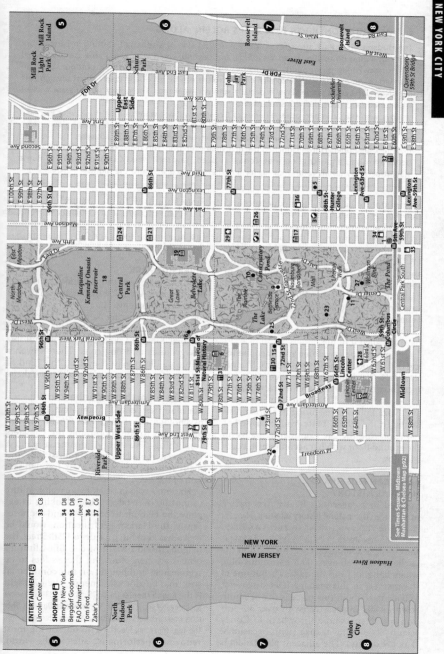

ENTERTAINMENT	
Lincoln Center	33 C8

SHOPPING	
Barney's New York	34 D8
Bergdorf Goodman	35 D8
FAO Schwartz	(see 1)
Tom Ford	36 E7
Zaba's	37 C6

OL' MAN (HUDSON) RIVER JUST KEEPS ROLLIN' ALONG

The **Hudson River Park** stretches up the entire west side of Manhattan, starting in Battery Park and continuing up to the Upper West Side and beyond. Lined with bike paths, the occasional café, grassy knolls, playgrounds, and renovated piers, this is one of the best outdoor spaces in Manhattan. An excellent place to picnic and stroll, it can be especially lovely when the sun sets over New Jersey. On warm days, especially summer weekends, the grassy sections are packed with toned (and not-so-toned) sunbathers.

Boys who like boys and other 'Friends of Dorothy' will not want to miss the 'Queer Pier' aka the **Christopher Street Pier** aka the 'bacon rack' (for all the shirtless men catching some rays while texting on their iPhones) and officially known as **Pier 45** (Map p82; Christopher St at West Side Hwy). In 1809 Robert Fulton launched the first steamship from this pier, but 160 years later is was better known as a gay cruising spot. Today it's been, how shall we say, cleaned up a bit? But it still attracts gay urban youth looking for a gathering place well into the night.

Side is home to bagel-loving media execs and *New Yorker* scribes.

Grand apartment buildings are among the architectural stunners in this part of town. One of the most famous is the **Dakota** (Map p96; 1 W 72nd at CPW), where John Lennon was shot and *Rosemary's Baby* was set. Completed in 1884, this was the first fashionable apartment building. Until then the elite all lived in private homes and considered apartments no better than tenements. Over the years Judy Garland, Leonard Bernstein and Boris Karloff have all called it home.

The other super-awesome apartment building in the 'hood is the **Ansonia** (Map p96; Broadway btwn 72nd & 73rd). This grand Beaux-Arts apartment boasts heavily ornamented facades, balconies, and towers. Babe Ruth, Igor Stravinsky and Nora Ephron are among its storied residents. In the 1970s, Bette Midler made her name playing the gay Continental Baths on the ground floor with her accompanist, Barry Manilow.

AMERICAN MUSEUM OF NATURAL HISTORY

Located in a cavernous Beaux-Arts palace of science, the **natural history museum** (Map p96; ☎ 212-769-5100; www.amnh.org; Central Park W & 79th St; adult/child/senior/student $16/9/12/12; ✆ 10am-5:45pm) is the classic academic expanse for, pardon the cliché, kids of all ages. The enormous blue whale hanging from the rafters is but one of the marvels in this menagerie of discovery. What's neat about this place is that it's both scientifically impressive (with over 30 million specimens) and a throwback to Coney Island–style extravaganza (with occasional faux taxidermy). The adjacent **planetarium** is more impressive for its architecture (a huge glass cube encasing a silver planet suspended within) than its truly enlightening exhibits (ho-hum moon rocks and 7th grade explanations of the universe).

RIVERSIDE PARK

A thin strip of parkland, **Riverside Park** (Map p96; Hudson River from 72nd to 125th Sts) bursts with flowers and cherry blossoms. Here Upper West Siders jog along meandering paths, eat their bagels and lox on benches overlooking the river, and let their kids and dogs run free in multiple playgrounds and dog runs. There's even a statue of Eleanor Roosevelt at the 72nd St entrance for you First Lady fetishists out there.

Harlem & Northern Manhattan

For many residents of Manhattan, the island psychologically ends at 96th St with Harlem being akin to the moon and the Cloisters something like the Andromeda galaxy. However, the adventurous tourist will find many reasons to enjoy this less-traveled section of the city.

Harlem's role in black history and culture cannot be overstated. Those looking to explore the Harlem Renaissance and more recently, the Harlem gentrification, would be well advised to hitch a ride to **125th Street**, the neighborhood's Main Street. Bill Clinton's offices are here now, but there's lots to be seen, eaten, and bought on this commercial strip that bustles with energy. The highlight is the **Apollo Theater** (Map p96; ☎ 212-531-5337; www.apollotheater.org; 253 125th St at Frederick Douglass Blvd; tours weekdays/weekends $16/18; ✆ tours 11am daily, 1pm Thu-Tue, 3pm Mon, Tue, Thu & Fri) one of the most renowned performance sites in the world.

Built in 1914, the music hall has welcomed the likes of Duke Ellington and launched the careers of such legends as Ella Fitzgerald and James Brown. Check out the website for a list of upcoming shows, but know that every Wednesday at 7:30pm is the classic 'Amateur Night' which is a rollicking good time.

Also up in this neck of the woods is the neighborhood of Morningside Heights, home to the **Cathedral of St John the Divine** (Map p96; ☎ 212-316-7540; www.stjohndivine.org; Amsterdam Ave at 112th St; ☀ 7am-6pm Mon-Sat, to 7pm Sun). The first stone of this, the largest church in the United States, was laid in 1892 – and it's still under construction! A century later, you can admire the largest stained glass window in the country and its altar designed by 1980s pop artist Keith Haring.

The other big institution in Morningside Heights is **Columbia University** (Map p96; ☎ 212-854-1754; www.columbia.edu; Broadway at 116th St), New York's contribution to the Ivy League. It was first chartered in 1754 as King's College. Highlights for the non-academic visitor are mostly in the central campus designed in 1897 by McKim, Mead and White in Italian Renaissance–style. Here you'll find the Low Library with its Grecian detailing and the Alma mater statue.

At the tip top of Manhattan in Fort Tryon Park is the Met's uptown annex known as the **Cloisters** (off Map p96; ☎ 212-923-3700; www.met museum.org; 99 Margaret Corbin Dr, Fort Tryon Park; adult/child under 12/student/senior $20/free/10/15; ☀ 9:30am-5:15pm Tue-Sun from Mar-Oct, to 4:45pm Nov-Feb). Constructed out of fragments of Spanish and French monasteries, the Cloisters houses the Met's collection of medieval frescoes, tapestries and paintings. In the spring and summer months, you can enjoy the more than 250 varieties of medieval flowers and herbs on view.

Brooklyn

Manhattan often gets the glory of fawning helicopter shots tracking over its skyline while the other four boroughs get short shrift. Brooklyn, however, has its own feisty attitude and in the last two decades it has become *the* place for certain know-it-all New Yorkers to live, eat, shop and drink copiously.

First settled in 1635 as New Netherlands (10 years after New Amsterdam), Breuckelen, one of five Dutch settlements on the island, was founded in 1646. It was its own city (called Brooklyn once the English took charge) for the next couple of centuries until New York City became incorporated in 1898.

Brooklyn is comprised of scores of individual neighborhoods. Unlike Manhattan, though, they tend to be much more spread out and walking between them can be arduous. That said, Brooklyn is very much worth exploring, especially for those interested in all things fashion-forward and trendy.

Brooklyn Heights, the city's oldest unchanged neighborhood, is a good stop for people interested in what New York used to be like. The first designated historic district is chock full of 19th-century brownstones ranging in style like Victorian Gothic, Romanesque, and neo-Greco. Truman Capote wrote *Breakfast at Tiffany's* at 70 Willow St and Cher's house from the movie *Moonstruck* ('Snap out of it!') is at 19 Cranberry St.

The main attraction in the neighborhood is the **Brooklyn Heights Promenade** (Map p82; near Furman St btwn Orange & Remsen Sts) at the river's edge, offering spectacular views of the harbor and Lower Manhattan. You've seen it a million times in the movies and we guarantee that it's even better in person, especially at dusk when the romance is high.

Williamsburg is the borough's mandated hipster reservation. Angular haircuts, funky clothes, groovier-than-thou attitude – they're all here in this gritty glam bohemian paradise. Until recently a fairly working-class neighborhood known for its pockets of Hasidic Jews, Dominicans, Puerto Ricans, and Italians, Williamsburg began its transformation in the late-1990s. Today it is an ideal place to

GREEN-WOOD CEMETERY

Over 550,000 interments dating from 1838 make this originally rural (now its smack dab in the middle of Brooklyn) **cemetery** (☎ 718-768-7300; www.green-wood.com; Fifth Ave at 25th St; ☀ 8am-5pm) a Victorian Gothic fantasy. The spectacular Gothic revival gatehouse by Richard Upjohn is but a taste of the deathly hallows in this bucolic 19th-century gem, the serene popularity of which led to the commissioning of Central Park. 'Boss' Tweed, Leonard Bernstein, and the Steinways are among the entombed. Historic trolley tours are offered every Wednesday and the last Sunday of each month at 1pm.

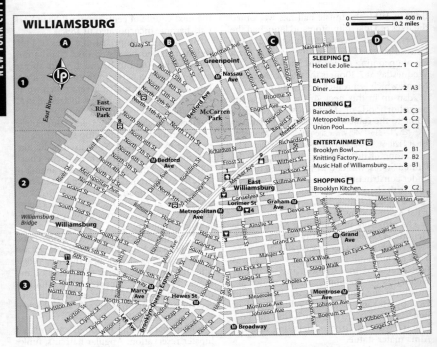

WILLIAMSBURG

SLEEPING 🏠
Hotel Le Jolie **1** C2

EATING 🍴
Diner **2** A3

DRINKING 🍷
Barcade **3** C3
Metropolitan Bar **4** C2
Union Pool **5** C2

ENTERTAINMENT 🎭
Brooklyn Bowl **6** B1
Knitting Factory **7** B2
Music Hall of Williamsburg **8** B1

SHOPPING 🛍️
Brooklyn Kitchen **9** C2

shop for vintage and vinyl, grab a Pabst Blue Ribbon and to kvetch about your digital media job. A Williamsburg bar crawl should be required for any self-respecting scenester visiting the city.

The stroller set has taken over **Park Slope** (Map p81) a beautiful area of brownstones bordering Prospect Park. With its large stoops and literary inclination, this is a section that caters to families where both parents have college degrees, if not PhDs, and the search for the perfect soy latte is an odyssey worthy of footnoted Homer. But with that hominess (bemoaned by singles, revered by families) comes great cafés, quiet coffeehouses, and offbeat yet practical stores. While it has a whiff of the upscale bourgeoisie, it retains an earthiness that is complemented by the world-class park next door.

PROSPECT PARK

You've probably heard of Central Park, but did you know it has a sexy cousin? Frederick Law Olmstead and Calvert Vaux, the famed designers of Manhattan's pride and joy, teamed up again to design this central Brooklyn park. Dating from 1866, **Prospect Park** (Map p79; ☎ 718-965-8999; www.prospectpark.org) has the expected gorgeous vistas, large playing fields, and hidden nooks. The **Audubon Center Boathouse** has visitor information and electric boat rides. Just north of here is the **Children's Corner** with a ride orphaned from Coney Island carousel, a small zoo, and ice rink.

BROOKLYN MUSEUM

Second in size only to the Met, the **Brooklyn Museum** (☎ 718-638-5000; www.brooklynmuseum.org; 200 Eastern Pkwy; adult/child/student/senior $10/free/6/6; 🕙 10am-5pm Wed-Fri, 11am-6pm Sat & Sun), at the northern end of Prospect Park, is often overlooked despite its impressive collections. In an 1897 Beaux-Arts building by McKim, Mead and White, it shows permanent exhibits of Egyptian and African art, and several Rodin sculptures. The free night – first Saturday each month – keeps the museum open until 11pm and is a rollicking good time with bands, screenings, and a beer and wine bar.

BROOKLYN BOTANIC GARDEN

A favorite of gardenistas, the **Brooklyn Botanic Garden** (☎ 718-623-7200; www.bbg.org; 1000 Washington

Ave; adult/child/student/senior $8/free/4/4; 8am-6pm Tue-Fri, 10am-6pm Sat & Sun Apr-Oct, to 4:30pm Nov-Mar), located within Prospect Park, sits on 52 acres and has over 10,000 species of plants. Turtles swim past a Shinto shrine at the Japanese Hill and Pond garden. There's a large pavilion with a variety of climates. In May, the Sakuri Matsuri is the cherry blossom festival that draws big crowds.

Queens

Queens doesn't get a ton of respect, despite the fact that it was named for Queen Catherine of Braganza (Charles II's wife). These days Queens is growing into its own as more and more of Manhattan's professional set make their homes there, especially in areas like Long Island City and Astoria, both of which are right across the East River.

Long Island City (Map p81) can feel somewhat like a corporate office park in places, what with its enormous glass condo building. **Astoria** (Map p81), on the other hand, feels a lot like the rest of Queens – slightly workaday homes and apartment buildings catering mostly to New York's middle class.

Yet interspersed among these areas are a couple of great museums including MoMA's not-so-secret annex dedicated to contemporary art. The **PS 1 Contemporary Art Center** (718-784-2084; www.ps1.org; 22-25 Jackson Ave at 46th Ave; adult/student/senior $10/5/5; 12-6pm Thu-Mon) is decidedly edgier than its Midtown cousin. You won't catch much impressionism in this former school building, but if you like video art then you will be in hog heaven. It's free if you've bought a MoMA ticket within 30 days. On summer Saturdays, the outdoor space is transformed into a well-attended party space with DJs, bands, and more.

The Bronx

'Ladies and gentlemen, the Bronx is burning!' exclaimed Howard Cosell during the 1977 World Series as he looked out from his announcer's box at Yankee Stadium and saw the borough in flames. Long a symbol of urban blight and poverty, the Bronx is more than the Yankees.

Anyone yearning for a good bowl of pasta should head to **Arthur Avenue** (Arthur Ave at 187th St), New York's 'real' Little Italy. Unlike the downtown Manhattan version that's about as authentic as your supermarket Ragu spaghetti sauce, Arthur Ave boils over with gastronomic

WARRIORS, COME OUT TO PLAY-EE-AY

Brooklyn's legendary boardwalk and beach is at **Coney Island** (Map p79; Surf Ave at Stillwell Ave or Ocean Pkwy). It's been a rough couple of years for the area with lots of classic amusements closing down as the city wobbles back and forth on how to preserve it. Summer 2010 brought some good news though, with the opening of **Luna Park** (www.lunaparknyc.com), a brand new amusement center with shiny rides and games. Add that to the **Cyclone** (www.coneyisland cyclone.com), the boardwalk's classic roller coaster and the nearby **NY Aquarium** (www.nyaquarium.com) and visitors with rambunctious kids should be more than pleased. If you haven't seen *The Warriors* you definitely should put this campy 70s film about a Coney Island gang on your Netflix queue.

markets and shops willing to shuck oysters for you on the sidewalk. A few restaurants like Roberto (p108) offer up lots of options for the hungry tourist. A recent visitor was overheard complaining to her waiter 'No one in the city speaks Italian' – that won't be a problem up here.

City Island is another funky and oft-forgotten corner, like a bizarre-transplant from Cape Cod. Amidst the Victorian clapboard houses you'll find a dizzying array of seafood shops like Johnny's Famous Reef Restaurant (p108) that fries just about everything before sending you outside to eat with the seagulls.

BRONX ZOO

The city's most famous **zoo** (Map p79; 718-367-1010; www.bronxzoo.com; 2300 Southern Blvd; adult/child/senior $15/11/13; 10am-5pm Mon-Fri, to 5:30pm Sat & Sun) is a kick to visit. The 265-acre menagerie has a variety of world habitats (African plains, Himalayan mountains, Asian rainforests) for its 4000 animals and is too big to be seen in a day, even if you take the monorail or shuttle rides around the grounds.

NEW YORK BOTANICAL GARDEN

Right near the Bronx Zoo is the wonderful **NY botanical garden** (Map p79; 718-817-8700; www.nybg. com; Bronx River Pkwy & Fordham Rd; adult/child/student/senior $6/1/3/3; 10am-6pm Tue-Sun). The garden (over 50 acres) has several lovely nooks and crannies and seems worlds away from the hustle and bustle of Gotham. The highlight is the Enid Haupt Conservatory, a grand, Victorian iron-and-glass edifice with several different climates controlled inside.

Staten Island

Oh, Staten Island (Map p79), New York's forgotten borough. If it weren't for its famous ferry (see p114), residents might forget about it entirely. By far New York's most suburban borough, it's more New Jersey than New York.

That said, you really should check out the **Snug Harbor Cultural Center** (☎ 718-448-2500; www.snug-harbor.org; 1000 Richmond Tce; gardens & galleries adult/child/student/senior $6/3/5/5; ☺ dawn-dusk). Formerly a retirement home for 'aged and decrepit sailors' (how hot is that?), this spectacular campus is full of gardens and 28 historic buildings constructed between 1831 and 1917 in Greek revival, Italianate, and Beaux Arts styles among others. There's a children's museum, and a Chinese Scholar Garden that comes with its own 'Moon Viewing Pavilion of Crispness.' Not making that last part up. Check it out – it's easily accessed via cab from the ferry.

NEW YORK FOR CHILDREN

This is a great town for kids. Most every major park in the city offers a playground. Most every museum has an angle for kids (OK, not the Frick which won't even let them in, but still…). The Disney shows on Broadway like *Lion King* are reliable extravagances. Here are five top hits we wouldn't let our kids miss:

Wollman Rink and Victoria Gardens (p94) Located in Central Park, in the winter it's a skating rink, in summer its an amusement park.

Books of Wonder (p112) Eager readers will revel in this children's bookstore.

FAO Schwartz (p112) The legendary children's emporium. Make sure to bring your credit card, though – this is the Tiffany of toy stores.

American Museum of Natural History (p98) The classic of NYC children's activities. Who doesn't love taxidermy?

Serendipity 3 (p107) More than a restaurant, this is the ultimate sweet shop for kids and their parents

TOURS

Oodles of tours are available in every shape and size. The best place to check out the options is at one of the NYC Tourist offices (p80) scattered about the city. Rest assured, you can do it by land, by sea, or by vintage checker cab.

City Sights (☎ 212-812-2700; www.citysightsny.com; 234 W 42nd St; tours adult/child from $44/34) Double-decker bus tours are a great way to see wide swaths of the city in a few hours. You can hop off the bus at dozens of predetermined locations from the West Village to Brooklyn and then hop on the next one. Tour guides narrate important sights and multilingual tours are available, too. City Sights isn't the only outfit offering this service, but it's a solid choice.

SEE ALL OF NEW YORK IN AN HOUR OR LESS

Queens has been the home of two World's Fairs, the first in 1939 and the second in 1964. Both times the event was held at **Flushing Meadows Corona Park** (Map p79; nr Grand Central Pkwy & Roosevelt Ave), and there are several leftover structures (mostly from the 1964 event) including the **Unisphere**, a marvelous globe that's 120ft high. If you're coming from the subway stop, you'll see mosaics by Andy Warhol and Salvador Dali as you meander along the walkway.

Queens Museum of Art

The real highlight of the park is the quirky and appealing **Queens Museum of Art** (☎ 718-592-9700; www.queensmuseum.org; admission adult/child/senior $5/2.50/2.50; ☺ 12-6pm) that boasts a fine collection of Tiffany glass and World's Fair memorabilia. Yet it is most renowned for the Panorama of New York City, a 9335-sq-ft miniature of New York City. Built first for the '64 Fair, the panorama replicates every building in NYC. Completely insane and fabulous, it was last updated in 1994 (though two prominent buildings were removed after September 11, 2001). This thing is so cool, and so wild, that it's definitely worth the trip out.

As an aside, if you're hungry after your spin around NYC, walk a few blocks into Corona and grab some tacos and margaritas at **Los Tres Potrillos** (☎ 718-505-1433; 111-16 Roosevelt Ave; meals $8-20; ☺ lunch & dinner) where Lady Gaga pours out of the jukebox and the food and drinks are cheap and exceptional.

Circle Line (☎ 212-563-3200; www.circleline42.com; Pier 83 at Twelfth Ave & 42nd St; adult/child/senior $35/22/30) One of several boat tours that circumnavigate the island of Manhattan. Traditional tours take you past the major bridges, all five boroughs, and the Statue of Liberty.

FESTIVALS & EVENTS

New York's always got something going on somewhere. Here are a few of our annual favorites:

Spring

Tribeca Film Festival (www.tribecafilmfestival.com) Robert De Niro heads this May film fest that gets bigger every year and has loads of interesting flicks.
Fleet Week (www.intrepidmuseum.org) The sailors dock in NYC and go 'on the town' in the last week of May.

Summer

Gay Pride Parade (www.nycpride.com) Drag queens, 'dykes on bikes,' Stonewall veterans, and go-go boys bring club music to the concrete canyons of lower Fifth Ave and the West Village. Always the last Sunday of June.
US Open Tennis Tournament (www.usopen.org) Tennis, anyone? August brings the Grand Slam tournament to Queens. Wildly fun.

Autumn

San Gennaro Festival (www.sangennaro.org) The streets of Little Italy come alive with sausages, games, rides and more for about two weeks in September.
our pick **Open House New York** (www.ohny.org) Architecture fans and those curious about hidden New York will *love* this October weekend when hundreds of sites from abandoned subway stations to ornate townhouses throw open their doors and offer tours. Totally awesome.

Winter

NY Botanical Gardens Holiday Train Show (www.nybg.org) Trains dip in and out of the flora and recreated NYC landmarks. Toy train enthusiasts will be in love.
New Year's Eve (www.timessquarenyc.org/nye) The famous ball drop. If you are insane and impervious to cold, then enjoy.

SLEEPING

New York City's hotels are notoriously pricey so anything under $200 a night should be considered a bargain. Rates are lower in the dead of winter and reach their peaks in spring and autumn, the heights of tourist season. Staying in the outer boroughs is trickier, but they all have the basic Hiltons and Radissons and Holiday Inns. Those exist on Manhattan,

---

FAMOUS FAT DAVE'S FIVE BOROUGH EATING TOUR

Very possibly the most fun we've ever had cabbing about NYC. Dave, a gourmand and licensed cabbie, picks you (and up to four more of your friends) in his **vintage checker cab** (www.famousfatdave.com; from $200) and takes you on a tour of New York's most out-of-the-way and unlikely epicurean highlights. He'll tailor the tour to your tastes while he chauffeurs you around New York's forgotten corners. He has standard tours, too, like the Midnight Munchies Tour, the Pickle Tickle Tour, and the Disappearing New York Tour. Ask to try the 'murder burger.'

---

too. But really, did you come to NYC to stay in a Holiday Inn?

Lower Manhattan & Tribeca

Duane Street Hotel (Map p82; ☎ 212-964-4600; www.duanestreethotel.com; 130 Duane St; d from $170) A perfectly decent place to hang your hat in Lower Manhattan at a comparatively bargain price. Rooms are cozy, but not cramped. And it's right around the corner from the brasserie Odeon (p105), a Tribeca institution.
   Tribeca Grand Hotel (Map p82; ☎ 212-965-2080; www.tribecagrand.com; 2 Ave of the Americas; d from $290) A lively bar and lounge scene on the ground floor of the atrium makes this a fun place to stay. It used to be the trendiest place in the 'hood but has been eclipsed a bit by newer entries.
   Greenwich Hotel (Map p82; ☎ 212-941-8900; www.thegreenwichhotel.com; 377 Greenwich St; d from $495) Robert De Niro's achingly chic hotel is a favorite among sophisticated travelers. A courtyard, gym with a pool, and plush drawing room will make you want to hole up in the hotel and forsake doing anything else.

Soho, Noho & Nolita

Soho Grand (Map p82; ☎ 800-965-3000; www.sohogrand.com; 310 W Broadway; d from $259) The leader of the Soho hotel boom, the Soho Grand has a prime location on West Broadway meaning shoppers will be close to all the retail action. Outdoor spaces and the lobby bar are popular with visitors and locals alike.
   our pick **Crosby Street Hotel** (Map p82; ☎ 212-226-6400; www.firmdale.com; 79 Crosby St; d from $495)

There's 86 high-style rooms with a quirky design sense that fill out 11 floors. Incredibly posh and brand-spanking-new, this place is ideal for those with a taste for perfection. Its new construction makes it one of NYC's first Green Hotels. A restaurant and bar below are filled with the owners' art collection, as is the lobby. A meadow suite offers your own personal rooftop prairie. Too tired to lift those shopping bags? The Crosby offers butler service. Jeeves!

Lower East Side & the East Village

East Village Bed & Coffee (Map p82; ☎ 917-816-0071; www.bedandcoffee.com; 110 Ave C; s/d from $125/135) Those looking for a boarding bargain and who like the 'urban realness' of Alphabet City should look into this lesbian-owned bed and breakfast.

Hotel East Houston (Map p82; ☎ 212-777-0012; www.hoteleasthouston.com; 151 E Houston St; s/d from $149/179) This is a new-ish boutique hotel with small but cozy, sexy rooms. The chocolate brown lobby is a good place to get away from busy Houston St.

Cooper Square Hotel (Map p82; ☎ 212-475-5700; www.thecoopersquarehotel.com; 25 Cooper Sq; d from $275) One of the newest additions to the East Village, at first its stark, modern tower seems out of place in the neighborhood. But once we stepped inside, we were in love. The second floor patio and bar are ideal for whiling away the afternoon. The rooms can offer spectacular unobstructed views of Manhattan and the central location makes getting around downtown a breeze.

I REMEMBER YOU WELL IN THE CHELSEA HOTEL

Anyone who fancies him or herself a fan of bohemian glamour and history will need to pay respects at the no doubt extremely haunted **Chelsea Hotel** (Map p92; ☎ 212-243-3700; www.hotelchelsea.com; 222 W 23rd St near Eighth Ave). Famed for its deaths (Dylan Thomas of alcohol poisoning), murders (Sid Vicious stabbed his girlfriend Nancy), ballads (Leonard Cohen paid homage with 'Chelsea Hotel #2' about Janis Joplin), and residents (Arthur C Clarke wrote *2001: A Space Odyssey* here). You can book a room, but the hotel primarily houses full-time New Yorkers. Sporadic tours are offered.

Greenwich Village & the West Village

Larchmont Hotel (Map p82; ☎ 212-989-9333; www.larchmonthotel.com; 27 W 11th St; s/d from $90/119) A 'European style' hotel means that for the cheap rates you get to share a bathroom. Rooms with private baths are available. The rooms are fine if not exactly luxurious, but you can't beat the location on leafy West 11th St.

Abingdon Guest House (Map p82; ☎ 212-243-5384; www.abingdonguesthouse.com; 13 Eighth Ave at 12th St; d $159-249) Nine rooms in these two 1850s townhouses come with four-poster beds and antiques will make you feel like a heroine from an Edith Wharton novel. It also offers a great location.

Chelsea & the Meatpacking District

Chelsea Pines Inn (Map p92; ☎ 212-929-1023; www.chelseapinesinn.com; 317 W 14th St; s/d from $169/199) This gay guesthouse has rooms named for Kim Novak, Ann-Margaret and the like. Blackglama fur posters line the walls. Some rooms have shared baths, but hey, that's how you get to know your neighbors. You don't have to be gay to stay here, but it helps.

ourpick Standard (Map p92; ☎ 212-645-4646; www.standardhotels.com; 848 Washington St; d from $295) This is a marvelous new hotel on the far west side towering above the Meatpacking District and the High Line. Views of Manhattan and the Hudson River are de rigueur from the sleek rooms with floor-to-ceiling windows. An exceedingly popular restaurant and a beer garden are downstairs. Stylish lounges are on the top floors.

Fashion 26 (Map p92; ☎ 212-858-5888; www.f26nyc.com; 152 W 26th St; d from $229) One of the new boutique hotels on the block; fashionistas of all sizes will enjoy this quirky new place in the garment district. Rooms are of average-to-medium size and have fun details like buttons on the door numbers and merino herringbone throws.

Union Square, Flatiron District & Gramercy Park

ourpick Ace Hotel (Map p92; ☎ 212-679-2222; www.acehotel.com; 20 W 29th St; d from $209) Arguably the hippest hotel downtown right now. Catering to Europeans and trendsetters, the prices start low with rooms with bunk beds (!) and inch up as you get more and more space. Charmingly utilitarian, this is ideal for youth and the young-at-heart. The lobby bar is packed with locals, as is its restaurant, the Breslin, currently one of the most talked about eateries in town.

Gramercy Park Hotel (Map p92; ☎ 212-920-3300; www.gramercyparkhotel.com; 2 Lexington Ave; d from $340) This is the latest Ian Schrager hotel, boasting interiors by Julian Schnabel. Maialino, the hotel's restaurant, is a trattoria that attracts the likes of Anna Wintour. Pricey, gorgeous, and worth it.

Midtown

Hotel QT (Map p92; ☎ 212-380-2700; 125 W 45th St; d from $205) The indoor pool in the lobby is but one of the quirky aspects of this very reasonably priced hotel. Rooms are basic but sexy with all the modern amenities like flatscreens and iPod docks. Tends to attract a youthful, boisterous crowd.

Flatotel (Map p92; ☎ 212-887-9400; www.flatotel.com; 135 W 52nd St; d from $208) This is a Midtown hotel that is very business-class in that it has large rooms, boring cream decor, and is ever so slightly threadbare. That said, they've got great prices, a terrific location, and should be a very satisfactory choice for the average traveler.

Algonquin Hotel (Map p92; ☎ 212-840-6800; www.algonquinhotel.com; 59 W 44th St; d from $399) Dorothy Parker and her cohorts would hardly recognize the rooms at this Midtown classic after the huge renovation shook off the cobwebs. Literary lions will still be pleased by the appealingly old-school Oak Room and lobby bar which are perfect places to read a little light verse and prose while sipping a sidecar.

Upper East Side

our pick **Mark Hotel** (Map p96; ☎ 212-744-4300; www.themarkhotel.com; 25 E 77th St; d from $830) A restaurant by top chef Jean-Georges is just one of the many amenities that make the Mark one of the most refined hotels in the city. Italian linens, black and white marble baths, and the divine Upper East Side locale just off Fifth Ave make this a study in elegance. If you have a question to pop or an anniversary to celebrate, this is the place.

Upper West Side

Empire Hotel (Map p96; ☎ 212-265-7400; wwww.empirehotel.com; 44 W 63rd St; d from $279) Fans of Gossip Girl will recognize the Empire as Chuck Bass's hotel. Right near Lincoln Center, the rooftop bar is a huge draw for locals, especially with

---

SO YOU WANT TO LEAVE TIMES SQUARE?

New York's not all about Fifth Ave, the Statue of Liberty and where Seventh Ave meets Broadway. Here's a few suggestions for some more offbeat restaurants, bars, and attractions:

- **Lady Mendl's Tea Salon** (p108) Sip tea and eat cucumber sandwiches in an elegant Gramercy Park parlor.

- **Panorama of New York City** (p102) All five boroughs are recreated in model form at the Queens Museum of Art.

- **Roll n Roaster** (p108) Deep in Brooklyn is this fast food throwback that is guaranteed to delight.

- **Ear Inn** (p108) New York's oldest bar is in Soho.

---

its iconic neon sign casting a red light over Broadway.

Brooklyn

Hotel Le Jolie (Map p100; ☎ 718-625-2100; www.hotellejolie.com; 235 Meeker Ave; d from $119) Popular with traveling bands, this very satisfactory Williamsburg hotel is just steps from all the hippest attractions in the 'Burg. While it isn't the ritziest place in town, it offers very nice rooms at an affordable price, with easy access via subway or car to Manhattan.

EATING

Dining out can be a contact sport in New York. Most top end recommendations, and many midrange ones, require reservations. The best place to grab dinner, in our opinion, is Greenwich Village, where cafés and bistros abound.

Lower Manhattan & Tribeca

Edwards (Map p82; ☎ 212-233-6436; 136 W Broadway; mains $13-24; ✦ breakfast, lunch & dinner) This quality continental restaurant has a large bar and bustling dinner scene late into the evening. Pizzas are on the menu, as well as blackened salmon and a smattering of traditional options like nicoise salad.

Odeon (Map p82; ☎ 212-233-0507; 145 W Broadway; mains $16-34; ✦ lunch & dinner) This brasserie was a pioneer in Tribeca before it was fashionable and upmarket. Still a classic, it's an ideal place for a martini and steak and frittes. Fans of *Bright Lights, Big City* will recognize the neon sign from the book jacket and enjoy its late night scene when it serves the brasserie menu until 2am on weekends.

Landmarc (Map p82; ☎ 212-343-3883; 179 W Broadway; mains $18-35; ⊙ lunch & dinner) Debonair bistro with a chic downtown clientele, offering a sophisticated menu with fun twists on oldies like pasta Bolognese with braised short rib. Top notch; should be well loved by meat-eaters.

Chinatown

Jing Fong (Map p82; ☎ 212-964-5256; 20 Elizabeth St at Canal St; dishes $3-15; ⊙ 9:30am-10pm) A massive dining room with scores upon scores of tables welcomes all sorts to this kooky dim sum palace in Chinatown with all your favorite dishes.

Great NY Noodletown (Map p82; ☎ 212-349-0923; 28 Bowery at Bayard St; dishes $4-12; ⊙ 9:30am-4am) A staple of Chinatown, what the place lacks in ambience is made up for in spades by the food. Just about everything you can think of is served at all hours of the day – and the handy menu has pictures.

Soho, Noho, & Nolita

Noho Star (Map p82; ☎ 212-925-0070; 330 Lafayette St; ⊙ breakfast, lunch & dinner) A sort of upscale diner, the Noho Star offers basics like porridge for breakfast and an array of salads and sandwiches for lunch, along with oddities like Viennese turkey schnitzel. Less thrilling, but still satisfying, for dinner it makes a good place to refuel during a downtown shopping spree.

Spring Street Natural (Map p82; ☎ 212-966-0290; 62 Spring St; mains $12-23; ⊙ breakfast, lunch & dinner) This café offers a wide selection of salads and entrees from sashimi to risotto that span the continents, many aimed at the vegetarian set. A favorite of editors from nearby Scholastic, it's a good place to talk shop about the book biz over microbrews.

Il Buco (Map p82; ☎ 212-533-1932; 47 Bond St; mains $22-35; ⊙ lunch & dinner) A new star on the foodie scene, Il Buco has a charming, dimly-lit rustic ambience that compliments the Italian-style cuisine. The menu changes daily so who knows what's on tap when you arrive. An expansive wine list is also on hand.

East Village & the Lower East Side

This Little Piggy Had Roast Beef (Map p82; ☎ 212-323-1500; 149 First Ave at 9th St; sandwiches $4-6; ⊙ 11am-4am) Moist and warm roast beef sandwiches topped with mozzarella and gravy or pastrami with coleslaw are the order of the day at this little hole-in-the-wall that has locals salivating.

Banjara (Map p82; ☎ 212-477-5956; 97 First Ave at 6th St; mains $12-18; ⊙ lunch & dinner) On 6th St between First and Second Aves you'll find Indian restaurant row. A little more upscale than some of the other options, Banjara has delicious, well-prepared Indian food without all the headache-inducing Christmas lights that festoon many of the other restaurants on the block.

Casimir (Map p82; ☎ 212-358-9683; 103-105 Ave B btwn 6th & 7th Sts; mains $14-25; ⊙ lunch & dinner) A café and bar with a French bent, this is a real romantic delight to find in the wilds of Alphabet City. Steak tartar and roast duck are expertly prepared, along with traditional standards like French onion soup.

Greenwich Village & the West Village

Bonsignour (Map p82; ☎ 212-229-9700; 35 Jane St at Eighth Ave; mains $7-12; ⊙ breakfast, lunch & dinner) Nestled on a quiet Village street, this sandwich shop offers dozens of delicious choices as well as salads, frittatas and a wonderful beef chili. Get a sandwich or a chicken curry salad to go and wander down the street to Abingdon Square for al fresco dining.

La Lanterna di Vittorio (Map p82; ☎ 212-529-5945; 129 MacDougal St at W 4th St; dishes $8-15; ⊙ 10am-3am, to 4am Fri & Sat) Primarily known as an intimate fireside and garden café with a wide selection of desserts, it also offers savory dishes. A great place for a nightcap before taking that special someone home to bed.

Sammy's Noodle Shop (Map p82; ☎ 212-924-6688; 453 Sixth Ave at 11th St); dishes $8-14; ⊙ lunch & dinner; 🕭) American-style Chinese fare gets served at this popular Village noodle joint. Among the better Chinese choices, it's a great bargain, especially if you can get there in time for the lunch special.

Alta (Map p82; ☎ 212-508-7777; 64 W 10th; dishes $4-12; ⊙ dinner) This tapas restaurant is a two-story Spanish gem hidden inside a precious Village townhouse and has great sangria along with superb dishes. Fried goat cheese with lavender honey is a hallmark of their ever-changing menu.

Smorgas Chef (Map p82; ☎ 212-243-7073; 283 W 12th St; mains $19-28; ⊙ lunch & dinner) This is a picturesque Scandinavian restaurant on a darling, cobblestone street. Outside tables are always inviting. If you have a taste for northern European cuisine, you should be quite pleased.

our pick **Blue Hill** (Map p82; ☎ 212-539-1776; 75 Washington Pl; mains $20-35; ☾ dinner) Dan Barber's farm-fresh restaurant is so widely admired that the Obamas dined here on one of their recent 'date nights' in NYC. The menu changes daily in response to what's available from their Westchester farm, Stone Barns. Never disappointing, this restaurant is elegant yet not overstated. Pure bliss. Reservations a must.

Spotted Pig (Map p82; ☎ 212-620-0393; 314 W 11th St; mains $14-30; ☾ lunch & dinner) This Michelin-starred gastro-pub is a favorite of Villagers. Two floors are bedecked in an old-timey decor that serve to make the experience both casual and refined. They don't take reservations, so there is often a wait for a table. But brunch and lunch are less packed and usually you can get a seat straight away.

Chelsea & the Meatpacking District

Crispo (Map p92; ☎ 212-229-1818; www.crisporestaurant.com; 240 W 14th St; mains $18-28; ☾ dinner) This is a fine Italian restaurant with a huge patio in the back. Funky 80s-style art adorns the walls. We recommend a prosciutto platter to start and the pasta is excellent, as are the carnivore entrees, like duck with figs and skirt steak.

our pick **Cookshop** (Map p92; ☎ 212-924-4440; www.cookshopny.com; 156 Tenth Ave; mains $20-33; ☾ lunch & dinner) Right at the terminus of the High Line at 20th St, this restaurant is one of the best in Chelsea, with superior entrees like braised meats and succulent vegetables that are topped off by great mixologists in an appealing contemporary setting.

Union Square, Flatiron District & Gramercy Park

Chat 'n' Chew (Map p92; ☎ 212-243-1616; 10 E 16th St; mains $9-17; ☾ lunch & dinner) Fried chicken and grilled cheese rule at this home-cookin' haunt. Rich and creamy and kickin'.

Pure Food & Wine (Map p92; ☎ 212-477-1010; 54 Irving Pl; mains $24-28; ☾ lunch & dinner) Raw food for fancy veggie and vegan lovers. Nothing is cooked. If this is your style then chow down!

Midtown

Angus McIndoe (Map p92; ☎ 212-221-9222; 258 W 44th St; mains $15-27; ☾ lunch & dinner) This is so one

of the best places to eat and/or drink in the Theater District. It's pub-esque – chops and fish and whatnot. After hours, when the ovations have died down, chorus kids and the occasional Broadway star get drunk on the third floor.

West Bank Café (Map p92; ☎ 212-695-6909; 407 W 42nd St; mains $16-23; ☾ lunch & dinner) Very good and off the beaten path, this is another Midtown option that promises the occasional star sighting (usually post-show) while you chow down on ravioli or a nice steak. Serves continental cuisine.

Upper East Side

Serendipity 3 (Map p96; ☎ 212-838-3531; www.serendipity3.com; 225 E 60th St; mains $15-23; ☾ lunch & dinner; ♿) This restaurant and sweet shop is adorned with Tiffany lamps in a really cute Eastside duplex that was a favorite of Andy Warhol. Kids are guaranteed to freak out over their signature dish, frozen hot chocolate.

Upper West Side

City Grill (Map p96; ☎ 212-873-9400; 269 Columbus Ave; mains $10-20; ☾ lunch & dinner) This place provides a plentiful bounty of salads, wraps and sandwiches, along with entrees that cater to the famished explorer fresh off the Dakota.

Ocean Grill (Map p96; ☎ 212-579-2300; mains $22-34; ☾ lunch & dinner) If you crave the tang of saltwater fare, this is your place. Settle down at the sidewalk tables or the plush lounge for great views of the Natural History Museum.

Brooklyn

Bark (☎ 718-789-1939; 474 Bergen St; dogs $5-7; ☾ lunch & dinner) This is the gourmet hot dog stand of your dreams. Extreme dogs are served to an eager public in Park Slope (Map p79).

DETOUR – BLUE HILL AT STONE BARNS

The only thing better than eating at Blue Hill, in the Village, is dining at their **farm restaurant** (www.bluehillfarm.com) 35 minutes north of Manhattan by train. Once in Tarrytown, a quick cab will whisk you to the quaint estate where a carefully prepared prix-fixe menu devised that day will make you want to quit your job and take up artisan farming. So heavenly you'll want to die. All the information for reservations and travel is at the website.

THINK & DRINK LIKE THE RICH

Is there anything more refined than sipping an expensive cocktail in a grand environment? We think not. Here are a few suggestions for getting your fancy drink on in Midtown Manhattan.

- **King Cole Bar** Home of the first Bloody Mary, here called the Red Snapper.
- **Bergdorf Goodman** (p111) The 7th-floor café has a bar and nibbles to go along with the striking views of Central Park.
- **Barneys New York** (p111) At Fred's on the top floor, ladies who lunch and their personal shoppers talk shop over lobster bisque and French wine.

Roll n Roaster (☎ 718-769-6000; Emmons & Nostrand Aves; sandwiches $3-7; ⏰ 11am-1am) Roast beef smothered in cheese is the house specialty at this Sheepshead Bay classic. It's a completely awesome throwback in a groovy old building.

Diner (Map p100; ☎ 718-486-3077; 85 Broadway; mains $15-20; ⏰ lunch & dinner) Simple, seasonal ingredients are the draw at this oh-so-Williamsburg eatery in an old diner car. No reservations are taken and the food is hearty and wonderful.

The Bronx

Johnny's Famous Reef Restaurant (☎ 718-885-2086; 2 City Island Ave; platters $10-12; ⏰ lunch & dinner) At the southern tip of City Island (Map p79) is this fried seafood shrine. Grab some clams or shrimp and head outside to eat with seagulls overlooking Long Island Sound.

Roberto (☎ 718-733-9503; 603 Crescent Ave; mains $19-26; ⏰ lunch & dinner Mon-Sat) Of all the restaurants in Little Italy in the Bronx (Map p81), this one is generally known as the finest.

DRINKING

Coffee and booze are to New York what oil is to Texas – the *ur*-fuel. Bars and gourmet coffee joints are everywhere, but the best ones tend to be downtown or in Brooklyn. Most bars are open until 4am.

Soho & Noho

Ear Inn (Map p82; ☎ 212-431-9750; 326 Spring St) Inside a building constructed in 1817, the Ear Inn is the oldest working bar in NYC. It serves quality pub food, too. Keep an eye out for the ghosts said to haunt the establishment.

Temple Bar (Map p82; ☎ 212-925-4242; 332 Lafayette at Houston) Spicy mojitos, sidecars and more dominate this high-end mixology joint.

East Village

McSorley's Old Ale House (Map p82; ☎ 212-473-9148; www.mcsorleysnewyork.com; 15 E 7th St) Slinging beers since 1854, this iconic Irish pub has only been allowing women in since 1970.

Boiler Room (Map p82; ☎ 212-254-7536; 86 E 4th St at Second Ave) This gay dive bar has a pool table, a great jukebox, and daily drink specials.

Heathers (Map p82; ☎ 212-254-0979; 506 E 13th St at Ave A) Hipster dive bar attracts bloggers and beards.

Greenwich Village & the West Village

Joe (Map p82; ☎ 212-924-6750; 141 Waverly Pl) Superb coffee is served at this always bustling joint located on bucolic Waverly Place in the heart of the Village. The lattes are particularly delicious.

Grounded Organic Coffee & Tea House (Map p82; ☎ 212-647-0943; 28 Jane St) We won't blame you for flashing back to the '90s and your grunge look when you step into this coffee house that seems as if it has been encased in amber since *Reality Bites*.

our pick Marie's Crisis (Map p82; ☎ 212-243-9323; 59 Grove St at Seventh Ave) Showtunes fans will be in hog heaven at this piano bar. It's like an Irish pub except that the liquored-up crowd sings *Les Miz* rather than Danny Boy. Ridiculously fun.

Gramercy Park

our pick Lady Mendl's Tea Salon (Map p92; ☎ 212-533-4466; 56 Irving Pl) High tea is served twice daily in this gorgeous little parlor in a plush townhouse. Reservations are required so call ahead.

Pete's Tavern (Map p92; ☎ 212-473-7676; 129 E 18th St at Irving Pl) O Henry wrote many of his works in this seriously old-school tavern.

Midtown

View Lounge (Map p92; ☎ 212-704-8900; 1353 Broadway at 46th St) High atop the Marriott Marquis is this fabulous revolving bar that's a tourist haven, but deservedly so for its epic Midtown vistas.

Sardi's (Map p92; ☎ 212-221-8440; 234 W 44th St) The famous theater joint has terrible food but a superior 2nd-floor bar overlooking Shubert Alley. A glass of pinot will afford you the opportunity to admire the thousands of celebrity caricatures including Liza and Kermit.

King Cole Bar (Map p92; ☎ 212-753-4500; 2 E 55th St at Fifth Ave) An elegant bar at St Regis, adorned with a Maxfield Parrish mural. Home of the first Bloody Mary, here called Red Snapper, this place is important for any cocktail lover.

Brooklyn

Williamsburg is a bar-hoppers paradise. Here are a few highlights, but there are dozens more.

Barcade (Map p100; ☎ 718-302-6464; 388 Union Ave) Microbrews and scores of 1980s vintage video games make this a prime destination for drunken gamers.

Union Pool (Map p100; ☎ 718-609-0484; 484 Union Ave) DJs and live music are a mainstay at this exceedingly hip bar inside an old pool store with a smoking patio.

Metropolitan Bar (Map p100; ☎ 718-599-4444; 559 Lorimer St) Williamsburg's first gay bar is still popular with gays, lesbians and their friends. The highlight of this divey place is their back patio with garden seating.

ENTERTAINMENT

It's pretty easy to find something to do in New York as it's buzzing 24 hours a day. Those who love sports should check out the **Chelsea Piers** (Map p92; ☎ 212-336-6666; 62 Chelsea Piers at 20th St) complex with ice-skating, golf, and a variety of other activities. If you prefer

---

GAY & LESBIAN NEW YORK

Despite the fact that NY State doesn't allow gay marriage, NYC remains at the forefront of all things homosexual. Gay bars and establishments can be found all over the city, but there are five primary neighborhoods that cater overwhelmingly to a gay clientele.

West Village
Stonewall Inn (p88) Where drag queens rioted. You can still buy a beer, but the establishment isn't quite the same as it was in 1969 (thank God).
Duplex (Map p82; ☎ 212-255-5438; 61 Christopher St) A Village stalwart, the first floor is a piano bar and the second floor has a lounge and a cabaret theater. In the summer, sidewalk seating is ideal for people watching.
Cubby Hole (Map p82; ☎ 212-243-9041; 281 W 12th St at 4th St) The premier lesbian dive bar.
Marie's Crisis The most awesome and appealing piano bar in the city – beloved by show queens.

Chelsea
Barracuda (Map p92; ☎ 212-645-8613; 275 W 22nd St) Chelsea's most popular dive bar, there are drag shows most weekday nights. Sexy bartenders help keep it packed on weekends.
Splash (Map p92; ☎ 212-691-0073; 50 W 17th St) This long-running club venue is great for dancing. An ideal place for out-of-towners.
Eagle (Map p92; ☎ 646-473-1866; 554 W 28th) The center of the leather and bear universe. Three floors and a roof deck make it appealing for everyone.

Hell's Kitchen
Therapy (Map p92; ☎ 212-397-1700; 348 W 52nd St) Upscale lounge with a bar menu, hosts shows on weekday nights. The big daddy of Hell's Kitchen.

East Village
Boiler Room They've been slinging drinks in this dive for ages. A great jukebox and pool tables provide entertainment other than cruising. Currently in the midst of a popularity upswing.
Phoenix (Map p82; ☎ 212-477-9979; 447 E 13th St at Ave A) Their long-standing dollar beer night on Wednesdays brings boys from all over the boroughs.
Eastern Bloc (Map p82; ☎ 212-777-2555; 505 E 6th St at Ave A) A tiny (or shall we say intimate?) place that brings in the hipster boys and their lesbian pals for DJs and go-go boys.

Williamsburg
Metropolitan Bar Brooklyn's most popular gay bar draws boho chic gays and lesbians. The back patio is smoky but relaxing.

just watching sports you can hardly go wrong with the 'Bronx bombers' at **Yankee Stadium** (Map p81; www.yankees.com) or the **Mets** (www.newyork. mets.mlb.com) at Citi Field (Map p79) in Queens.

All the kids love bowling and why shouldn't they? Hipsters can get their game on at **Brooklyn Bowl** (Map p100; ☎ 718-963-3369; 61 Wythe Ave) in Williamsburg while those who are a little more adventurous will enjoy **Leisure Time Bowl** (Map p92; ☎ 212-268-6909; 625 Eighth Ave) at the Port Authority Bus Terminal in Midtown. Despite its low rent surroundings, this is a surprisingly modern and groovy place to throw balls.

Cineastes will find just about every first run flick available around the city. The **Angelika** (Map p82; ☎ 212-995-2000; 18 W Houston St) is an indie-film staple to check out the latest in European art cinema. The new **IFC Center** (Map p82; ☎ 212-924-7771; 323 Sixth Ave) also offers cutting-edge movies.

Of course the theater is the pride and joy of New York and there are dozens and dozens of places to go to see it. The theater scene is usually divided between **Broadway** (500-plus seats), **Off-Broadway** (100-499 seats) and **Off-off-Broadway** (99 seats or less). Broadway is where you'll find the marquee shows like *La Cage aux Folles, Phantom,* and the other big musicals and major plays. These shows are exclusively in theaters around Times Square with a couple of far-flung locales like Lincoln Center or Studio 54. Off-Broadway is where you'll find edgier fare, like new plays and musicals that deal in more esoteric conceits from prominent writers. Off-off-Broadway is often where you'll find the most avant-garde types of theater, with results of variable quality. However, this is where you can discover emerging artists at a very low price (tickets are often only about $15). These are scattered all about the city.

UP ON THE ROOF

Drinking on the roof is many a New Yorker's favorite pastime. These hotels offer delightful places to booze it up while watching the twinkling lights of Manhattan:

- Empire Hotel (p105)
- Gramercy Park Hotel (p105)
- Standard (p104)
- Fashion 26 (p104)

See the boxed text for some advice on how to get tickets.

One place to check that's not as obvious to out-of-towners is the **Brooklyn Academy of Music** (☎ 718-636-4100; www.bam.org; 30 Lafayette Ave) hosting all sorts of exciting performances from movies to international theater to opera. Another big arts complex is **Lincoln Center** (Map p96; ☎ 212-875-5456; www.lincolncenter.org; 10 Lincoln Square) that houses the Metropolitan Opera, the New York Ballet, the American Ballet Theater, the NY Philharmonic, and usually a musical in the Mitzi Newhouse Theater.

Music that's of the non-musical theater variety is also a major pastime in New York City. Jazz lovers should try iconic venues like **Birdland** (Map p92; www.birdlandjazz.com; 315 W 44th St), the **Village Vanguard** (Map p82; www.villagevanguard.com; 178 Seventh Ave), or the funky **Arthur's Tavern** (Map p82; www.arthurstavernnyc.com) that is usually free as long as you buy some cocktails. See also the Apollo Theater (p98) in Harlem.

Rock and roll fans can find acts all over the city. Some of the premier joints are in Brooklyn: the **Music Hall of Williamsburg** (Map p100; www.musichallofwilliamsburg.com; 66 N 6th St btwn Kent & Wythe Aves); the **Knitting Factory** (Map p100; www.bk.knittingfactory.com; 361 Metropolitan Ave at Havemeyer St).

Crash Mansion (Map p82; www.crashmansion.com; 199 Bowery at Rivington), **Pianos** (Map p82; www.pianosnyc.com; 158 Ludlow St at Stanton St) and the **High Line Ballroom** (Map p92; www.highlineballroom.com; 431 W 16th St btwn Ninth & Tenth Aves) are among the many venues to see new music in Manhattan. Sadly CBGBs is now a John Varvatos store (albeit a cute one that has much of the seedy club's charms).

Classical music lovers should check out the aforementioned Lincoln Center or the famed **Carnegie Hall** (Map p92; ☎ 212-247-7800; www.carnegiehall.org; 881 Seventh Ave at 57th St) that you can get to with practice, practice, practice. Carnegie Hall offers a wide mix of acts, from highbrow opera singers to avant-garde performers like Laurie Anderson.

Again, this is just a smattering of the scores of venues. You can check for the current listings for theater and music in the *Village Voice,* the *New Yorker, New York Magazine,* and *Time Out New York.*

SHOPPING

Welcome to the consumer carnival that is New York. Get into your walking shoes and have your credit card ready.

CURTAIN UP, LIGHT THE LIGHTS

So you want to go see some theater. Good for you! It's cultural, it's edifying, it's *important*. But what show to see? There are so many choices. For our money, we like to avoid the shows like *Mamma Mia* or *Phantom of the Opera* that have grown a bit long in the tooth and are on their umpteenth casts. Better to see the newer shows, which tend to have a fresher energy. Since every season is different we can't really recommend what the hot new thing will be. The best way to find out what's hot is reading the *New York Times* (www.nytimes.com) for which Times Square is named. Loved and loathed for its ability to make or break a show with praise or withering disregard, the *Times* is the ultimate arbiter of what is good and bad. It is right more often than not – but don't just listen to the Gray Lady. Two other good resources are *New York Magazine* (www.nymag.com) and the *New Yorker* (www.newyorker.com).

So you've picked a show. If you chose *Wicked,* think again. It's probably sold out and it's over-rated anyway, so save your money. If you've chosen one of the scalding hot shows (usually those with big movie stars and/or rave reviews) you probably want to head straight to the theater's box office and be prepared to pay full price (usually about $125 a ticket for orchestra seats). If, on the other hand, you have something in mind that's a little less sought after, you can usu-ally find half-price day-of tickets at **TKTS** (www.tdf.org). The sparkling new **Times Square booth** (Map p92; 47th St btw Seventh Ave & Broadway) has a big wow-factor (and can be seen extensively in the Jay Z/Alicia Keys 'Empire State of Mind' video) but comes with long lines (though there is a 'Plays Only' window which moves faster). Clever theatergoers will check out the less-visited TKTS kiosks at the **South Street Seaport** (Map p82; cnr Front & John Sts) or in **Brooklyn** (cnr Jay St & Myrtle Ave in 1 MetroTech Center).

Those seeking a discount but unwilling to take their chances with the theater gods for re-mainder tickets should check out www.theatermania.com or www.playbill.com for discounts of about 30% for major shows. Finally, www.telecharge.com is the major ticket website, but you'll save almost 10 bucks a ticket if you drag your butt to the show's box office where there are no 'convenience' surcharges.

Department Stores

Bergdorf Goodman (Map p96; ☎ 212-753-7300; 754 Fifth Ave at 58th St) The gold standard of department stores, this is the place to pick up that ball gown you've been needing. Men's, women's, housewares – it's all here and it's all fabulous. The 7th-floor café has views of Central Park and the Plaza Hotel.

Barneys New York (Map p96; ☎ 212-826-8900; 660 Madison Ave at 62nd St) Hipper than Bergdorf's, with edgier fashions but still all the Armani you could want. Their top floor restaurant Fred's is an important stop on the society lunch circuit.

Bloomingdale's Soho (Map p82; ☎ 212-729-5900; 504 Broadway btwn Prince & Spring Sts) This is the downtown varietal of the mother ship up-town. Its shoe department is generally quite good and is known to focus on more youthful fashions.

Clothing & Accessories

Jeffrey New York (Map p92; ☎ 212-206-1272; 449 W 14th St) The ultimate in Meatpacking shopping. The shoe department alone inspires awe. Proenza

Schuler is but one of the cutting-edge design-ers represented.

Prada (Map p82; ☎ 212-334-8888; 575 Broadway at Prince St) There's more than one place to buy Prada's chic Milan designs in NYC, but this is the Rem Koolhaas–designed store with an impressive, swooping interior.

Eskandar (Map p82; ☎ 212-533-4200; 33 E 10th St) Located on one of the prettiest blocks in the Village, Eskandar offers women's fashions and chunky jewelry that would appeal to any Vassar professor of performance studies – mature and refined.

our pick Charles Nolan (Map p82; ☎ 212-924-4888; 30 Gansevoort St) All-American women's wear like crisp white shirts and tailored cocktail dresses. An appealing assortment of shoes, accessories and lovely housewares.

Behaviour (Map p92; ☎ 212-352-8380; 231 W 19th St) A terribly well-curated men's shop for the stylish dandy. From sunglasses to T-shirts, they are all excellent. Usually a dash of seer-sucker in the spring.

Nasty Pig (Map p92; ☎ 212-691-6067; 265 W 19th St) T-shirts, socks and underwear bearing the store's namesake, along with a bit of rubber and leather fetish wear, makes this an ideal stop for Chelsea boys and their admirers.

Lulu Guinness (Map p82; ☎ 212-367-2120; 394 Bleecker St) Any lady who loves a good purse will be hard-pressed not to go bonkers in this bright, fun store with loads of bags and clutches.

Jack Spade (Map p82; ☎ 212-675-4085; 400 Bleecker St) Men's wear in rustic plaids along with a spectacular array of man-bags make this a must for the urban gentleman.

Kesner (Map p82; ☎ 212-206-6330; 524 Hudson St) Been dying to pick up a pair of polka-dot Vivienne Westwood loafers? Those and more are available at this subtly slick store catering to witty men with a good credit rating.

our pick John Bartlett (Map p82; ☎ 212-633-6867; 143 Seventh Ave at Charles St) Rugby players and Ivy Leaguers will go gaga for the selection of extra-masculine clothing that comes with a wink at this underrated designer's Village shop. There's women's wear too.

Black Fleece (Map p82; ☎ 212-929-2763; 251 Bleecker St) If you've ever dreamed of playing polo in the Hamptons then check out this store with superb Brooks Brothers fashions for men and women.

Also recommended:

Tiffany & Co (Map p92; ☎ 212-755-8000; Fifth Ave at 57th St) Duh. It's Tiffany's. Buy your wife something nice.

Tom Ford (Map p96; ☎ 212-359-0300; 845 Madison at 70th St) The former Gucci impresario tailors exquisite shirts and suits for the well-heeled man.

Paul Smith (Map p92; ☎ 212-627-9770; 108 Fifth Ave at 15th St) The British designer brings his sartorial, quirky tailoring to Manhattan men. Exceedingly divine and fun.

Pippin (Map p92; ☎ 212-505-5159; 112 W 17th St) Vintage jewelry and accessories at great prices.

Children

Yoyamart (Map p82; ☎ 212-242-5511; 15 Gansevoort St) Totally awesome Japanese toy store with an excruciatingly hip selection of kids' clothes in the 5-12 range. Your kids will want the Ugly Dolls, you will want the French children's fashion magazine Milk.

Books of Wonder (Map p92; ☎ 212-989-3270; 18 W 18th St) A vast assortment of books for children and teens is available in this completely magical place. After you've picked out some fine literary selections, grab an ice cream or cupcake in the café. Aces.

Kidding Around (Map p92; ☎ 212-645-6337; 60 W 15th St) An excellent store with tons of toys, toys, TOYS! Lots of costumes, cooking play-sets, and stuffed animals are among the many, many options.

FAO Schwartz (Map p96; ☎ 212-644-9400; 767 Fifth Ave at 59th St) You don't have to have seen Big (though it helps) to fall in love with Manhattan's most iconic toy store that's more fantasyland than reality.

Comics & Magic

Abracadabra (Map p92; ☎ 212-627-5194; 19 W 21st St) It's not just a Steve Miller Band song, it's also an emporium of horror, costumes and magic. Those who like this sort of thing will be hard-pressed to leave without racking up some credit card bills.

Forbidden Planet (Map p82; ☎ 212-473-1576; 840 Broadway at 13th St) Comics, toys, manga – this is fanboy heaven. Geek out!

Housewares

our pick ABC Carpet & Home (Map p92; ☎ 212-473-3000; 888 Broadway at 19th St) Five floors of furniture make this a decorator's dream. Pillows, armoires, chandeliers, carpets, throws, chests, dining rooms, and more. A darling café on the ground floor and a new one on the roof make this a reminder of how lovely Ladies' Mile must have been.

Fishs Eddy (Map p92; ☎ 212-420-9020; 889 Broadway at 19th St) Dishes, more dishes, and then finally, even MORE dishes. Affordable prices make it hard to resist the novelty ceramics bearing Alice in Wonderland, Brooklyn vistas and more.

DDC (Map p92; ☎ 212-685-0800; 181 Madison Ave at 34th St) Domus Design Collection is the bees' knees of contemporary furniture. Some of it is outrageous, but much of it is sublime – like the cushy chairs with Paul Smith signature fabric. Swoon.

End of History (Map p82; ☎ 212-647-7598; 548½ Hudson St) Mid-century Scandinavian glass is the order of the day in this exquisite shop that also has other objects and furniture from the period.

Food & Kitchen

Chelsea Market (Map p92; 75 Ninth Ave at 15th St) An old Nabisco factory has been transformed into a paradise for gourmands. Cakes, pies, soups, seafood, wine, milkshakes, breads and more are available at the dozens of purveyors.

Murray's Cheese (Map p82; ☎ 212-243-3289; 254 Bleecker St) The finest fromage in town. You'll find all the moldy milk product you could want, and it offers classes to help make you a connoisseur.

Brooklyn Kitchen (Map p100; ☎ 718-389-2982; 100 Frost St) This Williamsburg kitchen store has all sorts of fancy utensils and cookware, along with a butcher, gourmet foods, and cooking classes.

Zabar's (Map p96; ☎ 212-787-2000; 2245 Broadway at 80th St) The be-all-and-end-all of Upper West Side food stores. Coffee, lox, bagels, and everything under the sun. Everyone loves Zabar's.

Myers of Keswick (Map p82; ☎ 212-691-4194; 634 Hudson St at Jane St) A traditional British grocery store that seems like it stepped out of Cornwall, or rather, we suppose, Keswick. All of your favorite treats from across the pond.

> **BROOKLYN FLEA**
>
> Perhaps the most popular marketplace in New York is the weekly **Brooklyn Flea** (Map p81; www.brooklynflea.com) with over 100 vendors selling their wares from antique jewelry to artisan cheese, and everything in between. On Saturday it's outside in **Fort Greene** (176 Lafayette Ave btwn Clermont & Vanderbilt; 🕑 10am-5pm Sat) while on Sunday the merchants set up camp in the tallest building in Brooklyn, the old **Williamsburg Savings Bank** (1 Hanson Pl at Flatbush Ave; 🕑 10am-5pm Sun) with its majestic vaulted ceilings.

GETTING THERE & AWAY

Air

The metro New York area is served by three major airports: JFK and LaGuardia in Queens and Newark in New Jersey; see p414. JFK and Newark are major hubs and handle most international travel while LaGuardia is primarily domestic. See also the details on travel to and from the airports.

Bus

Port Authority (Map p92) is the bus station in New York City that services all the major carriers. **Greyhound** (☎ 800-231-2222; www.greyhound.com) and **Peter Pan Trailways** (☎ 800-343-9999; www.peterpanbus.com) are the big ones, connecting to most major American and Canadian cities. Those traveling shorter distances will find **New Jersey Transit** (☎ 800-772-2222; www.njtransit.com) of use for getting to… wait for it… New Jersey.

Car & Motorcycle

The I-95 is the primary highway that connects all of the East Coast from Maine to Miami. But all roads lead to New York in this part of the country. Tunnels leading into Manhattan charge a fare, as does the George Washington Bridge. Bridges connecting Manhattan to the outer boroughs are free.

Train

New York is served by two primary train stations. Penn Station (Map p92) is the place to find national carrier **Amtrak** (☎ 800-872-7245; www.amtrak.com) as well as **Long Island Railroad** (LIRR; ☎ 718-217-5477; www.mta.nyc.ny.us/lirr/) that carries commuters and weekenders to points east in Brooklyn, Queens, and Long Island. You can also catch trains to New Jersey on **New Jersey Transit** (☎ 800-772-2222; www.njtransit.com). Another choice is the New Jersey **PATH train** (☎ 800-234-7284; www.panynj.gov/path) which connects downtown Manhattan with Northern NJ.

Grand Central Terminal (p91) is the place to find **Metro North Railroad** (☎ 212-532-4900; www.mnr.org) that services points north in Connecticut and the Hudson Valley.

GETTING AROUND

To/From the Airport

JFK is accessible by car, taxi, bus and monorail. **Taxis** from JFK to any destination in Manhattan cost a flat $45 plus tip and toll (if you go through the Midtown Tunnel). They'll take you back to the airport, too, but at a metered rate that may rise above $50 if traffic is heavy. Better to call a town car or 'gypsy cab' from **Tel Aviv** (☎ 212-777-7777) or **Carmel** (☎ 212-666-6666) that will charge about $48 (plus tip and toll).

The **Air Train** monorail connects JFK's terminals to Jamaica Station with subway and LIRR access for a $5 fee. It also goes to the Howard Beach subway stop.

Buses travel frequently from Port Authority to JFK on **NY Airport Service Express Bus** (☎ 212-875-8200; www.nyairportservice.com).

LaGuardia is also accessible via the NY Airport Service Express bus. Taxis or a car service will cost you about $40 as LaGuardia is closer to Midtown than JFK.

Newark Liberty Airport will cost about the same as JFK to reach by taxi or car service. Trains run every 20 minutes or so from Penn Station to the airport on NJ Transit. The **Newark Airport Express** (☎ 877-863-9275; www.usa coach.com) bus takes you to or from the airport via Port Authority.

Bicycle

Many New Yorkers bike about the city. With newly installed bike lanes popping up all over, it's not hard to see why. That said, unless you are an experienced urban biker, we'd recommend staying off the streets and avenues and sticking to the bike trails in Central Park or those along the Hudson River Park. Rentals are about $30 to $40 a day at most bike shops.

Boat

The **New York Water Taxi** (www.nywatertaxi.com) is a fun way to get around downtown Manhattan and over to Brooklyn for $3.50 per ride, though you can get a day pass and hop on/ hop off at different stops.

The **Staten Island Ferry** (☎ 311; admission free) leaves every 30 minutes from Battery Park (Map p83) for its trip across New York Harbor.

Bus & Subway

NYC's public transportation system is run by the **Metropolitan Transit Authority** (www.mta. info) which operates both the buses and the subways that run 24 hours a day. Rides cost $2.25 and you can transfer from one to the other at no additional charge when you swipe your Metrocard.

The subway is the ideal way to get around town, especially during the rush hour.

In Manhattan trains run 'Uptown' and 'Downtown.' Uptown trains tend to terminate in Queens or the Bronx while Downtown ones end up in Brooklyn. A particularly useful website is www.hopstop.com which plots your route, and accounts for any service changes, based on your starting and ending points.

Car & Motorcycle

Driving in Manhattan is complicated to say the least. Streets often go one-way only and are frequently jammed with traffic. Avoid Broadway which is closed to vehicles through much of Midtown. If you're looking to park, free parking can be found on neighborhood streets but chances are you'll have to leave the car in a garage. These can be pricey, particularly in Midtown and Lower Manhattan near Chinatown and Wall St. The best prices can be found at garages on the Far West and East sides of the island.

Taxis

Yellow taxis you can hail from the street corner are easily found south of 125th St in Manhattan. The fare is metered, with a base rate of about $2.50 (and surcharges late at night or during rush hour). At $0.40 per 1/5 of a mile (or per minute standing idle) it can add up quickly. Expect to pay about $10 to get from Midtown to Downtown. It can be $25 or more to get to destinations in Brooklyn, Queens, or the Bronx.

Car services are convenient if you are coming from the outer-boroughs into Manhattan. Try **Tel Aviv** (☎ 212-777-7777) or **Carmel** (☎ 212-666-6666). Locals in these areas tend to have other options, so make a point of asking.

New York State

It comes as a surprise to many visitors that New York State is so many things: a historically rich hub of river transportation, a bucolic enclave of farms and antiques, and a treasure trove of natural beauty. With the iconic Hudson River Valley as its original life source, New York City presided at the helm of America's greatest revolution: the Industrial Age. And the city's pulsing cultural energy has rubbed off on the entire state: you can't throw an apple and not hit an interesting cinema, theatre, art gallery or bookstore. Now that industry has largely moved on, it's the state's environment, tourism, arts, agriculture that shine.

Beyond the borders of NYC is a living canvas of lush forests, sapphire lakes and brooding hills. This harmony of form and color has inspired generations of artists – from the Hudson River School of painters to Jackson Pollock, whose creations can be found in the state's museums and Gilded Age mansions. This inspiration is best enjoyed outside: in a Hudson Valley apple orchard, atop the High Peaks of the Adirondacks, or beside the roar of Niagara Falls.

When George Washington viewed these scenes in the 18th century, he predicted that New York State would be the seat of the empire. But would he have predicted the wineries of the Finger Lakes, the Lake Placid Olympic village or the great Saratoga racetrack? Probably not. After all, New York State may be well known, but she's got plenty of tricks up her sleeves.

HIGHLIGHTS

- Watching 40 million gallons of water hurtling down at **Niagara Falls** (p204)
- Wowing your taste buds at the **Culinary Institute of America** (p137) in Hyde Park
- Living out your Great Gatsby-esque fantasies on Long Island's **Gold Coast** (p117)
- Screaming at the top of your lungs down the bobsled ride at Lake Placid's **Olympic Sports Complex** (p172)
- Betting the farm on horses at the **Saratoga Race Course** (p164) in Saratoga Springs
- Perfecting the art of poolside lounging at **Victoria Pool** (p161) in Saratoga Springs, the nation's oldest heated swimming pool
- Cruising the **wine trails** (p192) on the shores of Seneca, Keuka, and Cayuga Lakes
- Cooling off in the Finger Lakes with a double decker cone at **Not My Dad's Ice Cream** (p190) or the **Cayuga Creamery** (p193)

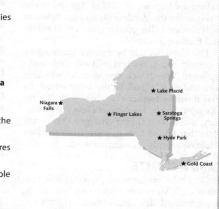

- POPULATION: 19,541,500
- AREA: 3,537,438 sq miles

HISTORY

From a riverbank along the Hudson, it's easy to imagine a New York of another era; when Amsterdam was the world financial center. When Manhattan itself was (by today's measure) a relatively small port and the skyline was dotted with tall buildings, some even reaching four or five stories. Picture masted ships sailing the wide river, which reminded German immigrants of their beloved Rhine, and muddy lanes cutting through small villages with stone fences, dairy farms and Victorian cottages. As the Dutch settled up the river, what was once farmland and the outskirts of civilization became the land of opulence, and extravagant mansions sprouted up – a reminder that fortunes could be made in this young nation. From then on, the rest of the state profited from New York City's burgeoning wealth, bringing factories to Syracuse, Buffalo and Rochester and government to Albany, while farming and smaller industries reigned elsewhere. Today, the industrial regions struggle to revitalize, while the bucolic Adirondacks, Finger Lakes and Thousand Islands area capitalize on their beauty by luring travelers from all over the world – and even New Yorkers out of their beloved city.

In the central part of the state, Civil Rights history and women's suffrage runs deep – Seneca Falls is the birthplace of the American women's rights movement. The area also played an important literary role – Mark Twain wrote some of his most infamous works in the region. Along the Hudson River Valley, the legacies of Gilded Age industrial tycoons like the Vanderbilts and Rockefellers exist alongside the gentler ghosts of Franklin and Eleanor Roosevelt.

The Catskills will be forever changed by a certain music festival in 1969 that made the word 'Woodstock' synonymous with free love and rock 'n' roll. In the same way, Lake Placid will be forever associated with Winter Olympics pride. Looking at New York's history, a common theme emerges: this is one state that knows how to learn from the past while constantly reinventing itself.

LAND & CLIMATE

Rolling hills, verdant valleys, fertile soil, dramatic cliffs, vineyards, high peaks, low valleys, apple orchards and endless miles of lake, river, and ocean coastline. And with 20 million people, you'd think there wouldn't be room for wildlife (think again). Whew. New York really does have it all.

While the Adirondacks' Lake Tear of the Clouds feeds the upper Hudson, the lower part of the river is actually a tidal estuary – so it contains more salt water than fresh water.

The entire state experiences four distinct seasons. Summers in the region are warm and muggy with temperatures soaring above 90°F, even in mountainous areas. Fall and spring are good times to visit, when humidity drops and temperatures are moderate. Autumn is particularly splendid when the myriad of trees put on a magnificent color show.

Winters are cold and snowy, especially in the mountains, although the snow does not fall there in as great a volume as it does in cities such as Buffalo and Syracuse, which are famous for a phenomenon known as 'lake effect snow.' And if you think those areas are cold, remember that the Adirondacks have nearly seven months of winter (just perfect for those winter sports competitors in Lake Placid.)

NATIONAL & STATE PARKS

For resources on national and state parks, contact the **New York State Parks office** (☎ 845-889-4100; www.nysparks.com). For $65, the Empire Passport gives unlimited day-use vehicle entry into most of the parks.

The Hudson River Valley is home to several spectacular parks. The **Hudson Highlands State Park** (☎ 845-225-7207; Rte 9D, Beacon; ☾ dawn-dusk; Ⓟ $8 for beach, free for hiking), a huge undeveloped preserve, has 25 miles of hiking trails, kayaking, fishing, a swimming beach and spectacular Hudson River views. Near Millbrook, **James Baird State Park** (☎ 845-452-1489; 122 Freedom Rd, Pleasant Valley; ☾ dawn-dusk) is a great day-use park that features an 18-hole golf course designed by Robert Trent Jones. **Clarence Fahnestock Memorial State Park** (☎ 845-225-7207; Rte 301, Carmel; ☾ dawn-dusk) has lake swimming, fishing, and camping. Nature trails include a portion of the Appalachian Trail.

The **Catskills region** (p143) includes the 1094-sq-mile **Catskill Park**, 40% of which is publicly owned and protected. The park includes the Catskill Forest Preserve where more than 200 miles of hiking trails meander. The **Catskill Mountains**, which are part of the Appalachian Range, are tallest are in the north – this area is home to downhill and cross-country skiing (p152). Both the Catskill Mountains and the older **Shawangunk Mountains** to the southeast are havens for hikers. Near the village of New Paltz are the **Mohonk Preserve** (p144) and the **Minnewaska State Park**. (p144). Both offer great rock climbing opportunities.

Highlights of the breathtaking **Adirondacks** (p166) include the **St Regis Wilderness Canoe Area** (p175); and the **High Peaks** (p172) is the most heavily visited region of the park because of its magnificent scenery: tall mountains clustered around Lake Placid and the Keene Valley.

Getting There & Away
AIR
The main airports in the region are LaGuardia in New York City (p414), Albany International Airport (p159) to the north and Buffalo Niagara International Airport (p203) to the west. **Stewart International Airport** (☎ 845-564-2100), to the south in Newburgh, is 20 miles from New Paltz and is the nearest airport to the Catskills, while **White Plains Airport** (☎ 914-995-4860; www.whiteplainsairport.com) is adjacent to the lower Hudson Valley.

TRAIN
Amtrak (☎ 800-872-7245; www.amtrak.com) runs to Saratoga Springs, Buffalo, Niagara Falls, and several other major destinations. **Short Line/ Coach USA** (☎ 800-631-8405; www.shortlinebus.com) offers good service to the region.

Getting Around
For motorists, the area is crisscrossed by interstates, and most regions are easily accessible by car: it's virtually essential for exploring the countryside and small towns.

Metro-North (☎ 212-532-4900, 800-638-7646; www.mta.info) Hudson Line runs from Grand Central Station in New York City to east-bank Hudson towns such as Tarrytown and Poughkeepsie.

Adirondack/Pine Hill Trailways (☎ 800-776-7548; www.trailwaysny.com) offers daily bus service to many towns across the state.

Greyhound (☎ 800-231-2222; www.greyhound.com) has a few routes within the region.

LONG ISLAND

Long Island, once a bastion of sleepy fishing towns, retains a bit of that original mystique, but today is in many ways a giant suburb of New York City, the black hole of the region that pulls all things towards it. However, nest led amongst the large swaths of middle-class housing are several points of interest, both romantic and historic as well as luxurious and, occasionally, very, very gay.

GOLD COAST
History
'So we beat on, boats against the current, borne back ceaselessly into the past.' Anyone who has thrilled to prose of F Scott Fitzgerald and the tragic elite of *The Great Gatsby* will be interested in exploring a collection of towns on the North Shore of Long Island in Nassau County. It is here on Long Island Sound that the East and West Eggs would have existed, amongst the glamorous mansions belonging to early-20th-century industrialist millionaires. Today, the area remains an upscale settlement with large houses and the occasional mansion. True manors, however, are of the historical variety and many can be toured.

Orientation
The Gold Coast is more of a concept than a singular destination. It is made up of several small towns stretching along the coves of the North Shore of Long Island. These include Great Neck, Roslyn, Oyster Bay, Port Washington, and Westbury. Route 25A will connect you to most of them.

Information
EMERGENCY
Ambulance, Fire, Police (☎ 911)

INTERNET
Great Neck Library (☎ 516-466-8055; 475 Great Neck Rd, Great Neck)

MEDICAL SERVICES
Nassau University Medical Center (☎ 516-572-3311; 2201 Hempstead Turnpike, East Meadow) Emergency room & full service hospital.

POST
Port Washington Post Office (☎ 516-883-1501; Port Washington Blvd, Port Washington; ☽ 7:30am-7pm Mon-Fri)

Sights & Activities
There are a variety of old manor house estates to visit along the Gold Coast, with most of them having been transformed into cultural institutions or nature preserves.

NEW YORK STATE

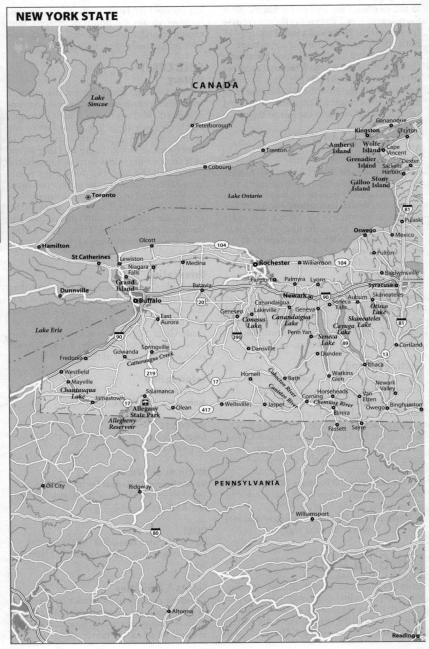

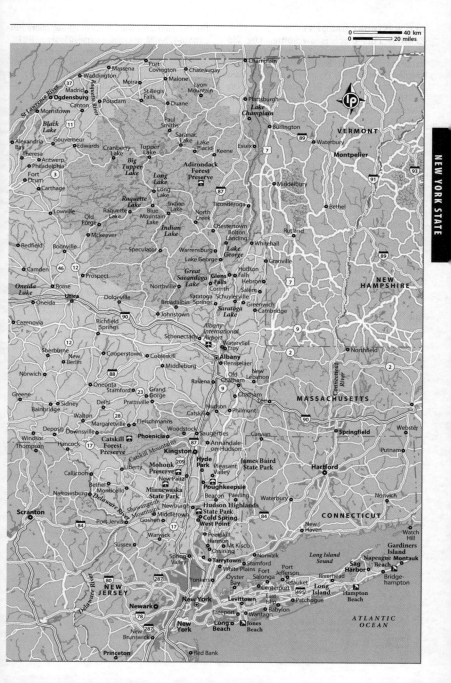

OLD WESTBURY GARDENS

ZOMG. This place is awesome. The **Old Westbury Gardens** (☎ 516-333-0048; www.oldwestburygardens.com; 71 Old Westbury Rd, Old Westbury; admission adult/child/senior $10/5/8; ☺ 10am-5pm Apr-Oct, closed Tue), built in the early 20th century, are on the 160-acre estate of the Phipps family. The Charles II–style house, boasting 23 rooms with lush interiors, can also be toured. The grounds include a walled garden, a cottage garden with children's playhouses, a primrose path, the spooky 'Ghost Walk', a boxwood garden and a lake. Completely magical and utterly jaw-dropping for its ornate beauty. Several special events are timed to coincide with the bloom schedules of the flora. Films such as *Love Story; North by Northwest; Age of Innocence; Cruel Intentions* and *To Wong Foo, Thanks for Everything, Julie Newmar* were all shot here.

SAGAMORE HILL

Driving through the secluded waterside spot of **Oyster Bay** brings reminders of robber barons and the Jazz Age. This quiet village – just one hour from New York City – is a refuge

for the rich and the location of **Sagamore Hill** (☎ 516-922-4788; www.nps.gov/sahi; 20 Sagamore Hill Rd, Oyster Bay; admission adult/child $5/free; ☺ 10am-4pm Mon-Sun Jun-Aug, 10am-4pm Wed-Sun Sep-May), the 23-room mansion built in 1885 by Theodore Roosevelt. Sagamore Hill eventually served as the summer White House during Roosevelt's tenure in office from 1902 to 1908; it was in this dark Victorian mansion that he brokered an end to the Russo-Japanese War, an effort for which Roosevelt won the Nobel peace prize.

Roosevelt was in many ways the first president of the modern era – he used a telephone (which is still on view in his study) to remain in contact with Washington. Though he was also the first chief executive to concern himself with conservation, animal rights activists will no doubt turn pale at the many mounted heads, antlers and leopard skins on display, along with the inkwell made from a rhinoceros foot.

Roosevelt died at Sagamore Hill in 1919 and is buried in a cemetery a mile away. A red-brick Georgian house on the grounds was later occupied by Theodore Roosevelt Jr, and is now a museum charting the 26th president's political career.

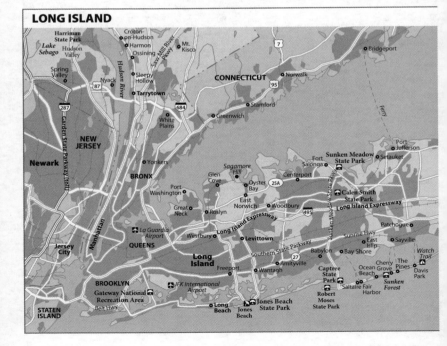

LONG ISLAND

NASSAU COUNTY MUSEUM OF ART

This appealing and quirky **museum** (☎ 516-484-9338; www.nassaumuseum.org; 1 Museum Drive, Roslyn Harbor; admission adult/child/senior $10/4/8; ⊗ 11am-4:45pm Tue-Sun; ⚓) is situated on the 145-acre **William Cullen Bryant Preserve**. Much of the art, sometimes featuring rotating shows with Joan Miro or Jean-Michel Basquiat, is located inside the Bryce-Frick Mansion, which was built in 1900 by General Lloyd Bryce and purchased 19 years later by Childs Frick. The real star of the show is the **sculpture garden**, which offers up a surprising array of contemporary works, from Richard Serra to Alexander Calder and Mark di Suvero. Many of the most interesting pieces are by artists with less brand-name recognition.

The preserve also offers eight **nature trails**, along with maps that make for excellent bird-watching – see if you can spot a great horned owl or a red-tailed hawk. On Sundays, the museum hosts a family fun day, with supervised art activities for kids as well as family-friendly gallery tours. The museum's **Art Space for Children** is open Tuesday through Sunday from noon to 4:30pm.

VANDERBILT MANSION & PLANETARIUM

Also known as Eagle's Nest, the **Vanderbilt Mansion & Planetarium** (☎ 631-854-5555; 180 Little Neck Rd, Centerport; www.vanderbiltmuseum.org; mansion/planetarium adult $8/7, student & senior $6/5, child $5/4, combo tickets available; ⊗ 10am-4pm Tue-Sun) used to be the estate of Willie Vanderbilt, one of the last major heirs to the Vanderbilt family's railroad fortune. Willie spent most of his life – and most of his money – collecting sea creatures and curiosities from around the South Pacific and throughout Egypt; many items of his collection are on display. In 1971 a planetarium was added to the grounds, featuring a 60ft 'Sky Theater' and telescope. The entire site is now owned by Nassau County, which holds community events on the 43-acre site.

Finding the Vanderbilt Mansion is tricky: heading east on Rte 25A look for a flashing yellow light in front of a fire department in Centerpoint, and turn left onto Park Circle; this road will bring you to the mansion. Please note that the mansion isn't recommended for small children and is not air-conditioned.

NEW YORK STATE

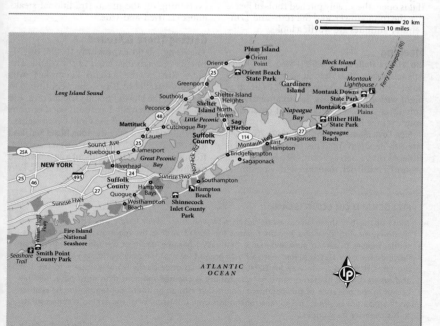

NEW YORK STATE

SANDS POINT PRESERVE & HEMPSTEAD HOUSE

Another former estate that's since been designated a nature preserve, Hempstead House (☎ 516-571-7900; www.sandspointpreserve.org; 127 Middle Neck Rd, Port Washington; admission $5 per car, free Wed; ⏰ 9am-4:30pm daily) looks like it got beamed here from the Scottish Moors or Cornwall. Built by Henry Gould, the estate was bought by Daniel and Florence Guggenheim in 1917. A massive stone castle, it perhaps is the easiest place to imagine the Jazz Age antics of real-life Gatsbys and Daisys playing croquet and swilling champagne with views of the Long Island Sound. That said, there's really not much to do here except look at the marvelous mansion and have a picnic before wandering the nature trails.

For $5 you can also occasionally get a tour of one of the few intact historic houses on the Gold Coast, the **Falaise**, which is designed to look like a 13th-century Norman manor house. It's located within the Sands Point Preserve and tends to be open in spring and summer, but budget cuts have made the opening hours unreliable, so it's best to call ahead. If it is open, the steeply pitched roofs of heave tile, the round tower, and the 16th- and 17th-century antiques are worth a look.

Sleeping

Inn at Fox Hollow (☎ 800-291-8090; 7755 Jericho Turnpike, Woodbury; d from $160) An all-suite boutique hotel with nifty landscaped grounds lit up at night with colored lights. Spa treatments and amenities such as a pool make it cuter than your average Radisson.

Glen Cove Mansion (☎ 516-671-6400; 200 Dosoris Lane, Glen Cove; d from $170) This 187-room hotel is situated on 55 acres. Rooms are both in and around a red-brick mansion with Corinthian

columns and a massive portico that once belonged to Charles Pratt. If you're staying in the area, the excellent grounds probably make this the top choice. There's also a pub with nice views of the estate.

Eating & Drinking

This area of Long Island is extremely developed and has lots of your favorite (or not so favorite) chain restaurants dotting the landscape. However, there are a couple of more interesting options.

Elaine's Asian Bistro (☎ 516-829-8883; 8 Bond St, Great Neck; mains $13-26) is a pan-Asian experience whose menu touches on Chinese, Japanese and Thai. There's probably some Vietnamese on there, too, but we lost track. Solid, if not exactly life-changing.

Peter Luger Steakhouse (☎ 516-487-8800; 255 Northern Blvd, Great Neck; mains $16-45) is probably the most famous steakhouse in New York. It has an outpost in Williamsburg, Brooklyn, too, but this location is the best place to play gentry after a day of touring mansions. The porterhouse is big here, but since they've been doing this for well over a century, just about everything on the menu (traditional steakhouse) is tried-and-true.

Getting There & Around

The Long Island Expressway (I-495, or L-I-E) cuts through the center of the island. The older Rte 25 (the Jericho Turnpike) runs roughly parallel to I-495, then continues to the end of the North Fork at Orient Point. Rte 25 and Northern Blvd are both good options that connect many of the Gold Coast sights.

While you can take the **Long Island Rail Road** (LIRR; ☎ 631-231-5477, 718-217-5477; www.mta.info/lirr) from Penn Station to just about any individual destination (there are stops in Great Neck, Port

---

FITZGERALD ON LONG ISLAND

'Most of the big shore places were closed now and there were hardly any lights except the shadowy, moving glow of a ferryboat across the Sound. And as the moon rose higher the inessential houses began to melt away until gradually I became aware of the old island here that flowered once for Dutch sailors' eyes-a fresh, green breast of the new world. Its vanished trees, the trees that had made way for Gatsby's house, had once pandered in whispers to the last and greatest of all human dreams; for a transitory enchanted moment man must have held his breath in the presence of this continent; compelled into an aesthetic contemplation he neither understood nor desired, face to face for the last time in history with something commensurate to his capacity for wonder.'

The Great Gatsby

Washington, Oyster Bay etc.) and catch a quick cab to any particular location, if you plan on traveling between towns it is best to have a car.

THE HAMPTONS
History
The Hamptons are what New York City dwellers call 'the country.' A collection of small villages and hamlets along eastern Long Island's South Fork, they were settled in the mid 17th century as bases for the fishing and whaling industries and today are a place where Hollywood titans and east coast elites find 'the simple life.' You can still get fresh fish and straight-from-the-farm fruit and veggies, but you can also get a $300 dinner or a $2000 pair of pumps at one of the luxury shops.

Despite the influx of big city money, the Hamptons have a pastoral and bucolic feel that residents work hard to maintain. The best way to describe the Hamptons is to point out their most prominent feature: the privacy hedgerow. Neatly manicured shrubs form a tall, impenetrable wall along what would otherwise be a scenic drive of majestic houses.

Pedigree used to be the only way to pass beyond the green fence to huge estates and mansions. But the Hamptons' exclusivity waned slightly as the nouveau riche started building bigger and bigger houses in the region. The easy money of the 1980s brought another influx of showier summertime visitors who made their fortunes in the fashion industry and on Wall Street.

Finally, in the late 1990s, Hollywood arrived in full force from the left coast and major celebrities like Stephen Spielberg and P Diddy began to be spotted in the cafes and bookstores – when not throwing extravagant parties on their massive lawns.

Many of the attractions, restaurants and hotels in the Hamptons close the last week in October and remain shut until late April. About two weeks after Labor Day, B&B prices drop and traffic jams along the Montauk Highway disappear. During the summer season, the place is packed and the rates and prices are high.

Hopefully this won't dissuade you from going, though, because the Hamptons really are exquisitely beautiful and well worth the trouble. Also, it's not nearly as clubby as some would make it out to be. You won't feel bad if you're not carrying a Fendi bag.

AND YOUR VERY FLESH SHALL BE A GREAT POEM

Anyone with a passing interest in the written word will know of Walt Whitman. America's greatest poet (or certainly most iconic) was born in Huntington in a small farmhouse in 1819. Today the **Walt Whitman Birthplace** (☎ 631-427-5240; www.waltwhitman.org; 246 Old Walt Whitman Rd, West Hills; admission adult/student/senior $5/4/4; 11am-4pm Mon-Fri, until 5pm Sat & Sun Jun 15-Labor Day, 11am-4pm Wed-Sun in winter;) is a National Historic site that offers tours, over 100 Whitman portraits, original manuscripts and letters, and even rare recordings of the poet's voice. Programs aimed at children are also available. It's neat stuff if you're a poetry aficionado.

Orientation
The Hamptons are comprised of several villages and hamlets clustered along the south fork of eastern Long Island. The first 'real Hampton' (locals don't count Hampton Bays) is Southampton. Continuing towards points east, along Montauk Highway (aka Rte 27), are Bridgehampton, East Hampton, Amagansett and finally Montauk. Sag Harbor is a few miles north of Bridgehampton. Within individual towns, Montauk Hwy is sometimes called Main St.

Information
BOOKSTORES
Bookhampton Southampton (☎ 631-324-4939; 93 Main St); East Hampton (☎ 631-324-4939; 20 Main St); Sag Harbor (☎ 631-725-8425; 20 Main St) A well-stocked favorite that also sells maps.

MEDIA
Dan's Papers (www.danspapers.com) A good place to find local listings for movies, music and special events.

MEDICAL SERVICES
Southampton Hospital (☎ 631-726-8420; 240 Meeting House Lane)

TOURIST INFORMATION
East Hampton (☎ 631-324-0362; www.easthampton.com; 79A Main St)
Montauk (☎ 631-668-2428; www.montaukchamber.com; 742 Montauk Highway, Montauk)

Southampton (☎ 631-283-8707; www.southampton
chamber.com; 76 Main St)

Sights & Activities
SOUTHAMPTON
Southampton, the oldest of the 'moneyed colonies,' has a bustling Main St with high-end shopping and galleries as well as several places to eat. It's easy to park the car and walk to various points of interest.

Southampton Historical Museum (☎ 631-283-2494) consists of, and operates, two historic homes in the village: **Rogers Mansion** (17 Meeting House Lane; adult/senior/student $4/3/2; ☽ 11am-5pm Tue-Sat, 1-5pm Sun, summer only; ☙), an 1840s Greek revival built by a prominent whaling captain, and the austere **Halsey Homestead** (249 S Main St; adult/senior/student $3/2/1; ☽ noon-5pm Fri & Sat, summer only), a saltbox house built in 1648, just eight years after the first European settlers arrived in the area. The Rogers Mansion has period rooms with Edwardian decor and a vintage toy collection. Photographs of the 1938 hurricane and its aftermath are quite interesting. Next to the Rogers Mansion is **Old Southampton Village** with twelve historic-style structures that re-create the colonial-era community.

The **Parrish Art Museum** (☎ 631-283-2111; 25 Jobs Lane; adult/child/senior/student $5/free/3/3; ☽ 11am-5pm Mon & Thu-Sat, 1-5pm Sun, open daily in summer) is just a short walk from Main St. It has been open to the public since 1898 and its gallery features the work of major artists including Roy Lichtenstein, who had a house nearby. The museum is truly a great little treasure to behold.

THE AMITYVILLE HORROR!
A gruesome detour for fans of the macabre is **112 Ocean Ave** in Amityville on Long Island's South Shore. It is in this Dutch colonial house that Ronald DeFeo Jr brutally murdered six family members in the 1970s. After the house sat empty for a while, George and Kathleen Lutz moved in with their family and promptly began experiencing paranormal activities that were detailed in the book *The Amityville Horror* by Jay Anson. The book is the basis for a whopping nine films (including the hilariously titled, if little seen, *Amityville Dollhouse*), with the most memorable being the 1979 James Brolin/Margot Kidder version.

BRIDGEHAMPTON
In **Bridgehampton**, the next town east, you'll find a homier Main St with a collection of shops and neighborhood eateries.

our pick The highlight of Bridgehampton is the **Dan Flavin Art Institute** (☎ 631-537-1476; www.diaart.org; Corwith Ave off Main St, Bridgehampton; ☽ noon-6pm Thu-Sun Apr-Oct, call for winter opening hours), an extra-groovy museum dedicated to the fluorescent light sculptures of Dan Flavin and run by the Dia Art Foundation. Located in an old firehouse-cum-Baptist chapel, the institute displays nine sculptures permanently and has rotating shows downstairs that change annually. A strange anomaly in the area, the institute helps remind visitors that much of the Hamptons was known as an artists' colony before it became the elite enclave it is today.

SAG HARBOR
About 7 miles north of Bridgewater is Sag Harbor, a popular, salty fishing port on the Peconic Bay. The more mellow vibe of fishing and surfers is more evident here than in, say, East Hampton. The **Sag Harbor Whaling & Historical Museum** (☎ 631-725-0770; cnr Main & Garden Sts; adult/child $5/3; ☽ 10am-5pm Mon-Sat, 1-5pm Sun May-Oct) celebrates the town's former industry.

EAST HAMPTON & AMAGANSETT
Currently the fanciest of all the Hamptons is **East Hampton**, where the billionaires and their brethren cavort in the summer months. Huge houses abound, and Main St is a luxury shopper's dream – this is typically what people visualize when they think of weekending on the East End.

Catch readings and art exhibitions at the **Guild Hall** (☎ 631-324-0806; www.guildhall.org; 158 Main St, East Hampton). Driving or biking down Main Beach along **Ocean Ave** will afford glimpses of the larger estates with water views. You can see some other grand (private) houses by turning right at **Lily Pond Lane** and peeking through the breaks in the high shrubbery. The book *Philistines at the Hedgerow* by Steven Gaines is an entertaining read about the private affairs that these homes have hosted.

LongHouse Reserve (☎ 631-329-3568; www.longhouse.org; 133 Hands Creek Rd, East Hampton; admission adult/senior $10/8; ☽ 2-5pm Wed & Sat May-early Oct; ☙) is a museum, garden and sculpture park unlike any other. Founded by Jack Larsen in 1970 in East Hampton's Northwest Woods, the estate is 16 acres of ornamental gardens

STAUNCH WOMEN

Fans of the cult-classic documentary *Grey Gardens* will know that Little Edie Beale accused East Hampton of being a 'mean, nasty Republican town' that could get you for 'wearing red shoes on a Thursday.' That may or may not be true, but anyone with a taste for eccentrics will want to check out this film by legendary filmmakers the Maysles brothers about Jackie Bouvier Kennedy Onassis's, um, *colorful*, cousins.

Big and Little Edie Beale while away their afternoons in East Hampton amidst a decaying mansion and infinite raccoons. A side of the Hamptons one rarely sees, this flick is wildly entertaining and has inspired an HBO movie with Jessica Lange and Drew Barrymore as well as a Broadway musical.

Fans of the film who want to see the real Grey Gardens can find it on the corner of Lily Pond Lane and West End Rd in East Hampton. Today it belongs to former Washington Post editor Ben Bradlee and his wife, Sally Quinn. No word yet on where to find that perfect 'Libra man.'

where landscape design is treated as an art-form. Studded with extreme sculpture like Yoko Ono's enormous chess set and Sol Lewitt's 'Irregular Procession High #7', the LongHouse is extraordinary and an attraction you don't want to miss.

Amagansett is basically an extension of East Hampton distinguished by the huge flagpole in the center of the Montauk Highway.

Northeast of town, on Rte 41, is the **Pollock-Krasner House & Study Center** (☎ 631-324-4929; www.pkhouse.org; 830 Springs Fireplace Rd, Amagansett; adult/child $10/free; ☼ Thu-Sat May-Oct), where Jackson Pollock and his wife Lee Krasner lived and worked. Pollock created his famous drip paintings here and the paint that extended beyond the canvas can still be seen. Call for the tour schedule.

MONTAUK

The landscape becomes windswept and grizzled as you approach **Montauk**, the furthest tip of the South Fork. This honky-tonk beach town is filled with shifting dunes, cheap beachside motels and T-shirt shops. After the beachgoers head back to school in September, Montauk fills up for sport-fishing season (blue fin tuna and bass are the main catches).

There are six public beaches (some charge parking fees) in Montauk, in addition to the beachfront property of many hotels and motels. Surfing, swimming and kayaking are all popular activities. If you're a cyclist looking for a challenge, peel off to the right of Rte 27 and take the Old Montauk Highway, an undulating ribbon of asphalt overlooking the ocean. **Montauk Downs State Park** (☎ 631-668-3781) has a fine public **golf course** (☎ 631-668-1234; in-/out-of-state residents $30/65). There are long waits in the summer, so call ahead to reserve a tee time.

Montauk is a feasible destination for those without a car. The LIRR station is at Edgemere St at Firestone Lane, a 10-minute walk to the center of town and the beaches.

Sleeping

The best way to stay in the Hamptons is at a pal's fabulous house, where you can prepare meals picked up from a farmers market in between doing laps in the pool and playing a few sets of tennis. If you don't travel in such circles (too bad for you!) there are still scores of options for the visitor unable or unwilling to rent a house for $10,000 (or more!) per week.

Rates are highest on summer weekends and lowest during winter weekdays. While it's decidedly less decadent during the winter, this can be a fine time to enjoy the pleasures of Long Island's East End because the scenery is still stunning and the crowds have died down. Autumn ain't half bad either.

Bridgehampton Inn (☎ 631-537-3600; 2266 Main St, Bridgehampton; d $145-390) offers rooms in something akin to a traditional Hamptons home – whitewashed with plank siding. It's a little more B&B than some might prefer, but you'll be hard-pressed to find a more central location from which to explore the various hamlets.

Hampton Maid (☎ 631-728-4166; www.hamtonmaid.com; 259 E Montauk Hwy, Southampton; d $145-620) The Hampton Maid seems a bit more of a motel than a hotel. It's Southampton – so it's obviously better than a Holiday Inn – but it's not a luxury spa. That said, it's completely darling and offers a great mix of locale and economy.

American Hotel (☎ 631-725-3535; www.theamericanhotel.com; 49 Main St, Sag Harbor; d from $245) The

NEW YORK STATE

American has the best beds ever, but this may deter you from leaving your bedroom to explore Sag Harbor. An old-world hotel (but still excellent and modern), it has a popular downstairs restaurant and bar that continues to be a center of the social scene all these years later. An ideal choice for any lover of European elegance and efficiency, you'll find fine accommodations all set in a superb location.

ourpick The Reform Club (☎ 631-267-8500; www.reformclubinn.com; 23 Windmill Lane, Amagansett; ste & cottages $375-2100) Swoon! This place is so slick and sweet and HOT that we're still sweating. Brand new and state-of-the-art, here you'll get an experience similar to those who rent or own houses. Lawns, privacy, elegance – even the Countess LuAnn would find it difficult to complain about the excellent accommodations of this classy inn. It's appealing even in winter, when it provides a perfect getaway from a hectic big-city lifestyle. You can even rent your own cottage.

Eating & Drinking

Candy Kitchen (☎ 631-537-9885; Main St at Hildreth St, Bridgehampton; mains $5-12; ☺ breakfast & lunch) Serving up ice-cream and classic diner eats since 1925, the Candy Kitchen is a staple of Hamptons living. It seems to have stepped out of the past, and the visitor can easily imagine previous regulars like Bette Davis and Truman Capote chowing down on burgers and milkshakes.

Amagansett Farmers Market (☎ 631-267-6600; Main St, Amagansett; ☺ 9am-5pm May-Oct) Fresh flowers for the porch table, corn for the beach clambake and something surprising for the afternoon luncheon – the sophisticated farm stand caters to all the locals' needs.

THE BARD OF LONG ISLAND

What Springsteen is to Jersey, Billy Joel is to Long Island – a rock poet, a maestro, and its favorite son. When you're cruising out in Montauk, find a copy of 'Downeaster Alexa,' a second-tier, but nonetheless first rate, song from Joel's catalog about the agony and ecstasy of the fisherman's life. You probably know his biggest hits, most of which reference specific Long Island restaurants, bars and locales. If not, buy his greatest hits and start with 'Piano Man.'

Lobster Roll (☎ 631-267-3740; Rte 27; mains $10-12; ☺ 11:30am-10pm summer) On Rte 27, between the towns of Amagansett and Montauk, a few roadside fish shacks like this institution pop up. With its distinctive 'Lunch' sign, the Lobster Roll serves the namesake sandwich as well as fresh steamers and fried clams.

Bobby Van's Steakhouse (☎ 631-537-0590; Main St, Bridgehampton; mains $10-30; ☺ lunch & dinner) A classic bar and grill, Bobby Van's has been serving Hamptonites in a French bistro-esque environment since 1969. We love this place.

World Pie (☎ 631-537-7999; 2402 Montauk Hwy, Bridgehampton; mains $15-25; ☺ lunch & dinner) Known for its pizzas, such as the Mr Tang with Asian duck, scallions, mozzarella and goat cheese, this place feels dark and clubby. An outdoor patio makes a perfect place to brunch. And don't worry – it offers more than pizza.

Driver's Seat (☎ 631-283-6606; 62 Jobs Lane, Southampton; mains $10-20; ☺ breakfast, lunch & dinner) is a casual but still appealing eatery with patio seating and crowned by a turquoise-stained glass window of a seascape. Chowders, sandwiches and seafood are mainstays.

Sen (☎ 631-725-1774; 23 Main St, Sag Harbor; mains $14-25; ☺ lunch & dinner) Sag Harbor's upscale Asian restaurant of choice, Sen is just steps from the American Hotel and will have that sushi you've been craving.

Meeting House (☎ 631-267-2764; 4 Amagansett Sq Dr, Amagansett; mains $12-30; ☺ dinner; 🕭) Located in the newly developed Amagansett Sq, the Meeting House offers dishes such as pan-seared scallops, chicken Milanese and vegetable curry. There's even a kids' menu for those traveling with young ones.

ourpick Stephen Talkhouse (☎ 631-267-3117; www.stephentalkhouse.com; 161 Main St, East Hampton; ☺ from 7pm) This concert venue has an active bar scene on nonperformance nights; Billy Joel and James Taylor have appeared here. In summers past, folks like Louden Wainwright III and Judy Collins sang here.

Shopping

If you're looking for Coach, Tiffany & Co., J. Crew or other such fancy chain stores, you'll find most of them lined up along Main St in East Hampton. Here are a few other choices, though some may be open only seasonally.

Mark Humphrey Gallery (☎ 631-283-3113; 95 Main St, Southampton) Jim Dine and Roy Lichtenstein were on view recently alongside Barbie photo panoramas and work by the owner himself. Very cool.

Vilebrequin Saint Tropez (☎ 631-204-1530; 42 Jobs Lane, Southampton) Colorful and fun board shorts for men and boys will guarantee you'll be stylin' at the Southampton Beach Club or the Maidstone. (Just kidding! You can't get into those places unless you're a member or the guest of one – so just wear the trunks at the public beaches and you'll still look supersexy.) They also have women's wear, but it's more limited.

Harmont & Blaine (☎ 631-287-6442; 38 Jobs Lane, Southampton) Great colorful clothes for yachting or relaxing on your Adirondack chairs. Relaxed, casual chic is on tap from this Italian design company that is still very 'East End'. Men are guaranteed to look good while driving with their Porsche's top down.

Jill Lynn Jewelry (☎ 631-287-1001; 66 Jobs Lane, Southampton) Handmade jewelry, mostly by Jill herself. Lovely beaded pieces are a highlight, though some might go for custom dog-bone jewelry from her 'Best Friends' collection.

Nancy Corzine (☎ 631-287-8606; 5 Main St, Southampton) Home furnishings fit for a princess come in creamy beach colors with high thread counts. Great bric-a-brac makes ideal Mother's Day presents.

Twist (☎ 631-287-7990; 46 Jobs Lane, Southampton) For young women, an upscale Hot Topic – and we mean that as a compliment!

Loaves & Fishes Cookshop (☎ 631-537-6066; 2422 Montauk Hwy, Bridgehampton) All things any Barefoot Contessa could need. It offers cooking classes, too, for adults and teens.

our pick **Maison 24** (☎ 631-537-2488; 2424 Main St, Bridgehampton) Super-hip and awesome boutique for the trust-fund hipster in all of us. Great housewares, as well as Japanese toys, modern design, and clothes by Fred Perry make this store a real treat.

Activities & Entertainment

Ideally your time in the Hamptons will be spent drinking Arnold Palmers poolside while working on that tan. But if you are hankering for a little outdoor excitement, there are a couple of possibilities, though dinner parties remain the prime social events.

The **Bridgehampton Polo Club** (☎ 631-537-8450; 849 Hayground Rd, Water Mill) hosts the **Mercedes Benz Polo Challenge** every July and the **Hampton Classic** horse show with show jumping and more every August, around Labor Day weekend.

Very fun, especially if you like equine events. Even if you don't, there's lots of fun to be had just by people watching.

Flying Point Surf School (☎ 516-885-6607; 220 Hampton Rd, Southampton; lessons from $125) offers one-on-one surf lessons seven days a week.

Guild Hall (☎ 631-324-0806; www.guildhall.com; 158 Main St, East Hampton) offers you live theater, special performances, movies and a museum all centered right in the middle of East Hampton.

Getting There & Away

Rte 27 (the Sunrise Highway) runs along the bottom of Long Island from the Brooklyn border and eventually becomes the Montauk Highway near Southampton, ending up at the South Fork's Montauk Point. A trip from New York City to the end of Long Island takes at least three hours, but on weekends traffic jams can turn it into a six-hour ordeal.

The **Hampton Jitney bus** (☎ 800-936-0440; www. hamptonjitney.com) leaves several times daily for Long Island's South Fork from four locations in Manhattan (40th St between Lexington and Third Aves; 59th St at Lexington Ave; 69th St at Lexington Ave; 86th St between Lexington and Third Ave). Drivers usually know ways of circumventing summer weekend traffic, making these buses a good alternative to driving a car.

The **Long Island Rail Road** (LIRR; ☎ 631-231-5477, 718-217-5477; www.mta.info/lirr) runs from New York City's Penn Station and stops at Southampton, Bridgehampton, East Hampton and Montauk.

SHELTER ISLAND

Nearly a third of quiet Shelter Island is dedicated to the **Mashomack Nature Preserve**, and there's an attractive town center in Shelter Island Heights, a cluster of Victorian buildings on the north side of the island. It's a perfect place to explore nature and a true respite from the crowds in the Hamptons.

Just beyond the Shelter Island Heights Bridge is **Picasso's Bike Shop** (☎ 631-749-0520; Bridge St). Bikes can be rented for the day, and are sturdy enough for a strenuous trek across Shelter Island, or take the ferry to Greenport to explore the North Fork and Orient Point. Call ahead in the summer to reserve bikes.

Sleeping & Eating

For such a small place, Shelter Island is well served by B&Bs, including **Ram's Head Inn**

(☎ 631-749-0811; Ram Island Dr; d with/without bathroom incl breakfast $250/135). A destination in itself, this waterfront hotel is moored to the mainland by a narrow causeway. The rooms are small but tidy and low-season rates are a bargain. All in all, the Ram's Head is a classic without being fussy, and the rambling grounds are big enough to host lawn games and lazy rendezvous with thick novels.

The dining choices on Shelter Island are very seasonal.

Dory (☎ 631-749-8871; mains $15-25; ⏲ 11am-9pm summer) Near the Shelter Island Heights Bridge, Dory is a well-scrubbed restaurant-bar named in honor of an early-17th-century boat invented in Massachusetts.

Shelter Island Pizza (☎ 631-749-0400; Rte 114; pizza $10-12) This simple pizza joint is just another choice in the off-season.

Getting There & Away

The **North Ferry Company** (☎ 631-749-0139; car & driver $7, additional passengers $1 per person) runs boats from the North Fork terminal (near the LIRR station in downtown Greenport) to Shelter Island every 15 to 20 minutes from 6am to 11:45pm. The trip takes seven minutes.

South Ferry Inc (☎ 631-749-1200; car & driver $7, additional passengers $1 per person) leaves from a dock in North Haven, 3 miles from Sag Harbor. To get to the dock go north on Rte 114 and follow the signs. Ferries leave from 6am to 11:45pm (to 1:45am Friday and Saturday).

FIRE ISLAND NATIONAL SEASHORE

Sandy beaches, saltwater marshes, evening sunsets and, best of all, no traffic. **Fire Island National Seashore** (☎ 631-289-4810; admission free), a car-free park, runs a narrow 32-mile-long barrier off the southern shore of Long Island. Within the protected zones are 15 hamlets that predated the National Seashore designation. With all this natural beauty, the crowds are a permanent fixture in the summer, and Fire Island is probably the country's leading gay resort area. The primary activity in these summer communities is relaxing on the beach, but as night falls, many communities such as Ocean Beach and the Pines also have a reasonable nightlife available for those looking to mingle. At the western end of the island, **Robert Moses State Park** (Map p120; ☎ 631-669-0470; Robert Moses Causeway) is better known as a family destination.

One of the primary wonders of this sandbar is the **Sunken Forest** (www.nps.gov/fiis) in Sailor's

Haven. A quick ride on the ferry from Sayville will deliver you to this rare maritime holly forest (which can only be found behind sand dunes on Atlantic ocean beaches from New Jersey to Massachusetts). In summer the area is supported by a visitor center and snack bar and is also a life-guarded beach. A real natural wonder, this is an easy day trip.

Sleeping

Camping spots include **Heckscher Park** (☎ 631-581-4433; camping $16-25) in East Islip, and **Watch Hill** (☎ 631-289-9336; www.watchhillfi.com; campsite $30) on Fire Island as part of the National Seashore.

The buildings on Fire Island don't always bear numbered signs. **Houser's Hotel** (☎ 631-583-7799; www.housersbar.com; Bay Walk, Ocean Beach; d $150-250) has 12 rooms. Another option is **Seasons Bed & Breakfast** (☎ 631-588-8295; 468 Denhoff Walk, Ocean Beach; d weekdays/weekend $125/300), open year-round.

Getting There & Away

By car you can get there by taking exit 53 of the Long Island Expressway and traveling south across the Robert Moses Causeway to the public parking facility. Alternatively you can take exit 58 (William Floyd Parkway) to the public parking lot in Smith Point County Park (on Fire Island). There are no cars or bikes allowed within the park.

The three ferry terminals are all close to the Bay Shore, Sayville and Patchogue LIRR stations (train fares from Penn Station are $8 to $12 one-way). The ferry season runs from early May to November; trips take about 20 minutes and cost an average of $12 for a round trip, with discounted seasonal passes available.

DANCERS FROM THE DANCE

The most famous of all the Fire Island communities are the two that cater primarily to the LGBT community: The Pines and Cherry Grove.

The **Fire Island Pines** (www.thepinesfireisland.com), along with Provincetown on Cape Cod, is the East Coast's sunny, gay playground. It's mostly men who summer here by its idyllic beaches in one of 700 or so houses that are often architectural stunners. No cars are allowed on the island, so the boys scamper back and forth from the beach to tea along boardwalks.

Currently the Pines is going through a major remodeling of its storied bars, clubs and hotel and so they might not have the same names as they did at the time of research. However, they are all clustered at the marina so you won't have any trouble locating them no matter what they are called. With that said, the traditions of the FIP are as ingrained as those at Buckingham Palace so it's the same every summer. Drinking begins in the mid-afternoon at low tea at the Blue Whale with boys in their speedos drinking vodka sodas as the ferry docks beside them. Action moves to middle tea later in the afternoon and centers around the pool at the Cantina, which also serves casual fare. Finally, high tea gets started around 7pm at the View Bar and goes until late with music pumping loudly out over the water.

Perhaps the best time to visit is July 4th, when the annual **Invasion of the Pines** takes place. On this occasion, a ferry arrives from Cherry Grove packed with drag queens that hoot and holler and cause general mayhem as they parade through the Pines commemorating a time when one of their sisters was denied service at a Pines bar. Once they've paraded around for all to see, they hop back on their boat and return to Cherry Grove, having proclaimed victory. Riotous and surreal, it is a wonder to behold.

In between the Pines and Cherry Grove is an area of undeveloped forest and dunes known as the 'meat rack' and if you can't imagine what goes on in the bushes after dusk, well then we're not going to ruin the surprise. This area was memorialized in the Village People's anthem 'Fire Island.'

Cherry Grove (www.cherrygrove.com) is much more family-oriented and attracts many lesbians as well as gays. Less pricey than its next-door neighbor, the Grove nonetheless has plenty of fun times. The town square of sorts is the Ice Palace, with its video bar and poolside sexy times. They also hold the annual 'Mr Meat Rack' competition.

FYI – it's a bit of trek, but one can easily walk between the Grove and the Pines via the beach, or, of course, by going through the meat rack.

Sleeping

Much like the Hamptons, the Pines and Cherry Grove are best experienced by renting or staying in someone's house. But if you can't commit to a whole summer, or even a week, there are options. As is to be expected, summer weekend rates are the highest, especially on holidays.

The Madison (☎ 631-597-6061; 22 Atlantic Walk; d from $260-500) is probably the nicest place to stay in the Pines, with its lovely and romantic rooms as well as a private pool. Expect to have a two- or three-night minimum on weekends during high season.

Hotel Ciel (☎ 631-597-6500; Pines Harbor; d from $178-1098) offers basic, but recently revamped, lodging in the Pines. The cheapest rooms have shared bathrooms with a neighboring room, but hey, it's a good way to meet the cuties next door.

Grove Hotel (☎ 631-597-6600; Cherry Grove Harbor; r from $40-500) is a very basic motel-style place that gains points for being attached to the always-bustling Ice Palace.

Tastes of Gay Fire Island

Andrew Holleran's 1978 novel *Dancer from the Dance* was an important work of gay fiction for its time and still resonates for its portraits of gay ennui. Much of the action takes place on Fire Island, making this perfect beach reading.

Others might enjoy logging onto YouTube to check out 'Party in the FIP' – a Miley Cyrus–approved re-imagining of her hit song 'Party in the USA', starring a handful of toned twinks cavorting in the Atlantic and on the boardwalks of Fire Island.

NEW YORK STATE

Most ferries depart in order to link directly with a train to/from New York.

Davis Park Ferry Company (☎ 631-475-1665) Travels from Patchogue to Davis Park and Watch Hill.

Fire Island Ferries (☎ 631-665-5045) Runs from Bay Shore to Saltaire, Fair Harbor and Ocean Beach.

Sayville Ferry Service (☎ 631-589-8980) Runs from Sayville to Cherry Grove, Sunken Forest and the Pines.

HUDSON VALLEY

Ah, the mighty Hudson. The Mississippi has its Huck Finn, its worldwide fame and its size, but you can't say the Hudson doesn't have soul – or history – in spades.

While the river's most important role in New York has been transportation and trade, its symbolic role can't be underestimated. The Hudson is what connected New York City to the rest of the state – both physically and culturally. Even Manhattan was once called Hudson New Amsterdam, a testament to the river's importance in the formation of the United States' most mythic city. Small towns dot the river, river traffic is abundant, and dairy farms, roadside produce stands and dirt roads adorn the landscape. This is the same landscape, by the way, captured in the luminous paintings by the famous artists of the Hudson River School. And with all of this natural bounty, don't forget that this valley fairly bursts with historic landmarks. Lately, the Hudson Valley is the site of a burgeoning ecomovement, from farming to wineries and butcher shops. Even choosy Manhattanites are known to day-trip up for dinner these days to one of the farm-to-table restaurants that are springing up in villages along the Hudson.

Striking a harmonious balance of urban and rural, overflowing with fresh air and pastoral delights, it seems impossible that a city of over 8 million is a stone's throw away. No wonder this land has been immortalized in so many paintings. The Hudson River Valley (*shhh!* the locals say) has become downright cool.

LOWER HUDSON VALLEY

Heading north from New York City, the lower Hudson Valley connects New York City suburbia with slower-paced villages. The big city buzzes here still (and yep, the rush hour traffic to go along with it) but the further away from what's universally referred to as 'the city,' lower-key delights begin to make themselves known.

Contact **Rockland County Tourism** (☎ 800-295-5723; www.rockland.org) for information on Nyack and Harriman and Bear Mountain State Parks. The folks at **Westchester County Tourism** (☎ 800-833-9282; www.westchestertourism.com) can help you out with Tarrytown and Peekskill resources.

Harriman & Bear Mountain State Parks

Just outside of New York City, Harriman State Park and the adjacent Bear Mountain State Park are Valhalla for outdoorsy city folks who sit in their cubicles dreaming about hitting the trails, beaches, and campgrounds come weekend. The Appalachian Trail passes through both parks.

Sprawling Harriman State Park is a good place for a hike or a swim on its sandy beaches. For free trail maps, visit the **Park Visitors Center** (☎ 845-786-2701; Palisades Parkway btwn exit 16 & 17; admission free; ◷ 8am-6pm summer).

HUDSON RIVER SCHOOL OF LANDSCAPE PAINTERS

Big soaring skies and little hamlets along the highway of the day: the Hudson River. The Hudson River School of painters captured the majestic and the ordinary. The expansion and prosperity that came in the first decades of the 19th century – especially after the completion of the Erie Canal in 1825 – gave the country a strong national consciousness and, along with it, the freedom to begin exploring distinctly American (that is, non-European) themes. The new artists shunned popular historical themes along with formal portraiture in favor of everyday life – romanticized to be sure, but with a detailed realism that was new to the American art scene around New York. Like Washington Irving, author of 'The Legend of Sleepy Hollow,' the romantic impulse was at work.

Thomas Doughty was the self-taught founder of the school, but its leading spirit was Thomas Cole, who was followed by Asher Durand, John Kensett and Frederick Church (who turned his home, Olana, into a 'real' landscape painting; see p142).

Inside the park, **Lake Tiorati** is a beautiful spot for hiking, swimming, boating, picnicking and, in winter, ice-skating. There's **camping** (☎ 845-947-2792; campsite $15) at Lake Welch.

Bear Mountain State Park (☎ 845-786-2701; admission free; ☼ 8am-sunset; ℗ $8) borders the western bank of the Hudson River. The stupendous view from Bear Mountain's peak (1305ft)

takes in the Manhattan skyline on a clear day. Hiking, fishing, spring-wildflower viewing, fall-foliage viewing and pool swimming (and even riding a merry-go-round) are the popular activities; in winter, cross-country skiing, sledding and ice-skating take over.

Lake Sebago Cabins (☎ 845-351-2360; cabin/cottage from $240/410; ☼ mid-Apr–mid-Oct; ♿) Take your

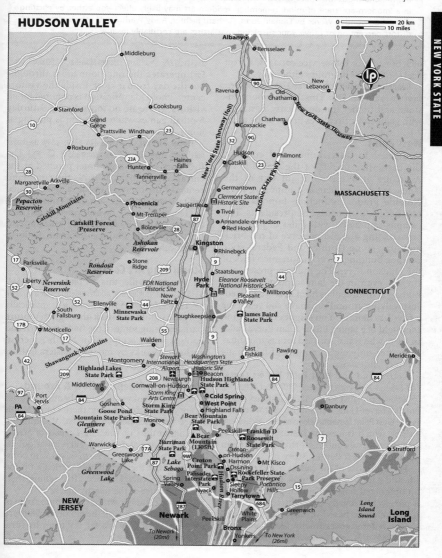

DETOUR – DIA:BEACON

The Manhattan-based museum Dia has staked out a satellite in the unlikeliest place: Beacon, a struggling, nearly forgotten industrial city north of Cold Spring. Now the art world (gasp!) treks up to this converted box factory. **Dia:Beacon** (☎ 845-440-0100; www.diaart.org; 3 Beekman St; adult/ student $10/7; ⏰ 11am-6pm Thu-Mon Apr-Oct, 11am-4pm Fri-Mon Nov-Mar) comprises 240,000 sq ft of exhibition space that is impressive in its own right: light streams through the skylights illuminating the enormous raw space of stark white walls. Before engaging the exhibits, first put yourself in a 'modern art' state of mind: remember, modern art may likely affect you either by eliciting disgust or wonder. Works by Donald Judd, Gerhard Richter, Andy Warhol and others alter space, distort perception or prove your suspicion that artists are certifiably insane.

pick of rustic or full-service cottages, a great deal for families or groups either way.

Bear Mountain Inn (☎ 845-786-2731; www.visitbear mountain.com; d from $99). This 1920s mountain-stone and timber inn oozes cozy nostalgia, with giant stone fireplaces in the lobby area.

West Point

Dedicated to duty, honor and country, the castle-like turrets of the US Military Academy at West Point jut out of the landscape in irregular and imposing tiers. Notable graduates include famous military heroes, astronauts and presidents. The campus impresses, with miles of pathways crisscrossing a grand preserve of red-brick and gray-stone Gothic- and Federal-style campus buildings over panoramic views of the Hudson River. The military presence is tireless, even in the landscaping; anything hinting at disorder has been neatly trimmed. Just walking around can make you yearn for a needless haircut. You might even imagine the plight of a young Edgar Allan Poe, a cadet in 1830, who was dismissed for insubordination after only eight months of less-than-military endeavors.

You'll find the **West Point Visitors Center** (☎ 845-938-2638; www.usma.edu; 2107 N South Post Rd; ⏰ 9am-4:45pm), just south of the military academy's Thayer Gate. Behind the visitors center is the **West Point Museum** (admission free; ⏰ 10:30am-4:15pm), which traces the history of warfare, famous generals and historical weapons, in addition to West Point history.

For a glimpse of the cadets' strict military life and a tour of the campus, you must join an organized bus-and-walking tour. This is a post-9/11 security procedure and is subject to change based on alert levels issued by the federal government. **West Point Tours** (☎ 845-446-4724; www.westpointtours.com; adult/child 2-11yr $12/9; ⏰ 10am-3:30pm Mon-Sat, 11:00am-3:30pm Sun) operates the one-hour tours throughout the day from a kiosk inside the visitors center. Photo identification is required for all visitors. There are no tours during Saturday football games when the team is playing at home.

Hotel Thayer (☎ 845-446-4731; www.thethayer hotel.com; inside Thayer Gate; r from $159; 🖥 🛜) The five-story Gothic-style hotel perched at the entrance gate looks as if it's the command center of the campus. Inside, a spit-polished military ambience prevails. Don't miss a drink in General Patton's Tavern; you can also dine at Edgar Allan Poe's Riverview Restaurant (formal) or the Thomas Jefferson Patio (a casual cafe).

Storm King Art Center

In Mountainville, this **art center** (☎ 845-534-3115; www.stormking.org; adult/student/senior $12/8/10; ⏰ 11am-5:30pm Wed-Sun Apr-Nov) is a dramatically gorgeous outdoor walk-through sculpture park featuring some of the finest modern and contemporary sculpture in North America, including works by modern masters Calder, Moore and Noguchi.

Tarrytown, Sleepy Hollow & Around

Don't let spooky childhood bedtime stories scare you off from visiting: there's more to this place than headless horsemen. Washington Irving, author of the *The Legend of Sleepy Hollow*, once stated that Tarrytown got its name from the Dutch farm wives who complained that their husbands tarried a bit too long at the village tavern after selling their farm produce at the nearby markets.

Historic Tarrytown has the appearance of a quaint village, but all the energy of a suburb of New York City – a far cry from its rural beginnings.

INFORMATION

Historic Hudson Valley (☎ 914-631-8200; www.hudsonvalley.org) This nonprofit organization maintains Sunnyside, Philipsburg Manor, Kykuit, Van Cortlandt Manor and the Union Church at Pocantico Hills.

SIGHTS & ACTIVITIES

Thanks to the endearing legacy of the Headless Horseman, Halloween is celebrated here with great enthusiasm.

Sunnyside

Washington Irving once described **Sunnyside** (☎ 914-591-8763; W Sunnyside Lane; adult/child/senior $12/6/10; grounds pass $5; ☺ 10am-5pm Wed-Mon Apr-Oct), his Hudson Valley home, as being 'made up of gable ends and full of angles and corners as an old cocked hat.' Today, it's easy to imagine Irving staring into the deep forests while envisioning the Headless Horseman of Sleepy Hollow chasing poor Ichabod Crane.

Lyndhurst

This marvelously landscaped **historic home** (☎ 914-631-4481; 635 S Broadway/Rte 9; adult/child/student/senior $12/free/6/10, grounds pass $5; ☺ 10am-5pm Tue-Sun mid-Apr–Oct; 10am-4pm weekends Nov–mid-Apr) is a classic 19th-century Gothic revival mansion overlooking the Hudson and originally built for the former mayor of New York City, William Paulding. Don't miss the rose garden.

Philipsburg Manor

Introduce the kids to farming, 17th-century-style, at this educational **manor** (☎ 914-631-3992; N Broadway/Rte 9; adult/child/senior $12/6/10; ☺ 10am-5pm Wed-Mon Apr-Oct; 10am-4pm weekends Nov-Dec). Kids toting iPhones and iPods marvel at farm workers in period dress performing the chores of the day with no technological assistance, from tending the vegetable garden to milking the cow. Other hands-on activities create great fodder for preteen Facebook brags like 'This is me shearing my first sheep.'

Old Dutch Church & Sleepy Hollow Cemetery

Across the road from Philipsburg Manor, this 1865 **church** (☎ 914-631-0081) was part of the original manor. Adjacent to the church is the **Sleepy Hollow Cemetery** (admission free; ☺ 8am-4:30pm). The eerie, mysterious air of the grounds reaches its apex on foggy mornings – the curvy lanes make getting lost seem like a prelude to a horror movie. Don't say we didn't warn you.

Kykuit

Rockefeller: just the name sounds iconic. Perhaps no family has had a larger influence on 20th-century American history than the Rockefellers, who have left their stamp on business, politics and international relations. By the time his landmark oil company was broken into 34 different companies by the US Supreme Court in 1911, John D Rockefeller had amassed a fortune worth more than $1 billion.

The Rockefeller's neoclassical mansion, built on a high bluff overlooking the Hudson,

---

Top 'I Can't Believe Manhattan is Only an Hour or Two Away' Moments

- Basking in the small town idylls of **Rhinebeck** (p138) and **Tivoli** (p141)
- Eating straight off the Farm at the CIA's **St Andrews Café** (p137)
- Hanging out at home with one of the original power couples at the Franklin D and Eleanor Roosevelt **historic sites** (p137)
- Getting spooked colonial-style at the **Sleepy Hollow Cemetery** (p133)
- Getting the Hudson River School aesthetic perspective by gazing out at the Hudson from Frederic Edwin Church's Moorish palace **Olana** (p142)
- Discovering tiny, storybook **Staatsburg** (p139)
- Shooting a pheasant (or just seeing one) in blue-blood **Millbrook** (p140)
- Hiking, swimming, camping and stargazing in **Harriman** and **Bear Mountain State Park** (p130)
- Watching a Shakespearian comedy (www.hudsonshakespeare.org) as sun sets over the lush riverside grounds and rose gardens of the **Boscobel Restoration** (☎ 845-265-3638; www.boscobel.org; Rte 9D, Garrison)

is known as **Kykuit** (☎ 914-631-9491; 2-hr tour adult/child $23/21; ☺ 9am-2:45pm Wed-Mon May-Nov) and was home to several generations of Rockefellers. It's almost impossible to imagine that people conducted day-to-day rituals inside a building more akin to a fine arts gallery than a house. Outside, the exquisite garden overlooking the Hudson River ('Kykuit' – keye-*cut* – is the Dutch word for 'lookout') is home to modern sculptures by Alexander Calder, Pablo Picasso and others.

Union Church at Pocantico Hills
This old stone **church** (☎ 914-332-6659; River Rd, Pocantico; admission $5; ☺ 11am-5pm Mon & Wed-Fri, 10am-5pm Sat, 2-5pm Sun, closed Jan-Mar) must be seen from the inside out. It's home to gorgeous stained-glass windows by Henri Matisse and Marc Chagall.

Rockefeller State Park Preserve
Three miles north of Sleepy Hollow lies the entrance to **Rockefeller Preserve** (☎ 914-631-1470; Rte 117; ☺ dawn-dusk; ⓟ $8), a peaceful and beautiful getaway with a rolling, woodsy expanse of solitude and old fields marked by low stone walls.

SLEEPING & EATING
While there are several mid-priced chains in town, the best independent options are the **Tarrytown House Estate and Conference Center** (☎ 800-553-8118; www.tarrytownhouseestate.com; 49 E Sunnyside Lane; r from $189; ☺) with lovely grounds and impeccable service, and the **Castle on the Hudson** (☎ 800-616-4487; www.castleonthehudson.com; 400 Benedict Ave; r from $220; ☺ ⓧ), a 100-year-old Medieval stone castle with wood-burning fireplaces, turrets, 4-star dining and awe-inspiring views of the Hudson.

Bella's Restaurant & Donut Shop (☎ 914-332-0444; 5 S Broadway at Main St; dishes $5-12; ☺ 6am-9pm Mon-Fri, 6am-5pm Sat, 7am-3pm Sun) Chocolate shakes. Wise-cracking waitresses. Philly cheesesteaks and Eggs Florentine. Bella's serves up goodness rumored to cure homesickness, heartbreak, or just hunger.

Lefteri's Gyro Restaurant (☎ 914-524-9687; 1 N Main St at Broadway; mains $4-15; ☺ 11am-10pm) Craving great homemade Greek food? Try a pita or a salad at this small, family-run business (and don't skip the baklava!).

Getting There & Away
Tarrytown is just off the Tappan Zee Bridge at the junction of Rte 9 and I-87. The **Metro-North** (☎ 212-532-4900, 800-638-7646; www.mta.info) line travels to NYC's Grand Central Terminal (45 minutes).

Peekskill
pop 24,000
Peekskill is a homely town with a big adorable heart and a thriving Ecuadorean community. Sound unique? It is. The active arts scene and great bookstore make up for what Peekskill might lack in that trendy faux-antique look. Amble down Division Street to peek into cafes and artsy shops, where locals seem incredibly laid-back considering that the big bad city is only an hour away.

Manhattan bibliophiles make the trek out here to visit **Bruised Apple** (☎ 914-734-7000; www.bruisedapplebooks.com; 923 Central Ave; ☺ daily, call for hours), an enchanting, funky used bookstore featuring floor-to-high-ceiling stacks of used,

---

FROM SING SING TO MAD MEN

Welcome to suburban angst, 1960s style. No, Ossining's not one of the prime tourists spots in the Hudson River Valley, but it's got a unique literary and cinematic backstory rivaled only by another story-worthy fact: it was once called Sing Sing, and is home to a notorious New York prison that, until the death penalty was abolished in 1965, was the primary facility for electrocution.

But back up. This strange little place was the longtime home of iconic American short story writer and novelist John Cheever (the 'Bard of Ossining'). It's also the mythic location for *Mad Men*, the critically acclaimed American TV show set in the early 1960s. In fact, Hollywood writer/producer Matthew Weiner used Cheever's novel *Bullet Park* as the namesake for the street where two of his star characters, Don and Betty Draper, live (and you'll have to watch the show to find out anything else). As with Cheever's novels, the whole place reeks of the American Dream gone wrong and curdled to a discontented yet utterly fascinating degree.

Visit the small **Ossining Visitors Center & Museum** (☎ 914-941-3189; 95 Broadway; admission free; ☺ 10am-4pm Mon-Sat) to see an old Sing Sing electric chair and get info on this mysterious town.

DETOUR – POUGHKEEPSIE RTE 9

Poughkeepsie (pooh-*kip*-see) is the largest town on the east bank of the Hudson and has suffered the same urban fate as many former factory towns in New York as industry moved out and decay moved in. There are, however, a few historic sites worth a detour. **Vassar College** (☎ 845-437-7000; www.vassar.edu; 124 College Ave at Raymond Ave), a well-respected liberal arts school where Meryl Streep studied theatre, offers tours of its 125-acre campus daily during the summer months. Vassar is also home to the **Francis Lehman Loeb Art Center** (☎ 845-437-5632; http://fllac. vassar.edu; admission free; ☷ 10am-5pm Tue-Sat, 1-5pm Sun) which contains several paintings from the Hudson River School.

Samuel FB Morse Historic Site (☎ 845-454-4500; Locust Grove, 370 South Rd/Rte 9; house entry adult/ senior/student $7/6/3, grounds free; ☷ house 10am-3pm May-Nov, grounds 8am-dusk) is a privately owned 1830 mansion that was the former home of telegraph inventor and artist Samuel FB Morse. The house, built in the Tuscan Villa style popular in the mid-19th century, has its picture windows designed to showcase the manicured grounds. Some of Morse's old telegraph equipment and paintings are displayed.

Come nightfall, head over to local legend **The Chance** (☎ 845-471-1966; 367 Main St; www.thechance theater.com), a club where many a rock band has kicked off their tour. Legend has it that The Police played a gig here back in the day, and only four people showed up. Hungry? People drive for miles for a heavenly taste of **Rossi Rosticceria Deli** (☎ 845-471-0654; 45 S Clover St; ☷ 7am-7pm Mon-Fri, 8am-5pm Sat) a longtime family-run Italian deli in the historically Italian waterfront district. In the end, this is an interesting blue-collar town. One local quipped, 'This is a funny place: the churches are on Hooker Avenue, but the hookers are on Church St.' Hmmm.

rare and out-of-print books – over 50,000 of them, actually. A selection of used LPs and CDs competes for your attention with a wildly eclectic selection of travel books, popular novels, philosophy, classics and esoterica.

Paramount Center for the Arts (☎ 914-739-2333; www.paramountcenter.org; 1008 Brown St) shows excellent international and independent films, and hosts concerts (from Ozomatli to Roberta Flack) and plays.

SLEEPING, EATING & DRINKING

Peekskill Inn (☎ 914-739-1500; 634 Main St; d from $116; ☐ ☒) This motel-inn is nothing fancy, but it's perched high on a bluff overlooking the river. Appalachian Trail hikers often stop for creature comforts (including a swim in the pool).

our pick **The Peekskill Brewery** (☎ 914-734-2337; 55 Hudson Ave; small/large plates $5-10/10-22; ☷ lunch & dinner, bar to 2am, to 3am Fri & Sat) On the Riverfront Green, this sophisticated brew-pub offers all-the-rage small plates like crispy pork belly, pulled pork sliders and cornmeal-crusted oysters, along with buttermilk fried chicken and steak frites.

Peekskill Coffee House (☎ 914-739-1287; 101 S Division St; ☷) This cozy coffee shop in a cool triangular building serves steamy cups of joe and hosts music and poetry readings under its pressed-tin ceilings.

Bean Runner (☎ 914-737-1701; 201 S Division St; mains $4-7; ☷) We dig this tranquil coffee and sandwich-soup-salad shop by day, hot jazz and Latin date-spot by night.

Getting There & Away

The **Metro-North** (☎ 212-532-4900, 800-638-7646; www.mta.info) Hudson Line reaches Peekskill from New York City's Grand Central Terminal in about one hour. By car, Peekskill is south of Cold Spring on Rte 9.

COLD SPRING
pop 2000

Set on a hill teeming with little boutiques, coffee shops and ice-cream shops angling down Main St, Cold Spring is a romantic town with prim townhouses lining the narrow streets, and quiet walks along the river in the shadow of Storm King Mountain. Many people take the train here from New York City for a weekend of antiquing, and the shops and cafes reflect this chi chi clientele.

This ivy-covered brick **Pig Hill Inn** (☎ 845-265-9247; www.pighillinn.com; 73 Main St; d $150-230 incl breakfast; ☷) sits smack on Main St and offers relaxing, antique-decorated rooms with exquisite beds.

our pick **Brasserie Le Boucon** (☎ 845-265-7676, 76 Main St; mains $18-26; ☷ dinner) In this colorful old

DID HE OR DIDN'T HE?

In a word: yes. There have been several American presidents about whose romantic lives – specifically, their extramarital affairs – have been wildly speculated upon. But as with JFK and Bill Clinton, there is little doubt whether or not Franklin D Roosevelt's notorious image as a ladies' man is true. Biographers generally agree that FDR and Eleanor Roosevelt's social secretary, Lucy Mercer, conducted an affair from around probably 1916 until the day of his death – where she was at his bedside. Was it secret? From the public, mostly. But after a devastated Eleanor found a bundle of love letters in 1918, she agreed not to divorce him under two conditions: that FDR stop seeing Lucy, and that he stop sharing his wife's bed. Only the latter condition he is rumored to have met. It's difficult to add up the cost of this heartbreak to Eleanor, who later discovered his broken promise. But some historians suggest that the emotional divide between this prominent couple only served to thrust Eleanor into her own spotlight as a champion of civil rights (so much that the Ku Klux Klan put a steep bounty on her head) and a woman – the author of 28 books and over 8000 articles – who proved nearly as admired and loved around the world as FDR himself, earning the nickname 'First Lady of the World.'

house decked out with a porch and fireplace, try five kinds of mussels (we like the provençal and the curry), Hudson valley duck confit, and homemade frites. This place pulls off an effortlessly sexy vibe, like an incognito French film star on vacation.

Cold Spring Depot (☎ 845-265-5000, 1 Depot Sq; dishes $10-18; ☽ lunch & dinner) The quintessential Cold Spring hangout, this fun-spirited restaurant and bar puts on quite a party in a converted train station. In summertime, sit on the umbrella-shaded outdoor tables, order a fresh fruit daiquiri and munch on American classics like chicken pot pie.

Cold Spring can be reached by train on the Hudson line of the **Metro-North** (☎ 800-638-7646; www.mta.info); the train station in Cold Spring is at the foot of Main St.

MID- & UPPER HUDSON VALLEY

You're not in the suburbs anymore. But don't mistake this area for country, either. There's a grand element of beauty and culture to this place that conjures the countryside on the edge of one of the world's great cities, where pastoral pleasures collide with urban appetites and celebrities roam farmers markets in their jeans, ignored by sophisticated villagers.

For insider news on culture and events, check www.ruralintelligence.com – it's everything a gossipy local would share.

The tourism boards in this heavily visited area are powerful forces of nature that can provide information and ideas on anything you could possibly want to know. **Dutchess County Tourism** (☎ 845-463-4000, 800-445-3131; www.dutchesstourism.com; Suite M-17, 3 Neptune Rd, Poughkeepsie)

covers Poughkeepsie, Red Hook, Rhinebeck, Hyde Park, Millbrook and Beacon. The **Hudson Valley Tourism** (☎ 800-232-4782; www.travelhudsonvalley.org) office provides a great free guide with information on regional special events. Look for the guide in county tourism offices located in towns along the Hudson.

Hyde Park
pop 20,000

Sure, there's more to Hyde Park than FDR and Eleanor, but the Roosevelt legacy still shines as the greatest attraction. History has catapulted FDR to saint-like status for his success in steering the country out of the uncertain events of economic collapse and world war. Highlights of FDR's legacy include his 'New Deal' programs, including the WPA (Works Progress Administration), unemployment insurance, and countless dams, roads, schools, turnpikes – even the Chicago subway. These radical policies were designed to pull the US out of the Great Depression, which had so devastated the nation at the time of his inauguration as banks were closed in a whopping 32 states.

While Franklin D Roosevelt is associated with the Depression Era and WWII, the rest of Hyde Park seems oddly stuck in the 1950s. As you drive along Albany Post Rd you'll pass a roller rink, a drive-in movie theater, a diner, old-fashioned ice-cream shops, and cute motels that look like they've harbored many a postwar honeymoon. It's actually kind of… well, fun. If you're game, Daddy-o, put on your saddle shoes and sock-hop over to this little town. You can have a whole 1950s era evening on this stretch, around where Albany Post Rd/ Rte 9G intersects with County Rd 40A.

FRANKLIN D ROOSEVELT NATIONAL HISTORIC SITE

Even in the staid environment of an historical monument, Franklin D Roosevelt's compelling and charming persona emerges. This **historic site** (☎ 845-229-9115; 4079 Albany Post Rd; adult/ child $14/free; ☺ 9am-5pm) includes FDR's home, library-museum, gravesite and rose garden.

Guided tours of FDR's home, **Springwood**, take visitors through a surprisingly ordinary home, outfitted with a hand-pulled elevator to transport FDR (who struggled with mobility after a bout with polio) and his chair to the 2nd floor.

The **Museum of the Franklin D Roosevelt Library** is the nation's first presidential library and the only one that was ever put to use by a sitting president. The museum features a special wing in memory of Eleanor Roosevelt, and FDR's famous 1936 Ford Phaeton car – equipped with special hand controls so he could drive despite the restricted mobility. His White House desk remains here, supposedly just as he left it on his last day at work prior to his 1945 death, less than a year after he was elected to a record fourth presidential term. Don't miss the map room, a small replica of a top-secret communication center that FDR had installed in the White House basement in 1942. How secret was it? Even the Secret Service was banned from entering.

Those more interested in behind-the-scenes political action might be keen to check

out Franklin D Roosevelt's private retreat. British monarchs and other world figures attended informal diplomacy meetings at **Top Cottage** (☎ 845-229-5320; 4097 Albany Post Rd; adult/ child $8/free; ☺ 10am, 1pm & 3pm Thu-Mon May-Oct). One widely reported event was when King George VI and Queen Elizabeth were served hot dogs at a picnic.

ELEANOR ROOSEVELT NATIONAL HISTORIC SITE

Better known as **Val-Kill** (Valley Stream; ☎ 845-229-9115; adult/child $8/free; ☺ 9am-5pm May-Oct, 10am-4pm Sat & Sun Nov-Dec & Apr), Eleanor Roosevelt used this cottage as a retreat from the main house at Hyde Park, in part to pursue her own interests and maintain her own identity.

It's obvious that Val-Kill was not meant to impress anyone. You can see the everyday chinaware and the plain water-glasses she used to entertain friends as well as statesmen, kings and queens.

VANDERBILT MANSION NATIONAL HISTORIC SITE

Want to really step back into the Gilded Age? Other than a time machine, this **mansion** (☎ 845-229-7770, 800-967-2283; Albany Post Rd/Rte 9; adult/child $8/free; ☺ grounds open dawn-dusk, guided tours 9am-5pm) 2 miles north of Hyde Park on Rte 9 is the second best option. It's one of the few such estates in the area to retain almost all of its original features, from interior furnishings to its lush outdoor landscape. This Beaux Arts monument – an eclectic mix of classical Greek, Roman and baroque lines –

SAMPLING CIA FARE

Food TV addicts, take heed: this is one of the best places to live out your *Top Chef* fantasies, or simply get your glutton on. Bearing the nickname 'CIA,' the **Culinary Institute of America** (reservations ☎ 845-471-6608; www.ciachef.edu; 1946 Campus Drive, Hyde Park) is the pre-eminent culinary school in the US. To sample the creations of America's next generation of chefs, you need reservations at one of the four restaurants on the gorgeous brick campus: Ristorante Caterina de' Medici (Italian), Escoffier Restaurant (French), American Bounty Restaurant and St Andrew's Café, where the farm-to-table craze has hit big. The airy, casual St Andrews offers locally-sourced, simple delicacies like free-range roast chicken and a beet, fennel and goat-cheese salad.

Business-casual attire is recommended and reservations are needed Monday through Friday. Lunch is served from 11:30am to 1pm, and dinner is served from 6:30pm to 8:30pm. Or try the casual counter service **Apple Pie Bakery Café** (☺ 7:30am-6:30pm Mon-Fri), a student-staffed eatery with to-die-for pastries.

It's a culinary delight to simply stroll around the hallways, where students clad in billowy chef's hats labor in open kitchens under the strict gaze of their supervising chefs. That kid chopping an onion with that huge knife? He could be the next Rick Bayless. Sigh. That's the charm of this place.

was painstakingly decorated to emulate the styles of European aristocracy.

STAATSBURGH STATE HISTORIC SITE
North of Hyde Park on Albany Post Rd (Rte 9) in Staatsburgh, this **historic site** (☎ 845-889-8851; www.staatsburgh.org; adult/child/student $5/free/4; ☺ 10am-5pm Sat, 11am-5pm Sun Apr-Oct) is an slightly decayed, but nonetheless ostentatious Greek revival–style mansion. At sunset this is an evocative place.

Sleeping & Eating
Mills-Norrie State Park (☎ 800-456-2267; www.reserveamerica.com; Rte 9, Staatsburg; campsite $15, cabins per week $340) Between Hyde Park and Rhinebeck, this 1000-acre park has camping, a marina, bicycling, sledding, kayaking, cross-country skiing, and nature trails. You'll also find Norrie Point Environmental Site, which has a small aquarium that replicates conditions of the Hudson River. Snag a cabin overlooking the river.

Roosevelt Inn (☎ 845-229-2443; fax 845-229-0026; 4360 Albany Post Rd/Rte 9; s/d from $70/85 incl breakfast; ☒) For 40 years, this friendly, immaculate family-run inn has been pleasing travelers with a cute diner-style breakfast room and rustic, knotty pine rooms.

Eveready Diner (☎ 845-229-8100; 4189 Albany Post Rd; dishes $4-14; ☺ breakfast, lunch & dinner) This busy art deco diner has a bit of everything, such as Brooklyn egg creams, malted waffles and pastrami sandwiches. Children are always welcome, although the menu quips 'No crybabies.'

WHAT THE...?

Even jaded New Yorkers who've seen it all probably haven't seen this: a children's playground smack in the middle of an old cemetery. Or is it a cemetery in the middle of a playground? In any case, the sight of crumbling Revolutionary War–era headstones poking out of a sandbox or right under a swing set is one of the weirdest things we've seen on the entire Eastern Seaboard. For a morbid chuckle, head to the **Reformed Dutch Church** (cnr Mill & South Sts, Rhinebeck) in the center of Rhinebeck. You'll see the cemetery (and the spooky playground) right behind the church.

RHINEBECK & AROUND
pop 7800

Don't be put off by the country club feel: this place has loads of personality and wit underneath that pretty face. A hundred miles north of NYC but a world away, blocks of proud Victorian homes and well-pressed residents create an idyllic small-town air normally found only on movie sets. While most residents aren't fabulously rich or famous, many of the townsfolk move comfortably in those circles. Sure, Rhinebeck appears to lack the messiness or chaos of ordinary life – and that's exactly why many of its Manhattan expat residents came here in the first place. Of course, before it became a getaway for well-heeled weekenders (and the site of Chelsea Clinton's highly speculated upon 2010 nuptials), the town was a stagecoach stop and still boasts the famous Beekman Arms (p139), America's oldest continuously operating inn. For a window into Rhinebeck culture, ask a local what they're most proud of, among the unique features of their town. Some will probably quip, 'the lack of a McDonald's.'

The energetic staff at the **Rhinebeck Chamber of Commerce** (☎ 845-876-5904; www.rhinebeckchamber.com; 23F E Market St, Rhinebeck; ☺ 9am-5pm Mon-Fri) is happy to offer advice on the area.

Sights & Activities
Sure, the Rhinebeck area is chock-full of historic attractions, but it's just as tempting to sleep in late, eat at a local see-and-be-seen restaurant and stroll the shops of the fetching downtown.

The good old days of summertime are at their peak at the **Dutchess County Fair** (☎ 845-876-4000; www.dutchessfair.com; adult/child under 12yr/senior $15/free/10) held every August in Rhinebeck: it's one of the best fairs in the state for all age groups.

OLD RHINEBECK AERODROME
Live out your wild Red Baron fantasies at the **Old Rhinebeck Aerodrome** (☎ 845-752-3200; www.oldrhinebeck.org; 9 Norton Rd, Rhinebeck; museum adult/child $10/8, teen & senior $8, air show adult/child $20/5, teen & senior $15; ☺ museum 10am-5pm mid-May–Oct, air shows 2pm Sat & Sun mid-Jun–mid-Oct). This high-adrenaline combination museum and air show features vintage planes from WWI and antique cars; you can even take a ride in an open-cockpit plane (but you have to provide your own scarf and goggles.)

BARD COLLEGE

If you happen to spy a bevy of young hipsters wandering dreamily along the road, you're probably approaching Bard College. The artsy, woodsy 600-acre campus is located near Montgomery Place on Rte 9G. Bard College's impressive **Richard B Fisher Center for the Performing Arts** (☎ 845-758-7900; www.fishercenter.bard.edu; Montgomery Place near Rtr 9G, Rhinebeck) was designed by Frank Gehry. It hosts opera, music and drama performances, including whimsical, uberbohemian Spiegeltent performances and the acclaimed Bard Music Festival every summer.

MONTGOMERY PLACE

In Annandale-on-Hudson, you'll find this 1805 neoclassical riverside **villa** (☎ 845-758-5461; River Rd/Rte 103; adult/student/senior $7/4/6, grounds pass $3; ☽ 11am-4pm Thu-Sun mid-May–Oct, grounds 9am-4pm). The house is impressive, but the grounds rank among the prettiest around. Among the 380 acres are gardens, a waterfall, walking trails through hemlock forests and views of the Catskill Mountains and the Hudson River. Montgomery Place lies north of Rhinebeck, just west of Rte 9G on River Rd, before the entrance to Bard College.

CLERMONT STATE HISTORIC SITE

Between Annandale-on-Hudson and Germantown off Rte 9G, this **site** (☎ 518-537-4240; 1 Clermont Ave, Germantown; adult/child/senior & student $5/free/4; ☽ 11am-5pm Tue-Sun Apr-Oct, 11am-4pm Sat & Sun Nov-Dec, Jan-Apr call for appt; grounds open dawn-dusk) is the early-18th-century Georgian home of the Scottish Robert Livingston family. The original manor was burned to the ground by the British during the Revolutionary War, but rebuilt soon after.

Try to come in spring, when the fragrant lilacs and linden trees bloom, or in early evening, as the sun sets across the river, over the Catskill Mountains.

Sleeping

Beekman Arms (☎ 845-876-7077; www.beekmandelameterinn.com; 6387 Mill St/Rte 9, Rhinebeck; r incl breakfast from $96; ☎ ☒) Since 1766, this inn has remained all candlelight and colonial ambience (even the heavy, wooden front door creaks appropriately when you enter). The lobby vividly recalls another era with this sign: 'Lodging 3 pence; with breakfast 4 pence; only 5 lodgers to a bed; no boots can be worn in

---

DETOUR – STAATSBURG

So you're cruising the pretty back roads down Old Post Rd, off Rte 9 N towards Rhinebeck, when a darling little library, church, firehouse and Italian restaurant seem to pop up in the veritable middle of nowhere (and a good-lookin' middle-of-nowhere at that). You're in the miniscule hamlet of Staatsburg (pop. 900). Stop in the bustling Italian restaurant, **Portofino** (☎ 845-889-4711; 57 Old Post Rd; mains $13-26; ☽ dinner, closed Mon) for a steal of a midweek prix-fixe dinner: four courses with wine for a wallet-happy $25.

---

bed.' The rooms in the original inn are exquisite, with big cozy beds and decanters of sherry. Don't miss the rough-hewn beamed and low-ceilinged **tavern**, so authentically colonial with its old stone hearth that it seems like Ben Franklin himself might wander in any moment.

The Looking Glass Bed & Breakfast (☎ 845-876-8986; www.thelookingglassbandb.com; 30 Chestnut St, Rhinebeck; d $140-190) With a relaxed, storybook feel and fanciful rooms, this colorful Victorian B&B lies in easy walking distance to downtown Rhinebeck.

ourpick Rhinecliff Hotel (☎ 845-876-0590; www.therhinecliff.com; 4 Grinnell St, Rhinebeck; d $200-320 incl breakfast; ☎) A legendary hotel with a notorious past (many locals admit to youthful shenanigans at this former music watering-hole), this LEED-certified hotel and restaurant has been lovingly renovated to its intended waterfront glory. Think antique plank floors, deep whirlpool tubs and bright-white rooms that usher in the sunsets over the Catskills like nobody's business. Downstairs, the original Victorian bar and brasserie-style restaurant (mains $14 to $23) has lost its licentious edge but none of its appeal. One of the best decks on the Hudson to sup, sip or swoon.

Eating

Rhinebeck Deli (☎ 845-876-3614; 112 E Market St, Rhinebeck; mains $2-10; ☽ breakfast & lunch) Mornings find this NYC-style deli full of retired so-called town criers who assemble around the simple tables for newspapers, coffee and gossip, while the stressed-out younger set clamors around the deli counter for take-away breakfast sandwiches ($2).

FARMERS FOR A DAY

The Hudson Valley has long been a rich agricultural area. Small farms are abundant, and gardening is a common activity. There are hundreds of local farms, produce stands and 'pick-your-own' farms in the region. Mid- to late summer is the best time to visit but check the harvest schedule; depending on the weather, rain and so forth, harvest times vary. Most farms are open daily during summer.

The pick-your-own system works like this: they give you a container (tray or basket), you pick what you want from the seasonal fruits and vegetables, then you weigh your pickings at the register and pay wholesale prices.

For info on local farmers markets and farm-to-table restaurants in Dutchess County, check out www.farmfresh.dutchesstourism.com. Want to apple pick? Peruse area orchards at www.allaboutapples.com.

Greig Farm (☎ 845-758-1234; www.greigfarm.com; Pitcher Lane, Red Hook; ⊙ 9am-5pm Apr-Dec, to 7pm summer) Between Rtes 9 and 9G, this farm is three miles north of Red Hook. It's a one-stop produce market with a bakery and education center. Popular produce pickings in the mid- to late summer include asparagus, peas, berries, pumpkins, and a dozen varieties of apples.

Old Chatham Sheepherding Company (☎ 888-743-3760; www.blacksheepcheese.com; 155 Shaker Museum Rd, Old Chatham; ⊙ 9am-5pm) Makers of locally famous cheese, the Old Chatham Sheepherding Company welcomes visitors to its 600-acre farm, the largest sheep dairy in the country. Stock up on fresh yogurt, ricotta and Hudson Valley camembert.

Bread Alone (☎ 845-876-3108; 45 E Market St, Rhinebeck; sandwiches $8-12; ⊙ breakfast & lunch, dinner Thu-Mon; ⑤) An outpost of the famed Woodstock bakery/cafe features toothsome pastries, soups and desserts. Try the open-faced tartine with poached salmon, avocado and dill crème fraîche.

ourpick Terrapin (☎ 845-876-3330; 6426 Montgomery St, Rhinebeck; bistro mains $7-16, dining room mains $19-28; ⊙ lunch & dinner; ⑤) A two-in-one showpiece of a converted church, with a casual bistro and bar on one side, and chi-chi dining with a stellar patio on the other. Soaring ceilings, fab woodwork, fantastic food (much of it locally sourced) and a carefree evening buzz reign on both sides. Solo diners: head to the chatty bistro bar, order a gooseberry mojito and a free-range turkey burger with wasabi aioli ($8), and chat up the locals who seem excited to have someone new in town. Parents will go gaga over the organic kids menu.

Calico Restaurant & Patisserie (☎ 845-876-2749; 6384 Mill St, Rhinebeck; lunch $8-10, dinner mains $18-25; ⊙ breakfast Wed-Sun, lunch & dinner Wed-Sat) This intimate, husband-and-wife-run bistro makes the best pastries in town. Think award-winning, CIA-schooled and French-inspired fare that's totally approachable. Crimson walls and local paintings woo diners off the street where they pause to ogle the pastry case before they eventually relent.

China Rose (☎ 845-876-7442; 1 Shatzell Ave, Rhinecliff; mains $12-18; ⊙ dinner Wed-Mon) On the waterfront in tiny, romantic Rhinecliff, this place buzzes with a party vibe, great bartenders, live music, and – oh, yeah – tasty Chinese classics like mu-shu pork. Beware of the mind-blowing sake margaritas, so deadly they make even the most wildly optimistic fortune cookie seem possible.

Cripple Creek Restaurant (☎ 845-876-4355; 22 Garden St, Rhinebeck; mains $16-25; ⊙ dinner Wed-Mon) Serving eclectic American cuisine, the restaurant features a long bar, a herb and floral garden courtyard for dining under the stars, and impressive artwork (check out the Chagall on the wall). The classical pianist is reason alone to come.

Getting There & Away

Rhinebeck's train station is 3 miles away in neighboring Rhinecliff. **Amtrak** (☎ 800-872-7245; www.amtrak.com) trains depart for NYC's Penn Station throughout the day (90 minutes).

Rhinebeck is north of Hyde Park on scenic Rte 9.

MILLBROOK & AROUND
pop 1500

Plenty of places compare themselves to the Hamptons, but Millbrook doesn't need to. Quicker than you can say 'old money,' you'll be breathing in the rarified air of this idyllic little downtown and the maze of back-road retreats, riding trails and genteel country homes that seem to appear and disappear among the sugar maples and the winding country roads. For an especially grand joyride, cruise Rte 22: it's one of the state's most bucolic corridors, dotted with farms and pastures.

Millbrook itself sports an immaculate village green and a shiny fire station. You'd never know that among its more famous visitors was one Timothy Leary, famed American psychologist and countercultural author who famously urged America to 'Turn on, tune in, and drop out' in the swinging 60s. Leary set up camp in this hoity-toity enclave to conduct experiments with LSD, a drug whose use he widely advocated. Controversial? You bet your love beads. While some townsfolk were scandalized, these days it only seems to lend this uber-perfect little place a bit of countercultural street-cred in an oasis of well-bred gentility.

To get to Millbrook by car, exit off of the Taconic Parkway on to Rte 44 east, which leads into town.

The awe-inspiring **Innisfree Garden** (☎ 845-677-8000; www.innisfreegarden.org; 362 Tyrell Rd, Millbrook; weekday/weekend $4/5; ☒ 10am-4pm Wed-Fri May-Oct, 11am-5pm Sat & Sun) is perhaps the most beautiful in the valley. When the great Irish poet William Butler Yeats wrote his poem 'The Lake Isle of Innisfree,' he described a spot in the imagination that is always alive. This 200-acre lakeside garden here lives up to that notion in meticulous fashion, evocative of ancient Chinese design principles.

Environmentalists and nature lovers should check out the world-renowned **Cary Institute of Ecosystem Studies** (☎ 845-677-5343; www.ecostudies.org; 2801 Sharon Turnpike/Rte 44; ☒ hiking trails dawn-dusk Apr-Oct). While the majority of the campus is set aside for research, visitors can explore several ecosystems by walking the lovely hiking trails across the 2000-acre grounds.

In a renovated Dutch dairy barn, **Millbrook Winery** (☎ 800-662-9463; www.millbrookwine.com; 26 Wing Rd, Millbrook; ☒ noon-5pm; 11am-6pm late May-Aug) has a lovely view of the vineyards and the undulating green hills.

Just outside town, the sparkling white **Cottonwood Motel** (☎ 845-677-3283; www.cottonwoodmotel.com; Rte 44; r weekday/weekend from $110/125, ste or cottage from $200) is set on panoramic grounds and offers attractive rooms with patios.

Offering up a bounteous breakfast (challah bread pudding, fresh herb omelets), the **Millbrook Country House** (☎ 845-677-9570; www.millbrookcountryhouse.com; 3244 Sharon Turnpike, Millbrook; r weekday $175-225, weekend $200-275) also serves afternoon tea in the lovely gardens. By night, have fantastical dreams on the 18th-century Venetian bed in the gold and red-walled Barocco room.

Millbrook Diner (☎ 845-677-5319; 3266 Franklin Ave, Millbrook; dishes $4-12; ☒ 6am-9pm) Near the village green, this 1929 town landmark serves basic diner fare such as eggs, waffles and Greek dishes. Let out your inner rockstar at the jukebox tables.

HUDSON
pop 8000

Upscale or downbeat? Antique or dilapidated? Hipster or hard times? Oh, Hudson, you're an enigma. Like a rockstar who's glamorous at night but bedraggled the next morning, Hudson seems to have a split personality: strung-out one minute, sexy the next, yet always interesting. This historic former whaling village is a study in contrasts, from stellar shopping and impressive architecture to its nefarious claim to fame as the country's original (and thankfully defunct) red-light district. Picture a riverfront town where elegant 18th

---

DETOUR – TIVOLI

A tiny, bewitching hamlet with an old steel water tower and lazily attractive cafes where artists, intellectuals and Bard students roam around pondering existentialism? No, it's not a bohemian's daydream of the perfect village: it's Tivoli, just west of Red Hook on Rte 9G.

Catch the mayor himself on the sunny patio chatting with locals at **Luna 61** (☎ 845-758-0061; 52 Broadway; mains $8-16; ☒ 5-10pm Tue-Sun), a cheerful, creative cafe offering from-scratch veggie comfort food such as sweet potato enchiladas. Warning: one bite of the signature banana-cream pie has been known to trigger a lifetime of cravings.

Across the street, funky **Santa Fe Restaurant** (☎ 845-757-4100; 52 Broadway; mains $15-25; ☒ 5-10pm Tue-Sun) does fresh, nouveau Mexican food for families, students and professional layabouts.

BAWDY, NAUGHTY HUDSON

Once called 'The Little Town with the Big Red Light District,' Hudson thrived as an epicenter of vice from the 1780s until the 1950s when state troopers raided the brothels, which never reopened. Until then, a so-called 'wink and nod' system had flourished on Diamond Street; as a sign of the times, the street has been renamed to the less flashy-sounding Columbia Street. These days, you're more likely to see a Soho antiques dealer than a madam cruising the main drag. Those who miss the good old days (and some old-timers confess to) keep in mind that Hudson's still got a gritty underbelly that makes the place a far cry from the bucolic village some city weekenders, locals say, seem intent on making the city. Maybe you could just say that Hudson's a bad girl who's changed her ways, but still has a wild (though hopefully legal) streak.

---

and 19th century Federal and Greek revival row houses line the main streets, then throw in a bunch of exiled city folks, friendly blue-collar locals, a gay pride parade or two, and plenty of tourists with antique fever, and you've got the idea. On Warren St, a small-town version of urban blight jostles with an ultra-cool New York City vibe, as young tattooed moms swerve their strollers to avoid hitting Martha Stewart's entourage. This is one complicated little town.

Pop in at the friendly **Columbia County Tourism Department** (☎ 518-828-3375; www.columbiacountytourism.org; 401 State St; ☽ 8am-4pm) and ask for a copy of the Hudson Antiques Dealers Association map, which provides method to the madness that is antiquing (and plain old shopping, and eating) on Warren St. Happy hunting.

Sights & Activities

An odd assortment of activities await in quirky little Hudson. When you're exhausted (or broke) from shopping, be sure to cruise the small country lanes around town that wind around shady creek beds, vista hills and gnarled apple orchards.

Lauded for its antiques district, Warren St is made for cruising for treasures, from funky knickknacks to opulent armoires with price tags that might make an average fashionista gasp. The best way to tackle this eclectic bounty is to dive in and walk it. Start at one end at First St, then circle back when you hit Eighth St and window-shop the other side of the street. You'll find vintage clothing stores and a few cozy bookshops nestled within this veritable paradise of furniture and antiques.

As you walk downtown, peek into the **Hudson Opera House** (☎ 518-822-1438; www.hudsonoperahouse.com; 327 Warren St; ☽ noon-5pm) a relic of the late-19th- and early-20th-century vaudeville and lecture circuit (Susan B Anthony

herself spoke here twice) that's in the process of being restored to its former glory. Check the schedule for performances and exhibits.

AMERICAN MUSEUM OF FIREFIGHTING

New York has a long and proud volunteer fire-fighting tradition, as evidenced by the stoic brick buildings in many towns, manned during the day by an assortment of local characters. This **museum** (☎ 877-347-3687; www.fasny firemuseum.org; 117 Harry Howard Ave; adult/child/under 5yr $5/2/free; ☽ 10am-5pm) is a one-of-a-kind exhibit displaying a vast array of historical fire engines, plus a memorial to the firefighters who lost their lives on 9/11.

OLANA

Using the stunning grounds around his home, **Olana** (☎ 518-828-0135; www.olana.org; Rte 9G; guided tour adult/child/senior & student $9/free/8; ☽ 10am-5pm Tue-Sun Apr-Oct; 11am-4pm Fri & Sat, from noon Sun Nov-Mar; grounds ☽ 8am-sunset year-round), as a canvas, landscape painter Frederic Edwin Church (1826 – 1900) set out to create an ambitious three-dimensional landscape painting. The Moorish architecture of the Persian-style villa is breathtaking.

Sleeping

Hudson City B&B (☎ 518-822-8044; 326 Allen St; r incl breakfast low-season $100-150, high-season 125-175; 🖵) You'll find spacious, tranquil bedrooms and great omelet breakfasts in this historic 1865 townhouse. The house itself is a history and architecture lesson, as is the surrounding neighborhood, which was built by the successful shipping magnates of the 1800s.

Thyme in the Country (☎ 518-672-6166; www.thymeinthecountrybandb.com; 671 Fish & Game Rd; d incl breakfast $130-155; 🖵) This ecofriendly country hideaway features delish organic breakfasts for veggies and carnivores alike. Luxuriate in the salt-filtered swimming pool or the lush organic gardens on the grounds of this 1880s farmhouse.

our pick **Union Street Guest House** (☎ 518-828-0958; www.unionstreetguesthouse.com; 349 Union St; ste incl breakfast $100-400; ☎) The most fun-loving member of the bunch, these boutique row houses offer quirky, antique-filled suites that would captivate your bookworm cousin or retro-obsessed hipster kid brother. We love the curl-up-and-read-all-night ambience of the divine Library Suite.

Eating & Drinking

Just walk down Warren St and follow your nose.

Le Gamin Country Café (☎ 518-828-2885; 609 Warren St; mains $8-12; ☑ 9am-5pm, closed Wed) On warm sunny days, this old pharmacy turned French rustic cafe goes from charming to heavenly. Couples, friends, and lone novel readers munch on savory crepes and drink citron pressé under vintage gas station signs on the street-side terrace.

Wunderbar & Bistro (☎ 518-828-0555; 744 Warren St; mains $8-21; ☑ lunch Mon-Fri, dinner Mon-Sat) Wunderbar breaks out from the pack of Warren St bistros with an $8 steal of a lunch special. Think straightforward American classics in portions that will defy your skinny jeans.

Baba Louie (☎ 518-751-2155; 517 Warren St; pizza $10-18; ☑ lunch & dinner) Great pizzas with mind-bending ingredients – think sweet potato, fennel and roasted garlic – seduce even those with a 'been there, done that' attitude towards pizza.

Red Dot Bar & Restaurant (☎ 518-828-3657; 321 Warren St; mains $10-26; ☑ lunch Mon-Fri, dinner Mon-Sat) A dinner-and-drinks mainstay of Warren Street that's as cozy as it is cool. Hang out at the warm wooden bar or out back on the leafy patio.

The Spotty Dog Books & Ale (☎ 518-671-6006; 440 Warren St; ☑ 11am-8pm Mon-Thu, to 10pm Sat, noon-6pm Sun) Underneath its dramatic ceiling and Medieval chandelier, this atmospheric little bookshop, bar, and lounge is bohemian yet down-to-earth.

Getting There & Away

Hudson's train station, on Allen and Front Sts, is within walking distance to downtown. **Amtrak** (☎ 800-872-7245; www.amtrak.com) runs frequent trains (2 hours) to NYC's Penn Station.

CATSKILLS REGION

Manhattan day trippers, hippies, Harley-Davidson bikers, hikers and skiers can all probably agree on something: the Catskills is an equal-opportunity outdoor playground with something for everyone. Cheaper than the Hamptons, more accessible than the Adirondacks and less crowded than the Hudson River Valley, you'll find a diverse array of weekend warriors and laid-back wanderers all blissing out on the vast trails. On a late summer afternoon, when the sun filters through the leafy trees and the shadows turn the surrounding hills a purplish hue, the understated beauty of the Catskills region becomes obvious. A land of lush rounded mountains and babbling brooks, the Catskills evoke an old-fashioned storybook land of sleepy, half-forgotten villages that are nonetheless magical. Just half a century ago an over-the-top resort destination, today the Catskills feels a bit left behind in the transition from one millennium to the next. Cool? No. Chill? Absolutely. Even in Woodstock, where Priuses zip around the village green and some complain it's become too commercial, it's still as funky as it is functional.

If you're searching for a once heavily beaten, but now forgotten path, the Catskills are worth exploring. This place isn't trying to be the next Hamptons (leave that to the other side of the Hudson), and it likes it that way.

EASTERN CATSKILLS

Encompassing everything from a cool college town and a decaying industrial enclave to a historic little city turning its sights towards urban renaissance, the west bank of the Hudson River along the Catskill Forest Preserve draws Manhattan and Brooklyn exiles looking for cheaper rents and fresh air.

NEW PALTZ
pop 6000

Farms. Orchards. Wineries. Great used bookstores. A cool record shop. And all nestled beneath the gorgeous Shawangunk Ridge where hiking and climbing adventures await. No wonder so many students have come to study at SUNY-New Paltz and never left. Yes, New Paltz is a college town with a hippie soul, but its roots go much further back than the Summer of Love. Founded by French Huguenot religious refugees in

1677, the town still shows off its original stone architecture on Huguenot St. Funky shops, ethnic and vegetarian restaurants, and plenty of friendly local eccentrics create an East Village vibe in the Catskills. For history, hiking, and a dash of hedonism, you can't beat it.

Nine miles west of the Hudson, New Paltz is easy to reach by car. Rte 299 turns into the town's main street.

The **New Paltz Chamber of Commerce** (☎ 845-255-0243; www.newpaltzchamber.org; 257 Main St; ☺ 10am-4:30pm Mon-Fri) has information about the town and surrounding areas.

Sights & Activities

Outdoor activities are big in New Paltz, but so is wandering around and checking out the historic architecture. Mosey down Church St to explore the fantastic new and used bookstores, but beware: you might while away the whole afternoon just browsing. Hikers and climbers can get outfitted right on Main St at **Rock and Snow** (☎ 845-255-1311; www.rockandsnow. com; 44 Main St), which specializes in climbing equipment.

HISTORIC HUGUENOT ST

To get the flavor of the original village, visit the **Huguenot Street Visitors Center** (☎ 845-255-1660; www.huguenotstreet.org; 18 Broadhead Ave; standard tour $9; ☺ 10:30am-5pm May-Oct, call for low-season hours). From here you can take a self-guided tour, or group tour of seven preserved stone houses dating back to the 1680s and a reconstructed French church.

MOHONK PRESERVE

A full-time conservation, education, research and recreation center, this wild **preserve** (☎ 845-255-0919; www.mohonkpreserve.org; 3197 Rte 44/55; admission for hikers/climbers $10/15; ☺ dawn-dusk) is located on 6400 acres of woods and is the second most-visited climbing spot in the nation after California's Joshua Tree National park. Picnicking, great rock climbing, hiking, biking and cross-country skiing abound. Ask about guided hikes.

MINNEWASKA STATE PARK

Very popular with rock climbers, this **state park** (☎ 845-255-0752; [P] $8; ☺ dawn-dusk) offers cross-country skiing (groomed trails), hiking,

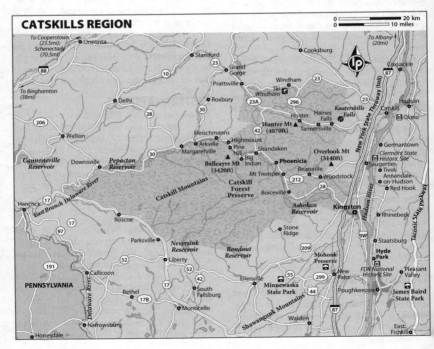

CATSKILLS REGION

snowshoeing, oodles of bike trails, picnicking, and swimming in the summer.

SAM'S POINT PRESERVE

South of both Mohonk Preserve and Minnewaska State Park, this preserve (☎ 845-647-7989; per car $7; ⏱ 9am-8pm, to 5pm during winter) is the highest point of the Shawangunk Ridge, a gorgeous spot that just happens to be home to one of the most outstanding collections of dwarf pine barrens in the world. This evocative place, full of cliffs, summits and ice caves, makes for a wonderful hike.

MOHONK MOUNTAIN HOUSE

Reminiscent of California's lavish Hearst Castle, this National Historic Landmark **resort** (☎ 845-255-1000; www.mohonk.com; 1000 Mountain Rest Rd; adult/child $10/8), 4 miles out of New Paltz, is a celebrity haunt and so exclusive that getting through the gate requires a reservation – or an uncanny resemblance to Robert de Niro. Once inside, the secluded location is a treasure trove of dramatic views of the cliff-lined Lake Mohonk, an imposing Victorian castle full of elaborate, old fashioned recreational activities like carriage rides, platform tennis, a vintage soda fountain, and a Victorian pavilion with ice-skating. Yeah, this place is dreamy. Buy a day pass (and remember to make a reservation!) to take advantage of the great hiking and cross-country ski trails. Rates include 3 meals and teatime. The fact that jackets are suggested evening attire for 'gentlemen over 12' will either appeal to your sense of nostalgia and formality, or not.

Sleeping, Eating & Drinking

In the evening, walk around and see which of the whimsical cafes and bars strike your fancy. Those looking for a frat bar scene should head towards the upper part of Main St, while countercultural types will dig the lower end.

New Paltz Hostel (☎ 845-255-6676; www.new paltzhostel.com; 145 Main St; dm $30, private r from $45) For clean, cheap accommodation (including airy private rooms) in a communal setting you can't beat the cheery New Paltz Hostel. The walls are filled with artwork, the owners are friendly and the spacious kitchen invites cooking.

Minnewaska Lodge (☎ 845-255-1110; www.min newaskalodge.com; 3116 Rte 44/55, Gardiner; r $135-259 incl breakfast; 🛜) Tranquil grounds, fantastic cliff views and a soaring, sunny great room. Ahh.

DETOUR – RTE 9W, EAST OF NEW PALTZ

From New Paltz head east on Rte 299 to Rte 9W, close your eyes and turn either right or left. Either way, you won't be disappointed. The road runs between the towns of West Park and Marlboro and is sprinkled with small wineries well-marked by signs. Get a copy of the Shawangunk wine trail map at www.gunkswine.com, or simply stop by the **Benmarl Winery** (☎ 845-236-4265; www.benmarl.com; 156 Highland Ave, Marlboro; ⏱ noon-5pm), which exudes a European feel and is the best known of the bunch.

So what if the comfy Arts and Crafts–style rooms are nothing spectacular? This is a comfy, sleep-like-a-rock place that takes its nature (and its breakfasts) seriously.

The Bakery (☎ 914-255-8840; 13A North Front St; ⏱ 7am-7pm) Stop here before a hike or a climb in the 'Gunks to grab fresh sandwiches and mini cheesecakes to reward yourself afterwards. Breakfast specials are a bargain at $2.99.

Hokkaido (☎ 914-256-0621; 18 Church St; ⏱ dinner, lunch Mon-Fri) In a small town bursting with good sushi, we have a soft spot for this quaint, intimate place with calming bamboo walls, fresh sushi and friendly service. Try the Mango Salmon roll.

Karma Road (☎ 914-255-1099; 11 Main St; ⏱ 8am-8pm) While it may seem too granola for some, even nonvegans will love the fresh smoothies (try the gingery Mango Stinger) and soups here.

Main Street Bistro (☎ 914-255-7766; 59 Main St; mains $6-9; ⏱ breakfast & lunch, dinner Fri & Sat) A breakfast lover's heaven, this cozy cafe with a whimsical disco ball is full of wooden booths where students, professors and hikers get down to breakfast specials like tropical French toast.

Bacchus Bar & Grille (☎ 914-255-8636; 4 South Chestnut St; mains $6-18) Belly up to the bar for a Magic Hat on tap or climb up to the loft for tasty Southwestern cuisine and more than 400 types of beer, including a good cider selection. Funky furnishings, like two huge stuffed dolls of drinking old ladies and a baby carriage hanging from the ceiling, lend this place a wacky yet lovable vibe.

36 Main Restaurant & Wine Bar (☎ 914-255-3636; 36 Main St; mains $25-30; ⏱ dinner) Featuring a locally-sourced menu that changes often and spotlights creative dishes like a sorrel and pea agnolotti and a lamb kofta kabob, this is one of the most stylish and fun spots around, with couches for wine sipping.

Getting There & Away

The **Adirondack Trailways** (☎ 845-255-6520; 139 Main St) bus station is next to the New Paltz Hostel. By car, take Rte 299 west from the NYS Thruway (I-87); it turns into New Paltz's Main St.

KINGSTON

pop 23,500

The 17th- and 18th-century streets of Kingston ooze with history, yet this town's no museum piece. The Catskills' largest town and the state's first capital for a brief period in 1777 when the British drove the provincial congress from New York City, Kingston is an eclectic mixture of longtime local families, blue-collar workers and NYC exiles – many of them artists – who dig the antique vibe and cheaper rent. If the words Federal, Greek revival, saltbox, Italianate and Queen Anne appeal to you, you'll like it here: it's an architectural gem. The town's layout is relatively simple – the two main tourist areas are Downtown (the Rondout Historic District) and Uptown (the Stockade District), separated from each other by a sometimes seedy stretch of Broadway, the city's main drag.

The best source of information, including free walking tour brochures and friendly advice, is the **Kingston Urban Cultural Park Visitors Center** Rondout Historic District (☎ 845-331-7517; 20 Broadway; ☾ 9am-5pm, weekends from 11am) Stockade District (☎ 845-331-9506; 308 Clinton Ave; ☾ 11am-5pm).

Fun events that showcase the city's artistic side include the annual Artists' Soapbox Derby, an outdoor sculpture biennial, the monthly First Saturday gallery openings, and the weekly Farmers Market.

Sights & Activities

STOCKADE DISTRICT

Filled with sedate stone buildings, including 21 homes built prior to the Revolutionary War (mostly converted into shops and restaurants), this district not only dates back to the 17th century. Authentic? Absolutely: it's one of the oldest neighborhoods in America. One remarkable intersection, the only in the US with 17th-century buildings on all four corners, is rumored to be standing because of a long-ago bread-making bargain. That's right: as Kingston was being torched by the British, one woman offered the soldiers fresh-baked bread in exchange for sparing the structures. (It worked.)

In 1777 the first New York State senate met briefly at the **Senate House State Historic Site** (☎ 845-338-2786; 296 Fair St; adult/child $4/3; ☾ 10am-5pm Mon-Sat year-round, 1-5pm Sun mid-Apr–Oct), dating from c 1635. The 1695 **Old Dutch Church & Cemetery** (☎ 845-334-9355; 272 Wall St; ☾ services Sunday) is quiet and shady, and the tombstones date back to the 1700s. Be sure to pick up a **walking tour** map at the visitors center.

RONDOUT HISTORIC DISTRICT

Once a bustling 19th-century terminal port of the Delaware and Hudson Canal, the Rondout today is thriving once again, speckled with seafood restaurants and intimate cafes in the shadow of a dramatic suspension bridge. Walk up the hill of Broadway to find a smattering of antique shops among the 19th-century storefronts, or stroll along the marina and fantasize about whether you'd rather sail this sailboat or that yacht into the sunset.

Within the historic district, the **Trolley Museum of New York** (☎ 845-331-3399; www.tmny.org; 89 E Strand St; adult/child $5/3; ☾ noon-5pm Sat & Sun late May–mid-Oct) offers rides on old trolleys and has some static dis-

---

TOP FIVE NATURAL HIGHS IN THE CATSKILLS

■ Skiing at **Windham** (p152), a town with cozy après-ski restaurants, one of the best lodgings in the Catskills and a mountain just outside town that provides some of the east's best ski runs.

■ Climbing in the **Mohonk Preserve** (p144) and **Minnewaska State Park** (p144) near the village of New Paltz – even if you don't climb, the setting is fantastic.

■ Tubing down **Esopus Creek** (p151), in Phoenicia, the busiest little town in the Catskills.

■ Chilling out 1960s-style on a sunny day in charming **Woodstock** (p149), with cool cafes, fun festivals and ample off-the-wall shops (free love optional).

■ Hiking to the impressive 260ft **Kaaterskill Falls** (p152).

plays of trolleys, subway cars and rapid-transit cars from both the US and Europe.

River life is celebrated at the **Hudson River Maritime Museum** (☎ 845-338-0071; www.hrmm.org; 50 Rondout Landing; adult/child $5/4; ⊗ 11am-5pm May-Oct). After you've got your fill of looking at ships, hop on one for a 15-minute ride on Rondout Creek to the Hudson River, where you can check out the 1913 Rondout lighthouse.

Sleeping

Rondout Inn (☎ 845-331-8144; www.rondoutinn.com; 79 Broadway; ste low/high season $145/175; ⊛) Three blocks from the waterfront in a 1920s Federal building housing an antique store downstairs, you'll find these two well-equipped, home-away-from-home suites with kitchens.

There are a number of chain hotels just off I-87 at exit 19. The best of the bunch is the **Hampton Inn** (☎ 845-382-2600; www.kingston.hampton inn.com; 1307 Ulster Ave; d $149; ⊛) which boasts a pool and exercise room.

Eating

Boice Brothers Dairy (☎ 845-340-2018; 62 Onell St) On hot summer nights it's hardly an exaggeration to say that half the town is here at this dairy store and ice-cream parlor with a modest profile but a fantastical array of flavors and concoctions.

Rondout Deli (☎ 845-331-1118; 21 W Strand; ⊗ breakfast & lunch) Grab a sandwich for a waterfront picnic at this NY-style (with a healthy twist) deli. Specials like the potato mushroom burger and summer gazpacho please all appetites.

Gabriel's Café (☎ 845-338-7161; 50 John St; ⊗ breakfast & lunch, dinner Fri) A vegan hideaway with pretty pink walls, hardwood floors and a palate- and health-pleasing array of soups, salads, and free-range delights.

Maxwell's at Community Gourmet (☎ 845-338-8315; 305 Wall St; mains $7-21) Al-fresco dining with a refreshing array of salads, sandwiches, pizzas and entrees, such as a herb-roasted salmon.

Armadillo Bar & Grill (☎ 845-339-1550; 97 Abeel St; mains $12-24; ⊗ dinner Tue-Sun, brunch & lunch weekends) The diverse menu at this colorful Rondout restaurant focuses on a sassy New York style Tex-Mex. Try the spicy shrimp cakes and the mole poblano chicken enchiladas. Margaritas on the patio are divine.

our pick **Mariners' Harbor** (☎ 845-340-8051; 1 Broadway; mains $18-25; ⊗ dinner) We like the sunny maritime vibe and the fresh seafood: try the

DETOUR – CATSKILLS

Has Catskill seen better days? Most definitely, and that's all part of its mythology. Yet history and beauty still mingle in the tiny town of Catskill, on the banks of the Hudson River at the mouth of Catskill Creek. Home of Thomas Cole, a painter from the 19th-century Hudson River School, Catskill also played an important role supplying booze to those who wanted it during prohibition. The rough terrain made for good hiding, both for moonshine and gangsters, when the law rolled in. (This hideaway became a favorite haunt of New York City thugs like Legs Diamond).

Cedar Grove, otherwise known as the **Thomas Cole House** (☎ 518-943-7465; www.thomascole.org; 218 Spring St; admission adult/student & senior $9/7; ⊗ 10am-4pm Thu-Sun May-Oct), features tours of the artist's lovely home and studio, along with changing exhibits on Hudson River School art and history.

ahi tuna, the shrimp fresca or the king crab mac and cheese. Sit on the open-air porch and watch the boats go by, or grab a drink at the outdoor bar, where come evening, the fountain gurgles and lights twinkle.

Le Canard-Enchaine (☎ 845-339-2003; 276 Fair St; dinner mains $22-28; ⊗ lunch & dinner Mon-Sat) A narrow, romantic French bistro with a just-right mix of elegance and comfort serving up adventurous classics like frog legs as well as reliable staples like beef bourguignon. We love the bar menu and the two-course lunch for $15.

Drinking

Bridgewater Irish Pub (☎ 845-339-9310; www.bridge wateririshpub.com; ⊗ dinner to midnight, bar to 2am) At the top of a footpath up from the Rondout waterfront you'll find an old church converted into a cozy pub. Grab a Guinness and take in the dramatic bridge views from the back patio.

Elephant Wine Bar and Bistro (☎ 845-339-9310; 310 Wall St; tapas $6-9; ⊗ 4-10pm Tue-Sat) Sipping Spanish wine at the window bar on Friday night in this sleek little Euro-feel tapas bar is one of Kingston's best evening pleasures. Small plates, like chorizo and chocolate on toast and lamb sliders, tease and delight.

Artie's Bar & Grill (☎ 845-331-0886; 44 N Front St; ⊗ 10am-midnight) An old-school Italian joint where tough customers with hearts of gold

---

GROOVIEST WOODSTOCK BUMPER STICKERS

- Welcome to Woodstock…Please don't squeeze the shaman.
- Refuse to Burn Out.
- Let's Shag!
- Woodstock: old beer, stale hippies and psychedelic rednecks.
- Woodstock: send more losers.
- PADD: Potheads Against Drunk Driving.
- If you lived here, you'd be om by now.
- Woodstock: Midlife crisis center of the north.
- Please don't hit me with that crutch, hippy beggarman.
- Welcome to Woodstock: you are now officially lost.

---

sidle up to the bar to discuss local gossip. Stella's, the adjoining restaurant, serves up Italian peasant fare (mains $14 to $26) in a homey atmosphere.

our pick **Stockade Tavern** (☎ 845-514-2649; 313 Fair St; ☽ from 4pm Wed-Sat) In the former Singer Factory, this brick speakeasy will take you back to the prohibition era. Sip classic cocktails under the ornate tin ceilings and wink at a tall dark stranger or a flask-toting dame.

Getting There & Around

Adirondack Trailways (☎ 800-858-8555) buses run hourly to New York City (two hours). Plan on a two-hour drive from Manhattan up I-87.

SAUGERTIES
pop 5000

A downscale, down-to-earth version of the perfect little New York town, Saugerties manages to strike a balance between cozy and off-the-radar cool. Quaint and charming, sure, but with enough of a rough edge so it feels like a charming slice of Brooklyn that got dropped off in the country. Saugerties' downtown, centered on Main and Partition Sts, is lined with historic red-brick buildings filled with antique stores, bookstores, and worth-the-trip restaurants that ooze ambience and – dare we say it? – fun.

Saugerties is 15 miles north of Kingston where Rte 212 meets Rte 9W. If it's hot out,

stop by the **Saugerties beach** (follow the signs from the 9W). You can cool off by swimming in a roped-off area in the river.

For crush-worthy grilled cheese sandwiches, great coffee and inventive breakfasts, stop by cute and cozy **Love Bites** (☎ 845-246-1795; 85 Partition St; mains $7-12). Try the addictive carrot-and-coconut French toast or the crab-cake sandwich.

Housed in an old 1864 tavern with wedding cake ceilings and tranquil outdoor seating, **Café Tamayo** (☎ 845-246-9371; 89 Partition St; mains $16-34; ☽ dinner Fri & Sat, Sun from May–October) serves prix-fixe menus of Hudson Valley–sourced American food with ethnic influences, including an asparagus risotto, braised rabbit and a to-die-for chocolate pot de crème. After dinner, retreat upstairs to one of the four simple, vintage **rooms** (r $110-190).

For an atmospheric trip to Morocco, duck into **Fez** (☎ 845-247-7198; 71 Partition St; mains $14-18; ☽ Wed-Sun) to dine on pistachio chicken breast, savory tagines, couscous and kabobs among deep orange walls and a lively vibe.

A delightful cafe whose warm-mustard and exposed-brick walls are lined with old books and aprons, **Miss Lucy's Kitchen** (☎ 845-246-9240; 90 Partition St; mains $8-9, dinner $17-24; ☽ lunch & dinner Wed-Sun) exudes a homey, feel-good cheerfulness that belies the fact that it doesn't mess around with its comfort food, like a cassoulet, grilled lamb chops or a vegetarian strudel.

Don't miss the cool-as-can-be **Inquiring Minds Bookstore** (☎ 845-246-5775; 65 Partition St; mains $10-18; ☽ 10am-9pm; ☏) that's rife with eclectic books, live music, a coffeehouse and plenty of room to curl up with a novel.

Grab a delish breakfast sandwich ($2.50) or afternoon snack at **Hudson Valley Dessert Company** (☎ 845-246-1545; 264 Main St; ☽ 8am-6pm), which offers a tempting array of biscotti and fanciful cookies to turn children positively starry-eyed.

NORTHERN CATSKILLS

There's more to these parts than Woodstock. Much of the rugged land here is part of the Catskill Forest Preserve and is rich with waterfalls, cliffs, fire towers, old farmsteads and rare plant species. So what if the tourists aren't flocking like they used to? Even the shabbier towns exude a cozy, lived-in vibe and at least one or two funky old cafes (and hopefully a token hippie or two).

DETOUR – THE REAL WOODSTOCK

From Monticello, head west on Rte 17B to the town of Bethel, where the infamous Woodstock Music Festival actually took place on Max Yasgur's farm in 1969 (see the boxed text, p149). The farm is off Hurd Rd and signs point the way from 17B to the gigantic green field. The site is marked by a stone marker near the road that reads: 'This is the original site of the Woodstock Music and Arts Fair held on Aug. 15, 16, 17, 1969.'

WOODSTOCK

pop 6000

Woodstock: the word alone conjures a smoky haze of half-naked long-haired hippies sprawled across a vast, muddy field, swaying to Jimi Hendrix and Joan Baez. Which is funny, because that celebrated Sixties event didn't actually happen here.

Although '60s nostalgia runs thick in Woodstock, the town's reputation as a legitimate arts colony dates back to the early 1900s. Most of today's residents appear to be artists, musicians or well-heeled folks from downstate who own summer homes here. You might be surprised by how modern and busy the village is on a Saturday morning, when city folks and locals all converge on the green for brunch and shopping in a very postmodern way that makes free love and bra-burning seem like ancient

concepts. With plenty of arts and culture – not to mention the mystique that this town has conjured worldwide – Woodstock is almost as weirdly enchanting as you hoped it would be.

In September the **Woodstock Film Festival** (☎ 845-679-4265; www.woodstockfilmfestival.com) draws movie aficionados and Hollywood celebrities to town.

Orientation & Information

With much of the town centered around the village green, Woodstock is easily negotiated on foot. A large parking lot off Tinker St, the village's main thoroughfare, in the center of town is a good place to drop off the car. **Golden Notebook** (☎ 845-679-8000; www.goldennotebook.com; 25 Tinker St; ☺ 10:30am-7pm) is an appealingly eccentric small bookstore with helpful staff knowledgeable about local attractions. (Got kids along? Check out the great children's store next door).

The active **Woodstock Chamber of Commerce** (☎ 845-679-6234; www.woodstock-online.com; ☺ 9am-5pm) has two staffed information booths: on Rock City Rd, just north of the village green, and at the junction of Tinker St and Mill Hill Rd on Rte 212.

Sights & Activities

Seeing Woodstock means strolling about town, enjoying the quirky feel of the place and meandering through the galleries and crystal shops.

THE WOODSTOCK FESTIVALS

About half a million people – many of them ticketless – descended on Max Yasgur's farm in Bethel, New York (40 miles southeast of the town of Woodstock), from August 15 to 17, 1969, for a music festival billed as 'Three Days of Peace & Music.' The lineup of musicians for the Woodstock Festival – Joan Baez; Joe Cocker & the Grease Band; Country Joe & the Fish; Crosby, Stills & Nash; Arlo Guthrie; Richie Havens; Jimi Hendrix; Santana; John Sebastian; Sha-Na-Na; Sly & the Family Stone; Ten Years After; and The Who – has never been matched.

Despite numerous setbacks ranging from broken toilets to a serious mud problem after a day of rain (earning the festival its 'Hog Farm' nickname), there were no riots and no violence. It was the most successful hippie gathering in the world. The most violent scene probably occurred when activist Abbie Hoffman ran on stage to make a speech, only to be greeted by The Who's Pete Townshend, who promptly bashed him over the head with his electric guitar.

At the Bethel Woods Center for the Arts (☎ 866-781-2922; www.bethelwoodscenter.org; 200 Hurd Rd, Bethel) you can attend concerts at a state-of-the-art performing arts center at the original Woodstock festival site: picture a huge stage, a 45,000-seat covered pavilion and a lawn accommodating over 10,000 people (free love not included). Artists who've played there in the past range from Sting to the Boston Pops. Stop by the fascinating onsite multimedia **museum** (adult/child $13/9; ☺ 10am-7pm Memorial Day-Labor Day, 10am-5pm Thu-Sun low season) that tells the story of the 1960s and Woodstock through artifacts, personal stories, and interactive exhibits. Groovy.

DOWNTOWN WOODSTOCK

Modern Mythology (☎ 845-679-8811; 12 Tinker St) stands out among Woodstock's New Age shops. It sells a plethora of jewelry (some of which is rather generic-looking), tasteful Woodstock T-shirts, Buddhas and lots of tarot cards and crystals.

About midway through town you'll find the **Center for Photography** (☎ 845-679-9957; www. cpw.org; 59 Tinker St; admission free; ☼ noon-5pm Wed-Sun). This attractive and serious gallery offers contemporary and historical exhibits, lectures and photography workshops year-round. It's well worth checking out.

BYRDCLIFFE ARTS COLONY & THEATER

For generations before the 1969 Woodstock Festival, artists and concertgoers traveled to **Byrdcliffe** (☎ 845-679-2079; www.woodstockguild.org; 34 Tinker St, Woodstock) to share their common vision of peace and justice. Today, the colony hosts artist residencies, craft demonstrations, exhibitions and performances at the Byrdcliffe Theater.

KARMA TRIYANA DHARMACHAKRA & OVERLOOK MOUNTAIN

A popular Buddhist center and Tibetan monastery, **Karma Triyana Dharmachakra** (☎ 845-679-5906; www.kagyu.org; 352 Meads Mountain Rd) regularly offers teachings ranging from introductory to advanced. Meditation instruction is available by appointment free of charge. Walk along the 2.4 mile trail from the monastery, where spectacular views can be found at the top of Overlook Mountain.

Sleeping

Saugerties-Woodstock KOA (☎ 845-246-4089; 882 Rte 212; campsites from $30, cabins from $55; ☼ Apr-Nov) Shady wooded sites and small rustic cabins make this campground appealing.

WHAT THE...?

Amazing man-made pathways, pools, steps and an obelisk are spread over 6.5 acres at **Opus 40** (☎ 845-246-3400; www.opus40.org; 50 Fite Rd, Saugerties; adult/child under 6yr/student & senior $10/free/7; ☼ 11:30am-5pm Fri-Sun Jun-Sep). Creator Harvey Fite, who meticulously carved and set the bluestone from an abandoned quarry, named it Opus 40 because he expected it to take 40 years to finish, though he toiled his whole life.

Twin Gables Guest House (☎ 845-679-9479; www. twingableswoodstockny.com; 73 Tinker St; d from $89) Not fancy but with tons of character, each room is decorated in a different color scheme with matching walls, floors and bedspreads. A superb location right in the center of town makes this a good quirky choice.

Woodstock Inn on the Millstream (☎ 845-679-8211; www.woodstock-inn-ny.com; 38 Tannery Brook Rd; d from $107) Tidy white walls and impeccable, comfy rooms with blonde-wood furniture create a relaxed vibe. A three-minute walk from downtown, each room comes with its own porch, the perfect spot for a warm afternoon.

Eating

At **Joshua's** (☎ 845-679-5533; 51 Tinker St, Woodstock; breakfast $7-10, mains $12-18; ☼ breakfast, lunch & dinner, closed Wed), breakfast is served until 3pm and there is a massive number of dishes to choose from. Try the Middle Eastern and Israeli dishes.

A Catskills chain, **Bread Alone** (☎ 845-679-2108; 22 Mill Hill Rd, Woodstock; mains $6-8; ☼ 7am-6pm) is a landmark for bread-lovers. Since most folks cannot live by bread alone, the shop also offers fine pastries, morning burritos and eggs and fresh salads and sandwiches.

There are several excellent restaurants just a short drive from Woodstock. Two miles west of the village green on Rte 212 is the small town of Bearsville, where you'll find **Bear Café** (☎ 845-679-5555; 295 Tinker St, Bearsville; mains from $20; ☼ dinner), serving American and French bistro fare in a rather serene brookside setting. The food is excellent and popular with local and New York City celebrities.

The adjacent **Little Bear** (☎ 845-679-8899; 295 Tinker St, Bearsville; mains $9-15), which shares the forest setting with Bear Café, serves amazing Chinese food in a lush setting. The menu offers a few Thai dishes too. In summer sit outside by the creek; in winter try the enclosed porch – there's a creek view.

Hip country gourmet food can be found at the **New World Home Cooking Co** (☎ 845-246-0900; 1411 Rte 212, Saugerties; mains $13-25; ☼ dinner) on Rte 212, halfway between Woodstock and Saugerties. The eatery specializes in a Caribbean-Thai-down-home mix featuring savory tapas, 'sexy' salads, spoonbread tamales and 'forbidden pleasure' like BBQ Korean pork belly. Try the *ropa vieja* (Cuban pot roast). Veggie offerings and vegan/nongluten desserts balance out the decadence.

Entertainment

Gone is the Tinker Street Café, where Bob Dylan often played during the early 1960s, but Woodstock continues to be home to a thriving arts and music scene.

our pick **Upstate Films Woodstock** (☎ 845-679-6608; www.upstatefilms.org; 132 Tinker St) Films at the Woodstock Film Festival are screened here. Other times of the year it features the best in recent and classic international and independent film.

Bearsville Theater (☎ 845-679-2100; www.bearsville theater.com; Rte 212, Bearsville) Next to the restaurants Little Bear and Bear Café, this venue puts on plays, concerts and stand-up comedy acts.

Byrdcliffe Arts Colony & Theater (☎ 845-679-2079; www.woodstockguild.org; 34 Tinker St, Woodstock) During summer this venue holds craft demonstrations, art exhibits and theatrical performances.

Maverick Concerts (☎ 845-679-7558; www.maverick concerts.org; Maverick Rd) Dating back to 1916, this is the oldest chamber-music series in the US, taking place in a lovely illuminated barn-like hall.

Getting There & Around

Adirondack Trailways (☎ 800-776-7548) goes to and from NYC several times daily (2½ hours). Motorists can reach Woodstock from I-87. Take exit 19 to Rte 28 west, then Rte 375 north.

PHOENICIA

pop 400

The place where Brooklyn hipsters come to risk their lives on inner-tube trips down capricious rapids, Phoenicia is also a down-to-earth, cheery little village of just a few vibrant blocks. Of all the small towns along Rte 28, Phoenicia offers the summertime visitor the most outdoor excitement.

Don't miss tubing on the **Esopus Creek** (the young, the cautious, or the fearful should wear helmets). Adrenaline junkies take note: the most exciting tubing starts 5 miles northwest of town.

Town Tinker Tube Rental (☎ 845-688-5553; www.towntinker.com; Bridge St; tube $12, life jackets $3; ☼ 9am-6pm mid-May–Sep), half a block south of Main St, is Phoenicia's most popular outfitter. You can rent wet suits and helmets.

The town is geared towards camping and has two good campgrounds. The **Phoenicia Black Bear Campground & RV Park** (☎ 845-688-7405;

> ### DETOUR – MT TREMPER
>
> In a bucolic spot halfway between Woodstock and Phoenicia, you'll find Mt Tremper (Map p144). Relaxing in the woods and sampling home-cooked authentic French cuisine are tiny Mt Tremper's main draws.
>
> **La Duchesse Anne** (☎ 845-688-5260; 1564 Wittenberg Rd; mains $18-25) is set in an old white wooden house and serves excellent dishes from France. The restaurant also has a few pleasant rooms ($80 to $230) available.
>
> Just around the corner from La Duchesse Anne, you'll find **Catskill Rose** (☎ 845-688-7100; Rte 212; mains $14-23; ☼ dinner Thu-Sun), one of the region's better-known restaurants and a fave among locals.

---

www.phoeniciacampground.com; 17 Bridge Rd; campsites $15 per person) offers shady sites right in town. Prices are based on two people and extra persons pay an additional $10.

Life is sweet indeed at **Sweet Sue's** (☎ 845-688-7852; 49 Main St; mains $7-12; ☼ 7am-3pm), at least during breakfast and lunch. If you can't decide among 25 kinds of pancakes, go for the colossal pecan-banana-coconut French toast.

See plays and classic films throughout the year at the vintage **Shandaken Theatrical Society** (☎ 845-688-2279; www.stsplayhouse.com; 10 Church St).

TANNERSVILLE & AROUND

pop 500

Named for the leather tanning industry that once thrived here, Tannersville and the surrounding areas are home instead to several exclusive residential developments. This little mountain village also has a rich Jewish history: in the 1920s, over 100 boarding houses in the area served kosher food (and as a result kept seven kosher butchers very busy!).

Visitors will be taken with the colorful downtown that's home to lots of restaurants and shops in an environment that feels at once rugged and refined. There's something about this place that just screams 'homey mountain town,' and feels blissfully far away from urban civilization.

Tannersville is located east of Hunter on Rte 23A; to reach the best hiking in the area continue heading east on Rte 23A to Haines Falls.

A dramatic inspiration for generations of painters and one of the original American tourist attractions, the 260ft **Kaaterskill Falls** are some of the highest in New York (Niagara Falls only measure in at 167ft) and actually make two plunges on Spruce Creek. Thomas Cole – one of the painters from the Hudson River school – was so impressed with the falls he immortalized them in his work *View of Kaaterskill Falls*.

To get to the base of the falls, drive 1 mile east of Haines Falls on Rte 23A; as the highway begins to dip, you'll see a small parking area on the right. Another fave subject of Thomas Cole and the Hudson River school painters, the state-run **North/South Lake area** (☎ 518-589-5058; Rte 23A; admission per vehicle $7, campsite $22; 🕑 9am-dusk May-Nov) is one of the most popular outdoor destinations in the Catskills. On a clear day, it's rumored that you can see five states at the site of the former Catskill Mountain House. On warm days, head to the sandy beach and rent a rowboat, go fishing, or explore the plethora of hiking trails before crashing at one of the 200 campsites.

SKI THE CATSKILLS

Ski bunnies, shake your tails. Okay, so it's not the Rockies. It's not even Vermont. But for proximity to New York City, a laid-back scene and (surprise!) plenty of decent runs even for experienced skiers, the Catskills bring it. You've got three main choices: Windham, Hunter Mountain, or Belleayre. Hunter Mountain is still the Catskills' best-known ski area, but Hunter itself is no longer looking so hot. By contrast Windham, just 10 miles away and also home to a ski resort, is much more upbeat with some very good restaurants and, even better, the Albergo Allegria Inn, which provides the best lodging value for money in the region.

The little town of Highmount attracts skiers who come to try out the slopes and trails of the **Belleayre Mountain Ski Center** (☎ 800-942-6904; www.belleayre.com; off Rte 28, Highmount). This state-owned resort has a 1404ft vertical drop in a rustic setting; the longest run is more than a mile.

Pine Hill Arms Hotel & Restaurant (☎ 800-932-2446; www.pinehillarms.com; Main St, Pine Hill; mains $14-20; r from $70; 🕑 dinner Tue-Sun) is a big brown barn-like structure with a cozy feel. We like the gleaming wood bar and the screened-in porch. There are seafood, Cajun and vegetarian specialties, and live music some weekends. Rooms are homey, with a vintage knotty pine motel feel.

Off Rte 23A, **Hunter Mountain** (☎ 800-486-8376; www.huntermtn.com) probably makes more snow than any other mountain in the US and attracts intermediate to advanced skiers. The resort draws people from all over the state to its three-mountain complex, which offers 15 lifts, a network of 50 trails and several restaurants and lodges.

When it's not snowing, adrenaline junkies will want to join up with **New York Zipline Adventure Tours** (☎ 518-263-4388; www.ziplinenewyork.com; from $19; 🕑 9am-4pm Jul-Oct) for what's purported to be the highest zipline canopy tours in the US.

The region's second-largest resort, **Windham** (☎ 800-729-4766; www.skiwindham.com) bills itself as a more relaxed experience than Hunter. It's quite a bit smaller than Hunter, but still operates a system of 40 trails and five lifts. These trails are open to mountain bikers in the summer. The resort is also the site of craft fairs, antique shows, mountain-bike races and festivals in summer and fall.

our pick **Albergo Allegria Inn** (☎ 518-734-5560; www.albergousa.com; 43 Rte 296, Windham; d from $93; wi-fi) is an immaculately decorated, unique B&B and is the best deal in the region. Walking in you'll be shocked that rooms here don't cost double what they do.

Possibly the strangest-looking hotel in the Catskills, **Scribner Hollow** (☎ 800-395-4683; www.scribnerhollow.com; Rte 23A, Hunter; half-board d per person from $115; wi-fi, swimming) is a cavernous place with huge atriums and a bizarre indoor grotto – you can swim through seven waterfalls in the heated pool or rejuvenate in the warm underground spa. Depending on the season and your tastes, you'll either love it or hate it. When it's empty it's a little creepy – think the mansion from *The Shining*. Each cathedral-ceilinged room is decorated in styles ranging from 17th-century Spanish adobe to 21st-century futuristic.

The decor at our pick **Chalet Fondue** (☎ 518-734-4650; Rte 296, Windham; mains from $16; 🕑 dinner) is a cross between ski-lodge hip and southwestern, with wood ceilings and rough white walls. Enjoy traditional German dishes such as sauerbraten and Wiener schnitzel, or try a Swiss fondue for two with veal and beef. Veggies beware, this place is geared towards carnivores.

FORGE THE DELAWARE!

And in a far better boat than George Washington had in 1776 to cross the river.

Narrowsburg is one of several points along the river that offers opportunities for watersports. **Lander's Delaware River Trips** (☎ 800-252-3925; www.landersrivertrips.com; boat/tube from $39/12 per person; ☺ Apr–mid-Oct) is a friendly, family-run operation that does raft, tube, kayak and canoe trips ranging from three to six hours, covering 5 to 10 miles of river (depending on river and weather conditions). The company also operates a campground ($16 per site).

Barryville is located at another especially beautiful part of the Delaware River where **Wild & Scenic River Tours** (☎ 800-413-6840; www.wildandscenic.com; ☺ May-Oct) offers rafting, canoeing and tubing trips.

A friendly family-run inn with a low-key resort vibe, staying at the **Villa Vosilla** (☎ 518-589-9886; www.villavosilla.com; 132 South Main St, Tannersville; r from $100/35 per adult/child incl meals; ☺) is like hanging out with a big, fun-spirited Italian family – one who cooks great pasta and has several swimming pools and two bocce courts, that is. We like the ecofriendly policies and the high-spirited nightclub shows. Those looking for other nostalgic throwbacks to the Catskills glory days, from all-inclusive meals to ping pong and shuffleboard (along with plenty of cocktails) will dig it here.

As the name suggests, the **Last Chance Antiques & Cheese Café** (☎ 518-589-6424; 6009 Main St, Tannersville; mains $8-20; ☺ lunch & dinner, tavern to 2am Fri & Sat) goes wild (as it has since 1971) for all things cheese: fondue, nachos and chili with cheese. Kids will dig the brass instruments hanging from the ceiling, beer fanatics will dig the international brews, and everyone will leave blissfully sated by comfort foods like chicken pot pie and French onion soup (smothered in cheese, naturally). Kick back to music on weekends.

Maggie's Krooked Café & Juice Bar (☎ 518-589-6101; Main St, Tannersville; mains $9-14; ☺ 7am-7pm) It's hard not to smile at this cheerful, funky cafe in the white house, especially when your breakfast (served all day) arrives. We like the cheeky 'SOB' (South of the Border) omelet and the cheekier Mother and Child Reunion (grilled chicken hash and veggies, topped with fried eggs).

Tannersville is the après-ski nightlife spot for those hitting the slopes at Windham and Hunter, with quite a few bars and dance clubs: ask the locals what's cool as of late.

SOUTHERN & WESTERN CATSKILLS

This area includes the infamous 'Borscht Belt' resorts that once were top-class tourist desti-

nations. These days, while some parts of this area may seem more shabby than sensational, this is still classic Catskills country with remnants of nostalgia for the good old days.

Borscht Belt

Have you seen *Dirty Dancing*? Hint: it's a 1987 American cult classic film, and perhaps the best pop-culture artifact to describe what this resort area used to be back when shuffleboard and the limbo ruled, Bermuda shorts were cool, and no one knew (or cared) where the Hamptons were.

In the southern foothills of the Catskill Mountains, the famous Catskill resorts evolved from the boardinghouses that sprang up here in the late 19th and early 20th centuries, when Jewish immigrants sought an escape from the poverty and crowded conditions of New York City. The area became known as the 'Borscht Belt,' and the small boardinghouses grew into enormous (although not especially graceful) resorts, offering guests every imaginable kind of activity, from swimming in Olympic-sized pools to skiing and golfing. As the resorts grew, so did the program of activities, which catered to whole families, from children and teenagers to parents and grandparents. Two major ingredients of the Borscht Belt experience were the food (and lots of it) and the comedians. Woody Allen captures some of this scene in his movies *Annie Hall* and *Broadway Danny Rose*.

With the advent of jet travel, the resorts went into decline and many closed as guests chose to travel to Florida, the Caribbean and Europe.

Kutsher's Country Club (☎ 800-431-1273; www.kutshers.com; Kutsher Rd, Monticello; r from $150 incl meals; ☺), off Rte 42, is one of the last surviving mega-resorts, it's a modern family-oriented place with a full activities program for children and adults. There are also indoor and outdoor pools, an 18-hole golf course, a health club and a lake. Kosher food, too.

CAPITAL DISTRICT & MOHAWK VALLEY

'Upstate' may be only 150 miles or so north of New York City, but any resident will tell you that it's not just a physical distance – it's a state of mind. It's a schizophrenic mixture of charming, vibrant towns, rolling hills, interstate highways and decaying industrial cities. The Mohawk Valley is named after the Mohawk Indians, an Iroquois tribe who were New York's first inhabitants.

When the game-changing Erie Canal was completed in 1825, the area became a manufacturing center employing thousands of European immigrants that flocked in search of jobs. During the industrial heyday this was the most densely populated region of the state, but as factories shut down and work moved overseas in the latter part of the 20th century, increased poverty became a sad reality. Today, the tourists go gaga for the region's idyllic small-town charms: charismatic Saratoga Springs, with the USA's oldest thoroughbred racetrack, and pristine Cooperstown, home to the National Baseball Hall of Fame. Feisty Albany is a paradox: it's a surprisingly photogenic state capital with interesting architecture and pleasant parks, yet it can't seem to shake its nefarious reputation (which only gets increasingly deserving the more state politicians get their hands dirty). While the main cities of the Capital District – tough politico Albany and resort paradise Saratoga Springs – could hardly be more different, nowhere else in the state (outside of New York City) do the descriptions 'charming' and 'gritty' so peacefully coexist.

ALBANY
pop 94,000
Say 'Albany' to many New York state voters – both upstate and downstate – and you may get a sigh or an eye roll. These days, the seemingly endless scandals among state politicians (not to mention massive budget deficits) mean that Albany rocks a somewhat deserving bad-boy reputation it can't seem to live down. Yet strolling around the historic parts of downtown, you'd never know it: much of the center city offers refreshing surprises, with plenty of wide-open green spaces. Flanking the west bank of the Hudson River, the state capital has managed to retain, and retrieve, the historic charm of an old and vibrant northeastern city – while keeping up its urban street-cred in spades. Reminiscent of Europe's grand cities, the architecture seems almost out of place in New York state – think ornate state buildings and brownstones gracing the downtown area. While some neighborhood streets are quiet and tree-lined, others are redolent of Brooklyn's chaotic energy.

As the seat of the nation's second-largest government, Albany escaped the economic devastation dished out to its Rust Belt neighbors. So while it's got its share of urban blight and issues, the city buzzes with excellent restaurants, revitalized neighborhoods, architectural gems and plenty of movers and shakers glad-handing and making (hopefully aboveboard) deals around town.

Orientation
Albany is hemmed in by the New York State Thruway (I-90), I-87 and I-787. The 98-acre Empire State Plaza sits at the center of the city. Packed with bars, retro shops, galleries and tattoo parlors in brightly painted brick townhouses, Lark St, between Madison and Washington Aves, has earned the saintly nickname of 'Greenwich Village North.'

Information
Used-book hunters will enjoy browsing the stacks at **Dove & Hudson** (☎ 518-432-4518; 296 Hudson St; ☺ 11am-7pm Tue-Fri). Check your emails with the wi-fi at the **Albany Public Library** (☎ 518-427-4300; 161 Washington Ave; ☺ 9am-9pm Mon-Thu, to 6pm Fri, to 5pm Sat, 1-5pm Sun; visitor computer pass $1).

You'll find the main **post office** (☎ 518-462-1359; 45 Hudson Ave; ☺ 8:30am-5:30pm Mon-Fri) at the corner of Pearl St.

The **Albany Heritage Area Visitors Center** (☎ 518-434-0405; www.albany.org; 25 Quackenbush Sq; ☺ 9am-4pm Mon-Fri, 10am-3pm Sat, 11am-3pm Sun) sports a vast assortment of brochures; check out the self-guided walking tour of the historic downtown area.

Sights & Activities
Albany has a multiple personality as capital, college town, arts hub and workaday blue-

collar city. The activities – and the architecture – reflect it.

EMPIRE STATE PLAZA

Futuristic, flashy or functional? This 98-acre behemoth of a public plaza inspires passionate opinions on the nature of its aesthetic statement. Between Madison and State Sts, you can't miss the brilliant white marble, glass buildings and sculpture gardens dwarfing everything in sight. The stuffy legislative offices, courtrooms and various state agencies are balanced by a collection of modern art and a performing arts center (p158), dubbed the 'Egg' because of its curvy, modern silhouette. Bring a picnic lunch and eat it by the long reflecting pool or peruse a collection of 92 modern-art sculptures and paintings scattered across the complex – including some by Alexander Calder and David Smith.

ALBANY INSTITUTE OF HISTORY & ART

This venerated **institute** (☎ 518-463-4478; 125 Washington Ave; adult/child/senior & student $10/6/8; ☺ 10am-5pm Wed-Sat, noon-5pm Sun) has a collection of period furnishings, silver and pewter, decorative arts and fine arts that beautifully illuminate the history and culture of the region. Don't miss the acclaimed works by Hudson River landscape painters.

NEW YORK STATE CAPITOL BUILDING

An imposing mixture of Italian, French Renaissance and Romanesque architecture, the late-19th-century **capitol** (☎ 518-474-2418; admission free; ☺ tours Mon-Fri) seems more redolent of Prague than New York. Venture beyond the pink granite facade to the famous Million Dollar Staircase, where you'll find 300 carved portraits of famous New Yorkers (along with a few of the sculptor's cronies).

WASHINGTON PARK

Perfect for strolling or picnicking, this park is a true urban oasis. Designed by Frederick Law Olmstead and Calvert Vaux in the 1870s, it consists of 81 acres of tree-lined grassy meadows. On the shores of the pretty lake is the **Washington Park Lake House** (☎ 518-434-4524); complete with pink floors and wrought-iron chandeliers, this amphitheatre hosts concerts and musicals every summer (bring a picnic).

NEW YORK STATE

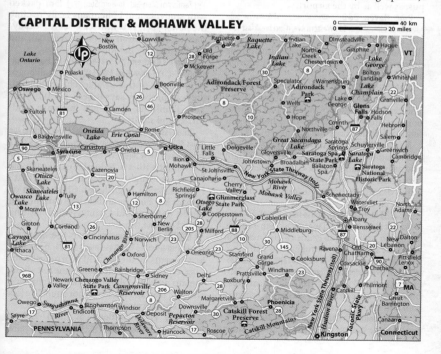

CAPITAL DISTRICT & MOHAWK VALLEY

NEW YORK STATE MUSEUM

An homage to this epic state, this **museum** (☎ 518-474-5877; www.nysm.nysed.gov; Madison Ave; admission free; ☼ 9:30am-5pm) highlights New York's political, cultural and natural history through installations and interactive exhibits. Don't miss the poignant exhibit on the tragic 9/11 World Trade Center attack and its aftermath.

Festivals & Events

Held the second weekend in May, the **Annual Tulip Festival** and **Pinksterfest** (☎ 518-434-1217; www.albanyevents.org) are three-day celebrations of the city's Dutch heritage, including food, crafts and the crowning of a Tulip Queen.

1st Friday Albany (www.1stfridayalbany.com) showcases local art galleries (along with local live bands) and takes place on the 1st Friday of each month.

Check www.albanyevents.org to get a headsup on other art, music, and cultural festivals that take place in this active town.

Sleeping

Budget and midrange chains cluster along Washington Ave near the SUNY-Albany campus, as well as by the airport.

Pine Haven B&B (☎ 518-482-1574; www.pinehavenbedandbreakfast; 531 Western Ave; d incl breakfast $69-109) Enjoy the old-fashioned front porch of this old house, furnished inside with antique dressers, iron bed-frames and other Victorian amenities.

State Street Mansion (☎ 518-462-6780; www.statestmansion.com; 281 State St; d incl breakfast from $95; ☎) This renovated downtown Neoclassical guesthouse is an airy, elegantly furnished former seminary with 12 unique rooms.

Mansion Hill Inn & Restaurant (☎ 518-465-2038; www.mansionhill.com; 115 Philip St; r from $125; ☎) Right downtown, this longtime classic offers simple rooms with dark-wood furnishings and a fine-dining restaurant featuring nouveau-American cuisine.

our pick Morgan State House Inn (☎ 518-427-6063; 393 State St; r $135-286; ☎) This grand 19th-century Victorian brownstone exudes a luxe mansion feel. Laze on the wonderful garden patio.

Century House Hotel & Restaurant (☎ 518-785-0931; 987 New Loudon Rd; d from $129; ☎ ☒ ⚛) This charming hotel in an 1810 Dutch farmhouse boasts exquisite grounds, including a nature trail and tennis courts.

The Desmond (☎ 518-869-8100; www.desmondhotels.com; 660 Albany-Shaker Rd; d from $180; ☎ ☒ ⚛) Short

of Paul Revere rushing in to announce that the British are coming, this colonial hotel feels like a trip back in a time-machine – albeit a trip with all the modern amenities, a posh restaurant and pub, landscaped atriums, and two nice pools.

Eating

If none of the following appeal, check out the eateries – with plenty of old-school Italian joints – on busy Central Ave downtown.

Kurver Kreme (☎ 518-459-4120; 1349 Central Ave; sundae $2-5; ☼ 11am-9pm Mon-Fri, from noon Sat, 1-9:30pm Sun) Under a vintage neon sign redolent of classic 1950s drive-ins, a rotating array of soft-serve ice-cream flavors and a million kinds of sundaes transform jaded adults into giddy children. See that line? It means it's *good*.

Cheesecake Machismo (☎ 518-427-7019; 293 Hamilton St; cheesecake & drink $5; ☼ noon-8pm Tue-Sat, to 10pm Fri) The tiny cheesecake shop with the funny name (yes, ladies are allowed) serves up adventurous flavors (PB & J, anyone?) under the watchful eye of saucy pin-up girls who seem to suggest that you *can* have your cake and eat it too.

Daily Grind Café (☎ 518-427-0464; 204 Lark St; ☼ 7am-9pm Mon-Sat, to 8pm Sun; ☎) Jam-packed with students and bohemians lazily reading the newspaper, this little cafe serves locally-roasted coffee, fresh soups, frozen chai, and sandwiches (try the Rueben).

Debbie's Kitchen (☎ 518-463-3829; 456 Madison Ave; mains $6-8; ☼ 10am-6pm Mon-Sat) The chalkboard sign outside of this lovable, cheery hole-in-the-wall probably says it best: *We Will Rock You*. Think out-of-the-box inventive sandwiches and salads.

Quintessence (☎ 518-434-8186; 11 New Scotland Ave; mains $7-15; ☼ 7am-midnight Mon-Wed, 7am-4am Thu & Fri, from 8am Sat & Sun; ☎) This trendy stainless-steel diner with a tuxedoed host sports a bar where one might expect a counter (that's right, cocktails reign here). Chow down on classics like burgers and shrimp scampi. Live music, dancing and Quintessential martinis round out the fun.

our pick Café Madison (☎ 518-935-1090; 1108 Madison Ave; brunch & lunch $7-9; dinner mains $17-26; ☼ breakfast, lunch & dinner) Oh, the brunch! (Carrot cake and raspberry oatmeal pancakes, a pine nuts-basil-tomato omelet.) Oh the twinkling lights over wrought iron and brick outdoor patio! We love this place morning, noon, and night.

Albany Pump Station (☎ 518-447-9000; 19 Quackenbush Sq; mains $9-20; ☼ 11:30am-10pm Mon-Thu,

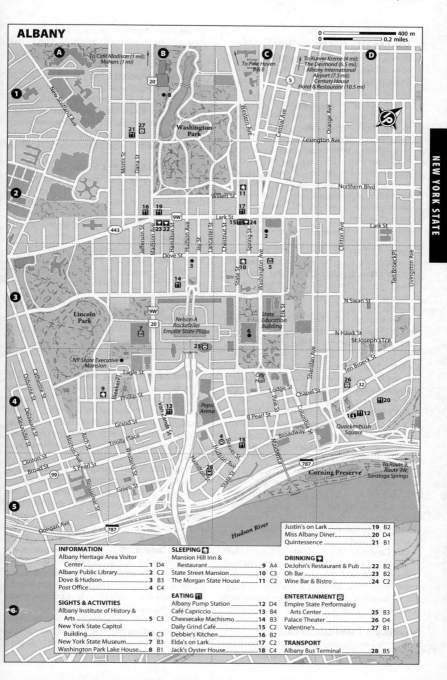

ALBANY

0 — 400 m
0 — 0.2 miles

NEW YORK STATE

INFORMATION
Albany Heritage Area Visitor
  Center 1 D4
Albany Public Library 2 C2
Dove & Hudson 3 B3
Post Office 4 C4

SIGHTS & ACTIVITIES
Albany Institute of History &
  Arts 5 C3
New York State Capitol
  Building 6 C3
New York State Museum 7 B3
Washington Park Lake House 8 B1

SLEEPING
Mansion Hill Inn &
  Restaurant 9 A4
State Street Mansion 10 C3
The Morgan State House 11 C2

EATING
Albany Pump Station 12 D4
Café Capriccio 13 B4
Cheesecake Machismo 14 B3
Daily Grind Café 15 C2
Debbie's Kitchen 16 B2
Elda's on Lark 17 C2
Jack's Oyster House 18 C4

Justin's on Lark 19 B2
Miss Albany Diner 20 D4
Quintessence 21 B1

DRINKING
DeJohn's Restaurant & Pub 22 B2
Oh Bar 23 B2
Wine Bar & Bistro 24 C2

ENTERTAINMENT
Empire State Performing
  Arts Center 25 B3
Palace Theater 26 D4
Valentine's 27 B1

TRANSPORT
Albany Bus Terminal 28 B5

NEW YORK STATE

THE CLASSIC AMERICAN DINER

The embodiment of down-home Americana, **Miss Albany Diner** (☎ 518-465-9148; 893 Broadway; mains $8; 🕑 7am-2pm Mon-Fri, from 9am Sat & Sun) was designed as an old railway car. Nostalgia and good home cooking are spooned up in equal parts. Known for its breakfasts – thick French toast with a pecan and cream cheese filling, topped with Irish whiskey butterscotch sauce; or the MAD eggs concoction (eggs on an English muffin with curry sauce) – it draws a loyal crowd. Some of the film based on William Kennedy's eponymous novel *Ironweed*– starring Meryl Streep and Robert De Niro – were shot here.

---

to 11pm Fri & Sat, noon-8pm Sun) An old warehouse converted into a hip brewpub and restaurant, with an artsy, industrial feel and plenty of exposed pipes. The eclectic entrees will please picky eaters, from Cajun shrimp and scallops to Polish pierogies.

Justin's on Lark (☎ 518-436-7008; 301 Lark St; mains from $10; 🕑 lunch & dinner, bar open to 4am) The dark brick and crystal chandeliers lend a sexy, offhand energy to the proceedings, whether it's brunch or dinner. Both the college crowd and the hip older set unwind with carefree abandon to hot jazz, free-flowing liquor and plenty of sultry sidelong glances.

Jack's Oyster House (☎ 518-465-8854; 42 State St; mains $12-40; 🕑 lunch & dinner) This 1937 Albany legend is worth its salt, with a divinely nostalgic atmosphere and decadent bar delicacies. It rarely disappoints.

Elda's on Lark (☎ 518-449-3532; 205 Lark St; mains $15-20; 🕑 4pm-4am) With a high-end, Prohibition-era supper-club feel, Elba's is perfect for those who want to sip martinis on the couches, dine on chicken Caruso or shrimp aphrodisiac, or have a reason to wear a dress and heels.

Café Capriccio (☎ 518-465-0439; 49 Grand St; mains $16-25; 🕑 dinner) Surrounded by dark red walls, you should cozy into one of the intimate booths for authentic regional Italian, like pollo alla Calabrese. Try the risotto with roasted duck leg.

Drinking & Entertainment

The city's best entertainment sources are the Thursday and Friday editions of the *Times-*

Union (www.timesunion.com) and *Metroland* (www.metroland.net), a free alternative weekly. Head to Lark St for hip and hedonistic nightlife.

DeJohn's Restaurant & Pub (☎ 518-465-5275; 288 Lark St; 🕑 3pm-2am weekdays, 11:30am-2pm weekends) Sure, you can dine on tasty classics here, but can you blame us if we prefer to drink? Something about the red walls, the low-slung pressed-tin ceilings and the seductive light endows a simple glass of wine with thrilling properties.

our pick **Mahars** (☎ 518-459-7868; www.itsonly beer.com; 1110 Madison Ave; 🕑 4pm-midnight Mon-Sat) Beer aficionados will want to make a stop at this intriguing narrow bar with a fireplace, board games, and a daily changing paper beer list that feels like a nostalgic pleasure to peruse. With so many fanatically loyal regulars, it doesn't need to advertise: in fact, the website quips 'Do we know you? We are not actively seeking new customers.' (Don't let that scare you off – they're perfectly cordial inside.)

Oh Bar (☎ 518-463-9004; 304 Lark St; 🕑 2pm-4am) At Albany's best gay bar, the party starts early and goes late. Dress up or down, shoot some pool, and enjoy the company of friendly (and, may we add, good lookin') guys – gals welcome too.

Wine Bar & Bistro (☎ 518-463-2881; 200 Lark St) This adorable cellar hideaway with a flowery stone patio and plenty of nooks and crannies in which to whisper sweet nothings (or just compare Pinot Noirs) thankfully resists the aesthetic minimalism that's all the rage these days. Thanks to good acoustics, conversations flow as much as wine here.

Empire State Performing Arts Center (☎ 518-473-1845; www.thegg.org; Empire State Plaza, cnr Madison Ave & Swan St) Albany's number-one arts venue has two theatres – a 982-seat main theater and a 500-seat intimate space – featuring eclectic concerts, dance, and theater performances.

Palace Theatre (☎ 518-465-3334; www.palacealbany. com; 19 Clinton Ave) A fanciful relic of the 1930s, this movie theater complete with a dreamy cloud-covered ceiling is home to the Albany Symphony Orchestra as well as being a venue for touring music and comedy acts.

Valentine's (☎ 518 432-6572; www.valentinesalbany. com; 17 New Scotland Ave) A grimy yet somehow lovable Albany legend, this is the place to rock out to local and touring acts.

Getting There & Around

Albany International Airport (☎ 518-242-2200; www.albanyairport.com; Albany-Shaker Rd) is a pleasant, low-key airport about 10 miles from downtown. Most major carriers serve the airport.

Adirondack Trailways (☎ 518-436-9651; www.trailwaysny.com) and **Greyhound** (☎ 518-426-9651; www.greyhound.com) depart from the **Albany Bus Terminal** (☎ 518-427-7060; 34 Hamilton St).

The **Amtrak station** (☎ 518-462-5763, 800-872-7245; www.amtrak.com; 525 East St, Rensselaer) is across the Hudson River in Rensselaer, about a 5-minute drive from downtown Albany.

Reliable **buses** (☎ 518-437-8300; www.cdta.org) around Albany cost $1.50. **Route 1** goes down Central Ave, from Washington & Lark to the Albany International Airport (25 minutes).

Albany is accessible via I-90 from western New York or Massachusetts and I-87 from southern or northern New York.

SARATOGA SPRINGS
pop 29,000

With a drop-dead gorgeous balance of culture and landscape, historic Saratoga Springs is a charming chameleon, wearing a swimsuit and sandals one minute and a little black dress and pearls the next. This is one happening resort town: shop in the morning, hit the mineral spas in the afternoon, dine with abandon, catch a ballet or opera in the evening, and have a nightcap with glitterati before heading back to your Victorian B&B – and you can do all of this with nary a car trip (see, there's this adorable old-fashioned trolley you can fashionably jump on or off). Summer in Saratoga provides a bewitching of world-class arts and culture – and that's not even talking about the racing season.

The whole town transforms into the Eastern Seaboard's answer to the Kentucky Derby for five weeks beginning in late July, when the thoroughbreds come to town – it's a thrilling, heart-pounding experience, even for those who bet on losing horses (okay, don't bet too much). With the horses come the crowds of hardcore horse people, rich society folks and others who simply dig the excitement. Sound over the top? Sure, dinner reservations become mandatory and hotel prices double, yet music and revelers fill the streets and the air is full of a palpable, electric magic. Ultimately, if you've ever wanted to live out the glamorous, beguiling debauchery of *The Great Gatsby*, racing season in Saratoga is your (hopefully winning) ticket.

Orientation

Walkable Saratoga Springs is just 35 miles north of Albany. Rte 9 goes right into town, where it becomes Broadway, the town's main drag, while the racecourse lies a few blocks east of Broadway off Union Ave.

Information

The **Lyrical Ballad Bookstore** (Map p162; ☎ 518-584-8779; 7 Phila St) is an inviting old bookstore. The **post office** (Map p162) lies on Broadway at the corner of Church St.

The **Heritage Area Visitors Center** (Map p162; ☎ 518-587-3241; www.saratogaspringsvisitorcenter.com; Drink Hall, 297 Broadway; ◷ 9am-4pm Mon-Sat year-round, 9am-4pm Sun Jul & Aug), across from Congress Park, provides maps and brochures. The helpful **Saratoga County Chamber of Commerce** (Map p162; ☎ 800-526-8970; www.saratoga.org; 28 Clinton St; ◷ 9am-5pm Mon-Fri) can set you up with information about lodging, events and promotions.

Sights & Activities

Mineral Springs and horseracing draw the crowds, but don't miss just strolling downtown or in the funky **Beekman St Arts District** (Beekman St & Grand Ave). Just west of Broadway off Washington, it is home to cutting-edge bistros and galleries.

DOWNTOWN SARATOGA SPRINGS

One of the most lively small-town downtowns in the country, Broadway Ave north of Congress Park is a something-for-everyone party that buzzes with a vibrant, fun-spirited energy. In summer, tables spill out onto the sidewalks while music fills the air and crowds pack the streets. The Victorian-style buildings are all immaculate, yet this town is no museum piece – it's a living, breathing downtown where work and play collide in the most delicious and decidedly elegant way. Don't miss the whimsical, almost life-size horse sculptures scattered around town.

Although at one time Broadway was lined with one grand hotel after another, sadly today only one remains. At 365 Broadway you'll find the beautifully appointed brown and cream Victorian **Adelphi** (p162), built in 1877. Continue north on Broadway through town and the hustle disappears. The road becomes thick with trees and lined with beautiful old homes on spacious lawns, until you eventually reach the tranquil, modern **Skidmore College** (Map p160; www.skidmore.edu)

campus, known for its strong arts programs, which sponsor fantastic not-just-for-students cultural programs and events. Notably, the acclaimed **Tang Museum** (☎ 518-580-8080; www.tang museum.org; 815 North Broadway) offers fun summer art openings and a rooftop jazz series, the **New York State Writers Institute** (www.albany.edu/writers -inst) hosts a renowned summer reading series, and the Skidmore Jazz Institute puts on jazz concerts by diverse professional musicians.

NATIONAL MUSEUM OF RACING & HALL OF FAME

Exhibits on the history of horseracing in England and America and on jockeys, thoroughbreds and breeding are displayed at this state-of-the-art, interactive **museum** (Map p160;

☎ 518-584-0400; www.racing.org; 191 Union Ave; admission adults/students $7/5; 🕙 10am-4pm Mon-Sat, noon-4pm Sun, 9am-5pm daily during racing season). Here you'll find the Agua Caliente trophy that Seabiscuit won in Mexico in 1938 (which was lost for about 50 years) and the leg brace worn by Red Pollard, his jockey, among thousands of artifacts. The adventurous can even race a horse (okay, so it's simulated).

MINERAL SPRINGS & BATHS

Public springs trickle throughout the town, and the taste of each and the purported medicinal effects vary greatly. Carry a cup for tasting, although you may not find it to rank among your favorite beverages (telling yourself that it's the 'fountain of youth' has been

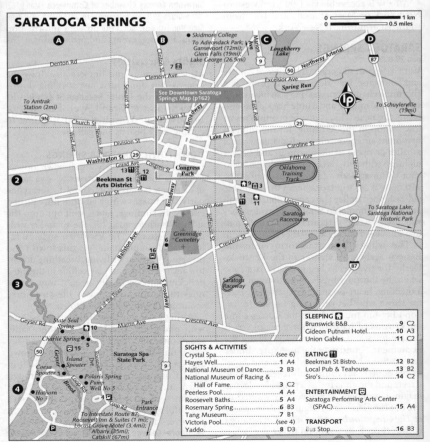

SARATOGA SPRINGS

SIGHTS & ACTIVITIES	
Crystal Spa	(see 6)
Hayes Well	1 A4
National Museum of Dance	2 B3
National Museum of Racing & Hall of Fame	3 C2
Peerless Pool	4 A4
Roosevelt Baths	5 A4
Rosemary Spring	6 B3
Tang Museum	7 B1
Victoria Pool	(see 4)
Yaddo	8 D3

SLEEPING 🏠	
Brunswick B&B	9 C2
Gideon Putnam Hotel	10 A3
Union Gables	11 C2

EATING 🍽	
Beekman St Bistro	12 B2
Local Pub & Teahouse	13 B2
Siro's	14 C2

ENTERTAINMENT 🎭	
Saratoga Performing Arts Center (SPAC)	15 A4

TRANSPORT	
Bus Stop	16 B3

known to significantly improve its palatability, however).

Don't miss the gorgeous, formally landscaped **Congress Park** (Map p162), on Broadway, home to Italian sculpture gardens and three springs, including **Congress Spring** (Map p162), which is inside a Greek revival–style pavilion. **Columbian Spring** (Map p162), a freshwater spring, also runs through the park. Inside the historic 1870 park casino, the **Saratoga History Museum** (Map p162; adult/student $5/4; ☾ 10am-4pm) offers a fascinating background on Saratoga. Check out photos of the 1920s 'drink halls', where the elite sat around drinking foul-tasting mineral water in a bar setting, and peek into the original, elegant High Stakes Gambling room where it's easy to imagine being a high-roller back in the day.

The **Old Red Spring** (Map p162) at the northern end of High Rock Ave, is high in iron and was called the 'beauty water spring' because it was said to be good for the complexion. The **Rosemary Spring** (Map p160), is behind the Crystal Spa at 120 S Broadway.

If you want to do more than taste the water, try the historic, chic, and beautifully remodeled **Roosevelt Baths** (Map p160; ☎ 518-452-7275; www.gideonputnamhotel.com; 39 Roosevelt Dr; admission from $25; ☾ 9am-4pm Jul-Aug, 9am-4pm Wed-Sun Oct-May, 9am-4pm Wed-Mon Jun-Sep) for a soak. The customary treatment here is to sit in the 97-degree effervescent water (which contains 16 minerals) for 20 minutes, and then relax on a table for another 20 minutes. Massages and facials begin at $55. Sandals and robes are provided.

The **Crystal Spa** (Map p160; ☎ 518-584-2556; www.thecrystalspa.net; 120 S Broadway; admission from $21; ☾ 8:30am-4:30pm) is the only private-bath facility in town, offering 15 luxurious soaking rooms with tile floors. The spa offers an array of soaks, massages and facials, which cost anywhere from $30 for a 'Fountain of Youth Rose Bath' to $110 for a lavender wrap or body scrub.

SARATOGA SPA STATE PARK

In the early decades of the 20th century, the state began constructing a complex of buildings, pools and bathhouses on the grounds of Saratoga's mineral springs, which were designed to rival those found in European health spas. The facilities opened to the public in 1935, and in 1962 the area officially became the 2000-acre **Saratoga Spa State Park** (Map p160; ☎ 518-584-2000; 19 Roosevelt Dr; parking $8). Despite an

air of faded elegance, the facilities still capture the kind of languid summer glamour that makes it the perfect place to lounge by the pool in dark sunglasses with a fruity drink. For drinks and a social resort scene, claim a chaise longue under the arched colonnades at **Victoria Pool** (Map p160; adult/child $8/4; ☾ 10am-6pm). If you're with kids, the **Peerless Pool** (Map p160; adult/child $2/1; ☾ 10am-6pm, closed Tue) will keep them better entertained. Both lie inside the park and are well marked with signs; they are open for swimming (and preening) during the summer months.

At one end of the park is the majestic **Ave of the Pines** and at the other end is **Loop Rd**, leading past half a dozen mineral springs, including **Hayes Well** (Map p160).

If you wander around this enchanting park you'll also find tennis courts, two golf courses, the Saratoga Performing Arts Center (p163) and the Gideon Putnam Hotel (p161).

YADDO

Once the stomping ground of that infamous literary couple, Sylvia Plath and Ted Hughes, this private **retreat** (Map p160; ☎ 518-584-0746; 312 Union Ave; admission to gardens free; ☾ 8am-dusk) east of the racecourse has been hosting writers, poets, artists and composers since the 1920s. The massive cut-stone mansion is off-limits to the public, yet the beautifully landscaped, mysterious gardens are open to visitors.

NATIONAL MUSEUM OF DANCE

This is the country's only **museum** (Map p162; ☎ 518-584-2225; www.dancemuseum.org; 99 S Broadway; admission $6.50; ☾ 10am-4:30pm May-Oct, closed Mon) dedicated to preserving the history and art of American dance, with a hall of fame and timely changing exhibits, like a tribute to Michael Jackson's dance career and a display of costumes from the TV show *Dancing With the Stars*.

Sleeping

Book ahead from late July through Labor Day, and plan to spend twice as much (or more) as other times of the year. High season rates quoted here refer to racing season.

The cheapest places to stay are the independently owned motels outside of town, between I-87 exits 12 and 13N, and along Rte 9/Broadway north of town.

Locust Grove Motel (off Map p160; ☎ 518-584-8038; 2838 Rte 9, Malta; r from $60; ☾ May-early Oct) 3 miles

DOWNTOWN SARATOGA SPRINGS

0   200 m
0   0.1 miles

NEW YORK STATE

INFORMATION
Heritage Area Visitors Center......1 A3
Lyrical Ballard Bookstore.............2 A3
Post Office....................................3 A2
Saratoga County Chamber of
   Commerce..................................4 A2

SIGHTS & ACTIVITIES
Columbian Spring.........................5 B3
Congress Spring...........................6 A3
Old Red Spring.............................7 C1
Saratoga History Museum...........8 B3

SLEEPING
Adelphi Hotel...............................9 A3
Fox N' Hound B&B......................10 C2
Saratoga Arms...........................11 A2
Saratoga Downtowner...............12 A2

EATING
Beverly's....................................13 B3
Circus Café.................................14 A3
Esperanto...................................15 A2
Forno Bistro...............................16 B1
Hattie's......................................17 B2
One Caroline Street Bistro.........18 B2
Ravenous...................................19 B3
Scallions....................................20 B2
Sperry's.....................................21 B2

DRINKING
9 Maple......................................22 B2
Caffé Lena.................................23 B3
Desperate Annie's.....................24 B2
Parting Glass Pub......................25 B2
Uncommon Grounds Coffee &
   Tea..26 A3
Virgil's House.............................27 B2

south of Saratoga, is the best cheap option – with kitchenettes and breakfast on the patio during track season – that puts you close to everything.

Roosevelt Inn & Suites (☎ 518-584-0980; www. rooseveltsuites.com; S Broadway; r from $80; ☼ May-early Oct) With nicely decorated rooms and a spa, it's an upscale bargain.

Saratoga Downtowner (Map p162; ☎ 518-584-6160; www.saratogadowntowner.com; 413 Broadway; d from $79/109 incl breakfast; ⓦ ☒ ⓖ) As convenient as the name suggests, this smack-dab-on-Broadway motel sports a cool atrium with a pool, simple, well-maintained rooms, and friendly owners. A good deal in racing season (book ahead).

ourpick Adelphi Hotel (Map p162; ☎ 518-587-4688; www.adelphihotel.com; 365 Broadway; r from $130; ☼ May-Oct) This hotel is old Saratoga (and vintage hotel heaven) personified – and the best deal in town. Built in 1877, the Adelphi is elegantly Victorian throughout. Strike a languid pose in the fern-filled vintage bar, order a fresh fruit daiquiri, party like it's 1929, and swoon to a barbershop quartet that just stepped off the street.

Brunswick B&B (Map p160; ☎ 518-585-6715; www. brunswickbb.com; 143 Union Ave; d incl breakfast low-/high-season from $100/$200; ⓦ) In a converted 1886 Victorian house across from the racetrack, this homey, funky place has a comfortable front porch, and a colorful clientele of racing fans.

Fox 'n' Hound (Map p162; ☎ 866-369-1913; www. foxnhoundbandb.com; 142 Lake Ave; d incl breakfast low-/high-season from $130/250; ⓦ) This B&B is in a sprawling and serene beautiful house with wonderful porches, fruit and crepes for breakfast, and afternoon tea.

Gideon Putnam Hotel (Map p160; ☎ 866-870-9458; www.gideonputnam.com; 24 Gideon Putnam Rd; d from $140/235; ⓦ) This gracious Georgian hotel has a resort-like feel and captures the vintage elegance of Saratoga, with a grand driveway, elegant common rooms, a quaint restaurant and bar, and an unbeatable location right in the middle of the lovely state park.

Union Gables (Map p160; ☎ 518-584-1558; 55 Union Ave; d incl breakfast low-season/high-season from $140/$300; ⓦ) Just before the racecourse, this Victorian hotel with 10 spacious rooms is one of the loveliest B&Bs in town.

Saratoga Arms (Map p162; ☎ 518-584-1775; www.saratogaarms.com; 497 Broadway; d incl breakfast low-season/high-season from $195/250; 🛜) For some serious luxury, this sprawling Victorian mansion has grand ornate staircases, fireplaces in each of the 16 rooms, and a wrap-around porch perfect for cocktails and merriment after the races.

Eating

You could come to Saratoga Springs, do nothing except eat and drink, and be as happy as a horse. Foodies will be in heaven, the indecisive in torment.

Esperanto (Map p162; ☎ 518-587-4236; 6 Caroline St; mains $4-8) Eat your way around the world on the cheap – Greece, Mexico, Thailand – at this funky little place. Walking out without trying a doughboy – chicken, three cheeses, scallions and spices baked in pizza dough – is a travesty.

Beverly's (☎ 518-583-2755; 47 Phila St; mains $7-12; 🍴 breakfast & lunch) A tiny cafe with big, fresh omelets, pancakes and salads, Beverly's has fanatical fans among both locals and tourists. Try one of the creative eggs benedict.

Local Pub & Teahouse (Map p160; ☎ 518-587-7256; 142 Grand Ave; mains $7-13; 🍴 lunch & dinner to midnight, brunch Sat & Sun) This cheerful local tavern with lovely architecture is full of chatty students and professionals who dig in to fish 'n' chips, shepherd's pie and welsh rarebit, alongside plenty of beers and organic teas.

Circus Café (Map p162; ☎ 518-583-1106; 392 Broadway; mains $8-20; 🍴 lunch & dinner; ♿) Got kids, or just act like one? Here's the three-ring circus with decadent comfort foods and desserts (and mojitos for the adults) you're looking for.

Ravenous (Map p162; ☎ 518-581-0560; 21 Phila St; crepes $10-12; 🍴 lunch Tue-Sat, brunch Sun) Savory and sweet crepes satisfy even picky eaters at this simple storefront that's a great place for a low-key, affordable meal. Sit at the window and people-watch while enjoying your ratatouille crepe.

Forno Bistro (Map p162; ☎ 518-581-2401; 541 Broadway; mains $10-22; 🍴 dinner; ♿) Arguably the most lovely and lush patio in town serves up well-prepared Italian classics to a sociable, wine-drinking crowd.

Scallions (Map p162; ☎ 518-587-4236; 44 Lake Ave; mains $10-25; 🍴 lunch & dinner Mon-Sat, lunch Sun) We adore this bright, bustling dining-room at lunch with its artsy feel, perfect crab-cakes, wonderful salads and soups (try the chilled peach). With all that, the fresh desserts still tempt.

our pick **Hattie's** (Map p162; ☎ 518-584-4790; 45 Phila St; mains $13-19; 🍴 dinner) Hattie's has been serving Southern fare since 1938. A Saratoga landmark that doesn't disappoint, Hattie's has a down-home kitchen feel in front, a sultry open-air patio in back, and mind-blowing fried chicken and Southern classics that promise to melt the hearts of even skeptical Yankees. Waiting in line's all part of the fun.

Beekman St Bistro (Map p160; ☎ 518-581-1816; 62 Beekman St; mains $14-26; 🍴 dinner Tue-Sun) Is this currently the best restaurant in Saratoga? That's the rumor 'round town, and a bold one among so much competition. One bite of the seared scallops over grapefruit and fennel and you may already believe it's true.

One Caroline Street Bistro (Map p162; ☎ 518-587-2026; 1 Caroline St; mains $19-26) This family-owned place succeeds with memorable food and ambience. In a chic, intimate setting, listen to live jazz and blues every night.

Sperry's (Map p162; ☎ 518-584-9618; 30½ Caroline St; mains $20-28; 🍴 dinner Tue-Sat) Red walls, racing decor and seafood dishes like Maryland crab-cakes with wasabi sauce. This is an understated Saratoga classic with a back courtyard perfect for dinner and drinks.

Drinking & Entertainment

Besides the listings here, there are plenty of bars and clubs on Broadway.

Saratoga Performing Arts Center (SPAC; Map p160; ☎ 518-587-3330; Saratoga Spa State Park) Drawing in folks from NYC and Boston and a local fave, 'SPAC' lives up to its reputation with world-class entertainment in the serene outdoor setting of Saratoga Spa State Park. In addition to being home for the New York City Ballet and the Philadelphia Orchestra, the outdoor amphitheater draws in big-name entertainment.

Caffe Lena (Map p162; ☎ 518-583-0022; www.caffelena.org; 47 Phila St) Iconic, historic, and cool before 'cool' meant *cool*, this is the oldest continuously operating coffeehouse in America. A wonderful throwback to the 1960s folk scene that's hosted legends like Ani DiFranco and Bob Dylan, it's an authentic Saratoga original. Dig it.

our pick **Parting Glass Pub** (Map p162; ☎ 518-583-2582; www.partingglass.pub; 9 Maple Ave) A feel-good Saratoga institution, this Irish pub draws loyal fans for its extensive beer selection, traditional Irish music, Monday night trivia and intense games of darts. Good pub food, too.

NEW YORK STATE

9 Maple Ave (Map p162; ☎ 518-583-1916; 40-42 Lake Ave) With an effortless *je ne sais quoi* that many speakeasies attempt but few master, this sultry bar features jazz on weekends and a menu of expertly shaken martinis that will put a swing in your step (or a stranger in your arms).

Desperate Annie's (Map p162; ☎ 518-587-2455; 12 Caroline St) Some people come to Saratoga to party with moneyed sophisticates, others to party with the hoi polloi and drunk college students. The latter group should head to DA's, as the tipsy call it.

Uncommon Grounds Coffee & Tea (Map p162; ☎ 518-581-0646; 402 Broadway; mains $4-6; ☺ 7am-midnight; ☻) A convivial morning or late-night spot for strong coffee, fresh bagels, sandwiches and yummy gelato. Inside are bright red walls, outside is a patio heavy on the flowers and wrought iron.

Virgil's House (Map p162; ☎ 518-587-2949; 86 Henry St; mains $4-6; ☺ 6:30am-9pm Mon-Fri, from 7am Sat, 7am-6pm Sun) You've got to love a cafe where cell phones, iPods and laptops are banned so that people can actually hang out and talk, listen to live music, read books, and play board games among the mismatched velvet couches. Salads,

wine, coffee – it's all good, but we come to escape technology.

Getting There & Away

Trains to NYC and Montreal depart from the **Amtrak station** (☎ 518-587-8354; cnr West Ave & Station Lane), where Greyhound and **Adirondack Trailways** (☎ 518-583-7490) buses also depart. The station is a couple of miles outside of town.

Saratoga is off I-87 at exit 13N.

Getting Around

See those old-fashioned trolleys rumbling down Broadway? CDTA Saratoga Springs runs open-air trolleys down Broadway, in a big loop from Skidmore College, through downtown and out to the state park.

COOPERSTOWN
pop 2000

As American as baseball and apple pie – in other words, a quintessential American town full of good, clean fun and plenty of baseball-crazed tourists – popular Cooperstown is a mix of kitsch and culture. Cooperstown was founded in 1786 by William Cooper, a wealthy land agent and the father of novelist James

---

A DAY AT THE RACES

Horse crazy: that describes this town from late July to August, as fans flock to the **Saratoga Race Course** (Map p160; ☎ 518-584-6200; www.nyra.com/saratoga; 267 Union Ave; admission grandstand/clubhouse $3/5; ☺ closed Tue), the oldest active thoroughbred racetrack in the US. Hotel prices soar, the streets are jammed with fancy cars, and the nights are long as gamblers celebrate or commiserate over their wins and losses. You don't have to be a high-stakes player to enjoy the racetrack – entry is still a steal and the minimum bet is just $1. On the way in pick up a copy of the *Post Parade*, which lists each horse's record and describes how to place bets.

Once inside, you can walk right up to the fence and stand a few thrilling feet from the horses as they charge past. Jazz and folk groups play daily, and the house Dixieland band guarantees that there is never a lull in the fast-paced, spirited atmosphere.

The biggest race of the season is Travers Day in late August. An entire festival, the Travers Festival, is organized in conjunction with this race and runs for a week with a line-up of daily events around town. The last weekend of the season is Final Stretch Weekend, characterized by lots of food and drink and live music downtown.

Parking near the track costs around $5. There is free admission from 7am to 9:30am, when many come to watch the horses' morning workouts and get a free tour of the stables. Splurge at the trackside cafe for a $12 breakfast buffet. As an alternative to typical concession stand food, you can eat at one of the several $15-minimum clubhouse dining rooms, but only if properly attired.

The most popular racetrack hangout, and the place to see and be seen, is **Siro's** (Map p160; ☎ 518-584-4030; 168 Lincoln Ave; ☺ dinner), adjacent to the track at the corner of Lincoln and Nelson Aves. Underneath a striped canvas tent you'll find a long bar where live bands play each evening, after which those with dinner reservations move inside to feast on tender cuts of steak or racks of lamb. Dinners aren't cheap – expect to pay about $150 for two people with drinks – but the atmosphere makes it worth it. Dress to impress.

Fenimore Cooper, author of books such as *The Last of the Mohicans* and *The Deerslayer*.

The **Cooperstown Chamber of Commerce** (☎ 607-547-9983; www.cooperstownchamber.org; 31 Chestnut St; ⏱ 9am-5pm) offers information on the attractions.

Sights & Activities
NATIONAL BASEBALL HALL OF FAME & MUSEUM
Baseball's national shrine, the **Hall of Fame** (☎ 888-425-5633; www.baseballhall.org; 25 Main St; adult/child 6-12yr $16.50/6; ⏱ 9am-9pm Jun-Aug, 9am-5pm Sep-May), houses all the important baseball artifacts, such as famous players' bats, gloves and uniforms and balls hit by Babe Ruth, Willie Mays and Reggie Jackson to name just a few.

DOUBLEDAY FIELD & BATTING RANGE
The oldest **baseball diamond** (☎ 607-547-5168; Main St) in the world was the site of the first official game in 1839. Next to the field is the **Doubleday Batting Range** (www.doubledaybatting.com; per batting round $2.25; ⏱ 9am-9pm daily May-early Sep, weekends only Apr & mid-Sep–Oct). Here you can test your batting skills against the same pitching machine used in the major leagues. (17 different kinds of pitches at various speeds).

FENIMORE ART MUSEUM
View the country's history through the lives of its literary figures at the **Fenimore Art Museum** (☎ 607-547-1420; www.fenimoreartmuseum.org; Lake Rd; adult/child $11/5; ⏱ 10am-5pm Jun-Sep, 10am-4pm Tue-Sun Apr-May & Oct-Nov) which displays an outstanding collection of folk art, Native American artifacts and masks, contemporary photography and paintings from the Hudson River. (Not to mention James Fenimore Cooper literary memorabilia.)

OTSEGO LAKE & GLIMMERGLASS STATE PARK
According to local lore, Judge William Cooper founded the village of Cooperstown in 1786 because of the pristine lakeside setting. His son, author James Fenimore Cooper, called the lake Glimmerglass in his novel *The Deerslayer*, describing it as 'a broad sheet of water, so placid and limpid that it resembled a bed of pure mountain atmosphere compressed into a setting of hills and woods.' Within a magical setting, there is swimming and fishing, public boat launches, and golf courses.

WHAT THE...?
Cooperstown's bizarre **Cardiff Giant** (☎ 607-547-1400; New York State Farmer's Museum, 100 Lake St, Cooperstown; ⏱ 10am-5pm high season, call for low season times) is a 2990lb carving that, in the 19th century, was once passed off as the petrified skeletal remains of a giant dug up in nearby Cardiff. In reality, cigar-maker George Hull had the giant sculpted out of gypsum. Even after the hoax was discovered people continued to line up – as they do today – to see the 'petrified giant.'

Glimmerglass State Park (☎ 607-547-8662; East Lake Rd; campsite $15) is at the northern end of the lake. Home to the Glimmerglass Opera, it's a serene green place and features a swimming beach, hiking and biking trails, a playground and a campground.

Sleeping
Lake 'n Pines Motel (☎ 800-615-5253; www.lakenpinesmotel.com; 7102 Hwy 80; r low-season/high-season from $55/90 incl breakfast; 🖧 🐾 ♿) A lakeside sundeck, an indoor and outdoor pool, whirlpool and paddleboats make this beachfront place appealing.

Cooperstown B&B (☎ 607-547-2532; www.cooperstownbandb.com; 88 Chestnut St; r $90-180; 🖧) This place has four rooms with beautiful linens and cheery colors. We like the airy 2nd-floor porch and the delish breakfast buffet, with homemade scones, fresh fruit and cinnamon buns.

Landmark Inn (☎ 607-547-7225; www.landmarkinncooperstown.com; 64 Chestnut St; d from $150 incl breakfast; 🖳 🖧) This delicate white mansion with magnificent stained-glass windows is set back from the road on a manicured lawn. Inside, classical music, hardwood floors and antiques greet guests.

our pick **Inn at Cooperstown** (☎ 607-547-5756; www.innatcooperstown.com; 16 Chestnut St; r low-season/high-season from $135/200) Once the posh Hotel Fenimore, you can still relive its gracious past by sipping lemonade and cookies served on the veranda every afternoon (yes, there are rocking chairs) at this friendly place. Antiques and oil paintings fill the rooms, and breakfasts may include fresh fruit salads and frittatas.

Otesaga Resort Hotel (☎ 607-547-9931; www.otesaga.com; 60 Lake St; s/d from $330/410; ⏱ May-Nov;

NEW YORK STATE

NEW YORK STATE

⚛ 🔋 ♿) Right on the lake, this beautiful 1909 Georgian resort sits majestically on manicured lawns. Play golf or tennis, fish, paddle a boat or swim from the resort's private dock. Rates include dinner and breakfast, plus teatime.

Eating

Cooperstown Diner (☎ 607-547-7901; 136½ Main St; mains $3-7; 🕐 6am-8pm, to 9pm Jun-Aug) The milkshakes. The enormous burgers that haunt our dreams with goodness. The cinnamon-roll French toast. How do such amazing tastes come out of this tiny brick diner?

our pick **Blue Mingo Grill** (☎ 607-547-7496; 6098 State Hwy 80; lunch $4-10, mains $19-26; 🕐 lunch & dinner late May-Sep; ♿) Along with plenty of locals and tourists, even TV host Rachael Ray likes this lakeside joint with its beautiful wooden veranda. The menu is eclectic, international and constantly changing – think corn-crusted shrimp, tortilla espagnol, sweet potato risotto and lobster.

Doubleday Café (☎ 607-547-5468; 93 Main St; mains $5-15; 🕐 breakfast, lunch & dinner) This friendly baseball-and-beer joint welcomes hungry families and imbibers alike.

Nicoletta's Italian Café (☎ 607-547-7499; 96 Main St; mains $10-22; 🕐 dinner) Outstanding pastas, savory classics and oh-so-garlicky garlic bread impress even jaded Manhattanites.

Drinking & Entertainment

Alice Busch Opera Theater (☎ 607-547-2255; www.glimmerglass.org; 7300 State Highway 80, Cooperstown; tick-

---

DETOUR – BINGHAMTON

Near the Pennsylvania border, 75 miles south of Syracuse, is Binghamton, a fab place for a sandwich stop. This place offers up a classic New York delicacy with a funny name. The town is the home of 'spiedies,' sandwiches made of pork, chicken or lamb in a special marinade, grilled and served on a hoagie roll. Binghamtonians all have an opinion on the best spiedie joint. While **Sharkey's** (☎ 607-729-9201; 56 Glenwood Ave; mains $6-12) gets points for being the original hole-in-the-wall complete with steamed clams and cheap beer, other locals claim that **Spiedie & Rib Pit** (☎ 607-722-7628; 1268 Upper Front St; spiedie $4-8) wins out flavorwise. You be the judge.

---

ets $26-126) Home of the summertime, crowd-pleasing Glimmerglass Opera, the theater is partially open to the outdoors. Chamber music concerts, lectures and plays are also staged here. Note: the box office is at 18 Chestnut St.

Taproom at the Tunnicliff Inn (☎ 607-547-9931; 34-36 Pioneer St) Cheap beers in 'the pit' – actually the basement of an 1802 inn – make this place a popular late-night hangout.

Getting There & Around

Pine Hills Trailways and **Adirondack Trailways** (☎ 800-776-7548 for both; www.trailwaysny.com) go daily to New York City.

By car from I-88, take exit 16 and then Rte 28 north for 18 miles to town. From I-90, take exit 30 to Rte 28 south for 28 miles to town.

THE ADIRONDACKS

So it's not the Rockies or the Alps, but who cares? The Adirondacks have their own inimitable charm, from the Olympic village of Lake Placid to the wilderness of rocky peaks ringing mirror-like lakes. The Adirondack National Park offers high-adrenaline outdoor activities and pinch-yourself-in-case-you're-dreaming storybook towns in an atmosphere so unspoiled that it's hard to imagine you're within easy driving distance of both New York City and Boston.

There aren't many places in the northeast where the vista from a mountain summit is of an undulating landscape of sleeping giants. And there aren't many places where land preservation is a cooperative between publicly and privately owned land. Adirondack Park is just such a place, showing the limits of language and ownership. Established in 1892, Adirondack Park isn't a park in the traditional sense that you pull up to a gate and pay an admission fee. Land rules over man here in the mighty 'Dacks, with 2000 miles of hiking trails, 6000 miles of rivers, and 46 mountains towering over 4000ft. Impressed? This is one of the most pristine – and powerfully evocative – landscapes in the nation.

INFORMATION

Words to the wise: seasonal hours are rampant in the 'Dacks, where many hotels and restaurants close from September or

October through May or even early June. Double-check by calling ahead to avoid disappointment.

Adirondack Mountain Club (ADK; ☎ 518-523-3441; www.adk.org; Lake Placid; ☼ 10am-5pm Mon-Fri) This club has been around since 1922 and maintains trails, promotes conservation and outdoor activities and publishes guides and maps to the Adirondacks. It also offers educational programs and operates campgrounds, lean-tos and lodges.

Adirondack Loj & ADK High Peaks Information Center (☎ 518-523-3441; Lake Placid) Operated by ADK, contact this center for lodging and hiking information for the High Peaks.

Department of Environmental Conservation (DEC; ☎ 518-402-9405; www.dec.ny.gov; 625 Broadway, Albany; ☼ 8:30am-4:45pm Mon-Fri) With regional offices throughout the Adirondacks, contact the DEC for trail and backcountry information and permit, fishing and hunting regulations and licenses.

LAKE GEORGE & AROUND
pop 3500

Welcome to tourist heaven. So what if it's a little too gaudy? Lake George is a pure shot of summertime fun, equal parts relaxation and good old-fashioned American excess, from mini-golf to dinner cruises. But with all of this man-made fun, don't underestimate the lake herself. A 32-mile-long breathtaking natural wonder – dotted with 365 islands – Lake George is often described as the 'Queen of America's Lakes,' in part for its deep blue, crystal-clear water and wild shorelines.

NEW YORK STATE

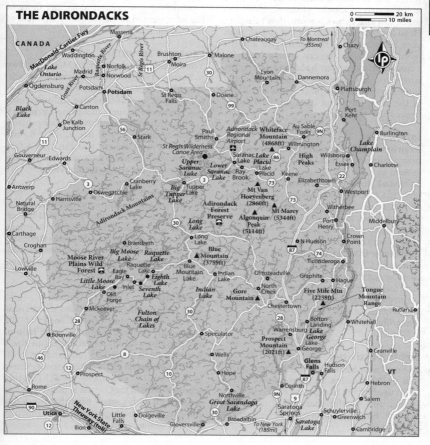

THE ADIRONDACKS

LAKE GEORGE HIKES

The north of Lake George is less developed and offers hiking, canoeing and kayaking. Adirondack Mountain Club Information Center (ADK) can give suggestions for this area.

Off Rte 9N, north of Bolton Landing, is the trailhead for hikes along the Tongue Mountain range, a peninsula that laps at Lake George. Deer Leap (3.4 miles round-trip, easy), Five Mile Mountain (7 miles round-trip, difficult) and Northwest Bay Trail (10.8 miles round-trip, moderate) offer vistas and shady glens within the Tongue Mountain area.

Over 60 miles of trails dissect the eastern side of the lake. Sleeping Beauty (7.8 miles round-trip, moderate) is a switchback trail with open ledges; Buck Mountain (4.6 to 6.6 miles round-trip depending on entrance, difficult) is a vigorous climb rewarded with an open summit with a panorama of Lake George.

At the southern edge of the lake you'll find Lake George village, a pleasant looking (albeit overbuilt and loud) tourist trap where bikers, families and retirees all head to, in search of kitschy pleasure. If it's too much fun and games for you, don't despair. Head to a lakeside patio spot at sunset: with your back turned to the neon lights and the motorcycle traffic, you can sit on a deck with a frozen drink in your hand and remember why Georgia O'Keeffe and Alfred Steiglitz came here in the first place – this is still one of the most gorgeous lakes on the Eastern Seaboard.

Information

Keep in mind that parking meters operate 24 hours daily, seven days a week. Useful organizations in town are:

Adirondack Mountain Club Information Center (ADK; ☎ 518-668-4447; www.adk.org; 814 Goggins Rd; ☻ 8:30am–5pm Mon–Sat) South of town, ADK's headquarters is the best source of information on the region's outdoor activities. The center is west of the I-87 overpass heading toward Lake Luzerne.

Lake George Chamber of Commerce & Visitors Center (☎ 518-668-5755, 800-705-0059; www.visit lakegeorge.com; Rte 9/Canada St; ☻ 9am–5pm summer) At the south end of the village opposite Prospect Mountain, on the east side of the street, this center distributes maps of French and Indian War sites.

Post office (☎ 518-668-3386, Canada St) A block north of Beach Rd.

Sights & Activities

History buffs, boating enthusiasts and divers will enjoy viewing the remains of seven boats used on the lake during the French and Indian, and Revolutionary Wars in the 18th century. For more information, contact the DEC (p167).

MILLION DOLLAR BEACH

This small sandy **beach** (☎ 518-668-3352; Beach Rd; admission free; ☻ 9am–6pm late-May–Labor Day) in Lake George Beach State Park is a short walk south of the town center along the shore of the lake, named for the wealthy clientele of the bygone era.

PROSPECT MOUNTAIN

You can drive up the Veterans Memorial Hwy to the top of **Prospect Mountain** (admission per car $8; 10am–7:30pm late-May–Oct), 2021ft above sea level, for dramatic views of the lake and surrounding mountain ranges, including Vermont's Green Mountains and New Hampshire's White Mountains. Off Rte 9, it's a 5-mile drive to a crest, where you can take a free air-conditioned bus to the summit or you can hike for even more spectacular views.

LAKE GEORGE CRUISES

A **cruise** (Jun–Labor Day) is a good way to enjoy the lake and take in the scenery along its shores. Several tour boats leave from the southern shore of the lake; we like **Lake George Steamboat Co** (☎ 518-668-5777; www.lakegeorgesteamboat.com), which offers scenic lake and romantic dinner cruises on its paddleboats.

Sleeping

Lake George village has dozens of inexpensive roadside motels lining Canada St, the main route through town. For more natural surroundings, cabins and cottages line Rte 9 heading north toward Bolton Landing.

Park Lane Motel (☎ 518-668-2615; www.parklaneon lakegeorge.com; 378 Canada St; d $69-229; ☒) This tidy representative of the Canada St motels has one large room with a small deck that overlooks the lake, with a postage stamp–sized beach at the foot of the motel.

Alpine Village (☎ 518-668-2193; www.alpinelg.com; 3054 Lakeshore Dr; d per day/week from $95/570, cabins per week from $795; ☒) Sleep in an authentic log cabin with a romantic porch just north of Lake George village. This shady spot faces a sandy lakeshore beach, and also features hotel-style doubles and a gorgeous Adirondack great room.

Melody Manor (☎ 518-644-9750; www.melodymanor.com; 4610 Lakeshore Dr, Bolton Landing; d low-/high-season $125/180; ☒) North of Lake George, this is one of the best views on the lake, sporting spacious rooms with balconies or patios, a small beach and a babbling brook running through the manicured property.

Eating

It's a common complaint: the food in Lake George village doesn't compare with the scenery, but that doesn't mean you can't find a tasty meal.

Prospect Mountain Diner (☎ 518-668-3650; 2205 Rte 9; ☺ 6am-3pm Mon-Thu, 6am-9pm Fri-Sun) This gleaming chrome-and-vinyl diner offers fully-fledged desserts masquerading as wholesome breakfasts, like pigs in a blanket (pancakes wrapped around sausage) or apple pancakes with whipped cream.

Caffe Vero (☎ 518-668-5800; 185 Canada St; ☺ 6:30am-6pm, to 8pm Fri & Sat) This authentic little cafe serves strong coffee, breakfast burritos and great pancakes.

Smokey Joe's Saloon & Grill (☎ 518-668-2660; 25 Canada St; mains $8-23; ☺ lunch & dinner) Solid barbecue and tasty sides with good prices and a view. What more could you want? Maybe log-cabin decor and friendly service? They've got that too.

Mario's (☎ 518-668-2665; 429 Canada St; mains $12-22; ☺ 4:30pm-late Mon-Sat, 3pm-late Sun, Thu-Sat Jan-Apr) In a rambling white house with flowerboxes, Mario's has been serving up honest Italian-American classics like chicken saltimbocca and seafood fra diavolo since 1954. After a few frozen drinks you'll feel like you own the place.

ourpick **Boathouse Restaurant** (☎ 518-668-2389; 3210 Lake Shore Dr; mains $13-27; ☺ dinner) Hidden up the road from town and right on the lake, the spirited ambience and classic steak and seafood captures the essence of summer.

Entertainment & Drinking

For sunsets or raucous late night fun, head to any of the lakeside patio bars.

Lake George Dinner Theatre (☎ 518-668-5762; Holiday Inn Turf, 2223 Canada St; tickets $53-58; ☺ shows 6:30pm Tue-Sat, 11:30am Wed & Thu mid-Jun–mid-Oct) Opposite the Tiki Lounge, this equity dinner theater does one play each summer, usually a Broadway or off-Broadway musical or comedy.

Adirondack Pub & Brewery (☎ 518-668-0002; 33 Canada St; ☺ noon-10pm) This brew pub-restaurant is a pretty blonde-wood place with amber lighting, low-key enough for families and singles.

Getting There & Away

In Lake George village **Adirondack Trailways** (☎ 800-776-7548) stops at the **Lake George Hardware Store** (35 Montcalm St) en route to Saratoga Springs and NYC.

From I-87, exit 21 lets you off at the south end of town on Rte 9.

BOLTON LANDING
pop 2000

Lakeside Bolton Landing is Lake George's more sophisticated elder sister: quaint instead of kitsch, refined rather than raucous, yet with a spirited summertime feel that recalls vintage postcards signed 'Wish you were here' in an elegant script.

The quirky **Marcella Sembrich Opera Museum** (☎ 518-644-9839; www.thesembrich.org; Lake Shore Dr;

NEW YORK STATE

LAKE GEORGE CAMPING

The State of New York maintains campgrounds on 92 of the islands in Lake George. For information and reservations in any New York state park, call the **camping reservation system** (☎ 800-456-2267; www.reserveamerica.com). All the island campsites are open from mid-May to mid-September. Canoeing parties sometimes get a tow at the marina to one of the islands, and then paddle around from there. Our faves include **Long Island** on the southern end of the lake, **Glen Island** in the narrows of Lake George and **Narrow Island**. Also try **Lake George Islands Public Campgrounds** (☎ 518-656-9426; campsite $16) on three islands in the middle of Lake George.

At the south end of town, **Lake George Battleground Public Campground** (☎ 518-668-3348, Rte 9; campsite $17; ☺ May–mid-Oct) has sites in a shady pine grove.

admission free; ⊙ 10am-12:30pm & 2-5:30pm Jun-Sep) was the home of opera singer Marcella Sembrich, best known for her role as Mimi in *La Bohème*, singing opposite Enrico Caruso. Her costumes and mementos charm.

Kayakers, note: you can paddle out for the day or set-up camp on two island groups in the northern part of Lake George, the Narrows and the Mother Bunch. **Lake George Kayak Co** (☎ 518-644-9366; www.lakegeorgekayak.com; 4973 Lake Shore Dr, Bolton Landing; kayak half/full day $44/54, canoe full day $59-69) rents kayaks and canoes and does guided tours.

For a stupendously scenic drive, take the 39-mile drive (via Rte 9N) along the western shore of Lake George. After passing Bolton Landing, you'll drive through the small towns of Silver Bay and Hague.

On a private island accessible by a bridge, the grand **Sagamore Resort** (☎ 866-385-6221; www.thesagamore.com; 110 Sagamore Rd; r from $200; 🛜) evokes an old-fashioned glamour that's more about refined elegance than flash. Built in the roaring twenties, this stunning hotel has a panoramic view of Lake George and a sweeping postcard-perfect veranda and huge pool along the water.

Bolton Beans (☎ 518-644-2106; Lake Shore Dr; dishes $6-9; ⊙ breakfast & lunch; ♿) The strongest coffee in the Adirondacks is paired with tasty breakfasts and lunches in a vintage dining-car that feels like a film set.

LAKE PLACID & AROUND
pop 2600

A welcome enclave of civilization, Lake Placid village – situated on **Mirror Lake** – hosted the 1932 and 1980 Winter Olympics. Only two other towns – Innsbruck in Austria and St Moritz in Switzerland – have hosted two Winter Games. Training still occurs in many of the Olympic facilities, and many special events and programs introduce visitors to the winter pursuits of bobsled racing, ice-skating and ski jumping.

While Lake Placid village rests on the shores of Mirror Lake, the eponymous Lake Placid is actually north of the village. Perched along the hills of the town are the summer homes of the people whose spending power keeps the resort alive.

Lake Placid became an Olympic center thanks to Dr Melvil Dewey, of Dewey Decimal System fame, who opened the Lake Placid Club in 1895 as place where outdoor enthusiasts could make, swim, camp, fish and play tennis and golf. At that time winter sports were so new to most Americans that Dewey had to import 40 skis and poles from Norway. His dedication paid off: by 1920, Lake Placid had transformed into a world famous winter resort, and the rest is Olympic history.

Information
The local biweekly newspaper is the *Lake Placid News* (www.lakeplacidnews.com).

Bookstore Plus (☎ 518-523-2950; 2491 Main St; ⊙ 9am-9:30pm Mon-Sat, 10am-6pm Sun)

NBT Bank (2483 Main St; ⊙ 8:30am-3pm Mon & Tue, to 5pm Wed-Fri)

Lake Placid Library (☎ 518-523-3200; www.lakeplacidlibrary.org; 2471 Main St; free computers & wi-fi; ⊙ 10am-5:30pm Mon, Wed & Fri, to 7pm Tue & Thu, to 4pm Sat)

Post office (☎ 518-523-3071; 2591 Main St)

Lake Placid (Essex County) Visitors Bureau (☎ 518-523-2445; www.lakeplacid.com; 49 Parkside Dr; ⊙ 8am-5pm Mon-Fri, 9am-4pm Sat & Sun)

Sights
When you begin asking yourself questions like 'am I too old to start training for the bobsled/figure skating/ski jumping events?' you know that Olympic fever has hit hard.

OLYMPIC SITES
If you're in town, don't skip these sites: they're just too much fun, regardless of whether you've ever harbored triple axel or luge fantasies.

The visitors bureau distributes weekly schedules for Olympic venue events. You can visit the following Olympic sites separately or all together on the all-inclusive **Summer Passport** (www.orda.org; $29; Jun-Oct). Most sites

---

DETOUR – THE HYDE COLLECTION

Skip the NY State Thruway traffic on your way from Lake George to Saratoga Springs. Take scenic Rte 9 instead. The pretty small town of Glens Falls has the **Hyde Collection** (☎ 518-792-1761; 161 Warren St; admission free; ⊙ 10am-5pm Tue-Sat, 12-5pm Sun), a remarkable collection of art on display in an atmospheric Florentine Renaissance mansion. View works from European and American artists spanning five centuries, from Rembrandt and Rubens to Matisse.

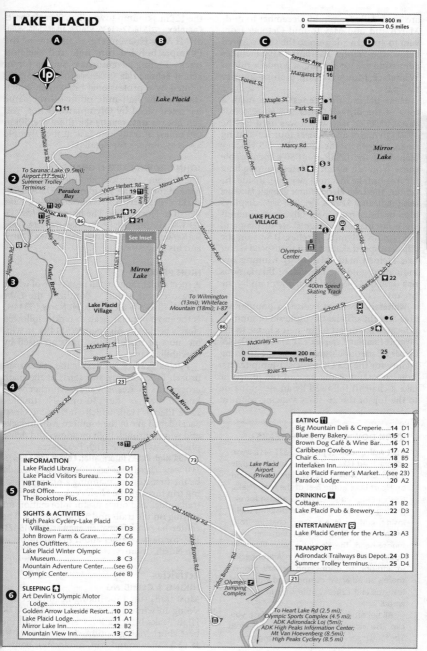

LAKE PLACID

0   800 m
0   0.5 miles

NEW YORK STATE

Lake Placid

To Saranac Lake (9.5mi);
Airport (17.5mi);
Summer Trolley
Terminus

Paradox Bay

Saranac Ave

Mirror Lake Dr

Mirror Lake Ave

Mirror Lake

See Inset

Mirror Lake

Lake Placid Village

To Wilmington
(13mi); Whiteface
Mountain (18mi); I-87

Saranac Ave

Margaret Pt

Forest St

Maple St

Pine St

Park St

Marcy Rd

Highland Pl

LAKE PLACID VILLAGE

Mirror Lake

Olympic Center

Cummings Rd

400m Speed Skating Track

School St

0   200 m
0   0.1 miles

McKinley St

River St

Lake Placid Airport (Private)

EATING 🍴
Big Mountain Deli & Creperie.....**14** D1
Blue Berry Bakery.........................**15** C1
Brown Dog Café & Wine Bar.....**16** D1
Caribbean Cowboy.....................**17** A2
Chair 6.......................................**18** B5
Interlaken Inn............................**19** B2
Lake Placid Farmer's Market....(see 23)
Paradox Lodge..........................**20** A2

INFORMATION
Lake Placid Library.....................**1** D1
Lake Placid Visitors Bureau........**2** D2
NBT Bank..................................**3** D2
Post Office.................................**4** D2
The Bookstore Plus....................**5** D2

SIGHTS & ACTIVITIES
High Peaks Cyclery-Lake Placid
  Village......................................**6** D3
John Brown Farm & Grave.........**7** C6
Jones Outfitters.........................(see 6)
Lake Placid Winter Olympic
  Museum..................................**8** C3
Mountain Adventure Center......(see 6)
Olympic Center.........................(see 8)

SLEEPING 🏠
Art Devlin's Olympic Motor
  Lodge.....................................**9** D3
Golden Arrow Lakeside Resort...**10** D2
Lake Placid Lodge.....................**11** A1
Mirror Lake Inn.........................**12** B2
Mountain View Inn....................**13** C2

DRINKING 🍷
Cottage.....................................**21** B2
Lake Placid Pub & Brewery.......**22** D3

ENTERTAINMENT 🎭
Lake Placid Center for the Arts...**23** A3

TRANSPORT
Adirondack Trailways Bus Depot..**24** D3
Summer Trolley terminus...........**25** D4

Cascade Rd

Chubb River

Sentinel Rd

Old-Military Rd

John Brown Rd

Olympic Jumping Complex

To Heart Lake Rd (2.5 mi);
Olympic Sports Complex (4.5 mi);
ADK Adirondack Loj (5mi);
ADK High Peaks Information Center;
Mt Van Hoevenberg (8.5mi);
High Peaks Cyclery (8.5 mi)

are open daily from mid-December to mid-March and mid-May to mid-October from 9am to 4pm. In addition to the sites covered below, the Winter Passport ($39) includes admission for ice-skating, a gondola ride at Whiteface Mountain and a cross-country trail pass.

Hear behind-the-scenes stories with a tour of the **Olympic Center** (800-462-6236; 2634 Main St; adult/child $8/6) which was used for the 1980 Olympics and houses four ice-skating rinks, one where the underdog US Hockey team beat the USSR in 1980's memorable game. You can watch athletes training here for free or take in a hockey game. Inside the center, the **Lake Placid Winter Olympic Museum** (adult/child/senior $11/8/8; ☺ 10am-5pm) displays memorabilia from past Olympics, including a fascinating vintage skate display and the famous Olympic torches. It was on the adjacent speed skating oval that speed skater Eric Heiden made history by winning five individual gold medals. Skate this famous **rink** (adult/child $7/5) and then warm up by the fire pit.

Whiteface (www.whiteface.com) a popular ski area and the official Olympic ski mountain, is located southeast of town. It's home to the **Olympic Jumping Complex** (☎ 518-523-2202; 5486 Cascade Rd; adult/child/senior $11/8/8), the training facility for the US Olympic ski-jump teams. You can stand at the base of the jumps or take a chairlift followed by an elevator ride to the top of the 26-story viewing room of

the 120m ski jump tower. The **Olympic Sports Complex** (☎ 518-523-4436; Rte 73; adult/child $8/6), at Mt Van Hoevenberg, is the site of the Olympic bobsled run, luge and skeleton tracks. Feeling adventurous? Suit up for an actual **bobsled ride** (adult/child under 12 yr $75/65) piloted by a professional brakeman, which starts at the half-mile point on the same icy track raced by Olympians. If not, you can always **cross-country ski**: there are 50km (30 miles) of trails here (ask at the Olympic Sports Complex for details).

JOHN BROWN FARM & GRAVE
The famous American abolitionist who was hanged for leading a raid on the US Arsenal at Harpers Ferry, WV, is buried outside Lake Placid in North Elba. The **historic site** (☎ 518-523-3900; John Brown Rd; ☺ 10am-5pm Wed-Sat & 1-5pm Sun May-Oct), off Rte 73, includes Brown's farm and his gravestone.

HIGH PEAKS
A spectacular range of tall peaks – 46 of which measure over 4000ft – dominate the Lake Placid–Keene Valley area. **Mt Marcy** (5344ft) is the most popular peak to tackle, followed closely behind by Algonquin (5114ft). In winter most of these hiking trails are used by downhill skiers.

Phelps Trail (9.5 miles) is the eastern approach to Mt Marcy and starts at the main crossroads in Keene Valley. Another well-known trail is the 130-mile Northville–Lake Placid Trail, which starts near Great Sacandaga Lake in the southern Adirondacks and winds through high meadows and dense pine forests into the High Peaks area.

ADK High Peaks Information Center (☎ 518-523-3441; www.adk.org; Adirondack Loj Rd, Lake Placid) should be the first stop for planning a hiking or skiing trip through the High Peaks. It has maps, trail guides and other useful information for staying on the trails and avoiding bears. The center has an **information number** (☎ 518-523-3518) for daily weather and trail conditions in the North Country.

Activities
HIKING & CLIMBING
Most trails (used for hiking in summer and skiing in winter) start at or near the ADK High Peaks Information Center. One of the best short hiking options in the area is **Mt Jo** (2.3 miles round-trip, moderate), named

---

BUNK DOWN AMID HIGH PEAKS

ADK Adirondak Loj (☺ 518-523-3441; www.adk.org; Heart Lake Rd/Adirondak Loj Rd; campsite $18-35, dm $54-64, d $159 incl breakfast) Sitting on Heart Lake at the feet of the High Peaks, this vintage lodge serves as a base for exploring the nearby hiking and skiing trails. Inside, curl up in a rocking chair in front of the stone fireplace presided over by a moose head. There's also a good library of books and magazines on the Adirondacks. In addition to dorms and private rooms, there's an adjacent campground with tent, lean-tos and canvas cabin sites in a pretty wood.

All Loj room rates include breakfast; you can also arrange dinner ($18) in advance. The food is served family-style at long tables.

in 1877 after Josephine Schofield, who was engaged to Henry Van Hoevenberg, but she died before they were to be married. The trail to the summit rises dramatically over Heart Lake. From the boulder ledge at the summit, you can see half a dozen of the High Peaks, including Mts Marcy and Algonquin.

Rock-climbers scale up Wallface Mountain in the High Peaks. For climbing resources and trips, contact **Alpine Endeavors** (☎ 845-658-3094; www.alpineendeavors.com).

Mt Van Hoevenberg (4.4 miles round-trip, moderate) is a healthy stroll through the woods garnering views of the High Peaks.

Want a guide? You can hire one, as well as getting outfitted with backpacks and books, at the **Mountain Adventure Center** (☎ 518-523-3764) in Lake Placid.

BICYCLING

The Lake Placid area is great bicycling country, and even hosts annual Iron Man competitions. In summer, the cross-country ski trails at Mt Van Hoevenberg and Whiteface Mountain are open to mountain bikers, both experienced and novice. Bikes and helmets are available to rent at the **High Peaks Cyclery** (☎ 518-523-3764; www.highpeakscyclery.com; 2733 Main St; per day $35) or at the **Mt Van Hoevenberg Olympic Sports Complex** (☎ 518-523-8972).

FISHING, CANOEING & KAYAKING

The west branch of the Ausable River (*oh-sable*) is one of the most fabled trout streams in the northeast. **Jones Outfitters** (☎ 518-523-3468; www.jonesoutfitters.com; 2733 Main St; fly-fishing half/full day $165/235) sells fishing licenses, along with leading courses and fly-fishing trips all year. Canoes and kayaks can also be hired.

Middle Earth Expeditions (☎ 518-523-7172; www.adirondackrafting.com) is a year-round outfitter specializing in whitewater rafting.

Sleeping

The press of the Olympic stamp is everywhere: yep, the prices are the steepest in the Adirondacks. Most of the cheaper motels extend along Saranac Ave, yet staying on Main St places you in walking distance of the shops, restaurants and Olympic sites.

Art Devlin's Olympic Motor Lodge (☎ 518-523-3700; www.artdevlins.com; 2764 Main St; r low-season/high-season from $68/110; ☒) This place screams vintage Olympic nostalgia. Bunk down in comfy, spacious rooms with tranquil Northwoods

lodge-style decor and fridges, and check out the 1950s ski-jumping trophies in the lobby (won by Art Devlin himself).

Mountain View Inn (☎ 518-523-2439, 800-499-2668; 140 Main St; d $87-145) This well-maintained, simple and independent inn is one of the best deals on Main St. The name is a bit misleading, as most rooms don't provide a room with a view experience.

our pick **Golden Arrow Lakeside Resort** (☎ 518-523-3353; www.golden-arrow.com; 2559 Main St; d $90-200; ☎ ☒ ♨) This ecofriendly hotel is right on the lake and has a beach, free canoes, heated pool, saunas, Jacuzzi and racquetball court.

Mirror Lake Inn (☎ 518-523-2544; www.mirrorlakeinn.com; 5 Mirror Lake Dr; d from $235; ☒ ☒ ♨) This is an Adirondacks classic and one of the most elegant retreats in upstate New York, with gracious white porches, crackling fires and afternoon tea. Swim on the private beach, canoe, or do yoga on the dock.

Lake Placid Lodge (☎ 518-523-2700; www.lakeplacidlodge.com; Whiteface Inn Rd; r from $400; ☒) The native and artisan-crafted furnishings and decor of this arts and crafts–style lodge are so authentic they almost seem unreal, as if the whole hotel was a Hollywood set for an Adirondacks adventure film. A grand 1880s hunting lodge converted into a lakeside romantic getaway, it's worth visiting for a drink in the sylvan-styled bar or a meal in the enchanting outdoor dining room – replete with fireplaces and afghans for chilly evenings. In winter ice-skating, and wood-burning stoves, create a festive nostalgia.

Eating

While Main St is the go-to dining spot, don't miss the gems off the main drag. Pick up fresh produce and picnic goodies at the **Lake Placid Farmers' Market** (Lake Placid Center for the Arts; 17 Algonquin Dr; ☼ 9am-1pm Jun-Oct).

Blue Berry Bakery (☎ 518-523-4539; 26 Main St) Addictive apple strudel, blueberry scones and linzer tortes.

Big Mountain Deli & Creperie (☎ 518-532-3222; 2475 Main St; mains $7-12; ☼ breakfast & lunch) How can you not love a deli that offers sandwiches in three sizes: Yeti, Sasquatch and Big Foot? In this casual storefront joint, you'll see folks noshing on savory and sweet crepes and delish breakfasts such as an egg, sausage, maple mayo and brie panini. Good coffee, too.

NEW YORK STATE

Brown Dog Café & Wine Bar (☎ 518-523-3036; 2409 Main St; mains $7-22; ☼ 11am-9pm) With 60 wines by the glass, savory bistro fare and an intimate, eclectic feel, this is the most authentically European cafe in Lake Placid.

Chair 6 (☎ 518-523-3630; 5993 Sentinel Rd; mains $8-20; ☼ breakfast, lunch & dinner Wed-Sun) Foodies, skiers, and bleary-eyed, bed-headed locals wander in to this simple dining room in a small house for sweet-potato pancakes, savory soups, fresh ravioli and pork saltimbocca with sage. We like the organic food and atmosphere.

our pick Caribbean Cowboy (☎ 518-523-3836; 2126 Saranac Ave; mains $17-28; ☼ 5-10pm) This rollicking restaurant offers a rotating eclectic menu of creative, spicy chicken, fish and vegetarian dishes in a convivial atmosphere intensified by the potent cocktails.

Paradox Lodge (☎ 518-523-9078; www.paradoxlodge. com; 76 Saranac Ave; mains $24-40; ☼ 6-8:30pm) Eating in the colorful dining room of this Victorian B&B is like visiting a charming friend's quirky house for a dinner party and then stumbling upstairs to your cozy room. Veal with morels and cognac fill the air with tantalizing aromas.

Interlaken Inn (☎ 518-523-3180; 15 Interlaken Ave; mains $25-30; ☼ dinner) This old Victorian house features a lovely, gleaming bar, creative seafood and poultry dishes, and desserts such as a phyllo-wrapped crème brûlée.

Drinking & Entertainment

A six-week season of concerts in July and August, the **Lake Placid Sinfonetta** (www.lakeplacidsin fonetta.org) includes free outdoor 'cushion concerts,' which some boaters attend by floating over to listen, at the **Lake Placid Center for the Arts** (☎ 518-523-2512; www.lakeplacidarts.org; 17 Algonquin Dr).

Fun bars and a few dance clubs line Main St. Peek in to see which vibe suits you.

our pick Cottage (☎ 518-523-2544; 26 Main St; dishes $8-12; ☼ 11:30am-10pm, cocktails to midnight) Just like it sounds: this cozy cottage right on the shores of Mirror Lake doubles as a cheerful lunch spot and the most laid-back (and, dare we say, fun) cocktail spot in town. Come for a drink and pub food at sunset: this place just oozes summertime relaxation.

Lake Placid Pub and Brewery (☎ 518-523-3813; 813 Mirror Lake Dr; ☼ 11:30am-2am) Salvaged church-stained glass presides over the social buzz at this award-winning local microbrewery. Try the Ubu Ale, a chocolate ale named after a chocolate Labrador who used to frequent the place (and drink the beer).

Getting There & Around

Adirondack Trailways (☎ 800-776-7548) stops at 326 Main St. Lake Placid is within reach of the **Adirondack Regional Airport** (☎ 518-891-4600; www.saranaclake.com/airport; 96 Airport Rd, Saranac Lake).

Placid Express (☎ 518-523-2597) runs a free, wheelchair-accessible trolley service during summer.

SARANAC LAKE
pop 5000

Lake Placid's shy twin sister may not be as flashy (or as famous), but she has nothing to be modest about: Saranac Lake is a delightful little place on its own, and a perfect base for exploring the High Peaks. Situated in the middle of a chain of lakes, including the Upper, Middle and Lower Saranac, the village of Saranac Lake was a major tuberculosis treatment center in the late 19th century. The first sanitarium for the treatment of tuberculosis was established here in 1884 as an alternative to the tuberculosis sanatoria of Europe.

If you're looking for a lot of faux-Alpine decor and a raucous après-ski (or après-anything) scene, you might be disappointed. Spend the day canoeing or kayaking on Saranac Lake, and then head to a bar or cafe, where you're more likely to chill out with locals than tourists. This is an authentic, refreshing place – not unlike the Adirondacks themselves.

Information

Several banks and ATMs are on Broadway, Church and Main Sts.

Adirondack Medical Center (☎ 518-891-4141; www. amccares.com; Lake Colby Dr) Northwest of downtown; the major hospital in the region.

Blue Line Sport Shop (☎ 518-891-4680; 82 Main St; ☼ 8:30am-5:30pm Mon-Sat, 9am-3pm Sun) It has hiking, fishing, and camping supplies, plus cross-country ski rental.

Saranac Lake Chamber of Commerce (☎ 518-891-1990; www.saranaclake.com; 30 Main St; ☼ 8:30am-5:30pm Mon-Fri, 10am-3pm Sat & Sun summer) Tourist info and resources.

Sights & Activities

The surrounding wilderness, while not as dramatic as the High Peaks region, is remote and secluded for hiking.

ROBERT LOUIS STEVENSON COTTAGE

The **house** (☎ 518-891-1462; 11 Stevenson La; adult/child $5/free; ☼ 9:30am-noon & 1-4:30pm Tue-Sun Jul–mid-Sep) was Stevenson's home for the winter of 1887–88, when he came to Saranac to 'take the cure' for tuberculosis. It's home to the largest collection of Stevenson memorabilia in the US.

COTTAGE ROW
The little-known historic 'cure cottages,' dating from the days when Saranac Lake was a mecca for people seeking a cure for tuberculosis, should be of interest to history buffs. The best-restored houses are on Park Ave between Catherine and Grove Sts.

SIX NATIONS INDIAN MUSEUM
About 14 miles north of Saranac Lake, this museum (☎ 518-891-2299; adult/child $2/1; ☉ 10am-6pm Jul-Sep) helps to preserve the culture of the Iroquois Confederation, and stands as a reminder to visitors that the Native American culture and history long predates their contact with Europeans.

CANOEING
Around Upper Saranac Lake, the **St Regis Wilderness Canoe Area** is prized by canoeists for its lack of motorized boats, cars or roads. This area is composed of 58 lakes and ponds where you can canoe for weeks, or put in for a leisurely afternoon. The tourist office, along with local outfitters, can recommend canoe trips to you.

There are many outdoor outfitters in the area that can help you organize a canoe trip. **Adirondack Lakes & Trails Outfitters** (☎ 800-491-0414; www.adirondackoutfitters.com; 541 Lake Flower Ave; ☉ 9am-5pm) gives guided tours and rents canoes, kayaks, skis and hiking and camping equipment.

Mac's Canoe Livery (☎ 518-891-1176; www.macs canoe.com; 5859 Rte 30, Lake Clear) offers canoes in summer (and cross-country skis and snowshoes in winter).

Sleeping
Saranac Lakes Islands Campground (☎ 518-891-3170; campsite $15) The 87 state-maintained campsites in and around Lower and Middle Saranac Lakes have tables, pit fireplaces and toilets. There's a fine little sandy beach reachable by an easy half-mile trail.

Adirondack Motel (☎ 518-891-2116, 800-416-0117; www.adirondackmotel.com; 23 Lake Flower Ave/Rte 86; d $90; ☉ 🖭) Strong coffee and homemade muffins greet you as the sun rises on the lake at this immaculate, quiet motel.

ourpick **Gauthier's Saranac Motor Inn** (☎ 518-891-1950; 143 Lake Flower Ave/Rte 86; r from $69; ☉ 🖭)

FORT TICONDEROGA
A strategic point during the French and Indian War, **Fort Ticonderoga** (☎ 518-585-2821; Rte 74; adult/child/senior $15/7/13.50; ☉ 9:30am-5pm May-Oct) straddles the southern end of Lake Champlain, which divides New York state and Vermont. Apparently the French thought it an ideal spot: they built the fort in 1755 to control the southern reaches of their conquests in America. While the fort is open, events include fife and drum concerts, historical drills and craft demonstrations. It's a picturesque and clear vantage point – no wonder it was fought over for so long.

In a 1950s fantasy world where everything is cute and comforting, this would be the fantasy vintage motel. The owners couldn't be friendlier, the rooms (with views) couldn't be cozier, and the kayaking straight from the waterfront lawn couldn't be easier.

Sunday Pond B&B (☎ 518-891-1531; www.sunday pond.com; Rte 30; d $50-89) Want rustic and comfortable, with hikes out the door? You got it: old quilts, antiques, screened-in porches and hearty meals (mains $10 to $25), too. There's great mountain-biking, fishing and canoeing from here.

Porcupine B&B (☎ 518-891-5160; 350 Park Ave; www. theporcupine.com; d from $155; ☉) This historic 1903 cure 'cottage' is comfortably luxurious, with a gorgeous staircase, porches, six fireplaces, a bar and a billiards table: it's hard to leave.

Eating
Little Italy (☎ 518-891-9000; 12 Main St; ☉ 7am-7pm Mon-Fri, 9am-6pm Sat & Sun) The guys tossing dough in the front window suggest this place is the real deal. One bite confirms it.

Lakeview Deli (☎ 518-891-2101; 102 River St; ☉ 7am-7pm Mon-Fri, 9am-6pm Sat & Sun) Facing the lake, this little deli serves excellent sandwiches made to order, along with its own fresh breads and soups.

Nori's Whole Foods (☎ 518-891-6079; 68 Main St; ☉ 9am-7pm Mon-Fri, to 5pm Sat, 10am-4pm Sun) Fresh produce and vegan/vegetarian items.

Eat n' Meet (☎ 518-591-3149; 139 Broadway; mains $6-12; ☉ noon-9pm Sun-Thu, to 10pm Sat & Sun) With Elvis on the porch and mini-golf on the upper lawn, this is a funky old house that cooks homestyle, locally sourced creative dishes to take away (or

NEW YORK STATE

DETOUR – ROUTE 22 TICONDEROGA TO ESSEX

This winding road curves along the shores of smooth, sculpted Lake Champlain. A twist here leads past meadows covered in Queen Anne's lace or freshly cut pastures bearing the mower's signature corduroy ribs. In the early morning, the road is as much a commuter route for people as it is for barn swallows and porcupines; in the evening, post-dinner strollers claim the unused lanes and wave politely at the passing cars. **Westport** and **Essex,** villages that face the lake and its attendant Green Mountains, seem more like satellites of Vermont, tidy and dignified – unusual exemptions from the brawny industrial towns typically found in the Adirondacks.

Browse the bookshop, have dinner and a glass of wine, and then walk upstairs to sleep in the Oscar Wilde or Marcel Proust room at the charming **Inn on the Library Lawn** (☎ 518-577-7748; 1234 Stevenson Rd, Westport; www.theinnonthelibrarylawn.com; d $71-139) an historic inn overlooking Lake Champlain.

---

eat at the tiny sit-down space while you watch the chefs in action).

our pick Blue Moon (☎ 518-891-1301; 55 Main St; mains $9-18; ☺ breakfast & lunch, dinner Tue-Sat) The best breakfast – and probably lunch – in town. At night, try Adirondack tapas and a beer.

Belvedere Restaurant (☎ 518-891-9873; 57 Bloomingdale Ave/Rte 3; dishes $10-22; ☺ lunch & dinner Tue-Sat) The 'Bel' is old-school Italian personified. Eat at the bar where all the action takes place among the local characters.

Waterhole No 3 (☎ 518-891-9502; 43 Main St) Across the street from the town hall, the Waterhole is a beer-and-whiskey kind of place that features local rock and folk.

Getting There & Away

Adirondack Regional Airport (☎ 518-891-4600; www.saranaclake.com/airport; 96 Airport Rd, Saranac Lake) is 5 miles from Saranac Lake. **Adirondack Trailways** (☎ 800-776-7548) stops at **Hotel Saranac** (101 Main St).

CENTRAL ADIRONDACKS

As you venture deeper into the Adirondacks, the outdoor recreation options expand, with paddling in the serene, remote-feeling Fulton Chain of Lakes a major high point.

BLUE MOUNTAIN LAKE & AROUND
pop 126

This town is a tiny, heavenly spot that's easy to miss if you've caught Adirondack Fever – where every view is so gorgeous you're liable to lose your bearings. Blue Mountain Lake is enclosed in demure mountains and dotted with heavenly blue ponds and lakes. Paddling through the quiet waterways to outcast islands

or pitching a tent in front of such a vista is awe-inspiring.

One of the finest regional museums in the US, the **Adirondack Museum** (☎ 518-352-7311; www.adkmuseum.org; Rte 30; adult/child/senior $18/8/17; ☺ 10am-5pm late May–mid-Oct) focuses on different aspects of Adirondack life. Wander through indoor and outdoor exhibits of rustic Adirondack furniture displayed in a restored Victorian cottage, a typical 19th-century luxury resort hotel room or a hermits' camp. Boating enthusiasts in particular will enjoy old boats, from dugouts and birch-bark canoes to speedboats.

Experience the rustic yet elegant summer life of the early 20th-century Vanderbilts at the **Sagamore Great Camp** (☎ 315-354-5311; www.sagamore.org; Sagamore Rd, Raquette Lake; r adult/child $279/139 for two nights incl meals; ☺ tours Jun-Oct, adult/child $10/4), which was one of many 'great camps' built between the end of the Civil War and the beginning of WWI. Staying here is a unique, family-oriented affair with communal meals and old-fashioned pastimes on Raquette Lake.

Blue Mountain (elevation 3759ft; 4 miles round-trip, difficult) is a popular family hike that starts out leisurely and morphs into a steady climb.

Midway between Inlet and Raquette Lake, **Eighth Lake Campground** (☎ 315-354-4120; www.reserveamerica.com; Rte 28, Eighth Lake; campsite $15; ☺ mid-Apr–mid-Nov) has pretty sites on Eighth Lake's shore and beach.

Families return year after year to rustic **Hemlock Hall B&B** (☎ 518-352-7706, 518-359-9065; d incl breakfast & dinner $150-200), which commands a spectacular view of Blue Mountain Lake. The main cedar and pine lodge has an enormous granite fireplace, window seats and an inviting porch. Swim off the beach or canoe before dinner.

An ideal spot for couples, the c 1903 **Big Moose Inn** (☎ 315-357-2042; www.bigmooseinn.com; 1510 Big Moose Rd, Eagle Bay; r $129-229) offers comfortable, vintage rooms, a boat dock and a classic lodge restaurant serving prime rib and seafood.

OLD FORGE & AROUND
pop 1600

The name says it all: Old Forge feels like a far outpost compared to Lake Placid. The western entry point to the Adirondacks, Old Forge (and the neighboring village of Thendara) is part *au naturel,* part amusement parks and pancake houses. It's the snowmobiling capital of the region during winter, while summer attracts canoe and hiking buffs.

Contact the Old Forge **tourist information center** (☎ 315-369-6983; www.oldforgeny.com; Main St; 8am-5pm Mon-Sat & 9am-5pm Sun), for a map of mountain-biking and hiking trails, plus fishing information. For hiking and camping equipment, go to the **Mountainman Outdoor Supply Company** (☎ 315-369-2300, Main St).

Most shops and businesses are along Rte 28 (Main St).

Sights & Activities

Although the town of Old Forge is straight-up Americana fun, the wilderness around the town is some of the most remote in the park.

The **Adirondack Scenic Railroad** (www.adirondackrr.com; adult/child/senior $30/17/27) operates vintage open-window coaches through some very pretty country between the old Thendara and Minnehaha stations, complete with fake weekly train robberies.

Made up of eight lakes – from the pond at Old Forge to Eighth Lake – the **Fulton** chain of lakes stretches for about 20 miles from Old

Forge to Raquette Lake. Old Forge to Third Lake is popular with boaters.

In September, the **Adirondack Classic** (☎ 518-891-2744) also known as the 90-miler, is a 90-mile race (and party) from Old Forge to Saranac Lake.

Good canoeing spots include **Nick's Lake**, **Third Lake**, **Seventh Lake**, and **Raquette Lake**. If you're an experienced canoer, try heading down the north branch of the Moose River.

Rent canoes at the marinas on most lakes, or try friendly **Tickner's Adirondack Canoe Outfitters** (☎ 315-369-6286; www.ticknerscanoes.com; 1 Riverside Dr, Old Forge; canoe hire per day $28).

Sleeping & Eating

There is no shortage of basic motels along Rte 28 between the towns of Blue Mountain Lake and Old Forge.

If you've got a boat it's possible to camp at **Alger Island Campground** (☎ 315-369-3224; campsite $15; May-Sep), a site only reachable by watercraft. To find **Nick's Lake Campground** (☎ 315-369-3314; 278 Bisby Rd; campsite $22; May-Sep) take Rte 28 through Old Forge, turn onto the road beside the school and follow the signs.

Van Auken's Inne & Restaurant (☎ 315-369-3033; www.vanaukensinne.com; 108 Forge St, Thendara; d from $80) This landmark across the street from the Adirondack Scenic Railroad station is a beautiful old white Victorian building with a long front porch for relaxing in this tiny town.

our pick **Woods Inn** (☎ 315-357-5300; 148 Rte 28; mains $12-18; d low-/high-season from $65/125) One of our favorite places in the Adirondacks, a rustically elegant turn-of-the-century 21-room hotel, restaurant and bar that oozes with old-fashioned summer nostalgia. The porches and grounds overlook serene Fourth Lake.

TOP FIVE WAYS TO RELAX IN THE 'DACKS

- At **Eighth Lake Campground** (p176), pitch a tent and stare at the stars then watch the sun rise over the placid waters
- Have a grand old-fashioned summer weekend at the **Sagamore Great Camp** (p176) or the **Woods Inn**
- Scale the High Peaks: **Mt Jo** (p172) is a stout peak with easy-to-reach views of wilderness anchored by darling Heart Lake.
- Glide across the pristine blue waters of **Saranac Lake** (p174) in a kayak: adventure has never been so relaxing.
- Stand at the top of the ski jump at Lake Placid's **Olympic Sports Complex** (p172), and take in the stunning vista.

Ozzie's Coffee (☎ 315-369-6246; 3019 Main St; ⏲ breakfast & lunch) Strong coffee, wooden booths and bagels imported daily from Brooklyn.

Tamarack Café & Movie House (☎ 315-357-2001; 153 Rte 28; ⏲ breakfast & lunch) Fantastic breakfast or lunch, then a matinee next door? Every little town should have a place like this.

Sisters Bistro (☎ 315-369-1053; 479 Rte 28; mains $10-20; ⏲ daily Jun-Sep, Sat & Sun Oct-May) Divine small plates and wine in this exquisitely restored vintage house with dramatic details.

Seventh Lake House Restaurant (☎ 315-357-6028; 479 Rte 28; mains $14-24; ⏲ daily Jun-Sep, Sat & Sun Oct-May) At the west edge of Seventh Lake, this is one of the best dinner spots west of Blue Mountain Lake. The owners call it 'civilized dining in the wilderness.'

THOUSAND ISLANDS & ST LAWRENCE SEAWAY

Be prepared for plenty of wistful sighs and smiles of delight. Dubbed the 'Garden of the Great Spirit' by the native Iroquois, the watery world of the Thousand Islands and St Lawrence Seaway is nothing short of fantastic. This is the kind of place where first-time visitors take one look and say, 'How come we haven't come here *before*?' Good question: somehow this stunning area, one of the premier vacation destinations for the Rockefellers and other tycoons during the Gilded Age, fell off the definitive American vacation map and has remained a well-kept secret to most of the country ever since.

The good news: this just means there's all the more for you to enjoy without the hassle of crowds and prices. Don't be surprised if you pinch yourself to make sure you're not dreaming: yes, you're really in New York. But you're also practically in Canada, just a bridge or a boat over the water. Best of both worlds? You bet.

Still not convinced? The stunning blue waters of Lake Ontario and the St Lawrence River provide a vivid backdrop to the small towns and villages, many with a weathered yet cozy feel, sprinkled throughout the region. The air is crisp and clean and breathtaking views are in abundance, with never-ending pink and purple sunsets and a distinct off-the-beaten-path allure. And then the finale: you stand on the waterfront and gaze out

at sunset towards countless little islands (all 1864 of them) that give this region its name. Is this place *real*?

If you arrive from crowded New York City or industrial Syracuse you'll feel as if you've stepped into another era – or even another world.

THOUSAND ISLANDS

While it would take a lifetime to visit all of the islands, the towns of the Thousand Islands – Alexandria Bay, Clayton, Cape Vincent and Sackets Harbor – are as manageable as they are charming. Each town is within easy driving distance of each other, so it's possible to stay in one, sightsee in the next and sup in the next before circling back. Driving here is a pleasure, with stunning views between the villages on the scenic Seaway Trail. Rte 12 itself is a road-tripper's dream, lined with small state parks, funky vintage motels and plenty of local color. While the towns listed below are relatively small, they each have a grocery store, post office, bank, gas station and ATM – oh, and a public waterfront for strolling and canoodling at sunset.

Keep in mind that many businesses shut down from October to April (or later) when the snow starts piling up.

ALEXANDRIA BAY & AROUND
pop 1100

With a tacky, old-fashioned feel that will make kids coo with delight and make jaded adults eat ice-cream cones and play mini-golf, Alex Bay, as the locals call it, is the crown jewel of tourism in the area. So what if the crown's ever so tarnished? Fading neon signs and boarded-up buildings share the

---

WHAT'S IN A NAME?

How were the Thousand Islands created? An Iroquois legend has it that the Great Spirit, or Master of Life, created a bountiful and beautiful land for the Indian nations that had agreed not to fight each other. When the nations broke their promise, the Great Spirit sent messengers to retrieve the paradise in a huge blanket. As the land was being lifted into the sky, it fell out of the blanket and broke into thousands of pieces, creating the Thousand Islands.

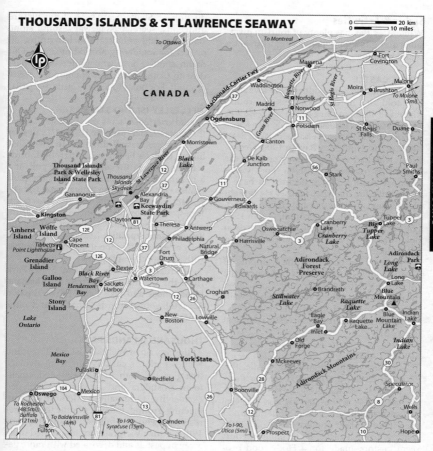

THOUSANDS ISLANDS & ST LAWRENCE SEAWAY

tree-lined streets with 1950s mom-and-pop stores, homegrown motels and kitschy souvenir shops. Come summertime, the party scene cranks up: expect sunburned 20- and 30-somethings shamelessly knocking back pirate-themed rum concoctions in the many bars. Be sure to stick around for the sunset – it's full-on gorgeous.

At the beginning of the 20th century, Alex Bay was a bustling resort town boasting several luxurious see-and-be-seen hotels. Today these grand hotels are gone (along with many of the uber-rich, who are probably now partying with Paris Hilton in Saint-Tropez) but many of the estates – built during the same time on privately owned islands – remain. The most jaw-dropping, gasp-inducing of these is

George Boldt's magnificent castle (p180) on the ironically named Heart Island.

Orientation & Information

The village's walkable commercial strip centers on James, Market and Church Sts: think shops, tour-boat companies, bars and restaurants.

The **Alexandria Bay Chamber of Commerce** (☎ 315-482-9531, 800-541-2110; 7 Market St; ⏰ 9am-5pm mid-May–early Oct, 9am-5pm Mon-Fri early Oct–mid-May) has information on the region. For a wider array of info on tourism along the St Lawrence River, stop by the **1000 Islands International Council** (☎ 315-482-2520, 800-847-5263; Collins Landing; ⏰ 8am-5pm Apr-Oct). It's under the Thousand Islands Bridge inside the New York State Welcome Center.

Sights & Activities

While Alex Bay has plenty of touristy diversions and gift shops, sightseeing focuses on island hopping.

BOLDT CASTLE

Billed as the site of the 'saddest true-love story ever told,' it's hard to skip this 127-room, Rhineland-inspired stone **castle** (☎ 315-482-9724; www.boldtcastle.com; adult/child $7/4.50; ☺ 10am-6:30pm mid-May–mid-Oct, to 7:30pm late-Jun–early-Sep) on **Heart Island**, across from Alex Bay. In 1900, George Boldt, who had worked his way up from the kitchen to ownership of New York City's Waldorf–Astoria Hotel, decided to have a castle built for his wife, Louise. He bought Heart Island and had it reshaped into a heart. As the castle was nearing completion in 1904 Louise unexpectedly died. A heartbroken Boldt halted work on the estate, and it was left to decay until 1977.

Romantic yet haunting, the tramping of hundreds of visitors' feet can't take away the cold, eerie feel the place gives off, especially in the upper rooms, where you'll find bare walls covered in graffiti from local ne'er-do-wells.

The only way to reach the castle is by boat (see p181).

SINGER CASTLE

Though far smaller than Boldt Castle, this 28-room **castle** (☎ 877-324-3275; www.singercastle. com; tours adult/child/senior $14/6/11; ☺ weekends mid-May–mid-Oct, daily mid-Jun–Labor Day, tours 10am-4pm) on **Dark Island** surpasses Boldt's interior ambience, if not its sheer mystery. Based on a 13th-century Scottish castle, its thrilling interiors seem custom made for a Hollywood pro-

duction of Shakespeare's *Macbeth*: picture dungeons, secret passageways, spiral stone staircases and subterranean labyrinths, all perfect for wandering around moaning 'Out damn spot!' Those who prefer sunny gardens to Gothic intrigue will enjoy the pretty grounds. For boats to Singer Castle, see p181.

WELLESLEY ISLAND STATE PARK

Spread over 2600 acres on Wellesley Island, this fantastic **state park** (☎ 315-482-2722; admission $7, $5 after 5pm) has all the bells and whistles: hiking trails, a beach, a campground, bird-watching, miniature and nine-hole golf, and a marina. At the southeast end of the park is **Minna Anthony Common Nature Center** (☎ 315-482-2479; admission free; ☺ 8:30am-4:30pm high season, 10am-4pm low season), which includes a museum and wildlife sanctuary. Consider joining the **Voyager Canoe Expedition** (adult/child $4/2, 1-2hrs), a daily ride in a 36ft canoe along river shorelines with a knowledgeable guide.

To reach Wellesley Island State Park from the US mainland, cross the **Thousand Islands Bridge** and take Exit 51. You'll pay a $2.50 toll going towards Canada, but it's free southbound.

THOUSAND ISLANDS PARK

At the very tip of Wellesley Island, Thousand Islands Park is a curious enigma of a village that gives off both an old-fashioned, small-town nostalgia and an air of privileged exclusivity. Originally a Methodist camp meeting-ground, today it's home to summer residents who carefully maintain elaborate 19th-century Victorian homes painted in an array of pastels and decorated with more gables than you can count. It's more restrained than opulent, but something about this place still screams 'old money.' Or maybe it just screams 'tourists go away.' Yep, the residents here don't exactly seem thrilled by outsiders' curiosity. Our advice? Ignore the snooty factor, and enjoy a stroll around: unlike the old days, visitors are blissfully free to wander around. The whole place is on the National Registry of Historic Places and features its own movie theater, playground, library and post office. Nice, huh?

And then there's the infamous golf club. The Thousand Islands Park was once a private golf club, and membership came with a hefty price tag – $100,000 for initiation. These days, golfers head over to **Wellesley State**

NEW YORK STATE

DETOUR – OGDENSBURG

North of Alexandria Bay and half-way to Massena, this town is the oldest (1748) settlement in New York. Visit the **Frederic Remington Museum** (☎ 315-393-2425; www.frederickremington.org; 303 Washington St; admission $6; ☺ 10am-5pm Mon-Sat, 1-5pm Sun May-Oct, 11am-5pm Tue-Sat, 1-5pm Sun Nov-Apr), which houses a large collection of Remington's bronze sculptures, oil paintings and pen-and-ink sketches, as well as many of the artist's personal effects. Remington is best known as a chronicler of the American Western experience.

Park Golf Course (☎ 315-482-9622), a historic – and challenging – nine-hole course just outside the village.

Tours

Get your sea legs on: the only way to reach the castles and islands in the St Lawrence River is by boat. We like **Uncle Sam Boat Tours** (☎ 315-482-2611, 800-253-9229; www.usboattours.com; 45 James St; adult/child $7.50/4.50; May-Oct), who run a shuttle on triple-deck paddle-wheelers to Heart Island every half-hour. Once there, stay as long as you like. The company also offers a variety of dinner and sightseeing tours around the islands, including Singer Castle and 'Millionaires' Row,' some of the more opulent island estates.

Shipshape adventurers might want to explore the islands independently. If you do, check **O'Briens U-Drive** (☎ 315-482-9548; 51 Walton St) for motor and pontoon boat rentals, which can be charged either by the hour, day or week.

Divers interested in checking out some of the hundreds of shipwrecks in the area (some dating back to the 1700s!) should contact the **Seaway Trail** (☎ 315-646-1000; www.seawaytrail.com).

Sleeping

The Ship Motel (☎ 315-482-9518; www.theshipmotel.com; 6 Market St; r low-/high-season from $60/80;) Small, clean, modern rooms near the harbor.

ourpick Maple Crest Motel (☎ 315-482-9518; www.maplecrestmotel.com; 11 Crossman St; r from $85) This charming little place is more European-style B&B than US-style motel, with a nice front porch and landscaped patio blooming with flowers.

Captain Thomson's Resort (☎ 315-482-9961; www.captthomsons.com; 47 James St; r low-/high-season from $59/126;) Right smack on the waterfront, this low-key place offers nicely updated rooms with balconies and two pools (one for the kiddies). Snag a room with a romantic view of Boldt Castle.

Edgewood Resort & Conference Center (☎ 315-482-9923; www.theedgewoodresort.com; 22467 Edgewood Park Rd; r weekday $79-99, weekend $109-139;) With beautifully landscaped grounds right on the river, and northwoods decor, locals swear by the smartly remodeled Edgewood. The beach and dock add to the laid-back resort experience.

The Captain Visger House (☎ 315-681-3422; www.captainvisger.com; 2 Church St; r $159-189, open year-round;) Luxuriate in a little bit of Gilded Age

elegance at this updated B&B with locally sourced, organic breakfasts.

Eating & Drinking

There's some decent eating among the tourist traps. Keep in mind that pickings may be slim in the low season.

Dockside Pub (☎ 315-482-9849; 17 Market St; mains $4-10) You'll find Canadian beer signs, chatty locals and decent pizzas in this waterside joint. Indulge in the poutine, a traditional Canadian dish of French fries, cheese and gravy (sounds terrible, tastes wonderful – ooh la la).

Brass Tacks (☎ 315-482-9805; 24 James St; mains $5-8) This low-ceilinged, low-key tavern serves salads and sandwiches to folks kicking back with a beer or two in the wooden booths.

ourpick Das Village Haus (☎ 315-482-2811; 5 Market St; mains $10-25;) This old cottage with the German name serves up tasty American and international dishes like Austrian wiener schnitzel in a cozy atmosphere. Dine on the flower-lined deck.

Cavallario's Steak & Seafood House (☎ 315-482-9867; 26 Church St; mains $18-22; dinner) Half a block south of James St, this steak-and-seafood joint goes buck wild with its medieval castle theme. If that's your thing, grab your sword and your armor and head over.

Getting There & Around

From the south, take I-81 to just before its northern terminus at the Thousand Islands Bridge taking the exit at Rte 12. Alex Bay is

---

FESTIVAL FEVER

The Thousand Islands area digs festivals so much that they seem to throw one practically every weekend during the summer. It's a perfect way to experience the local culture and kick up your heels (or practice your French) with the natives. Festivals worth checking out are:

- Can Am Festival (www.canamfestival.com; July)
- French Festival (www.capevincent.org; around Bastille Day on the second Saturday in July)
- Antique Boat Show and Regatta, Clayton (www.abm.org, early August)
- Sackets Harbor Oktoberfest (second week of October)
- Reenactment of the Battle of Sackets Harbor (www.sacketsharborbattlefield.org; end of July)
- The Great New York State Food and Wine Festival (www.nysfoodwinefestival.com; Clayton, mid-June)

NEW YORK STATE

then 4 miles to the east. From the northeast, take Rte 37 along the St Lawrence Seaway to Alex Bay.

CLAYTON
pop 1900

Finally, a cute small town where you can actually do what you came here for in the first place: relax. Does that mean there's nothing to do in Clayton? Absolutely not. From museums to fishing to strolling the pier, there's plenty. Yet something about this weathered-looking downtown, dotted with galleries and antique stores, gives off just the right lived-in, sleepy vibe that could relax even the most stressed-out tourist. Once a shipbuilding and lumbering port, Clayton's a fishing mecca for muskie, northern pike and largemouth bass. Stroll around the marina and pretend that cool sailboat is actually yours.

Downtown is just a few blocks of James St and Riverside Dr. The **Clayton Chamber of Commerce** (☎ 315-686-3771; 510 Riverside Dr; ☽ 9am-5pm Jul-Sep, 9am-4pm Mon-Fri Oct-Jun) can give you local maps, info on fishing licenses (you'll need one to fish), and a list of fishing guides.

Sights & Activities

Spend an afternoon poking around downtown; you'll find cute galleries and a great cheese shop.

ANTIQUE BOAT MUSEUM

The sight alone would make a small-craft boating fanatic salivate: 150 freshwater boats, ranging from a Native American dugout to birch-bark canoes, reside at this impressive **museum** (☎ 315-686-4104; www.abm.org; 750 Mary St; adult/child $12/6; ☽ 9am-5pm May-Oct). It's easy to

imagine cruising around the Great Lakes in one of the vintage St Lawrence skiffs or thickly varnished Kris-Kraft pleasure boats with the other millionaire summer residents back in the 1950s.

1000 ISLANDS MUSEUM

This **museum** (☎ 315-686-5794; 312 James St; adult/child $6/2; ☽ 10am-4pm May-Oct) is the home of the 'Muskie Hall of Fame,' the region's most prized fish. There's a replica of the world-record muskellunge, which weighed in at over 69lb when it was caught – one of the largest ever caught in the US.

BOATING & KAYAKING

While Alex Bay is the more popular departure point for boat tours, Clayton's waterfront is more relaxed. Try **Clayton Island Tours** (☎ 315-686-4820; www.claytonislandtours.com; 428 Riverside Dr) for daily boat tours to Boldt Castle and the islands, along with twilight bird-watching excursions.

Kayakers should check out **TI Adventures** (☎ 315-686-2500; www.tiadventures.com; 38714 Rte 12E), offering kayak instruction, rental and tours.

Sleeping

Bertrands Motel (☎ 315-686-3641; 229 James St; r from $67) A classic American motel smack in the middle of town: clean, big rooms, some with kitchenettes.

Wooden Boat Inn House & Motel (☎ 315-686-5004; www.woodenboatinn.com; 606 Alexandria St; r from $69, house rental low-/high-season $350/$1295 weekly) Oozing with nautical charm that's more cozy than cheesy, this excellent motel sports a fully equipped house that's perfect for groups and families.

our pick Thousand Islands Inn (☎ 315-686-3030; www.1000-islands.com; 335 Riverside Dr; r incl breakfast from $75; 🛜 ♿) Fans of that strange American condiment – the creamy orange stuff enigmatically called 'Thousand Islands' salad dressing – will be thrilled to know that it was allegedly invented in the restaurant of this hotel, a charming old brick place that has been hosting visitors for over 100 years. Check out its dizzying array of packages, including the wreck-diving excursions. Dine on fresh fish from the lake and Italian dishes in the classic restaurant (mains $16 to $29) and sip a beer in the atmospheric fisherman's bar.

Islander Marina and Lodge (☎ 315-686-1100; www.islandermarina.com; 500 Theresa St; r $125-150; ♿) The perfect spot for boaters, with dock rental, sunset views of the French Bay marina and comfy, remodeled rooms. Cook out on their gas grills.

Eating & Drinking
Clayton is high on small-town feel but low on pretension – and prices.

Bella's Bistro (☎ 315-686-2341; 602 Riverside Dr; mains $5-8; 🕐 7am-6pm Mon-Fri, Sun 8am-5pm) Stop in for fresh scones and soup-and-salad lunch specials. Snag a table by the window for a fab view of Calumet Island.

Koffee Kove (☎ 315-686-2472; 220 James St; mains $5-10) This down-home sandwich shop/diner serves up simple, super-filling meals (the stuffed meatloaf should keep you going for days) to families and fishermen.

ourpick The Lyric (☎ 315-686-4700; 246 James St; mains $6-23; 🕐 lunch Mon-Sat, dinner Tue-Sat) Renovating the old movie theatre and turning it into a warmly elegant coffee shop and cafe was one of this town's most brilliant ideas. Lunch on paninis and salads, sup on seared salmon, or just hang out with coffee and revel in the cinematic ambience.

The Clipper Inn (☎ 315-686-3842; 126 State St; mains $15-25; 🕐 dinner Tue-Sun) Where locals come for birthdays and Friday nights out, this is one of the best all-around dining spots in the region for fresh seafood and prime rib. Solo travelers, dine at the friendly bar.

Lost Navigator Bar (☎ 315-686-9809; 215 James St) This old-school tavern conjures long winters spent playing pool and drinking Yuengling on draft.

O'Briens (☎ 315-686-1110; 226 Webb St; 🕐 lunch & dinner, to 2am nightly) Chat up the friendly locals or get down to some live music in this big old clapboard house. Bar food served to 10pm.

CAPE VINCENT
pop 800
Sure, this town's small, but it hardly has a Napoleon complex. Cape Vincent has a strong French heritage that goes back to the 17th century, when French missionaries flocked here hoping to convert Iroquois and Onondaga natives to Christianity. More of their countrymen joined them in the 1790s, when French settlers fleeing Napoleon's notorious empire bought land. In a rather ironic twist, several of Napoleon's cronies (and his brother) emigrated here after their defeat at Waterloo; in fact, before the little tyrant died in exile, it was

---

CAMPING
Camping is wildly popular in the Thousand Islands. Take your pick from tons of campgrounds in both US and Canadian state parks on the various islands of the St Lawrence River. For general information, contact **New York State Parks** (☎ 315-482-2593; www.nysparks.com) or **Parks Canada** (☎ 613-923-5261; www.pc.gc.ca).

Wellesley Island State Park (☎ 315-482-2722; Rte I-81; campsite from $15) This is the largest US campground in the area. The park has 430 sites (including 10 cabins) and hot showers. See p180 for more info.

Cedar Point State Park (☎ 315-654-2522; campsite from $15) Park your boat in the marina of this great park 6 miles south of Clayton, with plenty of waterfront campsites. The vintage recreation hall with a stone fireplace, ping pong and a waterfront dining area feels like classic Americana, and it is: established in 1897, it's one of the oldest state parks in New York.

Keewaydin State Park (☎ 315-482-3331; Rte 12; campsite from $15; 🕐 May-Sep) Just west of Alex Bay, this is one of the prettiest parks in the region, with several old gazebos and 41 campsites.

St Lawrence Islands National Park (☎ 613-923-5261; 2 County Rd, RR 3 Mallorytown Landing, Ontario; campsite C$5-15) With about 9 sq km of land area this is the smallest national park in the Canadian system. Primarily water-based, its 21 granite islands and numerous tiny islets are a unique river landscape strewn along 80km of the upper St Lawrence River.

hoped he might seek refuge from the havoc in Europe in little old Cape Vincent.

Now the village celebrates its history with the colorful **French Festival** (www.capevincent.org; around Bastille Day on the 2nd Sat of Jul). Situated on the cape where the St Lawrence River meets Lake Ontario, Cape Vincent boasts stupendous scenery and a tiny, tranquil main street lined with towering trees and old houses. A drive around the roads reveals crashing waves, rugged coastline and outstanding sunsets. Past nightfall, driving out to the lighthouse is straight out of a scene from a Hitchcock film (hopefully minus the bad guys chasing you down the winding road).

Along with black-bass fishing, Cape Vincent is made for daydreaming and strolling along the waterfront.

Cape Vincent Chamber of Commerce (☎ 315-654-2481; www.capevincent.org; 175 James St; ☻ 9am-5pm Mon-Fri), near the ferry dock, can give information about fishing licenses and guides.

Sleeping & Eating

ourpick HI-AYH Tibbetts Point Lighthouse Hostel (☎ 315-654-3450; 33439 County Rte 6; dm with/without HI membership $20/23; mid-May–mid-Oct) This unique hostel is hands-down one of the most unusual and picturesque in the country. On the National Historic Register, it's situated on the grounds of an 1854 lakeside lighthouse that's still used by the coast guard. The dorms are comfy and relaxing, but for those in whom the word 'dorm' instills a fear of pillow fights or burnt popcorn, there are a couple of private rooms. At sundown, sit in the garden and listen to the waves crash against the point.

Buccaneer Motel and B&B (☎ 315-654-2975; 230 N Point St; d $70-185; open year round) Right on the river in a beautiful location, this four-room B&B features a summery lounge with the wicker couches facing floor-to-ceiling glass windows. Sit and watch the boats pass by, grill on the lawn, or lounge on the outdoor hammock. Next door, the cozy and classic motel sports a log cabin feel that's straight out of the 1950s (in a good way).

Taste of Design (☎ 315-654-2007; 288 E Broadway; ☻ from 7am weekdays, from 8am weekends) Across from the fire department, this charming coffee shop is the go-to spot in Cape Vincent for wi-fi, strong coffee and fresh pastries.

Aubrey's Inn (☎ 315-654-3754; 126 S James St; mains $5-18; ☻ breakfast, lunch & dinner) A warm, lovable spot with a lighthouse theme, Aubrey's is a diner by day, supper club by night. At sunset, unwind with the locals at the bar. At sunrise, the same folks gossip over coffee before work.

Getting There & Around

Cape Vincent is on Rte 12E, 28 miles southwest of Alex Bay.

Wolfe Island Ferries (☎ 315-783-0638; car/passenger $6/1; ☻ 8am-7pm May-Oct) makes 11 trips daily (weather permitting) each way between Cape Vincent and Wolfe Island, Canada. The ferry then continues from Wolfe Island to Kingston, Canada, which takes another 35 minutes and is free. The ferry dock in Cape Vincent is at the north terminus of James St.

STORIES OF THE THOUSAND ISLANDS

The **Price is Right Island** was given away on the *Price is Right* game show in 1964.

Longue View Island is the only artificial island; it was created by a doting husband wishing to build a luxurious home for his wife. His efforts were fruitless – his wife ended up running away with another man.

The Skull and Bones Society, a famous secret society at Yale University, owns **Deer Island**. President George W Bush was a member of this society when he attended Yale.

Grindstone Island was the home of the last existing one-room schoolhouse in New York State, which didn't close its doors until 1989. The schoolhouse accommodated children between kindergarten and the 6th grade in its one room.

Abbie Hoffman lived incognito on **Wellesley Island**, under the name Barry Freed, after jumping bail in 1974 on cocaine charges.

Church services are held in the water on the large crescent-shaped inlet that's **Half Moon Bay** in the St Lawrence River near Gananoque, Ontario. During July and August parishioners enjoy open skies as they sit in boats of every sort, while visiting ministers or local clergymen conduct the services on a natural stone pulpit. Ushers paddling about in their canoes pass out prayer books and hymnals to the floating congregation.

SACKETS HARBOR
pop 1400
Sackets Harbor is one of those places you stumble upon accidentally, only to be completely beguiled by its charm. Perched on a bluff overlooking the shores of Lake Ontario, it's a picturesque village with a strong sense of history, where kids ride bikes down Main St past the pretty 19th-century brick homes. When the sun is out the lake sparkles and in fall the trees blaze with color. It's a stunning place to photograph.

It's also a war site, yet with an unmistakable air of peace to it. The Americans won a key naval battle here at the expense of the British during the War of 1812 (see the boxed text). After the war, the harbor's strategic importance made it a major shipping point.

The small **Main St Historic District** starts at Main St, off N Broad. The town's most unusual neighborhood, however, is at the old **Madison Barracks**, a pretty landscaped compound of brick and stone buildings that functioned as military housing from the War of 1812 to WWII. They've been preserved – and transformed – into an idyllic little community with a post office, market and restaurants, all set among the lilac bushes overlooking the bay.

The **Sackets Harbor Chamber of Commerce** (☎ 315-646-1700; 301 W Main St; 🕑 10am-4pm Jun-Aug) can provide information on fishing guides and licenses. The **Sackets Harbor Heritage Area Visitors Center** (☎ 315-646-2321) shares the same building and hours as the chamber. In a pretty old limestone building, the **Seaway Trail Discovery Center** (☎ 1-800-732-9298; www.seawaytrail.com; cnr Ray & W Main Sts; adult/child/senior $4/2/3; 🕑 10am-5pm daily Jul-Aug, weekends May-Jun, Sep-Oct) offers outdoor resources.

The **Sackets Harbor Battlefield State Historic Site** (☎ 315-646-3634; www.sacketsharborbattlefield.org; cnr Main & Washington St; admission $1; 🕑 10am-5pm Wed-Sat year-round, 1-5pm Sun May-Aug) is a former naval base (which was maintained until the 1870s in case of a military attack by Canada) where two battles were fought during the War of 1812. Take a museum tour through the commandant's 1850s residence. Despite its dramatic past, the grounds are now a wonderfully peaceful place to stroll, with lovely harbor views.

On the windswept edge of the Battlefield Site, the **Candlelight Inn** (☎ 315-646-1518; www.imcnet.net/candlelight; 501 W Wasghington St; d incl breakfast $70-145) offers history with a view. Wake up in

THE WAR OF *WHAT*?
Don't feel bad if the phrase the 'War of 1812' doesn't conjure up the kind of iconic images of, say, Appomattox, Iwo Jima or Saigon. For most American and British people, the War of 1812 is skimmed over in history class. Sackets Harbor was once the center of American military operations on Lake Ontario; it was here that American forces staved off a surprise attack by the British in 1813. So who won this little war? One hint: look around you and listen to the accents…

this cozy brick house to the scent of baked-apple pancakes wafting up the stairs.

In the heart of town, you'll find the newly remodeled **Ontario Place** (☎ 315-646-8000; www.ontarioplacehotel.com; 103 General Smith Dr; r from $89, with Jacuzzi from $155; 🔲), a classy old waterfront hotel with 28 large rooms and 10 whirlpool suites.

ourpick **Tin Pan Galley** (☎ 315-646-3812; 110 Main St; mains from $10) is the perfect place for an afternoon cocktail by the fountain in the lush, atmospheric garden. Locals rightly rave about the nouveau twists on classics; we like it just as much for the deep red walls and the cozy old plank floors.

Sackets Harbor Brewing Company (☎ 315-646-2739; 212 W Main St; mains $10-26) Eat inside this former railroad station – now a gorgeous brewpub with a gleaming, dark wood bar – or eat outside at sunset, perched right on the harbor overlooking the marina. Seafood, steaks and salads shine, along with 15 craft beers brewed on site. This is one of the most atmospheric restaurants around. Order a War of 1812 Amber Ale and toast the losing side.

For a town this size, the **Lake Ontario Playhouse** (☎ 315-646-2305; www.playhousecomedy.com; 103 W Main St; 🕑 bar from 6:30pm, comedy shows 9pm Fri & Sat) is a total gem, with a comedy club, cafe and pub wrapped up in an old brick building.

ST LAWRENCE SEAWAY
In 1959, the long-sought joint effort of the Canadian and US governments to create a deepwater channel between the Atlantic Ocean and the Great Lakes paid off and the St Lawrence Seaway opened. The Canadians led the effort, and the US joined in when it became apparent that the canal might be built without its involvement – or benefit.

DETOUR – ATTRACTIONS IN CANADA

Once you've finished touring Wellesley Island, continue across the Thousand Islands Bridge into Canada and visit the **Thousand Islands Skydeck** (☎ 613-659-2335; www.1000islandsskydeck.com; Hill Island, Ontario; adult/child C$10/6; ☼ 9am-6pm Apr-May, 9am-8pm Jun-Aug, 9am-6pm Sep-Oct). Ride an elevator to the top of the observation tower, which offers excellent views of the islands and the river. To enter Canada, US citizens may be asked to show valid ID or a passport at the border; international visitors need a passport. When you're finished, continue across the bridge to the Canadian mainland and look for signs for the **Thousand Islands Parkway**. The parkway runs parallel to Hwy 401 for 25 miles between Gananoque and Brockville, and offers some of the most scenic coastline in the region. Breathtaking views pile up one after the other.

Now operated jointly by both countries, the seaway is a system of 15 locks that allows cargo vessels to travel 2350 miles from the Atlantic Ocean to Duluth, Minnesota, on Lake Superior. Along the way, the water level rises 602ft.

Throw out all notions of the images that the dreaded phrase 'driving in New York' may conjure, from city gridlock to packed Catskills mountain roads. The **New York State Seaway Trail** is the perfect antidote to all of that. Leisurely making its way through small towns and villages, it's a 450-mile scenic driving and bicycling route on a series of highways following the seaway through New York (and northern Pennsylvania) along the St Lawrence River, Lake Ontario and Lake Erie. Green and white 'Seaway Trail' signs help guide you along the historic route. Expect magnificent driving along the deep blue waters of Lake Ontario, sprinkled with colorful fishing boats, or meander through fields, across streams and past dilapidated red barns.

DWIGHT D EISENHOWER LOCK

Now there's an awesome sight you just don't see every day: a 700ft oceangoing ship (or 'laker') passing through a narrow canal, displacing 22 million gallons of water. The best place to see it happen is at Massena's **Eisenhower**

Lock Visitors Center (☎ 315-769-2049; Barnhart Island Rd; ☼ 8am-9pm Jun-Aug), just off Rte 37.

To make sure you get to see a ship passing through, call **Seaway Eisenhower** (☎ 315-769-2422) to hear a 24-hour recorded message giving the estimated arrival times of ships.

ROBERT MOSES STATE PARK

Wildlife enthusiasts will find plenty to gape at here. One of the prettiest **parks** (☎ 315-769-8663; admission $5; ☼ May-Oct) in the northeast, Robert Moses is spacious and serene. Situated on both the mainland and Barnhart Island, many animals call the habitat home. Kids will enjoy the beach and the nature interpretive center. Camp ($15 per campsite) or bunk down in a nice cabin with screened porches ($145 to $245 per week).

FINGER LAKES REGION

Hello, gorgeous. There's a word for this place: wow. Could this be one of the most underrated spots in the country? Picture green, undulating hills dotted with vineyards, wineries and charming villages, throw in 11 scenic lakes, a great college town, a bunch of environmental activists and just enough industry, farming and blue collar ethos to keep things real (along with a dose of savvy NYC sophistication, of course) and you've got the Finger Lakes.

Iroquois legend says the region's 11 lakes are actually the fingerprints of the Great Spirit, created when he reached out his hand to bless the land. Geologists have a different take: they say constant grinding from Ice Age glaciers created the lake valleys, among the deepest on the continent.

It can be daunting to navigate the overwhelming bounty of charming towns and wineries here; stop at, or call **Finger Lakes Tourism** (☎ 315-536-7488, 800-548-4386; www.fingerlakes.org; 309 Lake St, Penn Yan; ☼ 8am-4:30pm) for info on the region.

SOUTHERN TIER

This is the 'famous' part of the Finger Lakes, anchored by Ithaca (known for Cornell University and its gorges) and Corning (known for glass).

ITHACA
pop 30,000
You can't spend more than five minutes in Ithaca without spotting the slogan 'Ithaca is Gorges' on a bumper sticker or T-shirt. The slo-

gan doesn't lie: this is one of the most charming college towns in the country, as funky as it is fetching. Waterfalls and rocky gorges surround Ithaca, a college town dominated as much by a trademark artsy-hippie-outdoorsy vibe as it is by the distinguished Ivy-league ambience of Cornell University. When the students clear out (they double the population during the school year), the locals bust out their best party of the year, the **Ithaca Festival** (www.ithacafestival.org), four days in early June of arts, food, and live music capped off by a parade famous for its off-the-wall Volvo ballet.

Arrive on an early autumn evening, when there's a luxurious hint of chill in the air and you'll find this a magical place. The compact downtown pulses with life most nights, as eclectic crowds spill over sidewalk patios, mimes compete with guitar players for your attention, and window shoppers check out bookstores before rushing off to the theatre. Don't worry – Ithaca's not *too* perfect – but it's definitely close.

Orientation

Downtown Ithaca is dominated by Ithaca Commons, a pedestrian mall spread along State St. Jam-packed with restaurants, bars and upscale shops in late 19th-century buildings, the area stays hopping day and night. One block north of the Commons is the DeWitt Mall. Once a school building, it now houses shops and restaurants, the most famous of which is the Moosewood Restaurant. Perched high on a steep hill to the east is Cornell University. The surrounding streets, steep and narrow, comprise Collegetown. The campus is flanked by two gorges, both of which wind their way to Cayuga Lake.

Information

Buffalo Books (☎ 607-273-8246; www.buffalostreet books.com; DeWitt Mall, 215 N Cayuga St; 🕙 10am-8pm Mon-Sat, 11am-6pm Sun) Used, rare and out-of-print books and a rambling collection of contemporary prose, poetry, travel and children's books.

Ithaca/Tompkins County Convention & Visitors Bureau (www.visitithaca.com; 🕙 9am-5pm Mon-Fri year-round, 10am-5pm Sat & Sun Jun-Oct) Main branch (☎ 607-272-1313, 800-284-8422; 904 E Shore Drive, off Rte 13); Commons branch (☎ 607-273-7482; 171 The Commons).

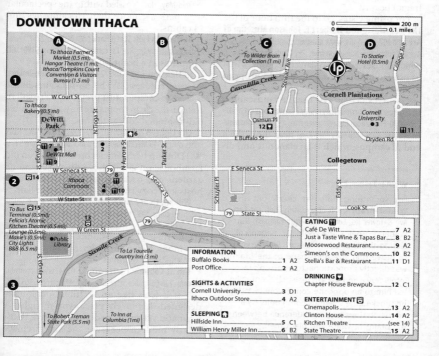

DOWNTOWN ITHACA

INFORMATION
Buffalo Books................................**1** A2
Post Office...................................**2** A2

SIGHTS & ACTIVITIES
Cornell University........................**3** D1
Ithaca Outdoor Store...................**4** A2

SLEEPING 🛏
Hillside Inn.................................**5** C1
William Henry Miller Inn.............**6** B2

EATING 🍴
Café De Witt...............................**7** A2
Just a Taste Wine & Tapas Bar.....**8** B2
Moosewood Restaurant...............**9** A2
Simeon's on the Commons...........**10** B2
Stella's Bar & Restaurant.............**11** D1

DRINKING 🍷
Chapter House Brewpub..............**12** C1

ENTERTAINMENT 🎭
Cinemapolis................................**13** A2
Clinton House............................**14** A2
Kitchen Theatre.....................(see 14)
State Theatre.............................**15** A2

Post office (☎ 607-272-5455; cnr Buffalo & Tioga Sts; 9am-5pm Mon-Fri, 9am-1pm Sat) Downtown.

Sights & Activities
The magnificent landscape around Ithaca provides opportunities for both serious hiking and simple strolls – plus the town is eminently walkable. If you forget shoes (or any other gear) pop into **Ithaca Outdoor Shop** (☎ 607-273-3891; 206 the Commons; 10am-8pm) who will likely have whatever you need.

CORNELL UNIVERSITY
Founded in 1865, **Cornell** (☎ 607-254-4636; www.cornell.edu) has a lovely, inviting campus, mixing old and new architecture, shaded Arcadian walkways and panoramic views of Cayuga Lake. The walks up to campus are so notoriously steep (especially in ice and snow) that students affectionately call the campus 'The Hill.' Be sure to walk across one of the two stupendous gorges on campus, **Cascadilla Gorge** and **Fall Creek Gorge**. Unfortunately, a recent rash of campus suicides means that the bridges are fenced in for safety, but you'll still get a sense of their dramatic (and potentially tragic) beauty.

For prime vistas, go to the fifth floor of the IM Pei–designed **Herbert F. Johnson Museum of Art** (☎ 607-255-6464; www.museum.cornell.edu; University Ave at Central Ave; admission free; 10am-5pm Tue-Sun), which houses a major Asian collection, as well as pre-Columbian, American and European exhibits.

Cornell's classic Ivy League landscaping includes the **Cornell University Plantations** (☎ 607-255-3020; Plantations Rd; admission free; 9am-4pm Mon-Fri Sep-Apr, 9am-4pm daily May-Aug) near the eastern end of campus, which is an elaborate and di-

verse complex with an arboretum, a botanical garden housing an array of poisonous plants and the ever popular 'weed garden.'

ITHACA AREA HIKING
Water tumbles down dramatically and forms 10 different waterfalls at **Buttermilk Falls State Park** (Map p193; ☎ 607-273-5761; car $5) 2 miles south of Ithaca on Rte 13. The park also features ragged cliffs, roaring rapids, a natural swimming hole, deep gorge trails and a campground with cabins. Walk the popular trail that climbs up to Pinnacle Rock and Treman Lake.

A gorgeous 3-mile gorge trail that passes 12 cascades, including Devil's Kitchen and Lucifer Falls, is the reason to visit **Robert H Treman State Park** (Map p193; ☎ 607-273-3440; car $5), on Rte 13 south of the city. This trail is part of the **Finger Lakes Trail** (www.fingerlakestrail.org) which connects the Appalachian Trail with Canada's Bruce Trail. The heavenly 776-mile footpath is bordered by waterfalls, glens and glacial lakes.

Sleeping
Robert H Treman State Park (☎ 607-273-3440; www.nysparks.state.ny.us; Rte 13; campsite $13, cabin $40; mid-May–Nov) Nestled within the spectacular state park are more than 70 campsites and 14 cabins.

Buttermilk Falls State Park (☎ 800-456-2267; www.nysparks.state.ny.us; Rte 13; campsite $15, cabin $190) 60 campsites in a beautiful setting.

Hillside Inn (☎ 607-272-9507; www.hillside-inn.net; 518 Stewart Ave; d from $65) This no-frills guesthouse is close to campus. Just pretend you're still in college: the clean rooms are tiny and resemble old-fashioned college dorms.

City Lights B & B (☎ 607-227-3003; www.theinnatcitylights.com; 1319 Mecklenberg Rd; d incl breakfast from $135;) Dine on herb-omelet breakfasts in an old farmhouse on a hill above town, set among gardens and trickling fountains with warm hosts and cozy suites with a dramatic flair.

William Henry Miller Inn (☎ 607-256-4553; www.millerinn.com; 303 N Aurora St; r/ste incl breakfast from $165/215;) Friendly host Lynette runs the classic Ithaca B&B, a stone's throw from the commons. Her evening desserts (and creative breakfasts) draw raves.

Inn at Columbia (☎ 607-272-0204; www.columbiabb.com; 228 Columbia St; r/ste incl breakfast from $165/205;) If it feels like an architect personally designed this lovely place, you're right. A dramatic yet restrained modern style that's utterly modern pervades the airy fireplace

WHAT THE...?

For something different check out the **Wilder Brain Collection** (Uris Hall, cnr East Ave & Tower Rd, Cornell University campus). Burt Wilder, Cornell's first zoologist, began collecting the brains in the late 1800s, trying to prove that size and shape of the brain was directly proportional to a person's race, intelligence and sex. His research eventually led him to an opposite conclusion: in 1911 he shocked the scientific community by announcing there was no difference between the brains of white and black men.

and skylit rooms, courtyards, decks and exotic gazebo suite.

Statler Hotel (☎ 607-257-2500, 800-541-2501; www.statlerhotel.cornell.edu; 130 Statler Dr; d from $180; 🛜) You can't say the staff at this top-notch hotel doesn't want to please you – they're majoring in hospitality at Cornell University's hotel management training school.

La Tourelle Country Inn (☎ 607-273-2734, 800-765-1492; www.latourelleinn.com; 1550 Danby Rd; d from $149; 🛜 🎱) Relaxing, unpretentious and inviting, La Tourelle sits on a hill with great views of Cayuga Lake, close to walking trails and has a great tennis court.

Eating & Drinking

Ithaca is an organic paradise for foodies. Start at the Ithaca Commons and stroll (or head to Collegetown for the college-bar thing). Most bars in Ithaca open in the mid to late afternoon and close, by county ordinance, at 1am (to the dismay of many Cornell students).

Ithaca Bakery (☎ 607-273-7110; 400 N Meadow St; sandwich $6-9; 👶) Eat in or take away: this is sandwich, soup and salad heaven. End of story.

our pick **Just a Taste Wine & Tapas Bar** (☎ 607-277-9463; 116 N Aurora St; tapas $3-6) Since 10 to 15 tapas change every night, dinner in this simple, candlelit dining room is always a delightful surprise. Gracious veteran servers know their food and wine backwards: ask for a recommendation.

Café DeWitt (☎ 607-273-3473; 215 N Cayuga St; mains $5-10; 🕓 8:30am-2:30pm Mon-Sat, brunch Sun; 👶) This is Ithaca's favorite breakfast and lunch spot, with homemade soups and desserts in a laid-back atmosphere inside DeWitt Mall.

Stella's Bar & Restaurant (☎ 607-277-1490; 403 College Ave; mains $8-18; 🕓 lunch & dinner to 1am, cafe 7am-1am) A striking Collegetown hangout with intellectuals hunkering down with dog-eared books in the casual cafe on one side while couples canoodle on the other. A chic yet bohemian vibe that's at once offbeat and a bit elegant makes this place unique.

Maxie's (☎ 607-272-4136; 635 W State St; mains $10-22; 🕓 4pm-midnight; 👶) A fun-loving restaurant bar with sexy red walls, where both dolled-up and dressed-down regulars joke with the bartender over oysters, key lime pie and other sultry Southern comforts. (PS: solo diners, y'all come on over.)

Simeon's on the Commons (☎ 607-272-2212; 224 W State St; mains $10-26; 🕓 dinner; 👶) Exuding a bright

THE FRESH FOOD REVOLUTION

Known for its beloved cookbook series, **Moosewood Restaurant** (☎ 607-273-9610; 215 N Cayuga St; mains from $8; 🕓 lunch & dinner) is a former 1970s cooking cooperative that rightly takes some credit for elevating vegetarian cooking to a loftier plane. Despite its veggie roots, Moosewood regularly offers a handful of inventive (and, not surprisingly, healthy and organic) dishes with meat. In recent visits, we've been wowed by their simplest offerings: perfectly dressed salad plates, fresh soups and sigh-inducing desserts.

vintage ambience, this beautifully laid-out restaurant features an ornate Victorian long bar with gilded mirrors and chandelier fans and an outdoor patio for Commons people-watching Try the Gorgonzola and pear salad.

Chapter House Brewpub (☎ 607-277-9782; 400 Stewart Ave) In Collegetown, dark wood paneling and a vast selection of beers evoke the ambiance of a cozy British pub.

Felicia's Atomic Lounge (☎ 607-273-2219; 508 W State St) Girls who like girls, along with just about everyone else in town, adore this friendly bar with its sleek interior and signature creative cocktails (a rhubarb martini and a ginger margarita).

Entertainment

Ithaca supports a thriving theater and performing arts scene. Call the **Ticket Center** (☎ 607-273-4497; www.ithacaevents.com; 171 E State St).

Cinemapolis (☎ 607-277-6115; www.cinemapolis.org; 120 E Green St) Foreign and indie film screenings just off the Commons.

Hangar Theatre (☎ 607-273-8588; www.hangartheatre.org; Rte 89) This popular professional summer

ARTSY ITHACA

About 50 local artists have banded together to form the **Greater Ithaca Art Trail** (☎ 607-273-5072; www.arttrail.com). Visitors call ahead to set up self-guided tours to the artists' studios, which feature everything from sculpture to handcrafted jewelry to pottery to photography – much of it high quality. Contact the visitors center for a map.

THE RONGOVIAN EMBASSY TO THE USA

If you grew up in the Finger Lakes region and were a teenager (or older) during the 1970s, you probably had had your first drink here – or seen your first live band. That's right, the 'Rongo,' as everyone calls it, is as much a coming-of-age ritual as it is a bar. In fact, you might say that the Finger Lakes' most legendary bar is hands-down the **Rongovian Embassy to the USA** (☎ 607-387-3334; 1 W Main St, Trumansburg). The centerpiece of this institution is the long wooden bar, cut from a single cherry tree that was carried into the bar by several of the town's strapping locals (the photo behind the bar proves it). For decades, this was the place to hear live music, and many national acts stopped in at this off-the-radar place. Be sure to order the signature drink, a Bastard ($5), which comes in three (successively more deadly) strengths depending on your mood: a Suffering Bastard, a Dying Bastard, and a Dead Bastard.

theater series presents classics and musicals and includes the Kiddstuff summer children's theater.

Kitchen Theatre Company (KTC; ☎ 607-272-4497; www.kitchentheatre.org; 417 W State/MLK) This well-respected company presents contemporary productions in an exciting new space.

State Theatre (☎ 607-277-7477; www.statetheatre ofithaca.com; 107 W State St) This landmark building showcases everything from West African drummers to punk rock to comedy.

Shopping

Ithaca Farmers' Market (☎ 607-273-7109; www.ithaca market.com; 535 3rd St; ☒ 9am-2pm Sat, 10am-2pm Sun Apr-Dec) Organic food and crafts overflow at this wonderful outdoor market: summer berries, autumn apples, Finger Lakes wines, bread and cookies just out of the oven…all with a host of idiosyncratic performers.

Getting There & Around

Tompkins County Airport (☎ 607-257-0456; www.fly ithaca.com; 72 Brown Rd, Ithaca) offers daily services to many East Coast cities.

The **bus terminal** (☎ 607-277-8800; 710 W State St at Fulton St) serves as a depot for **Adirondack Trailways** (☎ 800-776-7548) and **Greyhound** (☎ 800-231-2222).

At the crossroads of Rtes 13 and 96, Ithaca is about 55 miles southeast of Syracuse.

TRUMANSBURG
pop 1600

Tiny Trumansburg (Map p193), a friendly and fun-spirited village about 15 miles north of Ithaca on Rte 96, is the gateway to stupendous **Taughannock Falls State Park** (Map p193; ☎ 607-387-6739; campsite $13; ☒ camping late March–mid-October). The 215ft-high Taughannock Falls – 30ft higher than their more famous neighbor Niagara – drop down a steep gorge in a misty

cloud of thunder and are the highest straight falls this side of the Rocky Mountains. Walk the trails to see the lookout points, or just park and gape. It's a good family camping spot, with campsites, cabins, boat docks, a swimming beach, fire pits and a fun playground.

Trumansburg, a town of Cornell professors, activists and jacks-of-all-trades, has a lived-in community feel where everyone seems to know each other (and wants to know you). Stop for lunch or a drink at the Rongo (see the boxed text) and stroll this little one-street wonder's shops and cafes.

One of the most relaxing, sleep-like-a-baby inns in the region, the **Gothic Eves** (☎ 800-387-7712; www.gothiceves.com; 112 E Main St; d $159-259; ☒) strikes the perfect note of vintage farmhouse chic balanced by earthy touches (an outdoor wood-fired hot tub, sprawling herbal gardens and fresh organic breakfasts served on the sunny porch) that will delight both your inner sophisticate and your inner hippie.

Even foodies from restaurant-rich Ithaca go out of their way to dine at **Hazelnut Kitchen** (☎ 607-387-4433; 53 E Main St; mains $13-24; ☒ dinner Thu-Mon) a bewitching little candlelit bistro with checkered floors and a seasonal menu. Don't miss the glorious hazelnut butter cake with sea-salt caramel.

The great small-town ice-cream shop with the funny name, **Not My Dad's Ice Cream** (☎ 607-387-9596; 203 E Main St) serves tasty soft-serve, frozen yogurt and malts.

WATKINS GLEN
pop 2000

The kind of throwback small-town where teenage boys cruise around on dirt bikes and families hang out on picnic tables in front of ice-cream stands, Watkins Glen, at the southern tip of Seneca Lake on Rte 14, is famous for an unlikely duo of attractions: a world-class car-racing track and a spectacular natural gorge with waterfalls. The main drag of Franklin St combines an everyday scrappiness with genuine charm – but don't mistake this place for one of the storybook villages of the Finger Lakes. It's more about car-racing than wine tasting, and it likes it that way.

At the **Watkins Glen International Track** (☎ 607-535-2481; www.theglen.com; off County Rd 16; admission $10-50; ☼ Jun-Oct), cars used to race on a 6.6-mile course through town streets, but saner minds built a 2.3-mile course in its present location in 1956. Today it hosts major Nascar and grand prix races, including the Winston Cup Race in August.

Wow-inducing **Watkins Glen State Park** (Map p193; ☎ 607-535-4511; Franklin St btwn 10th & 11th St; ☼ May-Oct/Nov) had 19 waterfalls, grottoes, a swimming pool and a dramatic self-guided 1.5-mile gorge trail with 832 stone steps. You can camp here, too (campsites $15 to $20).

The smallest national forest in the country (and the only one in New York State), **Finger Lakes National Forest** (Map p193; ☎ 607-546-4470; off Rte 414; campsite $15) has more than 70 miles of hiking trails, fishing, ponds and a basic campground.

Glide past waterfalls and cliffs on moonlight, midnight, and regular old cruises with **Captain Bill's** (☎ 607-535-4541; foot of Franklin St; adult/child $8.50/4; ☼ mid-May–mid-Oct) on Seneca Lake.

The rustic **Seneca Lodge** (☎ 607-535-2014; south entrance of Watkins Glen State Park; cabin from $38, d from $63) is a tradition, with the chalet-style A-frames and cabins. We love the Adirondack-style log lodge with its big stone fireplace and outdoor patio.

In a distinctive pink-roofed Victorian with a wraparound porch and lovely grounds overlooking Seneca Lake, the **Idlewilde Inn** (☎ 607-535-3081; 1 Lakeview Ave; d $105-225 incl breakfast) has 16 charming rooms.

Right on the docks, **Seneca Harbor Station** (☎ 607-535-6101; Franklin St; mains $16-20) sports fabulous views of the lake. Listen to bands on the deck as you kick back and watch the sunset.

The Patio, at the new upscale **Watkins Glen Harbor hotel** (☎ 607-535-6116; 16 N Franklin St) is a good place to imbibe a cocktail in the outdoors.

HAMMONDSPORT
pop 700

Perfectly situated for wine tasting, tiny Hammondsport (Map p193) is a quaint Victorian town with a steepled white church, a

---

DETOUR – CORNING

Glass, glass and more glass. From the sculptors and shows at the Corning Museum of Glass to the downtown glass shops and artists' glassblowing studios, all this glass has helped make pleasant Corning a big tourist draw. The historic Market St area is perfect for strolling.

The **Finger Lakes Wine Country Visitors Center** (☎ 607-974-8271; 1 Museum Way; ☼ 9am-5pm Sep-Jun, 9am-8pm Jul & Aug) is located inside the Corning Museum of Glass.

Housed in a building made of giant sheets of glass, the astounding **Corning Museum of Glass** (☎ 800-732-6845; www.cmog.org; 151 Centerway; adult/under 19 yr $14/free; ☼ 9am-5pm Sep-Jun, 9am-8pm Jul & Aug) is a don't-miss attraction featuring 35 centuries of glass art. Exhibits range from Medieval to Tiffany to stained glass windows, plus the largest glass-sculpture gallery in the world.

Old American Western art, early examples of Steuben glass and antique toys are on display at the **Rockwell Museum of Western Art** (☎ 607-937-5386; www.rockwellmuseum.org; 111 Cedar St; adult/under 19yr/senior & student $6.50/free/5.50; ☼ 9am-5pm, to 8pm Jun-Aug) the largest collection of American Western art in the east.

Rosewood Inn B&B (☎ 607-962-3253; www.rosewoodinn.com; 134 E First St; d from $95) Corning's best sleeping option, the inn dates back to 1855 and is housed in an elaborately decorated Victorian house with seven rooms. Afternoon tea is served in an elegant parlor with antique rocking chairs.

On sunny days, the garden or rooftop patio at **Market Street Brewing Co** (☎ 607-936-2337; 63-65 W Market St; mains $6-18) is a blissful experience. The menu is exhaustive – you can order a $6 burger or an $18 steak. Wash it down with a fresh local brew.

The kids will go wide-eyed (and adults are advised to throw their diets away) at the sight of the **Old World Café & Ice Cream Parlor** (☎ 607-936-1953; cnr Market & Centerway St; mains $5-7) a vintage ice-cream parlor featuring all sorts of ice-cream, sundaes, shakes (from $3) as well as pink floral-patterned walls and plenty of sandwiches and salads to prevent a sugar meltdown.

gazebo and a nostalgia-invoking green square where you can actually spot people engaged in that old-fashioned activity: just sitting on a bench and enjoying the sunshine. Nearby, on the Keuka Lake waterfront, you'll find two nice public beaches.

For sleeping and eating check out the understated **Village Tavern & Inn** (☎ 607-569-2528; 39 Mechanic St; d from $79; mains from $15) on the town square. The restaurant is classy yet cozy, with a huge selection of Finger Lakes wines, more than 100 beers, and live piano music on weekends. The inn has eight studio/apartment-style rooms complete with kitchens.

For a posh downstairs bar scene and fun, stylish Italian food, head to **Union Block Italian**

FINGER LAKES WINERY TOUR

Finger Lakes vineyards come in all varieties: some have magnificent lake views. Others sit back off seemingly lost byways. A few are commercial enterprises with large tasting rooms, others are family-run affairs in the back of a faded barn. Sonoma and Napa Valley it's not, yet more and more vineyards have been cropping up in the region as it gains fame and respect among wine enthusiasts.

To find the wineries look for the 'Wine Trails' signs, but beware it will take months (and you will be very, very drunk) to visit every vineyard in the region. The major wine trails are **Seneca**, **Cayuga**, **Keuka** – visit **Finger Lakes Wine Country** (☎ 800-813-2958; www.fingerlakeswinecountry. com; Baron Steuben Place, 1 W Market St, Corning) to plan your route. Most wineries are open daily from late morning until 5pm and charge just a few dollars (or nothing) for a tasting of several wines. Call for low-season hours.

Perched high on a hill with a bird's-eye view of Keuka Lake, the sprawling **Bully Hill Vineyard** (☎ 607-868-3610; www.bullyhill.com; Rte 76, Hammondsport; ✷ 10am-6pm Mon-Sat, 11am-6pm Sun) is the most eccentric in the region – where else can you purchase women's thong panties with a glow-in-the-dark goat on them?

Between Hammondsport and the Rte 54 junction, the lovely **Dr Konstantin Frank's Vinifera Wine Cellars** (☎ 607-868-4884; www.drfrankwines.com; 9749 Middle Rd, Rte 76; ✷ 9am-5pm Mon-Sat, noon-5pm Sun) is home to some of the best wines in the region (Riesling, pinot noir and champagne) and to the vinifera revolution in Finger Lakes winemaking.

The **Glenora Wine Cellars** (☎ 607-243-5511; www.glenora.com; 5435 Rte 14, Dundee; ✷ 10am-6pm) has one of the most picturesque settings in the region with a commanding view of Seneca Lake. Besides the tasting room there is the **Veraisons Restaurant** (☎ 1-800-243-5513; breakfast & lunch $7-16, dinner $16-32; ✷ breakfast, lunch & dinner) and the **Inn at Glenora** (☎ 1-800-243-5513; r low/high from $119/179).

A winery for the party set, **Hazlitt 1852 Vineyards** (☎ 607-546-9463; www.hazlitt1852.com; Hector; ✷ 10am-6pm) is best known for its popular Red Cat wine, the best-selling domestic wine in NY State and the most notorious wine in the Finger Lakes due to its image as a 'hot tub wine' (whatever image that brings to mind is probably spot on). This 6th-generation winemaker has a rustic old barn of a tasting room where you can try good dry Riesling as jazz plays in the background.

A hip, young vibe rules at casual **Red Newt Cellars Winery** & **Bistro**, (☎ 607-546-4100; www. rednewt.com; Hector; tasting menu $60; ✷ 10am-6pm) which serves adventurous five-course chef's menus along with free tastings.

Experience an unparalleled synergy of wine and food at the **Sheldrake Point Winery** & **Simply Red Bistro** (☎ 607-532-9401; 7448 County Rd 153; www.sheldrakepoint.com; mains $10-15; ✷ lunch Thu-Mon, dinner Mon) featuring the cuisine of South African chef 'Mama Red' Samantha Izzo, who's locally known for her fiery red hair, larger-than-life persona and adventurous Southern comfort recipes. In addition to lovely views of the rolling hills leading down to Seneca Lake, the winery offers winemaker/chef's dinners that showcase local grapes as well as Finger Lakes produce.

It's crucial to eat well on the trail. On Seneca Lake, the former fruit stand turned **Stonecat Café** (☎ 607-546-5000; 5413 Rte 414, Hector; mains 8-24; ✷ lunch Thu-Sat, dinner Wed-Sun) is an ideal stop while cruising the wine trails, with a panoramic view of the vineyards, and local cuisine (with vegan and gluten-free options), such as pulled pork BBQ and a lemon-tahini falafel salad.

Just up the road, **Dano's Heuriger** (☎ 607-582-7555; 9564 Rte 414, Lodi; small plates $4-15; ✷ noon-

Bistro (☎ 607-246-4065; 31 Shether St; mains $8-12; 🍴) on the square.

Try the **Crooked Lake Ice Cream Co** (☎ 607-569-2751; 35 Shether St; mains from $3; 🍴) for lunch or great ice-cream (from $2) in an old-fashioned setting. Hammondsport lies on Rte 54A, just off Rte 54.

NORTHERN TIER

When visitors think of the Finger Lakes, this is usually a far cry from what they have in mind: small cities with rich urban and industrial histories, bursting with stately Greek revival mansions and a dash of failed 20th-century urban renewal. Cruise Rte 20,

9pm) is one unique restaurant – a standout in the state – with fun-spirited, casual, Viennese-style dining (small tasting plates, charcuterie, salads and homemade spreads and breads) in an architecturally dramatic setting on the lake.

Finally, don't miss the **Cayuga Creamery** (☎ 607-532-9492; 8421 Rte 89, Interlaken; small plates $4-15; ⏱ 11am-10pm) in Interlaken, with adventurous homemade flavors.

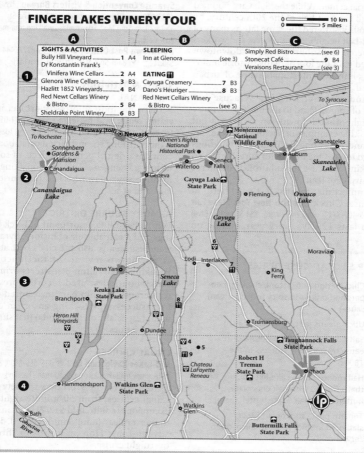

FINGER LAKES WINERY TOUR

0 ——— 10 km
0 ——— 5 miles

SIGHTS & ACTIVITIES
Bully Hill Vineyard **1** A4
Dr Konstantin Frank's
    Vinifera Wine Cellars **2** A4
Glenora Wine Cellars **3** B3
Hazlitt 1852 Vineyards **4** B4
Red Newt Cellars Winery
    & Bistro **5** B4
Sheldrake Point Winery **6** B3

SLEEPING
Inn at Glenora .... (see 3)

EATING 🍴
Cayuga Creamery **7** B3
Dano's Heuriger **8** B3
Red Newt Cellars Winery
    & Bistro .... (see 5)

Simply Red Bistro .... (see 6)
Stonecat Café **9** B4
Veraisons Restaurant .... (see 3)

NEW YORK STATE

which connects many of the towns and is considered among the loveliest drives in New York.

SYRACUSE
pop 141,000

With a Sicilian namesake and the snowiest winters of any US metro area, this medium-size city smack in the middle of the state has long been a crossroads of sorts, from the historic Underground Railroad to its current spot as an interstate and rail hub for the region. The salt industry that prospered here in the 19th century made Syracuse a working-class town at heart, and the completion of the Erie Canal solidified the city's image as an industrial center. While the 'Salt City' boomed through the first half of the 20th century, by the 1960s it suffered the same fate as many of its rust-belt neighbors; employers and workers discovered the suburbs and the downtown decayed with the loss of many historic buildings – all in the unfortunate name of 'urban renewal.'

Sound gloomy? Luckily, Syracuse has plenty of spunk. Head to the buzzing Armory Sq neighborhood downtown and check out the striking examples of Victorian Gothic, art deco and limestone Romanesque buildings around town. One thing's for sure: there's no mistaking Syracuse for suburbia. This fierce little city's got soul.

Summertime means festivals here in Syracuse. Check out the **New York State Fair** (☎ 315-487-7711; www.nysfair.org; 581 State Fair Blvd) which lasts 12 days every year, ending on Labor Day weekend, and featuring food, music, amusement rides and livestock competitions. Jazz fans will dig the annual **Syracuse Jazz Fest** (☎ www.syracusejazzfest.com; 4585 W Seneca Turnpike, Onondaga Community College; admission free) in late June that brings in performers from all around the world.

Orientation & Information

Clinton Sq, where Erie Blvd meets Salina St, marks the heart of downtown Syracuse. The city's main business district lies just south of the square; downtown sights are easily walkable. Syracuse University is on a hill to the southeast. I-81 and I-690 pass right through town.

Syracuse Convention & Visitors Bureau (☎ 315-470-1910; www.VisitSyracuse.org; 572 S Salina St; ◷ 8:30am-5pm Mon-Fri) Provides walking tour maps of downtown.

Downtown Post Office (☎ 800-275-8777; 444 S Salina St; ◷ 8am-5pm Mon-Fri, 9am-1pm Sat)

Sights & Activities

ERIE CANAL MUSEUM

Perhaps the most impressive artifact in this **visitors center** and **museum** (☎ 315-471-0593; 318 Erie Blvd E at Montgomery St; admission free; ◷ 10am-5pm) is the 65ft-long reconstructed canal boat that contains original personal effects of some of its first passengers, like a heartbreaking letter by an Irishwoman who had just buried her husband at sea.

ARMORY SQUARE DISTRICT

With a beguiling assortment of brick buildings and a palpable air of history, Syracuse's trendiest area is also the city's best attempt at downtown revival. At the junction of Franklin and Walton Sts, streets brim with funky boutiques, used record stores, chic restaurants and hip bars in restored buildings, successfully rocking an urban excitement (especially on weekends) that surprises many visitors.

CANAL CRUISES

Mid-Lakes Navigation Co (☎ 315-685-8500, 800-545-4318; www.midlakesnav.com; Dutchman's Landing; ◷ mid-Apr–early Nov), off Rte 370, offers a variety of Erie Canal cruises, from 50-minute sightseeing excursions (adult/child $12/7) to champagne dinner cruises (adult/child $47/38). Feeling adventurous? Hop on a two- or three-day overnight cruise.

TOP 5 LOCAL 'CUSE DISHES

- Chicken riggies (rigatoni, chicken, peppers and onions in spicy tomato-cream sauce)
- Utica greens (a spicy escarole dish)
- Salt potatoes (a boiled potato dish eaten by salt-mine workers in the 1800s)
- Half moons (a big cake-like cookie that's frosted with half chocolate buttercream, half white buttercream)
- Tomato pie (a square-cut pizza slathered in thick tomato sauce, often served cold)

ONONDAGA HISTORICAL ASSOCIATION MUSEUM

This county **museum** (☎ 315-428-1864; www.cny history.org; 321 Montgomery St; admission free; ☒ noon-4pm Wed-Fri, 11am-4pm Sat & Sun) might be one of the best small museums in the state. It covers the entire scope of New York history from the Onondaga Nation to the Erie Canal and the salt industry.

MILTON J RUBENSTEIN MUSEUM OF SCIENCE & TECHNOLOGY

Housed in the grand old armory, the **Museum of Science & Technology** (MOST; ☎ 315-425-9068; www.most.org; cnr Franklin & W Jefferson St; adult/child $6/5, with IMAX ticket $11.50/9.50; ☒ 11am-5pm Wed-Sun) has several hands-on exhibits designed to wow kids, plus a great planetarium and an IMAX Omnitheater.

Sleeping

Oneida Shores Campground (☎ 315-676-7366; www.OnondagaCountyParks.com; 9248 McKinley Ridge Rd, Brewerton; campsites from $20) Sure, it's 15 miles north of downtown, but for the lakeside beach location (right on huge Oneida Lake) you can't beat the scenic appeal in summer and fall.

HI-AYH Downing International Hostel (☎ 315-472-5788; www.hiayh.org/hostels/newyork/syracuse.cfm; 535 Oak St; dm $14; ☒) With a gorgeous antique staircase that lures budget travelers up to its airy dorm and private rooms, this hostel a mile northeast of downtown offers major ambience for the money. Curl up with a movie in the library, or cook dinner in the big basement kitchen. Bonus: the residential neighborhood is safe for women and solo travelers.

Bed & Breakfast Wellington (☎ 315-474-3641, 800-724-5006; www.bbwellington.com; 707 Danforth St; d $125-165; ☒) Located on a quiet residential street, this 1914 Tudor-style B&B offers delish breakfasts such as pear Hawaiian French toast, along with ecofriendly policies and festive cheer (especially around the holidays). Play chess in front of the fireplace or kick back on one of four porches.

Jefferson Clinton Hotel (☎ 315-425-0500; www.jeffersonclintonhotel.com; 416 S Clinton St; r from $155; ☒) Nice: the Armory Sq location, the omelet breakfast bar, and the elegance coupled with a nostalgic whimsy (rubber ducks in the bathrooms). Brilliant: complimentary valet parking, Tuesday happy hour, and a DVD library for snowy Syracuse nights.

Eating & Drinking

Check the Armory Sq district for the most tempting array of options.

Sugarpearl (☎ 315-422-7464; 600 Burnet Ave; mains $4-8; ☒ 8am-4pm Mon & Sun, to 8pm Tue & Wed, to 11pm Thu-Sat; ☒) Between the AYH hostel and downtown, this slick veggie-friendly cafe with great breakfasts belies its shabby corner.

Strong Hearts Café (☎ 315-476-4937; 719 E Genesee St; mains $5-12; ☒ 8am-6pm Mon, to midnight Tue-Thu, to 2am Fri & Sat, 10am-midnight Sun) Between the Syracuse campus and downtown, this cafe's slogan, '100% Vegan, 100% Delicious,' doesn't exaggerate. Try the pesto pizza or the deluxe milkshakes with historical names, like the Harriet Tubman (maple, vanilla, oreo).

L'Adour (☎ 315-475-7653; 110 Montgomery St; breakfast & lunch $7-16, dinner $24-36) A cozy French bistro in a funky triangular building.

ourpick Pastabilities (☎ 315-474-1153; 311 S Franklin St; mains $5-25; ☒ lunch Mon-Fri, dinner daily) Bustling at lunch and buzzing at night, this happening eatery makes a wide variety of homemade pastas in unusual flavors such as Southwestern Chicken Lasagna and Spinach Feta Manicotti. Cozy up in a booth or at the bar; music in a garden courtyard adds to the summertime atmosphere.

Alto Cinco (☎ 315-475-1111; 238 W Jefferson St; mains $6-14) Mouthwatering Mexican in a funky, bright space with a copper bar, where an energetic crowd downs catfish burritos like they're going out of style. Fresh, veggie-friendly and open until 2am every night? Si, por favor.

Dinosaur Bar-B-Que (☎ 315-476-4937; 246 W Willow St; mains $9-23; ☒ lunch & dinner, to midnight Mon-Thu, to 1am Fri & Sat) The quintessential Syracuse spot, packed with a motley crew of tourists, bikers, tattooed waitresses, and business professionals. With live blues most nights, it's always a people-watching party. The food (try the Big-Ass Pork plate and fried green tomatoes) is almost as fun as the bizarre decor.

Entertainment

Syracuse Symphony Orchestra (☎ 315-424-8200; www.syracusesymphony.org; John H Mulroy Civic Center, 411 Montgomery St) Classical and popular music concerts are performed from October to May.

Landmark Theatre (☎ 315-475-7980; www.landmarktheatre.org; 362 S Salina St) A flourishing 1928 architectural leftover from Hollywood's make-believe tropical-vaudeville movie-palace days, now showcasing everything from touring stage shows to classic films.

NEW YORK STATE

WHAT THE...?

Head to Syracuse's oldest Irish neighborhood, Tipperary Hill, to see the country's only upside-down traffic light found at the intersection of Tompkins and Lowell Sts. Legend has it that when the traffic light was first installed (right-side up), residents were so outraged that British red was placed above Irish green they immediately destroyed the light's lenses. Realizing this was a battle they could not win, city officials reversed the lenses to placate the neighborhood.

Syracuse Stage (☎ 315-443-3275; www.syracusestage.org; 820 E Genesee St) The area's only professional theater, presenting a mix of contemporary and classical drama.

Getting There & Around

Hancock International Airport (☎ 315-454-4330; http://.syrairport.org) offers daily services by a number of major airlines.

On the north side of town, the **William F Walsh Regional Transportation Center** (RTC; ☎ 315-478-1936; www.centro.org; 220 Cortland Ave) houses both the bus and train station, served by **Greyhound/Trailways** (☎ 800-231-2222; www.greyhound.com) and **Amtrak** (☎ 800-872-7245; www.amtrak.com).

Driving to Syracuse is a piece of cake as two major highways cross it: I-81 and I-90 (the NY State Thruway).

SKANEATELES
pop 2600

Like the glossy cover of a magazine, Skaneateles ('skinny-atlas') draws you in immediately with its good looks and evocative charm. Rough around the edges? Edgy? No, and that's exactly why vacationers come here, to leave their cares (and, perhaps, reality?) behind. At the top of one of the prettiest, deepest and smallest of the Finger Lakes, Skaneateles is definitely the most camera-ready little town in the Finger Lakes region. It's about strolling and dining and sunsets on the beach, and thus it attracts a well-heeled crowd that (gasp!) may even dress up a (tiny) bit for dinner.

The town centre covers just a few blocks around Genesee and Jordan Sts, which are packed with shops, chic restaurants and bars.

Since 1807, the classic choice for lodging has been the **Sherwood Inn** (☎ 315-685-3405; www .thesherwoodinn.com; 26 W Genesee St; d from $100; mains $18-25), a classic New York colonial inn that dates back to 1807 when it was a stagecoach stop. We love that none of the 20 tranquil, richly-colored and antiques-filled rooms are the same (snag the one with the window seat!). Downstairs, laze away the evening, dining and wining as the glorious sunset seeps through the lakefront windows.

For a classic summertime Skaneateles experience (and a must with kids), head to **Doug's Fish Fry** (☎ 315-685-3288; 8 Jordan St; mains under $12): it's good, greasy, loud and cheap, with fresh fish trucked in from Boston daily. Try the steamed clams and fish sandwiches. Kids will dig the yummy frozen custard, the aquarium, and the model train that runs on a track around the restaurant.

Skaneateles Bakery (☎ 315-685-3538; 19 Jordan St; mains under $10; ☒ 6:30am-4pm Mon-Sat, 7am-3pm Sun) a green striped awning marks this from-scratch bakery, where standouts include gruyere cheese sandwiches with grilled onions and apples. Kids will like the homemade pop-tarts.

SENECA FALLS
pop 6800

As you pass through this quiet little town just 3 miles west of Cayuga Lake, it's hard to imagine that it was once home to some of the most radical women in US History: the original suffragettes. No, that's not an all-girl rock band – we're talking about the women who initiated the struggle towards women's rights and suffrage in the United States. Rich in both abolitionist and women's suffrage history, Seneca Falls was the home of Elizabeth Cady Stanton and the 1848 women's rights convention she organized.

Today, Seneca Falls quiet streets are lined with stately homes. The downtown, more workaday than picturesque, centers around Fall St. For area information, stop by the **Heritage Area Visitors Center** (☎ 315-568-2703; 115 Fall St; ☒ 10am-4pm Mon-Sat, noon-4pm Sun), which also houses exhibits on the town's history and women's suffrage.

Explore interesting exhibits on the historic 1848 Women's Rights convention at the **Women's Rights National Historical Park** (☎ 315-568-2991; 136 Fall St; admission $3; ☒ 9am-5pm) which traces the movement's leaders and what life was like in the times in which they lived.

Bird-watchers, don't hesitate to head towards the **Montezuma National Wildlife Refuge**

(☎ 315-568-5987; 3395 Rtes 5 & 20E; admission free; ☽ dawn-dusk Apr-Nov), which is a major stop-over point for waterfowl on their way south from Canada and a must-see (315 species!) for bird lovers.

The best budget option in town is camping at **Cayuga Lake State Park** (☎ 315-568-5163; Rte 89; campsite $17; ☽ May-Nov), which has almost 300 campsites.

In an 1855 gingerbread Gothic revival home, you'll find **Hubbell House B&B** (☎ 315-568-9690; www.hubbellhousebb.com; 42 Cayuga St; r from $135-155 incl breakfast), which offers four elegant rooms and a wonderful wraparound screened porch overlooking Van Cleef Lake. Swim or take a rowboat off the private dock.

A jewel of a mod hotel in an old brick building, the **Clarence Hotel** (☎ 877-788-4010; www.hotelclarence.com;108 Fall St; r from $129, ste from $149; ☒) boasts luxe linens, chandeliers over every bed, and a sleek bar and **restaurant** (☎ 315-712-4000; lunch $7-25; ☽ breakfast, lunch & dinner) serving baked oysters and flaming rum punch.

For 50 years, the classic **Mac's Drive In** (☎ 315-539-3064; 1166 Waterloo-Geneva Rd, at US 20 & NY 5, Waterloo; mains $2-6; ☽ 10:30am-10pm Tue-Sun) has been serving its diehard fans hand-cut fries, hot dogs and cheeseburgers along with its signature homemade rootbeer in frosted mugs.

At sunrise, come to **Zuzu's Cafe** (☎ 315-586-2205; 107 Fall St; mains $4-7; ☽ 7am-4pm Tue-Sat) for coffee, pastries, and breakfast delights like the sconewich (eggs, tomato and cheese in a savory dill scone). At lunchtime, salads (a Southern cobb) and sandwiches continue to delight.

GENEVA
pop 14,000

Geneva's a little dull, sure, but boy is she easy on the eyes. Located at the northern tip of Seneca Lake, you'll find stately homes, gracious trees, and the **Hobart and William Smith College** campus sharing the pleasant Main St. For tourist information, contact the **Geneva Area Chamber of Commerce** (☎ 315-789-1776; www.genevany.com; 1 Lakeside Drive; ☽ 9am-4:30pm Mon-Fri, daily from late May).

If there is one reason to go to Geneva, it's to visit the amazing **Belhurst Castle** (☎ 315-781-0201; www.belhurstcastle.com; 4069 Rte 14S; r low-season/high-season from $80/$140), south of town. Belhurst is a sprawling, red 1889 Medina stone house. Rooms glow with polished woodwork, solid oak doors and gas fireplaces. Think beautiful

grounds, a winery, a lakeview dining room resplendent with mosaic fireplaces, and a cozy bar.

PENN YAN
pop 5200

Welcome to Finger Lakes farm country. The area around Penn Yan, at the northern tip of Keuka Lake on Rte 54, is replete with corn fields, grain silos and red barns, while the tiny village consists of just a few shops and restaurants.

For a truly old-fashioned farmers market experience, check out the **Windmill Farmers' Market** (☎ 315-536-3032; www.thewindmill.com; 8am-4:30pm Sat May-Dec) on Rte 54 about 6 miles south of downtown. Mennonites, who still travel by horse and buggy, come to sell produce, jams, molasses and baked goods at this fabulous indoor-outdoor farmers' market.

Luxuriate in an evocative Greek revival mansion (and play a game of billiards) at the **Fox Inn** (☎ 315-536-3101; www.foxinnbandb.com; 158 Main St; d from $280-350), which has five rooms and a lovely rose garden.

Campers, head to **Keuka Lake State Park** (☎ 315-536-3666; 3370 Pepper Rd, Bluff Point; campsite $15; ☽ May–mid-Oct) features a swimming beach, boat launches, hiking, cross-country skiing and campsites with lake views.

For swoon-worthy gastropub food under pressed-tin ceilings, the **Red Dove Tavern** (☎ 315-781-2020; 30 Castle St; mains $10-21; ☽ lunch Thu-Sat, dinner to 1am Tue-Fri, to 2am Sat) offers unique small and big plates like pork shank with cheddar grits and baked ricotta with endive. Resistance to the chocolate-orange bread pudding is futile.

ROCHESTER
pop 208,000

Rochester's a wily New York enigma, half-way between a small city and a big town, an arts hub and a victim of post-industrial

---

WHAT THE...?

Looking to have an extremely intimate wedding? Say, one where there's not even room for, well, your mother-in-law? Rumored to be the world's smallest church, the Cross Island Chapel (Sconondoa Rd, off Rte 365) in Oneida (Map p155) only fits a bride, a groom, and a minister. Oh, and it's in the middle of a pond, accessible only by boat.

NEW YORK STATE

suburban flight. Yet somewhere between its rep as uncool and misunderstood lies a vibrant town with buzzing cafes and a fantastic music scene fed by the world-class Eastman School of Music. Posh mansions are a reminder of the city's industrial glory days, long before Kodak made snapshot cameras that changed photography (and Rochester) forever. A drive around town proves it's a place with equal parts shabby and grand, lively and bland, and totally worth a second look (make sure to snap a few photographs for posterity, of course).

Orientation & Information

The central downtown area of Rochester is encircled by the 'Inner Loop,' part of I-490. Park Ave, a popular restaurant and shopping district, is just east of downtown. East Ave is Rochester's museum and mansion row.'

Brownbag Bookshop (☎ 716-271-2494; 678 Monroe Ave; ☾ 9am-6pm) Sells used books.

Greater Rochester Visitors' Association (☎ 585-546-3070; www.visitrochester.com; 45 East Ave; ☾ 8:30am-5pm Mon-Fri, 9am-5pm Sat, 10am-3pm Sun) Good information about the area.

Main post office (☎ 716-272-5952; 1335 Jefferson Rd; ☾ 9am-5pm Mon-Fri, 9am-1pm Sat)

Sights & Activities
GEORGE EASTMAN HOUSE & INTERNATIONAL MUSEUM OF PHOTOGRAPHY & FILM

The **house** (☎ 585-271-3361; www.eastmanhouse.org; 900 East Ave; adult/child/senior/student over 12yr $10/4/6/8; ☾ 10am-5pm Tue-Sat, to 8pm Thu, 1-5pm Sun) that Kodak built is a palatial 1905 colonial revival mansion, but more than its architecture, it's impressive for its contents: the world's largest collection of historic films, photographs, cameras and books about photography and film with rotating exhibits of original photographs and equipment. Photography lovers will be in two kinds of heaven: black and white *and* color.

Visitors can also step outside to take in the restored gardens on this 12-acre estate.

STRONG MUSEUM

A stupendously fun hands-on history center for children and kids-at-heart, and a must for anyone into vintage Americana, the **Strong National Museum of Play** (☎ 585-263-2700; www.museumofplay.org; cnr Chestnut St & Woodbury Blvd; adult/child 2-15 yr $11/9; ☾ 10am-5pm Mon-Thu, 10am-8pm Fri & Sat, noon-5pm Sun) boasts the largest collection of toys, dolls and games in the world. A working 1918 carousel and an old farmhouse kitchen where kids can pump water and churn butter set the tone for a whimsical and interactive learning environment.

SUSAN B ANTHONY HOUSE & MT HOPE CEMETERY

The **Susan B Anthony House** (☎ 585-235-6124; www.susanbanthonyhouse.org; 19 Madison St; adult/child under 12 yr $6/3; ☾ 11am-5pm Tue-Sun) was the famous feminist's home from 1866 to 1906. The exhibits trace her life and the many political reforms (abolitionism and temperance, along with suffrage) into which she invested her remarkable passion and commitment.

DETOUR – CANANDAIGUA

The late Victorian–flavored town of Canandaigua sprawls around bustling Main St. Full of stately homes and Greek Revival buildings, The town sits on the northern tip of Canandaigua Lake. The name Canandaigua comes from the Seneca 'kanandarque,' which means 'chosen spot,' and the site was the main village in the Seneca Nation. This was where Susan B Anthony was tried for voting in the 19th century, found guilty and fined $100, which she refused to pay.

Among the finest Victorian gardens in the US, the **Sonnenberg Gardens and Mansion** (☎ 716-394-4922; www.sonnenburg.com; 151 Charlotte St; adult/student $10/5; ☾ 9:30am-5:30pm May-Oct) includes nine formal gardens around an 1887 stone mansion, an arboretum and the Finger Lakes Wine Center.

Lay your head at the friendly, colorful **Miami Resort Motel** (☎ 585-394-7800; www.visitinnonthelake.com; 4126 Rtes 5 & 20; d from $130; ☒) with the area's best deal with Jacuzzi rooms and retro furnishings in a spruced-up motel that's more mod than odd. You can't miss the vintage neon sign.

For an atmospheric Northwoods feel in the Finger Lakes, cozy up to the aptly named **Chalet of Canandaigua** (☎ 585-394-9080; www.chaletbandb.com; 3770 State Rte 21; ste from $235) which features to-die-for suites with cast-iron stoves, fireplaces, soaking tubs and wood-beamed ceilings. Sleeping in feels like an adventure here (but don't miss the three-course breakfast on the deck).

Sleeping

Decent, and usually cheaper, motels are outside town near the highways.

Dartmouth House B&B (☎ 585-271-7872; www.dartmouthhouse.com; 215 Dartmouth St; d from $145) This English Tudor B&B with friendly hosts is ideally within walking distance of several restaurants and museums.

Strathallan Hotel (☎ 585-461-5010; www.strathallan.com; 550 East Ave; d from $129; ☒) This 150-room hotel set among gracious mansions features excellent service and a rooftop bar. Most rooms have balconies.

Eating, Drinking & Entertainment

Inviting eateries cluster along Monroe Ave.

Dogtown (☎ 585-271-6620; 691 Monroe Ave; mains $10-16; ☒ 11am-11pm, to midnight Fri & Sat) Locals go wild for this cool stand that does regional versions of hot dogs, from Cincinnati Reds to a Chicago Bull Dog, in regular and veggie styles.

Café Cibon (☎ 585-461-2960; 688 Park Ave; mains $10-16; ☒ 11am-midnight) Munch on a dynamic, light menu of pizzas, pastas and salads at this casually alluring Euro cafe with martinis and music come evenings. Near the Eastman House.

Richardson's Canal House (☎ 585-248-5000; 1474 Marsh Rd, Pittsford; lunch $9-12, dinner $19-32; ☒ lunch Mon-Fri, dinner Tue-Sat) Richardson's is a Rochester institution in a restored 1818 Erie Canal tavern, where French and American cuisine is served by candlelight.

The Geva Theatre Center (☎ 585-232-4382; www.gevatheatre.org; 75 Woodbury Blvd) At the corner of Clinton Ave S, this is Rochester's premier professional theater.

Little Theatres (☎ 585-258-0400; 240 East Ave; admission $3) Revivals and new independent movies are shown on five screens in a classic art deco building in the East End district.

Eastman School of Music (☎ 585-274-1100; 26 Gibbs St) One of the world's leading music schools stages over 700 jazz and classical concerts by students and visitors a year.

Getting There & Around

Greater Rochester International Airport (☎ 716-464-6000; Brooks Ave), at I-390 exit 18, is served by most major American carriers.

The **bus terminal** (☎ 800-295-5555; 187 Midtown Plaza) is on the corner of Broad and Chestnut Sts. Trains from the **Amtrak train station** (☎ 585-454-2894, 800-872-7245; 320 Central Ave) go to Buffalo and NYC.

> **WHAT THE...?**
>
> Curious about the history behind that most bizarre of American desserts, Jell-O? Visit the hometown of the carpenter who invented it in 1897 to find out. Thirty minutes southwest of Rochester in Le Roy (Map p200), the **Jell-O Gallery** at the **LeRoy House Historic Museum** (☎ 585-768-7433; 23 E Main St, Le Roy; admission adult/child $4/1.50; ☒ 10am-4pm Mon-Sat, 1-4pm Sun, closed weekends Jan-Mar) tells the story of this original bit of Americana. Don't forget to pick up your Jell-O mold or Jell-O shot glass in the gift shop.

If you're coming by car, Rochester is about 10 miles north of I-90.

WESTERN NEW YORK

In a state that's decidedly East Coast, going west is a whole different world – and one, to the surprise of many city slickers, that's hardly the hinterlands. The magnificent Niagara Falls are not the only reason to visit this part of the state – don't forget about the vibrant city of Buffalo. In a state of revival, it is home to numerous art galleries, fascinating architecture – some of which was designed by Frank Lloyd Wright – and a thriving theater scene. It's also the home of Buffalo wings and Buffalo Bills football. South of Buffalo, the iconic Chautauqua Institution hosts a well-known summer retreat, which includes lectures, performances, and educational programs meant to inspire the spirit and expand the intellect in a lovely community setting.

BUFFALO
pop 277,000

Famous for its winter snowfalls (which, contrary to rumor, are *not* the heaviest in the US), Buffalo turns heads as an outpost for art, theater and architecture. Grand streets lined with palatial mansions pay homage to Buffalo's industrial glory days, yet turn a corner and a block away the view shifts to a decidedly rough-and-tumble world of urban struggle and heartbreak. This is a human city, where you're never far away from 'real life,' whether hopeful or bleak. As Buffalo tries to pull itself out of its maligned image as a snowy, poor rust-belt city surrounded by bleak industrial wastelands, it's impressive what kind of scrappy optimism gets cooked up here. Hang out in the Allen Street area or on Elmwood Ave, and you might sense that this town's still growing into its coolness – although its edgy grit has never been in question.

Orientation

With Lake Erie to the west and south, most of the city's major streets begin in the downtown area and run to the north and the east. A Metro rail public transportation line runs up the center of Main St and this car-free pedestrian area is designated 'Buffalo Place.'

North of downtown is the historic district of Allentown. Between Allen and North Sts in Allentown is the Elmwood strip, a trendy and lively area of shops, eateries and bookstores.

Information

Rust Belt Books (☎ 716-885-9535; www.rustbeltbooks. com 202 Allen St) is an eclectic bookshop in the Allentown neighborhood.

The **Greater Buffalo Convention & Visitors Bureau** (☎ 716-852-0511; www.visitbuffaloniagara.com; 617 Main St; ⏰ 8am-5pm Mon-Fri) houses a visitors center in the Market Arcade.

The local newspaper is the *Buffalo News* (www.buffalonews.com). *ArtVoice* (www. artvoice.com) is the arts paper in town and a good source of information for culture and entertainment.

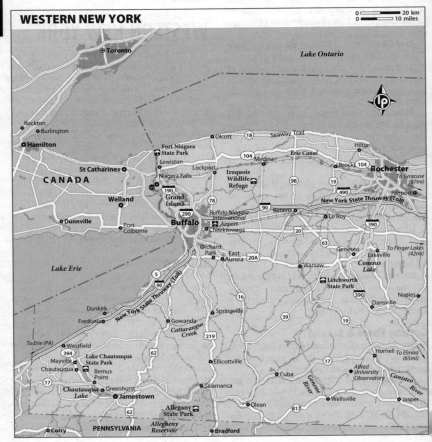

WESTERN NEW YORK

Sights & Activities
ALBRIGHT-KNOX ART GALLERY
Housed in a wonderful Greek revival building north of downtown, this **museum** (☎ 716-882-8700; 1285 Elmwood Ave; adult/child/student & senior $12/free/8; ☺ 11am-5pm Tue-Sat, noon-5pm Sun) is the heart of Buffalo's art scene. Renowned for its contemporary art, it was the first US museum to purchase works by Picasso and Matisse. Other 20th-century works cover the gamut from Rothko and Pollock to Gauguin and Toulouse-Lautrec.

THEATER DISTRICT
The restored Theater District (www.theateralliance ofbuffalo.com) is a 20-block area downtown, buzzing with a half-dozen theaters, along with restaurants, galleries and shops. The crown jewel is the opulent 1926 **Shea's Performing Arts Center** (☎ 716-847-0580; www.sheas.org; 646 Main St), full of 15ft Tiffany chandeliers, marble floors and a European opera-house feel.

Also worth checking out are the **Ujima Theater Co** (☎ 716-883-0380; www.ujimatheatre.org; TheaterLoft, 545 Elmwood Ave) and the **Alleyway Theatre** (☎ 716-852-2600; www.alleyway.com; 1 Curtain Up Alley), a small, intimate theater company that showcases new plays. The **Irish Classical Theatre** (☎ 716-853-4282; www.irishclassicaltheatre.com; 625 Main St) performs in a state-of-the-art theatre-in-the-round and focuses on Irish and international playwrights.

PEDALING HISTORY BICYCLE MUSEUM
This **museum** (☎ 716-662-3853; www.pedalinghbicyclemuseum.com; 3943 N Buffalo Rd, Orchard Park; adult/child $7.50/4.50; ☺ 11am-5pm Mon-Sat, 1:30-5pm Sun Apr–mid-Jan, closed Tue-Thu mid-Jan–Mar) is the only one in the country dedicated exclusively to bicycles.

Tours
Theodore Roosevelt Inaugural National Historic Site (☎ 716-884-0095; Wilcox Mansion, 641 Delaware Ave) offers self-guided audio walking tours of Buffalo's architectural sites.

Buffalo Bar Crawls (☎ 716-462-4385; www.buffalobarcrawl.com) To explore Buffalo like the party-loving locals, join up with a bar crawl, held each spring along a Chippewa St stretch of 20 bars. Get a bargain $10 wristband, plunge into the debauchery, and say 'When in Buffalo…'

Sleeping
Chains abound off the interstates and near the airport in Buffalo.

> **WHAT THE…?**
>
> The only **metal kazoo factory** (☎ 716-992-3960; 8703 S Main St, Eden; admission free; ☺ 10am-5pm Tue-Sat, noon-5pm Sun) in the world is a one-of-a-kind place: a combo factory, museum and gift shop. Established in 1916, the factory paid $5000 for its first kazoo patent and still makes the instruments in the same way – using sheet metal and die presses.

Hostel Buffalo (☎ 716-852-5222; www.hostelbuffalo.com; 667 Main St; dm $22, d $51) In the heart of the Theater District, this big, airy hostel is in a historic building and has 52 beds in immaculate dorms.

Honu House (☎ 716-886-2397; www.elmwoodvillageinn.com; 893 Elmwood Ave; r $95-130; ☺) In the hip Elmwood neighborhood, this 1891 house has a relaxed, sunny elegance and fetching rooms, including a richly-colored Middle Eastern room.

Beau Fleuve B&B (☎ 716-882-6116; www.beaufleuve.com; 242 Linwood Ave; s/d from $120/140; ☺) With themed rooms celebrating the ethnic heritage of Buffalo's original immigrants, this historic inn is rich with nostalgic luxury. We like to

> **BUFFALO ARCHITECTURE**
>
> You can explore Buffalo's architectural treasures in greater depth if you take advantage of one of the excellent self-guided or guided architectural **tours** sponsored by the Theodore Roosevelt Inaugural National Historic Site.
>
> The largest concentration of Frank Lloyd Wright homes is north of the downtown area near Delaware Park, which was designed by landscape architect Frederick Law Olmsted. The impressive **Darwin Martin House** (☎ 716-856-3858; www.darwinmartinhouse.org; 125 Jewett Pkwy; adult/student $15/10; ☺ tours 10am-3pm hourly May-Oct, call for other times) has been beautifully renovated to showcase its forward-thinking modern interiors, like a plant-filled conservatory, sleek pergola and modern kitchen.
>
> Literary types should check out **F Scott Fitzgerald's childhood home** at 29 Irving Place. **Mark Twain** lived at 472 Delaware Ave while working for the *Buffalo Morning Express*.

say *guten nacht* in the German room, whose sleigh bed and electric stove seem made for chilly Buffalo nights.

Embassy Suites (☎ 716-842-1000; www.embassy suites1.hilton.com; 200 Delaware Ave; r from $139; 🛜 🖵 ♿) This spanking new hotel offers tempting amenities including a fitness center, complimentary breakfast, and an evening cocktail-hour spread. Starbucks addicts can seek a fix in the lobby.

Mansion on Delaware Avenue (☎ 716-886-3300; www.themansionondelaware.com; 414 Delaware Ave; d from $195; 🛜) Hip, but not hipper-than-thou. Ultra-swanky, the 134-year-old mansion has 28 rooms and dramatic parlors that are divine for complimentary happy hour cocktails,

DOWNTOWN BUFFALO

NEW YORK STATE

INFORMATION
Greater Buffalo Convention &
  Visitors Bureau.........................1 B1
Rust Belt Books...............................2 C2

SIGHTS & ACTIVITIES
Alleyway Theatre.............................3 B1
F Scott Fitzgerald's House..............4 D2
Irish Classical Theatre....................5 B1
Kleinhans Music Hall.......................6 C2
Mark Twain's House.........................7 C3
Shea's Performing Arts Center.......8 B1
Theater Loft--Ujima Theater Co...9 C1
Theodore Roosevelt Inaugural
  National Historic Site...............10 D2

SLEEPING
Beau Fleuve B&B...........................11 D1
Embassy Suites..............................12 C4
Hostel Buffalo...............................13 B1
Mansion on Delaware Ave...........14 C3

EATING
Allen St Hardware..........................15 C2
Anchor Bar....................................16 D2
Bacchus...17 A2
Betty's...18 C3
Left Bank.......................................19 C1
Merge.....................................(see 20)

DRINKING
Founding Fathers..........................20 D3

ENTERTAINMENT
Babeville..21 C3
Nietzsche's....................................22 C2

TRANSPORT
Metro Transportation Center.....23 D4

reading, or just lounging and pretending you own the place. Who says that drop-dead gorgeous can't have personality?

Eating

Feeling spontaneous? Head to Elmwood St, Delaware Ave or Allen St, and explore. Pick up snacks and picnic supplies at the **Lexington Coop** (☎ 716-886-2667; 807 Elmwood Ave).

Sweetness 7 Café and Gallery (☎ 716-883-1736; 220 Grant St; mains $5-8; 7am-9pm Mon-Sat, 7am-3pm Sun; ☞) Connected to the Grant St Gallery, this bohemian feel-good cafe is as charming as it is friendly. Sit at the big wooden communal table adorned with fresh flowers and munch on fresh paninis, almond biscotti and great hibiscus lemonade with a diverse crowd reading or playing cards.

our pick Allen Street Hardware (☎ 716-882-8843; 245 Allen St; mains $7-12; lunch & dinner) Deep red walls, great woodwork, and excellent pub food with an eclectic (tattoo artists, lawyers, musicians) clientele make this one of Buffalo's best bar-restaurant combos.

Bacchus (☎ 716-854-9463; 54 Chippewa St; small plates $7-15; dinner Tue-Sat, to midnight weekends) This swanky wine bar and nouveau restaurant is perfect before or after the theater.

Merge (☎ 716-842-0600; 439 Delaware Ave; mains $8-16; 11:30am-midnight Tue-Sat) Posh vegetarian, vegan and raw food in a stylish setting. Try the raw pad Thai.

Betty's (☎ 716-362-0633; 370 Virginia St; mains $8-19; dinner) A pretty bar leads to a bustling restaurant and patio. Packed at brunch, the healthy menu offers delicious twists on comfort food like a veggie shepherds pie.

Left Bank (☎ 716-882-3509; 511 Rhode Island St; mains $11-19; dinner) The romantic brick interior, fabulous outdoor patio, wine list and 'bourgeois' and 'peasant' fare like fondue and fresh focaccia is downright sigh-inducing.

Drinking & Entertainment

You won't suffer in Buffalo from a lack of entertainment – or beer. The Chippewa District downtown is the traditional party-hearty central (people do shots here), while the entertainment in Allentown historic district is more diverse.

Nietzsche's (☎ 716-886-8539; 248 Allen St) This is an old standby where the crazy interior invites free association, ennui and plenty of rock 'n' roll nihilism. Rock out to all kinds of live music, or just come along to participate

> ## ANCHOR BAR
>
> Your vocabulary need only consist of four words at Buffalo's most famous restaurant – mild, medium, hot or suicidal. The **Anchor Bar** (☎ 716-886-8920; 1047 Main St; mains $6-15; lunch & dinner, to midnight Fri & Sat) claims to have invented Buffalo chicken wings in 1964. If you're feeling adventurous (or tipsy), don the spongy buffalo head and get your photo snapped.

in that consummate cold-weather activity, drinking.

our pick Founding Fathers (☎ 716-855-8944; 75 Edward St) Pay homage to Buffalo's historic past by toasting Grover Cleveland or another of the long-ago US presidents celebrated at this old-school tavern. Even expats may feel patriotic here – especially after the third beer.

Kleinhans Music Hall (☎ 716-885-5000; www.bpo.org; 3 Symphony Circle; 370 Pennsylvania Ave) One of five acoustically perfect concert halls in the country, this is the home of the Buffalo Philharmonic Orchestra.

Lancaster Opera House (☎ 716-683-1776; www.lancopera.org; 21 Central Ave, Lancaster) This early-20th-century 'town hall' style theater presents plays, musicals and concerts.

Buffalo Bills (☎ 716-649-0015; www.buffalobills.com; Ralph Wilson Stadium, 1 Bills Dr, Orchard Park) Once notorious for being both OJ Simpson's team and for its knack of losing championship games, rabid fans come in droves to cheer this NFL team.

Getting There & Around

Buffalo Niagara International Airport (☎ 716-630-6000; www.buffaloairport.com; 4200 Genesee St) is about 16 miles from downtown.

New York Trailways (☎ 800-776-7548; www.trailwaysny.com), **Greyhound** (☎ 800-231-2222; www.greyhound.com) and **NFTA** (☎ 716-285-7211; www.nfta.com) operate out of the **Metro Transportation Center** (cnr Ellicott & Division Sts), with buses each day to Niagara Falls. The **Buffalo Metro Rail** runs down Main St from the HSBC stadium to the University of Buffalo.

Amtrak (www.amtrak.com) stops in Buffalo at the downtown **Buffalo Exchange Station** (☎ 716-683-8440; cnr Exchange & Oak Sts).

Reach Buffalo by I-90 or I-190 from Niagara Falls. The Peace Bridge over the Niagara River connects Buffalo to Ontario.

NIAGARA FALLS & AROUND

Straddling Canada and the US, Niagara Falls has long attracted travelers, daredevils and honeymooners to its misty shores.

NIAGARA FALLS

pop 56,000

With 40 million gallons of water per minute hurtling downward and extending outward into a cloud of mist, Niagara Falls is western New York's most revered tourist attraction. Honeymooners, daredevils, artists and families all traipse through the Niagara Reservation State Park to stare at the power and magnificence of the falls.

Note that there are actually two cataracts, or high waterfalls. The Canadian **Horseshoe Falls** are the larger and more impressive of the two, while the smaller **American Falls** are 1100ft across and fall 180ft. Sometimes referred to as a separate cataract, **Bridal Veil Falls** actually forms the western portion of the American Falls. **Goat Island** sits in the middle of the Niagara River, which is the international border between Canada and the US – the longest unprotected border in the world. Check out the falls at night, when they're illuminated at sunset. Unfortunately, while the falls themselves are amazing, the towns of Niagara Falls fit every cliché in the book – cheesy, tacky and 1950s kitsch.

Orientation

There are actually two towns of Niagara Falls: Niagara Falls, NY, and Niagara Falls, Ontario (Canada), situated across from one another on the opposite banks of the Niagara River. In Niagara Falls, NY, most major attractions are south of Niagara St, along the river.

Information

The **Niagara Falls State Park Visitors Center** (☎ 716-278-1796; Prospect Park; ⊗ 8am-10:15pm) is adjacent to the falls.

Sight & Activities

Here's the question: which side offers the better view? The answer: check out both sides. (For the best panoramic view, cross over to the Canadian side.) On the other hand, the American side allows you (you have no choice) to feel the immense power of the

falls. You can easily walk or drive to Canada across **Rainbow Bridge** (car/pedestrian $3.25/$0.50). Be prepared to go through customs for both countries; have your passport ready.

Hikers will want to explore the **Niagara Gorge Trail System**.

NIAGARA RESERVATION STATE PARK

The oldest state **park** (www.niagarafallsstatepark.com) in the country includes **Goat Island**, a half-mile-long island connected to the US mainland by free pedestrian and car bridges. From the island you can walk to **Three Sisters Islands**, a series of rapids approaching Horseshoe Falls. You can also walk down to **Terrapin Point**, the closest viewing point to Horseshoe Falls.

To experience the falls up close, take an elevator down from Goat Island to the **Cave of the Winds** (☎ 716-278-1730; adult/child $11/8; ⊗ Jun-Oct), where you'll walk along wooden walkways within 25ft of the cataracts.

SENECA NIAGARA CASINO

Gamblers will want to check out this high-octane **casino** (☎ 877-873-6322; www.senecaniagaracasino.com; 310 4th St), with tons of slot machines and tables for blackjack, craps and poker along with a theater, a nightclub and restaurants.

Tours

Although you can view the falls on foot, many prefer to take a narrated bus tour. Typically, tours include stops on both sides of the border and include a boat ride and visits to Prospect Park and Goat Island.

Since 1846, Niagara Falls' biggest tourist attraction has been a boat ride on the **Maid of the Mist** (☎ 716-284-8897, Canada ☎ 905-358-5781; adult/child $13.50/8; ⊗ 9am-6pm May-Oct), which leaves from the base of the Prospect Park Observation Tower. If you only have time for one attraction, this should be it. They'll hand you a big yellow raincoat before heading for the base falls.

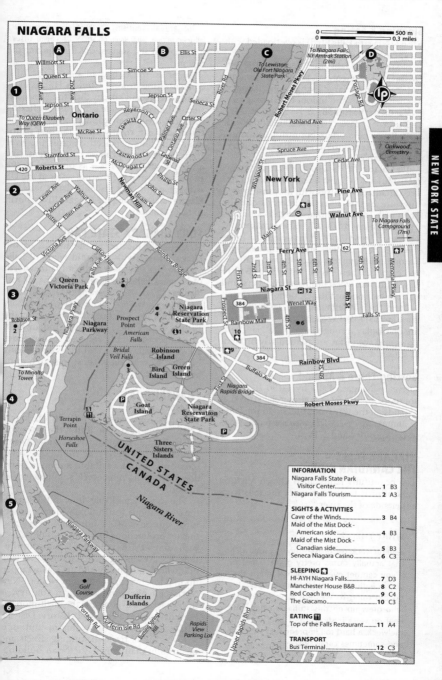

NIAGARA FALLS

NEW YORK STATE

INFORMATION

Niagara Falls State Park
Visitor Center...................................1 B3
Niagara Falls Tourism....................2 A3

SIGHTS & ACTIVITIES

Cave of the Winds..........................3 B4
Maid of the Mist Dock -
American side..............................4 B3
Maid of the Mist Dock -
Canadian side..............................5 B3
Seneca Niagara Casino..................6 C3

SLEEPING

HI-AYH Niagara Falls.....................7 D3
Manchester House B&B.................8 C2
Red Coach Inn................................9 C4
The Giacomo.................................10 C3

EATING

Top of the Falls Restaurant........11 A4

TRANSPORT

Bus Terminal................................12 C3

NEW YORK STATE

Sleeping & Eating

Rte 62 (Niagara Falls Blvd) is overloaded with inexpensive motels.

HI-AYH Niagara Falls (☎ 716-282-3700; 1101 Ferry Ave; dm $20) This Georgian home features dormitory rooms, a large living room, laundry, kitchen facilities and indoor bike storage.

Manchester House B&B (☎ 716-285-5717; 800-489-3009; 653 Main St; d $90; 🛜) This 1903 home with friendly owners offers bountiful breakfasts like apple French toast, as well as a wonderfully walkable location.

The Giacamo (☎ 716-299-0200; www.thegiacomo.com; 222 First St; r from $175, with Jacuzzi from $195; 🛜) Art deco architecture mixes with Mayan-inspired interiors in this 38-room luxury boutique hotel with Jacuzzis and luxe details.

Red Coach Inn (☎ 716-282-1459; www.redcoach.com; 2 Buffalo Ave; d from $179; 🛜) This delightful 1920s Tudor-style inn offers suites furnished with European antique reproductions and dramatic red carpets. Their restaurant (mains $10 to $34) with faux wood beams, chandeliers, and oak tables is one of the best options in town.

Top of the Falls Restaurant (☎ 716-278-0337; Goat Island; mains $10-15) Excellent views of the falls are on display through large plate-glass windows and the vistas are particularly brilliant at sunset.

Getting There & Around

Drive to Niagara Falls by I-190 from the south, or by Rte 62, a commercial strip that extends all the way from Buffalo to the falls.

Amtrak (☎ 716-285-4224; www.amtrak.com) stops at Lockport Rd and 27th St.

NIAGARA FALLS – THE CANADIAN SIDE

The beautifully landscaped Queen Victoria Park affords the best view of the falls from either side of the river.

WHAT THE...?

Beef on weck: the gross-sounding sandwich that actually tastes pretty good – that is, if you can get over the mental image that you're eating something called 'weck.' It's no big thing to Western New York folks, who grew up on this stuff. So what is it? Beef on weck is sliced roast beef on kummelweck, a hard roll impregnated with salt and sometimes caraway seeds.

Niagara Falls Tourism (☎ 800-563-2557; www.niagarafallstourism.com; 5400 Robinson St; 🕙 9am-5pm) offers information and suggestions for enjoying the region.

Surprise: the Canadian side of the falls, concentrating around Clinton Hill, is even more touristy and kitschy than the American side. While the US side can boast of offering the most thrilling proximity to the falls, the Canadians can rightly claim the best panorama. The long perspective across the river from **Queen Victoria Park** is magnificent, like a long leisurely breath – as opposed to the powerful gasp of the roaring water at the US vantage point. For a scenic drive, take the **Niagara Parkway** along the Niagara River, north to Lake Ontario.

FORT NIAGARA STATE PARK

Strategically located at the mouth of the Niagara River with splendid views of Lake Ontario, this state park is about 15 miles north of Niagara Falls town, and contains **Old Fort Niagara** (☎ 716-745-7611; www.oldfortniagara.com; adult/child $10/6; 🕙 9am-5pm). The fort was built by the French in 1726, but was captured by the British during the French and Indian War. The impressive, fully restored fort includes a French castle and a well that's supposedly haunted by a headless ghost in search of its head.

CHAUTAUQUA

Pop 4700

65 miles southwest of Buffalo on lovely Chautauqua Lake, you'll find the township of Chautauqua (pronounced sha-*taw*-kwah). While few live here year-round, the town blossoms into a veritable summer paradise during the nine-week summer tourist season.

The most remarkable draw to this area is the Chautauqua Institution, which hosts lectures, concerts, workshops and dance and theater productions for thousands of visitors each summer. This venerated summer institution deserves its legendary status as an icon of intellect, spirituality and art – all wrapped up in a lovely resort setting in western New York's bucolic wine and farm country. A throwback to a bygone era, the institution has been designated a National Historic District. Inside its gates, the sprawling institution is a 'town' full of tranquil winding streets and beautifully maintained Victorian buildings and gardens. Between attending lectures and concerts, swimming and biking around the grounds, visitors loll about on front porches and garden benches or stroll the locust-tree-covered grounds. Cars are banned (except for loading and emergencies), and given its 'Sunday School' roots, alcohol is permitted but it is not sold, and no drinking is allowed in public. Life here is as unstructured as you wish to make it. The psychologist William James, brother to Henry James, referred to Chautauqua – in a less than complimentary tone – as a 'middle-class paradise, without a sin, without a victim, without a blot, without a tear.'

You can visit in one day, but most visitors arrange for stays of a weekend, a week or longer (and many return each year). A weekly gate pass is $375, a full day pass is $60, and an evening only (4pm-midnight) pass runs at $36. Call or peruse the online resources at the **Chautauqua Institution** (☎ 716-357-6200; www.ciweb.org) to look into lodging, entertainment, and other programs.

Located in the Welcome Center at the Chautauqua Institution main gate, the **Chautauqua County Visitors Bureau** (CVB; ☎ 716-357-4569, 800-908-4569; www.tourchautauqua.com; Main Gate; ◷ 9am-5pm Jun-Aug) is another source of information.

Sights & Activities

The **lecture series** at Chautauqua enjoys national renown. President Franklin D Roosevelt gave his 'I Hate War' speech at the Chautauqua amphitheater in 1936. Nine other US presidents, from Ulysses S Grant to Bill Clinton, plus Leo Tolstoy, have lectured here.

There are morning Christian religious services most days of the week. On Sunday, visiting theologians such as Jesse Jackson, Elie Wiesel and Mrs Coretta Scott King inspire with their sermons.

Since 1929, the American and international musicians of the **Chautauqua Symphony Orchestra** have performed on the grounds; also worth hearing is the chamber music series, guest recitals and student recitals. Along with the **Chautauqua Opera**, acclaimed pop, rock and folk concerts and other high-profile performances (featuring anything from ABBA to Salman Rushdie) take place in the 5000 seat, open-air amphitheater. And don't forget the renowned **Chautauqua Dance Company**'s modern dance and ballet perform-

DETOUR – JAMESTOWN

Do you love Lucy? If so, drive 90-minutes south from Buffalo to check out Jamestown, where comedienne Lucille Ball was born in 1911. A working-class city with a touch of elegance, Jamestown's love affair with its favorite daughter is everywhere. Tribute is paid at the **Lucy-Desi Museum** (☎ 716-484-7070; www.lucy-desi.com; 2 W 3rd St; adult/child $10/7; ◷ 10am-5pm Mon-Sat, 11am-4pm Sun Apr-Oct). At 15, Lucille took a bus to New York City, landed a job as a Broadway chorus girl, and met Desi Arnaz in 1940. The rest is history.

ances, or the **Chautauqua Theater Company**, whose resident company and conservatory students present a repertory of three plays each season.

Along with boasting the oldest continually running **book club** in the nation, Chautauqua offers fascinating **lectures** by a diverse range of artists, politicians, journalists and writers, from the *New York Times*' David Brooks to Jim Lehrer to the US Poet Laureate, Billy Collins.

Sports fanatics and recreational junkies, don't fear: Chautauqua offers plenty for the body as well as the spirit and mind. Along with the usual suspects (swimming, tennis and a fitness center) there's golf, sailing, kayaking, canoeing and programs for kids. No wonder people hang out here for at least a week.

Sleeping & Eating

The **Chautauqua CVB** can assist you in finding housing for your stay at the institution. Many of the following options offer guest rooms as well as apartments with kitchen facilities, and all offer weekly rates. Many people dine in the village at various hotels; ask at the CVB for dining options.

ourpick Chautauqua Inn (☎ 716-357-3885; www.chautauquainn.com; 15 Roberts Ave; r from $89) Relax in the flowery back garden of this remodeled Victorian house with 17 rooms, all with private baths.

Athenaeum Hotel (☎ 716-357-4444; s/d incl meals from $212/317) For many, this ornate Victorian hotel defines the Chautauqua experience. Overlooking the lake, it's the perfect place to step back in time: ladies dress in their

NEW YORK STATE

DETOUR – ALLEGANY STATE PARK

Popular year-round, this **park** (☎ 716-354-9121) is particularly fantastic in the winter when you can indulge in ice-fishing, snow-mobiling and cross-country skiing. About 25 miles east of Chautauqua, the 65,000-acre park offers great hiking trails, two sandy beaches, horseback riding, biking, fishing, and year-round camping with winter (brrr!) cabins.

---

loveliest and men in their jackets and ties for formal five-course dinners, while the languid breeze on the grand veranda conjures nostalgia itself.

Gleason Hotel (☎ 716-357-2595; www.gleasonhotel.com; 12 N Lake Drive; s/d weekly $550/950) This sprawling lakefront house has four lovely porches complete with wicker rocking chairs. Guests can cook in the kitchen.

Ashland and Vera Guesthouses (☎ 716-357-3436; www.chautauquaguesthouse.com; r without/with bathroom from $565/645 per week) Two multiple story Victorian guesthouses with front porches on every floor offer kitchens and views. From the Vera's porch, you can hear the symphony orchestra performing at the nearby Chautauqua Amphitheater.

Redline Drive-In (☎ 716-753-5550; Rte 394, Mayville; mains $7-10) Rock out to 1960s classics as waitresses skate over to bring your Philly cheese steak or strawberry milkshake.

New Jersey

Go ahead, crack jokes. Take your best shots. Jersey can take it. New Jersey has been a national punchline since at least the 1800s and, according to one 2002 study, the funniest joke in the world is about Jersey. The state is, by turns, venal, greedy, smelly, rude, hopelessly corrupt and hilariously inept.

So why is New Jersey one of the top-10 states in tourist spending? If Jersey's so bad, why do so many people vacation here? Why do so many people want to *live* here? The truth is New Jersey is much more than it's cracked up to be. Yeah, sure, it earns its reputation in a thousand ways every day, but the state is as complex and diverse as America offers and about the size of a toaster oven. It's a mighty, pugnacious little dynamo.

Consider these contrasts: It's the nation's most densely populated and urbanized state, yet over 40% of it is forested and the Pine Barrens are the largest preserved coastal habitat between Boston and Richmond; it has the most roads per square mile, as well as the second-highest percentage of farmland; state citizens enjoy the nation's highest per capita income and the highest taxes, and are one of the most ethnically diverse, immigrant-rich groups.

Most visitors come to New Jersey for its famous beaches and boardwalks – for Atlantic City's casinos, Cape May's Victorians and Asbury Park's clubs. Yet there's high culture in Princeton, New Brunswick and, get this, Newark. The Delaware Water Gap and the canals of Lambertville provide lovely canoeing and hiking. There's American Revolution history, sculpture parks, amazing pizza, gourmet cuisine and, oh: Did you hear the one about the guy…

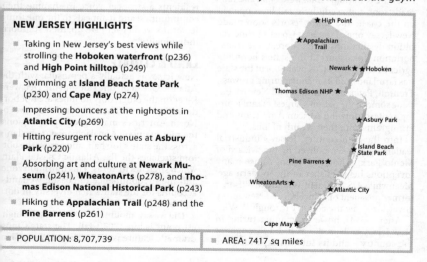

NEW JERSEY HIGHLIGHTS

- Taking in New Jersey's best views while strolling the **Hoboken waterfront** (p236) and **High Point hilltop** (p249)
- Swimming at **Island Beach State Park** (p230) and **Cape May** (p274)
- Impressing bouncers at the nightspots in **Atlantic City** (p269)
- Hitting resurgent rock venues at **Asbury Park** (p220)
- Absorbing art and culture at **Newark Museum** (p241), **WheatonArts** (p278), and **Thomas Edison National Historical Park** (p243)
- Hiking the **Appalachian Trail** (p248) and the **Pine Barrens** (p261)

★ High Point
★ Appalachian Trail
Newark ★ ★ Hoboken
Thomas Edison NHP ★
★ Asbury Park
★ Island Beach State Park
Pine Barrens ★
WheatonArts ★
★ Atlantic City
Cape May ★

- POPULATION: 8,707,739
- AREA: 7417 sq miles

HISTORY

New Jersey has always been a place with identity issues, a state of division and diversity ever since its founding. In 1674, Lord John Berkeley and Sir George Carteret were given the land grant for the territory, and they soon divided it into East Jersey (whose capital was Perth Amboy) and West Jersey (capital in Burlington). The dividing line ran from the state's northwest corner south to the coast's Little Egg Harbor, below Long Beach Island; adjusted slightly, this still marks today's cultural divide between North Jersey and South Jersey.

This division persists due to geography: New Jersey – sandwiched between New York City and Philadelphia, colonial America's two biggest cities – was, and is, a vital transportation corridor between them. This proximity to commercial hubs, immigration gateways and easy transportation attracted a diverse mix of settlers and led to the state's economic importance.

Geography is also why New Jersey was the main battleground during the American Revolution. The British held Manhattan, the patriots were headquartered in Philadelphia, and their armies met most often in the middle – New Jersey saw over 600 battles and skirmishes (see p36). After the war, East and West Jersey were made whole, and the state capital moved to Trenton.

In the 1830s, the Morris Canal and the Delaware & Raritan Canal were built, and railroads soon followed; these rail lines opened up the coast, and shore resorts soon made New Jersey one of the East Coast's prime vacation destinations. Even more, these transportation links spurred the state's booming agriculture (in the 1870s over 60% of the state was farmland) and its manufacturing prowess. Trenton, Paterson, Camden and Newark became some of the nation's largest manufacturing centers, drawing African Americans and immigrants with their wealth of jobs.

Into the 20th century, Jersey's industrial leadership was symbolized by the 'wizard of Menlo Park,' Thomas Edison, whose many inventions helped usher in the modern age. Meanwhile, US President Woodrow Wilson – former president of Princeton and New Jersey governor – saw the country through WWI.

After WWII, however, manufacturing in New Jersey collapsed – as it did throughout the country – and its suburbs expanded like wildfire. This in-migration was spurred by massive road-building whose epitome was the NJ Turnpike, completed in 1951 and dubbed 'the greatest highway of all.' Yet industry left behind a slew of toxic-waste sites and abandoned factories, and NJ's once-thriving cities became scarred by poverty and crime.

Beginning in the 1970s, New Jersey shifted from muscle to mind, from blue collar to white collar, as it led the telecommunications revolution and focused on services and high-tech research, particularly in medicine. Jersey today contains wealthy exurbs of New York and Philadelphia, it's home to numerous corporate headquarters, and it is a continuing magnet for immigration, particularly from India, the Dominican Republic, the Philippines and Latin America.

In addition to these things, Jersey is also known for its ethically challenged government and its high taxes – both of which have roots in the sacred cow of state politics, 'home rule.' This is the term for the peculiar division of the state into 566 municipalities (some of them only a few sqare miles), each with its own mayor, police and fire departments and school system. These services are expensive, which accounts for the taxes, and they make for an extremely localized political culture that has encouraged, perhaps, the 'pay-to-play' shenanigans, the kickbacks and bribes between contractors and city officials (and the mob), that keep state prosecutors so busy. Home rule, though, gives residents a stronger voice in shaping their communities, and it appeals to the one thing Jerseyans won't ever give up, their stubborn individuality.

LAND & CLIMATE

New Jersey is actually a peninsula: with the Atlantic Ocean on one side and the Delaware River on the other, only 48 miles are not bordered by water. The state includes two of North America's major geographic regions: the mountainous Appalachian system slants across the state's top half, and across the bottom stretches the flat Atlantic Coastal Plain, which stretches to Texas. This transition zone and the predominance of coastal wetlands accounts for the state's rich diversity in flora and fauna.

Did we say 'mountains'? New Jersey's highest point is but 1803ft tall. The state's most dramatic feature is the Delaware Water Gap

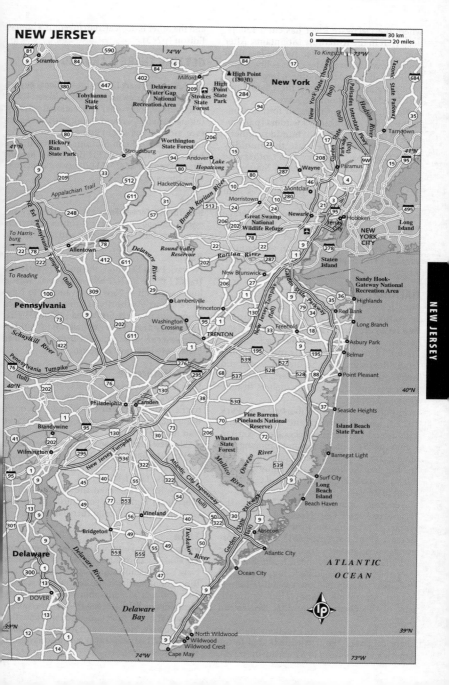

NEW JERSEY

where the Delaware River has cut a 1300ft-deep cleft in the Kittatinny Mountains. After that, the state is pretty flat, mostly less than 400ft above sea level. The coast is lined with barrier islands, and the southern interior contains a wetlands wilderness, the 1.1-million-acre Pinelands National Reserve.

New Jersey experiences all four seasons to the fullest – with snowy winters (particularly in the north) and hot humid summers. Atlantic Ocean breezes ease the humidity along the coast, but they don't otherwise bring down state temperatures. Statewide, average temperatures are 31°F in January, 50°F in April, 74°F in July and 54°F in October. However, summer highs can average over 84°F and winter lows can average below 20°.

New Jersey gets a lot of rain – 47in annually, which is 50% greater than the national average. The heaviest months are July and August.

NATIONAL & STATE PARKS

New Jersey has 45 state parks, forests and recreation areas, and all are managed by the **New Jersey Division of Parks and Forestry** (☎ 609-984-0370, 800-843-6420; www.njparksandforests.org). About 19 parks and forests offer camping (individual sites $20); all include water and toilets and most include showers. Some have other options, from lean-to shelters to fully equipped cabins.

Highlights include Liberty State Park (p239), with access to Statue of Liberty and Ellis Island ferries; the Delaware & Raritan Canal (p258), with hiking and canoeing; the state parks accessing the Appalachian Trail (p248); and the beaches and nature walks at Island Beach State Park (p230) and Cape May Point State Park (p275).

Federally managed lands include the Delaware Water Gap National Recreation Area (p247) and the Pinelands National Reserve (Pine Barrens; p261), which incorporates several state parks. For more birding and wildlife-watching, head to the Edwin B Forsythe National Wildlife Refuge (p262) and the Great Swamp National Wildlife Refuge (p246). Meanwhile, Sandy Hook (p213) is part of the Gateway National Recreation Area.

New Jersey has two excellent national historical parks: the first is dedicated to the American Revolution in Morristown (p245),

and the other is dedicated to inventor Thomas Edison (p243).

GETTING THERE & AROUND
Air
In Newark, **Newark Liberty International Airport** (☎ 973-961-6000; www.panynj.gov/airports/newark-liberty.html) is the region's other international gateway (along with JFK). From the airport, AirTrain (see airport website) runs a 24-hour service to Newark Penn Station; it's free if you buy a NJ Transit or PATH ticket. The **Newark Airport Express** (☎ 877-863-9275; www.coachusa.com) runs buses to New York.

Boat
New York Waterway Ferry (☎ 800-533-3779; www.nywaterway.com) runs ferry routes between Hoboken, Liberty State Park and Manhattan.

Bus
Newark Penn Station is the hub for **New Jersey Transit** (☎ 800-772-2222; www.njtransit.com), whose buses serve all of New Jersey and go to New York's Port Authority terminal. Other regional bus lines are **Greyhound** (☎ 800-231-2222; www.greyhound.com), **Peter Pan Trailways** (☎ 800-343-9999; www.peterpanbus.com) and **DeCamp Bus Lines** (☎ 800-631-1281; www.decamp.com).

Car & Motorcycle
New Jersey has the most roads per square mile of any state in the US, which means the most traffic and road repair too (though no one's done the math). For updates, call ☎ 511 or visit www.511nj.org.

The **New Jersey Turnpike** (I-95; www.state.nj.us/turnpike) and the **Garden State Parkway** are the major north–south toll roads. Going east–west from New York, take I-80 or I-78.

New Jersey invented the 'jughandle': on most local highways, you must exit on the right to make a lefthand turn. Go figure.

Train
From Newark Penn Station, **New Jersey Transit** (☎ 800-772-2222; www.njtransit.com) runs trains to New York's Penn Station, down the shore, and throughout northern and central Jersey; trains also connect Philadelphia to Atlantic City. New Jersey **PATH** (☎ 800-234-7284; www.panyny.gov/path) trains connect downtown Manhattan with Newark, Hoboken and Jersey City. **Amtrak** (☎ 800-872-7245; www.amtrak.com) also connects through Newark.

JERSEY SHORE

Whether traveling north or south, in Jersey you always go 'down the shore.' And chances are – if you're traveling *to* Jersey, not *through* it – that's where you're headed. From Sandy Hook to Cape May, the Jersey coast is nearly 130 miles of sandy beaches and barrier islands, of clanging boardwalks and too-hot-to-eat funnel cakes. It is a summertime escape valve for state residents as well as for overheated Manhattanites and Philadelphians – who in the humid haze of July suddenly remember that, gosh, Jersey does have something to recommend it.

Diversity defines New Jersey, and the shore is no exception. Perhaps you've seen the reality TV show *Jersey Shore,* and think it's just copper-hued Jersey girls and muscle-headed goombahs looking to party, right? Not quite. You can certainly find that – in Seaside Heights, for one – but it won't prepare you for the serene natural beauty of Island Beach State Park and Sandy Hook. It doesn't account for the clean-cut, family-friendly dry towns of Ocean Grove and Ocean City. It doesn't apply to old-money resorts like Spring Lake or middle-class vacation spots like Long Beach Island. Nor does it encompass Cape May's preserved Victorian splendor or Wildwood's doo-wop nostalgia. It doesn't even fit bohemian, gay-friendly Asbury Park, buzzing with new energy.

Of all shore destinations, Atlantic City is the most visited – because of its casinos, of course – and it lends the shore an urban vibe, as well as urban problems. The Jersey shore encompasses a multitude, and it must accommodate one as well. That, ultimately, is the thing to remember: reserve ahead and start driving early, because you won't be alone.

Indeed, the shore is so big it's split between two sections: everything south of Long Beach Island is under Southern New Jersey (p259).

SANDY HOOK

Sandy Hook is perfectly named – it's a crooked peninsula reaching into the Atlantic Ocean, hooking the masses as the first beachworthy destination on the Jersey shore. Most come to sunbathe and swim, and to admire Brooklyn in the hazy distance, but Sandy Hook's marshes and dunes make for great hiking and bird-watching. You'll also find a historic fort and lighthouse, and the biking, ocean fishing and windsurfing are tops.

Sandy Hook is part of the **Gateway National Recreation Area** (www.nps.gov/gate), which includes districts on Staten Island and Brooklyn's Rockaway Peninsula. Sandy Hook's **visitors center** (☎ 732-872-5970; ✆ 10am-5pm, park 5am-10pm), about 2 miles past the toll plaza, has park information and a small museum dedicated to the US Lifesaving Service, which began in 1848 at Sandy Hook's Spermaceti Cove.

The entrance fee ($10 per car from Memorial Day to Labor Day) applies to beach parking; if you're only biking or birding, entrance is free. On summer weekends, arrive by 10am, though, or the lots may be full and the park closed; it reopens when enough cars leave (usually early afternoon). Sandy Hook has no camping.

Sights
FORT HANCOCK & SANDY HOOK LIGHTHOUSE

One day, Sandy Hook may be an island: tides continually shift sand south to north, and the tip has grown so much the Sandy Hook Lighthouse, built in 1764, is now 1.5 miles from shore. Meanwhile, the strategic importance of the peninsula, which guards the entrance to New York Harbor, has been evident since the Revolutionary War. Various forts and gun emplacements were built over the years, particularly from 1890 to 1904. In 1895, it was designated Fort Hancock, which today contains over a hundred century-old brick buildings.

Admission to all these sights is free. The **Fort Hancock Museum** was closed in 2010 for renovations, but should reopen in 2011. The **Sandy Hook Lighthouse** (✆ 1-4:30pm Mon-Fri, noon-4:30pm Sat & Sun Jun-Aug) conducts guided climbs every half hour and has a small museum and movie. Tours of Battery Potter and

NEW JERSEY

WHAT THE...?

Tried to fill up your own tank, didn't you? Well, New Jersey is one of only two states that doesn't allow self-serve gas stations (Oregon is the other). So just pull up to the pump, stay in the car and hand over your credit card (or cash) to the attendant through the window. As the T-shirt says, 'Jersey girls don't pump gas.'

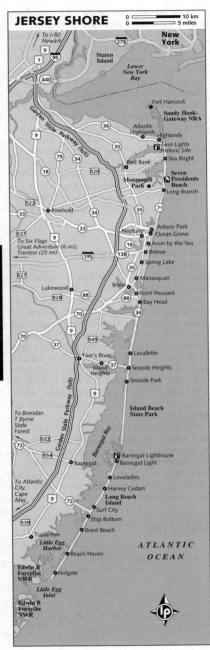

JERSEY SHORE

Battery Gunnison are conducted on summer weekends.

BEACHES & ACTIVITIES

Along the Atlantic Ocean, Sandy Hook's 7 miles of sand contain five excellent swimming beaches with parking, lifeguards and concessions; Beach D even has a **restaurant** (☎ 732-872-0025; www.seagullsnest.info). Far and away the most popular, however, is **Gunnison Beach** – aka Jersey's only official nude beach. Doff your duds and enjoy some nude volleyball, but note the beach's unofficial motto – 'get naked or get lost' – applies particularly to gentlemen.

Windsurfers and kiteboarders head for Sandy Hook Bay opposite Beach C, and Area F is reserved exclusively for fishing. Leisurely, scenic bike trails weave through Fort Hancock, and bikes can travel the main roads. In addition, mainly on summer weekends, the park conducts guided hikes and canoes, seining in the coves, sunrise lighthouse climbs and more. Call the visitor center for schedules and reservations.

SANDY HOOK BIRD OBSERVATORY

Sandy Hook is part of the East Coast's migratory flyway and a major bird-watching destination. For information, books and optics, visit the NJ Audubon Society's **bird observatory** (☎ 732-872-2500; www.njaudubon.org; Fort Hancock Officer's Row, Bldg 20; ☷ 10am-5pm Tue-Sat, 10am-3pm Sun Jun, 10am-5pm Tue-Fri Jul & Aug).

Festivals & Events

Free summer beach **concerts** (☎ 732-291-7733; www.sandyhookfoundationnj.org; ☷ 6pm Wed) happen on Wednesday from late June through early August. The All-Women Lifeguard Tournament is in late July.

Getting There & Away

Most people drive to Sandy Hook, and traffic backups entering and leaving are legendary; call ☎ 511 or 866-511-6538 (say 'Traffic' and 'Route 36') for updates. In recent years, ongoing bridge construction (replacing the old drawbridge) has made traffic worse; the scheduled completion is 2011.

From Manhattan, **Seastreak** (☎ 800-262-8743; www.seastreak.com; adult/child $40/16) offers limited daily ferry service to Sandy Hook in summer. **New York Water Taxi** (☎ 212-742-1969; www.nywatertaxi.com) offers summer weekend service.

HIGHLANDS & ATLANTIC HIGHLANDS
pop 5300

As they flee to the sea, most folks drive straight past the northern Highlands area. But if hunger strikes, or you need a view, or you want to add a Manhattan ferry ride to a Jersey vacation, pull over as you speed along Hwy 36.

Sights & Activities
TWIN LIGHTS HISTORIC SITE

The twin towers of this historic **lighthouse** (☎ 732-872-1814; admission free; ☼ grounds 9am-sunset, museum 10am-4:30pm Wed-Sun), also known as Navesink Light Station, command an almost aerial view of Sandy Hook, with New York on the horizon. The grounds provide some of this, but arrive during museum hours to ascend the north tower and get the real deal.

The current structure dates from 1862, but lighthouses have stood on this site since 1756. Navesink has an interesting history, well-represented in the museum exhibits, as an 'early adopter' of navigational equipment – it was the first to be powered by kerosene, and later by electricity. It was also the sight of the first wireless telegraph tower, set up by Guglielmo Marconi in 1899. Also on display is the south tower's 'first order' lens – measuring 9½ft and weighing 10 tons.

To reach the lighthouse from Route 36 east, make a right onto Portland Rd (just before the bridge to Sea Bright/Sandy Hook), then take an immediate right onto Highland Ave. Go uphill, and follow signs, making a left onto Lighthouse Rd.

FISHING

Shore fishing trips for bluefish and flounder are quite popular; boats must stay pretty close to the shore. **Schupp's Landing** (☎ 732-872-1479; www.schuppslanding.com; 12 Bay Ave, Highlands; ☼ 6am-8pm Apr-Nov) rents fishing boats ($75 to $225 per day) and sells bait, tackle, ice and food.

Sleeping & Eating

Atlantic Highlands is a quaint town whose main drag, First Ave, is lined with cute shops and eateries. Highlands is the place to pull over for a seafood feast as you wait for the evening traffic jam to unknot itself.

Blue Bay Inn (☎ 732-708-9600, 888-708-4666; www.bluebayinn.com; 51 First Ave, Atlantic Highlands; r midweek/weekend from $139/199; ☼ ☐ ☼) These 27 uniquely decorated rooms aim to please

Manhattan businessfolk, yet the immaculate digs are a bargain compared to equivalent shore spots – nary a scratch or sand pebble. Service is excellent if corporate formal.

Memphis Pig Out (☎ 732-291-5533; www.memphis pigout.com; 67 First Ave, Atlantic Highlands; mains $14-24; ☼ 4-9pm) Nothing fancy, just good BBQ; some say the best ribs in Jersey.

Copper Canyon (☎ 732-291-8444; www.thecopper canyon.com; 51 First Ave, Atlantic Highlands; mains $15-30; ☼ lunch & dinner Mon-Fri, dinner only Sat & Sun) Attached to the Blue Bay Inn, this restaurant focuses on upscale Southwestern fare like chile rellenos and shrimp-and-jalapeno risotto. The tequila bar, with 150 varieties, specializes in margaritas.

Windansea (☎ 732-872-2266; www.windanseanj. com; 56 Shrewsbury Ave at Bay Ave, Highlands; mains $18-25; ☼ 11:30am-9pm Mon-Sat, from noon Sun) Windansea has an attractive vantage and interior, plus its open, breezy bar gets hopping at night as folks cool off with frozen drinks and live entertainment.

Bahr's (☎ 732-872-1245; www.bahrstogo.com; 2 Bay Ave, Highlands; mains $19-30; ☼ 11:30am-9:30pm daily, to 10:30pm Fri & Sat) This classic lobster house and fishermen's bar sits in the shadow of the bridge. For seafood that's cheap, fried and easy, cross the parking lot to its down-market sibling, Moby's, with takeout only and a deck full of picnic tables.

Doris & Ed's (☎ 732-872-1565; www.dorisandeds.com; 348 Shore Dr, Highlands; mains $28-44; ☼ dinner Wed-Sun) This much-lauded, gourmet shore institution maintains high standards and makes a worthy romantic meal. It has both classic and contemporary seafood preparations and an attractive three-course prix fixe; dress up and toast summer at the shore.

Getting There & Away

Both Highlands and Atlantic Highlands are served by **Seastreak** (☎ 800-262-8743; www.seastreak. com; round-trip adult/child 5-12yr $40/16), which runs passenger-only ferries from Manhattan (Pier 11 and E 34th St). Weekday ferries run about 10 times a day; weekends run half as often and only to Highlands.

To drive, take Hwy 36. For Atlantic Highlands, exit at 1st Ave, which leads directly to downtown and the ferry terminal. For Highlands, exit at Bay Ave (just before the bridge), which is the main drag. Follow signs for the ferry terminal; from Bay Ave, take a left on Miller St, then a right on Shore Dr.

NEW JERSEY

NEW JERSEY

THE ONLY SHORE HANDBOOK YOU'LL EVER NEED

First time going down the shore? There's so much to learn. Here's a primer to jump start your education:

- Summer high season is Memorial Day to Labor Day. Further south, high season doesn't start till mid-June. Lots of shore business are only open weekends until the high season, and then close soon after.

- For the best room rates, book early and be flexible. Hotel rates function like algorithmic equations of desire – fluctuating constantly to reflect the specific arc of summer, the day of the week, the popularity of events, a view's swoon-worthiness and the carting distance to the beach.

- On summer weekends, most hotels require a two- or three-night stay.

- Most motels provide parking for one car only.

- Statisticians have proven it: the busiest times to drive to the shore are from 3pm to 8pm Friday and 9am to 2pm Saturday; returning, it's after 4pm Sunday and Monday morning. For parkway updates, visit www.511nj.org.

- Nearly every Jersey beach requires a beach badge or tag. These usually cost $5 to $8 per day and can be purchased from lifeguards or beach-entrance 'taggers.' For annual badges, visit the town's city hall.

- Fun Fact! In north-shore towns, a summer tourist is called a 'Benny' (an acronym for Bayone, Elizabeth, Newark and New York). In the south, they're a 'Shoobie.'

- To get sand off your feet: sprinkle them with baby powder, or put a splash of conditioner in a water jug (and let it warm all day in the trunk).

- Freeze your water bottles overnight.

- Put several large plastic bags in your beach bag – for easy end-of-day cleanup and to hold wet suits.

RED BANK
pop 11,800

Perched inland on the Navesink River, Red Bank is a hip town with a rich musical heritage that provides a happening, vibrant music scene. The walkable downtown (along Broad and Maple Sts and adjoining lanes) is a warm-and-fuzzy mix of boutiques, restaurants, funky home decor, comic shops and coin exchanges – most proudly displaying racks of *Weird NJ* magazines. On summer nights, it's almost a block-party atmosphere, as people and music spill onto the sidewalks.

For info and maps, visit the **Red Bank Visitor Center** (☎ 732-741-9211; www.visit.redbank.com; 20 Broad St, 2nd fl).

Sleeping

Molly Pitcher Inn (☎ 732-747-2500; www.themolly pitcher.com; 88 Riverside Ave; r $150-210; ⊠ ▣ �fan ▣) These spacious, tidy, modestly Victorian-style rooms have some nice river views and a scenic pool (plus a private dock for boaters), but mainly it's the location – within walking distance of downtown and the theaters – that elevates this above other choices.

Eating & Drinking

Downtown (☎ 732-741-2828; www.thedowntownnj.com; 10 W Front St; salads & small plates $10-16; ☼ lunch & dinner) Recently reopened, the Downtown is a multifaceted restaurant, bar, live-music venue that lets you know through thrown-open windows what's going on. The menu is a trendy mix of sushi, sliders and small plates.

Jamian's (☎ 732-747-8050; www.jamiansfood.com; 79 Monmouth St; mains $10-19; ☼ 11am-2am) The menu is a mashup of Caribbean, Hawaiian and Creole influences, but it's the specialty cocktails, along with the DJs and world music, that draw crowds to this tiny space near the Count Basie Theatre.

Basil T's Brewery Pub & Italian Grill (☎ 732-842-5990; www.basilt.com; 183 Riverside Ave; mains $14-25; ☼ dinner) For the most fun, order your dinner at the bar and enjoy one of Basil T's award-winning brews (try the dry stout!). The Italian food is fine, but it's not why this place has the largest 'mug club' in the state. After 9pm, musicians add to the festive mood.

our pick **Siam Garden** (☎ 732-224-1233; www.siam gardenrestaurant.com; 2 Bridge Ave, in the Galleria; mains $15-22; 🕑 11:30am-9:30pm Mon-Sat, noon-9:30pm Sun) A soothing Thai restaurant where dishes are as delicious as they are attractive. Tongue-tingling curries, piquant coconut-milk soups and a gracious decor make this a standout.

Bistro at Red Bank (☎ 732-530-5553; www.the bistroatredbank.com; 14 Broad St near Front St; mains $16-30; 🕑 lunch & dinner) Combine upscale sushi, wood-fired-oven pizza and interesting pastas with a sidewalk-friendly, brick-walled bistro atmosphere, and you get this casual, lively restaurant.

Entertainment

Count Basie Theatre (☎ 732-842-9000; www.countbasie theatre.org; 99 Monmouth St) Count Basie hailed from Red Bank, and his namesake historic theater has never looked better – recently renovated inside and out. The diverse programming brings in rock stars and orchestras, Broadway and ballet.

PNC Bank Arts Center (☎ 732-203-2500; www.artscenter.com; Garden State Parkway exit 116, Holmdel) Attending a gig here is a rite of passage for Jersey youth – it's just not summer at the shore without at least one fuzzy memory of a concert. All the top acts cycle through. It's just north of Red Bank, signed off the Parkway.

Two River Theater Company (☎ 732-345-1400; www.trtc.org; 21 Bridge Ave) Across from the Galleria, this theater produces a year-round slate of plays and musicals.

Shopping

Galleria (☎ 732-530-7300; www.thegalleriaredbank.com; cnr W Front St & Shrewsbury Ave; 🕑 10am-6pm Mon-Sat, 10am-5pm Sun) This indoor mall, surrounded by antiques shops, has restaurants and upscale home decor and boutiques. It also hosts a farmers' market on Sundays, 9am to 2pm, from May through November.

Jack's Music Shoppe (☎ 732-842-0731; www.jacks musicshoppe.com; 30 Broad St; 🕑 10am-7pm Mon-Tue, 10am-9pm Wed-Sat, 11am-5pm Sun) A legendary music store that has it all: new and old vinyl, CDs, sheet music, instruments, and guitars signed by the Boss and Bon Jovi.

Jay & Silent Bob's Secret Stash (☎ 732-758-0508; www.jayandsilentbob.com; 35 Broad St; 🕑 11am-6pm Mon-Sat, noon-5pm Sun) NJ filmmaker Kevin Smith flies the freak flag at his hushed temple for comic geeks.

LONG BRANCH
pop 32,600

Like all Jersey shore towns, Long Branch has had its booms and busts. It first made a name for itself in 1870, when it opened Monmouth Park, a racetrack that had gamblers flocking to the resort. The most famous was President Ulysses S Grant, whose entourage of politicians and celebrities titillated the masses and helped make Long Branch a posh, elegant destination equal to any on the East Coast. Six other US presidents – including William McKinley and Woodrow Wilson – vacationed here.

Gambling had its detractors, however, and when New Jersey made gambling illegal in 1897, the racetrack shut down, the gambling halls shuttered and the town declined. Through the 20th century, Long Branch sought to remake itself as a middle-class resort with an amusement-rich boardwalk, but it struggled with urban problems and beach erosion. In 1987, a huge fire decimated the boardwalk, and instead of rebuilding the amusements, the city decided to redevelop the town itself.

The results of the regentrification haven't been without controversy, and remain incomplete. Today, the beach scene is anchored by the upscale **Pier Village** (www.piervillage.com) condo and retail complex, which contains an attractive mix of stores, restaurants, bars and nightclubs. In its own quiet way, Long Branch is becoming hip again, in part because it has preserved its best asset: that long, long pretty stretch of sand. In fact, just north of Long Branch on Rte 36, Seven Presidents Beach makes another excellent destination for those seeking only the sea.

For more information on Long Branch, visit www.long-branch.net.

Monmouth Park

New Jersey's nicest racetrack, **Monmouth Park** (☎ 732-222-5100; www.monmouthpark.com) is 2 miles inland from Long Branch on Rte 36. Monmouth is considered one of the best-run tracks in the Northeast, and it's far superior to the two New York racetracks and the Meadowlands in North Jersey. For a sunny day at the races, head here.

The main racing season is from Memorial Day to Labor Day (with a smaller fall season), but the big event is August's $1 million Haskell Invitational, which usually fields one or more Triple Crown race winners. There are about 12 races a day from Friday to Sunday, with the first post time at 12:50pm. Admission is $3 for grandstand and $2 for parking.

NJ Transit (☎ 973-275-5555; www.njtransit.com/monmo uthpark) runs a 'Monmouth Park Thoroughbred Package' between the park, Newark Penn Station and New York Penn Station ($15 one-way; 85 minutes). Driving from Long Branch, take Route 36 west for 2 miles into Oceanport and follow signs.

Sleeping

Bungalow Hotel (☎ 732-229-3700; www.bungalowho tel.net; 50 Laird St; rooms $250-700; ❍ ▢ 🖭) In Pier Village, this new boutique hotel has designer bona fides: it was a creation of Bravo channel's *9 by Design* team, and exudes an aggressively hip, neo-Hawaiian vibe, with rhino skulls and feathered lampshades in the lobby. The 24 co-piously sized, amenity-rich rooms are coolly spare meditations in white, accented by faux cowhide rugs, low-slung couches, fireplaces, and surfer portraits. Request Little Pipeline, with its open bedside bathtub. The only thing the Bungalow lacks is a view.

Eating & Drinking

our pick **Max's** (☎ 732-571-0248; www.maxsfamous hotdogs.com; cnr Ocean Blvd & Matilda Terrace; hot dogs from $4.50; ❍ daily Apr-Oct, call for hr) Just consider the wall of fame: Frank Sinatra, the Boss, the Fonz, Hulk Hogan, Sean Connery, Norman Fell – all giving props to a hot-dog joint! In fact, owner Celia Maybaum is the Jersey shore's official 'Hot Dog Queen' (by state proclamation). Jerseyans, see, appreciate quality and person-ality in equal measure, and these legendary split, blackened dogs overwhelm your taste buds the way they overwhelm the bun. Enjoy. Max's is a few blocks south of Pier Village.

Sawa Steak House & Sushi (☎ 732-229-0600; www. sawasteakhouse.com; Pier Village; mains $20-30; ❍ lunch & dinner, daily in summer) This contemporary, stylish Japanese restaurant satisfies all desires with sushi, hibachi, teriyaki and tempura. Restful and tasty, and steps from the boardwalk.

Avenue (☎ 732-759-2900; www.leclubavenue.com; 23 Ocean Ave; mains $22-36; ❍ lunch & dinner, nightclub to 2am) A sign of changing times: this vaulted, sleek, contemporary space, with marble floors and long metal bars, serves dedicated French cuisine (*steak frites, moules, steak au poivre*) – smack on the boardwalk. The midweek prix fixe ($29) is a great deal.

Avenue Nuit (☎ 732-759-6700; www.leclubavenue. com; 23 Ocean Ave; ❍ 10pm-2am Thu-Sat) A rooftop club above Avenue restaurant, this fun place has a shimmering pool, hip DJs and a supper-club-meets-nightclub atmosphere. Whatever you wear, dress to impress.

Getting There & Away

NJ Transit (☎ 800-772-2222; www.njtransit.com) trains and buses stop at the station on 3rd Ave be-tween N Bath Ave and Morris Ave. Long Branch is reached via Garden State Pkwy exit 105.

ASBURY PARK
pop 16,600

For the past 40 years, Asbury Park has seemed a crumbling wreck of its former self, a bleary-eyed shell of a town that had stumbled far from its glory days as a preeminent amuse-ment boardwalk. Today, though, steady op-timism is replacing broken-hearted nostalgia. You'll find a returning sense of hope and of bawdy, unrestrained fun.

Asbury Park was founded in 1871 by James Bradley, a devout Methodist with an enter-tainer's flair. He created a bustling ride-filled boardwalk and appealed to middle-class vaca-tioners. Eventually, this grew into the famous Palace Amusements – with its hall of mir-rors, ferris wheel, Looff carousel, bumper cars, and Tillie, the smiling devil-haired clown boy that became the town's trademark. In 1903, landscape architect Frederick Law Olmstead redesigned the entire boardwalk, and for the next 50 years Asbury Park was the funhouse of the shore.

Then in the 1950s, as the automobile changed vacation patterns, business declined. The mood turned ugly in 1970, when race riots shook Asbury Park, damaging property and the town's reputation. Despite the 1970s emergence of the 'Asbury Park sound' – led by Bruce Springsteen and the Stone Pony night-club – and despite the ongoing schemes of developers, all the amusements were eventu-ally sold off, and even the Stone Pony shut its doors. Asbury Park couldn't seem to recover.

Couldn't, that is, until now. Instead of amusements, the boardwalk is today lined with a growing collection of trendy, con-temporary restaurants, bars and clubs. The resurrected, thriving music scene is hands-down the best in the state. Plus, the revital-ized downtown district is humming with boutiques, galleries, an art-house cinema and more restaurants. The sense of faded grandeur remains, as do the empty lots, abandoned construction sites and gritty neighborhoods. Yet embracing this with a playful bohemian swagger is an artsy, gay-friendly community that is remaking Asbury Park into an inviting image of itself.

Information

The **Asbury Park Boardwalk** (www.apboardwalk.com) maintains an excellent website that covers the town. The central shore's main daily newspaper is the *Asbury Park Press* (www.app.com). Asbury Park has a very active and out gay community; for information and events (such as June's Gay Pride Parade), visit www.gayasburypark.com.

Sights & Activities

The **beach** (badges $5 per day) is a clean, well-kept, pretty strand with good surfing and volleyball and safe swimming (there are lifeguards). Parallel to Ocean Ave (between Asbury Ave and 5th Ave), the boardwalk is anchored on the north end by Convention Hall, which bustles with eateries and shops, and on the south end by the dramatically abandoned carousel and casino house. In summer, Wednesday is fireworks night.

The boardwalk lacks a traditional arcade, but it's got the **Silverball Pinball Museum** (☎ 732-774-4994; www.silverballmuseum.com; 1000 Ocean Ave; half hr/hr $7.50/10; ⏰ 11am-9pm, to 11pm Fri & Sat). This 'pinball hall of fame' has 200 classic machines from the 1930s through the 1980s, all set to free play. Can you say 'pinball wizard'?

The downtown district is along Cookman Ave near Main St (Rte 71) and Mattison Ave. Here, make sure to visit **Paranormal Books & Curiosities** (☎ 732-455-3188; www.paranormalbooksnj.com; 627 Cookman Ave; ⏰ noon-6pm Wed-Sun, to 7pm or 8pm Fri & Sat), a funky bookstore that contains the small but moody **Paranormal Museum** (adult/child 8-12yr $5/3; ⏰ from noon Thu-Sun). Exhibits change, but the Jersey Devil is always here; see p220. Guided **Ghost Walks** (adult/child $10/5; ⏰ 8pm Thu-Sat) take in downtown and the boardwalk.

Sleeping

Berkeley Ocean Front Hotel (☎ 732-776-6700; www.berkeleyhotelnj.com; 1401 Ocean Ave; r midweek $100-190, weekend $150-230; ❄ 🖥 🛜 🍽) This imposing, 250-room hotel has been given a boutique

makeover. Rooms are coolio crash pads with jungle-stripe carpets, oversized leather headboards, marble showers and just-so beige-and-lime tones. A stylish bar and restaurant opened in 2010. Still, the cranky elevators and occasional scuffs remind you that this hotel is a survivor of a bygone era.

Empress (☎ 732-774-0110; www.asburyempress.com; cnr Asbury & Ocean Aves; r midweek $130-190, weekend $180-260; ❄ 🖥 🛜 🍽) This 101-room hotel has stylish, well-kept accommodations that will appeal to anyone. However, it's a destination for Asbury Park's gay community, with a poolside bar and nightclub that can pulse late into the night, making noise an issue on weekends.

our pick **Hotel Tides** (☎ 732-897-7744; www.hoteltides.com; 408 7th Ave; r midweek $140-180, weekend $160-205; ❄ 🖥 🛜 🍽) On a suburban street off the main drag, this art-infused 20-room boutique hotel successfully mixes luxurious digs with a friendly B&B atmosphere. Sleek black-and-white designer decor, luxe mattresses and glass-walled, river-rock showers define spacious rooms stocked with amenities. The pool, lounge and spa services make it easy to forget about going out.

Eating

Sunset Landing (☎ 732-776-9732; 1215 Sunset Ave; dishes $5-8; ⏰ 7am-2pm Tue-Sun) Maui transplants have created the perfect breakfast-style surf shack, with longboards on the ceiling and pet geese hanging by the sunny deck overlooking Deal Lake. Fluffy omelets, Hawaiian sweetbread French toast and coconut-sprinkled pancakes are highlights – but no Spam!

Bistro Ole (☎ 732-897-0048; www.bistroole.com; 230 Main St at Mattison Ave; tapas $7-14, mains $16-25; ⏰ lunch & dinner Tue-Sun) This refreshing Latin fusion, updating Spanish and Iberian favorites, features sizzling tapas, rich soups, and grilled meats and seafood. The crisp black-and-white decor and kicking Latin music set a festive mood. A BYOB, Ole will happily turn your wine into sangria. Near Taka.

our pick **Langosta Lounge** (☎ 732-455-3275; www.kitschens.com; 1000 Ocean Ave at 2nd Ave; mains $16-25; ⏰ lunch Mon-Sat, dinner nightly) The current Asbury Park renaissance owes a debt to restaurateur Marilyn Schlossback, who's led the culinary charge with exuberant places such as Langosta Lounge (and the taqueria-style Pop's Garage, next door), right on the boardwalk. The menu borrows and steals from the world's

NEW JERSEY

KATHY KELLY: STALKING THE JERSEY DEVIL IN ASBURY PARK

In 1909, thousands of New Jersey residents reported seeing a strange winged creature they couldn't identify but believed to be the Jersey Devil. In 2009, to celebrate the centennial anniversary of this famous mass sighting, Kathy Kelly created the Paranormal Museum, a small exhibit space attached to Paranormal Books & Curiosities (p219) – which, to the horrified incredulity of visitors, displays the legendary beast's *actual skull and intestines*.

Kelly says with a smile, 'I had a limited idea of who would be interested in this, and people have educated me. Interest in the paranormal transcends any demographic.'

Since then, Kelly has become something of an expert in Jersey Devil lore. Originally dubbed the 'Leed's Devil,' it was said to be born in the Pine Barrens to one Mrs Leed, the wife of a prominent businessman, who issued a curse on her unborn child that she lived to regret. But in fact centuries before, the Lenni Lenape Indians told a similar story of a winged beast in the Pine Barrens, which they dubbed the 'Land of the Dragon.' It's the universal pull of this ancient mythology that draws Kelly.

'It's not about commercializing the Jersey Devil. It's about the story of it, the folklore and the history. I love the families that come in, and I see them bond over this in a way they might not bond otherwise. Their reaction is 'Eeeuw, that's really gross. How cool!' A father and son asked me, 'Can you tell us how to get to where the Jersey Devil was born?' They knew they were stepping into history, and going to explore parts of New Jersey they had never seen before, and they knew they were going to do it *together*. I think the Jersey Devil could become a unifier for all of New Jersey, north and south.

'I don't know what the Jersey Devil is, but I know it exists in our folklore. It's entirely possible that through genetic mutation something now looks like not what it's supposed to look like. Cryptozoologists – aka 'monster hunters' – believe it's a real animal.'

Kelly says her personal fascination isn't devils or ghosts per se, but 'the survival of personality after death. I'm a skeptic, but I've seen enough to keep me looking. I've spent time in darkened basements, but I haven't had that 'holy cow' moment – yet.'

So why set up shop in Asbury Park? She says, 'I grew up in North Jersey, and I chose Asbury Park because of its uniquely decadent and dark history. It's easy to tell a ghost story here.' Kelly's infectious enthusiasm for Asbury Park now infuses her walking tours, which are steeped in the town's authentic history, making them just as much 'ghost tours' of 'where things used to be. Some things needed to be let go of, like the carousel. Palace Amusements needed to be torn down. The amusements aren't coming back. And eventually,' she says, referring to the Asbury Park of today, 'all this will be gone.'

Ghost stories of the future.

cuisines in inventive ways, while emphasizing farm-to-table freshness. Make reservations.

Taka (☎ 732-775-1020; www.takaapnj.com; 632 Mattison Ave at Bond St; mains $16-30; ✲ dinner Tue-Sun) Downtown, Taka is a modern take on Japanese cuisine and sushi, a delectable fusion of tastes, textures and styles. Gorgeous inside, with appealing streetside dining, it's so cool it has river-rock chopstick rests. BYOB.

Stella Marina (☎ 732-775-7776; www.stellamarina restaurant.com; 800 Ocean Ave; mains $18-29; ✲ lunch & dinner) Another stylish newcomer on the boardwalk, Stella Marina offers contemporary, upscale Italian cuisine, along with sunny, 2nd-floor deck seating, sleek cocktails, and some of the best calamari, octopus and designer salads around. It's a hot ticket.

Drinking & Entertainment

Since 2006, the **Wave Gathering** (www.wavegathering.com) music festival draws everyone for three days in June.

Stone Pony (☎ 732-502-0600; www.stoneponyonline. com; 913 Ocean Ave) Reopened in 2000, the Pony is the dean of Asbury Park rock. The black walls crowded with signed guitars and drumheads will give you goosebumps, but more importantly, great music again commands the stage.

our pick **Asbury Lanes** (☎ 732-776-6160; www. asburylanes.com; 204 4th Ave) A carnival-esque atmosphere pervades this bowling alley re-envisioned in a punk cum lounge-lizard aesthetic. Marching bands might blast the stage in the middle of the lanes, while bowlers play through the legs of stiltwalkers. Or not.

Sometimes it's just a friendly all-ages crowd chatting quietly among the devil grrl paintings and red velvet curtains. Ya never know.

Wonder Bar (☎ 732-502-8886; www.wonderbarasburypark.com; Ocean at 5th Ave) Tillie smiles again on the Wonder Bar, with a roomy stage and dance floor inside, and a patio and sand pit outside.

Paradise at the Empress (☎ 732-988-6663; www.paradisenj.com; 101 Asbury Ave; ☻ from noon) The Paradise combines your typical black-wall mirror-ball gay nightclub with an outdoor tiki-hut pool bar to make any weekend a raucous event.

Chico's House of Jazz (☎ 732-774-5299; www.chicoshouseofjazz.com; 631 Lake Ave; ☻ Wed-Sat) New in 2010, Chico's brings live jazz to this music-rich town four nights a week.

Revision Theatre (☎ 732-455-3059; www.revisiontheatre.org) In summer and fall, the abandoned Carousel House becomes the stage for this theater troupe's musical shenanigans, such as revivals of the Who's *Tommy* and the *Rocky Horror Picture Show*.

Paramount Theatre (☎ 732-897-8810; www.apboardwalk.com; Convention Hall, boardwalk at 5th Ave) The biggest names appear on Asbury Park's biggest stage.

Getting There & Away
The **NJ Transit** (www.njtransit.com) train and bus station is at the Transportation Center on Cookman Ave and Main St. Asbury Park is off Garden State Parkway exits 100A or 100B.

OCEAN GROVE
pop 4400
A lovely little seaside town that makes the perfect family-friendly destination, Ocean Grove has taken as its slogan, 'God's square mile at the Jersey shore.' Indeed, Ocean Grove is as sober, conservative and quaint as Asbury Park is loud, scraggly and hungover.

These two neighbors didn't start out as opposites. Both were founded by devout Christians, but Ocean Grove always aimed to be something special. It was founded in 1870 by the Ocean Grove Camp Meeting Association as an experimental spiritual community and the site for summertime revival meetings. These were so successful – at times drawing over 300,000 people – that its temporary tent cottages became a permanent fixture and Victorian homes sprouted in abundance. Through the 20th century, Ocean Grove maintained an insular character, epitomized

by its moral codes and bylaws – such as banning alcohol, and no swimming or driving on Sundays. The driving ban lasted until 1979, when the state Supreme Court ruled the town's charter was unconstitutional and the camp meeting's control of local government ended.

Ocean Grove's highlights today – its well-preserved Victorian architecture and its completely commercial-free boardwalk – are the result of its long disdain for the trappings and traps of modern life. The town is now more diverse, and it eagerly welcomes vacationers every day of the week. But walking the narrow side streets crowded with century-old architecture or taking in a concert at the Great Auditorium, conjures up the flavor of a more civilized era.

Information
Chamber of commerce (☎ 800-388-4768; www.oceangrovenj.com) A source of local information.
Ocean Grove Camp Meeting Association (☎ 732-775-0035; www.oceangrove.org) Maintains an information booth at the Great Auditorium in summer.

Sights
GREAT AUDITORIUM
This 6000-seat wood **auditorium** (☎ tickets 800-965-9324; www.oceangrove.org) was built in 1894 and stands in the center of town at the western end of Ocean Pathway. An acoustic marvel, it still holds weekly Sunday services and has twice-weekly free organ recitals (7:30pm Wednesday and noon Saturday, July to August). In addition, Memorial Day kicks off a summer concert series, mainly on weekends, that ranges from classical singers to Johnny Mathis and ABBA tribute bands.

TENT CITY
Visitors to Ocean Grove in the 19th century set up hundreds of tents around the great auditorium, and 114 of them are still clustered here. The tents actually front small wooden cabins, with a kitchen and bathroom. Want to stay in one? You need to join the Camp Meeting Association, and they rent for $2500 to $3000 a season. Oh, and there's a 15-year waiting list.

Sleeping
Ocean Grove has a wealth of historic inns and B&Bs, but overall, properties are not as posh as in Cape May. Most are family run and a

little homespun, offering simple continental breakfasts. Very few offer parking.

Shawmont Hotel (☎ 732-776-6985; www.shawmont. com; 17 Ocean Ave; r high $110-255, low $65-140; ✕ ♿) An affordable option for families is this clean and friendly 28-room hotel. Rooms lack Victorian flavor – just attractive motel-style decor. Some have balconies and efficiencies; right across from the beach.

Carriage House (☎ 732-988-3232; www.carriage housenj.com; 18 Heck Ave; r high $125-180; low $100-140; ✕ 🛜) A very beautiful, quiet eight-room Victorian B&B run by a lovely couple who put a lot of heart into their place. Kathi makes a full gourmet breakfast, and rooms are cozy, immaculate and nicely decorated; five have gas fireplaces. To maintain the peace, they prefer children to be 10 or older.

Laingdon Hotel (☎ 732-774-7974; www.laingdon hotel.com; 8 Ocean Ave; r high $159-289, low $99-239; ✕ 🖳 🛜) Restored in 2004, the Laingdon has a handsome Victorian flair, with big hand-carved mahogany beds, old-fashioned phones, pleasing bathrooms and terraces overlooking the ocean. The enclosed porch is a great touch; prefer children over 10.

Majestic Hotel (☎ 732-775-6100; www.majestic oceangrove.com; 19 Main Ave; high $205-325, low $140-270; ✕ 🛜) Inside this impressive Victorian mansion are 15 thoroughly modern rooms with only a faint whiff of Victoriana. French art posters, stylish furniture and cool lighting create a sense of contemporary (and slightly corporate) luxury. Breakfast is buffet; no children under 10.

Eating

Ocean Grove is no culinary hothouse, but plenty of simple, midrange eateries, cafes and coffeehouses ensure no one goes away hungry. Simple walk along Main Ave.

Starving Artist at Days (☎ 732-988-1007; www. thestarvingartist-og.com; 47 Olin St at Central; dishes $5-9; ☺ 8am-3pm Mon-Tue & Thu-Sat, 8am-2pm Sun) A block off Main Ave, this cute café serves tasty salads, pastas and quiche in an artsy dining room or on a big outdoor porch, where, if you aren't careful, live theater might happen.

Nagle's Ice Cream & Apothecary Cafe (☎ 732-776-9797; 43 Main Ave; mains $5-12; ☺ 8:30am-9pm Wed-Mon) No, the diner-style menu in this old-fashioned, Victorian-era apothecary ('here since the beginning of time') is nothing special, but it's delightfully nostalgic dining. If nothing else, grab a scoop or two of delicious ice cream.

Seagrass (☎ 732-869-0770; www.seagrassnj.com; 68 Main Ave; mains $16-29; ☺ lunch & dinner daily summer) Definitely the nicest restaurant in town, and well-loved by locals for its emphasis on locally sourced, creatively prepared seafood. Modern art inside, attractive sidewalk dining outside.

Getting There & Away

By train, take **NJ Transit** (☎ 800-772-2222; www. njtransit.com) to Asbury Park and walk through the Ocean Grove gateway two blocks away. Ocean Grove is reached via Garden State Parkway exit 100A.

BELMAR & AROUND
pop 5900

Belmar was once another version of Seaside Heights, or Florida's Fort Lauderdale: a rowdy 20-something booze-up at the shore. This started in the 1970s, when cheap rentals were abundant, and it reached its nadir in 1992, when an enormous rap concert descended into an actual riot of over 100,000 people. Since 2004, local authorities have clamped down on dissolute youth (note the 'no tolerance' noise signs leading from the beach), and today, with one notable exception, those hard-partying days are mostly memories.

Belmar's boardwalk is free of amusements, though it is evenly spaced with pavilions containing restaurants. An equally attractive beach can be found just north in quiet Avon by the Sea.

Belmar's downtown retail district is six blocks off the beach, along Main St/Hwy 71. Belmar's local **chamber of commerce** (☎ 732-681-1176; www.belmar.com) offers information on events and activities.

Activities

Besides the beach, the most popular activities are **boating** and **fishing**. The most common catch is bluefish, along with mackerel, whiting and tuna. Boats leave the busy **Belmar Marina** (☎ 732-681-6137; www.belmar.com/marina; Marina & 10th Aves) daily, with most trips offered from April to November; see the website for charters. To rent a boat, stop by **Fisherman's Den tackle shop** (☎ 732-681-5005; www.fishermansdennj.com; ☺ from 6am). There are more charters offered on River Rd next to Klein's, such as **Promise Charters** (☎ 732-280-1704; www.promisecharters.com).

If you prefer unmotorized travel, rent a kayak from **Shark River Kayak** (☎ 732-749-0490; www.sharkriverkayaks.com; Belmar Marina; kayaks per 2hr $30, surfboards per day $25); it rents surfboards, standup paddle boards, and offers surfing lessons.

Sleeping

Belmar's accommodations are nothing special. To overnight, nearby Avon by the Sea, where these two inns are located, is a much more pleasant stay.

Avon Manor Inn (☎ 732-776-7770; www.avonmanor. com; 109 Sylvania Ave, Avon by the Sea; r high $130-285, low $85-225; ✿ ✿) This friendly, homey B&B offers nine relatively plain but pleasant rooms. The public rooms have some Victorian flourishes, but overall, the owners encourage unfussy relaxation with lots of thoughtful touches. Included is a full hot breakfast, beach badges, access to a pool, loaner bikes and even a wee putting green.

Our pick Cashelmara Inn (☎ 732-776-8727, 800-821-2976; www.cashelmara.com; 22 Lakeside Ave, Avon by the Sea; r high $180-289, ste $300-375, low season $80 less; ✿ ✿) Nestled a half block from the beach, Cashelmara Inn is a stunning Victorian retreat that's a riot of antiques, ornate wallpapers and carved four-poster beds. Of the 15 romantic rooms, the three suites are delicious velvet palaces with Jacuzzi tubs. Decor on the 3rd floor gets more beachy, and bathrooms are tiny. There are free beach badges, a full breakfast and (can we move in?) a plush, full-screen Victorian movie theater. As you enter the front door, your heart slows down to match the gently ticking grandfather clock.

Eating

Klein's (☎ 732-681-1177; www.kleinsfish.com; 708 River Rd; mains $15-26; ✿ 11:30am-10pm, market from 8am) With a fresh fish market, a sitdown restaurant, and a wide dockside patio positioned for sunset, Klein's typifies the classic Jersey shore seafood

shack. It's a lively local institution serving an excellent range of sushi, on top of the usual broiled, baked and grilled suspects.

Matisse (☎ 732-681-7680; www.matissecatering.com; 1300 Ocean Ave at 13th; mains $18-30; ✿ dinner nightly Jul-Aug, Wed-Sat low season) This boxy, strangely white-columned building on the boardwalk used to be a McDonald's, but don't worry: Matisse offers surprisingly sophisticated dining with excellent service (and ocean views!). The three-appetizer special ($24) and the prix fixe ($22) are great deals. Enjoy fine renditions of clam chowder with smoked bacon, tuna tartar and salmon with grilled asparagus. BYOB.

Vivas Classic Latin Cuisine (☎ 732-681-1213; www. vivasrestaurant.com; 801 Belmar Plaza, btwn 8th & 10th Aves; tapas $10-13, mains $26-32; ✿ lunch Tue-Fri, dinner daily) In a grungy mall near the train station, Vivas is another surprise – a nuevo Latino fusion restaurant, with bold orange walls and live Latin music on weekends. Whether ordering tapas or entrees, expect gourmet renditions of steak cubano with mojo, seafood ceviche, duck with orange zest sauce, and rice and beans.

Drinking & Entertainment

Bar Anticipation (☎ 732-681-7422; www.bar-a.com; 703 16th Ave, near F St) For a taste of Belmar's good ole bad days – there's only one place to go. A massive, warrenlike complex, 'Bar A' packs in more muscle and miniskirts than any *Jersey Shore* reality show could handle. Seemingly every young single – or those wishing they were young (or wishing they were single) – tanned body within 50 miles crowds in for live bands, DJs, a couch-filled sand pit and multiple bars.

Getting There & Away

The train station is at 10th Ave and Belmar Plaza, between 9th and 10th Aves behind

---

DETOUR: SIX FLAGS AMUSEMENT PARK

It ain't the shore, but no question – the best amusement park in New Jersey is **Six Flags** (off Map p214; ☎ 908-928-1821; www.sixflags.com/greatadventure). A veritable city, and the largest of Six Flags' parks, this is three parks in one: the Great Adventure amusement park, with 75 rides and 13 state-of-the-art roller coasters; the Safari Theme Park, known for its drive-through African-animal encounter; and the Hurricane Harbor water park, with slides that dwarf what you'll find down the shore. Add in wandering costumed characters, summer concerts and various performances, and this park could hold its own in Orlando.

Each park has its own prices, schedule and hours, which vary weekly. The amusement park and safari are open late March to early November; the water park from late May to Labor Day. All are open daily in summer. Six Flags is at I-195 exit 16; get here by either the NJ Turnpike exit 7A, or Garden State Parkway exit 98.

Belmar Mall, one block east of Route 35. To drive, take Garden State Parkway exit 98 to Rte 138 east.

SPRING LAKE
pop 3500

Spring Lake was developed as a 19th-century resort around the lake that gives the town its name. Town fathers, wanting to avoid the crush of middle-class tourism swamping shore towns elsewhere, banned carousels and amusements, zoning the boardwalk to maintain its noncommercial character. Instead, behemoth oceanfront resorts opened that appealed to the upper classes and wealthy urbanites, and tony Spring Lake came to be known as the 'Irish Riviera.'

By the mid-20th century, these massive hotels started dying, and one by one in the 1970s, they were either torn down or turned into condominiums. With each decade, tourism in Spring Lake has shrunk, a process that accelerated after 9/11, and only a couple dozen hotels and inns remain. To many longtime residents, that's just fine. They prefer their community's quiet charm. Who wants to be the summertime home for harried New Yorkers?

Indeed, Spring Lake makes a staid place to enjoy the sand and get away from the hubbub. Spring Lake's attractive downtown is along 3rd Ave, between Passaic and Washington Aves; it contains all services. For information and maps, visit the **chamber of commerce** (☎ 732-449-0577; www.springlake.com; 302 Washington Ave; ◷ 11am-3pm Mon-Sat). Beach tags cost $8 per day.

Sleeping & Eating

Sandpiper Hotel (☎ 732-449-6060; www.sandpiper.com; 7 Atlantic Ave; r high $170-330, low $130-260; ◷ Jun-Oct; ✷ ♨) The spacious, airy sitting room, done in powder blue, sets the gracious seaside mood in this grand three-story hotel. The breezy feeling is sustained in the 15 clean, well-cared-for rooms, which sport iron bedframes, modern furnishings, pastel decor and bright tall windows. Breakfast is included, and there's a heated pool in a covered gazebo. Children under 14 are discouraged.

Hewitt Wellington Hotel (☎ 732-974-1212; www.thehewittwellington.com; 200 Monmouth Ave; r high $220-320, low $110-210; ✷ ☍ ♨) One of the old-style Spring Lake resort hotels, this was renovated in 2009 and is now partially reserved for

condominiums. Suites are large and attractive, with a nice Victorian flavor. Breakfast is included.

Spring Lake Inn (☎ 609-449-2010; www.springlakeinn.com; 104 Salem Ave; r high $230-400, low $180-300; ✷ ☍) This stately 1888 home is done-up in full Victorian style, with gorgeous antiques and thoughtful decor in all 16 rooms. The lovely wraparound porch is a bonus. Breakfast is a gourmet feast.

Black Trumpet (☎ 732-449-4700; www.theblacktrumpet.com; 1505 Ocean Ave, Grand Victorian Hotel; mains $24-31; ◷ lunch & dinner) For playful gourmet cuisine in a low-key atmosphere, Black Trumpet serves creative takes on classics like lobster bisque, grilled scallops and lamb chops.

Whispers (☎ 732-974-9755; www.whispersrestaurant.com; 200 Monmouth Ave; mains $28-38; ◷ dinner) The on-premises restaurant at the Hewitt Wellington, Whispers offers formal fine dining on rose china, with all the right cutlery and proper service. It serves classic refined meals with contemporary twists, such as broiled sea bass with bok choy.

Getting There & Away

The train station is at Railroad Plaza and Warren Ave, one block east of Rte 71. To drive, take Garden State Parkway exit 98 to Rte 138 west, then Rte 71 south.

MANASQUAN
pop 6200

South of Spring Lake, Manasquan has a long, amusement-free beach and one of the better **surfing** spots in the state. Manasquan Inlet Beach is at the southern end of town, immediately north of the jetty on the north side of Manasquan inlet. Local surfers flock here, and signs remind newcomers to follow proper surfer etiquette (and to have a beach badge, $8 per day). From Hwy 71, take Main St south to 1st Ave, and follow 1st Ave south till it ends.

If you get hungry, Manasquan has a very pleasant downtown corridor; from Hwy 71, turn north on Main St – it's the four blocks right here. At the corner of Broad St is the **Squan Tavern** (☎ 732-223-3324; www.squantavern.com; 15 Broad St; ◷ 11am-11pm Tue-Sat, noon-11pm Sun), a local institution for pizza and classic Italian fare, and Manasquan's watering hole of choice for over 40 years.

If, perchance, night falls and you're itching for something louder and younger, head back down to the beach to the **Osprey Hotel**

(☎ 732-528-1800; www.ospreynightclub.com; Main St & 1st Ave; ☾ Fri-Sun Jun-Aug). This sprawling nightclub has multiple bars, DJs and live music.

POINT PLEASANT
pop 5400

From the north, Point Pleasant is the first skee-ball-and-tilt-a-whirl amusement boardwalk on the Jersey shore. It is also the northernmost community on the Barnegat Peninsula, a narrow 22-mile barrier strip between the Atlantic and Barnegat Bay, one that ends in the pristine beauty of Island Beach State Park.

In 1877, Point Pleasant was originally designed as a vacation resort, but it didn't really take off until 1895, when the railroad arrived – a story common to most shore towns. Interestingly, until 1915, Point Pleasant's wooden boardwalk was movable: each winter it was dismantled into sections and stored away.

In another common story, storms and fires occasionally damaged the boardwalk and pavilions. The storm of the century hit Point Pleasant in 1938, and afterward, the section south of New Jersey Ave was never rebuilt. The Point Pleasant boardwalk is now a mix of commercial and noncommercial sections: for quietude, walk north.

Indeed, if clanging amusements leave you rattled, you can really escape by driving just south to Bay Head, a quiet town with a serene beach and no boardwalk at all. How do they keep the tourist hordes at bay? By leaving daytrippers almost no place to park.

Orientation & Information

The **chamber of commerce** (☎ 732-899-2424; www.pointpleasantbeachnj.com; 517-A Arnold Ave) has tons of information; it can help you find a room, too. For info, also visit www.pointpleasantbeach.com. The **post office** (410 Arnold Ave) is within sight of the train station, at Arnold Ave and Cincinnati Ave/Rte 35. North of the train station along Arnold Ave is the six-block commercial district, with all services.

The streets nearest the boardwalk are exclusively 24-hour metered parking, and they fill up early. Aim for the enormous parking lot at Arnold and Ocean Aves, but even this gets full on high summer weekends.

Sights & Activities

JENKINSON'S PAVILION & AQUARIUM

Aimed at families with younger kids, **Jenkinson's Pavilion** (☎ 732-892-0844; www.jenkin

sons.com; ☾ Memorial Day to Labor Day) is on the boardwalk near the intersection with Arnold Ave. It offers several dozen rides, most of which will delight the under-12 set, but few will excite their teenage siblings. Tickets are $1, and rides cost multiple tickets, but Tuesday and Friday offer wristband deals. The boardwalk also has indoor arcades (open year-round), a funhouse, a huge minigolf course and **Jenkinson's Aquarium** (☎ 732-899-1659; adult/child $10/6; ☾ 10am-10pm high, 10am-5pm low). This makes the perfect, pint-sized encounter with seals, sharks, penguins and alligators. Feeding times are popular (and frequent), and best of all, admission comes with unlimited in/out privileges – come and go all day as you like.

BEACHES

Point Pleasant has the unusual distinction of having two privately owned, adjacent beaches along its boardwalk. Each charges its own fee ($7 per day) – so you have to choose.

Jenkinson's Beach (☎ 732-892-3274) runs from Trenton Ave north to the Manasquan River, and it fronts the amusement park. Jenkinson's provides a small bathhouse.

South of Trenton Ave is **Risden's Beach** (☎ 732-892-8410). This is a much shorter strand, and the boardwalk here contains no amusements, just some concessions. Risden's provides its own large **bathhouse** (☎ 732-892-9743, 732-892-9580; ☾ 9am-5pm), but there is an extra charge to use the lockers.

FISHING & BOATING

The beaches here are long enough for good surf casting, and the inlet has several marinas; drive along Channel Dr to survey your options. Closest to the beach is **Ken's Landing** (☎ 732-892-9787, 732-899-5491; www.kenslanding.net; 30 Broadway); party charter boats and sightseeing cruises are lined up here, with posted departure times and costs. A larger charter operation is **Norma K Fleet** (☎ 732-496-5383; www.normak.com); for sightseeing cruises, try the scenic paddlewheeler **River Belle** (☎ 732-528-6620, 732-892-3377; www.riverboattour.com). For sailing lessons, visit the **New Jersey Sailing School** (☎ 732-295-3450; www.newjerseysailingschool.com).

Sleeping

Most motels are strung along Broadway between Chicago and Boston Aves and on the southern end of Ocean Ave. Most places are seasonal – opening just before Memorial Day and closing soon after Labor Day – but the motels below are open year-round.

Mariner's Cove (☎ 732-899-0060; www.mariners covemotelnj.com; 50 Broadway; r high $150-350, low $80-180; ✷ ☎ ✷ ♿) In 2010, the Mariner's 38 rooms got a complete makeover, with new mattresses, flat-screen TVs, minifridges and a restful tan-and-beige color scheme; suites are quite large. A well-managed, well-maintained property, it's just walkable to the beach. Free beach tags and parking.

Surfside Motel (☎ 732-899-1109; www.surfside -motel.com; 101 Broadway; r high $170-290, low $80-130; ✷ ☎ ✷ ♿) Another crisp, clean, dependable choice; all 32 rooms are well-maintained and have a minifridge. Bathrooms have nice tiled showers, and two rooms with king-sized beds have fantastic Jacuzzi tubs worth requesting. Management is on the ball; no pets, but free beach tags and parking.

Windswept Motel (☎ 732-899-1282; www.wind sweptmotel.net; 1008 Ocean Ave; r high $170-295, low $100-170; ✷ ☎ ✷ ♿) At the southern end of Risden's Beach, and within walking distance of the amusements, Windswept has 46 rooms in three buildings. All are clean, good sized and decorated with a typical sea-green-and-coral seaside decor, but the ocean-view rooms, with balconies facing the sea, are far superior. Free parking and beach tags.

Eating

Amusement-filled boardwalks are packed with easy eats – pizza, burgers and fried seafood. Ocean Ave, paralleling the boardwalk, contains some simple delis and cafes.

our pick **Spike's Fish Market & Restaurant** (☎ 732-295-9400; 415 Broadway; lunch $9-12, mains $18-25; ✷ 11:30am-8:30pm Sun-Thu, 11:30am-9:30pm Fri & Sat) Spike's embraces its seafood shack-ness so fully that it verily defines the genre. The owner even calls his no-pretensions, picnic-bench hut a 'dive,' but that goes too far: Spike's serves great, fresh seafood with 'nothing deep-fried.' Gorge on lobster bisque, a bucket of steamers, and jambalaya, and choose from a raft of fresh-caught fish, either Cajun or blackened.

Jack Baker's Wharfside (☎ 732-892-9100; www. wharfsidenj.com; mains $17-23; ✷ 11:30am-9:30pm Mon-Thu, 11:30am-10pm Fri & Sat, 11:30am-9pm Sun) A more typical and casual dockside surf-and-turf eatery compared to its sibling, the Shanty, which can be found next door.

Jack Baker's Lobster Shanty (☎ 732-899-6700; www.jackbakerslobstershanty.com; 81 Channel Dr; mains $19-32; ✷ dinner Wed-Sun, lunch Sun) Presents upscale interpretations of seafood classics – like bisque, stuffed flounder, and seared ahi – along with a raw bar and whole lobster. The formal dining room has great inlet views.

Latitude 40N (☎ 732-892-8553; www.latitude40n.com; 16 Arnold Ave; mains $23-30; ✷ dinner) A bit hidden on the west side of downtown, Latitude 40N reflects more personality in its Caribbean-accented menu. The delicious tempura tuna is a signature dish, and the black bean soup with lobster is excellent. If only the plain bistro dining room was more romantic.

Entertainment

The Point Pleasant boardwalk isn't all about the kids. **Martell's Tiki Bar** (☎ 732-892-0131; www. tikibar.com) makes sure of that singlehandedly. If you're on the beach, aim for the neon-orange palm trees, or follow the twang of amplified guitars; live bands play on weekends in May, twice daily in summer. Pitchers of margaritas flow copiously on the pier, and inside is a multipart eatery, with both takeout and sit-down options.

Shopping

Point Pleasant's downtown has a number of antique stores. **Point Pleasant Antique Emporium** (☎ 732-892-2222, 800-322-8002; cnr Bay & Trenton Aves; ✷ 11am-5pm) has over 125 dealers under one roof.

Getting There & Away

The **NJ Transit** (www.njtransit.com) train and bus station is at Route 35 north and Arnold Ave. Driving, take Garden State Parkway exit 98 then Rte 34 south to the traffic circle leading to town.

SEASIDE HEIGHTS & AROUND
pop 3300

For better and worse, Seaside Heights has become inextricably linked with the reality TV show *Jersey Shore*, which dropped a handful of self-professed 'guidos' and 'guidettes' into what has long been the shore's most raucous, debauched singles scene – and captured every embarrassing drunken moment. For a town already dubbed 'Sleeze-side' – and this by locals who *enjoy* the action – this might seem par for the course, but it does Seaside Heights an injustice. As locals point out, the TV show primarily reflects the behavior of bennies (summer tourists) rather than that of residents. And it reduces Seaside Heights to an unflattering stereotype, when the amusement-rich boardwalk is as family-friendly as any.

Well, during the day. While the sun shines, everyone crowds the busy wooden piers, which rattle mightily and punctuate the air with thrill-ride screams. The beach is also packed, an all-ages mix of strolling string bikinis and grandparents guiding toddlers to the water's edge.

Once the sun sets, and the bands start, and the nighttime promenade begins, that's when the evangelical 'Life in the Son' booth opens, preachers reaching out to the flirting, drinking, 20-something passersby, hoping to guide them away from the media-hyped infamy of Snooki, the Situation and J-Woww.

Orientation & Information

The main **visitor information booth** (☎ 800-732-7467; www.seasideheightstourism.com) is on the boardwalk at Webster Ave; a second booth is at Fremont Ave. Another useful website is www.seasideheights.net. The best place for metered

parking is on Central Ave, two blocks off the beach (and parallel to the Boulevard); it can be quicker to park and walk than to search closer for that elusive spot.

Most of the town's bars and restaurants are along 'the Boulevard,' the main drag a block off the beach. Ten minutes south of Seaside Heights, Seaside Park is the gateway to Island Beach State Park, with several motels and restaurants.

Activities

The Seaside Heights boardwalk has two amusement piers and a waterpark, in addition to being stuffed end-to-end with arcades and games of chance. Surfing and bicycling (early or late) are also popular.

The **beach** (badges per day $5) is wide and long. It's easy to reach the slightly quieter northern end: ride the sky tram from Casino Pier.

Funtown Pier (☎ 732-830-7437; www.funtownpier. com) is the southern pier and has go-carts, a Ferris wheel and more kiddie rides. **Casino Pier** (☎ 732-793-6488; www.casinopiernj.com; 800 Ocean Terrace) is the northern pier; it's bigger, with more thrill rides and stomach-churning bungee

NEW JERSEY

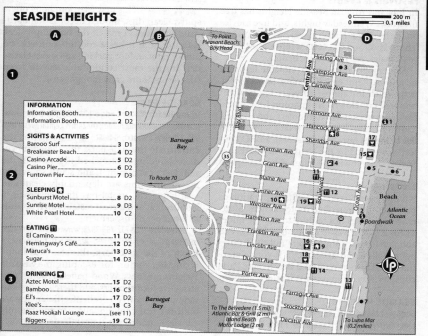

SEASIDE HEIGHTS

0 — 200 m
0 — 0.1 miles

INFORMATION
Information Booth 1 D1
Information Booth 2 D2

SIGHTS & ACTIVITIES
Barooo Surf 3 D1
Breakwater Beach 4 D2
Casino Arcade 5 D2
Casino Pier 6 D2
Funtown Pier 7 D3

SLEEPING
Sunburst Motel 8 D2
Sunrise Motel 9 D3
White Pearl Hotel 10 C2

EATING
El Camino 11 D2
Hemingway's Café 12 D2
Maruca's 13 D3
Sugar 14 D3

DRINKING
Aztec Motel 15 D2
Bamboo 16 C3
EJ's 17 D2
Klee's 18 C3
Raaz Hookah Lounge .... (see 11)
Riggers 19 C2

flings, plus several coasters and a log flume. In the adjacent Casino Arcade is the historic **carousel**, with carved animals from the 1890s and a 1923 Wurlitzer organ. All rides take tickets, with various wristband deals offered midweek; rides run April to September, but daily only July to August.

Across from Casino Pier is Jenkinson's **Breakwater Beach** (www.breakwater-beach.com; pass $19-30), at Sherman and Ocean Aves. Though not enormous, the water park has slides and splash zones for every age. Combo slide-and-ride tickets are offered.

For surfboard rentals, head to **Barooo Surf** (☎ 732-793-9009; www.baroosurf.com; 1520 Boulevard at Hiering Ave; surfboards per half-day $15-20). In addition, it rents bikes ($15 per day), surreys ($22 to $30), wetsuits, beach umbrellas and more. A full range of surf lessons ($50 per hour) includes multiday surf camps for kids.

Or, have your bicycle delivered: **Summer Bikes** (☎ 206-279-4472; www.summerbikes.com; bikes per day/week/month $10/20/75) will deliver anywhere from Seaside Heights to Point Pleasant; great rates for long-term rentals.

Festivals & Events

In July and August, Seaside Heights has free fireworks Wednesday nights, and free movies on the beach (at Hiering Ave) on Sundays and Thursdays. See the **town website** (www.seaside heightstourism.com) for a full schedule.

September contains two notable festivals: in mid-September is **Clownfest** (www.clownfest. com), which for almost 30 years has brought hundreds of clowns from around the world for a long weekend of tomfoolery and a surreal 'clown parade.' The other is late September's **Que by the Sea** (www.quebythesea.com), a BBQ contest sanctioned by the Kansas City Barbecue Society that crowns the state's BBQ champion.

Sleeping

No one rues Seaside Heights' reputation as party central more than motel owners. Many make a point of not renting to anyone under 21 (or 25), as a way to maintain a family- and couples-friendly atmosphere (all the listings below follow this age policy). If you're more interested in visiting Island Beach State Park, consider staying in nearby Seaside Park.

SEASIDE HEIGHTS

Sunburst Motel (☎ 732-793-2889; www.sunburstmotel. com; 1020 Boulevard at Hancock Ave; r high $135-200, low

$90-170; 🅿 🛜 🔲 🚭) You won't call it stylish, but it's comfortable. There are 36 clean, well-kept rooms in two buildings, including 28 with decent-sized efficiency kitchens. There's a guest laundry, and Sunburst II has a protected deck with BBQ grills.

Luna Mar (☎ 732-793-7955; www.lunamarmotel. com; cnr Ocean Ave & L St; r high $150-200, low $100-180; 🅿 🛜 🔲 🚭) Super plain and nothing fancy, this is nevertheless a well-managed motel that was fully renovated in 2010. The 24 rooms include a mix of efficiencies and apartments, and it's right on the beach, south of the boardwalk but within walking distance. Open from May to October.

Sunrise Motel (☎ 732-793-7471; www.visitsea sideheights.com; 202 Boulevard; r $150-180, luxury ste $240 summer, $70-120 off-season; 🅿 🛜 🔲) At this extremely well-run motel most of the 40 rooms have nicely laid-out efficiency kitchens (but BYO cookware and cutlery), with tile floors that make for easy cleaning. The roomy luxury suites are ideal for longer stays. A 2nd-floor sundeck with grills, and free beach tags, are a plus.

White Pearl Hotel (☎ 732-830-4242; www.thewhite pearlhotel.com; 201 Sumner Ave; r high $150-200, low $100-160; 🅿 🛜 🔲) This new 34-room hotel offers spiffy, clean digs, though decor is standard-issue and doesn't match the building's sleek exterior. Still, it has a rooftop sundeck, an indoor pool, indoor parking and a guest laundry. It's the most comfortable stay in town (the *Jersey Shore* crew thought so).

SEASIDE PARK

Island Beach Motor Lodge (☎ 732-793-5400; www. islandbeachmotorlodgenj.com; cnr 24th & Central Aves; r high $95-270, low $52-160; 🅿 🔲 🚭) Literally at the entrance to the state park, this two-story cement building is stretched like taffy in the sun. Decor is minimal, and scuffs show, but the small rooms are dependably clean and well-kept. The motel has its own beach, a laundromat and a great restaurant; it appeals to families and fishermen.

Belvedere (☎ 732-793-7373; www.seaside-park.com; cnr 13th & Central Aves; 🅿 🛜 🔲 🚭) A few blocks north of the state park, this standard motel is another option for escaping the Seaside Heights madness. Wood-paneled rooms have attractive tiled showers, and there's a gorgeous new pool. Its five excellent efficiencies are built for real cooking; another good family choice. Laundromat is next door.

Eating

On the boardwalk, the bright-yellow Midway Steak House pumps out sausages and peppers that win raves. Note that restaurants have shorter hours, and can close midweek outside summer.

Sugar (☎ 732-793-7900; www.justaddsugar.net; 22 Boulevard at Dupont Ave; items $1.50-5; 🕑 7am-1pm & 7-11pm) Hip coffeehouses are in short supply in Seaside, and Sugar fills the void. Get bakery delights, ice cream and 'designer cupcakes' worthy of a Food Network show. Watch your back, *Cake Boss*.

El Camino (☎ 732-830-2470; www.theelcamino.com; Boulevard at Grant Ave; mains $11-13; 🕑 dinner) This stylish, BYOB Mexican restaurant has a short menu of homemade favorites – tacos, enchiladas, burritos and chimichangas – served in generous portions. Its nice outdoor patio is shared with Raaz Hookah Lounge.

Maruca's Pizza (☎ 732-793-0707; www.marucaspizza. com; cnr boardwalk & Porter Ave; plain pie $16; 🕑 daily year-round) Maruca's makes probably the best pie on the shore (an honorific not bestowed lightly). It specializes in crisp-crust South Jersey pies that are light as air, the essence of simplicity.

Hemingway's Cafe (☎ 732-830-1255; www.heming waysnj.com; 612 Boulevard near Sumner Ave; mains $20-30; 🕑 dinner, bar to 3am) Wrought-iron railings and open streetside dining lend a Bourbon St feel to this contemporary American restaurant. The menu offers the full range of steaks, pasta, chicken and seafood. After dinner, the two bars host DJs and live music on weekends, making this a popular watering hole.

Atlantic Bar & Grill (☎ 732-854-1588; www.atlan ticbarandgrillnj.com; cnr 24th & Central Aves, South Seaside Park; mains $27-35; 🕑 dinner) Romantic, gourmet dining – in Seaside Heights? Nope. Come instead to Seaside Park and the Atlantic Grill. The soothing modern green-and-black decor is counterbalanced by huge windows taking in the dunes and sea. You'll find a full raw bar, and a cocktail bar, and the menu is awash in Asian and Pacific Rim fusion, such as peppercorn-crusted ahi and scallop ceviche with seaweed. Steaks, too.

Drinking & Entertainment

On the boardwalk, two old-school Seaside haunts with cover bands grinding out the hits are **EJ's** (☎ 732-793-4622; boardwalk at Sheridan Ave) and the **Aztec Motel** (☎ 732-793-1010; boardwalk at Sherman Ave).

In town, most bars and clubs are on the Boulevard between Sumner and Dupont Aves. **Rigger's** (☎ 732-830-9600; 519 Boulevard; 🕑 7am-2am) is a year-round neighborhood bar, as is **Klee's** (☎ 732-830-1996; www.kleesbarandgrill.com; 101 Boulevard at Dupont Ave), which in addition to live music on weekends has Irish sing-alongs on Sunday. One of the most popular nightclubs currently is **Bamboo** (☎ 732-830-3660; www.bamboobar.com; cnr Lincoln Ave & Boulevard).

For something completely different, sidle into **Raaz Hookah Lounge** (☎ 732-793-6300; www. raazjerseyshore.com; 715 Boulevard at Grant Ave; hookah $15-20), which is dripping with sinful blood red and has devilish black leather couches. There's no liquor, just hookahs (with dozens of flavors) and smoothies, and a trancey DJ vibe.

Getting There & Away

NJ Transit (☎ 800-772-2222; www.njtransit.com) runs buses from New York City and Philadelphia to Seaside Heights. To drive, take Garden State Parkway exit 82 to Rte 37 west, which leads into downtown. Or, from Point Pleasant, take Rte 35 south.

TOM'S RIVER & AROUND
pop 94,900

In and around Tom's River are three excellent reasons to stop. Tom's River is inland and due west of Seaside Heights, right off Garden State Parkway exits 81 and 82 (and the Rte 37 turnoff for the barrier island).

First, there's **Insectropolis** (☎ 732-349-7090; www.insectropolis.com; 1761 Lakewood Rd/US 9; admission $7; 🕑 10am-3pm Tue-Sun, also Mon in summer), a fantastic creepy-crawly 'bugseum' so amusing you *almost* forget to be grossed out. Whimsical murals and dioramas are perfectly designed for school-age sensibilities, but any age will gape at the over 60 live tarantulas, plus scorpions, millipedes, hissing cockroaches and live bee, termite and ant colonies. The welcoming staff is hands-on. From Garden State Parkway exit 83 take Rte 9 north 1.8 miles; look for the Ozane Exterminating sign on the right.

Second, the **Nelson Sailing Center** (☎ 732-270-6510; www.nelsonsailingcenter.com; 12 Lake Dr, Island Heights; 🕑 9am-6pm Thu-Tue May 1-Oct 3) has the biggest sailing fleet in the tri-state area, and accomplished sailing instructors. It rents mostly 19ft to 35ft keel boats ($100 to $415 per day); reservations are required for first-time customers

NEW JERSEY

(add $50 orientation fee). For lessons, the center certifies sailors through ASA. It's at the Island Heights marina, east of Tom's River; get directions online, as it's easy to get lost.

Finally, if you agree breakfast is the most important meal of the day, then go to ourpick **Shut Up and Eat!** (☎ 732-349-4544; 290 W Water St, Tom's River; breakfast $3-9, sandwiches $8-10; ✆ 6:30am-2:30pm), a cheeky, genuinely warm café that will start your day laughing. Waitresses wear matching PJs (wear yours for a 13% discount), tablesettings are mismatched garage-sale finds, the walls are festooned with flotsam, hula hoops await hips, and the menu is a riot of jokes and misspellings. Did we mention that breakfast is great? The stuffed French toast will keep you going till dinner. Take Rte 166/Main St through downtown Tom's River, turn right on Water St, then the first left after the post office.

ISLAND BEACH STATE PARK

Island Beach is one of New Jersey's most beautiful natural areas, and its white-sand beaches and windswept, rustling dunes are a shore highlight. This 3000-acre state park takes up the southern third of Barnegat Peninsula, stretching about 9 miles south of Seaside Park. The land was bought in 1926 by Henry Phipps, a Pittsburgh steel millionaire, for development as a resort, but the stock-market crash put a stop to the scheme. The tract of land remained untouched until the state bought it in 1953 and opened the park six years later, representing one of New Jersey's first efforts at conservation.

Reasons to come are many: the road makes a wonderful bike ride, the shore fishing is legendary, the marshes at the southern end are a paradise for hikers and bird-watchers, kayaking is wonderful, and the swimming beach is without peer. As a result, as at Sandy Hook, it's best to arrive before 10am on summer weekends. Once the parking lots are full, the entrance is closed – only to reopen later once enough people leave.

Orientation & Information

The park is divided into three sections: two natural areas at either end, and a recreational zone/swimming beach in the middle. In summer, parking costs $6/10 weekday/weekend, and $5 low season. Bikers can get in free (there is limited public parking just outside the park). The park **information center** (☎ 732-793-0506; www.state.nj.us/dep/parksandforests/parks/island. html; ✆ 8am-dusk) is at the entrance gate; stop here for maps and program schedules. Other useful websites are www.islandbeachnj.org and **Friends of Island Beach State Park** (www.friends ofislandbeach.com), who publish a visitor guide.

The park has no public transportation and doesn't allow camping, and the only concessions are at the swimming beach.

About 7 miles into the park is the newly expanded **Interpretive Center** (☎ 732-793-1698, ✆ noon-6pm Fri-Sun summer), with small exhibits. It runs a slate of guided hikes and outdoor programs (like surf-fishing clinics and kayak trips).

Activities

For **swimming**, the Jersey shore doesn't offer a more heart-stopping stretch of white sand. Despite having 10 miles of beaches, only the 1-mile strip in the recreational zone has lifeguards and allows swimming (10am to 6pm). There are concessions, showers and changing rooms.

Head to the southern natural area for **hiking** and **bird-watching**. A handful of short scenic trails lead through the marshes and wetlands. The Bird Blind Trail (signed on the road) leads to what it promises: a chance to sight egrets, herons, ibises and other migratory birds. An osprey relocation program has been so successful the island now boasts 30 nesting pairs, one of which is usually here. The longest, best hike is to walk from the end of the road to the peninsula's tip, where you can admire 'Old Barney' lighthouse.

Biking is restricted to the paved roadway, making for an 18-mile roundtrip.

Anglers can't get enough of the **surf fishing**. Bluefish and striped bass are caught year-round, and flounder and kingfish in summer. In Seaside Park, visit **Grumpys Tackle** (☎ 732-830-1900; www.grumpystackle.com; 906 NE Central Ave) for gear, bait and advice. You will need to register for saltwater fishing (see p404).

For **kayaking**, visit **Yakkity Yak Kayaks** (☎ 732-830-1835; www.yakskayakrental.com; cnr 24th & Bay View Aves) in the marina in Seaside Park; it has rentals and runs kayak tours within Island Beach State Park.

LONG BEACH ISLAND

Long Beach Island is an 18-mile-long barrier island that is almost entirely settled, with a series of small towns interspersed with residential neighborhoods of summer homes. As Jersey bumper stickers indicate, LBI is a favorite spot. In particular, it's where many families like to spend their summer vacation, returning year after year, and the sense of community is palpable. LBI has fantastic beaches and a wide array of activities, nightlife, restaurants and things to do – the main one being, nothing at all.

LBI is connected to the mainland by a single causeway at its halfway point – the town of Ship Bottom. On the north side of Ship Bottom is Surf City, and together these towns form LBI's largest commercial district. Beach Haven on the southern end is the other main town with the most services. Heading north, Harvey Cedars and Barnegat Light also have small commercial centers.

Orientation & Information

Long Beach Blvd is the island's main – and in some stretches only – north–south street; its name changes to Bay Blvd in Beach Haven and Central Ave in Barnegat Light. The speed limit is actually lowered from 40mph to 35mph in summer. While it's time-consuming driving from end to end, don't give in to temptation and speed; the police make a lot of money from impatience.

The **chamber of commerce** (☎ 609-494-7211, 800-292-6372; www.visitlbiregion.com; 265 W 9th St; ◷ 10am-4pm Mon-Fri, plus 10am-2pm Sat & Sun summer) is two blocks in from the causeway; Rte 72 becomes 9th St once it reaches the island. The chamber offers tons of informational brochures – on beach badges, public toilets, activities and more – and it maintains lists of available hotel rooms. Another excellent website to find local businesses is www.lbisland.com.

The *Beach Haven Times* is the island's weekly newspaper. For entertainment and event listings, pick up the free weeklies the *Sandpaper* (www.sandpaper.net) and the *Summer Times Islander* (www.app.com/islander).

There are several post offices on Long Beach Blvd, including branches at 6th St, Beach Haven; and at 18th St, Ship Bottom.

Atlantic Books (☎ 609-492-2068; www.atlanticbooks.us; cnr Bay Ave & 5th St, Beach Haven; ◷ 9am-6pm) is the best bookstore, with magazines, newspapers, local guides and kids' books and toys.

A 24-hour laundromat is on Long Beach Blvd at 22nd St, Ship Bottom.

Sights & Activities
BARNEGAT LIGHTHOUSE
At the northern tip of LBI, in the town of Barnegat Light, is the famous and stately **'Old Barney' lighthouse** (☎ 609-494-2016; admission $1; ◷ 10am-4pm Memorial Day-Labor Day, Sat & Sun May, Sep & Oct). It's a Jersey shore icon and the signature of the 31-acre Barnegat Light State Park, with short nature trails, picnic benches and a long strollable seawall.

Built in 1859, Old Barney was originally 900ft from the shore and has been rescued several times from being undermined by erosion. It's 165ft tall, and climbing the tower's 217 steps provides a sweeping panorama of the interplay of bay, ocean and barrier islands. The park is a popular place to watch the sunset. Drive north on Central Ave till it ends.

MUSEUM OF NJ MARITIME HISTORY
A fun highlight, this **museum** (☎ 609-492-0202; www.museumofnjmh.org; admission free; ◷ 10am-4pm Jun-Aug, Fri-Sun Sep-May) is a neat, orderly paean to nautical life and lore, with a particular fascination with maritime disasters. Not only that, it has a cool historic postcard collection. It's in Beach Haven at Dock Rd and West Ave, on the bayside.

FANTASY ISLAND & THUNDERING SURF
LBI doesn't have a boardwalk, but to the relief of antsy children and their parents, Beach Haven does have **Fantasy Island** (☎ 609-492-4000; www.fantasyislandpark.com; 320 W 7th St; ◷ rides 6-11pm late Jun-early Sep), a small amusement park and arcade with children's rides, skee ball and other favorites. The indoor arcade is open from noon May to August.

Next door is **Thundering Surf** (☎ 609-492-0869; www.thunderingsurfwaterpark.com; adult/child $26/24; ◷ 10am-6pm Jun–mid-Sep), a modest waterpark with a sizable minigolf course. Completing the trifecta, this amusement complex is next to the Bay Village shopping mall.

LONG BEACH ISLAND FOUNDATION OF THE ARTS & SCIENCES
In the town of Loveladies, the **foundation** (☎ 609-494-1241; www.lbifoundation.org; 120 Long Beach Blvd, Loveladies; ◷ 9am-5pm Mon-Fri, 9am-3pm Sat & Sun) has small art galleries and exhibits and offers courses in ceramics, jewelry, painting, silkscreening and other crafts. It also schedules lectures, children's programs, nature walks and science programs (www.lbiscience.org).

NEW JERSEY

Loveladies is between Harvey Cedars and Barnegat Light.

FORSYTHE NATIONAL WILDLIFE REFUGE

The undeveloped southern tip of LBI is part of this **refuge** (☎ 609-652-1665, ext 11; www.fws.gov/northeast/forsythe). Called the Holgate District or the Brigantine Wilderness Area, it's an important nesting site for endangered piping plover, least terns and black skimmers. Though closed to the public from April 1 to August 31, rangers run popular guided walks in the refuge on summer weekends; call or check the refuge information board. From September 1 to March 31, the refuge is open to hikers, but not swimming. Drive south on Long Beach Blvd till it ends.

BEACHES

The beaches are excellent on LBI. They get very wide in the north near Barnegat Light, the result of jetties built to protect Barnegat Lighthouse from erosion. Elsewhere, beaches are a short walk from the end of the street to the water.

Despite so much choice, it helps your pocketbook to pick a beach and stick to it. LBI's five main towns – in order, Barnegat Light, Harvey Cedars, Surf City, Ship Bottom and Beach Haven – each have separate beach badges (all $5 per day except Surf City, which is $7 per day). All other beaches use Long Beach Township badges. Buy your badges from lifeguards on the beach or from each town's borough hall; LBI's visitors' center has a list.

SURFING & WATERSPORTS

LBI has over 20 designated surfing beaches (the visitors' center has a list), and they are generally well-regarded.

The most comprehensive rental shop is **Island Surf & Sail** (☎ 609-494-5553; www.island surf-sail.com; 3304 Long Beach Blvd at 33rd St, Brant Beach). A fixture for 25 years, it sells and rents equipment for surfing (including standup paddle), windsurfing, wakeboarding and kayaking. It is also the only NJ store selling kiteboarding gear. And it offers excellent lessons in all the above watersports.

The **Acme Surf Company** (☎ 609-492-1024; www.lbi.net/skates; Long Beach Blvd at 13th St, Beach Haven) is another good watersports rental company, with surfboards, body boards, kayaks and wetsuits. It can arrange private surf lessons.

SAILING

Most sailing is done in the bay. **Harvey Cedars Marina** (☎ 609-494-0111; 6318 Long Beach Blvd near Atlantic Ave; ☯ closed Wed & Sun) rents Hobie sailboats (from $60 for two hours) and kayaks, and provides sailing lessons. The shop sells boating and fishing supplies.

The visitors' center has a brochure listing LBI's boating options. Another place to look is www.longbeachisland.com/boat.html. Dedicated sailors might also consider driving to Nelson Sailing Center (p229) near Tom's River.

FISHING & CRUISES

With its many small marinas and long stretches of unoccupied beach, Long Beach Island is ideal for anglers, whether they prefer party boats or casting from shore. The visitor center has a full list of options. Also, for a list of captains and fishing resources, visit the website www.beachhavencharterfishing.com.

The main place for charter boats is **Barnegat Light Yacht Basin** (☎ 609-494-2094), at the end of 18th St on the bay, in Barnegat Light. This is next to **Viking Village wharf** (☎ 609-494-7211; www.vikingvillage.net), which also conducts tours of its commercial dock on Fridays in summer.

At the Beach Haven dock, at Center St and West Ave on the bay, is the **Miss Beach Haven** (☎ 609-978-9951; www.missbeachhaven.com), which runs half-day fishing trips and one-hour sunset cruises. Also here, **Black Whale Cruises** (☎ 609-822-8849; www.blackwhalecruises.com) conducts paddlewheel cruises to Atlantic City, sunset cruises, and has a dress-up pirate ship adventure for kids (daily July to August).

BICYCLING & ACTIVITY RENTALS

Finding a bike on LBI is about as hard as locating the sun. The biggest rental place is **Faria's** (☎ 800-332-7427; www.fariassurf.com), which has three locations along the main boulevard: in Beach Haven at **Taylor Ave** (☎ 609-492-0200); in Ship Bottom at **28th St** (☎ 609-494-7368); and in Surf City at **5th St** (☎ 609-494-8616). It rents bikes, surries, surfboards, body boards, kayaks, cribs and more.

Specializing in everything the unprepared family might need is **Surf Buggy** (www.surfbuggylbi.com) with two locations: in **Surf City** (☎ 609-361-3611; 1414 Long Beach Blvd) and **Brant Beach** (☎ 609-361-0100; 3801 Long Beach Blvd). In addition to bikes and surries, they rent joggers, trailers, cribs, high chairs, linens and assorted beach gear.

Festivals & Events

As you can imagine, LBI's calendar is stocked. The visitors' center has a list, and check out www.visitlbiregion.com. In mid-June, one standout is the **Jersey Shore Fine Arts Festival** (www.jerseyshoreartfest.com), a nationally regarded art show that's tops in the state.

LBI's signature festival is October's **Chowderfest** (www.chowderfest.com). For over 20 years this has been the ultimate chowder competition (with coveted bragging rights). What makes it really fun is that judging is open to all ticketholders. That's a lot of chowder!

Sleeping

The liveliest town is Beach Haven, which has the greatest concentration of B&Bs and nightlife. As a rule, accommodations are more expensive here and in the middle of the island than at the quieter ends. Unless you like driving, stay where you want to play; listings are arranged north to south by town. Hotels are open year-round except where noted. In Beach Haven Victorian-themed B&Bs line Engleside Ave and Centre St, from Bay Ave to the beach, all of which is within walking distance of the main commercial district.

North Shore Inn (☎ 609-494-5001; www.north shoreinn.com; 806 Central Ave, Barnegat Light; r high $130-165, low $70-130; ☽ Apr-Nov; ✖ ☎ ♿) This standard, pastel seaside motel is very clean and well-managed and has great summer rates. Half the 28 rooms have cramped but still workable kitchenettes. Free beach badges.

Surf City Hotel (☎ 609-494-7281, 800-353-3342; www. surfcityhotel.com; 800 Long Beach Blvd at 8th Ave, Surf City; r high $160-240, low $90-180; ☽ Apr-Oct; ✖) This attractive two-building hotel has pleasant, well-cared-for rooms; the only drawback is the late-night noise from its popular bar. To avoid this, request a room in the newer building out back. Free beach tags.

Drifting Sands (☎ 609-494-1123, 877-524-7866; www.dslbi.com; 119 E 9th St, Ship Bottom; r high $219-360, low $110-260; ✖ ☎ ♿) At this large 100-room hotel done in standard yellow-and-blue shore hues, opt for the renovated, very clean oceanfront buildings (with tiny efficiencies), which sit at the dunes' edge. The older back building is musty and neglected. Free beach tags.

Daddy O (☎ 609-361-5100; www.daddyohotel.com; 4401 Long Beach Blvd, Brant Beach; r high $240-395, low $178-318; ✖ ☐ ☎) LBI's biggest splash in recent years has been Daddy O, an urban-chic 22-room boutique hotel (and restaurant).

Designer rooms soothingly mix textures and tones – faux fur throws and wood-slat window shades, marble baths and Murano glass wallpaper, with nary a tacky clamshell in sight. Technology-rich, amenity-laden rooms lack only a view; for that, sunbathe on the rooftop deck.

Magnolia House (☎ 609-492-2226; www.magnolia houselbi.com; 215 Centre St, Beach Haven; r high $170-300, low $140-230; ✖ ☎) New owners are breathing fresh air into this rambling 1867 Victorian home. All 12 rooms are idiosyncratic, deliciously romantic little antique cornucopias with teeny private bathrooms. Public rooms are sumptuous, and full breakfast and afternoon tea (and beach tags) are included. No children under 10.

Engleside Inn (☎ 609-492-1251; www.engleside. com; 30 Engleside Ave, Beach Haven; r high $250-375, low $125-290; ✖ ☒ ♿) Overall, this is a very well-kept 71-room property; ocean-view rooms are excellent and have been recently updated with flat-screen TVs. Though decor is motel standard, it eschews seaside tackiness. All have minifridges, but efficiencies are disappointing – they're small and need facelifts. Kids under 14 free.

Lorry's Island End Motel (☎ 609-492-6363; www. lorrysmotel.com; 23 Washington Ave, Holgate; r high $110-200, low $60-150; ✖ ☎) At the island's south end, this no-muss, no-fuss 12-room motel invites families for long, restful stays with full refrigerators and a huge, fenced outdoor picnic area with multiple BBQs. Management is friendly and on the ball. New tiled showers, breeze-catching screen doors and weekly deals are pluses. Free beach tags.

Eating

On LBI, you never have to worry about finding ice cream, breakfast or clam chowder, while a recent influx of upscale dining has improved the dinner scene. Listings in this section are arranged north to south by town.

Mustache Bill's (☎ 609-494-3553; 8th & Broadway, Barnegat Light; mains $8-14; ☽ 6am-3pm Fri-Sun) A classic silver-sided diner and longtime LBI favorite. Omelets and pancakes draw raves, and Bill's draws everyone: it's a warm community meeting place, so come early and be prepared to wait.

Plantation Restaurant (☎ 609-494-8191; www. plantationrestaurant.com; 7908 Long Beach Blvd near 80th, Harvey Cedars; mains $21-32; ☽ 11:30am-9pm) Next door to Harvey Cedars Shellfish, Plantation makes for a romantic night out. Excellent preparations take a contemporary Caribbean-accented approach (like blackened seafood, cheese grits, Cajun and Creole sauces, coconut shrimp), but aren't above a retro wedge salad. A fireplace, wicker chairs and a pressed-tin ceiling lend a Key West vibe, which the lively bar scene enhances.

Harvey Cedars Shellfish (☎ 609-494-7112; www. harveycedarsshellfishco.com; 7904 Long Beach Blvd at 79th, Harvey Cedars; mains $19-23; ☒ dinner summer only) For casual picnic-table dining under a roof, this place has been an LBI institution for 35 years. Extremely fresh and simply prepared, just the way you remember it.

Yellow Fin (☎ 609-494-7001; www.yellowfinlbi.com; 104 24th St at Beach Ave, Surf City; mains $22-35; ☒ dinner Thu-Sun) The most refined meal on LBI may be at Yellow Fin, the place that started LBI's gourmet trend. Small, with simple but romantic decor, the focus is entirely on seafood, with creative, accomplished Asian-French-influenced preparations. Make reservations, dress up and BYOB.

our pick Daddy O (☎ 609-494-1300; www.daddyorestaurant.com; 4401 Long Beach Blvd, Brant Beach; mains $14-29; ☒ lunch & dinner) Are we still on LBI? Daddy O's stylish restaurant and bar seem airlifted from Philly, which might be the point. High-backed red leather chairs, scalloped banquettes and coral-like starburst chandeliers make a hip setting for designer cocktails and top-notch world-fusion cuisine. Start with piquant flatbreads, then move on to porcini-dusted scallops, nori-wrapped ahi, and steak frites.

Chicken or the Egg (☎ 609-492-3695; www.492fowl. com; 207 N Bay Ave, Beach Haven; dishes $6-15; ☒ 7am-9pm, 24hr summer) All hens on deck! The long menu – packed with egg-scrutiating puns and well-made, well-priced diner classics – satisfies everyone, at any hour. Naturally, this diner takes pride in its wings (don't miss Wednesday nights!); choose from 15 hot sauces.

Show Place (☎ 609-492-0018; www.theshowplace. org; cnr Centre St & Beach Ave, Beach Haven; ice cream $3-9; ☒ 6pm-midnight summer) Ice cream is just ice cream unless you have to sing for it – and sing you will, along with the harmonizing, theatrical 'waitri,' who put on a bona fide cabaret. Come at least once.

Drinking & Entertainment

Check the free *Summer Times Islander* (www. app.com/islander) and *Sandpaper* (www. sandpaper.net) for music and entertainment listings.

Surf City Hotel Beach Club (☎ 609-494-7281; www. surfcityhotel.com; 800 Long Beach Blvd at 8th Ave, Surf City) A popular place for live music most summer nights; from July to August, the Wednesday night 'Long Beach Idol' contest is a must (your applause decides the winner!).

Buckalew's (☎ 609-492-2252; www.buckalews.com; cnr Bay Ave & Center St, Beach Haven) This place draws a Boomer crowd for '50s, '60s and '80s cover bands, plus Irish and piano music. It's also a full restaurant.

Joe Pop's (☎ 609-494-0558; www.joepops.com; Long Beach Blvd at 20th St, Ship Bottom; ☒ Fri-Sun) For 20-somethings, Joe Pop's is a big lemon-yellow box of happiness. DJs and bands keep the energy high; outside is a separate tiki-themed bar and stage.

Surflight Theatre (☎ 609-492-9477; www.surflight. org; cnr Engleside & Beach Aves, Beach Haven) Surflight has been presenting Broadway's well-loved musical chestnuts every summer for 60 years. It also has a Monday night concert series and a children's theater (shows Wednesday to Sunday). What to do when the sun goes down? Go to *Oklahoma!*

Shopping

Bay Village (9th St, Beach Haven) and **Schooner's Wharf** (9th St, Beach Haven) are shopping complexes overflowing with beachwear, gifts, chowder, fudge and hermit crabs.

Historic **Viking Village** (☎ 609-494-7211; www. vikingvillage.net; cnr 19th St & Bayview Ave, Barnegat Light) is a string of shops in renovated fishermen's shacks, with some upscale boutiques mixed in with standard gift shoppes.

Hand's (☎ 609-492-2385; 1400 Bay Ave, Beach Haven) is an all-purpose department/hardware store you'll need at least once – for sauce pans, cutlery, bathing suits, board games, Adirondack chairs and whatever else you forgot.

Mod Hatter (☎ 609-492-0999; 1103 Bay Ave at 11th St, Beach Haven) specializes in stylish woven hats for men and women. Styles range from beachwear to churchwear, plus baskets, bags and jewelry.

Positioned near the base of the causeway, you can't, and shouldn't, miss **Ron Jon** (☎ 609-494-8844; www.ronjons.com; 201 9th St at Central Ave, Ship Bottom). This surfer store sells all the latest gear (including magazines and DVDs), plus it has the 'world's largest surfboard' and cheap board rentals.

NEW JERSEY

Getting There & Around

The island is reached via Garden State Parkway exit 63 along Rte 72.

During the summer, the only on-island shuttle service is Trolley Tours' **LBI Dial-a-Ride** (☎ 609-548-4970; www.trolleytoursinc.com/lbi_dial-a-ride. htm; per person $10; ⏰ 5:30pm Fri & Sat Jun, Tue-Sat Jul-Aug). For one ticket, you get unlimited rides all night.

NORTHERN NEW JERSEY

It takes about 90 minutes, without traffic, to drive from Hoboken or Newark to the Delaware Water Gap. In that short trip across the state's forehead, you encounter almost everything that makes New Jersey such a bewildering package of contrasts.

You travel, most obviously, from the state's most densely populated counties (Hudson and Essex) to one of its least densely populated (Sussex) – from areas with over 13,000 people per sq mile to one with less than 230. You go from an ethnically diverse, sometimes impoverished industrial/urban stew to a region of predominantly white rural villages tucked in forested mountains. In between, you pass by some of New Jersey's wealthiest suburban towns – like Montclair and Morristown – and through much of the farmland that earns the state's nickname, the Garden State.

You will have a chance to experience world-class fine arts and symphony orchestras,

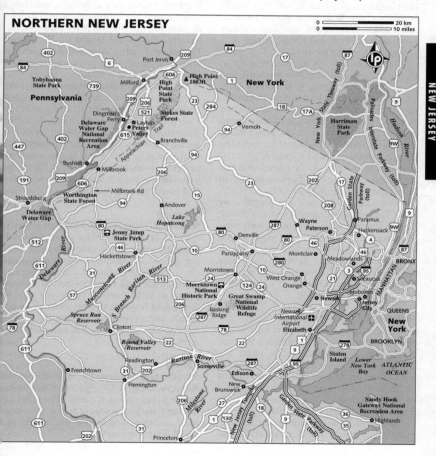

NORTHERN NEW JERSEY

Revolutionary War history, Iberian cuisine, the Appalachian Trail, the birthplace of the movies, a Giants football game, a corn maze, Frank Sinatra's hometown, and to climb New Jersey's highest peak and get a ferry to the Statue of Liberty. Not all in one day, mind you. That'd be crazy. But Northern Jersey, in a nutshell, is like that.

HOBOKEN
pop 40,600

Wander Hoboken in the dusky orange of early evening – passing narrow gentrified streets of well-preserved brownstones, as Wall Street dads push strollers with one hand and lead collies with the other, as hipster moms smoke pipes while biking with their kids – and you can't help feeling that this is New York's sixth borough, a mini-Brooklyn across the Hudson. Ask a Manhattanite, and they'll grudgingly agree, adding, 'Yeah, but it's still Jersey.'

Seriously, we can't win.

There is, in fact, an ongoing tension in Hoboken between longtime residents and those young, interloping New Yorkers looking for cheap(er) rent and an easy Manhattan commute. You just don't feel it as a visitor. Instead, Hoboken presents itself like a warm amalgam of all types and classes, a town riding a resurgent wave of trendy cool yet rooted in genuine community and history.

Hoboken was actually first developed as a recreation resort for New Yorkers. In 1846 in one of those welcoming parks, Elysian Fields, the first game of baseball was played – by New Yorkers needing more space. Frank Sinatra was also born and got his start here. The young singer, yearning for bigger stages, eventually left New Jersey; he must have been tantalized by Hoboken's waterfront panorama of the Big Apple, the greatest city on earth. Skyscrapers aglow at sunset, it's a perspective you don't get on the island.

Orientation & Information

Hoboken is tiny, about a square mile, and is easily explored on foot. Washington St – running north–south parallel to the water – is the main drag, and it's lined top-to-bottom with shops, restaurants and bars. It's busiest at the south end, where short side streets lead to the ornate, historic Erie Lackawanna Train Terminal, where the PATH train arrives.

Parking in Hoboken is a headache, especially at night and on weekends. Parking po-

lice ticket aggressively, so don't take chances. Keep an eye on your meter or pay for a parking lot.

Hoboken has no tourist office, but it's not hard to find event information and free newspapers around town. Good websites include www.hoboken411.com and www.hobokennj.org. Northern Jersey's daily newspaper is the *Star-Ledger* (www.nj.com).

The **main post office** (River St) is between Newark and 1st Sts. **Symposia** (☎ 201-963-0909; www.symposia.us; 510 Washington St; ☎ 9am-9pm Mon-Sat, from noon Sun) sells intellectual used books and acts as a community space.

Sights

Hoboken's waterfront parks – and their Manhattan views – are a highlight, including a new 2-acre kids' playground at Pier C Park on an island in the Hudson River (near 3rd St); just stroll along Frank Sinatra Dr. The original Elysian Fields, site of baseball's first game, no longer exists, but there is a commemorative plaque at 11th and Washington Sts.

Small **Hoboken Historical Museum** (☎ 201-656-2240; www.hobokenmuseum.org; 1301 Hudson St at 13th St; admission $2; ☎ 2-7pm Tue-Thu, 1-5pm Fri, noon-5pm Sat & Sun) presents evolving, city-focused exhibits that make good use of the museum's vast collection of historic photos. There is no permanent Sinatra exhibit, but it has an excellent, self-guided walking tour of Sinatra sights (the home he was born in was torn down) and of Hoboken's historic buildings.

Sleeping

W Hotel (☎ 201-253-2400; www.whotels.com; 225 River St; r $250-500; 🕸 💻 📶) W has recently planted its flag in Hoboken, which otherwise lacks sleeping options. A self-consciously hip boutique chain that oozes designer flair and big-city prices, with mod furniture and bold hues, it tries to be an event as much as a place to sleep. And it succeeds. The views alone ensure it, not to mention the spa, the sunken lounge, the restaurant… Internet deals drop rates $50 to $80.

Eating

Schnackenberg's Luncheonette (☎ 201-659-9836; 1110 Washington St; items $2-4.50; ☎ 8:30am-4:30pm Thu-Tue) Order an egg cream or a malted and soak up the time-warp atmosphere at this old-school soda fountain. The food is forgettable, but you'll fight to spend $10.

Carlo's Bakery (☎ 201-659-3671; www.carlos bakery.com; 95 Washington St; pastries $3-7; ⊙ 7am-7:30pm) What's a bakery doing with lines requiring sidewalk barriers and a sign warning that by entering you agree to appear on TV? Why, it's the home of TLC's *Cake Boss*! Frankly, waiting 45 minutes for a cannoli is a bit much, no matter how great. But Buddy's here, and his cakes *are* amazing.

Stacks Pancake House & Cafe (☎ 201-710-5777; www.stacksofhoboken.com; 506 Washington St; mains $6-9; ⊙ 6am-10:30pm Mon-Thu, 24hr Fri & Sat, to 10pm Sun) A newcomer, Stacks has been an instant hit, and why not? It serves incredibly scrumptious pancakes from an original (and secret!) recipe, prepares them in oodles of fruit-a-licious ways, and is open 24 hours on weekends.

Bin 14 (☎ 201-963-9463; www.bin14.com; 1314 Washington St; small plates $6-15; ⊙ 10am-11pm Mon-Thu, to 1am Fri & Sat, 9am-10pm Sun) Everything works at this upscale wine bar, whose extensive array of small plates and wines (in 2oz or 6oz pours) allows you to invent your own tasting menu. The wood-fire grill is put to excellent use, and the industrial space, dominated by a red-brick wall, verily hops with excitement at night.

La Isla (☎ 201-659-8197; 104 Washington St; lunch $7-11, mains $14-19; ⊙ 7am-10pm Mon-Sat, 10am-3pm, 5-9pm Sun) In this unpretentious diner – with 14 counter stools and six tables – the nuevo Cuban cuisine will have you shouting ¡No! Expect lively service, upbeat music and extremely satisfying versions of pan Cubano,

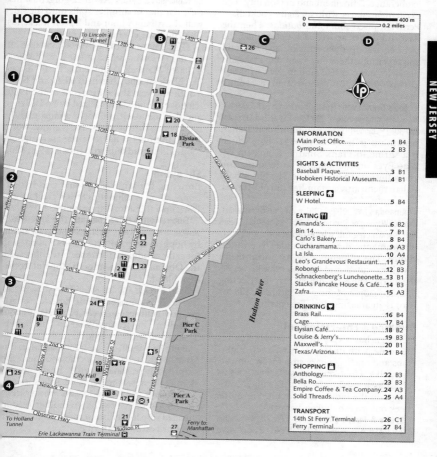

HOBOKEN

0   400 m
0   0.2 miles

NEW JERSEY

fried plantains, churrasco with chimichuri sauce, batidos and more. *Si, Si!*

Robongi (☎ 201-222-8388; www.robongi.com; 520 Washington St; mains $15-24; ☿ 11am-11pm) This sushi bar is best appreciated at night, when the neon, black lights, house music and jumble of fishing nets, shark heads and mounted marlins vibrates like a futuristic, neo-Tokyo fever dream. The extensive menu highlights rock-star sushi – big, dramatic rolls with robust flavors.

our pick **Cucharamama** (☎ 201-420-1700; www. cucharamama.com; 233 Clinton St at 3rd St; tapas $9-12, mains $20-26; ☿ dinner Tue-Sun, also lunch Sun) This atmospheric neighborhood gem presents a gourmet fusion of a continent's worth of cuisine – mixing the entire South American palette with exuberance, refinement and personality. The excitement starts with specialty cocktails – Peruvian pisco sours and *batidas*. Then the flavorful dishes arrive, each better than the last – corn soup, duck tamales, ceviche – and you're warning the waiter away: don't take this plate! Its more casual sibling, Zafra (phone 201-610-9801; 301 Willow Ave), is around the corner.

Leo's Grandevous Restaurant (☎ 201-659-9467; www.leosgrandevous.com; 200 Grand St at 2nd St; mains $20-30; ☿ dinner) This neighborhood Italian restaurant is legendary for its bar, which is a shrine to Frank Sinatra. Crank up Ol' Blue Eyes on the jukebox, order a martini and admire the Sinatra wall. The old-school Italian menu attracts families and old-timers. Cash only.

Amanda's (☎ 201-798-0101; www.amandasrestaurant. com; 908 Washington St; mains $20-30; ☿ dinner, plus brunch Sun) For an elegant, white-tablecloth-and-candles romantic dinner, Amanda's is an ideal choice. The contemporary American menu is well-executed, and warm service preserves the mood. The early-dinner prix fixe (seating 5pm to 5:30pm Monday to Saturday, $28 for two) is an amazing deal. Free parking.

Drinking & Entertainment

Hoboken has a very lively, walkable nightlife scene, with dozens of bars, a few nightclubs and one legendary stop for live music, Maxwell's. Hoboken's music scene isn't as robust as it used to be, but it's still a destination on the indie-band circuit. For more, check out www.hoboken-bar.net.

Louise & Jerry's (☎ 201-656-9698; 329 Washington St near 3rd St) A basement-level, old-school dive

bar in the best way, when you just need a beer and a pool table.

Texas/Arizona (☎ 201-420-0304; www.texasarizona. com; 76 River Rd) Across from the PATH station, TX/AZ provides fantastic people-watching as the bridge-and-tunnel crowd come and go. A good start to an evening.

Cage (☎ 201-216-1766; www.thecagehoboken.com; cnr Newark & River Sts) A friendly, popular neighborhood gay bar, with DJs, drag nights, bingo and karaoke.

Elysian Cafe (☎ 201-798-5898; www.elysiancafe.com; cnr Washington & 10th Sts) This atmospheric 1896 café and bar has been beautifully restored. It feels like a movie set, and in fact appeared in *On the Waterfront*. Get a cocktail, ya bum.

Brass Rail (☎ 201-659-7074; www.thebrassrailnj.com; cnr Washington & 2nd Sts) Another gorgeous, historic bar that in summer spills onto the sidewalk. Busy happy hour and DJs on weekends. The 2nd floor is a full restaurant.

our pick **Maxwell's** (☎ 201-798-0406, showtimes 201-653-1703; www.maxwellsnj.com; cover $8-25; cnr Washington & 11th Sts) Maxwell's punk rock, East Village-like black shoebox has held REM and Sonic Youth and was at the forefront of the 1980s 'Hoboken Sound,' epitomized by Yo La Tengo and the Bongos. It still rocks almost nightly, often with a slate of bands, and is always worth a visit. In front is a full restaurant serving soul food–influenced pub grub (mains $9 to $20).

Shopping

Browsing the funky shops and trendy boutiques along Washington St is a great way to work up a thirst for happy hour.

Empire Coffee & Tea Company (☎ 201-216-9625; www.empirecoffeetea.com; 338 Bloomfield Ave at 4th St) Run by hopped-up extroverts, this is a must-stop for caffeine addicts, with specialty coffees like the Obama Blend, 'a smooth, hopeful, confident blend.'

Solid Threads (☎ 201-484-0529; www.solidthreads. com; 365 1st St at Grand St) Come here for smartass, pop-culture logo-wear, particularly about Hoboken and Jersey. Wear a 'The Boken' T-shirt and show some local pride!

Bella Ro (☎ 201-222-6833; www.shopbellaro.com; 521 Washington St near 6th St) A chic boutique with surprisingly reasonable prices: floaty blouses skimpy dresses, handbags and accessories.

Anthology (☎ 201-610-1000; www.shopanthology. com; 704 Washington St near 7th St) Another recommended stop for stylish women's clothes, with great prices and a fun vibe.

Getting There & Away

The **PATH train** (www.panynj.gov/path) from Manhattan stops at the Erie Lackawanna Train Terminal in Hoboken.

Traveling by car from Manhattan, take either the Holland or Lincoln Tunnels and follow the signs.

From the NJ Turnpike/I-78, take exit 14C (Holland Tunnel exit); get in the far left lane. At the bottom of the ramp, take a left at the first light, Jersey Ave. Follow this as it bears right (under the overpass), and merge onto Observer Hwy (the town's main streets are on your left). Or take exit 16E (Lincoln Tunnel exit), bear right at the Hoboken exit and continue to the bottom of the ramp; turn right onto Park Ave, left onto 14th St.

New York Waterway Ferry (☎ 800-533-3779; www.nywaterway.com) runs several ferry routes between Hoboken and Manhattan: weekdays only between Hudson St (near the Lackawanna Terminal) and Lower Manhattan, and seven days between Hoboken's 14th St and Midtown Manhattan. Service varies but is frequent all day; trips take less than 15 minutes and cost $5.50 to $8.50 one-way.

JERSEY CITY
pop 241,100

Sadly, as you emerge from the Holland Tunnel from Manhattan, your first impression of the state is formed by Jersey City, and it's not pretty. Merge onto the Pulaski Skyway, perhaps the ugliest bridge in America (actually the nation's first superhighway in 1932), and the derelict, steaming landscape seems an un-ending industrial blight. No wonder people joke and keep driving.

Further, Jersey City has been historically notorious for its ineffective (and periodically indicted) local politicians. Even though the city has improved in recent years, it doesn't hold much to draw travelers – with the significant exception of Liberty State Park. This incredible reclamation project is the well-deserved pride of the city: a stretch of once-abandoned, rotting piers transformed into a sparkling green oasis, with expansive lawns, vibrant marshes and a first-class science museum – and all so close to the Statue of Liberty you could reach out and touch her hem.

Liberty State Park

This beautiful **park** (☎ 201-915-3440; www.libertystatepark.org; admission free; ☺ grounds 6am-10pm) first opened in 1976 (for the nation's bicentennial celebration) and has since grown from 35 acres to over 1100. It is a departure point for ferry trips to Ellis and Liberty Islands, which both sit just offshore, with lower Manhattan silhouetted behind them. It's a vantage you could admire all day, and people do – biking or jogging the paved, meandering multi-use trails and enjoying the grassy meadows, picnic areas and playgrounds.

The ferry ticket office and main visitors' center are inside the gorgeous, restored train terminal, known officially as the **Central Railroad of New Jersey Museum** (☎ 8am-5pm). Beyond a few small displays, the 'museum' is the building itself, but it provides restrooms, concessions and free two-hour parking (in addition to a paid, all-day lot for ferry trips). On a grassy hill outside the terminal, the unfinished 9/11 memorial 'Empty Sky' guides onlookers to the 'empty' space in the skyline where the Twin Towers once stood.

In the middle of the park is a small **Interpretive Center** (☎ 201-915-3409; admission free; ☺ 8am-3pm). Attractive exhibits explain the Hudson River wetlands ecology, with touch exhibits and a cool periscope for peeks at Lady Liberty. Meanwhile, at the park's south end, you'll find the park's administrative offices, more parking, shady picnic areas, monuments to WWII and Christopher Columbus, and a walkway over the water with even more tremendous views.

The park is ideal for concerts, and 2008 inaugurated New Jersey's largest rock music festival: **All Points West** (www.apwfestival.com), held annually in early August.

By car, take NJ Turnpike/I-78 exit 14C and follow the signs. The NJ Transit Liberty State Park Shuttle runs through the park and connects to the Hudson–Bergen Light Rail line. Also, the **Liberty Landing Ferry** (☎ 201-604-5799; www.libertylandingferry.com; roundtrip $14) connects the park directly with Manhattan's financial district; weekdays year-round, plus weekends in summer.

STATUE OF LIBERTY TOURS

Ferries (☎ 201-435-0499, 877-523-9849; www.statuecruises.com; adult/child 4-12yr $12/5) depart Liberty State Park for the Statue of Liberty and Ellis Island every day except Christmas Day. The trip takes 15 minutes, and the boats are less crowded than those leaving from Lower Manhattan. That doesn't mean the islands are

NEW JERSEY

WHAT THE...?

That smell. On the Turnpike. Near Elizabeth. You know what we mean, right? Coming from that staggering *Blade Runner*-esque, smoking, flaming monstrosity? It's the Bayway Refinery – happily converting crude oil into gasoline, jet fuel, diesel, heating oil, propane and more since it was first founded by Standard Oil in 1909. Today, it is the largest refinery on the East Coast. Now roll up the windows.

less crowded; to see both sites depart before noon. For more on the monuments, see p84.

Liberty Science Center

Within the state park is this spectacular, state-of-the-art science **museum** (☎ 201-200-1000; www.lsc.org; adult/child 2-12yr $16/11.50; ⏱ 9am-4pm Mon-Fri, 9am-5pm Sat & Sun). It's chockful of kid-focused hands-on experiments and multimedia experiences (focusing on biology, energy, communication and invention), plus both 3-D and Imax movies and regular live science demonstrations. The 3rd-floor Hudson River ecology exhibit – with fishtanks and get-wet waterplay – is a standout, with a fantastic view deck of Manhattan. Most stunning of all, though, is the skyscraper exhibit, an oversized, immersive exploration of these technological marvels: walk an I-beam, work a scale-model crane and digger, survive a curtain-wall test, design a city and much more. Naturally, a cafe and cool museum shop round out a visit.

NEWARK
pop 279,000

New Jersey's largest city, and home to the metropolitan area's second-largest international airport, Newark is a gateway for regional visitors, but one they rarely pause to explore. This is because Newark has long had a bad but well-earned reputation for poverty and crime. Yet after several decades of trying, Newark seems to be turning itself around. Today it contains an ever-growing number of excellent reasons to check it out.

Many people consider effusive Mayor Cory Booker a key reason for the renaissance. Re-elected to a second term in 2010, Booker has lowered the crime rate, attracted major businesses and inspired renewed pride. For a firsthand look, check out the compelling 2009 Sundance Channel documentary series *Brick City*, which follows Booker and Newark residents as they doggedly revitalize their city.

To a degree, tourism first shifted when the beautiful NJ Performing Arts Center (NJPAC) opened in 1997, followed two years later by the Newark Bears minor-league baseball stadium. In 2007, the Prudential Center (aka the Rock) was unveiled – an 18,000-seat pro-hockey arena and concert venue, which will host pro basketball's NJ Nets in 2011–12. Next door, a huge Marriott hotel is currently under construction – the first new downtown hotel in 40 years – and in 2011, the Children's Museum of NJ hopes to cut the ribbon on its new three-story home next to the train station.

Meanwhile, art galleries are springing up (following the artists, who follow cheap rents), and they complement the state's long-standing preeminent art museum, the Newark Museum.

Steadily, these attractions are forming an expanding hub of tourism mostly within walking distance of Newark Penn Station and close to what has been Newark's most vibrant immigrant community, the Ironbound, a Latino enclave that is Newark's restaurant district.

Orientation & Information

Downtown Newark can be reached from either I-78 or I-280; attractions are well-signed in town. From Newark Penn Station, it's an easy walk to the Ironbound and the Prudential Center. For reasons of distance and safety, driving is preferred to NJPAC and the Newark Museum; both have their own parking.

For information, the **city website** (www.gonewark.com) provides transportation, event and business information. For a great website about Newark's past, visit **Old Newark** (www.oldnewark.com).

Newark Public Radio's **WBGO** (88.3FM; www.wbgo.org) is a great jazz station and a staple for city news.

Sights

The **Ironbound District**, which runs for 10 blocks along Ferry St east of Penn Station, attracted Portuguese immigrants beginning in the 1950s. Their influence is still felt in the neighborhood's Iberian restaurants, but today Brazilian and Latin American newcomers set the tone. So, get a paper cup fruit ice from a sidewalk cart, and enjoy the friendly barrio vibe of Latin music, import stores, Portuguese bakeries and family restaurants.

NEW JERSEY PERFORMING ARTS CENTER

The sixth-largest performing arts center in the US, **NJPAC** (☎ 888-466-5722; www.njpac.org; One Center St) is the home of the NJ Symphony Orchestra and an internationally recognized cultural center. Its two theaters – the 2700-seat Prudential Hall and the 500-seat Victoria Theater – are glittering, polished, breathtaking venues. Programming pulls in the finest in ballet, modern dance, and classical and popular music from around the world. They also have children's programs, educational workshops, and in summer 'Sounds of the City' on Thursday nights. These alfresco concerts on the front lawn shouldn't be missed; they are the closest thing Newark has to a community block party.

NJPAC has two restaurants, **Theatre Square Grill** and **Theatre Square Bistro** (☎ both 973-642-1266); reservations are advised. It also has several parking lots within a block; see the website for advance-purchase vouchers.

NEWARK MUSEUM

Founded in 1909, the **Newark Museum** (☎ 973-596-6550; www.newarkmuseum.org; 49 Washington St at Central Ave; suggested donation adult/child $10/6; ❧ noon-5pm Wed-Fri, 10am-5pm Sat & Sun) is a jewel among New Jersey's cultural institutions, with an impressive, sweeping arts collection and a strong

NEW JERSEY

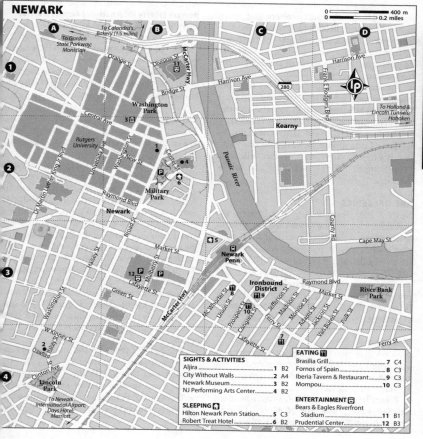

NEWARK

SIGHTS & ACTIVITIES
Aljira	1 B2
City Without Walls	2 A4
Newark Museum	3 B2
NJ Performing Arts Center	4 B2

SLEEPING
Hilton Newark Penn Station	5 C3
Robert Treat Hotel	6 B2

EATING
Brasilia Grill	7 C4
Fornos of Spain	8 C3
Iberia Tavern & Restaurant	9 C3
Mompou	10 C3

ENTERTAINMENT
Bears & Eagles Riverfront Stadium	11 B1
Prudential Center	12 B3

lonelyplanet.com

focus on the natural sciences. In addition, it's notably family-friendly, not just through children's programming, but by interspersing displays that translate the main exhibits for young minds (and hands), thus integrating kids into the adult art world, as it were.

The museum's 80 galleries span every era from antiquity to the present day, and the collections touch every continent and world culture, including Africa, the Americas and the Pacific, from the pre-Columbian era to today. The most jaw-dropping is the **Tibetan collection**, the best in the US. Its shimmering Buddhist altar was consecrated in 1990 by the Dalai Lama.

Another highlight is the **American art collection**, with significant pieces from the Hudson River school and a veritable roll call of major artists: Moran, Bierstadt, Sargent, Stella, Rothko, Thiebaud, Rauschenberg and much more. The large **Decorative Arts collection** features glass, ceramics and textiles from the Renaissance to the present, while the **Ballantine House** re-creates the Victorian era in eight period rooms.

The natural-science collection includes a **planetarium** (separate admission) and the **Victoria Hall of Science**, which somehow crams in everything, plus some exciting taxidermy.

The museum is in the University Heights section of downtown Newark and has parking. It's best to drive, as it's a far walk from Penn Station. Take I-280 exit 15 and follow the signs.

ART GALLERIES

Newark has a burgeoning arts community and gallery scene. The **Newark Arts Council** (www.newarkarts.org) is the main source for information and events; it publishes a gallery map (in most galleries). Across from NJPAC, **Aljira** (☎ 973-622-1600; www.aljira.org; 591 Broad St; ☽ noon-6pm Wed-Fri, 11am-4pm Sat) is a stalwart of contemporary happenings; another intriguing space is **City Without Walls** (☎ 973-622-1188; www.cwow.org; 6 Crawford St; ☽ noon-6pm Wed-Fri, 1-6pm Sat).

Sleeping

Newark has two good options downtown, and when the Marriott is completed, it will have three. Most other Newark hotels serve travelers near the airport.

Robert Treat Hotel (☎ 973-622-1000; www.rthotel.com; 50 Park Place; r from $120; ❋ ▣ ☞) Directly across from NJPAC, this hotel looks snazzy

after a 2008 renovation. Rooms are small, but they attractively mix beige/brown tones and have nice furniture and amenities, like flat-screen TVs. Rates vary by event, not location, so ask for higher floors to sneak a tiny view. It offers shuttles from the train.

Hilton Newark Penn Station (☎ 973-622-5000; www.newarkpennstation.hilton.com; One Gateway Center; r weekend/midweek from $120/240; ❋ ▣ ☞) Directly connected to Penn Station, the Hilton is the preferred choice for businessfolk. Rooms are dependably attractive and shipshape.

If you need to overnight before or after a Newark Airport flight, consider the following:

Days Hotel-Newark Airport (☎ 973-242-0900; www.dayshotelnewark.com; 450 Rte 1 & 9 South; r from $80; ❋ ☞) An inexpensive, plain option for a clean bed. Ask for a renovated room; these have had attractive makeovers. Older rooms are tired. Free airport shuttle.

Newark Liberty International Airport Marriott (☎ 973-623-0006; www.newarkairportmarriott.com; 1 Hotel Rd, Newark Airport; r weekend/weekday from $90/210; ❋ ▣ ☏) It doesn't get closer to the runway than this Marriott within the airport circle road. Lobby screens display flight times, and the 600 rooms are top-quality chain nice and surprisingly quiet. Upper floors score Manhattan views. Free airport shuttle.

Eating

Except for the bakery, all the listings below are in the Ironbound District, along or near Ferry St.

Calandra's Bakery (☎ 973-484-5598; www.calandrasbakery.com; 204 First Ave at Bloomfield Ave; items $3-6; ☽ 6am-9pm) It's a trek, no question, but for Jersey's best bread and cannolis, Calandra's is worth it. It supplies restaurants as far south as Atlantic City. Stock up on pastries and cookies too. From downtown, take Broad St north to Bloomfield Ave, and keep going.

Mompou (☎ 973-578-8114; www.mompoutapas.com; 77 Ferry St; tapas $7-14; ☽ noon-2am Mon-Fri, 5pm-3am Sat, 5pm-1am Sun) A wine bar, Mompou attracts a younger crowd with delicious, contemporary versions of classic Spanish tapas and, in particular, live jazz, flamenco and bossa nova. The pretty courtyard is ideal on warm evenings.

Brasilia Grill (☎ 973-589-8682; www.brasiliagrill.com; 99 Monroe St; mains $15-21, rodizio $25; ☽ 11:30am-11pm Mon-Sat, noon-10pm Sun) Rodizio is a Brazilian meat-fest, an all-you-can-eat grilled BBQ extravaganza. Families crowd this casual sit-down restaurant for this and other Brazilian dishes.

Iberia Tavern & Restaurant (☎ 973-344-7603; www.iberiarestaurants.com; 80-84 Ferry St; mains $19-24; ☻ 11am-2am Tue-Sat, from noon Sun) The low wood-beamed ceiling and brick walls make this Iberian icon feel like a castle cellar. The dishes aren't refined, but it's a fun night out over robust Spanish cuisine.

Fornos of Spain (☎ 973-589-4767; www.fornosrestaurant.com; 47 Ferry St; mains $20-32; ☻ 11:30am-10:30pm Mon-Fri, noon-11pm Sat & Sun) Considered the best of the Iberians, but it's a matter of degrees. The culinary shtick is similar, but the atmosphere is more formal and the food is generous and satisfying.

Entertainment
In addition to shows at NJPAC, you can catch the biggest names in popular music at the **Prudential Center** (☎ 973-757-6000, tickets 201-507-8900; www.prucenter.com; 165 Mulberry St), as well as Jersey Devils pro hockey, Seton Hall college basketball and NJ Nets pro basketball for the 2011 and 2012 seasons (before the Nets move to Brooklyn). 'The Rock' is walkable from Newark Penn Station and quite safe on show/game nights.

At **Bears & Eagles Riverfront Stadium** (☎ 866-554-2327; www.newarkbears.com; 450 Broad St) the minor-league-baseball Newark Bears play 70 home games from April to August. Take I-280 exit 15 and follow the signs.

Getting There & Away
For information on Newark International Airport, see p212.

Amtrak (☎ 800-872-7245; www.amtrak.com), PATH and **NJ Transit** (☎ 800-772-2222; www.njtransit.com) all arrive at Newark Penn Station (not to be confused with New York's Penn Station). Driving, downtown Newark is well-signed from I-280 and I-78.

MEADOWLANDS
This 750-acre **sports complex** (☎ 201-935-8500; www.visitmeadowlands.com) was first built in 1976, but has evolved today into a dubiously managed array of attractions (whose managing agency, the Sports Authority, is $800 million in debt).

On the positive side, the NFL Giants and Jets christened a brand-new football stadium in 2010. It's a $1.6-billion, 82,500-seat state-of-the-art monster that includes four 118ft by 30ft video boards and has dazzled fans and the league.

On the less positive side, the complex contains the **Meadowlands Race Track** (www.thebigm.com), which is lobbying to add slots, so that it might turn a profit. It includes the Izod Center, which lost the NJ Devils and the NJ Nets to Newark, leaving its calendar empty except for circuses and concerts. And it contains the shell of the long-delayed pleasure palace Xanadu: a tremendous indoor mall/entertainment center whose completion date remains unknown.

The complex is accessed by Rte 3 off the NJ Turnpike (Meadowlands exit) and by public transportation from the Port Authority Bus Terminal in New York City.

Secaucus Outlet Center
This legendary collection of over 50 **brand-name discount outlets** (☎ 877-688-5382; www.harmonmeadow.com) is spread over several industrial parks in the Meadowlands. The indoor Harmon Cove mall is the outlet epicenter, with dozens more outlet stores on surrounding streets. It's the real deal, with prices 20% to 50% off (plus: no NJ sales tax on clothes and shoes!) from names such as Calvin Klein, Gucci, DKNY, Eileen Fisher, Lenox, Samsonite and many more. It also has a regular retail mall, entertainment, dining – and free parking. Pick up a map before exploring (online or at Harmon Cove).

The Outlet Center is signed off Rte 3. From the Secaucus train station, several buses and a **Harmon Meadows shuttle** (www.meadowlink.org) get you here.

MONTCLAIR & AROUND
pop 38,000
An upscale New York commuter town, Montclair is a cute place to eat and shop in between visiting the area's notable sights: particularly Thomas Edison National Historical Park, but also a surprisingly good art center, baseball museum and zoo. For local info, visit www.destinationmontclair.com.

Sights
THOMAS EDISON NATIONAL HISTORICAL PARK
We'd be in the dark without Thomas Edison. Need convincing? Just visit his **labs** (☎ 973-736-0550; www.nps.gov/edis; cnr 211 Main St & Lakeside Ave, West Orange; adult/child under 16yr $7/free; ☻ 9am-5pm Wed-Sun, Glenmont 11:30am-5pm Fri-Sun), which reopened in 2009 after a stunning six-year renovation.

NEW JERSEY

Edison had an overwhelming practical genius. He didn't just invent the lightbulb – he also built power stations, new batteries for electric cars and invented cement. He didn't just create the phonograph – he also built the first record changer and dictaphone. He invented sprocketed celluloid film, the first motion-picture studio and the first movies with sound. Touring this complex is like visiting the birthplace of our modern, media-saturated 21st century.

Edison's enormous, red-brick labs, meanwhile, feel captured in *medias res* – as if the grease-stained 'muckers' have only stepped away from their Rube Goldberg–esque belt-driven machines on a lunch break. A re-

THE NEW JERSEY HALL OF FRIGGIN' FAME

Yeah, New Jersey's got a Hall of Fame. Ya gotta problem with that? Jersey may not have the Rocky Mountains or a Grand Canyon. It may not have an international city like New York or Philadelphia, or even Pittsburgh, for cryin' out loud. It has no architectural monument or natural wonder to make you stop in goggle-eyed incredulity. What it has is personality – its people. What it has is a certain knack for fostering the human qualities that lead to greatness.

Bruce Springsteen (who hails from Freehold) tried to capture this when he inducted good friend Danny DeVito (Asbury Park) into the NJ Hall of Fame in 2010, saying in his raspy growl: 'They call New Jersey the Garden State. No one believes that. New Jersey is the F you state, right? Right? It's a place where we proudly fly the state bird.'

What he meant was – and what all that year's inductees tried to express, albeit less profanely, from Judy Blume (Elizabeth) to Carl Lewis (Willingboro) to Susan Sarandon (Edison) – was that growing up in Jersey is to live with a chip on your shoulder. It's a home that keeps you humble. New Jersey is a place of massive contradictions and diversity – of wealth and poverty, ethnicity, language, class – crammed in more tightly than Jon Bon Jovi (Perth Amboy) into leather pants. Many Jerseyans are immigrants, all are underdogs and everyone rubs elbows.

Several signature traits emerge: one is 'fierce loyalty,' to quote Frankie Valli (Newark). Another is what Jack Nicholson (Neptune) called the state's 'iconoclast nature,' epitomized by the fact that 'Jersey is the only state that voted against Abraham Lincoln – twice!' Another, as Springsteen himself exemplifies, is an unpretentious embrace of the arts, particularly creativity in service of the practical, for everyday people. Other signature traits are the egalitarian tolerance and sense of social justice seen in the lives of Woodrow Wilson (Princeton), Supreme Court Justice William Brennan (Newark) and suffragette Alice Paul (Mt Laurel).

What New Jersey has is a **Hall of Fame** (www.njhalloffame.org), and this abridged list of other inductees gives a sense of why. For more on these people, see the website, because what the Hall of Fame needs now is a friggin' building.

- Clara Barton (Bordentown)
- Count Basie (Red Bank)
- Thomas Edison (West Orange)
- F Scott Fitzgerald (Hackensack)
- Althea Gibson (East Orange)
- Jerry Lewis (Newark)
- Vince Lombardi (Englewood)
- Paul Robeson (Princeton)
- Philip Roth (Newark)
- Frank Sinatra (Hoboken)
- Norman Schwarzkopf (Trenton)
- Meryl Streep (Bernardsville)
- Walt Whitman (Camden)
- William Carlos Williams (Rutherford)

creation of the 1893 Black Mariah sits on its circular track, the movie set ready and needing only actors. In the chemistry lab, glass jars contain brightly colored powders, and beakers await the flame. The gorgeous ornate library is a symphony of Victorian-era splendor, yet here, at Edison's desk, is where he helped will the next age into being.

The audio tour ($5) is highly recommended; it makes generous use of the park's extensive sound archives. In addition, Edison's ornate home, Glenmont, is nearby and open for half-hour guided tours; no reservations, so come early.

Take I-280 exit 10 turn right on Northfield Ave, then left on Main St; the parking lot is opposite the lab.

MONTCLAIR ART MUSEUM

Near downtown Montclair, this sophisticated **fine art museum** (☎ 973-746-5555; www.montclairart museum.org; S Mountain Ave at Bloomfield Ave/Rte 506; adult/ child $12/10; ☺ noon-5pm Wed-Sun) is among New Jersey's best. It has major works by late-19th-century American painters like George Inness, Thomas Cole, Benjamin West and Charles Wilson Peale. It also has a major American Indian collection, with both modern and traditional art, and galleries dedicated to today's head-scratchingly bizarre abstract works.

YOGI BERRA MUSEUM

If you can't make it to Cooperstown (p165), come to the **baseball museum** (☎ 973-655-2378; www.yogiberramuseum.org; 8 Quarry Rd, Montclair State University; adult/child $6/4; ☺ noon-5pm Wed-Sun) Yogi Berra built. Yogi has, you might say, a few souvenirs from his illustrious career as one of the New York Yankees' all-time greats, and they will send any fan over the moon: the 10 World Series rings, the championship trophies, his catcher's mitt from Don Larsen's perfect game, and more – all lovingly displayed in a gorgeous modern museum. Take Hwy 46 east to the Valley Rd exit, turn right onto Valley Rd and follow signs into Montclair State University.

TURTLE BACK ZOO

The state's best **zoo** (☎ 201-731-5800; www.turtle backzoo.org; 560 Northfield Ave, West Orange; adult/child $9/6; ☺ 10am-4:30pm Mon-Sat, 11am-5:30pm Sun) is this 16-acre park, with plenty of kid-sized exhibits and a petting zoo, pony rides, carousel and train ride. Take I-280 exit 10 and go north on Northfield Ave.

Eating

Montclair Center is a pedestrian-friendly downtown area loaded with shops and restaurants; the hub is Bloomfield Ave at Church St.

Raymond's (☎ 973-744-9263; www.raymondsnj. com; 28 Church St at Fullerton St; lunch $7-10, dinner $10-18; ☺ breakfast, lunch & dinner) Montclair's social center is this old-fashioned soda fountain remade into a stylish New American restaurant. Families pack the place for its creamy grits, upscale mac & cheese, steak frites, homemade meatloaf – and for breakfast, the killer French toast.

Bistro 18 (☎ 973-233-0800; www.bistro18nj.com; 18 S Fullerton; mains $21-26; ☺ 4:30-10pm Mon, 11:30am-10pm Tue-Sat) This BYOB prepares updated Italian classics with an international flair. It offers thoughtful, eclectic deliciousness, with great service, but it can get crowded (and noisy); make weekend reservations.

MORRISTOWN & AROUND
pop 19,300

Similar to Montclair, Morristown is a wealthy, medium-sized town with a genuine history of its own. Travelers will find it most useful as a base for exploring nearby natural and historic parks, or even for Delaware Water Gap day trips.

Sights
MORRISTOWN NATIONAL HISTORICAL PARK

Dedicated to the American Revolution, this **national park** (www.nps.gov/morr) contains two main sites. Early in the war, in 1777–78 and in 1779–80, General George Washington twice chose to winter the Continental Army at Jockey Hollow in the Watchung Mountains, while he commandeered a mansion in nearby Morristown where he plotted next spring's military maneuvers. Today at **Washington's Headquarters** (☎ 793-539-2016; www.nps.gov/morr; Washington Pl, Morristown; adult $4; ☺ 9am-5pm), you can tour the restored Ford Mansion where Washington strategized and, yes, slept. Meanwhile, the recently renovated museum sparkles with three packed exhibits: a domestic room looking at household life; a military room bristling with cannons, swords and rifles; and the stunning historic documents room, containing a wealth of letters and Revolutionary pamphlets by Thomas Paine, John Adams and others – aka the 18th century's bloggers. There's also a 2009 movie about Morristown's role in the war; mansion tours are on the hour from 10am to 4pm.

The soldiers lived considerably less well at **Jockey Hollow** (☎ 973-543-4030; admission free; ✆ visitors' center 9am-5pm, park 8am-8pm). In fact, the worst winter in a century hit in 1779–80 – much more vicious than at Valley Forge (see p38). Ultimately, up to 13,000 soldiers gutted out the winter in a thousand huts, which by population made it the would-be nation's fifth-largest city. Nothing remains except some re-created huts, the old farmstead and pretty wooded trails where you too can watch for the advancing British army.

Washington's Headquarters is between Morris St and Lafayette Ave in Morristown; take I-287 exit 36 and follow the signs. Jockey Hollow is south of town along Western Ave; take Morris St south to Washington St, and then left on Western.

GREAT SWAMP NATIONAL WILDLIFE REFUGE

Not 20 minutes from Newark Airport and Elizabeth's refineries is this 7700-acre wilderness, home to over 240 bird species, a wealth of reptiles and amphibians and dozens of mammal species, such as muskrat, beaver, red fox and coyote. The Great Swamp, as the name implies, is mostly marshland, and it's the local mecca for bird-watching. It also contains miles of muddy wilderness trails for urban hikers seeking to escape.

The place to start is the brand-new **Helen C Fenske Visitor Center** (☎ 973-425-9510; www.fws.gov/northeast/greatswamp; 32 Pleasant Plains Rd; ✆ noon-4pm Thu & Fri, 10am-4pm Sat & Sun), which has maps, good exhibits, a kids' discovery area and an excellent bookstore. The **Refuge Headquarters** (☎ 973-425-1222; ✆ 8am-4:30pm Mon-Fri), further south along Pleasant Plains Rd, has information but isn't staffed to handle the public. The refuge itself is open dawn to dusk. For more information, visit www.greatswamp.org and www.friendsofgreatswamp.org.

The **Wildlife Observation Center**, off Long Hill Rd, is the primary area for wildlife- and bird-watching, with long boardwalks leading through the swamp and the cacophony of birdsong to bird blinds. It has interpretive

---

OF FARMS, FOOD, & CAMERA PHONES

The Garden State takes its food very seriously. Doesn't matter if we're talking pizza or fois gras, lobster bisque or disco fries – in Jersey there's always an opinion (or 12), sharply worded and deeply felt. In fact, there seems nothing that Jerseyans like better than traversing their state and blogging about their culinary discoveries.

It's just part and parcel of the overall renaissance in Jersey dining, as ever more restaurants join the larger farm-to-table, locavore trend. Shouldn't be hard. This is the Garden State, after all.

So here's a small sampling of Jersey's dining blogosphere and a few of those legendary farms:
The Artful Diner (www.artfuldiner.com) Jersey-born son of a chef; reviews won a James Beard award.
Ed Hitzel (www.edhitzel.com) Hitzel's radio show, magazine and newsletter cover south Jersey.
A Food Coma (www.afoodcoma.com) Mostly young PA & NJ foodies on a budget; recipes too!
Jersey Bites (www.jerseybites.com) A comprehensive, true Jersey 'quest for food with attitude.'
John and Lisa are Eating in South Jersey (www.johnandlisaareeatinginsj.blogspot.com) Not critics, but 'enthusiasts' who eat out – a lot.
The Munchmobile (www.nj.com/munchmobile) Star-*Ledger* food writer Pete Genovese, the man in the van.
The Restaurant Guys (www.restaurantguysradio.com) Francis Schott and Mark Pascal, the click and clack of Jersey food critics.

For a statewide list of farmer's markets and farms, visit **Jersey Fresh** (www.jerseyfresh.nj.gov). Here are some northern Jersey pick-your-own farms with hayride and corn maze fun in fall:
Abma's Farm (www.abmasfarm.com; Wyckoff)
Alstede Farm (www.alstedefarms.com; Chester)
Hillview Farms (www.hillviewfarmsnj.com; Gillette)
Ort Farms (www.ortfarm.com; Long Valley)
Sun High Orchard (www.sunhigh.com; Randolph)
Stony Hill Farm Market (www.stonyhillgardens.com; Chester)
Wightman's Farm (www.wightmansfarms.com; Morristown)

displays and restrooms; on most weekends volunteers open an information booth and set up telescopes for bird-watching. Separate wilderness trails are highly recommended, but they can be wet and buggy year-round; wear waterproof shoes and insect repellent. Early morning and late afternoon are best.

To reach the visitor center, take I-287 exit 30A onto N Maple Ave, turn left on Madisonville Rd, and follow signs to Pleasant Plains Rd. Continue south on Pleasant Plains Rd to White Bridge Rd; turn left to reach Long Hill Rd (turn left for the Observation Center); turn right to reach the Raptor Trust.

Raptor Trust

Within the Great Swamp, the nonprofit **Raptor Trust** (☎ 908-647-2353; www.theraptortrust.org; 1390 White Bridge Rd, near Pleasant Plains Rd; suggested donation $2; ☻ 9am-dusk) is dedicated to rehabilitating injured birds of prey and returning them to the wild. However, they also have some 50 raptors who, for various reasons, are permanent residents, and these magnificent birds are on display to the public in large outdoor cages. Get eyeball to eyeball with snowy owls, bald eagles, hawks, falcons, vultures and more.

Sleeping & Eating

Morristown Hyatt (☎ 973-647-1234; www.morristown.hyatt.com; 3 Speedwell Ave, Morristown; r weekend/midweek from $110/230; ⛶ 🖥 🛜 🏊 ♿) has stylish decor and technologically up-to-date business-traveler amenities. Best of all, it's within walking distance of the many downtown restaurants and shops.

Olde Mill Inn (☎ 908-221-1100; www.oldemillinn.com; 225 Route 202; r weekend/midweek $125/159; ⛶ 🖥 🛜 ♿) Closer to the Great Swamp in Basking Ridge, this inn is like a top-quality chain hotel with a B&B feel; pleasing rooms and great service.

South Street Creamery (☎ 973-267-8887; www.southstreetcreamery.com; 146 South St; items $6.50-7.50; ☻ 8am-8:30pm Mon-Fri, 11am-9:30pm Sat, noon-8:30pm Sun) A go-to spot in Morristown for a fresh, light meal of panini, soups and salads. At night, families line up for the delicious ice cream.

Origin Thai (☎ 973-971-9933; www.originthai.com; 10 South St; mains $15-25; ☻ lunch & dinner Tue-Sat, dinner Sun) This top-notch French/Thai fusion restaurant is a satisfying choice for a nice dinner. Choose from Thai standards or try wild boar, ostrich and French dishes such as *steak au poivre*.

DELAWARE WATER GAP NATIONAL RECREATION AREA

The Delaware Water Gap is the enormous, 1300ft-deep cleft that the Delaware River has cut through the Kittatinny Mountains running along the northwestern edge of New Jersey. The Gap is the signature feature of a rugged, forested region that constitutes New Jersey's most popular outdoor destination for hiking, canoeing, mountain biking, fishing and camping. Because the Delaware River forms the state border with Pennsylvania, the 37-mile-long National Recreation Area encompasses both states, and in fact the NRA's primary Delaware River access points, recreation areas, services and camping are on the Pennsylvania side (see p398). These are, however, also quite easy to reach from New Jersey.

On the Jersey side, most of the recreation opportunities people seek when they 'go to the Gap' are in state parks, which are described in the Skylands section (p248). You can drive the length of the river on the Jersey side, but north of the Kittatinny Point Visitor Center and Worthington State Forest, this is the DWG's quiet side.

The **Kittatinny Point Visitor Center** (☎ 908-496-4458; www.nps.gov/dewa; ☻ 9am-5pm Memorial Day to Labor Day, Sat & Sun fall) is closed entirely in winter and spring. When open, it provides full park information and sells outdoor guides. Take I-80 exit 1 and turn left under the overpass. Turn right to continue to Worthington State Forest and the rest of the national park.

At the visitors' center are restrooms, picnic areas, parking and a sandy beach that are accessible even when the visitors' center is closed. On the Jersey side, this beach is the most popular spot for wading and sunning along the river (no lifeguards), and it has a canoe and boat launch (most guided canoe trips start on the PA side).

Twelve miles north of the visitors' center, at the intersection of Rtes 606, 615 and 602, is the park-run **Millbrook Village** (☎ 908-841-9531), a small historic village and mill staffed with docents on summer weekends.

For a guided trip, consider **Urban Escapes** (☎ 212-609-2547; www.urbanescapesnyc.com), which creates fun Delaware River and wine trips based out of Philly and Manhattan.

The only camping allowed on federal lands on the New Jersey side is at the canoe-in-only sites along the river.

NEW JERSEY

SKYLANDS & THE APPALACHIAN TRAIL

The New Jersey **Skylands** (www.njskylands.com) encompasses the state's northwest region. Through this gently mountainous terrain winds the 74-mile New Jersey portion of the Appalachian Trail. The AT is officially part of the NPS, but here, as in all states, the trail is mostly contained within a series of state parks and forests. For more information on these, visit www.njparksandforests.org.

The park descriptions here go south to north. All of these parks (except Jenny Jump) contain access points to the Appalachian Trail, making it easy for day hikers to experience. (For more on the AT, see p66.)

Jenny Jump State Park

For several reasons, **Jenny Jump** (☎ 908-459-4366) is one of New Jersey's most popular state parks. First, since it's not within the Kittatinny Mountains, its modest, kid-friendly trails provide absolutely gorgeous views of them. Second, it is haunted by spooky legends concerning places like Ghost Lake and Shades of Death Rd that, for aficionados of *Weird NJ* magazine, are must-visit places. Third, a local astronomy club runs Saturday night stargazing from April to October. Last but not least, it's developed camping and cabins are top-notch. The campground ($20 per night, April to October) has well-kept showers and toilets, while eight basic but roomy cabins ($40 per night year-round; reserve ahead) sleep four in two bunks and have a wood-burning stove.

Take I-80 exit 12 then a slight left onto CR 521 for 1.3 miles to Hope. Turn left onto CR 519 (at the blinking light); at the third right, turn onto Shiloh Rd, and it's a mile further.

Worthington State Forest

This 5878-acre **forest** (☎ 908-841-9575) begins just north of the DWG's Kittatinny Point Visitor Center, and it has camping along the Delaware River. In summer, it's scenic, steep, short trail to the top of 1527ft Mount Tammany, and the 4-mile section of the Appalachian Trail between the Dunnfield Creek Trailhead and Sunfish Pond, are easily the busiest hikes. Fishermen love this park and jockey like mad for the 23 wooded, tent-only riverside campsites ($20 per night). Facilities are just as nice as those at Jenny Jump; the second camping area, however, is a grassy meadow that lacks privacy.

To get here take I-80 exit 1 and veer right along Old Mine Rd/Rte 606. You reach the Worthington visitors' center after about 3 miles.

CAMP TAYLOR & LAKOTA WOLF PRESERVE

Near Worthington's eastern edge is **Camp Taylor** (☎ 908-496-4333, 800-545-9662; www.camptaylor.com; 85 Mt Pleasant Rd, Columbia; tent/RV from $25/33), a private campground with clean wooded sites and a full range of amenities – store, swimming pond, RV hookups, pets OK – as well as trail access to Worthington and DWG.

Worth visiting even if you aren't camping is the attached **Lakota Wolf Preserve** (☎ 908-496-9244, 877-733-9653; www.lakotawolf.com; adult/child $15/7; ☒ 10am & 3:30pm Tue-Sun). Home to over 30 wolves in large, wooded, fenced enclosures, the preserve runs twice-daily 'wolf watches,' where you get up close and personal with these splendid canines. The animals were raised in captivity and are habituated to humans. Reservations are required midweek (to avoid school groups); cash only. Campers get a discount.

Take I-80 exit 4 on 94N (toward Blairstown); after 3.5 miles, turn left on Benton Rd. Turn right on Frog Pond Rd, and take the first left on Wishing Well, and keep driving till you see signs.

Stokes State Forest

Stokes State Forest (☎ 973-948-3820; cars summer midweek/weekend $5/10) follows the Appalachian Trail along the crest of Sunrise Mountain; indeed, the trail to the mountain is one of the best day-hike access points for the AT, particularly in fall. Trails within the Tillman Ravine are also recommended. All Stokes trails are multi-use, making them a destination for mountain bikers. Stony Lake has swimming in summer.

Tent camping ($20 per night) is nice, with decent facilities, but the popular cabins (with half/full bathroom $45/85; one-week minimum in summer) get booked up 11 months in advance.

The forest is signed along Hwy 206, near the intersection with Rte 521.

PETERS VALLEY

This historic village near Stokes is a non-profit craft education center. The **gallery store** (☎ 973-948-5202; www.petersvalley.org; Kuhn Rd at Rte 615; ☒ 10am-6pm Thu-Tue May-Dec, closed Mon-Wed Jan-

---

MOUNTAIN CREEK SKI RESORT

In Vernon off Rte 94, **Mountain Creek** (☎ 973-827-2000; www.mountaincreek.com) is the closest ski resort to New York City. It has three mountains (typically open December to March), dozens of trails and excellent terrain parks for snowboarding, in addition to lodging and restaurants. In summer, activity shifts to an outdoor waterpark with bumper cars and amusements.

However, ownership changed hands in 2010, and supposedly big changes are afoot: a new indoor waterpark, more hotels and retail, and a 'rain forest.' While there's no reason to doubt the improvements, the same thing happened a decade ago: then known as Vernon Valley/ Great Gorge ski resort and Action Park waterpark, it was a dilapidated enterprise and statewide punchline before it went bankrupt (The action never stops… at Traction Park!). A decade later, the renamed Mountain Creek was still financially struggling, and the town of Vernon is openly hoping that the new owners (who own area golf courses) can finally create a resort destination like Lake George, New York.

For now, call ahead before making plans; with changes come new rates, schedules and so on.

Apr) sells the work of the center's professional students and local artists, including gorgeous woodwork, blown glass, ceramics, jewelry and photography. In summer, it holds weekly **auctions** (☯ 1:30pm Sun), where you might snatch up artworks for a song. The craft workshops are open to the public, and on weekends from May to September (2pm to 5pm, Saturday and Sunday) you can observe working blacksmiths, metalworkers, carvers and potters.

Peters Valley is along Rte 615, about 12 miles north of Millbrook Village; follow the signs. From Stokes, take Hwy 206 north, then left onto Rte 521, and left onto Rte 615.

WALPACK INN
Walpack Inn (☎ 973-948-3890; www.walpackinn.com; Rte 615, Walpack Center; mains $22-44; ☯ 5-10pm Fri & Sat, Sun 1-8pm) is a locally famous restaurant buried deep in the Gap. Folks come for the prime rib, the all-you-can-eat salad bar, and to watch animals at the deer lick outside. It's signed on Rte 615, about 8.5 miles north of Millbrook Village and 3.5 miles south of Peters Valley.

High Point State Park
Snug in the state's northwest corner, this is another extremely popular **state park** (☎ 973-875-4800; cars Memorial Day to Labor Day midweek/weekend $5/10), particularly with families, for its wide range of activities and easy access. It is named after 1803ft High Point Peak, the highest elevation in New Jersey. No, it's not Mt McKinley, but you get to lord it over the undulating spine of the Kittatinny Ridge and admire, in all directions, a rippled wooded panorama barely scratched by civilization. From here, you wonder: 'What population density?'

Peak-bagging High Point is a breeze, too: you can drive right to the top. Of course, pretty trails reach it, and most are mountain bike–friendly. Meanwhile, **Lake Marcia** (☯ 10am-6pm) is a spring-fed lake with a swimming beach in summer and a concessions building with changing rooms. In winter, the building becomes a **cross-country ski center** (☎ 973-702-1222), renting skis and snowshoes. Plus there are playgrounds, picnic areas and an **interpretive center** (☎ 973-875-1471).

If that weren't enough, the park's Sawmill Lake campground ($20 per night) is the epitome of lakeside camping: protected, wooded sites ring an absolutely gorgeous, tranquil lake. Facilities include water and toilets; no showers or lake swimming.

High Point is 4 miles south of Port Jervis, NY; take I-84 exit 1 to Rte 23 south. From New Jersey, take Rte 23 north.

CENTRAL NEW JERSEY
Culturally speaking, there is no 'central' Jersey. Either you're from North Jersey or South Jersey. Either you root for the New York teams (Mets, Yankees, Giants, Jets) or the Philadelphia teams (Phillies, Eagles). Either you buy subs at 7-Eleven and get sprinkles on your ice cream, or you get hoagies at Wawa and ask for jimmies on your cone.

Where is the dividing line between the more urbanized North and the more rural South? It depends on who you ask. Many place it at the Garden State Parkway's Driscoll Bridge over the Raritan River, near New Brunswick. Others draw a line between Princeton and Long Beach Island, and say everything north is North.

NEW JERSEY

Trenton, the state capitol, is almost always considered South. Thus we drew the boundaries for this chapter, encompassing New Jersey's amorphous cultural transition zone.

Interestingly, one of the highlights of this region is culture: from the theaters and museums of New Brunswick, home of Rutgers University, to the museums and history of Princeton, home of Princeton University. Plus, there are major Revolutionary War sights and one of the most bucolic sections of the Delaware River near Lambertville.

NEW BRUNSWICK
pop 51,100

The home of Rutgers University, New Brunswick is a modest university town with a collection of top-notch theaters and one destination-worthy museum. The compact downtown area has a pleasant scruffiness that really comes alive on busy weekends when the theaters are full.

For information and events, contact **New Brunswick City Market** (☎ 732-545-4849; www.new brunswick.com).

Rutgers University

The well-regarded state **university** (☎ 732-445-4636; www.rutgers.edu) has a handsome campus right in town; in particular, the Old Queens Campus section, at George and Hamilton Sts, exudes the historic ambience you expect of a college founded in 1766 in the colonial era.

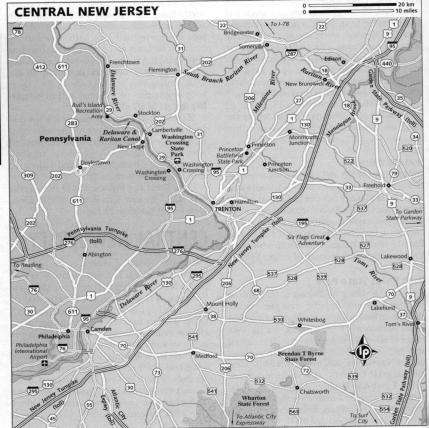

CENTRAL NEW JERSEY

Fittingly, this is where you'll find the **Zimmerli Art Museum** (☎ 732-932-7237; www.zimmerlimuseum.rutgers.edu; cnr George & Hamilton Sts; admission $3; ⌚ 10am-4:30pm Tue-Fri, noon-5pm Sat & Sun). The unexpected cornerstone of its permanent collection is the renowned Dodge Collection of 20th-century nonconformist Soviet art, which is unmatched in the world. Fashioned from over 10,000 works by 900 artists, it creates a vivid, awe-inspiring portrait of dissident social commentary and political struggle in Russia from the Cold War to Glasnost. Excellent displays put the era and artists into historical context, but the vivid artworks need no interpreter. In addition, the Zimmerli displays Russian art from other periods, and it has galleries of contemporary American art, European art, printmaking and special exhibits. Don't miss it.

Nearby, the **Geology Museum** (☎ 732-932-7243; http://geologymuseum.rutgers.edu; Geology Hall, Old Queens Campus; admission free; ⌚ 9am-5pm Mon-Thu, 9am-4pm Fri, 10am-2pm Sat) is like a Victorian-era 'hall of curiosities.' Its small, eclectic displays include a massive mastodon skeleton, an Egyptian mummy, dinosaur tracks, petrified wood, gems and minerals, and more.

Sleeping

Heldrich (☎ 866-609-4700; www.theheldrich.com; 10 Livingston Ave; r weekend/midweek from $100/140; 🔣 💻 🛜 🐾) This stately property anchoring downtown, and across the street from the theaters, exudes an elegant cool. Rooms sport mesh lampshades, frosted armoire doors, and smooth sky blue and brown tones; deluxe rooms add a view. It has an indoor pool, fitness center, restaurant and bar.

Eating & Drinking

For the cheapest eats, make like a student and head for Rutgers' Grease Trucks. At College Ave and Hamilton St, a half-dozen food trucks (with names like 'RU Hungry') serve sandwiches and meals ($4 to $6) from 7am to the wee hours. Get-and-go or sit at picnic tables.

Harvest Moon Brewery (☎ 732-249-6666; www.harvestmoonbrewery.com; 392 George St; burgers $9, mains $15-25; ⌚ 11:30am-10pm) A lively microbrewery serving decent pub food to a mixed crowd of students and locals.

Skylark Fine Diner (☎ 732-777-7878; www.skylarkdiner.com; 17 Wooding Ave at Rte 1, Edison; mains $11-23; ⌚ 7am-1am) A few minutes north of New Brunswick along Rte 1, this place boasts the classic, sleek '50s moderne diner decor, but its menu is the creation of one of Jersey's gourmet kings, Craig Shelton. Dishes take a bistro approach to diner favorites, creating flavorful upscale comfort food. Short ribs with egg noodles is delish. There's a full bar.

Makeda (☎ 732-545-5115; www.makedas.com; 338 George St; mains $13-25; ⌚ noon-9pm Mon-Thu, to 11pm Fri & Sat, 1-9pm Sun) Ethiopian cuisine is a rich palette of ginger, lentils, peppers and cardamom, and it's heaven for vegetarians and carnivores alike. You won't find it better in New Jersey; order a sample plate and enjoy the contemporary, African-accented dining room and live music on weekends.

Delta's (☎ 732-249-1551; www.deltasrestaurant.com; 19 Dennis St at Hiram Square; mains $19-26; ⌚ 5pm-midnight Tue & Wed, 5pm-2am Thu-Sat, 1-8pm Sun) New Brunswick has several upscale date-night restaurants. Delta's is the most fun, with gourmet renditions of southern standards and live music on weekends.

Court Tavern (☎ 732-545-7265; 124 Church St; ⌚ 11am-2am Mon-Sat, to 8pm Sun) A dive bar and punk-rock club that's a local institution and the heart of Rutgers' music scene.

Entertainment

New Brunswick has a thriving cultural scene. **New Brunswick Cultural Center** (☎ 732-247-7200; www.newbrunswickarts.org; 11 Livingstone Ave) has all the information.

Three major venues sit shoulder to shoulder on Livingston Ave: the **State Theatre** (☎ 732-246-7469; www.statetheatrenj.org; 15 Livingstone Ave) hosts visiting pop stars, comics and performers; **George Street Playhouse** (☎ 732-246-7717; www.georgestplayhouse.org; 9 Livingston Ave) premieres new plays and musicals; and **Crossroads Theater Company** (☎ 732-249-5560; www.crossroadstheatrecompany.org; 7 Livingstone Ave) is a nationally renowned African American theater company and won the 1999 Tony for Outstanding Regional Theatre. In addition, New Brunswick has the state's premier ballet company, **American Repertory Ballet** (☎ 732-246-1254; www.arballet.org; 80 Albany St).

Getting There & Away

From Garden State Parkway exit 9, follow Rte 18 north and follow signs for downtown (New St exit). New Brunswick is also accessible by train from Philadelphia and New York City via **NJ Transit** (☎ 800-772-2222; www.njtransit.com) or **Amtrak** (☎ 800-872-7245; www.amtrak.com).

NEW JERSEY

PRINCETON
pop 13,400

Princeton is a quintessential East Coast Ivy League town – steeped in history, home to one of the nation's premiere universities, and by turns wealthy, intellectual, sophisticated and sophomoric. No place with 5000 undergraduates doesn't have pranksters.

Princeton is the sort of place where, in the 1930s and 1940s, you might run across Albert Einstein window-shopping along Nassau St. Today, it could be scholar Cornel West or novelist Joyce Carol Oates, who both teach at the university. Without question, the expansive Princeton campus is the highlight of any visit: you feel smarter just strolling the grounds. Its imposing grandeur and historical significance conjure moments when the universal human search for knowledge is palpable.

When that passes, Princeton has some great restaurants, shops and pubs, and some lovely places to stay.

Information

The **Princeton Regional Convention & Visitors Bureau** (☎ 609-924-1776; www.visitprinceton.org) maintains the town's website and will send visitor packets. In town, get info at the **Historical Society of Princeton** (☎ 609-921-6748; 158 Nassau St; Bainbridge House). For university information, contact **Orange Key** (☎ 609-258-3060; www.princeton.edu; Clio Hall).

Labyrinth Books (☎ 609-497-1600; www.labyrinthbooks.com; 122 Nassau St; ☉ 9am-8pm Mon-Fri, 10am-6pm Sat, 11am-6pm Sun) Two floors of the most sophisticated reading possible, plus a nice children's section.

Post office (Palmer Sq)

Princeton Public Library (☎ 609-924-9529; www.princetonlibrary.org; 65 Witherspoon St; ☉ 9am-9pm Mon-Thu, 9am-6pm Fri & Sat, 1-6pm Sun) Gorgeously renovated; free internet access.

Sights

If you want to know about Albert Einstein's life in Princeton, oddly enough the best place is the woolen shop **Landau's** (☎ 800-257-9445; www.landauprinceton.com/einstein-museum; 102 Nassau St; ☉ 9:30am-5:30pm Mon-Sat, 11:30am-4:30pm Sun), which has an Einstein Museum in the back. Einstein's house is a private residence (112 Mercer St), and closed to the public.

PRINCETON UNIVERSITY

Princeton was established in 1746 as the College of New Jersey in Elizabeth, the fourth-oldest college in the country. The university campus that we know today was built in 1756 on 10 acres of donated land. Princeton is currently home to about 5000 undergraduates and 2000 graduate students, the majority of whom pursue degrees in liberal arts or engineering.

Princeton has a long list of famous graduates, including US presidents James Madison and Woodrow Wilson (who also served as the university's president), actor James Stewart and current First Lady Michelle Obama. The faculty is equally noteworthy: over two-dozen Nobel Prize winners – including novelist Toni Morrison – have made Princeton their academic home.

Free tours of the campus are offered by **Orange Key** (☎ 609-258-3060; ☉ tours 11:15am, 1pm & 3:30pm Mon-Sat, 1pm & 3:30pm Sun); reservations not necessary. Tours are led by students, who discuss university history as well as campus life. Weekday tours leave from Clio Hall; weekend tours leave from **Frist Campus Center** (☎ 609-258-1766; www.princeton.edu/frist; ☉ 8am-5pm summer, to 2pm winter), a good source of information.

Anyone is free to stroll around the beautiful campus. Make sure to visit the following highlights.

Princeton University Art Museum

In New Jersey, the **art museum** (☎ 609-258-3788; http://artmuseum.princeton.edu; McCormick Hall; admission free; ☉ 10am-5pm Tue-Sat, to 10pm Thu, 1-5pm Sun) is without equal in terms of its extensive antiquities collection: exhibits cover ancient Rome, Greece, Egypt, Mesoamerica, China and the Orient, and are packed with sculpture, mosaics, pottery and artifacts. There is also a notable collection of Impressionist painters and a smattering of contemporary works. Free guided tours at 2pm on Saturday and Sunday.

Princeton Chapel

The stunning Gothic revival **chapel** (www.princetonchapelchoir.com), completed in 1928, hosts free afternoon **organ concerts** (☉ 12:30-1pm Thu) once a week during the school year, which fill the vaulted space with sound. The choir rehearses twice weekly and performs during Sunday services. It also has a slate of evening concerts.

Firestone Library

Only students get into the stacks, but if you have kids, don't miss the **Cotsen Children's Library** (☎ 609-258-1148; www.princeton.edu/cotsen; ☉ 9am-5pm

Mon-Fri, noon-5pm Sat & Sun), a fantastical space with reading nooks inside Winnie-the-Pooh's tree, Jack's well and oversized chairs. Meanwhile, bibliophiles (guilty!) shouldn't miss the **gallery** (same hours), whose vast collection of rare and antique books is hard to grasp, encapsulating a decent percentage of the literate Western world.

BAINBRIDGE HOUSE

The home of the Historical Society of Princeton, this Georgian-style **house** (☎ 609-921-6748; www.princetonhistory.org; 158 Nassau St; admission free; ☺ noon-4pm Tue-Sun) contains a few small exhibits focusing on Princeton's celebrated residents and local history. The shop has an excellent selection of local histories and a self-guided tour of historic homes ($1). It also offers a two-hour walking tour of Princeton (including the campus) at 2pm Sunday ($7).

MORVEN

This historic 1750 **mansion** (☎ 609-924-8144; www.morven.org; 55 Stockton St/Rte 206; adult $5; ☺ 11:15am-2:15pm Wed-Fri, 12:15-3:15pm Sat & Sun) is only accessible through 45-minute guided tours, which leave on the quarter hour. Exhibits focus on the lives of the original occupants, including Declaration of Independence signer Richard Stockton and Robert Wood Johnson (founder of Johnson & Johnson).

DRUMTHWACKET

The official residence of the New Jersey governor, this Civil War–era **home** (☎ 609-683-0591; www.drumthwacket.org; 354 Stockton St/Rte 206; adult $5) is theoretically open to the public for tours each Wednesday. However, tours do not always operate. Call ahead, as reservations are required; the state police frown on drop-ins.

PRINCETON BATTLEFIELD STATE PARK

About a mile from downtown, **Princeton Battlefield State Park** (500 Mercer St; admission free; ☺ dawn to dusk) commemorates the historic battle of Princeton, fought on January 3, 1777. George Washington's victory over the British here was one in a series of battles that marked an early turning point in the American Revolution. Today, conjuring the scene takes a real leap of the imagination. The battlefield is but a grassy meadow with a few

NEW JERSEY

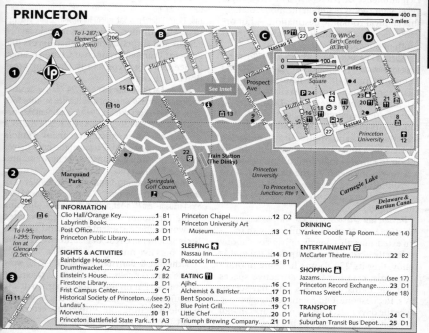

PRINCETON

0 ____ 400 m
0 ____ 0.2 miles

0 ____ 100 m
0 ____ 0.1 miles

plaques and a grave marker tucked behind free-standing white columns.

Also here is the faded **Thomas Clarke House** (☎ 609-921-0074; admission free; ☺ 10am-noon & 1-4pm Wed-Sat, 1-4pm Sun). A portion of the house is furnished in colonial dress, and on weekends docents give tours; a weaponry exhibit – with muskets, bayonets and cannonballs – gives a whiff of Revolutionary-style carnage. For more information, visit www.saveprinceton battlefield.org.

Sleeping

Princeton contains no budget lodging. However, Rte 1 outside of town is lined with a mix of midrange and top-end chain hotels catering to the area's corporate headquarters and business travelers.

Inn at Glencairn (☎ 609-497-1737; www.innat glencairn.com; 3301 Lawrenceville Rd/Rte 206; r $160-210; ☒ ☺) Few historic inns so flawlessly blend the original property with the presence and comforts of modern life, but everything mixes beautifully at Glencairn. Local art graces the walls, and the comfortable, relaxing Great Room, with its huge open hearth, evokes a rich ambience of years past. The five simple yet elegant rooms maintain the mood, making this an ideal romantic destination. A hot organic breakfast is included. It's about 3 miles south of downtown.

our pick **Peacock Inn** (☎ 609-924-1707; www. thepeacockinn.com; 20 Bayard Lane; r $250-320; ☒ ☺) Reopened in 2010, this historic property has been remade into a stylish 16-room art-infused boutique hotel. Luxuriate on four-poster beds with luscious sheets and top-quality mattresses; sleek baths have glass-walled showers and Molton Brown toiletries. There isn't a hint of dusty Victoriana. In addition to a new restaurant, the inn is adding a wine-tasting cellar in the basement, once a Prohibition-era speakeasy. Best of all, it's within walking distance of downtown and the campus.

Nassau Inn (☎ 609-921-7500; www.nassauinn.com; Palmer Sq; r $260; ☒) A 1756 building with modern extensions, this dowdy university standby is directly across from campus. Finally, it is renovating its 250 rooms to contemporary standards, creating fresh, attractive spaces with tile baths, new beds and flat-screen TVs. Request one. Old rooms feel unchanged since the days Fidel Castro and Indira Ghandi stayed here. Parking is $20 per day.

On Rte 1 closest to Princeton, consider the following:

Courtyard by Marriott (☎ 609-716-9100; www. marriott.com; 3815 Rte 1 at Mapleton Rd; r weekend $110-160; midweek $145-180; ☒ ☐ ☺)

Westin Princeton (☎ 609-452-7900; www.westin. com/princeton; 201 Village Blvd, Forrestal Village; r weekend $115-140, midweek $190-220; ☒ ☐ ☺) Forrestal Village also contains recommended restaurants and bars.

Homewood Suites Princeton (☎ 609-720-0550; www.homewoodsuites.com/princeton; 3819 Rte 1 S; r weekend/midweek from $116/140; ☒ ☐ ☺) All rooms are suites with kitchens.

Eating & Drinking

Princeton's downtown makes for lovely strolling on its own, and it has a wide selection of eateries – from cheapies catering to coed budgets to posh culinary standard-bearers.

Little Chef (☎ 609-924-5335; www.littlechefpastries. com; 8 S Tulane St; pastries & tarts $2-6.50; ☺ 7am-5pm, to 8pm Thu-Sat) Run by a Haitian-born pastry chef who makes the flakiest croissants this side of Paris, plus delectable tarts and hand-held cakes. Buy some before walking the campus.

Bent Spoon (☎ 609-924-2368; www.thebentspoon. com; 35 Palmer Sq; scoops $3.50-5; ☺ 11am-10pm Mon-Thu, 11am-11pm Fri & Sat, noon-10pm Sun) Last things first: after dinner, enjoy exquisite locavore gelatos and sorbets with designer flavors like grapefruit campari, sour cream, blood orange, lychee and other constantly changing creations. Cash only.

Whole Earth Center (☎ 609-924-7421; www.whole earthcenter.com; 360 Nassau St near Harrison St; items $6-9; ☺ deli 8:30am-6pm Mon-Sat, 10am-4:30pm Sun) An organic grocery with a vegetarian café that's a destination for unrepentant crunchy-granola types, young and old. Fresh-made hot entrees (falafel, quesadilla, soups) to eat here and pre-wrapped food to go.

Triumph Brewing Company (☎ 609-924-7855; www.triumphbrewing.com; 138 Nassau St; mains $11-26; ☺ 11:30am-1am Mon-Sat, noon-midnight Sun) The yang to the Tap Room's yin: a loud, bright, vaulted brewpub where students relax and dish on their teachers. Great beer and pretty good food, plus live music on weekends.

Alchemist & Barrister (☎ 609-924-5555; www. theaandb.com; 28 Witherspoon St at Nassau St; burgers $12-14; ☺ dinner) Eat on the outdoor patio, stick to the juicy burgers and draft beers, and enjoy people-watching the university crowd. A mainstay for a low-key meal.

Yankee Doodle Tap Room (☎ 609-688-2600; www.yankeedoodletaproom.com; 10 Palmer Sq; mains $13-19; ✆ 7am-10pm) Order a drink, eavesdrop on professors and soak up the flavor of this Princeton institution – with Norman Rockwell's *Yankee Doodle* mural over the bar, the photo wall of graduates (Ralph Nader, Don Rumsfeld, Brooke Shields), and the graffiti-scarred tables. The full menu is only average.

Ajihei (☎ 609-252-1158; 11 Chambers St; mains $20-28; ✆ lunch & dinner Tue-Fri, dinner Sat & Sun) Below street level and tiny, with Formica tables and a cheesy mural, Ajihei nevertheless dazzles with absolutely fresh, fat, bright-flavored sushi – no gimmicks, no fancy rolls. A full menu of Japanese meals as well. Expect a line.

Blue Point Grill (☎ 609-921-1211; www.bluepointgrill.com; 258 Nassau St; mains $20-38; ✆ dinner) You'll only find fresher fish at the shore, with a long list of well-prepared choices and a raw bar with excellent oysters. The airy space, with pressed-tin ceilings and tall windows, makes for a lively dinner scene. Reservations only taken midweek. BYOB.

our pick **Elements** (☎ 609-924-0078; www.elementsprinceton.com; 163 Bayard Lane/Rte 206; mains $26-36; ✆ lunch Mon-Fri & Sun, dinner nightly) For cuisine and decor as refined as anything in Manhattan or Philly, reserve a table at Elements. The modern space features stacked slate, exposed beams, bare wood risers and fabric walls – contrasting visual textures with a gracefulness the chef matches, and then some. The six-course tasting menu ($80) is recommended, but true foodies should reserve the nine-course menu at special tables in the kitchen itself. About a mile north of downtown, off Nassau St.

Entertainment

Check the *Princeton Weekly Bulletin*, available from campus buildings and newspaper bins around town, for the latest calendar of events.

Princeton University's **McCarter Theatre** (☎ 609-258-2787; www.mccarter.org), on campus near the train station, stages plays, musicals and concerts. During the school year, the university has a full range of **sporting events** (☎ 609-258-4849; www.goprincetontigers.com).

Shopping

Palmer Square (www.palmersquare.com) and its surrounding streets are the places for upscale shopping: Ann Taylor, Ralph Lauren, Kate Spade, Dandelion and more.

Princeton Record Exchange (☎ 609-921-0881; www.prex.com; 20 S Tulane St) Since 1980, a Princeton institution for vinyl, CDs and DVDs.

Thomas Sweet (☎ 609-924-7222; www.thomassweet.com; 29 Palmer Sq) Gourmet chocolates and truffles to melt the heart of the one you love.

Jazams (☎ 609-924-8697; www.jazams.com; 25 Palmer Sq) Kid stuff for the *Yo Gabba Gabba!* generation: smart, sophisticated toys and books and knowledgeable staff.

Getting There & Away

NJ Transit (☎ 800-772-2222; www.njtransit.com) and **Amtrak** (☎ 800-872-7245; www.amtrak.com) offer several daily trains to Princeton Junction. Passengers then cross over to a smaller train (known as 'the dinky') to make the five-minute trip to Princeton itself. The dinky stops on the south end of Princeton campus.

Driving from New York, take NJ Turnpike exit 9 to Rte 1 south, then exit on Washington Rd/Rte 571 to Nassau St. From Philadelphia, take I-95 north to Rte 206 north, which leads directly to Nassau St.

Getting Around

Street parking is mostly metered and vigilantly enforced; park in a lot. Hullfish St has a convenient parking lot; www.princetonparking.org has a parking map. Late afternoon traffic (4:30pm to 6:30pm) is a nightmare; just keep shopping.

A new, university-run bus service is **Tiger Transit** (☎ 609-258-3157; www.princeton.edu/transportation). It's free and runs weekdays only; routes connect the train station, campus and downtown. Regional NJ Transit buses stop near Palmer Sq.

For a taxi, use the ecovehicles of **A Amigo Taxi** (☎ 609-452-2121).

TRENTON
pop 88,675

'Trenton Makes – The World Takes.'

When Trenton adopted this slogan in 1910, it was hardly a boast. By then, Trenton was one of America's major manufacturing centers for steel, rubber, linoleum and ceramics. Indeed, by the late 19th century, over half of the pottery companies in the US were in Trenton, including the fine china maker Lenox. Ever since 1935 the slogan has glowed in neon from Trenton's main bridge over the Delaware River.

Trouble is, Trenton is not much of a manufacturing powerhouse anymore. It's home to

NEW JERSEY

the state legislature, and for all the taxes the state takes, residents have grown frustrated with how little Trenton makes with it, particularly during the recent recession. Interestingly, the governor's official residence is in Princeton, and this has long symbolized the divide in state government between New Jersey's weaker legislature and its stronger executive – as well as a class divide between the towns.

Despite being a seat of power, Trenton is predominantly a working-class city. While the downtown district around the statehouse is clean, attractive and safe – the city itself isn't much of a tourist destination. It has a handful of interesting historical sites and museums, and one stunning sculpture park, which travelers can easily visit as a day trip from Princeton, Lambertville or Philadelphia.

Information

Trenton Visitors Center (☎ 609-777-1770; www. trentonnj.com; cnr Lafayette & Barrack Sts; ⌚ 10am-4pm) In the Old Masonic Lodge across from the Old Barracks.

Sights & Activities

STATE HOUSE

The **New Jersey State House** (☎ 609-633-2709; www. njleg.state.nj.us) was built in 1792, and remodeled and expanded extensively after an 1885 fire, to become the grand building that lords it over W State St in downtown Trenton. The only way to see it is on a free 45-minute **tour** (☎ 10am-3pm Mon-Fri, noon-3pm Sat); these leave on the hour. Reservations aren't required, but call ahead, if only to avoid school groups.

Before or after your tour, cross the street to admire the **World War II Memorial**, a circular plaza surrounded by panels that trace the entire course of the war's Pacific and European theaters.

OLD BARRACKS MUSEUM

After the state house, school groups migrate to this Revolutionary War **museum** (☎ 609-396-1776; www.barracks.org; 101 Barrack St; adult/child $8/6; ⌚ 10am-5pm). As the name suggests, it is a former soldiers' barracks – built by the British around 1760 for the French and Indian War. During the Revolution it housed British-hired Hessian mercenaries – that is, until George Washington routed them and drove them out on December 25, 1776, after his crossing of the Delaware River.

Guided tours begin on the hour, led by engaging docents in period dress who admirably conjure up the times. The barracks' interiors are entirely re-created, but the freshness makes it easier to imagine what the soldiers' lives were like.

NEW JERSEY STATE MUSEUM

Next to the state house, **New Jersey State Museum** (☎ 609-292-6464; www.newjerseystatemuseum.org; 205 W State St; admission free; ⌚ 9am-4:45pm Tue-Sat, noon-5pm Sun) has an eclectic collection. Strongest are the ethnography exhibits on indigenous cultures in the Americas, but it also has modest displays on American painting, dinosaur fossils and Trenton-made porcelain. There's also a planetarium ($5).

TRENTON CITY MUSEUM

The **Trenton City Museum** (☎ 609-989-3632; www. ellarslie.org; admission free; ⌚ 11am-3pm Tue-Sat, 1-4pm Sun) is housed in Ellarslie, a pretty 1850 Italianate villa, in Cadwalader Park. The 1st floor is gallery space devoted to local artists, and the 2nd floor focuses on Trenton's ceramics industry. From State Museum, follow W State St for a mile, turn right on Parkside Ave, and follow signs into Cadwalader Park.

NJ STATE POLICE MUSEUM

Think about it. In a state known for organized crime, shouldn't it have a really cool **police museum** (☎ 609-882-2000, ext 6401; www.njsp. org; ⌚ 10am-4pm Mon-Fri)? Crisp exhibits show how, through the years, NJ state troopers dealt with Prohibition moonshiners and caught mobsters. The best display unravels the famous Lindberg baby-kidnapping trail, with period newsreel footage. It also has a fake murder to solve and a confiscated gun case with a mounted anti-tank cannon. The question is: How did the *police* get it?

The museum is south of Trenton. Take I-95 exit 1 to Rte 29 south, make a left at the first light and follow signs to state police headquarters. Tell the guard you're visiting the museum.

GROUNDS FOR SCULPTURE

There are sculpture gardens, and then there's **Grounds for Sculpture** (☎ 609-586-0616; www.grounds forsculpture.org; 18 Fairgrounds Rd, Hamilton; adult/child 6-17yr $12/8; ⌚ 10am-6pm Tue-Sun), a tremendous 35-acre manicured landscape woven with 250 modern sculptures and two huge indoor art galleries, plus a café, shops and a renowned restaurant. Founder Seward Johnson (a Johnson & Johnson heir) likes to re-create Impressionist paintings in life-sized dioramas – creating whimsical 3-D encounters with art's most famous scenes. The effect is enchanting and thought-provoking and, at sunset, sublime. Take I-295 exit 65B/Sloan Ave, and follow the signs.

TRENTON THUNDER
The Trenton Thunder are the AA minor-league affiliate of the New York Yankees, and they play in attractive **Mercer County Waterfront Park** (☎ 609-394-3300; www.trentonthunder. com; 1 Thunder Rd; seats $9-12; ☺ Apr-Aug). See future Yankees today; Joba Chamberlain pitched here before getting called up.

Sleeping & Eating
Note that most Trenton restaurants are not walkable from the downtown area, which is so quiet at night it's not a place for strolling.

Trenton Marriott at Lafayette Yard (☎ 609-421-4000; www.trentonmarriott.com; 1 W Lafayette St; weekend $100, midweek $110-150; ✷ ▯) Serving business travelers and political types, and around the corner from the state house, this Marriott is spiffy clean and comfortable. Offers a free shuttle from the train station, but charges for extras like parking, internet and breakfast.

BOYS OF SUMMER: BASEBALL IN NEW JERSEY

New Jersey and baseball go way back – really, all the way back to the very beginning. In 1846, when the New York Knickerbockers (who invented the modern game) wanted to play their first 'match game' with another club, the New Yorks, they chose Elysian Fields in Hoboken. Unfortunately for the Knicks, they got their bats handed to them, losing 23-1 to a bunch of former cricket players, but no matter: baseball had arrived.

In the 1870s, when baseball formed the first professional leagues, New Jersey fielded its own teams, as many as 15. The most successful were in Newark, Jersey City and Trenton. In the 1930s and 1940s, the Newark Eagles were one of the most successful Negro League teams, and in 1946, before Jackie Robinson broke major-league baseball's color barrier with the Brooklyn Dodgers, he played his first pro game in the minor leagues – in New Jersey.

Soon after this, the Negro Leagues folded, along with, incredibly, all of New Jersey's baseball teams. From 1950 to 1994, the state had no professional baseball.

Over the last decade, along with the general resurgence in the minor leagues, as many as eight minor-league teams have started. The state will probably never have a major-league team – not with New York and Philly teams controlling regional markets – but New Jersey hasn't had pro baseball like this in 70 years.

New Jersey minor-league baseball encompasses both affiliated leagues (those connected to MLB teams) and independent leagues, which are a separate product. If you've never been, the main thing to know is that minor-league games are cheap, fun, relaxed, intimate, family-friendly events – much closer to baseball's origins than the wallet-gouging major leagues today. Seats typically cost $10 to $12, teams fill game days with promotions, fireworks and lots of between-innings slapstick – along with a chance to see tomorrow's stars today. Plus, Jersey stadiums are practically brand-new brickfull, 6000-seat beauties with sometimes great views.

For the full story of New Jersey baseball, read *No Minor Accomplishment* by Bob Golon. For more on minor-league baseball, visit www.minorleaguebaseball.com. Here are five of New Jersey's teams, all in north and central Jersey.

Newark Bears (☎ 866-554-2327; www.newarkbears.com) An independent team that plays in the Atlantic League at Bears & Eagles Riverfront Stadium. See p243.

Somerset Patriots (☎ 908-252-0700; www.somersetpatriots.com; Bridgewater) An independent team in the Atlantic League at Commerce Bank Ball Park.

Trenton Thunder (☎ 609-394-3300; www.trentonthunder.com) Double-A minor-league Yankees affiliate that plays at Mercer County Waterfront Park. See p257.

Camden Riversharks (☎ 866-742-7579; www.riversharks.com) An independent team in the Atlantic League that plays at Campbell's Field. See p261.

Lakewood BlueClaws (☎ 732-901-7000; www.blueclaws.com; Lakewood) Single-A minor-league Phillies affiliate that plays at FirstEnergy Park, Lakewood.

De Lorenzo's Tomato Pies (☎ 609-695-9534; www
.delorenzostomatopies.com; 530 Hudson St at Swan St;
pies $12-16; ☺ 4-9pm Thu-Sun) Trenton is an old-
school pizza town. The best thin-crust pie in
the city, and maybe the state, is made here, and
it's an experience: no slices, no bathrooms, no
credit cards, no decor. Just a tiny rowhouse
on a rundown street. If you've come this far,
don't miss it.

Delorenzo's Pizza (☎ 609-393-2952; 1007 Hamilton
Ave; pies $12-16; ☺ lunch & dinner Tue-Sat) Similar
name, owned by relatives, but different crisp-
crust pie and a nicer sit-down atmosphere.
Some like it better; you decide!

ourpick Rats (☎ 609-584-7800; www.ratsrest
aurant.org; 16 Fairgrounds Rd; mains $20-35; ☺ 10am-9pm
Tue-Sun) Within the Grounds for Sculpture's
magical setting, Rats paints French-influenced
culinary canvases that would please Monet.
Francophiles will appreciate chef Kevin
Sbraga's accomplished renditions of *moules*,
escargot, *vichyssoise* and *steak frites*, but
other dishes playfully mix locavore and international touches with delicious results.
Surrounded by beauty and art, it's as memorable a meal as Jersey offers.

Getting There & Away

NJ Transit (☎ 800-772-2222; www.njtransit.com) trains
run from New York's Penn Station to Trenton.
Amtrak (☎ 800-872-7245; www.amtrak.com) also runs
several lines that stop at Trenton en route
to New York, Washington and Philadelphia.
During peak hours, **SEPTA** (☎ 215-580-7800; www.
septa.org) operates a light rail/train service between Trenton and Philadelphia.

By car, both Rte 1 and Rte 29 lead directly
to downtown; access these from I-95, I-295
or I-195.

LAMBERTVILLE & AROUND
pop 3700

Sophisticated Lambertville and its bohemian sister across the Delaware River,
Pennsylvania's New Hope (p314), together
make a lovely, antique- and arts-filled destination for romantic getaways and wider explorations of this pretty region. A scenic bridge
connects the towns and straddles the wide,
majestic Delaware River. Though George
Washington found it made for a dangerous
crossing during wartime, the beautiful river's
soothing heartbeat inspired a renaissance in
American Impressionist painting about a
century later.

For more information, contact the
Lambertville Chamber of Commerce (☎ 609-397-0055;
www.lambertville.org); shops in town carry area
maps and information brochures. The main
drag through town is Bridge St, which leads
from Rte 29 to the bridge with New Hope.

Sights & Activities
WASHINGTON CROSSING STATE PARK

About 7 miles south of Lambertville along
Rte 29, this **park** (☎ 609-737-0623; www.njparksand
forests.org; admission summer weekends $5; ☺ visitors'
center 8am-4:30pm, park dawn-dusk) commemorates where General Washington made his
Christmas-night river crossing in 1776 to
surprise the sleeping British-led forces in
Trenton. This marked the beginning of a fortnight of American advances and victories that
changed the early course of the war, and the
crossing is reenacted every year at Christmas.

The expansive park is a lovely spot for picnicking, hiking and biking in summer. The
visitor centers' **museum** is jam-packed with
historic artifacts and weapons, and the **Ferry
House**, where Washington rested post-crossing
to plan the Trenton attack, re-creates a colonial household, with craft demonstrations.

Across the river in Pennsylvania,
Washington Crossing Historic Park (p314)
also highlights these events.

DELAWARE & RARITAN CANAL
STATE PARK

This long, narrow **park** (☎ 609-924-5705; www.
dandrcanal.com; ☺ dawn-dusk) runs about 70
miles: first along the Delaware River from
Frenchtown to Trenton, and then inland
along the Raritan Canal past Princeton to
New Brunswick. The old towpath along the
D&R Canal makes a hugely popular hiking
and biking trail. Along the river, canoeists
get to enjoy a rare roundtrip: paddling in the
river downstream and returning upstream in
the adjacent canal. The park is also a great
fishing spot.

The Delaware River here is the essence of
bucolic; the towpath parallels Rte 29 and has
tons of access points. One of the biggest is
Bull's Island Recreation Area (☎ 609-397-2949; 2185
Rte 29, Stockton), with shaded picnic areas and
playgrounds, and a scenic pedestrian suspension bridge. Bull's Island has the only camping
along the D&R Canal. The **tent-only sites** (per
night $20; ☺ Apr-Oct) are some of the best in the
state: pretty, wooded, right along the river,

with full facilities. Bull's Island is just over 7 miles north of Lambertville along Rte 29.

For bike rentals, call **Greenway Bike Rentals** (☎ 908-581-5780; www.greenwaybikerentals.com; bike per day $35; ◷ 10am-dusk Sat & Sun, weekdays by appt); it sets up on River Dr within Washington Crossing Park next to the bridge; it also provides a shuttle service along the river.

For leisurely tubing and canoeing, see **Delaware River Tubing** (☎ 866-938-8823; www.del awarerivertubing.com; 2998 Rte 29; tube $18-23, canoe/kayak $30-60), in Frenchtown north of Bull's Island. Rentals include lunch with the 'Hot Dog Man,' who operates from a skiff in the river.

GOLDEN NUGGET FLEA MARKET

A mile south of Lambertville is New Jersey's best **antique and flea market** (☎ 609-397-0811; www. gnmarket.com; 1850 River Rd/Rte 29; ◷ 8am-4pm Wed, Sat & Sun). It's a fun community scene as folks paw through acres of genuine antiques and garage-sale treasures – from accordions, tin toys, brass telescopes, a 1908 edition of Dickens and Civil War knives to rusted garden tools, faded VHS tapes and ceramic ballerina lamps.

Sleeping

Stockton Inn (☎ 609-397-1250; www.stocktoninn.com; 1 Main St/Rte 29 at Bridge St, Stockton; r weekday $95-170, weekend $135-195; ⌘) Four miles north of Lambertville in Stockton, this historic inn has 11 rooms in three buildings. All have a funky, atmospheric charm that mixes antique and modern furnishings without attempting to be Victorian simulacrums; most have fireplaces. Bathrooms are small. It also has a recommended restaurant and bar.

Inn at Lambertville Station (☎ 609-398-8461; www. lambertvillestation.com; 11 Bridge St; r midweek $125-135, weekend $160-220; ⌘ ▯ ⌘) Another attractive option. It's a more standard hotel, but with the antique-filled flavor of an inn. It's well-located near downtown.

York Street House (☎ 609-397-3007; www.yorkstreet house.com; 42 York St, Lambertville; r weekday $125-150, weekend $185-250; ⌘ ⌘) This gorgeous, six-room B&B in a stately, brick house provides luxurious accommodations, with lacy four-poster beds, stunning tiled bathrooms and cozy quilts. Some have Jacuzzis. The candlelight gourmet breakfast is a highlight.

Eating & Drinking

Sneddon's (☎ 609-397-3053; 47 Bridge St; mains $4-8; ◷ 6am-2pm, plus 5-8pm Fri) A bit of old-school

Lambertville, this gathering place for breakfast is where gossip and politics get hashed out over diner-style egg and pancake dishes.

Lilly's on the Canal (☎ 609-397-6242; www.lillys gourmet.com; 2 Canal St; lunch mains $10-20, dinner $16-30; ◷ lunch & dinner Wed-Sun) A gorgeous restaurant right on the towpath that whips up sophisticated meals meant to satisfy Philly food snobs. Lunchtime sandwiches, like the fried oyster po boy, are incredible. Wine by the bottle or BYOB.

Hamilton's Grill (☎ 609-397-4343; www.hamiltonsgrill room.com; 8 Coryell St; mains $18-38; ◷ lunch Sat & Sun, dinner nightly) Seafood and steaks done over a wood-fired grill with bright Mediterranean flavors have made Hamilton's a long-standing favorite. Focus on the day's market specials; this is the place to try the local shad (fish). The hidden, relaxed canalside setting is tops. BYOB.

Boathouse (☎ 609-397-2244; 8½ Coryell St; ◷ from 4pm) Across from Hamilton's, the century-old building houses a two-story cocktail bar that's crammed floor-to-ceiling with so much nautical hoo-ha you feel like you're floating in the canal. It's actually down an alley off Coryell St.

River Horse Brewing Company (☎ 609-397-7776; www.riverhorse.com; 80 Lambert Lane; ◷ noon-5pm Fri-Sun) Way at the north end of Lambert Lane (off Bridge St) is River Horse. Self-guided tours and tastings on weekends are so darn friendly, and the samples are so generous ($1 for four!), it's like happy hour at the brewery.

SOUTHERN NEW JERSEY

Southern Jersey has a noticeably more rural character. Gone is the north's syncopated rhythm of city and suburb. The vast pine forests of the Pine Barrens dominate the flat interior, which otherwise is made up of quiet towns and farmland. Camden, in the shadow of Philadelphia, forms a gritty urban sprawl to the west. Along the shore, Atlantic City is the casino capital of the East and the state's most popular tourist destination, while south of Atlantic City are some of Jersey's best shore towns: Wildwood, Ocean City and Cape May.

CAMDEN
pop 79,400

Across the Delaware River from Philadelphia, Camden is a troubled city with a rich history. Many of the 19th-century industrialists built their grand homes in Camden; Walt Whitman lived here from 1873 until his death in 1892; and the Campbell Soup Company was founded here in 1869 (the factory closed in 1999). However, despite the state's efforts, Camden remains bedeviled by poverty and crime.

The one positive exception has been the development of the waterfront, near the Ben Franklin Bridge. With several interesting attractions within walking distance of each other, the waterfront is both safe and worth a day trip, particularly on busy weekends. It makes for an all-American afternoon: visit the Walt Whitman House, an aquarium, a battleship and take in a minor-league baseball game.

Sights & Activities

WALT WHITMAN HOUSE

This humble brick **row house** (☎ 856-964-5383; 330 Mickle Blvd at 4th St; admission free; 10am–noon & 1–4pm Wed-Sat, 1–4pm Sun) is where Walt Whitman spent the last 20 years of his life. The first edition of his seminal book *Leaves of Grass* was published in 1855, but he continued revising it until his death. America's greatest poet, he is buried in Camden, and his home contains his letters and personal belongings. The free 45-minute tours require reservations; staff is limited. This is the only site not along the Camden Waterfront.

CAMDEN WATERFRONT

First created in the mid-1990s, and expanded since, the **Camden Waterfront** (www

SOUTHERN NEW JERSEY

.camdenwaterfront.com) flows south from the base of the Ben Franklin Bridge. There are several large paid parking lots; it's easiest to park and walk.

Next to the aquarium, the **Camden Children's Garden** (☎ 856-365-8733; www.camdenchildrensgarden. org; 3 Riverside Dr; adult/child 3-12yr $6/3; ☺ 10am-4pm Fri-Sun) is a fenced, landscaped playground with a carousel and a small train ride, perfect for little ones.

At the waterfront's south end is **Susquehanna Bank Center** (☎ 856-365-1300), a 25,000-seat outdoor amphitheater. Summer concerts bring big names in pop music; there's a smaller indoor stage for theater and family shows.

ADVENTURE AQUARIUM

The state's biggest aquarium, **Adventure Aquarium** (☎ 856-365-3300; www.adventureaquarium. com; 1 Riverside Dr; adult/child 2-12yr $22/18; ☺ 9:30am-5pm) has a crowd-pleasing shark tank, a hippo room, nice touch tanks and enough colorful exhibits to fill a day. The truly adventurous can literally swim with the sharks and get up-close with the seals (reserve ahead). A huge cafeteria and gift shop round out the experience.

BATTLESHIP NEW JERSEY

The *New Jersey* is the country's most decorated **battleship** (☎ 856-966-1652; www.battleship newjersey.org; adult/child 6-11yr $18.50/14; ☺ 9:30am-5pm). Self-guided tours include audio; guided tours are unscheduled and infrequent. You climb in and around the 'Big J' and get up close to the 16in guns, with nice exhibits on the sailor's life.

CAMDEN RIVERSHARKS

The minor-league baseball **Riversharks** (☎ 866-742-7579; www.riversharks.com; 401 N Delaware Ave; tickets $5-15; ☺ Apr–mid-Sep) play at Campbell's Field, a gorgeous red-brick stadium framing the Ben Franklin Bridge and the Philly skyline.

Getting There & Away

Camden is on the NJ Turnpike just before the Ben Franklin Bridge.

RiverLink Ferry System (☎ 215-925-5465; www.river linkferry.org; adult round-trip $7) links Philadelphia's Penn's Landing with the Camden waterfront. Ferries run once an hour from 9am to 6pm. Service is daily from Memorial Day to Labor Day; weekends in May and September; and closed the rest of the year.

PINE BARRENS

Officially the Pinelands National Reserve, the region's 1.1-million protected acres were dubbed 'Pine Barrens' by the region's 18th-century settlers because the sandy, acidic soil wouldn't support traditional agriculture, and the name stuck. It is, indeed, a daunting landscape, a scruffy pine forest and wetlands ecology that doesn't lend itself to human enterprise. Not only is its beauty something of an acquired taste, it can exude a moody menace: this is the land of the Jersey Devil, a legendary winged beast with a horse's head, forked tale and hooves (see p220).

Yet people have always made a home here – melting sand into glass, filling bogs with cranberries, scrabbling together their own proud 'Piney' culture – and the region rewards travelers with New Jersey's most unexpected face: not turnpikes or beaches but raw wilderness.

The Pinelands Reserve is a patchwork of state forests and private lands, and includes several coastal national wildlife refuges. For the best hiking, canoeing and camping, head for Wharton and Bass River State Forests; bird-watchers should aim for Edwin B Forsythe NWR. For more on the Pinelands, visit the **NPS** (www.nps.gov/pine), the **NJ Pinelands Commission** (www.nj.gov/pinelands) and the nonprofit **Pinelands Alliance** (www.pinelandsalliance.org). For local culture, visit www.pineypower.com.

Wharton State Forest

This 115,000-acre state forest contains the two main visitors' centers for the Pinelands – at Batsto and Atsion – and between them they have the most popular trails, canoeing and camping.

BATSTO

Batsto provides the best all-in-one experience of the Pine Barrens. The **Batsto visitors' center** (☎ 609-561-0024; ☺ 9am-4pm) contains an updated, interesting nature center surveying Pine Barrens history and ecology, as well as a great bookstore stocked with wildlife guides and Jersey Devil lore. Batsto also contains a **historic village** (☎ 609-561-3262; www.batstovillage. org), once a glass- and iron-making center that made ammunition for the Continental army during the American Revolution. The village (with free phone audio tour) has over 30 historic buildings, including a mansion, charcoal kiln, piggery, and blacksmith and wheelwright shops. On summer weekends, there's a $5 car fee; admission is free otherwise. Batsto is signed along Rte 542, about 11 miles west from Rte 9.

From the visitors' center, you can access several easy one- to three-hour **hikes**, in addition to the Pine Barrens' signature hike, the 50-mile **Batona Trail**, one of the state's great trails. The most popular stretch is between the Carranza Memorial and Apple Pie Hill, which at 205ft is the highest point in the Pine Barrens; a graffiti-covered firetower allows for an unparalleled panorama of this unending pine forest. You can drive to the trailhead and the firetower; get directions at the visitors' center.

The Mullica River runs past Batsto, offering excellent **canoe** trips. The region's biggest outfitter is **Bel Haven** (☎ 800-445-0935; www.belhavenpaddlesports.com), on Rte 542 about 3 miles east of Batsto; it rents canoes, kayaks, inner tubes and rafts, and leads guided trips.

Near the Carranza Memorial is the recommended, hike-in-only Batona campground (per person $2), with toilets and drinking water.

ATSION

Signed along Rte 206, north of Hammonton, **Atsion** (☎ 609-268-0444; cars summer weekday/weekend $5/10) is extremely popular for its sandy **swimming lake** (with lifeguards and concessions); on summer weekends, arrive before 11am or the lots may be full. Popular canoe trips also leave from here; for rentals, **Adams Canoe** (☎ 609-268-0189; www.adamscanoerental.com) is at the park entrance. Atsion has a large drive-up campground (per site $20) and nine cabins (one-week minimum in summer $315 to $595) with kitchens and bathrooms; cabins get booked up a year in advance.

Bass River State Forest

Like Atsion, **Bass River** (☎ 609-296-5456; cars summer midweek/weekend $5/10) is popular for its swimming lake (with lifeguards and concessions) and attractive drive-up campground (per site $20), plus primitive shelters and cabins ($30 to $65). From the Garden State Parkway, take exit 50 from the south or exit 52 from the north and follow the signs.

Edwin B Forsythe National Wildlife Refuge

A mecca for birding, this 47,000-acre wildlife refuge protects a range of coastal wetlands that are a vital migratory flyway for water birds and raptors. Refuge **headquarters** (☎ 609-652-1665; www.fws.gov/northeast/forsythe; cars $4; ⏱ 10am-3pm, grounds dawn-dusk) has information, binocular rentals, short nature walks and an 8-mile wildlife drive. Depending on the season, you might see sandpipers, egrets, owls, osprey, bald eagles and snow geese.

From Garden State Parkway exit 48, take Rte 9 south for 6 miles to Oceanville. The refuge entrance is signed; follow Great Creek Rd east.

ATLANTIC CITY
pop 39,400

In 2005, the Miss America pageant left Atlantic City. Atlantic City invented the Miss America pageant and proudly hosted its parade for over a century. But it's now in Las Vegas, and there is no clearer snapshot of the shift in stature between America's two great casino-resort cities. Whatever its struggles, Atlantic City could always say it crowned the most beautiful woman in America. How can you lose that and not feel a little less lovely?

This sense of loss shadows the conversations of longtime residents. They are upbeat about the future, and with reason, despite AC's ongoing struggles with poverty, mismanagement and crime. Yet they know they will never again be America's darling, when their amusement pier was unparalleled, the true epitome of entertainment – one that, in its era, outshone all of AC's casinos combined.

Today, Atlantic City is a puzzle of contradictions: beside empty lots and boarded-up buildings tower glittering resorts. The homeless panhandle along a boardwalk thick with middle-class vacationers. Visitors spend nearly $4 billion annually in the casinos, and yet the casinos remain precarious enterprises, regularly falling in and out of bankruptcy. The city is New Jersey's biggest vacation destination, with 33 million tourists a year, but Atlantic City's schools are underfunded, and poverty and unemployment are high.

On the other hand, when it comes to tourism, Atlantic City and its casinos get it: steadily, they are imitating Vegas. The resorts are increasingly fashioning themselves as 'experiences,' as over-the-top themed 'events,' and it's working. Ever since the Borgata opened in 2003, the surge in fine dining, trendy bars and nightclubs, top-notch entertainment and chic shopping has been phenomenal, so much so that gambling has become almost secondary. In fact, maybe for the first time since casinos arrived in 1978, it's possible to skip gambling entirely and still have a great time.

History

Atlantic City began in 1793 as a tiny settlement on Absecon Island. Inspired to create a resort, Dr Jonathan Pitney, with the help of a group of businessmen, had a railroad line built and a city designed from scratch. 'Atlantic City' was incorporated in 1854 – like Las Vegas, a resort in the sand dreamed up by speculators.

Serendipity smiled on Atlantic City when, spurred by hotel owners complaining of guests tracking in sand, the city built the world's first wooden boardwalk in 1870. Considered a street name, and thus capitalized, the Boardwalk's flirtatious 'parade' drew visitors by the ton. The Boardwalk got longer, and longer, to accommodate the crowds, culminating with the 1898 addition of the Steel Pier.

This massive, two-level structure contained everything: a theater, a dance pavilion, an aquarium, thrill rides, and whatever wild entertainment the day's promoters could imagine: a diving bell, boxing kangaroos, the human cannonball and, most famously, the high-diving horse. For the next 40 years, the Steel Pier was host to America's best performers – Glenn Miller, Abbott and Costello, Jackie Gleason – and was known as the 'Showplace of the Nation.'

A steady decline set in after WWII, when jet travel and middle-class prosperity made it easier to vacation in Florida or the Caribbean. By the 1970s, the drop in tourism led to intractable economic woes and high crime, and Atlantic City's once-vibrant African American community, originally drawn to the city for its job opportunities, had been drawn into poverty.

Boosters argued that casinos would save the city, and state voters legalized gambling in 1976. In 1978, the Resorts casino opened, and for the next two decades, Atlantic City once again became one of America's top destinations. Yet somehow the city itself still struggled. Despite the success of the casinos, Atlantic City hasn't reaped the benefits.

Today, competition from Las Vegas and from gaming in neighboring states threatens to undermine AC's casinos. The Sands was imploded in 2007 to make way for a megaresort, then financing evaporated, leaving an empty lot. At the Boardwalk's north end, the Revel casino sits half-built, awaiting a new backer. AC's own impresario Donald Trump almost lost his three properties – the Marina, Plaza and Taj Mahal – to bankruptcy in 2010. This is Atlantic City's pickle: it fights to support the casinos it now can't live without.

Orientation

If you've played Monopoly, you will recognize Atlantic City street names, since they were the basis for the game. Arranged on a grid, they are easy to navigate: the principal avenues paralleling the Boardwalk are Pacific and Atlantic. While Pacific is the main thoroughfare accessing the casinos, it's a tawdry street lined with sketchy motels and nude dancing. Cross-streets perpendicular to the Boardwalk are mostly avenues named after states. If you come into town via the Atlantic City Expressway, it leads directly to the Walk

---

DETOUR: BOGS & BERRIES

One of New Jersey's most dramatic harvest spectacles is the blood-red cranberry bogs in the Pine Barrens. The cranberries start to turn color in late September, and within a month the harvest is in full swing. On the third weekend of October, the **Chatsworth Cranberry Festival** (☎ 609-726-9237; www.cranfest.org) draws upwards of 100,000 people to celebrate. Drive about 3 miles south of Chatsworth on Rte 563 to reach working commercial bogs. While you're here, stop at **Chatsworth General Store** (☎ 609-894-4415; intersection of Rtes 563 & 532; ☀ 10am-3pm Thu-Sun); it's the site of Buzby's Cafe, which John McPhee made famous in his classic The Pine Barrens. Today, it's a lovely gift shop for local jams and home of **Pine Barrens Press**.

Drive north to **Whitesbog** to visit the home of the cultivated blueberry, invented by Elizabeth White. The atmospheric **general store** (☎ 609-893-4646; www.whitesbog.org; ☀ 10am-4pm Sat & Sun Feb-Dec) has information and jams, and the road is lined with more cranberry bogs. The **Blueberry Festival** is in late June. From Rte 70, turn onto Rte 530 for 1 mile, then right on Whites Bog Rd.

shopping mall and Caesar's. To reach the Marina District casinos, take Virginia Ave west to Absecon Blvd to Brigantine Blvd, and follow signs.

Information

The **Visitors Information Center** (☎ 888-228-4748; www.atlanticcitynj.com; ⏱ 9:30am-5:30pm May-Oct, closed Tue & Wed Nov-Apr) is on the Boardwalk in Boardwalk Hall; in addition to brochures, it'll help you find a room. There is also a Boardwalk information booth near Illinois Ave, and you'll find a staffed desk in the Convention Center.

The best free weeklies for news and entertainment are *Atlantic City Weekly* (www. acweekly.com) and *At the Shore* (www.press ofatlanticcity.com).

The main **post office** (1801 Atlantic Ave) is between Indiana and Ohio Aves. **Atlantic City News Agency** (☎ 609-344-9444; cnr Pacific & Illinois Aves; ⏱ 24hr) has an international selection of magazines and newspapers, plus gambling guides and cigars.

Atlantic City Free Public Library (☎ 609-345-2269; www.acfpl.org; 1 N Tennessee Ave; ⏱ 10am-8pm Mon-Wed, 9am-5pm Thu-Sat, noon-5pm Sun) is a nice space, with 40 internet terminals; get a free three-month computer card (bring photo ID).

Sights & Activities

CASINOS

Atlantic City's 11 casinos are obviously the city's main attraction. If you've been to Las Vegas, all but a few may pale by comparison, but in aggregate, they form an intriguing portrait of the industry's evolution: from gambling-focused money pits to themed and theme park–like pleasure palaces where gambling is just one amusement. Still, spending time at the blackjack and craps tables remains an essential part of the fun.

Gone, though, are the showers of silver winnings, the cups of quarters. Today, slots don't take coins, they use casino-issued cards, and players win credits as they push buttons. The sign of the serious slot player is a lanyard dangling five to six plastic cards. Always get the casino's card, as it comes with perks (like free parking).

You must be 21 years old to gamble or be on the casino floor. Casinos allow smoking, but only in designated areas. All casinos, despite their differences, offer the same basic package: casino floors with slots, gaming tables and card rooms; buffets and gourmet restaurants; bars, a nightclub and a theater (or two); and at least 500 hotel rooms – most double or quadruple that.

Finally, casinos come and go. The unfinished Revel will, most likely, be finished, but maybe not. Below, AC's casinos are listed in their recommended order of interest.

Borgata (☎ 609-317-1000, 866-692-6742; www. theborgata.com; 1 Borgata Way) When it opened in 2003, the first new casino in 13 years, the Borgata completely changed the playing field, and everyone else is still catching up. Dale Chihuly chandeliers lend a classy, contemporary, designer feel that doesn't have a gimmick – except to be chic and sexy. The Borgata's name-brand gourmet dining – with outposts for Wolfgang Puck, Bobby Flay, Michael Minna – started the trend. The gaming tables are lively, with AC's largest poker room, and the boutique hotel the Water Club is attached.

Harrah's Resort Atlantic City (☎ 609-441-5000, 800-242-7724; www.harrahsresort.com; Brigantine Blvd) Harrah's calling card is the Pool, a domed atrium filled with towering palms, cabanas, and multiple luscious pools and hot tubs. For guests only during the day, it becomes an open-to-the-public club at night. The decor – with oversized butterflies and fish tanks backing the front desk – is contemporary and stylish. The brand-new Viking Cooking School (www.vikingcookingschool.com) gives classes, and Harrah's teams with the Food Network for events.

Bally's Atlantic City & the Wild Wild West (☎ 609-340-2000, 800-225-5977; www.ballysac.com; cnr Park Place & Boardwalk) Two casinos: the original Bally's and the newer Wild Wild West next door. A true Vegas-style themed gaming palace, Wild Wild West has a vaulted interior that re-creates a (literally) false-fronted Virginia City: mining cars on railroad tracks, stagecoaches, and gold miners hanging out brothel windows. The anachronistic frisson of the Old West in Jersey, not Nevada, is swell.

Tropicana Hotel & Casino (☎ 609-340-4000, 800-257-6227; www.tropicana.net; cnr Iowa Ave & Boardwalk) The Trop recently added 'the Quarter,' a retail/restaurant/entertainment corridor that evokes 1950s Havana with flickering streetlamps, tiled walkways and spinning palm-frond fans. It's a Vegas-quality fantasy detached from the casino, which shares the kitschy Cuban decor.

ATLANTIC CITY

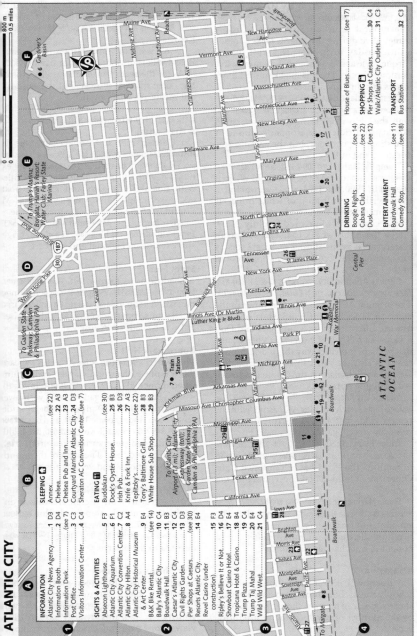

INFORMATION
Atlantic City News Agency.....................1	D3
Information Booth..................................2	D4
Information Desk.............................(see 7)	
Post Office...3	C3
Visitors Information Center...................4	C4

SIGHTS & ACTIVITIES
Absecon Lighthouse..............................5	F3
Atlantic City Aquarium..........................6	F1
Atlantic City Convention Center...........7	C2
Atlantic City Hilton...............................8	A4
Atlantic City Historical Museum	
& Art Center...................................9	E4
B&K Bike Rental.............................(see 14)	
Bally's Atlantic City............................10	C4
Boardwalk Hall....................................11	B3
Caesar's Atlantic City..........................12	C4
Civil Rights Garden..............................13	D3
Pier Shops at Caesars....................(see 30)	
Resorts Atlantic City...........................14	E4
Revel Casino (under	
construction)...................................15	F3
Ripley's Believe It or Not....................16	D4
Showboat Casino Hotel.......................17	E4
Tropicana Hotel & Casino....................18	B4
Trump Plaza..19	C4
Trump Taj Mahal.................................20	E4
Wild Wild West...................................21	C4

SLEEPING
Annex...(see 22)	
Chelsea..22	D4
Chelsea Pub and Inn...........................23	A3
Courtyard Marriott Atlantic City.........24	D3
Sheraton AC Convention Center...(see 7)	

EATING
Buddakan......................................(see 30)	
Dock's Oyster House...........................25	B3
Irish Pub...26	D3
Knife & Fork Inn.................................27	A3
Teplitzky's...................................(see 22)	
Tony's Baltimore Grill.........................28	B3
White House Sub Shop.......................29	B3

House of Blues..............................(see 17)		

SHOPPING
Pier Shops at Caesars..........................30	C4
Walk/Atlantic City Outlets...................31	C3

TRANSPORT
Bus Station...32	C3

DRINKING
Boogie Nights...............................(see 14)	
Cabana Club.................................(see 12)	
Dusk..(see 14)	

ENTERTAINMENT
Boardwalk Hall..............................(see 11)	
Comedy Stop..................................(see 18)	

NEW JERSEY

Showboat Casino Hotel (☎ 609-343-4000, 800-621-0200; www.showboatac.com; cnr Delaware Ave & Boardwalk) The modest Bourbon Street theme really comes alive during the 'Mardi Gras parade,' a thrice-a-day roving carnival with surreal Cirque-style acrobats, spangly costumes, live music and beads. The attached House of Blues has its own hip casino area.

Caesar's Atlantic City (☎ 609-348-4411, 800-443-0104; www.caesarsac.com; cnr Arkansas Ave & Boardwalk) Only the lobby really brings it, with oversized statuary and ridiculous Roman columns. A nice shopping corridor, but the gaming area doesn't stand out.

Trump Taj Mahal (☎ 609-449-1000, 800-825-8786; www.trumptaj.com; cnr Virginia Ave & Boardwalk) When it opened in 1990, the Taj Mahal overwhelmed, the exterior a confection of white minarets and glinting gold, the casino festooned with crystal chandeliers mirrored brightly. Now, it feels like a throwback to the tacky glitz of yesteryear. It keeps adding sexy bars to stay hip, and has the second-largest poker room in the city.

Resorts Atlantic City (☎ 609-340-6000, 800-438-7424; www.resortsac.com; cnr N Carolina Ave & Boardwalk) The original AC casino. The 'Entrance of the Stars' includes cement handprints of Dean Martin, Cher, Liberace, Tom Jones and Don Rickles – a roll call of yesteryear's headliners that perhaps indicates why this old-fashioned resort is also the most financially troubled. Despite its rich history, the casino is a standard, clanging noise pit.

Atlantic City Hilton (☎ 609-340-7100; Boardwalk btwn Boston & Pacific Aves) A smaller AC casino, with the typical gold, marble and mirrors decor. No real draw except gambling.

Trump Plaza (☎ 609-441-6000, 800-919-8786; www.trumpplaza.com; cnr Mississippi Ave & Boardwalk) In a nod to families, the Plaza has a Rainforest Cafe. Otherwise, it needs a makeover, and the Don knows it.

Trump Marina (☎ 609-441-2000, 800-677-7378; www.trumpmarina.com; cnr Huron Ave & Brigantine Blvd) The smallest and least interesting casino. It's actively for sale, dirt cheap. Jimmy Buffet almost bought it, but changed his mind.

BOARDWALK

The Boardwalk is over 4 miles long, and old-school arcades, boardwalk games and trinket shops squeeze in between the casinos. Judging by the number of psychics, the future in AC is clear.

In summer, bicycles are only allowed till 10am; for rentals, **B&K Bike Rental** (☎ 609-344-8008; Boardwalk & N Carolina Ave; per hr $8) is next to Resorts.

Don't want to walk? Hire a push cart, a Boardwalk tradition; it's $5 for five blocks.

As for the **beach**, north of Steel Pier erosion has taken most of it away, but the sand fills out nicely as you go south.

Atlantic City Historical Museum & Art Center

On Garden Pier at Connecticut Ave, the **Historical Museum** (☎ 609-347-5839; www.acmuseum.org; ☉ 10am-4pm) has attractive, fascinating exhibits devoted to AC's glory days. It's filled with nostalgic flotsam and jetsam: posters, poker chips, Miss America dresses, Mr Peanut, historic photos and a great movie.

Also here, the **Art Center** (☎ 609-347-5837; www.acartcenter.org; ☉ 10am-4pm) is a clean, bright space featuring regional and local art.

Steel Pier

A shadow of its former self, this **amusement pier** (☎ 866-386-6659; www.steelpier.com) is no longer the nation's showplace. It's just a collection of small amusement rides that wouldn't raise a pulse in Seaside or Wildwood.

Boardwalk Hall

The former site of the Miss America pageant, this was one of the world's largest auditoriums when it opened in 1929, and it still holds the world's biggest pipe organ – a beast with seven keyboards and 33,000 pipes. It's been under renovation since the late 1990s, and **organ tours** (☎ 609-348-7000; www.acchos.org; adult $20) are highly recommended (reservations required). Held on the first and third Tuesdays of the month, they are 2½ hours and very hands on.

Ripley's Believe It or Not

If the creatures on the Boardwalk aren't fascinating enough, step inside this **museum** (☎ 609-347-2001; www.ripleysatlanticcity.com; Boardwalk at New York Ave; adult/child 5-12yr $16/10; ☉ 11am-8pm) devoted to the bizarre.

Pier Shops at Caesars

You can't miss this green-glass behemoth fronting Caesar's. An upscale **shopping mall** (☎ 609-345-3100; www.thepiershopsatcaesars.com) with gourmet restaurants, it also has 3rd-floor views from Adirondack chairs in scalloped sand pits. The water fountain music-and-lights show is fun, too.

ATLANTIC CITY CONVENTION CENTER
The $300-million **Convention Center** (☎ 609-449-2000; www.accenter.com) is above the train station and connected to the Sheraton Hotel. It is also the north end of the Walk, Atlantic City's outdoor outlet mall. Altogether, this makes an attractive, safe, walkable corridor between the train station and the Boardwalk.

CIVIL RIGHTS GARDEN
Behind the Carnegie Library at Illinois and Pacific Aves is this outdoor sculpture garden commemorating the Civil Rights Movement. It's a peaceful space offering food for thought in a city with a strong African American legacy.

ABSECON LIGHTHOUSE
Ironically, New Jersey's tallest **lighthouse** (☎ 609-449-1360; www.abseconlighthouse.org; 31 S Rhode Island Ave; adult/child $7/4; ☺ 11am-4pm Thu-Mon) is now dwarfed by casinos. It's still stately and offers nice views.

GARDINER'S BASIN
Next to the marina is the tiny **Atlantic City Aquarium** (☎ 609-348-2880; www.acaquarium.com; adult/child 4-12 $8/5; ☺ 10am-5pm daily), designed for small kids. You'll find a picnic area, several restaurants, kayak rentals and in summer a 'crafters village' of shops.

Festivals & Events
Without the Miss America Pageant, AC's calendar doesn't feel the same. A fun tradition is the Polar Bear Plunge in January. The St Patrick's Day Parade is in early March, and the Puerto Rican Day Parade in July. The Atlantic City Marathon is in October. See www.atlanticcitynj.com for dates.

Sleeping
The accommodations service the visitors' center uses is **Central Reservations** (☎ 800-524-1706, 888-227-6667; www.accentralreservations.com); it buys room blocks and often has deals.

Staying at the casinos (see p264) can be either extremely affordable or a wallet-gouging outrage – it just depends on the season and *especially* the day of the week. As summer heats up, prices rise, but whatever the season, the weekday rate will at least double on Friday

and might triple on Saturday. In other words, a $90 room on Thursday might become $220 on Friday and $280 on Saturday – or even $350 if occupancy is high. Simply put, the weekends are when AC and its nightclubs are happening.

Also, the fancier the casino, the higher its rates: the Borgata discounts less because it doesn't have to. A room at Resorts or the Marina will be cheaper, and considerably less interesting. Bally's, Harrah's, the Tropicana, Taj Mahal and Caesar's are all attractive, decent places to stay, but unless you're in a high-roller suite, the rooms aren't going to blow you away.

Finally, Pacific Ave is lined with budget motels, but these are not, as a rule, recommended; many have terrible reputations for safety and, as well, being working motels.

Rates below are for high season (summer); low-season rates are steeply discounted.

NON-CASINO HOTELS
our pick **Chelsea Pub and Inn** (☎ 609-345-4700; www.chelseapubandinn.com; 8 S Morris Ave; r midweek $60-70, weekend $100-150; 🅿 💻 🛜) This rambling 1880 building is a casual European-style, 30-room B&B, meaning its imperfections enhance its genuine personality. Floors creak, rooms are funky but exceptionally clean, and all have private bath, no matter how small. Decor is charmingly eclectic: from a life-sized photo of a Philadelphia Eagles running back to Victorian-style red velvet curtains to the classic sky-blue, wicker seaside. Moreover, parking is free, breakfast is included and loaner bikes are available.

Courtyard Marriott Atlantic City (☎ 609-345-7070; www.courtyardatlanticcityhotel.com; 1212 Pacific Ave; r weekday $80-120, weekend $160-280; 🅿 💻 ♿) The old building was gutted, then reopened in 2008, so this 206-room Courtyard is a fresh, attractive stay with historic AC photos and a stylish lobby that avoids chain blandness. Rooms have minifridges, flat-screen TVs and good-sized bathrooms, plus there's a guest laundry and a fitness center with a large Jacuzzi. Parking is $12 per day.

Sheraton AC Convention Center (☎ 609-344-3535; www.sheraton.com/atlanticcity; 2 Convention Blvd; r weekday $125-152, weekend $190-340; 🅿 💻 ♿) The Sheraton has a stylish art deco theme and a lobby exhibit dedicated to Miss America. Many rooms have nice views, and they are dependable, top-quality chain nice, with flat-screen TVs, marble sinks and great desks. Within walking distance of the Boardwalk. Parking is $12 per day.

ourpick Chelsea (☎ 609-884-6567, 800-548-3030; www.thechelsea-ac.com; 111 S Chelsea Ave; r midweek $120-160, weekend $220-340; ☒ ▭ ☎ ☒) Hey hip-daddy, here's the boutique hotel you're looking for. Over 300 designer rooms are playfully tripped out in cheetah-print armchairs, parrot lamps and sea-green velvet curtains; rainfall, glass-wall showers are egregiously nice, as are the lush beds. It's right on the Boardwalk, and best of all, it has two pools, two restaurants, a tony spa and its very own nightclub scene – no need to go out! Quoted rates reflect standard internet deals; rack rates add $50 to $120. Parking is $5 per day.

Annex (☎ 609-884-6567, 800-548-3030; rooms midweek $110 to $150, weekend $140 to $340) Chelsea's recently renovated is attached to the Chelsea. It's slightly cheaper, and offers upscale motel, not boutique hotel, decor. It's clean, updated and cozy, and has access to all the Chelsea's amenities – but alas, no leopard prints or flatscreen TVs.

Water Club (☎ 609-317-8888, 800-800-8817; www.thewaterclubhotel.com; r midweek $150-180, weekend $240-380; ☒ ▭ ☎ ☒) Owned by the Borgata, the Water Club is its own experience. While it's hard to call a 43-story, 800-room hotel 'boutique,' the 'designer lifestyle' sensibility infuses the rooms completely. Gleaming natural woods are contrasted with marble, glass and metal; a mixture of chocolate-and-cream tones predominates; views are tremendous; and no technological need is missing. You are here, as well, for the five pools, indoor and out, and the spa. Like the Borgata, the mood is sexy-cool.

Eating

In the last seven years, Atlantic City dining has been transformed by the emergence of gourmet celebrity-chef restaurants in the casinos. These stylish places create a heady atmosphere of event dining unlike anything AC has been known for, and more are opening continually. Because casino restaurants are easy to find, we've focused on non-casino dining.

Also, casino buffets remain alive and kicking. A cheap, belt-busting meal is not hard to come by. The better ones, which transcend the typical cafeteria assembly line, are at Borgata, Harrah's and Caesar's. Depending on the meal, they run $15 to $28; the cheapies cost less.

Irish Pub (☎ 609-344-9063; www.theirishpub.com; 164 St James Pl, near the Boardwalk; dishes $4-7; ☺ food to 3am, bar 24hr) Another old-AC holdout, the atmospheric Irish Pub is the anti-nightclub spot, a dive bar that isn't divey at all, just an unpretentious, friendly place for a seriously inexpensive bite, a few Irish drafts and conversation. Walls are plastered with historic photos, and the low pressed-tin ceiling, wood bar and tiffany lamps make it feel like 2am any time.

Tony's Baltimore Grill (☎ 609-345-5766; www.baltimoregrill.com; 2800 Atlantic Ave at Iowa; dishes $5.50-10; ☺ restaurant 11am-3am, bar 24hr) For a time-warp to old AC, get a plain or sausage crisp-crust pizza at Tony's – one of the best pies on the shore. Nothing's changed in 50 years, not the Formica tables, the yellowed drop ceiling, the menu, the tabletop jukeboxes or the brusque, whiskey-voiced waitresses. But ask them if they miss the Miss America parade, and they get downright soft-hearted. Cash only.

ourpick White House Sub Shop (☎ 609-345-8599; 2301 Arctic Ave at Mississippi; subs half $6.50-7.50, whole $12.50-15; ☺ 10am-9pm) A sub landmark, a cheesesteak icon – everyone loves it. It's worth waiting for an orange-vinyl booth so you can admire the wall of fame: Elvis, Burt Lancaster, Guy Fieri, Ellen DeGeneres. When ordering to go, the counter guys get friendlier the faster you decide, so here's what you want: a half Italian with everything and oil. Say yes to peppers. Or get a half cheesesteak. A whole feeds a family of four. Cash only.

Teplitzky's (☎ 609-428-4550; Chelsea & Pacific Aves; dishes $9-12; ☎ 7am-8pm Sun-Thu, 7am-11pm Fri, 7am-midnight Sat) This retro '50s-style diner in the Chelsea (p268) stands out as a rare interesting breakfast spot in AC. A short menu of breakfast favorites and classic sandwiches is nicely prepared. Later, the back patio is a sunny place for a beer and a daily special ($15).

ourpick Dock's Oyster House (☎ 609-345-0092; www.docksoysterhouse.com; 2405 Atlantic Ave; mains $25-46; ☺ from 5pm) Since 1897, Dock's has been a top seafood restaurant in AC, and if anything, it's even better today. The oyster bar is a standout, and seafood preparations are both robust and refined; listen well to the market-fresh specials. Service is great, there's piano music, and the crisp dining room is lively and loud with conversation. Make reservations.

Buddakan (☎ 609-674-0100; www.buddakanac.com; Pier Shops, 3rd fl; mains $26-35; ☻ 11am-3:30pm, 5-10pm Mon-Fri, noon-11pm Sat & Sun) This Stephen Starr creation almost needs no introduction: the towering Buddha presides over a 24ft communal table, and the sophisticated French/Asian fusion cuisine delights the senses. Event dining at its best. It's in the Pier Shops on the Boardwalk, which has more good choices.

Knife & Fork Inn (☎ 609-344-1133; www.knifeandforkinn.com; cnr Atlantic & Pacific Aves; mains $28-45; ☻ from 5pm) This AC institution provides an ideal combination: a historic, beautiful dining room and bar with a contemporary gourmet menu – featuring seafood like crab and avocado terrine, tuna tartare and whole lobster. Don't let the faded exterior fool you. This is an elegant romantic meal with an old-world feel, courtesy of the fireplace, leaded-glass windows and trompe l'oeil mural.

Entertainment

As with dining, the casinos are now attracting younger crowds with chic, dress-to-impress nightclubs, trendy bars and top-flight music concerts, featuring all the big names, from Lady Gaga and the Black-Eyed Peas to Sting and Jay-Z. Post-show celebrity spotting is a club staple. While bars are open nightly, nightclubs are typically weekends only.

BARS & NIGHTCLUBS

Many casinos have lounge bars with fog-and-laser sexy dancer shows within their gambling areas, such as at Wild Wild West and the Taj Mahal. Three beach bars actually pull folks outside: the AC Hilton, Trump Plaza and Bally's, where Sammy Hagar has brought his Cabo Wabo style.

For nightclubs, dress to the nines or you may not get past the bouncers. The Borgata's mur.mur and Mixx (recently redone) remain the epitome of see-and-be-seen destinations. Caesar's Dusk also enjoys its share of after-hours celebrity visitors.

Coming on strong is Harrah's After Dark at the Pool, where you swim and preen at Joanna Krupa 'bad girl' parties and the like. Less manic DJ-led poolside happenings also define Borgata's Water Club and the Chelsea's Cabana Club – really, they're hard to resist.

The best thing Resorts has going for it is free-wheeling Boogie Nights, a retro paean to the '70s; club dancers sport white suits, stratospheric afros and include Rollergirl.

THEATERS

Headliners fill AC theaters year-round. The top venues are Borgata's Event Center; the **House of Blues** (☎ 609-343-4000; www.hob.com) in the Showboat casino, on the Boardwalk near Maryland Ave; and **Boardwalk Hall** (☎ 609-348-7000; www.boardwalkhall.com) on the Boardwalk between Florida and Mississippi Aves. In addition, the Taj Mahal, the AC Hilton and the Tropicana have large showrooms.

Comedy Stop (☎ 609-822-7353; www.thecomedystop.com; Pacific Ave in Tropicana Casino; admission $23-28), within the Tropicana, is AC's only comedy club, with a range of comedians nightly.

Shopping

In addition to the upscale shops in the casinos, Atlantic City has two shopping destinations.

The **Walk**, or **Atlantic City Outlets** (☎ 609-872-7002; www.acoutlets.com), is an outdoor outlet mall. Get name brands like Nike, Tommy Hilfiger, Donna Karan, Banana Republic and a hundred more at 20% to 50% off.

The **Pier Shops at Caesars** (☎ 609-345-3100; www.thepiershopsatcaesars.com), on the Boardwalk, is defined by trendy boutiques and decidedly undiscounted upscale stores.

Getting There & Away

AIR

Atlantic City International Airport (☎ 609-645-7895; www.acairport.com) is at AC Expressway exit 9. **Spirit Airlines** (☎ 800-772-7117; www.spiritair.com) and **AirTran** (☎ 800-247-8726; www.airtran.com) connect to Boston, Detroit, Atlanta and several Florida cities.

The **Royal Airport Shuttle** (☎ 609-748-9777; www.royalairportshuttle.com) and **AC Airport Car Service** (☎ 609-748-8853; www.609shuttle.com) offer daily services to New York, Newark and Philadelphia airports.

BUS

NJ Transit (☎ 800-772-2222; www.njtransit.com) runs buses from New York City and Philadelphia to the depot on Atlantic Ave between Michigan and Ohio Aves. For a better deal, check out the casino buses from New York and Philadelphia; they include food vouchers and slot credits.

For transport from New York's Port Authority, contact **Academy** (☎ 800-442-7272; www.academybus.com) or **Greyhound** (☎ 800-231-2222; www.greyhound.com). Academy's buses go directly to several casinos.

NEW JERSEY

CAR & MOTORCYCLE

Atlantic City is reached via exit 38 on the Garden State Pkwy. The Atlantic City Expressway runs directly from Philadelphia to Atlantic City.

TRAIN

NJ Transit runs trains from Philadelphia to Atlantic City; the trip takes about an hour. It also has direct trains from New York Penn Station on **Aces** (☎ 877-326-7428; www.acestrain.com); trips take under three hours.

Getting Around

The Atlantic City **Jitney** (609-344-8642; www.jitneys.net; ride $2.50) runs 24-hour buses along a few main corridors, such as Pacific Ave and Michigan Ave to the Convention Center/train station. Lines are color-coded; the Green Line runs to the marina-area casinos.

Along the Boardwalk, you can get rides in either rolling chairs or the tram.

For a taxi, call **Atlantic City Yellow Cabs** (☎ 609-344-1221). Casinos also arrange cab services to Margate and Cape May.

NEW JERSEY

AROUND ATLANTIC CITY

Renault Winery

This bucolic, 130-year-old **vineyard** (☎ 609-965-2111; www.renaultwinery.com; 72 N Bremen Ave), in Egg Harbor City, is known for its blueberry champagne. Guided tours ($3; from 10:30am to 4pm) of the historic winery include tastings and a museum highlighting antique wine glasses and goblets, some dating to the Middle Ages. At summer's end, the winery hosts a lighthearted grape-stomping festival. It has a restaurant and a golf course.

Take Route 30 west from Atlantic City for 16 miles to Bremen Ave, turn right and continue for 2½ miles to the winery.

Margate

pop 8500

A pleasant beach town just 3.5 miles south of Atlantic City on Absecon Island, Margate (www.margate-nj.com) is best known for its famous landmark – Lucy the Elephant. It also has a great beach and several popular restaurants.

From Atlantic City, take Atlantic Ave south several miles to Washington St; Lucy the Elephant is at this intersection. Head one block west on Washington St for Margate's main drag, Ventnor Ave; if you're looking for restaurants, keep going to the bayside to reach the restaurant strip.

LUCY THE ELEPHANT

A National Historic Landmark and a six-story zoomorphic delight, **Lucy the Elephant** (☎ 609-823-6473; www.lucytheelephant.org; adult/child 2-12yr $6/3; 🕒 10am-8pm Mon-Sat, to 5pm Sun, closed Mon-Tue & Sun winter) was built in 1881 as a promotional attraction to sell real estate. She went on to become a tavern and a summer home for an English doctor, but never a hotel. In 2009, the old girl got a new paint job, and she looks fab: with gleaming white tusks, toenails polished, eyes bright, her red-and-yellow blanket fluffed. Tours inside reveal her gleaming wood interior, thrilling views from the howdah and a peek out her eyeballs. A short video includes surreal footage from when she was moved down Atlantic Ave.

EATING

Tomatoes (☎ 609-822-7535; www.tomatoesmargate.com; 9300 Amherst Ave at Washington Ave; mains $26-36; 🕒 dinner) The menu is 'California eclectic' and the circular copper bar and wood booths enhance the LA vibe, giving Tomatoes a fun, trendy feel. It offers a sushi bar and separate tavern menu ($13 to $20).

Steve & Cookie's by the Bay (☎ 609-823-1163; www.steveandcookies.com; 9700 Amherst Ave at Monroe Ave; mains $27-36; 🕒 dinner) Should you wish for a romantic seafood extravaganza, with white tablecloths and live piano music, one graced with bayside views, this would be the place. Lobster, bouillabaisse and steaks draw raves.

OCEAN CITY

pop 14,700

Ocean City has perhaps the cleanest, friendliest, most pleasant boardwalk on the Jersey shore. Another beach community founded by Methodists, it remains a dry town, but that doesn't mean it's dowdy and too serious – just the opposite. Undeniably a family destination Ocean City knows how to have fun, and its wry playfulness appeals to everyone. Plus, the beaches are gorgeous.

On Rte 52 just past the inlet bridge into town, the **Chamber of Commerce Welcome Cente**[r] (☎ 609-399-2629, 800-232-2465; www.oceancityvacation.com; 16 E 9th St at Simpson Ave; 🕒 9am-5pm Mon-Fri, 10am-4pm Sat, 10am-2pm Sun) has complete information; the website tracks lodging availability, and the center will help you book a room. For more visit www.ocnj.us.

Ocean City's calendar is packed with quirky delights. Things really get lively in August, which has a sandcastle contest, the famous Miss Crustacean Pageant (a Miss America spoof), the Baby Parade (held for over a century), and then Weird Week, a bunch of 'Wacky But Not Tacky' goofiness. In April is the bassethound Doo Dah Parade, in May the 'Businessperson's Plunge,' and in late July 'Night in Venice,' one of the world's largest boat parades.

The local free weekly is the *Sandpaper* (www.oceancitygazette.com/sp). The main retail corridor is along Asbury Ave between 6th and 11th Sts, which parallels the amusement section of the boardwalk. From Garden State Parkway exit 30, take Rte 52 directly into town.

Sights & Activities

Ocean City's **boardwalk** is packed with the quintessential arcades and rides, but the teenage barkers aren't microphoned, so the atmosphere is less frantic. Minigolf is a standout: play around grimacing tiki, sharks, octopuses and reggae apes flying a helicopter. The two amusement centers are pint-sized perfection: **Castaway Cove** (www.oceancityfun.com) and castlelike **Gillian's Wonderland** (☎ 609-399-7082; www.gillians.com) have an ideal mix of rides for young kids, plus **Gillian's Waterpark** (www.gillianswaterpark.com). In July and August, the **Music Pier** hosts a series of music concerts and children's shows, courtesy of the **Stockton Performing Arts Center** (☎ 609-652-9000; www.intraweb.stockton.edu/pac).

And don't miss the oddball **Discovery Seashell Museum** (☎ 609-398-2316; www.shellmuseum.com; 2721 Asbury Ave at 27th St; ♥ 9am-7pm Mon-Sat Jun-Aug), a half-museum, half-store with an unbelievable collection of over 10,000 species. It's tucked away in a residential neighborhood.

Sleeping & Eating

Beach Club Hotel (☎ 609-399-8555; www.beachclubhotel.com; 1280 Boardwalk; r high $90-230, low $160-350; ♥ May-Sep; ✖ 🔲 🞫 🐕) Another well-kept standard hotel, right on the boardwalk. There's a laundry, pool and free beach tags; also has an onsite restaurant.

Forum Motor Inn (☎ 609-399-8700; www.theforummoc.homestead.com; Atlantic & Ocean Aves; r high $134-88, low $82-114; ♥ May-Sep; 🔲 🞫 🐕) This very clean, ship-shape motel has 55 rooms, all with fridge and microwave. Heated pool, guest laundry, outdoor shower and free beach tags make it ideal for families.

Flanders Hotel (☎ 609-399-1000; www.theflandershotel.com; 719 E 11th St; r from high $260-340, low $150-200; ✖ 🔲 🞫 🐕) The Flanders is more of a condotel, every room is essentially an immaculate, well-decorated furnished apartment with full kitchen and in-room laundry. Ideal for families and groups for extended stays. It's on the boardwalk, with a pool and free beach tags.

Cafe Beach Club (☎ 609-398-7700; www.cafebeachclub.com; mains $5-15; ♥ breakfast, lunch & dinner summer) Part of the Beach Club Hotel, this decent restaurant offers breakfast and Italian dinners.

701 Mosaic (☎ 609-398-2700; 701 E 4th St at Ocean Ave; mains $15-22; ♥ 8am-2pm & 5-9pm) The Jamaican owners have created the ideal shore restaurant – a soothing space with lively cuisine. The delectable jerk chicken is a family recipe, and the menu is a Caribbean fusion, with plantains, curry, fish and even a pasta putanesca.

Mack & Manco's (☎ 609-399-2548; www.mackandmancos.com; pie $17) In the shore pizza wars, this is the only pizzeria where staff twirl dough over their heads. Not the absolute 'best,' but very good. Three locations on the boardwalk; the 9th St location is open year-round.

WILDWOODS
pop 5300

The Wildwoods are three towns – North Wildwood, Wildwood and Wildwood Crest – steeped in the architectural doo-wop nostalgia of their 1950s hey-day and offering the biggest, most exciting collection of waterparks, roller coasters and amusement rides on the shore. Families and teens flock here, and there's a modest nightlife scene catering to the Eastern European exchange students who work the amusements.

In the '50s and '60s, as car and jet travel killed summer resorts further north, the Wildwoods embraced the future and thrived. Drive-up motels advertised with neon-lit space-age signs, plus the town appealed to rock 'n' roll–loving youth, booking the day's hippest musicians – Little Richard, Chubby Checker and more. Cruise along Wildwood Crest's Ocean Ave and time seems to have stood still – signage is a riot of sloops, angles and tropical fantasies. It's vintage roadside Americana. Yet youth is still served: in today's riotous boardwalk and the memories of parents.

DON'T MISS: BOARDWALK TREATS

Rides, shmides. Jersey boardwalks are about food. Here are five treats we can't live without:

- **Kohr's soft-serve ice cream** Cools you down from the inside out; found everywhere.
- **Saltwater taffy** A Jersey invention. In Ocean City, **Shrivers** (☎ 609-399-0100; www.shrivers.com); in Atlantic City, **Fralinger's** (☎ 800-938-2339; www.fralingers.com).
- **Curley's Fries** Hot and fresh – they're the best! A specialty in Wildwood and Ocean City.
- **Pizza** Don't miss Maruca's, Seaside Heights (p229); Tony's Baltimore Grill, Atlantic City (p268); Mack's Pizza and Sam's Pizza, Wildwood (p274); or Mack & Manco's, Ocean City (p271).
- **Hot dogs** In Long Branch, Max's (p218); in Wildwood, Maui's Dog House (p274); in Cape May, Hot Dog Tommy's (p279).

Orientation & Information

The **Wildwoods Information Center** (☎ 609-522-1407, 800-992-9732; www.wildwoodsnj.com; ☼ 10am-8pm in season, 10am-4pm after Labor Day) is on the boardwalk at Schellenger Ave. Another welcome center is on Rte 47, just before the inlet bridge. For more information, contact the **Greater Wildwood Chamber of Commerce** (☎ 609-729-4000; www.gwcoc.com).

The **post office** (3311 Atlantic Ave) is between Wildwood and Oak Aves.

Street parking is metered. It's easiest to use the large lot at Rio Grande and Ocean Aves, but arrive early.

In central Wildwood, the main downtown corridor is along Pacific Ave, between Wildwood and Rio Grande Aves. The doo-wop motels are primarily in Wildwood Crest, along Ocean Ave from Rio Grande Ave south. North Wildwood is the quiet north end of town.

Sights & Activities

GEORGE F BOYER HISTORICAL MUSEUM

This lovingly tended city **museum** (☎ 609-523-0277; www.funchase.com; 3907 Pacific Ave at Spicer Ave; admission by donation; ☼ 9am-2pm Mon-Sat summer, Thu-Sat low season) is a treasure trove of historic photos and boardwalk artifacts, which the congenial docent Bob Bright brings to life in a heartbeat. Definitely peruse the terrific website.

DOO-WOP MUSEUM

Across from the Convention Center, and fronting a picnic-friendly grassy park, is the new **Doo-Wop Museum** (☎ 609-523-4000; www.doowopusa.org; cnr Ocean & Burke Aves; free admission; ☼ 10am-noon & 5-10pm Fri-Sun), in a refurbished diner. Hours are limited, but the orgy of neon should not be missed. It has self-guided doo-wop tour brochures and conduct fantastic 90-minute trolley tours (adult/child $12/6) of the motels. Call for a schedule; summer only. For more doo-wop motel history, visit www.wildwooddoowop.com.

Adjacent to the museum is Wildwood's **Vietnam War Memorial**, unveiled in 2010. It's a scale re-creation of the Washington DC black wall.

HEREFORD INLET LIGHTHOUSE

In North Wildwood, this **lighthouse** (☎ 609-522-4520; www.herefordlighthouse.org; 111 N Central Ave at 1st Ave; adult/child $4/1; ☼ 9am-5pm summer, call in winter) is more of a historic-home tour focusing on the life of a lighthouse keeper. It's a modest testament to a bygone era.

BOARDWALK & BEACHES

Many Jersey beaches have erosion problems. Wildwood's beach is growing, and it's so wide near the amusement boardwalk it's a quarter mile to reach the water – but once there, the pretty sand is gently sloped and soporific. Wildwood Crest and North Wildwood beaches are normal size and much quieter; North Wildwood also has a cement seawall jogging path. Another plus: all Wildwoods beaches are free.

Three enormous all-ages amusement piers define Wildwood's boardwalk, which starts at the Convention Center on Montgomery Ave and goes north to around 23rd Ave. All are run by **Morey's Piers** (www.moreyspiers.com): Surfside Pier at 25th Ave with Ocean Oasis waterpark; Mariner's Landing at Schellenger Ave with Raging Waters waterpark; and Adventure Pier at Spencer Ave with the shore's best roller coaster, the Great White. The piers are open April to September, with varying hours and a slew of unlimited-ride wristband options. Typically, every day has a $20 to $30 ride deal.

A third, separately run waterpark is **Splash Zone** (☎ 609-729-5600; www.splashzonewaterpark.com; Boardwalk at Schellenger Ave; ⏱ Jun-Aug). If that's not enough, the boardwalk is choked with go-karts, an aquarium and win-a-prize carnival fun. If you brought marbles, dust off a National Marbles Tournament platform at Wildwood Ave and have at it.

Bicycles are allowed on the boardwalk till 11am; get rentals from **Surf Bikes** (☎ 609-729-5147; Ocean & Leaming Aves; bikes per hr from $7).

BOATING & FISHING

For fishing charters and sightseeing cruises, the Wildwood marina just past the inlet bridge on Rte 47 (look for the great white shark) has several options. **Royal Flush Fishing** (☎ 609-522-1395; www.royalflushfishing.com) runs four-hour fishing trips three times a day. **Adventurer Fishing** (☎ 609-729-7777; www.fishbox.tv/adventurer) runs six-hour trips. Join a dolphin-watching cruise on a speedboat, the **Silver Bullet** (☎ 609-522-6060; www.silverbullettours.com; adult/child $26/13). Or tear up the bayside on a waverunner from **Mocean Waverunners** (☎ 609-522-3159; www.moceanwaverunners.com; half/full hr $65/110). Mocean shares space with **No Bones Bait & Tackle** (☎ 609-522-3017), with fishing advice, tackle and more charters.

To rent a kayak or try your hand at crabbing, go to **Canal Side Boat Rental** (☎ 609-522-7676; cnr 18th & Delaware Aves; ⏱ May-Oct). You'll catch 'em, but they sell live crabs too.

SURFING

The Wildwoods have two dedicated surfing beaches that are perfect for beginners. Get advice and rentals from **Wild Ocean Surf Shop** (☎ 609-729-0004; Ocean & Leaming Aves; surfboards per day $25).

Festivals & Events

Like Ocean City, Wildwood's calendar is silly with events. Some highlights are Memorial Day weekend's International Kite Festival, with stunt kite and indoor kite competitions; late June's National Marbles Tournament; a super July 4 celebration; and July's NJ State BBQ Championship. Motocross and monster-truck races in the sand are popular, and naturally, the Fabulous '50s Weekend in October is the doo-wop highlight of Wildwood's year.

Sleeping

Even in the '50s, the unique signage was a showman's distraction from the modest sameness of motel rooms. Wildwood has over 200 motels, yet most have undistinguished accommodations. Rates vary by proximity to the boardwalk and the level of renovations.

Marlane Motel (☎ 609-522-7463; www.marlanemotel.com; 4310 Atlantic Ave; r high $110-140, low $85-115; ⏹ ⏹ ⏹) This family-owned, 25-room motel lacks retro chic, but that's about it. Rooms are well-cared-for, affordable jewels; kitchenettes are the most newly renovated. Friendly, on-site owners keep the atmosphere adult (not teen crazy); apparently, Canadians love it and book far in advance. Just within walking distance of the boardwalk.

Heart of Wildwood Motel (☎ 609-522-4090, 888-522-2248; www.heartofwildwood.com; 3915 Ocean View Ave; r high $130-270, low $100-190; ⏹ ⏹ ⏹) If location and cleanliness are everything, come here. Three buildings hold 74 rooms in a wealth of configurations. One building fronts the boardwalk; from its rooftop pool, you can hear the screams from the thrill rides and can watch the ferris wheel spin. Easily cleaned tile floors and sturdy, bland furniture define the decor.

Riviera Motel (☎ 609-522-5353; www.gotowildwood.com; Spicer & Ocean Aves; r high $150-200, low $105-150; ⏱ Apr-Sep; ⏹ 🛜 ⏹ ⏹) Next door, the Riviera is a very similar family-focused option if you want to make the most of your wristbands. It runs the adjacent Sea-n-Sun Motel, giving it 57 standard, well-kept, clean motel rooms only steps from the fun.

Caribbean Motel (☎ 609-522-8292; www.caribbeanmotel.com; 5600 Ocean Ave, Wildwood Crest; r high $150-205, low $80-150; ⏱ Apr-Oct; ⏹ 🛜 ⏹ ⏹) This renovated, retro doo-wop gem has rooms so bright they might keep you awake: lime-green walls, canary-yellow furniture, and mint-green with pink bathrooms. Wow. Also stylin' is the rainbow-arch pool, the angle-windowed 2nd-floor lounge, the plastic palm trees and the shuffleboard. Summer weekend events make it a party.

ourpick Summer Nites B&B (☎ 609-846-1955, 866-762-1950; www.summernites.com; 2110 Atlantic Ave at 22nd Ave; r high $155-280, low $115-230; ⏹ 🛜) Designed to break the hearts of romantic Boomer couples, this B&B is a paean to the '50s. Eight themed rooms are filled with classic photos and posters, signed memorabilia and some outrageously cool murals – of '50s TV stars, Marilyn Monroe and *(sigh)* Elvis. Several places have whirlpool tubs. Breakfast is in a perfectly re-created diner with jukeboxes. Summer lovin', indeed. Look for the cherry-red Bel-Air.

StarLux (☎ 609-522-7412; www.thestarlux.com; 305 E Rio Grande Ave; r high $200-305, low $100-200; ☒ ☎ ☒ ☒) This classic doo-wop motel's magnificent profile contains 36 rooms to match: with wiggly mirrors and curved furniture, googie-print fabrics and stainless-steel bathroom sinks. Kitchenettes have full fridges and decent space. There's a heart-shaped pool, loaner bikes and helpful 'beachgear porters' for families. Two Airstream trailers are icing on the cake.

Eating

Fine dining is not Wildwood's strong suit. Stick to shore favorites, and head to Cape May for that nice evening out.

Maui's Dog House (☎ 609-846-0444; www.mauis doghouse.com; 806 New Jersey Ave at 8th Ave; hot dogs $3-4.50; ☒ 11am-4pm Apr-Oct, to 8pm summer) This only-in-Jersey, off-the-beach shack serves some of the shore's best hot dogs in dog bowls, with a heaping side of sarcasm. The horseradish mustard really bites and the spicy fries are friggin' awesome, as are their 'salty balls.' Try one! Look for the orange-striped awning. Cash only.

Wildwood's famous pizza battle is between **Mack's Pizza** (☎ 609-522-6166; Boardwalk at Wildwood Ave) and **Sam's Pizza Palace** (☎ 609-522-6017; www. samspizzawildwood.com; Boardwalk at 26th St). Both are thin crust, but Mack's adds cheddar cheese. They're within six blocks of each other, so you decide. If looks count, pinkalicious Mack's wins by a nose. Cash only.

Getting a good-quality diner-style breakfast is easy: just go to the corner of Pacific and Andrews Aves. On one corner is **Uncle Bill's Pancake House** (☎ 609-729-7557; 4601 Pacific Ave; mains $6-9; ☒ 7am-2pm), with a long menu and all the basics (cash only). On the opposite corner is **Key West Cafe** (☎ 609-522-5006; 4701 Pacific Ave; mains $4.50-10; ☒ 7am-2pm), which adds tropical decor.

For dinner, skip Wildwood's tired seafood joints and find **Dominic's Place** (☎ 609-522-2630; www.dominicsplace.com; 5209 Pacific Ave; main $19-27; ☒ from 4:30pm Wed-Sun), a tiny casual Italian place offering well-prepared classics and a few pastas. BYOB.

Entertainment

At night, **Luna** (☎ 609-729-0120; www.lunanj.com; 3800 Pacific Ave at Garfield Ave; ☒ Tue-Sun) turns from a restaurant into a nightclub catering to young Eastern Europeans with 'Bulgarian Nights' and Russian Standard vodka. There are three or four more bars within a block.

At Schellenger and Atlantic Aves are another cluster of bars, of which **Stardust** (☎ 609-522-8503; www.myspace.com/stardustnightclub) is the most lively club, with two floors and several DJs.

Getting There & Around

The **bus stop** (☎ 609-522-2491) is at New Jersey Ave (between Davis and Burk). **NJ Transit** (☎ 800-772-2222; www.njtransit.com) runs buses from New York City (two hours) and Philadelphia (90 minutes).

Driving, take Garden State Parkway exit 4 to Rio Grande Ave, which runs east to Wildwood's beachfront.

'Watch the tram car, please.' Don't know this phrase? You will. It's the boardwalk's **Sightseer Tram** (☎ 609-523-8726; 1-way $2.50), running from 10am to 1am in summer. The **Wildwood trolley** (☎ 609-884-5230; www.gatrolley.com; one-way $2.50) runs along Ocean and Atlantic Aves, from Schellenger Ave in Wildwood to Jefferson Ave in Wildwood Crest, in summer.

CAPE MAY
pop 3700

At the southern tip of New Jersey, Cape May is one of the oldest seashore resorts in the US. Like Wildwood, it plays off nostalgia, but it reaches back four times as far. With over 600 gingerbread Victorian homes, the entire town is designated a National Historic Landmark. The pace is slower, the mood more genteel. Cape May likes to remind visitors that it resides below the Mason-Dixon Line, making it technically part of the South. If the whole point of a shore vacation is relaxation, no place succeeds as well as Cape Maybe, locals quip, where everything gets done… eventually.

Victorian B&Bs and gourmet dining define Cape May, but it's a natural beauty too. Dreamy white strands stretch around the point, which is a major migratory flyway for shorebirds and a home for whales and dolphins. An 18th-century whaling center, Cape May remains a major commercial fishery, ranking 13th in the nation. Through the 19th century, four US presidents vacationed here, and it was one of the East Coast's toniest resorts, rivaling Newport, Rhode Island. Then a massive 1878 fire decimated the town center, and it never quite regained its stature. Most of the historic architecture dates from this time.

Still, Cape May possesses a certain magic that's hard to quantify. How charmed is a place where 'diamonds' wash up on the beach and you can toast both sunrise and sunset over the water? It may not be the South, but it doesn't seem like Jersey either.

Orientation & Information

Three municipalities occupy the island. From east to west they are Cape May, the main commercial center; West Cape May, a largely residential area; and Cape May Point, with the state park and Sunset Beach. In downtown Cape May, Washington St between Ocean and Perry Sts is a pedestrian mall.

The **Cape May Welcome Center** (☎ 609-884-5508; www.capemaychamber.com; ☺ 9am-5pm) is in the transportation center building at Lafayette and Ocean Sts; it has comprehensive information and tracks accommodations availability online. For more, visit www.capemaytimes. com. At Ocean St on the Washington Street Mall is also a staffed information booth

This Week, published by the Mid-Atlantic Center for the Arts (www.capemaymac.org), lists the week's events. *Exit Zero* (www.exit zero.us), another free weekly, also doubles as the defacto social pages, providing a humorous window into local life. **Gables** (www.gables capemay.com) covers Cape May's gay community.

There's a **post office** (700 Washington St), and the main bookstore is **Atlantic Books** (☎ 609-898-9694; www.atlanticbooks.us; 500 Washington St Mall; ☺ 9:30am-5:30pm).

Cape May Public Library (☎ 609-884-9568; cnr Ocean St & Hughes Ave; ☺ 9am-5pm Mon-Fri, to 8pm Tue & Thu, 9am-4pm Sat) provides internet terminals; get a $10 annual card for unlimited access. **Washington Commons** (cnr Ocean & Lafayette Sts) has a large grocery store and bank; it allows free 40-minute parking.

Sights & Activities

EMLEN PHYSICK ESTATE

This elegant, well-preserved 18-room **mansion** (☎ 609-884-5404; www.capemaymac.org; 1048 Washington St; adult/child $10/5; ☺ 10am-5pm) was built in 1879; 45-minute tours leave hourly. This is also the home of the Mid-Atlantic Center for the Arts. Book trolley tours here and browse the nice

gift shop. The **teahouse** (☺ 11:30am-3pm) offers a civilized way to wait for your tour.

SUNSET BEACH

This beach enjoys sunset over an unobstructed horizon of water, and it's a beauty. The daily sunset celebration begins with a flag-lowering ceremony (Memorial Day through October), using the casket flags of veterans and accompanied by the national anthem. Then everyone toasts the sun and resumes exploring the pebbly beach for 'Cape May diamonds' – bits of crystal quartz that tumble down the Delaware River and wash up here. Polished and faceted, they indeed resemble jewels.

Just offshore is the crumbling remains of an experimental **concrete ship**, built during WWI. This deteriorating avant-garde wreck is one reason there's no swimming.

For sunset times, call the **gift shop** (☎ 609-884-7079; www.sunsetbeachnj.com; ☺ 8:30am-dusk), which runs a beach grill and minigolf. For a view from altitude, visit the nearby **Fire Control Tower** (www.capemaymac.org; Sunset Blvd; adult/child $6/2.50; ☺ 10am-4pm), built during WWII to watch for enemy ships. At 71ft, it's half the height of the lighthouse.

CAPE MAY POINT STATE PARK

This **state park** (☎ 609-884-2159; 707 E Lake Dr; ☺ museum 8am-6pm summer, to 4pm winter, park dawn-dusk) has pretty trails and platforms for observing the millions of migratory birds who arrive annually, while from its gorgeous (nonswimming) beach you can often watch dolphins frolicking offshore. A small museum has live turtles and snakes and interesting displays on the point's erosion.

Also here, the red-and-white, 157ft **Cape May Lighthouse** (☎ 609-884-5404; www.capemaymac. org; adult/child $7/3; ☺ 9am-8pm summer, call low season), built in 1859, has 217 steps to the top, where you'll get a panoramic vista.

CAPE MAY BIRD OBSERVATORY

Birding in Cape May is unparalleled, and the **Bird Observatory** (☎ 609-884-2736; www.birdcapemay. org; 701 E Lake Dr; ☺ 9:30am-4:30pm Apr-Oct, closed Tue Nov-Mar) is 'bird central.' It runs programs and conducts tours year-round (spring and fall are best). One of the most dramatic events is in May, when thousands of shorebirds swarm bayside beaches to feed on horseshoe crab eggs. Also in May is the World Series of Birding, and in October the Raptor Watch. The center

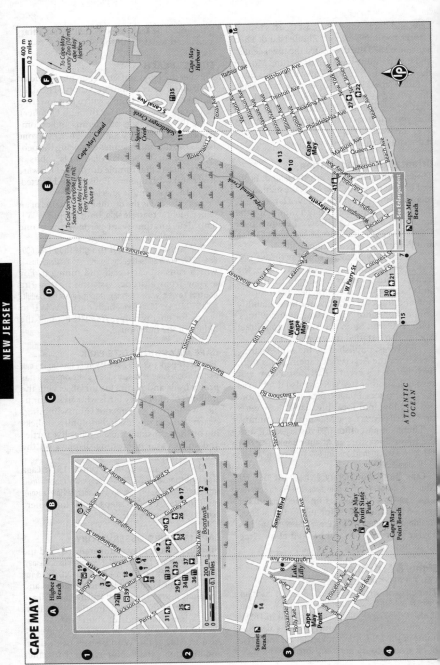

sells every imaginable birding and nature book and the best optics money can buy. It's off Lighthouse Ave, the road to the state park.

NATURE CENTER OF CAPE MAY

Affiliated with the Audubon Society, the **Nature Center** (☎ 609-898-8848; www.njaudubon. org/centers/nccm; 1600 Delaware Ave at Brooklyn Ave) is another good resource for birding and kid-friendly nature explorations. It has a few small exhibits, but don't trek to the center unless you've booked a trip. Weekends are busiest, with bike tours, kayak trips, seining in the harbor, and more. Call for hours and fees. It's north of downtown, on Cape May Harbor.

SWIMMING BEACHES

Long, narrow **Cape May Beach** is an idyllic gleaming strand (tags $5). At the west end, past the fishing jetty, is an area dubbed 'the Cove,' with the best bodyboarding. To escape the crowds, walk east. The boardwalk has only one small amusement arcade.

In West Cape May is free **Higbee Beach**. A quiet, secluded local's spot (without lifeguards), the beach is backed by fragrant dunes and littered with driftwood. It's frequented by dog walkers and napping sunbathers. From Sunset Blvd, take Bayshore Rd/Rte 607 north, turn left onto New England Rd/Rte 641, and follow till it ends.

HISTORIC COLD SPRING VILLAGE

Designed for kids, **Cold Spring Village** (☎ 609-898-2300; www.hcsv.org; 720 Rte 9; adult/child 3-12yr $8/6; ☿ 10am-4:30pm Tue-Sun late Jun-Labor Day) re-creates early-19th-century life in South Jersey, with historic buildings and docents in colonial dress. It's also open some weekends in June and September. From Cape May, take Lafayette St/Rte 109 north, left on Sandman Blvd/Rte 9, and follow signs.

CAPE MAY COUNTY PARK & ZOO

Far north of town, **Cape May County Park & Zoo** (☎ 609-465-5271; www.capemaycountyzoo.org; admission by donation; ☿ 10am-4:30pm) is a pleasant surprise. The spacious park has picnic areas and playgrounds for kids to run loose, and the adjacent zoo is an attractive facility. Shady, raised boardwalks make great perches to admire giraffes, zebras, lions and tigers, and the aviary is a walkthrough treat. Families pack the place on weekends. Take the signed Garden State Parkway exit 11.

WHALE-WATCHING

Cape May Whale Watcher (☎ 609-884-5445, 800-786-5445; www.capemaywhalewatcher.com; 2nd Ave & Wilson Dr) has three trips daily, including a three-hour whale tour (adult/child $38/25) and a two-hour dolphin tour ($28/20). Sightings are 'guaranteed.'

FISHING & BOATING

Popular fishing jetties are at the west end of Beach Dr. Offshore fishing often pulls in tuna and blue marlin in summer and varieties of shark year-round. Party boats leave daily from the **Miss Chris Marina** (☎ 609-884-3351; www.miss chrismarina.com; 3rd Ave & Wilson Dr), which also rents kayaks and crabbing boats.

NEW JERSEY

NEW JERSEY

TENNIS

Next to Emlen Physick, **Cape May Tennis Club** (☎ 609-884-8986; www.capemaytennisclub.com; 1020 Washington St; ☺ 8am-dusk) has 16 pretty courts, enclosed by vine-covered fences, open on a first-come, first-serve basis (walk-on $12 per person). It loans rackets and sells tennis balls.

BICYCLING

For surreys and all types of bikes, head to **Shield's** (☎ 609-898-1818; 11 Gurney St; ☺ 8am-6pm) and **Village Bike Shop** (☎ 609-884-8500; Lafayette & Ocean Sts; ☺ 9am-5pm Mon-Fri, 7:30am-7pm Sat & Sun); rates are $10 to $15 per day.

Tours

The **Mid-Atlantic Center for the Arts** (☎ 609-884-5404, 800-275-4278; www.capemaymac.org; 1048 Washington St) offers an enormous range of Cape May walking and trolley tours, plus a few boat tours. Most leave from the Washington St pedestrian mall at Ocean St, where there's a ticket booth. Tours take in the town's Victorian architecture, gardens, wineries, nature, the wharf, WWII history and more. The Cape May ghost and moonlight tours are popular and the most fun. Most tours are $10; those involving boats and food cost more.

Festivals & Events

Cape May has events year-round; visit www.capemaymac.org for schedules. The mid-April **Cape May Jazz Festival** (www.capemayjazz.com) is a highlight. Birders won't want to miss mid-May's **World Series of Birding** (www.birdcapemay.org/wsob.shtml). In both March and November, Sherlock Holmes Weekend involves an interactive mystery. And the town pulls out the stops for October's Victorian Week.

Sleeping

Cape May is defined by its gorgeous Victorian B&Bs and inns, but in summer, even standard motels charge a premium. Most places are open year-round.

BUDGET

Seashore Campsites (☎ 609-884-4010, 800-313-2267; www.seashorecampsites.com; 720 Seashore Rd; sites without/with hookups high $53/62, low $31/35; ☺ mid-Apr–Oct) A pristine full-service campground on 90 wooded acres. It caters to RVs, but has plenty of wooded tent sites. The complex includes a swimming lake, pool, sports courts, convenience store and laundry. From Cape May, take Rte 626 (Broadway) north; it's about a mile past the Rte 109 intersection.

MIDRANGE

our pick Abbey Inn (☎ 609-884-4506; www.abbeybedandbreakfast.com; 34 Gurney St; r high $130-200, low $95-170; ☒ ☞) No place in town can match the Victorian phantasmagoria and quirky, unpredictable charm of this rambling mansion. Jay, the owner, is an incorrigible raconteur, ensuring guests enjoy themselves. The seven rooms revel in funky, unpolished splendor, each uniquely memorable, with standing harps, crystal chandeliers, clawfoot tubs, pull-chain toilets and on and on. It won't please the tea-and-doilies crowd, and Jay couldn't care less.

Victorian Motel (☎ 609-884-7044; www.victorianmotelnj.com; 223 Congress Place; r high $155-195, low $80-140; ☒ ☞ ☒ ☒) This recently renovated standard motel has new furniture, tiled baths and pleasing brown tones that avoid seaside cliches. Most of the 38 rooms have workable efficiencies, the staff is very friendly, and the 2nd-floor sundeck lets you people-watch the Washington St parade.

DETOUR: WHEATONARTS

For a stunning experience of glass-making artistry, detour to Millville's **WheatonArts and Cultural Center** (☎ 856-825-6800, 800-998-4552; www.wheatonarts.org; 1501 Glasstown Rd, Millville; adult/child $10/7; ☺ 10am-5pm Tue-Sun Apr-Dec, Fri-Sun Jan-Mar). Its Museum of American Glass displays a magnificent collection, unmatched anywhere, of historical glass from the earliest American bottles to art nouveau lamps, Edison Christmas lights, glass caskets and a mind-blowing paperweight collection. Breathtaking modern pieces defy comprehension. Professional artists give glass-making and ceramic demonstrations; it has a one-on-one make-your-own glass-making program ($55 to $135; reserve ahead), and the cultural Down Jersey Folklife Center. Too bad it doesn't have a gift shop – it has five.

From Cape May, take Rte 47 north to Rte 55, then continue north to exit 26. Turn left onto Rte 555/Main Rd, then left onto Wade Blvd. The entrance is a half mile further, on the right.

Buckingham Motel (☎ 609-884-4073; www.bucking hammotel.com; 1111 Beach Ave; r high $158-177, low $75-145; 🔀 🛜 ♿) A perfectly located, friendly, no-frills motel, with 19 plain-but-clean rooms and seven workable efficiencies. Families enjoy the grassy BBQ area and being steps from the sand.

Sea Crest Motor Inn (☎ 609-884-4561; www.sea crestinn.com; 101 Beach Ave; r high $145-275, low $80-175; 🌛 Apr-Nov; 🔀 🛜 🖵) This well-kept, 55-room, family-owned motel restricts children to 12 and older to maintain an adult mood, particularly around the pool. Request a renovated ocean-front room, with wood floors, tiled baths, picture windows and breezy screens. Decor has a contemporary seaside vibe.

Carroll Villa Hotel (☎ 877-275-8452; www.carrollvilla. com; 19 Jackson St; r high $180-260, low $100-200; 🔀 🛜) This pretty 22-room, 1882 hotel feels like an unpretentious B&B. Ornate wallpapers, period photos, framed lace, and antiques mixed with modern touches create a relaxed Victorian atmosphere. Perfect downtown location, breakfast vouchers for the Mad Batter downstairs, and free off-site parking.

TOP END

ourpick **Mission Inn** (☎ 609-884-8380, 800-800-8380; www.missioninn.net; 1117 New Jersey Ave; r $215-310; 🔀 🛜) Escape smothering Victoriana at this refreshing, artistic B&B. Each of the eight rooms are playfully reimagined using immersive trompe l'oeil murals inspired by California's Spanish missions. They include spa tubs, fireplaces and flat-screen TVs. Public spaces and porches are just as soothing, immaculate and beautiful, and your gracious hosts serve a gourmet breakfast.

Beach Shack (☎ 877-742-2507; www.beachshack.com; 205 Beach Ave; r high $300-350, low $170-240; 🌛 May-Oct; 🔀 🛜 🖵 ♿) This 66-room motel has been remade into a stylish boutique property designed to appeal to families. Tangerine-colored rooms have plush linens, cool furniture and flat-screen TVs; efficiencies are functional. The pool is nice, but the 'sand pit' is nicer, an outdoor lounge and firepit next to the Rusty Nail (p280).

Columbia House (☎ 609-884-2789; www.thecolumbia house.com; 26 Ocean St; ste weekly high $1600-2900, nightly low $150-350; 🔀 🛜) An alternative to B&Bs, the four spacious suites in this guesthouse let you indulge in Victorian splendor. Ornately furnished with stunning antiques, wallpapers and decor, each has a full kitchen, dining area and living room, plus a shared outdoor garden.

It doesn't get better for secluded romantic getaways. In summer, weekly rentals only.

Congress Hall (☎ 609-884-8421, 888-944-1816; www.congresshall.com; cnr Perry St & Beach Ave; r high $360-460, low $140-290; 🔀 🛜 🖵 ♿) Cape May's grandest landmark, the lemon-yellow, white-columned Congress Hall is a wedding favorite. It gets knocks for noise and sometimes distracted service, but stylish, contemporary rooms will fulfill your elegant seaside fantasies. Gorgeous tile-and-marble bathrooms, cool blue decor and false, wood-slat hall doors add beachy charm. Great pool and spa, and several bars/restaurants on-site.

Other highly recommended, posh Victorian B&Bs are:

Queen Victoria B&B (☎ 609-884-8702; www.queenvictoria.com; 102 Ocean Street; r high $230-320, low $150-280; 🔀 🛜)

John Wesley Inn (☎ 609-884-1012, 800-616-5122; www.johnwesleyinn.com; 30 Gurney St; r high $265-345, low $150-250; 🔀 🛜)

Saltwood House (☎ 609-884-6754; www.saltwood house.com; 28 Jackson St; r high $135-330, low $100-295; 🔀 🛜)

Eating

In a quirk of NJ liquor laws, most of Cape May restaurants are BYOBs. Conversely, all of the bars under Drinking & Entertainment serve budget-friendly, no-regrets restaurant meals.

BUDGET & MIDRANGE

ourpick **Hot Dog Tommy's** (☎ 609-884-8388; www.hot dogtommys.com; Jackson St at Beach Ave; hot dogs $2-4; 🌛 9:57am-6:01pm) Tommy is the wise-cracker in the hot dog hat; like he says, 'Relish today, ketchup tomorrow.' Try Mary's homemade cranberry coleslaw on an all-beef dog with a frozen soda; better yet, try two. Hole-in-the-wall hot-dog stands don't get much better.

Mad Batter (☎ 609-884-5970; www.madbatter.com; 19 Jackson St; breakfast $8-12.50, dinner $13-29; 🌛 8am-3pm & from 5pm) A great Cape May moment: sitting under the Mad Batter's yellow-and-white-striped awning, enjoying the excellent crab eggs benedict or blueberry pancakes, while the breeze carries the sounds of morning. Dinner is fine, the bar is social, but breakfast is the star. The back patio isn't bad either.

Blue Pig Tavern (☎ 609-884-8422; 251 Beach Ave, Congress Hall; mains $15-32; 🌛 7:30am-2pm & 5pm) Casual, and attractive patio, plus upscale comfort food all day, and nightly 'blue plate specials' of prime rib and linguini in clam sauce.

Sean's Restaurant (☎ 609-898-0017; www.seansrest aurant.com; 314 Beach Ave; dinner mains $22-33; ☼ 7-11am Fri-Sun, 11am-10pm Mon & Thu-Sun) This casual BYOB pulls out tablecloths and candles for dinner and uses plastic beach pails as wine buckets. Focus on market-inspired specials: typically fresh seafood with peppery, Pacific Rim accents, like spicy shrimp with mango salsa or scallops with Thai chili sauce. Great bisque and crab cakes. Gregarious Sean likes to circulate front of house.

TOP END

Lobster House (☎ 609-884-8296; www.lobsterhouse.com; 906 Schellengers Landing Rd at Lafayette St, Fisherman's Wharf; mains $21-48, takeout $10-20; ☼ restaurant 11:30am-10pm, market 8am-7pm) Yes, it's touristy, and you have to fight like a seagull for a wharfside table, but it's a quintessential shore experience: enjoy sunset next to moored boats, slurping oysters and cracking lobsters. The restaurant is calmer but not as much fun. A fresh fish market and schooner bar rounds out the scene. Come early; no reservations.

ourpick 410 Bank Street (☎ 609-884-2127; www.410bankstreet.com; 410 Bank St; mains $28-42; ☼ dinner) The spinning fans and green lamppost inside the covered patio provide a romantic whiff of French Quarter atmosphere, along with playful crayon-and-paper tops. The cuisine emphasizes perfectly done mesquite-grilled fish and meats, which are ladled with robust Caribbean and Creole sauces, along with gumbos and bisques. A long-standing favorite, the cuisine isn't innovative, but little in Cape May is. Instead, 410 is fun, social, delicious and satisfying.

Ebbitt Room (☎ 609-884-5700, 800-732-4236; www. virginiahotel.com/ebbitt.html; 25 Jackson St, Virginia Hotel; mains $28-45; ☼ dinner) The chefs may change, but the Ebbitt Room continues to set Cape May's gourmet standard. The seasonal menu emphasizes farm-to-table freshness and refined, French-influenced preparations, with a smattering of international flavors. Extensive wine list and good service, though it doesn't always match the cuisine and the formal setting.

Drinking & Entertainment

Carney's (☎ 609-884-4424; www.carneyscapemaynj.com; 411 Beach Ave) is an unpretentious social fixture, with entertainment nightly. The same can be said of the **Ugly Mug** (☎ 609-884-3459; 426 Washington St at Decatur), where locals gather to gossip and sing 'Sweet Caroline' at midnight on Tuesday.

A breezy beachside choice is the **Rusty Nail** (☎ 609-884-0017; 205 Beach Ave, Beach Shack); finagle a 'sand pit' seat and enjoy live music nightly.

Congress Hall has a hip hotel bar, the **Brown Room** (☎ 609-884-8421; www.congresshall.com), and a basement-level nightclub, the **Boiler Room** (☼ Fri & Sat), an industrial-chic place to dance, with stone walls, metal tables and fuzzy red lamps.

An excellent regional theater, **Cape May Stage** (☎ 609-884-1341; www.capemaystage.com; cnr Bank & Lafayette Sts) presents around eight shows from May to December, from world premiere's to Samuel Beckett's *Happy Day*s to Broadway musical revues.

Shopping

The Washington St pedestrian mall makes for a pleasant stroll for fudge, ice cream, clothes and seaside gifts. To bring some beachy decor home, visit **Wanderlust** (☎ 609-884-0488; 609 Jefferson St near Columbia), stocked with seagrass rugs and retro signs.

The hippest logo-wear in town says **Exit Zero** (☎ 609-770-8479; www.exitzero.us; 109 Sunset Blvd), which also publishes glossy photo books on the history of the area.

Getting There & Away

BUS

NJ Transit (☎ 201-762-5100, 800-772-2222; www.njtran sit.com) runs buses from New York City and Philadelphia. They arrive at the **Cape May Transportation Center** (☎ 609-884-9562) at Lafayette and Ocean Sts.

BOAT

The **Cape May-Lewes Ferry** (☎ 800-643-3779; www.cmlf. com) runs daily between North Cape May and Lewes (pronounced 'Lewis'), Delaware. The 17-mile trip across Delaware Bay takes about 85 minutes. It can be convenient for drivers heading south, or for day-trippers wanting to visit Delaware's Lewes and Rehoboth beaches; buses complete the journey.

Ferries run daily year-round, but the number of trips varies from four in winter to 14 in summer. The one-way fare for vehicle and driver runs $30 to $44; foot passengers adult/child aged six to 13 $10/5.

North Cape May's ferry terminal is on Rte 9 west of the Garden State Parkway.

CAR & MOTORCYCLE

Take the Garden State Parkway to exit 0 and keep going.

Philadelphia

The City of Brotherly Love, once the stomping ground of Benjamin Franklin and Thomas Jefferson, is the home of the Liberty Bell and the birthplace of the US Constitution. It's a city famous for its pop-culture icons: for Springsteen ballads, and for Rocky getting into fighting shape on the steps of the art museum. It's also the city responsible for cream cheese, cheesesteaks and gargantuan fireworks displays on the Fourth of July.

Despite its rich cultural history, Philadelphia is a city that was notorious just a short time ago for crime, pollution and financial woes. With his much-quoted statement, 'I'd rather be dead than live in Philadelphia,' WC Fields gave voice – and a scathing comic edge – to the public opinion of Pennsylvania's largest city. In the early '90s, Mayor Ed Rendell took the bull by the horns, determined to transform the city and restore its original luster; today's bustling metropolis is a testament to his efforts.

Of course, the recent renaissance didn't solve all of the big city's problems, but it did make Center City into a supremely beautiful and livable urban center, an oasis almost unimaginable in 1990. Some of the outer neighborhoods still suffer from urban blight; others, like University City and Northern Liberties, are thriving cultural centers. Some can't believe their eyes when they see the changes; others debate whether this gentrification is really so desirable. After all, they suggest, Philly wasn't so bad – even WC Fields changed his mind. Before he died in 1925, he jokingly suggested his own epitaph: 'I would rather be living in Philadelphia.'

PHILADELPHIA

HIGHLIGHTS

- Eating the best Philly cheesesteak at **Pat's King of Steaks** (p309) or **Geno's** (p309)
- Being thankful for your freedom at the **Eastern State Penitentiary** (p298)
- Riding the **Fairmount Park** (p299) bike trails
- Listening to live acoustic music at the **World Cafe Live** (p309)
- Looking for creative inspiration at **Philadelphia's Magic Gardens** (p296)
- Heading to the **Reading Terminal Market** (p294) for coffee, croissants and people-watching
- Marveling at the wonder of modern sound technology at the **Kimmel Center** (p295)

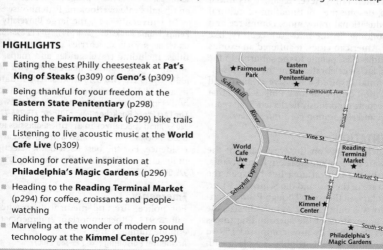

- POPULATION: 1,447,400
- AREA: 159 sq miles

HISTORY

William Penn made Philadelphia his capital in 1682, naming it after the Greek phrase for 'brotherly love.' A survivor of London's Great Fire of 1666, Penn oversaw the plans for the city that included a grid system with wide streets, not the narrow, winding maze that caused so much havoc in England's capital. This format was the inspiration for most American cities.

Philadelphia quickly grew to become the second largest city (after London) in the British Empire, before ceding that title to New York City. Opposition to British policy in the colonies became focused here, and colonial leaders met to plan their course of action. The end result was the Declaration of Independence, and in 1790 the city became the temporary capital of the new United States before Washington, DC, got the job in 1800. The US Constitution was drawn up and first read here in 1786. Philadelphia became a center of exciting new developments in the world of arts and science, led by the amazingly talented Benjamin Franklin.

Between 1793 and 1820 the citizens suffered five yellow fever epidemics, which killed thousands but led to the construction of the nation's first city water system.

Philadelphia's fortunes declined in the 1800s as New York City took over as the nation's cultural, commercial and industrial center. Philly never regained its initial status, despite the continuation of cultural and educational innovation, commerce and shipbuilding. In the mid-20th century, like many American cities, it suffered an exodus of middle-class people to the suburbs. In the 1970s, lavish celebrations for the nation's bicentennial inspired a massive cleanup and renovation campaign for a Philadelphia that had become notoriously neglected. That renovation and restoration continues today.

ORIENTATION

Philadelphia sits on the west bank of the Delaware River in southeastern Pennsylvania. Most of the central area lies between the Delaware in the east and the Schuylkill River, a tributary, in the west. Though Penn's original city was only about 2 sq miles in size, the 1854 annexation of the surrounding towns means that the city now comprises 159 sq miles. Think of Philadelphia as a place with extents so large that it contains both its city and its suburbs. While most of these other 157 sq miles aren't frequented by tourists, they make up a defining part of Philadelphia.

You can drive in Philadelphia, to be sure: this isn't Manhattan. But it goes without saying that driving here is a pain when you're downtown and/or during rush hour. Luckily, the city is easy to get around: it's laid out in a grid. East–west streets are given names. North–south streets are mostly numbered, except for Broad St, the main north–south street (and the equivalent of 14th St), and Front St (the equivalent of 1st St). Market St is the main east–west route and divides the city's center between north and south. Downtown Philly is laid out around public squares, with City Hall more or less at the center in Penn Sq. The other squares are: Washington Sq, near Society Hill; Rittenhouse Sq, west of Broad St; Franklin Sq, near Independence Hall; and Logan Sq at the southeast end of Benjamin Franklin Pkwy. Other central areas of interest are University City (in West Philadelphia), Fairmount Park (northwest of downtown) and South Philadelphia.

INFORMATION

Bookstores

Borders (Map p286; ☎ 215-568-7400; 1727 Walnut St), near Rittenhouse Sq, has a wide selection of titles on most subjects and a busy cafe upstairs; nearby, **Barnes & Noble** (Map p286; ☎ 215-665-0716; 1805 Walnut St; ☼ 8am-10pm Mon-Fri, 9am-10pm Sat, 10am-9pm Sun) also has a program of events and an upstairs cafe overlooking Rittenhouse Sq.

In University City, the large **University of Pennsylvania Bookstore** (Map p301; ☎ 215-898-7595; cnr Walnut & S 36th Sts) carries general-interest titles, including travel guides and maps, in addition to textbooks. **House of Our Own** (Map p301; ☎ 215-222-1576; 3920 Spruce Street), situated in an old Victorian home, stocks political books and highbrow literature. Not far away, **The Last Word Bookshop** (Map p301; ☎ 215-386-7750; 220 S 40th St) specializes in art titles, classics and used books – there's also a friendly cat in residence. For the best used-book selection in the city, try **The Book Trader** (Map p292; ☎ 215-925-0511; 7 N 2nd St).

Emergency

For police, fire and medical emergencies call ☎ 911. Other important emergency telephone numbers are:

Accidental Poisoning (☎ 215-386-2100)
Dentist (☎ 215-925-6050)
Travelers' Aid Society (☎ 215-546-0571)

PHILADELPHIA

Internet Resources

There are a number of helpful web resources covering Philadelphia events and listing general information. A good place to start is the Philadelphia Convention & Visitors Bureau official website at www.philadelphiausa.travel; here, international travelers can download the *Philadelphia International Visitors Guide* in 10 different languages. Another great page with lots of links to attractions, accommodations, dining, entertainment, transportation and news are the official visitor site at www.visitphilly.com.

The Philadelphia Inquirer has an online version at www.philly.com, while the free entertainment newspaper *Philadelphia Weekly* has a dynamic page at www.philadelphia weekly.com. For happenings in University City, try www.universitycity.org. The LGBT crowd can check out the *Philadelphia Gay News* at www.epgn.com.

Libraries

The **Free Library of Philadelphia** (Map p286; ☎ 215-686-5322; www.freelibrary.org; 1901 Vine St; ☷ 9am-9pm Mon-Thu, 9am-6pm Fri, 9am-5pm Sat, 1-5pm Sun) was the country's very first lending library. It now houses over 6 million books, magazines, newspapers and recordings, and it hosts feature films, concerts, lectures and children's programs.

Other libraries include Library Hall (p285; in Independence National Historic Park), the Civil War Library & Museum (p294) and

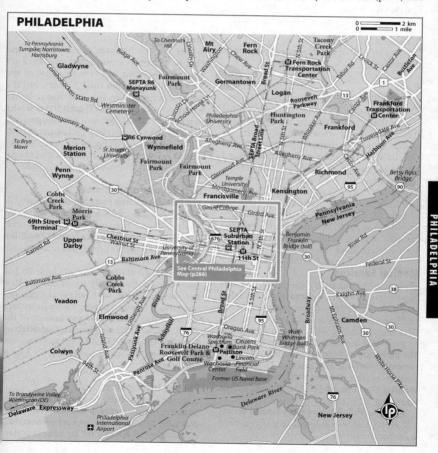

PHILADELPHIA

PHILADELPHIA IN ONE, TWO OR THREE DAYS

If you only have one precious day to spend in Philadelphia, you might choose to stay in the historic center. Make sure you hit the **Liberty Bell Center** (p289) and **Independence Hall** (p285), then head over to **Reading Terminal Market** (p294) for a casual lunch and some colorful people-watching. Stop at the **National Constitution Center** (p289) in the afternoon, then swing into nearby **Continental Restaurant + Martini Bar** (p307) for happy hour. In the evening, stroll down South St and pick a sidewalk cafe, do some window shopping at the boutiques and cafes around posh **Rittenhouse Square** (p293) before finishing your Philly whirlwind with a cold microbrew and mussels at **Monk's Cafe** (p308).

Have another day to spare? Venture into South Philadelphia, stopping first at **Philadelphia's Magic Gardens** (p296), before picking up gourmet cheese and chocolate at the **Italian Market** (p296). Stop at **Pat's King of Steaks** (p309) for the obligatory cheesesteak, then work it off by spending the afternoon in **Fairmount Park** (p299) atop a bicycle. Finish off the evening with a concert at the **Kimmel Center** (p295) or the **Tin Angel** (p310). Making a long weekend of it? Wander the creepy deserted hallways of the **Eastern State Penitentiary** (p298) on a guided tour, then head over to University City for lunch and acoustic music at the **World Cafe Live** (p309).

the Rosenbach Museum & Library (p293; in Center City), all of which are covered later in this chapter.

Maps

Free, excellent-quality paper maps of Center City are available at the Independence Visitor Center. Excellent city maps are available for free download at www.visitphilly.com. As well as these, the maps in the *Philadelphia Official Visitors Guide* (available free around town) are useful; or get hold of *Streetwise Philadelphia*. It's a laminated folding map with more thorough coverage of downtown, University City, and the SEPTA rail and bus system. Pick one up at any large bookstore or order one ahead of time online. For similar map offerings, stop by the University of Pennsylvania Bookstore (p282).

Medical Services

Philadelphia has many hospitals, including the country's first, **Pennsylvania Hospital** (Map p286; ☎ 800-789-7366; www.pennmedicine.org/PAHOSP; 800 Spruce St), founded by Ben Franklin. The same number will connect you to the branch in University City, the **Hospital of the University of Pennsylvania** (Map p301; www.pennmedicine.org/hup; 3400 Spruce St). In the city's center is the **Thomas Jefferson University Hospital** (Map p286; ☎ 215-955-6000; www.jeffersonhospital.org; 111 S 11th St).

Call the **Philadelphia County Medical Society** (☎ 215-563-5343; www.philamedsoc.org) if you need a doctor to visit you.

Money

ATMs are readily available at banks and shopping centers around the city. There are exchange bureaus in every terminal of the Philadelphia International Airport, but the best rates are generally available at banks in the city. Try **American Express Travel Service** (Map p286; ☎ 215-587-2300; www.americanexpress.com/travel; 1600 John F Kennedy Blvd; ☼ 9am-5pm Mon-Fri). US-dollar traveler's checks are accepted like cash at larger restaurants, hotels and shops, but smaller businesses often refuse them.

Post & Communications

The **Philadelphia Main Post Office** (Map p286; ☎ 215-895-8980; 2970 Market St; ☼ 6am-midnight) is impressively old and massive, occupying several city blocks, while the **B Free Franklin Post Office** (Map p292; 316 Market St) postmarks stamps with Franklin's signature.

Internet access is widely available in hotels – usually for a daily fee of about $10 – but you'll find free wi-fi access at cafes and restaurants around town. Complimentary access is also available at any branch of the Free Library of Philadelphia: the **Central Library** (Map p286; ☎ 215-686-5322; 1901 Vine St; ☼ 9am-9pm Mon-Thu, to 6pm Fri, to 5pm Sat, 1-5pm Sun) is the largest and grandest.

Tourist Information

Near the Liberty Bell, the city of Philadelphia operates the stellar **Independence Visitor Center** (Map p292; ☎ 800-537-7676; www.independencevisitorcenter.com; cnr 6th & Market Sts) to help travelers arrange accommodation and develop itineraries. Here you can get detailed information not only on Philadelphia but also on Bucks, Montgomery and Chester counties, and grab a copy of their *Official Visitors Guide*. Similar offerings can be found at the **City Hall Visitor Center** (Map p286; ☎ 800-537-7676; cnr Broad & Market Sts).

DANGERS & ANNOYANCES

Certain sections of the city are best avoided at night, especially the quiet, often poorly lit streets of North Philadelphia and West Philadelphia to the west of University City. Downtown, the area around Walnut and S 13th Sts gets a bit sleazy at night, particularly on weekends when you may see a few police around.

Use caution on the subway, particularly at night, by watching your wallet or purse and concealing expensive electronics. To be on the safe side, keep your car doors locked when driving as well as when parked.

SIGHTS

Historic District

Start by picking up information at the Independence Visitor Center (Map p292) and when you need a break from the grand tour, kick back on a park bench in **Independence Square** (Map p292), where the Declaration of Independence was first read in public on July 8, 1776.

INDEPENDENCE NATIONAL HISTORIC PARK

This **park** (Map p292; ☎ 215-597-8787; www.nps.gov/inde; 9am-5pm Tue-Sun) combined with the rest of Old City forms 'America's most historic square mile.' The L-shaped park includes essential sights like Independence Hall and the Liberty Bell; many of the following monuments are considered part of the park. Free admission to the park and all sites within it.

CARPENTERS' HALL

Founded in 1724 to teach architectural skills to its members, the Carpenters' Company, America's oldest trade guild, had a lot of influence on Philadelphia's development; its members gave advice on building techniques and worked as architects on many projects around the city. The Georgian-style **Carpenters' Hall** (Map p292; ☎ 215-925-0167; www.carpentershall.org; 320 Chestnut St; 10am-4pm; closed Tue in Jan-Feb) was designed in 1770 by Robert Smith and it served as the site of the First Continental Congress in 1774. The exhibits are all carpentry-related and include a scale model of the building during its construction, early tools and some Windsor chairs used by Congress delegates.

SECOND BANK OF THE US

Modeled after the Greek Parthenon, this 1824 marble-faced Greek revival masterpiece used to be home to the world's most powerful financial institution until its charter was dissolved by President Andrew Jackson in 1836 – he didn't approve of the bank's conservative policies. The gorgeous old bank is now home to the **National Portrait Gallery** (Map p292; 420 Chestnut St; 10am-5pm Mon-Fri), with several pieces by Charles Willson Peale, America's top portraitist at the time of the American Revolution – the people he painted were among the most prominent men of the day.

LIBRARY HALL

Worth a visit to see a copy of the Declaration of Independence (handwritten by Thomas Jefferson), first editions of Darwin's *On the Origins of the Species* and Lewis and Clark's field notes, this **library** (Map p292; ☎ 215-440-3400; 105 S 5th St; 10am-5pm Mon-Fri) sits on the site of the first subscription library in the US. The present building was constructed in 1959, and its facade is an exact reproduction of the original.

INDEPENDENCE HALL

A World Heritage Site, this **hall** (Map p292; ☎ 215-597-8974; Chestnut St btwn 5th & 6th Sts; 9am-7pm) is the birthplace of the US government. It was built between 1732 and 1756 and started life as the colony's headquarters – the Second Continental Congress met here from 1775 to 1783. The Assembly Room saw a lot of action: the delegates from the 13 colonies met in it to approve the Declaration of Independence (July 4, 1776) and the design of the US flag (1777); the Articles of the Confederation (1781) were drafted here, and the Constitutional Convention produced the US Constitution (1787) within its walls. Later, the assassinated body of President Abraham Lincoln lay in state here on April 22, 1865. One of the country's best examples of Georgian architecture, the hall's simple, understated

CENTRAL PHILADELPHIA

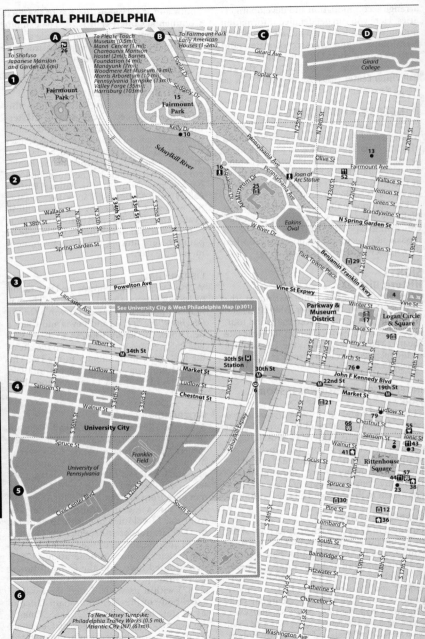

To Please Touch
Museum (0.5mi);
Mann Center (1 mi);
Chamounix Mansion
Hostel (2mi); Barnes
Foundation (4 mi);
Manayunk (7mi);
Woodmere Art Museum (9 mi);
Morris Arboretum (10 mi);
Pennsylvania Turnpike (13mi);
Valley Forge (35mi);
Harrisburg (103mi)

To Shofuso
Japanese Mansion
and Garden (0.6mi)

To Fairmount Park
Early American
Houses (1-2mi)

Girard
College

Fairmount
Park

Fairmount
Park

Schuylkill River

Joan of
Arc Statue

Eakins
Oval

See University City & West Philadelphia Map (p301)

Parkway &
Museum
District

Logan Circle
& Square

University City

30th St
Station

University of
Pennsylvania

Franklin
Field

Rittenhouse
Square

Civic Center Blvd

To New Jersey Turnpike;
Philadelphia Trolley Works (0.5mi);
Atlantic City (NJ) (61mi)

Grays Ferry Ave

E
To Cliveden (5mi); Ebenezer
Maxwell Mansion (5mi); Germantown (5mi);
Upsala (5mi); Wyck (5mi);
Earth Bread & Brewery (7mi);
Chestnut Hill (6.5mi)

F

G

H

0   400 m
0   0.2 miles

Girard Ave

Ridge Ave

North St

Vernon St

N 18th St

Fairmount
Fairmount Ave

Broad St

N 15th St

N 13th St

N 12th St

N 11th St

Cambridge

W Wildey St

Poplar St

Brown St

Culvert St

N Lawrence St

N Orianna St

N American St

N Hancock

N 2nd St

31

63

Spring
Garden
Spring Garden St

Buttonwood St

Green St
14

Spring Garden St

Spring
Garden
Station

To Barbary (0.5mi);
Trenton (NJ) (3mi);
New York City (NY) (94mi)

Callowhill St

N 16th St

Wood St

Vine St

Race St

51

N 5th St

Ridge Ave

Race-
Vine

N 13th St

N 12th St

Willow St

Green St

N 7th St

N 6th St

N 5th St

N 4th St

68

Callowhill St

67
58

Delaware Expwy

Front St

Columbia Blvd

SEPTA
Suburban
Station

JFK
Plaza

22

Broad St

Juniper St

Pennsylvania
Convention Center

Franklin
Square

50

See Historic District & Waterfront Map (p292)

Race St

15th St
City Hall

20

24 Reading
Terminal
Market

Chinatown

Cherry St

69

Appletree St

N 6th St

Arch St

Independence
Mall

N 3rd St

Benjamin
Franklin
Bridge

Penn
Square

11

S Pennsylvania Sq

13th St

Filbert St

28

32
78

Market St

Filbert St
Market
East
Station

11th St

Market St

8th St

5th St

Filbert St

2nd St

74

35

56 70

45

54

77

Chestnut St
7

Sansom St

Ranstead St

Market St

Old
City

Columbus Blvd (Delaware Ave)

Market St

42

48

Walnut-
Locust St

Locust St

8

49

47

72 62

19

40

59

Walnut St
Washington
Square West

71

Jeweler's
Row

37

Independence
National
Historical Park

Washington
Square

Locust St

N 2nd St

Penn's
Landing

Delaware River

Spruce St

34

60

65

Historic Antique Row

Clinton St

5

Locust St

Spruce St

Dock St

Society
Hill

USS Olympia
& Becuna

Lombard-
South St

S 15th St

Broad St (Avenue of the Arts)

Lombard St

Seger Park

27

South St

Pine St

Addison St

Gaskill St

18

S 2nd St

Shackam

64

Bainbridge St

Fitzwater St

Rodman St

39
53

75

46

South St

Bainbridge St

5

Catharine St

Webster St

Christian St

To Gloria Dei
Church (0.5 mi)

To Fante's Kitchen
Wares Shop (0.5 mi)
To Italian Market (100ft); The Samuel S
Fleisher Art Memorial (100ft);
Geno's (1 mi); Pat's King of Steaks (1 mi);
Paradiso (1 mi); Citizen's Bank Park (3mi);
Lincoln Field (3mi);
Wachovia Center (3mi)

Monroe St

To Mario Lanza
Museum (0.5 mi)

American St

To Mummers
Museum (3mi)

33

To Philadelphia
International
Airport (7mi);
Wilmington
(DE) (30mi)

1

2

3

4

5

6

INFORMATION
American Express
  Travel Service **1** E4
Barnes & Noble **2** D5
Borders **3** D5
City Hall Visitor Center ....(see 11)
Free Library of
  Philadelphia **4** D3
Pennsylvania Hospital **5** F5
Philadelphia Main Post
  Office **6** C4
Thomas Jefferson
  Hospital **7** F5

SIGHTS & ACTIVITIES
Academy of Music **8** E5
Academy of Natural
  Sciences Museum **9** D4
Boathouse Row **10** B2
City Hall **11** E4
Civil War Library &
  Museum **12** D5
Eastern State
  Penitentiary **13** D2
Edgar Allan Poe
  National Historic Site **14** G3
Fairmount Park **15** B1
Fairmount Water Works
  Interpretive Center **16** C2
Franklin Institute
  Science Museum **17** D3
Head House Square **18** G6
Historical Society of
  Pennsylvania **19** E5
Kimmel Center for the
  Performing Arts ....(see 60)
Macy's ....(see 73)
Masonic Temple **20** E4
Mütter Museum **21** D4

Pennsylvania Academy of the
  Fine Arts **22** E4
Pennsylvania Hospital ....(see 5)
Philadelphia Art Alliance **23** D5
Philadelphia Center for
  Architecture **24** F4
Philadelphia Museum of Art **25** C2
Philadelphia Zoo **26** A1
Philadelphia's Magic Gardens **27** F6
Reading Terminal Market **28** F4
Rodin Museum **29** D3
Rosenbach Museum & Library **30** D5
Shrine of Saint John
  Neumann **31** H2
Space 1026 ....**32** F4
Spirit of Philadelphia **33** H6

SLEEPING
Alexander Inn **34** F5
Hotel Palomar Philadelphia .**35** E5
La Reserve B & B **36** D5
Morris House Hotel **37** F5
Rittenhouse 1715 ....**38** D5
Seventh Street B&B **39** F6
The Independent **40** E5
The Rittenhouse **41** D5

EATING
Alma de Cuba **42** E5
Argan Moroccan Cuisine **43** D5
Barclay Prime **44** D5
Fogo de Chão Churrascaria ..**45** E5
Jim's Steaks **46** G6
La Viola **47** E5
Le Bec-Fin **48** E5
Monk's Cafe **49** E5
Nanzhou Hand Drawn Noodle
  House **50** F4
Sabrina's Cafe **51** E3

Zorba's Taverna **52** D2

DRINKING
L'Etage **53** G6
McGillin's Olde Ale House......**54** E5
Tria **55** D4

ENTERTAINMENT
Chris' Jazz Cafe **56** E5
Curtis Institute of Music........**57** D5
Electric Factory Concerts.......**58** G3
Forrest Theatre **59** F5
Kimmel Center for the
  Performing Arts **60** E5
Lincoln Financial Field **61** E2
Merriam Theater **62** E5
Ortlieb's Jazzhaus **63** H2
Philadelphia Clef Club of
  the Performing Arts **64** E6
Philadelphia Orchestra **65** E5
Roxy Theater **66** D4
Shampoo **67** G3
Silk City Diner & Lounge........**68** G3
Trocadero **69** F4
Upstages **70** E5
Walnut St Theatre **71** F5
Wilma Theater **72** E5

SHOPPING
Macy's **73** E4
Shops at Liberty Place **74** E4
South St Antiques
  Market **75** G6

TRANSPORT
Avis **76** D4
Enterprise **77** F5
Intercity Bus Terminal **78** F4
Hertz **79** D4

PHILADELPHIA

lines show the Quaker influence of Philadelphia's early days. British troops used the furniture in the 1st-floor's two rooms and the large central hallway for firewood when they occupied the city from 1777–78. What you see today are examples from the period.

The **Supreme Court Chamber** is to your right as you enter. The Pennsylvania coat of arms, dating from 1785, hangs over the judge's chair. It replaced King George III's coat of arms, which was burned outside in Penn Sq (near the site of today's City Hall) on July 8, 1776, the day the Declaration of Independence was read in public for the first time. The **Assembly Room**, across the hall, is where most of the building's notable events took place, and you can see original fixtures, including the chair George Washington used during the Constitutional Convention. To join a free tour of the building, you need to get a ticket from the NPS desk in the Independence Visitor Center (p284) at

least a half an hour before heading over to Independence Hall. It's a good idea to get your tickets before 2pm on busy days.

The West Wing of Independence Hall houses a small exhibit containing some blockbuster artifacts: the copy of the Declaration of Independence that was first read to the public (by John Nixon in Independence Sq), a copy of the Constitution edited by Washington, and a copy of the Articles of Confederation covered with congressman Elbridge Gerry's notations.

CONGRESS HALL
When Philadelphia was the nation's capital, this Federal-style **hall** (Map p292; ☎ 215-597-8974; S 6th & Chestnut Sts) is where the US Congress met from 1790 to 1800. Here, the Bill of Rights (the first 10 amendments) was added to the Constitution, the US Mint was established, George Washington was inaugurated for his second term, and Vermont, Kentucky and Tennessee were admitted to the Union.

Beautifully restored and still with some of its original furnishings, the various chambers, offices and committee rooms look much like they did 200 years ago.

OLD CITY HALL

Built in 1791, **Old City Hall** (Map p292; S 5th & Chestnut Sts) was home to the US Supreme Court until 1800, when Philadelphia ceased to be the nation's capital. It became City Hall when the federal government moved to Washington, DC. In 1901, the local government moved over to Center Sq. Today the hall contains exhibits on the early Supreme Court and the daily life of Philadelphia's late-18th-century citizens.

LIBERTY BELL CENTER

Philadelphia's top tourist attraction, the Liberty Bell, is housed in this good-looking new **center** (Map p292; ☎ 215-597-8974; 6th & Market Sts; ◷ 9am-7pm). Commissioned to commemorate the 50th anniversary of the Charter of Privileges, this 2080lb bronze bell was made in London's East End in 1751. The bell's inscription, from Leviticus 25:10, reads: 'Proclaim liberty through all the land, to all the inhabitants thereof.' For more on the big bell, see the boxed text p290.

NATIONAL CONSTITUTION CENTER

This **museum** (Map p292; ☎ 215-409-6600; www.constitutioncenter.org; 525 Arch St, Independence Mall; adult/child $12/8; ◷ 9:30am-5pm Mon-Fri, 9:30am-6pm Sat, noon-6pm Sun) accomplishes the near-impossible: it makes the United States Constitution seem sexy and interesting for a general audience. (It's a good thing, too, since, as the folks at the NCC will tell you, embarrassingly few American citizens can name the basic freedoms guaranteed by the 1st Amendment.) Housed in a massive building whose scale is intended to overwhelm, the NCC's central exhibit, 'The Story of We the People,' comprises more than 100 interactive displays and a 350-seat theater in the round, where an enveloping screen and single live actor bring to life the evolution of the Constitution through history. Other attractions include a blue screen that creates the illusion of visitors being sworn in as president, mock voting booths, and Signer's Hall, which contains life-like bronze statues of the signers in action. Excellent temporary exhibits and a bustling cafe add to the center's drawing power.

FRANKLIN COURT

This **complex** (Map p292; Market St btwn 3rd & 4th Sts; ◷ 10am-5pm Mon-Sat), a tribute to Benjamin Franklin, is built on the site where he lived and worked. Entry to the court from Market St is through the miraculously preserved brick archway that Franklin and his carriages once used. The court itself is a void occupied by three steel frame 'Ghost Buildings,' designed by Robert Venturi, that outline the long departed shapes of Franklin's house (it was razed by his heirs in 1812) and his print works. Inscribed in the ground throughout the court are quotations from correspondence between Franklin and his wife, Deborah. An **Underground Museum** sits on the west side of Franklin Court and displays Franklin's various inventions, revealing just how much this genius managed to contribute to 18th-century science and technology. Franklin's **printing office and bindery** (320 Market St) has working demonstrations of reproduction colonial equipment. One of the coolest spots in Franklin Court is the **fireproof building** (318 Market St) that Franklin designed with inspiration from the Great Fire of London and was one of the rental properties that he built along this street.

DECLARATION HOUSE

Thomas Jefferson drafted the Declaration of Independence in rented rooms on this **site** (Map p292; ☎ 215-597-8974; Market & S 7th Sts; ◷ 10am-noon Wed-Sun). The 18th-century house was demolished in 1883 and reconstructed in 1975 for the Bicentennial. There's an exhibition of Jefferson memorabilia, an eight-minute documentary film about him called *The Extraordinary Citizen* and replications of his two upstairs rooms with period furnishings, including reproductions of the chair and desk he used to write the declaration.

CHRIST CHURCH

This beautiful Episcopal **church** (Map p292; ☎ 215-922-1695; www.oldchristchurch.org; Church & N 2nd Sts; admission by donation; ◷ 7am-6pm) was built in 1744. George Washington, Benjamin Franklin and Betsy Ross all worshiped here, and the signatories of the Declaration of Independence came to the church to pray together on July 5, 1776. The church was built in 1744, and its white steeple – which dominated the city skyline at the time – was added in 1754.

ELFRETH'S ALLEY

Believed to be America's oldest residential street, this **picturesque alley** (Map p292) connects N Front St with N 2nd St. Along the alley, 33 privately owned houses date back to between 1728 and 1836. The small **Mantua Maker's Museum House** (Map p292; ☎ 215-574-0560; www.elfrethsalley.org; adult/child $2/1; 126 Elfreth's Alley) has period furniture and changing exhibits.

BETSY ROSS HOUSE

Some uncertainty surrounds Betsy Griscom Ross (1752–1836), an 18th-century upholsterer and seamstress. Although it's now known that she didn't design the American flag, she may or may not have sewn the first US flag for the early federal government. This is either the house where she lived or it's next to the site where her house once stood. Though sparsely furnished, inside the two-story **house** (Map p292;

RING MY BELL

Ask the two million annual visitors to the Liberty Bell why it is famous and 80% will shrug their shoulders. Some 18% will say because 'it's a symbol of liberty' but not know exactly why. And 2% will say the bell rang on July 4, 1776, to announce the signing of the Declaration of Independence.

Well, the Old State House Bell – now known as the Liberty Bell – is indeed a universally recognized symbol of American independence. But it did not ring on July 4. As a matter of fact, the Continental Congress voted for independence from Great Britain on July 2, 1776. The vote was 12 colonies for the break, with New York abstaining while it awaited instruction from home. (It soon joined in the vote.) On July 4, Congress issued an eloquent explanation to the world of why it was breaking ties to Britain. One historian has described the Declaration of Independence as a 'press release.'

The Liberty Bell did not ring on either July 2 or July 4. However, on July 8, all of the city's church bells rang for hours to announce a public reading of the declaration. No one can say for sure if the State House Bell joined the chorus. There is doubt, because the wood steeple was rotted at the time, so it may have been too dangerous to ring the bell for hours on end. But the bell did not become a beloved symbol of freedom until the late 1830s – some 60 years after the revolution.

Ordered from an English foundry in 1752 by Pennsylvania's colonial assembly, the bell carries a biblical inscription that reads 'proclaim Liberty thro' all the land to all the inhabitants thereof.' Since no one in 1752 knew a revolution was coming, historians believe the verse commemorates William Penn's liberal constitution for the colony of Pennsylvania called 'the Charter of Privileges.'

The fist time the bell was rung, it cracked. The bell was broken up and recast by local foundry owners, Pass and Stowe, who put their names on it. The new bell's sound was so poor that Pass and Stowe recast it again. The third casting is the Liberty Bell we see today. The bell may have cracked in 1845 (no one is sure of the date). A repair was made by drilling out the hairline crack. This is the famous visible crack. A newspaper account tells us the thin hairline crack continued to expand, finally silencing the bell for good on Washington's birthday, February 23, 1846.

So why is the bell famous? In the late 1830s those working to abolish slavery began using the image of the bell in their literature and referring to the old State House Bell as 'the Liberty Bell.' Abolitionists liked its inscription proclaiming liberty 'to ALL the inhabitants.'

But what really made the bell an icon was a fanciful tale that appeared in the *Saturday Courier Magazine* in 1847 by writer George Lippard. The fictional story tells of an elderly bell ringer waiting in the belfry on July 4, 1776 – doubtful that Congress had the nerve to break with Britain. Finally, the old man's cute little grandson – who had been listening to the great debate at the door – shouts 'Ring, Grandfather, ring.'

This tale was taken as truth and soon reprinted in newspapers and 19th-century history books. It is doubtful that the Liberty Bell would be today's famous symbol of liberty and independence without George Lippard and his tale of the old bell ringer.

☎ 215-686-1252; 239 Arch St; suggested donation $2; ☺ 9am-6pm Mon-Sat), built in 1740 (but restored to how it appeared in early 1777), you can see Betsy's sewing machine and other tools.

US MINT

The **US Mint** (Map p292; ☎ 215-408-0112; www.usmint.org; cnr Arch & Market Sts; admission free; ☺ 9am-4:30pm Mon-Fri) is the world's largest, and the fourth mint built on this site (the current building dates from 1969). It makes coins (including over one million Lincoln pennies a day!) and medals, performs designing and engraving, and processes mutilated coins. During the self-guided tour, visitors can see real coin production and check out exhibits about the history of the US Mint, its coinage history, and its current programs.

FIREMAN'S HALL

North of Elfreth's Alley, this restored 1876 firehouse is a **museum** (Map p292; ☎ 215-923-1438; www.firemanshall.org; 147 N 2nd St; admission by donation; ☺ closed Sun & Mon) that portrays the history of fire fighting in America with a terrific collection of fire-fighting memorabilia, graphics, photographs, film and restored early models of pumpers and rolling stock. The 1st floor covers the rise of an organized volunteer department led by Ben Franklin, while the 2nd floor deals with the inception of the paid department. Exhibits include models of early equipment, large fire trucks, and a re-creation of typical firefighters' living quarters.

Other recommended sights in the district include the following:

Arch St Meeting House (Map p292; ☎ 215-627-2667; 320 Arch St; admission $1; ☺ 10am-4pm Mon-Sat) Built in 1804 on land donated by William Penn, this is the country's largest Quaker meeting house.

Congregation Mikveh Israel (Map p292; ☎ 215-922-5446; www.mikvehisrael.org; 44 N 4th St; ☺ 8am-7pm) Founded in 1740, it's the oldest congregation in Philadelphia and the second oldest in the country. Among the artifacts is a thank-you letter to the congregation from a newly elected George Washington.

National Museum of American Jewish History (Map p292; ☎ 215-923-3811; www.nmajh.org; 55 N 5th St; free admission; ☺ 10am-5pm Sun-Fri) Set to reopen in a grand new building in late 2010, this is the country's only museum devoted to the role of Jews in American history.

Philadelphia Exchange (Map p292; S 3rd & Walnut Sts; ☺ 10am-5pm Sun-Fri) Site of the country's first stock exchange, which opened here in 1834 and operated until the Civil War.

Waterfront & Society Hill

On the waterfront is Penn's Landing, the once-busy port area that became an underused and unattractive stretch of land in the 1960s and '70s. After large-scale renovations, the neighborhood once again buzzes with activity: locals jog or walk along the water's edge, music lovers show up with picnic blankets for outdoor concerts, and families flock to the Independence Seaport Museum. A block or two away from the Delaware River, Society Hill is a pretty residential neighborhood dominated by 18th- and 19th-century architecture and named after the Free Society of Traders, a group of businesspeople who settled here with their families in 1683 at the behest of William Penn. It's a pleasant place for a stroll through narrow side streets lined with colonial and contemporary homes, renovated warehouses converted into art galleries and high-end apartments.

BENJAMIN FRANKLIN BRIDGE

The world's longest suspension **bridge** (Map p292) when it was completed in 1926 at a cost of $37 million, this 1.8-mile long, 800,000-ton bridge crosses the Delaware River between Philly's Old City and Camden, NJ. The bridge, designed by Paul Cret, dominates the skyline here, especially at night when it's beautifully lit – each cable is illuminated by computer in a domino-like effect to follow the trains as they cross. Pedestrians can enjoy a picturesque walk over the bridge during the day, with views of the waterfront piers below.

INDEPENDENCE SEAPORT MUSEUM

This kid-friendly **museum** (Map p292; ☎ 215-925-5439; www.phillyseaport.org; 211 S Columbus Blvd; adult/child $12/7; ☺ 10am-5pm; ♿) offers a range of exhibits and interactive displays. Sound a series of signals such as foghorns and a steam whistle, climb into an immigrant's steerage compartment, or learn about shipbuilding history at the 'What Floats Your Boat' exhibit. Your admission ticket also gains you access to board the nearby American warships USS Becuna and USS Olympia.

USS BECUNA & USS OLYMPIA

Today it's a floating **museum** (Map p286) – but the USS Becuna was once a 1944 Balao-class

PHILADELPHIA

submarine that led General MacArthur's Southwest Pacific Fleet, destroyed three Japanese vessels in WWII and patrolled the Java and China seas. The USS Olympia was one of the US Navy's first steel ships and the flagship of Commodore Dewey in 1898's Battle of Manila Bay (during the Spanish-American War.) Later, the Olympia carried the body of the Unknown Soldier from France to Arlington National Cemetery.

IRISH MEMORIAL

Dedicated to the victims of the 'Great Hunger' that claimed a million Irish lives between 1845 and 1850 and caused a million more to emigrate to the US, the centerpiece of this **memorial** (Map p292; Front & Chestnut Sts; www.irishmemorial.

org) is a massive bronze sculpture by Glenna Goodacre. Measuring 30ft long, 12ft wide and 12ft high, it portrays 35 life-sized figures in a thematic progression from starvation to emigration.

PHYSICK HOUSE

This **house** (Map p292; ☎ 215-925-7866; www.phila landmarks.org/phys.aspx; 321 S 4th St, Society Hill; adult/child $5/4; ☺ tours noon-4pm Thu-Sat, 1-4pm Sun) was built in 1786 by Henry Hill, a wine importer, and it later became the home of Dr Philip Syng Physick, known as the father of American surgery (and whose patients included Andrew Jackson). It was restored in the 1960s, and today it is the only freestanding Federal-style mansion remaining in Society Hill. As well

as its architectural importance, it is also one of the few sites still displaying original neo-classic furnishings.

Washington Square & Rittenhouse Square

On the northwest edge of Society Hill, this Washington Sq is one of those in William Penn's original city plan – and, notably, the location of the **Tomb of the Unknown Soldier**, the country's only monument to the unknown American and British dead of the Revolutionary War. Once an upper-class residential district, and in the 19th century the center of Philadelphia's publishing industry, the neighborhood is now a mixture of high-end and low rent. The character varies greatly: some blocks are shabby, others ritzy; some are packed with dive bars, those along Antique Row fill with shoppers during the day, others, around the hospitals, are eerily empty at night.

Rittenhouse Sq, in contrast, is thoroughly fashionable and contains some of the most expensive apartments in the city – the square even feels safe at night, thanks to the constant activity at sidewalk bars and restaurants. As the architecture suggests, the district was settled around the end of the 19th century by Philadelphia's aristocratic class. Though Penn allocated space for the square when he planned the city 250 years earlier, it wasn't much more than a patch of grass until the upper crust started building their mansions here. It was named after David Rittenhouse,

the 18th-century astronomer, mathematician and clockmaker.

MÜTTER MUSEUM

Don't plan on a three-course lunch after a visit to this **museum** (Map p286; ☎ 215-563-3737; www.collphyphil.org; 19 S 22nd St; adult/child $14/10; ☽ 10am-5pm) at the College of Physicians & Surgeons. This collection of pathological and anatomical specimens and medical artifacts was established in the late 19th century to educate medical students: it features a fascinating but often gruesome collection of exhibits, including the double liver shared by 19th-century Siamese twins Chang and Eng Bunker, the tumor removed from President Cleveland's cancerous jawbone and numerous skeletons of dwarves and unusually tall people.

ATWATER KENT MUSEUM

Over 300 years of the city's social history and local culture are represented at this **museum** (Map p292; ☎ 215-685-4830; www.philadelphiahistory.org; 15 S 7th St; adult $5; ☽ 9am-5pm Mon-Fri), which boasts a collection of more than 75,000 artifacts – including military uniforms, dolls, model ships and radios – that depict ordinary daily life in Philadelphia's past. It's set to undergo major renovations, so check that the museum is open before planning a visit.

ROSENBACH MUSEUM & LIBRARY

Bookworms delight in the rare book collection at this petite **museum** (Map p286; ☎ 215-735-1600; www.rosenbach.org; 2010 Delancy Pl; adult/child $10/5;

PHILADELPHIA

noon-5pm Tue & Fri-Sun, noon-8pm Wed-Thu). Look for the original handwritten manuscript of James Joyce's *Ulysses*, the first four pages of Bram Stoker's *Dracula*, Joseph Conrad manuscripts and original illustrations by author Maurice Sendak.

HISTORICAL SOCIETY OF PHILADELPHIA

This **library** (Map p286; ☎ 215-732-6201; www.hsp.org; 1300 Locust St; adult/child $8/5; 12:30-5:30pm Tue-Thu, 10am-5:30pm Fri) is more of a serious academic center than a tourist attraction, but the collection contains a few historic gems, like William Penn's political papers and letters, George Washington's desk and the first draft of the Constitution.

Other recommended sights in this district include the following:

Civil War Library & Museum (www.cwurmuseum. org) Closed at the time of research and awaiting a move to a new building; in the meantime, Civil War buffs can see the stuffed head of Old Baldy and other unique artifacts on temporary exhibits at the African American Museum and National Constitution Center – see website for details.

Philadelphia Art Alliance (Map p286; ☎ 215-545-4302; www.philartalliance.org; 251 S 18th St; adult/child $5/3; 11am-5pm Tue-Sun) This stately mansion hosts rotating exhibits; back in the '30s Frank Lloyd Wright, Le Corbusier and Martha Graham spoke here.

Center City & Avenue of the Arts

Philadelphia's center of creativity, commerce and culture, Center City contains the city's tallest buildings, the financial district, big hotels, museums, concert halls, shops and restaurants. At its center sits Penn Sq and City Hall, covered in Alexander Milne Calder's sculptures and topped with a ridiculously large statue of William Penn. During the day, tourists ride to the top of the City Hall tower for excellent views of the city.

Cutting straight through the center is the Avenue of the Arts (Broad St), lined with many of Philadelphia's most important houses of culture, from the Ballet to the Kimmel Center. The Broad St art scene got its start back in the 1850s when the city's grand opera house, the Academy of Music, was built. At the time the Broad St site was chosen because it was a relatively quiet spot on the edge of the city; today it's a busy boulevard dominated by classic theaters, mammoth music halls, and well-dressed locals and tourists hurrying to catch a Broadway show or a Philadelphia Orchestra performance.

CITY HALL

Considered by many to be Philadelphia's architectural highlight, **City Hall** (Map p286; cnr Broad & Market Sts; free admission; tours 12:30pm Mon-Fri, observation deck 9:30am-4:15pm) took 30 years to build and was completed in 1901. The elaborately designed building was constructed without a steel framework, so the 22ft-thick granite walls at the base support the central tower. It was the city's tallest building until the completion of Liberty Place in 1987. The 548ft-high City Hall is crowned by a 27-ton, 37ft-high bronze statue of William Penn. Before Liberty Place, a 'gentlemen's agreement' had limited the height of Philadelphia's buildings to the hat on Penn's statue.

PENNSYLVANIA ACADEMY OF THE FINE ARTS

This **academy** (PAFA; Map p286; ☎ 215-972-7600; www.pafa.org; 118 Broad St; adult/child $10/8; 10am-5pm Tue-Sat, from 11am Sun) was founded in 1805 and boasts a prestigious art school and museum. Its present home is a magnificent Victorian Gothic–style building dating from 1876; the collection includes American paintings and sculpture by such noted early American painters as Charles Willson Peale (1741–1827), Gilbert Stuart (1755–1828) and Thomas Eakins (1844–1916).

READING TERMINAL MARKET

This large indoor **market** (Map p286; ☎ 215-922-2317; www.readingterminalmarket.org; 12th & Arch Sts; 8am-6pm Mon-Sat, 9am-5pm Sun) is a feast for the senses. Started in 1893, the colorful marketplace overflows with some of the city's best pretzels, hoagies and farmers' produce, in addition to casual food stands selling everything from jambalaya to sushi to Amish-made shoofly pie. It's a terrific place to come for breakfast, lunch or a snack.

ACADEMY OF MUSIC

The oldest grand opera house still used for its original purpose, the neo-baroque **Academy of Music** (Map p286; ☎ 215-893-1999; www.academyofmusic. org; Broad & Locust Sts) was designed by LeBrun and Runge in 1855 and hasn't changed much since it first opened. The beautiful murals on the ceiling still exist, though the 5000lb chandelier is no longer raised and lowered by hand, much to the delight of today's stage workers. The Academy is home to the Opera Company of Philadelphia and the Pennsylvania Ballet.

AMERICAN LEGEND: BENJAMIN FRANKLIN

Born in Boston, the son of a soap maker, Franklin (1707–90) joined the workforce at the age of 12 as an apprentice at his brother's printshop. He moved to Philadelphia in 1723 and founded the *Pennsylvania Gazette*, which soon became the colonies' top newspaper. He became involved in local politics by helping to launch public-works projects to pave, clean and light Philadelphia's streets. He founded America's first circulating library, the American Philosophical Society, and an academy that would later become the University of Pennsylvania. While still in his 20s, he invented flippers for swimming, and in 1743 he invented a heat-efficient stove to warm houses. In 1748, he retired from the newspaper business to study electricity. In a famous experiment, he verified the identity of electricity in lightning by using a kite and in the process invented the lightning rod.

By now a political leader in Pennsylvania, Franklin sailed to Britain in 1757 to represent the colony. He became an agent for several other colonies and the de facto ambassador for all 13. He had supported a united empire, but was disillusioned by the corrupt ways of the British political and aristocratic scene. He gradually became opposed to British taxes on the colonies, and when he returned to America in 1775 he caused a stir by declaring his support for independence.

Franklin worked with Thomas Jefferson to draft the Declaration of Independence, served in the Continental Congress, then sailed to France in 1776 to become ambassador to the court of Louis XVI. Dressed in simple Quaker clothes, he made quite an impression in his extravagant surroundings as a great speaker. His popularity helped him persuade the French king to stand by the 1778 Treaty of Alliance, saving the struggling American Revolution from certain bankruptcy. Franklin remained in France for five years, playing a pivotal role in the important European side of the struggle.

Returning to America in 1784, he was involved in the final draft of the US Constitution in 1787. Shortly before his death, his final public act was to sign a memorial to Congress urging the abolition of slavery.

Among the other public enterprises Franklin either launched or helped create were the first fire-fighting company in America, the first fire-insurance company, street lighting and paving, the reorganization of the town watch, a local militia, the post office and the country's first hospital.

It also stages Broadway shows. The main box office is at the Kimmel Center.

KIMMEL CENTER FOR THE PERFORMING ARTS

Very few pieces of architecture achieve instant critical recognition as superior works: the **Kimmel Center** (Map p286; ☎ 215-790-5800; www.kimmelcenter.org; Broad & Spruce Sts; tickets $18-80; ☯ 10am-6pm (open later on performance evenings) is one of the few. Opened in 2001, Rafael Viñoly's design is a stunning technological and aesthetic achievement. The shell of the building is a 400ft-long glass vaulted ceiling exposing the sky overhead. Inside are two theaters with exemplary acoustics and sight lines: Verizon Hall, a 2500-seat, cello-shaped concert hall, and the Perelman Theater, containing 650 seats and a rotating stage. It's also the home of the Philadelphia Chamber Music Society. Other recommended sights in this area are as follow:

Masonic Temple (Map p286; ☎ 215-988-1917; 1 N Broad St) Headquarters of the Grand Lodge of Free & Accepted Masons of Pennsylvania; George Washington and other Founding Fathers were members. The seven lodge halls are designed in different architectural styles.

Macy's (Map p286; ☎ 215-241-9000; Market & Juniper Sts) Built between 1902 and 1910, this elegant department store is a landmark and boasts a large bronze eagle and a 30,000-pipe organ in the concourse.

South Street & Around

South Street is simultaneously cool and seedy, offbeat but trendy, ugly and beautiful. Teenagers, tourists, artists and punks alike are drawn to this neighborhood crammed with record and art-supply stores, thrift shops, ethnic eateries and upscale BYOBs specializing in organic food. The Street attracted an alternative crowd from the get-go: the freeway was slated to bulldoze here, and rents for the doomed area dropped to just above zero, bringing in artists and squatters. Even

PHILADELPHIA

after the ramp scheme was dropped, rental rates remained low because the neighborhood had become a ghost town. When galleries and underground clubs started opening, South Street started taking shape.

HEAD HOUSE SQUARE
Named after the fire-engine houses (once called 'head houses') that once circled it, this attractive **square** (Map p286; 2nd & Pine Sts) was built in the early 19th century. The main firehouse escaped demolition and was restored; it still has its original cupolas, alarm bells and a fire officers' social club. The shed between Lombard and Pine Sts was one of several built in 1745 for street trading; also restored, it's home to an open-air craft market on summer weekends.

MOTHER BETHEL AME CHURCH
Founded by two local freed slaves in 1787, this **church** (Map p292; ☎ 215-925-0616; www.mother bethel.org; 419 S 6th St; admission free; ☒ 10am-3pm Tue-Sat & after services Sun) is South Street's major historic building and is regarded as the birthplace of the African Methodist Episcopal (AME) order. As a stop on the Underground Railroad, the church and its pastor, Richard Allen (entombed within the church), hid hundreds of fugitive slaves here prior to the Civil War. The church is also the oldest piece of real estate owned by African Americans; a museum inside tells the story.

ST PETER'S CHURCH
Robert Smith, also responsible for Christ Church (p289) and Carpenters' Hall (p285), built this beautiful **church** (Map p292; ☎ 215-925-5968; www.stpetersphila.org; 313 Pine St; admission free; ☒ 8am-4pm) between 1758 and '64. Apart from the mid-19th-century steeple, the church looks much as it did when George Washington and his family worshiped here. Buried in the graveyard are artist Charles Wilson Peale and the chiefs of seven Indian tribes who died in Philly during the 1793 smallpox epidemic, while meeting with Washington for a peace council.

PHILADELPHIA'S MAGIC GARDENS
Strolling down South Street, it's hard to miss the whimsical mosaics and tilework splashed across building exteriors and crawling up doorframes. Isaiah Zagar is the man behind it and this delightful park and indoor-out-

door **museum** (Map p286; ☎ 215-733-0390; www.philly magicgardens.org; 1029 South St; adult/child $4/2, tours $6-10; ☒ 11am-6pm Sun-Thu, 11am-8pm Fri & Sat; ☒) is his headquarters. Enter the fantastical man-made garden to wonder at scores of murals and mosaics made from bits of broken mirrors, bicycle wheels, dolls heads, broken dishes, and wine bottles – to name a few – and learn about the community's most outrageous artist, at once brash, childlike, and devoted to urban aesthetics.

South Philadelphia
South Philadelphia is the birthplace of the cheesesteak, and the neighborhood is still known for its blue-collar Italian immigrant roots: walking down these streets, you'll see gritty 24-hour diners, sidewalks without trees, crazy traffic, plain brick row-houses, auto-body shops and unpretentious restaurants where the portions are big and the sauce is red. Most of area's sights – the Mummers Museum, the Mario Lanza Museum and the Italian Market – reflect the neighborhood's Italian-American heritage, though new waves of Mexican and Asian immigrants have arrived, adding *taquerias* and Vietnamese markets to Washington Ave and 8th St.

ITALIAN MARKET
The country's largest outdoor **market** (off Map p286; www.phillyitalianmarket.com; 9th St btw Wharton & Fitzwarer Sts; admission free; ☒ 9am-5pm Tue-Sat, 9am-2pm Sun) teems with Italian goodies, fresh produce and gourmet treats. Highlights include huge stuffed olives, artisan cheeses, handmade pastas, Italian-style water ice, potent espresso and buttery pastries. Don't miss a visit to the butcher stands, where you can purchase sausage that's 10% garlic by volume. Like the neighborhood itself, the marketplace has a rough-and-tumble charm.

SAMUEL S FLEISHER ART MEMORIAL
Founded in 1898 by Samuel Fleisher, a wealthy businessman and art enthusiast who wanted 'the world to come and learn art,' this exhibition space and **art school** (off Map p287; ☎ 215-922-3456; www.fleisher.org; 719 Catharine St; admission free; ☒ 11am-5pm Mon-Fri, 10am-3pm Sat) offers free art classes and workshops to the public. Check the website for details. The Fleisher compound also features intriguing temporary exhibits and permanent installations, like a Romanesque revival church de-

signed by Furness with stained glass windows by La Farge.

MARIO LANZA MUSEUM

This small and friendly **museum** (off Map p286; ☎ 215-238-9691; www.mario-lanza-institute.org; 712 Montrose St; admission free; ☺ 11am-3pm Mon-Wed, Fri & Sat) pays homage to Mario Lanza (1921–59), a famed tenor singer and film actor born in the neighborhood. The place, full of photos, movie stills, film posters, childhood memorabilia and a knowledgeable staff willing to give tours, showcases the varied talents of the Italian-American opera singer, a local legend who died of a heart attack at the age of 38.

GLORIA DEI (OLDE SWEDES') CHURCH

Before the arrival of William Penn, the 'town' of Philadelphia was settled by Swedish Lutherans; they built log cabins and a basic wooden **church** (off Map p286; ☎ 215-389-1513; www.nps.gov/glde/; 916 S Swanson St; admission by donation; ☺ 9am-4pm, closed Mon Sep-May). The log structure, built in 1643, was replaced in 1700 by the current brick version, which is still considered the oldest church building in Philadelphia. Surrounded by a graveyard and other 18th-century buildings, it's a worthwhile point of reference for history buffs interested in the pre-Penn days.

MUMMERS MUSEUM

Anyone who thinks of Philadelphia as a staid historic city should hold off judgments and step into this lively **museum** (off Map p286; ☎ 215-336-3050; www.mummersmuseum.com; 1100 S 2nd St; adult/child $3.50/2.50; ☺ 9:30am-4:30pm Wed-Sat, 9:30am-9:30pm Thu May-Sep). The exhibits explain the background and culture of the mummers, the city's most colorful citizens, who spend every day of the year planning, costume designing and practicing for an enormous masquerade on New Year's Day. Check out their extravagant costumes, a video of the most recent parade and a digital clock that counts down the days to the next January 1.

Chinatown & Northern Liberties

Though it lacks the energy of its sister neighborhoods in New York and San Francisco, Philly's Chinatown is the fourth largest in the nation. Started in the 1860s, the area remains a center for immigrants; note the decorative Chinese Friendship Gate on N 10th St, built in 1984 as a joint project between Philadelphia

and its Chinese sister city, Tianjin. On these streets you'll find restaurants, Chinese bakeries, shops full of Hello Kitty merchandise and hungry locals seeking spring rolls and noodles.

Further north – and with decidedly more character – Northern Liberties has emerged as a hipster enclave in recent years. A one-time brewery district, the neighborhood became a refuge for artists, musicians and spendthrifts fleeing the increasingly expensive southern neighborhoods. Now, you can hit a dive bar here or go out for a stylish Sunday brunch. While it's gentrifying quickly, the slightly grimy Northern Liberties is still something of a fringe destination.

THE AFRICAN-AMERICAN MUSEUM IN PHILADELPHIA

This excellent **museum** (Map p292; ☎ 215-574-0380; www.aampmuseum.org; 701 Arch St; adult/child $10/8; ☺ 10am-5pm Tue-Sat & noon-5pm Sun) contains one of the country's best collections on black history and culture, with displays on African heritage through slavery, emancipation, the civil rights movement and beyond. Exhibits have included an outstanding collection of photojournalism documenting Dr Martin Luther King Jr and another outlining the history and symbolism of black dolls (for example, black china dolls were 'intended to be the slave and servant playmates of white dolls').

PENNSYLVANIA HOSPITAL

Founded in 1751 by Benjamin Franklin and Dr Thomas Bond, this historic **hospital** (Map p286; ☎ 215-829-3370; www.pennmedicine.org/pahosp/; 800 Spruce St; admission free; ☺ 9am-5pm Mon-Fri) was the country's first. Ask at the information desk in the contemporary wing for the booklet offering a self-guided walking tour. Inside the 8th St entrance, you'll find the History of Nursing Museum, Historic Library of Pennsylvania Hospital (containing important collections on the history of medicine) and North America's oldest surgical amphitheater for medical students. Outside is the tranquil Physic Garden, where plants used in the 18th century as herbal remedies are grown.

SHRINE OF SAINT JOHN NEUMANN

Entombed in a glass case beneath the main altar, the preserved body of the nation's first saint is now a **shrine** (Map p286; ☎ 215-627-3080; www.stjohnneumann.org; 1019 N 5th St; admission free; ☺ 7:30am-6pm Mon-Sat, 7:30am-5pm Sun) at St

Peter's Catholic Church. Born in 1811, St John Neumann served as a Catholic bishop, founded the nation's first Archdiocesan school system and established an order of nuns. He was canonized in 1977. Parishioners still show their devotion to the church's namesake saint, pressing their hands against the altar's glass in prayer.

EDGAR ALLAN POE NATIONAL HISTORIC SITE

'For the most wild, yet most homely narrative which I am about to pen, I neither expect nor solicit belief…' America's most famous 19th-century horror-story writer dreamed up *The Black Cat* and other works on this **site** (Map p286; ☎ 215-597-8780; www.nps.gov/edal; 532 N 7th St; admission free; ⊙ 9am-5pm Wed-Sun). A legendary poet and editor, Poe lived in this modest brick house from 1843 to 44; he lived in other buildings in Philadelphia over the years, but this is his only surviving residence in the city. In the museum, you'll find related exhibits on his life and work.

SPACE 1026

On the edge of Chinatown, this cooperative studio and **gallery** (Map p286; ☎ 215-574-7630; www.space1026.org; 1026 Arch St; admission free) is run by a group of artists (many from Rhode Island School of Design) who present fantastic exhibits of other peoples' work on First Fridays. Some past shows include Andrew Kuo's screen prints, the work of installationists and a flipbook festival. For the daring, it's pretty easy to drop by the studio during the week; someone friendly is awake by noon. Be sure to check out their store of silk-screen items – all cool, all for sale.

Parkway & Museum Area

Back in 1907, Philadelphia tastemakers were inspired by the urban designs introduced in the World's Columbia Exposition in Chicago.

So the city's fathers installed a quasi-Parisian boulevard – the Benjamin Franklin Parkway – which runs diagonally from the northwest quadrant of Center City through to Fairmount Park. Along it are many of the city's most-visited museums. At one end of the parkway, the large frogs and turtles of Alexander Stirling Calder's Swann Memorial Fountain perpetually spit water in Logan Sq; in summer, kids wade among the water-spouting creatures in the large fountain and nobody – including the police – seems to care that this activity is illegal.

The northern section of this neighborhood stretches up along Pennsylvania Ave. Though many blocks are run-down, the impressive, castle-like Eastern State Penitentiary is here: don't miss a fascinating tour of this bleak monument, or a drink at one of the neighborhood bars afterwards.

EASTERN STATE PENITENTIARY

Al Capone was once behind bars at this eerie Gothic-revival **penitentiary** (Map p286; ☎ 215-236-3300; www.easternstate.com; Fairmount Ave). Built in 1829, the prison's design featured a forbidding exterior intended to frighten would-be criminals and a wheel-like design that allowed guards to practice 'central surveillance' – a structure that was copied afterwards in prisons all over the world. Since the facility was guided (for a while, at least) by the Quaker belief in reform through strict isolation, each prisoner had his own individual cell and little contact with the outside world. Today, the decaying place feels haunted; admission to the crumbling castle includes an excellent audio tour, special guided tours and access to rotating art installations

ACADEMY OF NATURAL SCIENCES MUSEUM

The country's oldest natural history **museum** (Map p286; ☎ 215-299-1000; www.ansp.org; 1900 Benjamin

---

NEW KIDS IN TOWN

The first large wave of immigration from the 1820s through 1850 was Irish. The only two groups to settle in Philadelphia in large numbers at the end of the 19th century were Italian and Jewish. Relatively small numbers of Slavs, Poles, Greeks, and other Eastern Europeans chose Philadelphia.

Because most jobs in Philadelphia required some skills, British and German craftsmen continued to arrive into the 1920s. A good cricket match with a visiting English team could attract 15,000 fans, even in the 1920s. A Puerto Rican community established itself in North Philadelphia in the 1950s and '60s. More recently, thousands of immigrants from Cambodia, Vietnam, China and India have settled in the city.

ROCKY WAS HERE

The Constantine tapestries and Renoir's oil paintings are great – but the Philadelphia Museum of Art is perhaps most famous for its association with the boxing champ of the silver screen, Rocky Balboa. Sylvester Stallone ran up the stairs in front of the museum in the original *Rocky* movie and the film won an Oscar for best screenplay. In the early 1980s, a bronze statue of the fictional boxer was erected outside the museum for the filming of Rocky III, and after moving around to a few locations, the Italian Stallion's figure has found a permanent home at the foot of the famous museum staircase. To relive that cinematic moment, do as Rocky did and sprint up the steps, then turn to look out over the glorious city skyline (or just stick around and count how many tourists do exactly this before raising their arms in the air and yelling 'Adrian!' at the top).

Franklin Pkwy; adult/child $12/10; 10am-4:30pm Mon-Fri, 10:30am-5pm Sat & Sun;), was founded in 1812. The prizewinning skeleton in its terrific Dinosaur Hall is a 7.5-ton *tyrannosaurus rex*; there's also an interactive exhibit called 'The Big Dig,' in which kids can 'dig' for fossils in a simulated New Mexico field station. The museum also features a hands-on nature center and well-curated halls on Africa, Asia and North America.

FRANKLIN INSTITUTE SCIENCE MUSEUM

Founded in 1824, this world-class **museum** (Map p286; 215-448-1200; www.fi.edu; 222 N 20th St; adult/child $15.50/12; 9:30am-5pm;) moved into this Greek revival building in 1934 and became one of the pioneering hands-on science museums. Attractions include the walk-through, 4-ton, two-story papier-mâché replica of a beating heart, the new and extremely kid-friendly Train Factory exhibit, the futuristic Space Command center and flight simulator, and the innovative art and physics exhibits at Sir Isaac's Loft. For an additional charge, there are also fascinating films shown in the four-story IMAX Theater.

RODIN MUSEUM

A must-see for fans of the French figurative sculptor, this noteworthy **museum** (215-568-6026; www.rodinmuseum.org; Benjamin Franklin Pkwy & 22nd St; suggested donation $5; 10am-5pm Tue-Sun) is home to the largest collection of Auguste Rodin's works outside Paris. These include his famous *The Burghers of Calais* and *Gates of Hell* and a bronze replica of *The Thinker*. The museum is about to undergo major renovations, so expect construction.

Fairmount Park

Fairmount Park (Map p286) is the nation's largest urban green space – it occupies 10% of the city's land and is many times the size of New York's Central Park (but who's counting?) This leafy retreat is immensely popular with locals who love to picnic, bike or run, but the park is also a cultural attraction in its own right: this is the home of the old waterworks, the Victorian-style Boathouse Row, a Japanese teahouse and a large zoo. The southern section stretches some 4 miles northwest from the Philadelphia Museum of Art to the Falls Bridge.

PHILADELPHIA MUSEUM OF ART

Degas, Renoir, Manet, Van Gogh, Duchamp, Stieglitz, Picasso, Dali – a long list of masters are represented at the country's third largest art **museum** (Map p286; 215-763-8100; www.philamuseum.org; adult/child $16/12; 10am-5pm Tue-Sun, to 8:45pm Fri), home to over 300,000 paintings, sculptures, drawings, prints and decorative arts. The collection showcases mostly Asian, European and American art, with excellent permanent exhibits of Constantine tapestries and Chinese snuff bottles; you'll also find a French cloister, a Japanese teahouse and a reception hall from 17th-century China. In the Great Stair Hall just past the 1st-floor entrance, look for the 1892 statue of the nude huntress Diana by Augustus St Gaudens. It was brought here from New York in 1932 after being saved from the demolished Madison Sq Garden.

FAIRMOUNT WATER WORKS INTERPRETIVE CENTER

When the Fairmount Water Works were built in 1815, Mark Twain praised their beauty, calling the system 'no less ornamental than useful.' A National Historic Engineering Landmark, today's **complex** (FFWIC; Map p286; 215-685-0723; www.fairmountwaterworks.org; 640 Waterworks Dr; admission free; 10am-5pm Tue-Sat, 1-5pm

PHILADELPHIA

Sun; ⓖ) comprises the waterworks – built in 1815 to pump 4 million gallons of water daily from the Schuylkill River to a reservoir on the site now occupied by the Philadelphia Museum of Art – and a family-friendly interpretive center. To educate the public about watersheds, the center has a helicopter simulator and hands-on activities for kids.

PLEASE TOUCH MUSEUM

A perennial hit with kids, the highly regarded **Please Touch Museum** (off Map p286; ☎ 215-581-3181; www.pleasetouchmuseum.org; 4231 Av of the Republic; all ages $15; ⓣ 9am-5pm Mon-Sat, 11am-5pm Sun; ⓖ) emphasizes learning through playing. Its interactive exhibits feature a mock TV studio with a working camera, a real SEPTA bus and a miniature supermarket. In the Sendak area children meet oversize creatures from books such as *Where the Wild Things Are*. Outside is a science park, jointly administered with the Franklin Institute Science Museum. It's an interactive learning area where exhibits include a miniature golf course and a radar detector.

BOATHOUSE ROW

This picturesque row (Map p286) of Tudor-style Victorian buildings lined up along the east bank of the Schuylkill River are a distinctive Philadelphia landmark. The boathouses are home base for the 'Schuylkill Navy,' a collection of high-brow rowing clubs; the structures date from the late 19th and early 20th centuries. Boathouse Row is a lovely enough sight during the day, but after dark it's illuminated to marvelous effect.

EARLY AMERICAN HOUSES

Fairmount Park features a number of fine early American houses, many which stand on their original grounds, that are open for public tours. The 19th-century Federal-style **Lemon Hill Mansion** (off Map p286; ☎ 215-232-4337; Sedgeley & Lemon Hill Drs; adult/child $5/3; ⓣ 10am-4pm April-Dec & by appt) was owned by financier Robert Morris and is furnished with period artifacts. Currently closed for repairs, the largest house in the park, **Strawberry Mansion** (off Map p286; ☎ 215-228-8364; www.historicstrawberrymansion.org; 2450 Strawberry Mansion Dr; adult/child $5/2) features an antique doll exhibit, Tucker porcelain, and mixture of Empire, Federal and Regency furniture.

The Philadelphia Museum of Art now administers two of the houses, **Cedar Grove** (off

Map p286) and **Mt Pleasant** (off Map p286), the latter of which was described by John Adams as 'the most elegant seat in Pennsylvania.' Log onto the museum website (www.phila museum.org/parkhouses) for details; while you're in the historic house circuit, keep your eyes open for other worthwhile stops like **Laurel Hill** (off Map p286; E Edgely Dr) and **Woodford** (off Map p286; 33rd & Dauphin Sts), a Georgian mansion with lovely colonial furniture and decorative art.

SHOFUSO JAPANESE HOUSE & GARDEN

A gift of the American-Japan Society of Tokyo, the authentic 17th-century-style upper-class **Japanese house** (off Map p286; ☎ 215-878-1373; 4301 Lansdowne Dr; adult/child $6/3; ⓣ 10am-4pm Wed-Fri, 11am-5pm Sat & Sun May-Sep) provides a peaceful retreat from the city bustle. Shofuso is set in beautiful Japanese gardens beside a stream and is open for guided or self-guided tours as well as tea ceremonies and origami demonstrations. The house and gardens are part of the 22-acre Horticultural Center.

PHILADELPHIA ZOO

West Fairmount Park's 42-acre **zoo** (Map p286; ☎ 215-243-1100; www.philadelphiazoo.org; 3400 W Girard Av; adult/child $18/15; ⓣ 9:30am-5pm; ⓖ) is the country's oldest, opened in 1874 and containing over 1800 furry and feathered creatures. Despite its age and Victorian touches, the zoo has been modernized and features many 'natural' habitats. The latest attractions (some involving extra fees) add even more kid-friendly appeal to the zoo and include a hand-carved Amazon rainforest carousel, a camel safari and swan boat rides.

University City & West Philadelphia

As the name suggests, University City buzzes with 30,000 students – all working on degrees at the University of Pennsylvania and Drexel University – but despite all the budget-friendly bars and crowded coffee shops, the neighborhood's not only about college kids. University City also has significant architectural sites and museums, not to mention an interesting neighbor: the much larger region of West Philadelphia.

For most of the last several decades, University City suffered from its position within blighted West Philly, and it wasn't very hard to find a house boarded shut or falling down directly across the street from the university. But in past years, University City has spruced itself up: the pedestrian-friendly streets near the campus have attracted a pair of movie theaters, numerous boutiques and a bunch of restaurants.

30TH ST STATION
Built by Graham, Anderson, Probst & White in 1934, this station (Map p301) deserves a visit, even if you're not catching a train. The massive neoclassical station's main concourse, with its refined ceiling treatment, is one of Philly's most romantic public spaces. The grand exterior, with Corinthian columns and beautiful floodlighting, can be seen across the river from John F Kennedy Blvd and Market St Bridge. It's worth noting that this is the busiest train hub in America outside of New York City.

UNIVERSITY OF PENNSYLVANIA
Philadelphia's contribution to the Ivy League traces its roots to Benjamin Franklin's Public Academy of Philadelphia, which opened its doors in 1751. The fifth-oldest college in the colonies, it stood out from its antecedents be-

cause they were concerned with the education of religious figures, while Penn's curriculum focused on nonsectarian instruction. The college became the nation's first university in 1779 and moved to this 260-acre campus, west of the Schuylkill, in the 1870s.

The central portion of the campus, Levy Park (also known as The Green), is well-landscaped and provides comfortable, shady spaces to laze about in the summer. On Locust Walk, College Hall was the first building and a classic example of the 'collegiate Gothic' style. The **Ann & Jerome Fisher Fine Arts Library** (Map p301; 220 S 34th St), generally referred to as the Furness Library as it was designed by renowned local architect Frank Furness, was an important contribution to innovative library design.

MUSEUM OF ARCHAEOLOGY & ANTHROPOLOGY
A magical place with interesting archaeological treasures from around the world, this famous **museum** (Map p301; ☎ 215-898-4000; www.penn.museum; 3260 South St; adult/child $10/6; ⏰ 10am-4:30pm Tue-Sat, 1-5pm Sun) houses one of the world's largest crystal balls (a 55-pounder which may have

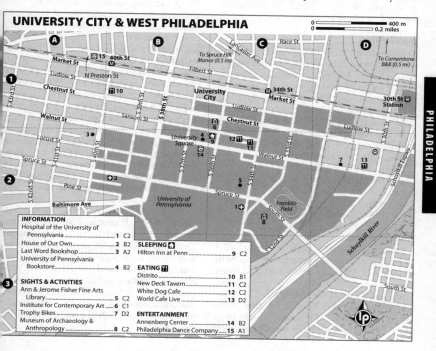

UNIVERSITY CITY & WEST PHILADELPHIA

| 0 | 400 m |
| 0 | 0.2 miles |

INFORMATION

PHILADELPHIA

belonged to the Empress Dowager of China), samples of the oldest writing ever found (from Sumeria), a waterproof parka made from the throat lining of sea lions, bronzes from Benin in Nigeria, and a 12-ton granite Sphinx of Rameses II, c 1293–1185 BC, from Egypt.

INSTITUTE FOR CONTEMPORARY ART

Philadelphia's principal contemporary art venue, this **museum** (ICA; Map p301; ☎ 215-898-7108; www.icaphila.org; 118 S 36th St; admission free; ☺ 12-8pm Wed-Fri, 11am-5pm Sat & Sun) features regularly changing exhibitions of up-and-coming artists, film screenings, art classes and seminars, and avant-garde theater performances. The ICA's claim to fame is Andy Warhol, whose first important show was held here; the museum has also displayed the works of Robert Mapplethorpe, Robert Morris, Patti Smith and Charles LeDray.

Northwest Philadelphia

Well worth a visit if time permits are the genteel Northwest Philadelphia suburbs of Chestnut Hill, Manayunk and Germantown, 4 to 6 miles northwest of downtown, as well as Merion, where you'll find the prestigious Barnes Foundation Gallery.

MANAYUNK

With its steep hills and Victorian row-houses overlooking the Schuylkill River, Manayunk – from a Native American expression meaning 'where we go to drink' – still remains a good spot to accomplish this activity. The gentrified Main St, a National Historic District with chic boutiques, art galleries, restaurants and bars – is an appealing place for a stroll. Back before railroads took over, canal systems like this one in Manayunk were a primary means of moving cargo in the first half of the 19th century. Today the Manayunk system is in picturesque ruins, and you can stroll along its former **Tow Path**, peering at rail lines, derelict canal locks, old textile mills and remnants of buildings.

CHESTNUT HILL

Chestnut Hill got its start in the colonial period as a farming community, and both British and American forces marched along the town's main road as they went to and from the Battle of Germantown. The town underwent serious change in the 1880s when Henry Howard Houston bought large tracts of land to develop for wealthy families.

Over several decades, a few hundred beautiful homes were built (and many survive) in styles ranging from Queen Anne to the Arts and Crafts movement. Most of these homes are stone, made from schist quarried in the Wissahickon. The area was mostly farmland until the Pennsylvania Railroad connected it with downtown Philadelphia at the end of the 19th century. Along Germantown Ave and its cobblestoned side streets you'll find fashionable shops, cafes and restaurants; you'll also encounter the 92-acre **Morris Arboretum of the University of Pennsylvania** (off Map p286; ☎ 215-247-5777; www.business-services.upenn.edu/arboretum; 100 Northwestern Ave) and the **Woodmere Art Museum** (off Map p286; ☎ 215-247-0476; www.woodmereartmuseum.org; 9201 Germantown Ave; admission free; ☺ 10am-5pm Tue-Sat, 1-5pm Sun) with its collection of 19th- and 20th-century American and European art.

To arrive by car, head north along Broad St, turn left onto Pike St then right onto Germantown Ave, which takes you through Germantown and Mt Airy to Chestnut Hill.

GERMANTOWN

Established on land deeded by William Penn to 13 German-speaking families in 1683, Germantown, 6 miles northwest of downtown, became a papermaking, printing and publishing center. It's also the site of Philadelphia's only revolutionary battlefield and a former country retreat for the upper crust who needed to flee from outbreaks of yellow fever or escape the city's oppressive summer heat. When George Washington was president and serving his term in Philadelphia, he joined the migration of the wealthy; thus Germantown became the de facto national capital. Germantown is also famous as an important stop on the Underground Railroad: Harriet Tubman led freed slaves along the Wissahickon to a Germantown Ave station, the **Johnson House** (☎ 215-438-1768; www.johnsonhouse.org; 6306 Germantown Ave; adult/child $8/4; ☺ 10am-4pm Thu-Fri, Sat from 1pm).

Today, an identity crisis looms over Germantown. It contains several excellent history-related attractions, but monuments are underused and sit along a seedy commercial corridor with check-cashing places, convenience stores and pawn shops. But you'll also find blocks of well-loved, well-preserved (and huge) Victorian mansions on grassy lawns and tree-lined streets – a clear reminder of Germantown's days as a supremely affluent community.

Some historic and architectural gems open to the public (all charge $6 to $10 admission and are usually open on Thursday and Sunday afternoons from April to December) are the Victorian Gothic **Ebenezer Maxwell Mansion** (off Map p286; ☎ 215-438-1861; www.ebenezermaxwell mansion.org; 200 W Tulpehocken St), built in 1859; **Cliveden** (off Map p286; ☎ 215-848-1777; 6401 Germantown Ave), a Palladian-style Georgian house dating from 1763; the 1750s Federal-style **Upsala** (off Map p286; ☎ 215-842-1798; 6430 Germantown Ave); and the charming **Wyck** (off Map p286; ☎ 215-848-1690; www.wyck.org; 6026 Germantown Ave), a Quaker home built in 1690.

To arrive by car, head north along Broad St, turn left onto Pike St, then take a right onto Germantown Ave.

MERION
About 6 miles northwest of downtown, Merion sees a steady stream of visitors thanks to the wonderful **Barnes Foundation** (off Map p286; ☎ 610-667-0290; www.barnesfoundation.org; 300 N Latch's Lane; adult $15; ☼ 9:30am-5pm Thu-Sun Sep-May & Wed-Sun Jun-Aug). The art collection is set to move to a new location on the Benjamin Franklin Parkway; for now the Merion location houses the world's largest private collection of impressionist, post-impressionist and early French modern paintings. The gallery contains works by Cezanne, Degas, Matisse, Manet, Monet, Modigliani, Picasso, Renoir, Rousseau, Seurat and Van Gogh. Art and craftwork from around the world, including antique furniture, ceramics, hand-wrought iron and Native American jewelry, are also major draws. The adjacent arboretum boasts a wide diversity of plants.

If you're driving, follow the Schuylkill Expressway northwest then turn left at the City Ave turnoff. Follow City Ave then turn right onto Lancaster Rd; Latch's Lane is the fourth turn on the left.

ACTIVITIES
The huge Fairmount Park is the city's main center for outdoor activities. With around 100 miles of jogging, cycling and bridle paths and the Schuylkill River and Wissahickon Creek within its borders, the park is very popular with city residents. For details of what's available in the park call **Fairmount Park Information** ☎ 215-685-0000).

For walking, jogging and bicycling, a paved 8.2-mile loop from the Philadelphia Museum of Art heads along Kelly Drive on the east bank of the Schuylkill River to the Falls Bridge, then returns to the museum via West River Drive. Further north, Forbidden Drive is a 5.5-mile traffic-free gravel path on the west bank of Wissahickon Creek with some spectacular scenery. Bike rentals are available around town; try **Trophy Bikes** (Map p301; ☎ 215-592-1234; www.trophybikes.com; 3131 Walnut St). For a map of city bike trails, visit the website of the **Bicycle Coalition of Greater Philadelphia** (www. bicyclecoalition.org/resources/maps).

Rowing and canoeing are popular on the Schuylkill River. Fairmount Park also has 115 tennis courts open free to the public and five outdoor swimming pools, as well as six 18-hole public golf courses. Weekends tend to be fully booked.

TOURS
A variety of tours exist to help you explore the city. They can be booked directly with the operators, through your hotel reception, at the Independence Visitors Center (p284) or with a travel agent.

Walking Tours
Free audio walking tours are offered by the park rangers at Independence National Historic Park (p285); check with the Independence Visitors Center for the current schedule.

The specialized tours at **Philadelphia Urban Adventures** (☎ 215-280-3746; www.philadelphiaurban adventures.com; Independence Visitor Center; tours $20-59) are highly recommended; offerings include full city treks as well as half-day tours like 'Essence of South Philly.' Architecture buffs line up for 'Emergence of a Modern Metropolis', a design-focused walking tour run by the **Philadelphia Center for Architecture** (Map p286; ☎ 215-569-3186; www.philadelphiacfa.org; 1218 Arch St; adult/child $15/5; ☼ 2pm Tue, Thu & Sat Apr-Nov, 2pm Sat Dec-Mar). After dark, the candlelit **Ghost Tour of Philadelphia** (☎ 215-413-1997; www.ghosttour.com/philadelphia.html; purchase tickets at Independence Visitor Center; adult/child $17/8; ☼ 7:30pm nightly Apr-Oct, Fri & Sat only Nov, Dec & Mar; select dates in Jan-Feb) takes curious visitors through the shadowy back streets and gardens of Society Hill and the historic center.

Trolley Bus & Carriage Tours
Take in the city sights with **Philadelphia Trolley Works & 76 Carriage Company** (☎ 215-389-8687; www. phillytour.com; adult/child from $27/10), whose popular

tours include sightseeing in motorized 'trolley' buses, trips on a London double-decker bus, horse-drawn carriage outings, the 'Philly by Night' tour and the popular 'Franklin's Footsteps' walking tour of Old City. Purchase tickets online or at Independence Visitor Center (p284).

Cruises

To see the skyline from the water, climb aboard the **Spirit of Philadelphia** (Map p286; ☎ 866-455-3866; www.spiritofphiladelphia.com; Penn's Landing; adult $37-84), which offers popular lunch, dinner and sunset cruises along the Delaware River. Good views of the river and city are also possible on the Riverlink ferry to the New Jersey State Aquarium. Kids love the adventures run by **Philadelphia Duck Tours** (☎ 215-629-1131; www.philadelphia.ridetheducks.com; Independence Visitors Center; adult/child $27/17) – you'll tour the historic district aboard a WWII DUKW amphibious vehicle, then splash into the river for a boat ride around the city.

FESTIVALS & EVENTS

The highlights of the Philadelphia events calendar are listed below:

January

Mummers Parade (www.mummers.com) January 1 is the day to see many thousands of mostly Italian-American men strut around in fancy handmade costumes with makeup and banjos. See the boxed text.

February/March

Philadelphia Flower Show (www.theflowershow.com; Convention Center) The world's largest and most prestigious flower show makes for a spectacular week – unless, of course, you're allergic to pollen.

April

Philadelphia Antique Show (www.philaantiques. com; West Philadelphia) More then 50 dealers and their objects gather for the country's premier show of American antiques and decorative arts.

May

Philadelphia Festival of World Cinema (www. filmadelphia.org) A 10-day festival celebrated at venues across the city, it features the best independent films from around the world.

Aberdeen Dad Vail Regatta (www.dadvail.org) The largest collegiate regatta in the US draws thousands of rowers and spectators to the Schuylkill River.

June

Odunde (www.odundeinc.org) One of the country's largest and oldest African-American festivals, Odunde draws over 200,000 spectators to South Street. Derived from a West African spirit festival, the event features visiting dignitaries and a boatload of food vendors and dance performances.

Pride Day (www.phillypride.org) The colorful LGBT Pride Parade and Festival is held in June, International Gay Pride Month.

July

Welcome America (www.americasbirthday.com) A series of Independence Day celebrations with parades, concerts and fireworks during the first week of the month. Often preceded by the Taste of Philadelphia food festival on Penn's Landing.

Xponential Music Festival (www.xpn.org) A three-day celebration of singer-songwriters and bands such as Yo La Tengo and Cowboy Junkies, thrown by Penn's WXPN radio station. There's also a full schedule of kids' activities.

August

Pennsylvania Dutch Festival (www.readingterminalmarket.org) The Reading Terminal Market comes alive with Amish festivities, from buggy rides to bluegrass music and shoofly pie contests.

Philadelphia Folk Festival (www.pfs.org) One of the city's most famous events, the three-day festival features a first-class lineup; recent performers included Bonnie 'Prince' Billy and Jeff Tweedy.

September

Live Arts Festival & Philly Fringe (www.pafringe. org) From serious dance and theater to uncouth vaudeville and drag acts, the highly acclaimed Fringe Festival puts on hundreds of shows in a two-week period at diverse venues around the city.

Feria del Barrio (www.tallerpr.org) A lively celebration of Latino art and culture, this family-friendly *feria* (festival) features spicy street food and Spanish-language music performances.

October

Terror Behind the Walls (www.easternstate.org/halloween) As if the Eastern State Penitentiary wasn't creepy enough to begin with: around Halloween, the deserted prison morphs into a full-fledged haunted house-style attraction that's 'high-startle and low-gore.'

November

Thanksgiving Day Parade The country's oldest Thanksgiving parade, with floats and bands along Market St and Benjamin Franklin Pkwy.

December

Christmas Holiday Tours (www.fairmountpark.org/tours.asp) Get into the holiday spirit with tours of seven historic houses in Fairmount Park dressed up for Christmas.

SLEEPING

Whether you'd like to hang your hat in a family-friendly hotel or a character-filled B&B, there's no shortage of accommodation options in Philadelphia. During holidays, summer weekends, convention center events, university graduations or football games, popular hotels are often booked up well ahead of time. If you're staying downtown, be aware that overnight garage parking can drive up the price of your stay. Many hotels and B&Bs also add a hefty tax onto the nightly rate.

Historic District & South Street
BUDGET

Apple Hostel (Map p292; ☎ 215-922-0222; www.applehostels.com; 32 Bank St; dm/d $31/79; ☒ ☎) This clean and simple hostel has shared dorms and doubles. Complimentary offerings include coffee all day, luggage storage, Thursday pub crawls, laundry soap, and a fully equipped communal kitchen.

our pick **Seventh Street B&B** (Map p286; ☎ 215-238-9042; http://mysite.verizon.net/lu72; 702 S 7th St; d without/with bathroom from $105/120, 2-night min stay; ☎ ☒) A warm, family-friendly inn located in a turn-of-the-century brick townhouse, the Seventh Street B&B is centrally located but wonderfully quiet. There's just a handful of rooms and suites, so book ahead – with such a thoughtful host, appealing public areas and fair prices, this place won't stay under wraps for long.

Thomas Bond House B&B (Map p292; ☎ 215-923-8523; www.thomasbondhousebandb.com; 129 S 2nd St; d $115-190; ☒ ☎) Featured on the *Today Show* and in the *Washington Post*, this historic B&B dates from 1769. The restored townhouse still boasts a marble fireplace, so

---

MUMMERS' PARADE

Said to be the country's oldest continual folk festival, it isn't known for sure how the Mummers' Parade started. It may have originated from a Swedish and Finnish custom of celebrating a 'Second Christmas' with wandering minstrels, or from the English Mummery Play, a kind of burlesque with harlequins dressed in silk and satin. In German, Mummerkleid means 'fancy dress' and Mummenspiel means 'masquerade.' Philadelphia's first Mummers appeared in the 1700s parading in the Washington Ave area, and the bands grew in size until, in 1901, an official site at Broad St from South Philadelphia to City Hall was ordained for the parade. The South Philadelphia headquarters and the Mummers' association with the neighborhood have helped give the parade a distinct Italian-American flavor.

Staged each New Year's Day, participants number over 25,000, with most of the participants being heterosexual men wearing sequins, feathers, makeup and outrageous costumes. Women dress up too, and they all strut their way along Broad St. They're accompanied by bands that are traditionally limited to accordions, saxophones, drums, violins, banjos, bass fiddles, glockenspiels and clarinets.

As with Mardi Gras, the extravagant costumes are the highlight of the show. The Mummers are members of clubs that represent different city neighborhoods. They spend all year (and a lot of money) designing and creating their costumes, not to mention practicing the music and choreographing their routines. Each year features different themes, such as fairy tales or Broadway shows.

The parade starts at 7am and can last as long as 12 hours. Despite the low temperatures, there's always a large, enthusiastic and often hard-drinking turnout. If you miss the parade, you can catch the Mummers' bands performing at the Mummers' Museum and at other special performances. To catch them in all their glory, though, you really need to see them on New Year's Day.

The parade's theme song is 'Oh Dem Golden Slippers,' written by James Bland (1854–1911) in 1879. He was born of free African-American parents in Flushing, NY, and studied at Howard University. He worked for a while as a page in the House of Representatives and later became a successful minstrel in England where he gave a command performance for Queen Victoria. He wrote about 700 songs, including 'Carry Me Back to Old Virginny,' but was only credited with 37. Around the turn of the 20th century he settled in Philadelphia where he died in poverty.

cozy, complimentary wine and cheese every evening and a kitchen baking fresh muffins every morning – not to mention the killer breakfast spread put out on weekends. Simpler rooms have wrought-iron beds while fancier doubles have Chippendale furnishings and whirlpool tubs.

MIDRANGE & TOP END

Alexander Inn (Map p286; ☎ 215-923-3535; www.alexan derinn.com; 12th & Spruce Sts; s $119, d $129-169; 🔀 🤶) If period furniture and chess boards aren't your thing, make a beeline for this contemporary boutique hotel where 48 rooms are filled with splashy artwork and good-quality bath products and linens. Even though the antique building has been renovated, it still has its original stained glass and marble tilework – and with B&B-style extras like an all-day complimentary fresh fruit and pastry bar, you get the best of both worlds.

Morris House Hotel (Map p286; ☎ 215-922-2446; www.morrishousehotel.com; 225 S 8th St; d/ste from $179/249; 🤶) Just a block away from Washington Sq, Morris House is charming through and through. The building, dating from 1787, is a registered national historic landmark, with antique decor, hardwood floors and a daily afternoon tea. But for all its grace, the place isn't stuck in the past – standard amenities include Godiva chocolate squares on your pillow and 600-thread-count cotton sheets.

our pick Penn's View Hotel (Map p292; ☎ 215-922-7600; www.pennsviewhotel.com; Front & Market Sts; d $149-299; 🔀 🤶) Another lovely boutique hotel, Penn's View is known for its beautiful rooms – the premium king room has a marble Jacuzzi, fireplace and views over the Delaware River – but perhaps even more so for its fabulous wine bar. With the largest wine preservation system in the world, the bar at Ristorante Panorama boasts a vast selection of wines by the glass, not to mention a romantically lit place in which to savor them.

Rittenhouse Square & Center City

BUDGET & MIDRANGE

La Reserve B&B (Map p286; ☎ 215-735-1137; www.la reservebandb.com; 1804/1806 Pine St; d/studio from $80/115; 🤶 👶) This B&B comprises a pair of pretty townhouses dating from the 1850s. Inside you'll find a grand piano, decorative candlesticks, floral brocades and antique furnishings. Studio rooms come with kitchenettes, ideal if you're traveling with a baby or small

child; breakfast is served in a formal dining room and the main parlor is a great place to kick back with a good book.

The Independent (Map p286; ☎ 215-772-1440; theindependenthotel.com; 1234 Locust St; d/ste from $170/197; 🤶) This sleek boutique hotel, housed in a restored Georgian revival building, contains 24 fashionable rooms with hardwood floors, first-class bedding and wool rugs from New Zealand – not to mention extras like flat-screen TVs and wine and cheese receptions on weeknights. The impressive Queen Loft Suite has two floors and a dining room with fireplace.

our pick Hotel Palomar Philadelphia (Map p286; ☎ 215-563-5006; www.hotelpalomar-philadelphia.com; 117 S 17th St; d/ste from $239/319; 🔀 🤶 👶) Stylish, inviting and ecofriendly, the Hotel Palomar – like others from the Kimpton line – isn't a typical chain hotel. The amenities at this upscale boutique-style place set it apart: it has pet-friendly facilities, a slick fitness center, a complimentary wine hour each evening, an organic coffee bar, in-room spa services and welcome kits for kids.

TOP END

The Rittenhouse (Map p286; ☎ 215-546-9000; www.ritt enhousehotel.com; 210 W Rittenhouse Sq; d/ste from $275/599; 🔀 🤶) The very picture of Philadelphia-style sophistication, the Rittenhouse was recently named the number-one hotel in the city by *Travel & Leisure* magazine. The sumptuous downtown building features 98 rooms and suites with classic mahogany furnishings, luxurious linens, marble bathrooms, feather-down pillows and huge HD TVs with iPod hook-ups. The property also includes two fine dining establishments, the Mary Cassatt Tea Room and a gorgeous full-service spa – it's enough to make you forget about Benjamin Franklin and stay in the hotel all day.

Rittenhouse 1715 (Map p286; ☎ 215-546-6500; www.rittenhouse1715.com; 1715 Rittenhouse Sq St; d/ste from $249/459; 🔀 🤶) For lavish lodgings in a more intimate setting, try this romantic boutique hotel: on a quiet side street, Rittenhouse 1715 contains 23 guest rooms with marble baths, oversized plasma TVs, designer bath products and old-world charm. The Drawing Room serves fine wines in the evening and the complimentary breakfast is an event in itself.

Fairmount Park & University City

Chamounix Mansion (off Map p286; ☎ 215-878-367 www.philahostel.org; 3250 Chamounix Dr, W Fairmount Park dm $23;) Once a grand country house, this elegant old mansion is now a basic but atmospheric hostel in the center of Fairmount Park. There are free bikes for exploring the area, a communal kitchen, a front porch for lazy afternoons, and a picnic area; the dorm-style accommodations are less impressive than the house, but functional nonetheless.

Spruce Hill Manor (off Map p301; ☎ 215-472-2213; www.sprucehillmanor.com; 3709 Baring St; d $150-175;) In a Victorian mansion dating from 1879, Spruce Hill has lovely gardens, original woodwork and homelike rooms with private baths and convenient kitchenettes. It's a kid-friendly establishment (at least for guests over nine years' old) and there's free parking and luggage storage. Breakfast is all-natural and organic.

Cornerstone B&B (off Map p301; ☎ 215-387-6065; www.cornerstonebandb.com; 3300 Baring St; d $165-205;) With a picturesque wraparound porch, colorful stained glass windows and brightly painted walls, this urban inn consists of several beautifully illuminated rooms. Each has a flat-screen TV, refrigerator, fine linens and a private bathroom. The weekend breakfast spread is memorable.

The Hilton Inn at Penn (Map p301; ☎ 215-222-0200; www.theinnatpenn.com; 3600 Sansom St; d from $199/429;) Smack dab in the middle of the Penn campus is this elegant inn outfitted with a wine bar, fitness center and contemporary guest rooms characteristic of the Hilton chain. There's a wine bar and an Italian restaurant, but with so many restaurants and watering holes nearby in the student neighborhood, it might not matter.

EATING & DRINKING

Overstuffed cheesesteaks, freshly baked pretzels, ice-cold microbrews, hoagies heaped high with Italian salami and cheese – anyone hungry yet? Eating is a one of the city's finest pastimes, from the budget-friendly Italian market and ethnic dives of South Philly to the refined bistros and wine bars of Rittenhouse Sq. Generally speaking, bars get going around happy hour (5pm) and shutter around 2am, with a few exceptions.

Historic District & Center City
Nanzhou Hand Drawn Noodle House (Map p286; ☎ 215-923-1550; 927 Race St, Chinatown; mains $6-15) This Chinatown staple is the local pick for wonderfully savory soups made with long, chewy homemade noodles and reasonably authentic southwest Chinese cuisine (pig ears, anyone?) It's a no-frills joint, accepting cash only, but it's cheap and unbeatable in the neighborhood – and perhaps in the city, as well.

our pick Continental Restaurant + Martini Bar (Map p292; ☎ 215-923-6069; www.continentalmartinibar.com; 138 Market St; mains $6-13) This retro martini bar and eatery is packed round-the-clock, thanks to the stylish atmosphere, central location, well-mixed vintage cocktails and simple but gourmet international dishes like pad thai with jumbo lump crab and Mexican-style pizza. The bar stays open till 2am.

Amada (Map p292; ☎ 215-625-2450; www.amadarestaurant.com; 217 Chestnut St; tapas $5-12; closed for lunch on weekends) Amada's known for authentic Spanish tapas; the rustic-chic setting; with a long bar stretching along one side of the room and candlelit wooden tables for two, is a cozy place to sample lamb meatballs or clams & chorizo.

Fork (Map p292; ☎ 215-625-9425; www.forkrestaurant.com; 306 Market St; mains $10-28) Praised in *Food and Wine*, this sophisticated New American bistro turns out classic dishes based on local and seasonal produce. The wine list is excellent, as is the leisurely Sunday brunch – it's hard to go wrong with quiche lorraine and a spicy, fresh Bloody Mary.

PHILADELPHIA

THE HOAGIE, CHEESESTEAK & PRETZEL
The hoagie, a sub-style sandwich filled with Italian cold cuts and sliced cheeses on French bread, got its name from the city's Hog Island Shipyard. The workers there used to call their lunchtime staple 'hoggies' before today's name stuck. Cheesesteaks, a sandwich of sliced steak and melted cheese, were also invented in Philadelphia, and several places claim to make the best, including archrivals Pat's King of Steaks (p309) and Geno's (p309), both located near the Italian Market.

Soft pretzels are another specialty. Locals say that you should buy them from the Amish at Reading Terminal Market, they should be stuck together and rectangular or they're not the real thing, and you should eat them with mustard.

Zento (Map p292; ☎ 215-925-9998; www.zentocontemporary.com; 138 Chestnut St; sushi & sashimi platter $25-35; ⓨ closed for lunch Sun) This petite sushi bar is a peaceful lunchtime hideaway near the historic sites. Share a sushi and sashimi platter with a friend or opt for the king crab miso (a steal at $5) on a chilly afternoon. Zento's signature roll is the fresh-tasting 'square sushi' with eel, avocado and plum sauce and tuna or salmon. Bring your own sake: the eatery is BYOB.

Union Trust Steakhouse (Map p292; ☎ 215-925-6000; www.uniontruststeakhouse.com; 717 Chestnut St; mains $25-50; ⓨ closed for lunch Sat & Sun) An upmarket steakhouse located in a cavernous, ultra-glamorous old bank, Union Trust wins major points for atmosphere. But it's not only the glitter and soaring ceilings and polished chrome that make the restaurant a fine spot for a special occasion: Union Trust also serves up monster-sized Argentinian steaks, decadent seafood towers stacked high with raw oysters and king crab legs, and killer cocktails (with prices to match.)

L'Etage (Map p286; ☎ 215-592-0656; www.creperie-beaumonde.com; 6th & Bainbridge Sts; cocktails $7; ⓨ closed Mon) A vintage-chic cocktail lounge and performance space a few blocks south of Washington Sq, L'Etage is the spot for story slams, acoustic music, or after-dinner drinks in one of the bar's cozy nooks. The lovely Beau Monde creperie downstairs is open until 11pm most nights.

Beneluxx Tasting Room (☎ 267-318-7269; www.beneluxx.com; 33 S 3rd St; drinks $6-14) Casually gourmet but unpretentious, this subterranean beer and wine bar offers glass-washers at every table, sampler menus, asiago cheese fondues and chocolate tastings served by a well-informed staff. It's a lesser-known watering hole in the neighborhood; if you're up for a bar hop, head to Beneluxx's sister bar, the famous (and always crowded) Eulogy Belgian Tavern, nearby at 136 Chestnut St, or Triumph Brewing Company, a few doors down at 117 Chestnut St.

Rittenhouse Square
BUDGET & MIDRANGE

Argan Moroccan Cuisine (Map p286; ☎ 215-873-6552; 132 S 17th St; mains $6-12; ⓨ closed Sun, closed for dinner Mon) With quick service and delicious baba ghanouj, Argan is an ideal lunch locale when you're in the neighborhood. The place is famous for spicy lamb sandwiches, mint tea, and vegetarian-friendly pita and hummus platters.

Monk's Cafe (Map p286; ☎ 215-545-7005; www.monkscafe.com; 264 S 16th St; mains $8-15) This good-looking and immensely popular brasserie is famous for an excellent list of Belgian beers and top-notch comfort food like savory mussels and juicy burgers with perfectly crispy pommes frites.

La Viola (Map p286; ☎ 215-735-8630; 253 S 16th St; mains $10-15) Planning a night at the theater? Make a night of it by scoring reservations at this intimate Italian spot. With just a handful of tables and a short but authentic menu, La Viola is the real deal – it's cash-only and BYOB.

Alma de Cuba (Map p286; ☎ 215-988-1799; www.almadecubarestaurant.com; 1623 Walnut St; mains $16-32) This low-lit, contemporary Cuban eatery is a seductive locale for a pair of icy mojitos and lime-infused lobster ceviche. The cuisine is innovative, to be sure, but the dramatic ambience is the real scene-stealer.

McGillin's Olde Ale House (Map p286; ☎ 215-735-5562; www.mcgillins.com; 1310 Drury St; beer sampler $8.50) A rollicking Irish pub that pulls in a near-nightly crowd of college kids and 20-somethings craving wings and budget-friendly pitchers of beer and wine by the glass, McGillin's also serves up decent roast beef sandwiches. A lively spot to knock back a few; try Monk's Cafe or Beneluxx for something mellower.

Tria (Map p286; ☎ 215-972-8742; www.triacafe.com; 18th & Sansom Sts; snacks $3-10) This cool, laid-back bar is billed as a 'wine, cheese and beer cafe.' Need we say more? Many of the microbrews are local, the list of wines by the glass is extensive, the tapas-style appetizers are well-priced, and the staff know their stuff: they also run wine courses and the popular Tria Fermentation School.

TOP END

Barclay Prime (Map p286; ☎ 215-732-7560; www.barclayprime.com; 237 S 18th St; steaks $41-56) The same ambitious restaurateur behind Alma de Cuba dreamed up this chic update on a classic steak house. The look is elegant with a funky twist – crystal chandeliers, polished wood and lime green modernist furniture – and the dry aged porterhouse is positively mouthwatering.

Fogo de Chão Churrascaria (Map p286; ☎ 215-636-9700; www.fogodechao.com; 1337 Chestnut St; lunch/dinner $33/50; ⓨ closed for lunch on weekends) With sizzling skewers of spicy beef, pork, chicken and sausage delivered to your table, killer cocktails and a fabulous salad bar, this classy Brazilian steakhouse – though one of the better branches of a US–Brazil chain – is a carnivore's dream come true.

Le Bec Fin (Map p286; ☎ 215-567-1000; www.lebec fin.com; 1523 Walnut St; prix fixe lunch $55, 4-course dinner $80) A Philadelphia institution that earns a mention partly for its famous reputation, the Parisian-inspired Le Bec Fin boasts an elegant, highly decorative interior, first-rate service – the younger crowd might find it a bit on the stuffy side – and rich, traditional French cuisine. But this landmark restaurant is clearly looking to appeal to a new generation: the downstairs Le Bar Lyonnais hosts a happy-hour special on weekday evenings with classy cocktails (like the Hemingway, a snappy concoction of rum, grapefruit, and maraschino liqueur) priced at just $6.

University City & Museum Area

As in any student neighborhood, University City overflows with budget-friendly pubs, late-night cafes, basic diners and ethnic eateries with bargain lunch buffets.

BUDGET & MIDRANGE

Sabrina's Cafe (Map p286; ☎ 215-636-9061; www.sabrina scafe.com; 1804 Callowhill St; mains $7-18; ☺ closed for dinner Sun & Mon) Known for spot-on breakfast dishes like banana pancakes and caramelized challah French toast, this pretty cafe also has locals (and tourists around for the art museum) lining up later in the day for cobb salad, garlic chicken wraps, and ahi tuna.

Zorba's Taverna (Map p286; ☎ 215-978-5990; 2230 Fairmount Ave; mains $8-12; ☺ closed for lunch Sun) This friendly family-run Greek restaurant is traditional and satisfying: mural paintings of the island of Santorini cover the walls, and on the menu you'll find excellent gyros and Greek salads topped with crumbled fresh feta cheese.

our pick **World Cafe Live** (Map p301; ☎ 215-222-1400; www.worldcafelive.com; 3025 Walnut St; mains $8-15) This cool performance space and theater offers fresh American fare – salads, wraps, sandwiches – but more importantly, you can lunch here while listening to acoustic music, part of the Live at Noon concert series. The venue hosts a lighthearted happy hour, gourmet beer tastings, film screenings and children's events.

Distrito (Map p301; ☎ 215-222-1657; www.distrito restaurant.com; 3945 Chestnut St; mains $9-16) Billed as 'modern Mexican,' this eatery specializes in tasting menus and small bites like shrimp and chorizo tacos. The place is perhaps more well-known for its ambience, which tows the line between minimalist and funky; you'll find a slick cantina cocktail bar with hot-pink barstools and 60s-style sofas alongside campier decor, such as a child's swingset and a taxi dining booth reminiscent of the table where John Travolta and Uma Thurman dined in *Pulp Fiction*.

New Deck Tavern (Map p301; ☎ 215-386-4600; www.newdecktavern.com; 3408 Sandom St; mains $10-18; ⚘) With delicious half-pound burgers and comfort food like shepherd's pie, a solid beer selection, a kids' menu and a lively happy hour, this Irish pub has something for families and college students alike.

White Dog Cafe (Map p301; ☎ 215-386-9224; www. whitedog.com; 3420 Sansom St; mains $15-36) Founded by the highly respected community activist Judy Wicks, the environmentally conscious White Dog is housed in three Victorian brownstones and specializes in organic international cuisine made with seasonal produce. It's renowned for its charm and innovation.

South St & South Philadelphia

South Street crawls with ethnic eateries and stylish bar-restaurants that seem to come and go with the seasons: it's fun to just take a stroll down the avenue and see which sidewalk table or bar stool looks good. But starting here and into South Philly, you'll also find the city's longtime cheesesteak institutions. Ask any of the city's natives: everyone proclaims loyalty to one of the following establishments. At these historic – and wonderfully atmospheric – takeaway joints, the lines are long, the hours run late, and the house special currently sets you back around $7.50.

Take your pick from the following:

Jim's Steaks (Map p286; ☎ 215-928-1911; www.jims steaks.com; 400 South St)

Pat's King of Steaks (off Map p286; ☎ 215-468-1546; www.patskingofsteaks.com; 1237 E Passyunk Av)

Geno's Steaks (off Map p286; ☎ 215-389-0659; www. genosteaks.com; 1218 S 9th St)

ENTERTAINMENT

The Avenue of the Arts is Philly's premier cultural destination, while more bohemian neighborhoods like South Street and Northern Liberties are popular for drinking, dancing and live music. For current events, check the

'Weekend' section of Friday's *Philadelphia Inquirer* and other recommended internet resources (see p283). You can buy tickets for most entertainment from **Ticketmaster** (☎ 215-336-2000) or from **Upstages** (Map p286; ☎ 215-569-9786; 1412 Chestnut St) in Center City, where you can buy full price tickets or half-price on the day of the performance.

Theater

Philadelphia has a rich and varied theater scene that ranges from Broadway shows to community theater and from experimental drama to student repertory. Check www.theatrealliance.org or www.theatermania.com/philadelphia for more information and listings.

   The Walnut St Theatre (Map p286; ☎ 215-574-3550; www.walnutstreettheatre.org; 825 Walnut St), at 9th St, established in 1809, stages mostly mainstream drama, dance and musical productions, while the **Forrest Theatre** (Map p286; ☎ 215-923-1515; www.forrest-theatre.com; 1114 Walnut St) puts on big Broadway musical hits and the **Wilma Theater** (Map p286; ☎ 215-546-7824; www.wilmatheater.org; Spruce & Broad Sts) provides excellent avant-garde drama and comedy.

   At the University of Pennsylvania, the **Annenberg Center** (Map p301; ☎ 215-898-6701; www.pennpresents.org; 3680 Walnut St) comprises several theaters and stages theater, dance and children's shows.

Dance

The acclaimed **Pennsylvania Ballet** (www.paballet.org) performs at the Academy of Music (see p294) and the **Merriam Theater** (Map p286; www.merriam-theater.com; 250 S Broad St) at the University of the Arts. The **Philadelphia Dance Company** (Map p301; ☎ 215-387-8200; www.philadanco.org; 9 Philadanco Way), also known as Philadanco, explores the black experience through modern dance and ballet at the Annenberg Center and other venues.

Cinema

Philadelphia has a large selection of cinemas showing mainstream movies. For a mix of mainstream, limited-release and foreign films downtown, try arthouse-style cinemas like the downtown **Ritz at the Bourse** (Map p292; ☎ 215-925-7900; 400 Ranstead St). Near Rittenhouse Sq, the charming **Roxy Theater** (Map p286; ☎ 215-923-6699; 2023 Sansom St) shows classic cult US and foreign films.

Classical Music & Opera

The world-class **Philadelphia Orchestra** (www.philorc.org) performs at the Academy of Music (see p294) and the **Mann Center** (off Map p286; ☎ 215-893-1999; www.manncenter.org; 5201 Parkside Av) in Fairmount Park. The high-tech **Kimmel Center for the Performing Arts** (Map p286; ☎ 215-790-5800; www.kimmelcenter.org; Broad & Spruce Sts; ☼ 10am-6pm) also hosts classical and jazz concerts. You can also catch performances at the **Curtis Institute of Music** (Map p286; ☎ 215-893-7902; www.curtis.edu; 1726 Locust St), where many classical music students do their training. For large-scale operatic productions with international stars, there's the **Opera Company of Philadelphia** (☎ 215-732-8400; www.operaphila.org), performing at the Kimmel Center and the Academy of Music.

Jazz, Blues & Gospel

Philadelphia has a strong jazz and blues tradition, its own sound and some terrific venues. The **Philadelphia Clef Club of the Performing Arts** (Map p286; ☎ 215-893-9912; www.clefclub.org; 738 Broad St) is part of the Avenue of the Arts. It's a nonprofit organization that promotes jazz by hosting public performances, keeping records of its history and training musicians. The earthy **Ortlieb's Jazzhaus** (Map p286; ☎ 215-922-1035; www.ortliebsjazzhaus.com; 847 N 3rd St) is the city's oldest venue, housed in a restored brewery north of the Old City. **Chris' Jazz Cafe** (Map p286; ☎ 215-568-3131; www.chrisjazzcafe.com; 1421 Sansom St) is another cool jazz club worth a visit.

Rock & Indie

Electric Factory Concerts (Map p286; ☎ 610-784-5400; www.electricfactory.info; 421 N 7th St) dominates the independent music scene with a range of venues from the Theater of the Living Arts (TLA) to the Electric Factory Nightclub and the more commercial Tweeter Center. Log onto the website for schedules and details. You'll find free noon concerts and a dynamic schedule of indie singer-songwriters performing at World Cafe Live (see p309) and indie shows in a restored burlesque theater at the **Trocadero** (Map p286; ☎ 215-922-6888; www.thetroc.com; 1003 Arch St) Another appealing bohemian concert venue and cocktail bar is the **Tin Angel** (Map p292; ☎ 215-928-0770; www.tinangel.com; 20 S 2nd St).

   For bigger-name acts and conventional stadium concerts, there's the **Mann Center** (off Map p286; ☎ 215-893-1999; www.manncenter.org; 5201 Parkside Ave) and the **Wachovia Center** (off Map p286; ☎ 215-336-3600; www.wachoviacenter.com; 3601 S Broad St).

Clubbing

Clubs come and go; for the time being, night owls can hit the dance floor in Northern Liberties. At the hipster-friendly **Barbary** (Map p286; ☎ 215-634-7400; http://thebrbry.blogspot.com; 951 Frankford Av), rock, electronica and DJ-spun house music dominate. **Silk City Diner & Lounge** (Map p286; ☎ 215-592-8838; www.silkcityphilly.com; 435 Spring Garden St) offers a unique concept: after you work up a sweat on the dance floor, you can slide into a diner booth and order scrambled eggs or a grilled cheese sandwich. At the slightly cheesy but lighthearted **Shampoo** (Map p286; ☎ 215-922-7500; www.shampoooonline.com; 417 N 8th St) a diverse crowd from college girls to gay men take to three dance floors for '80s and retro music.

Cover charges vary – expect to pay anywhere between $5 and $15.

Sports

Philadelphia's professional and college sports teams enjoy an enthusiastic following. Most tickets can be bought from **Ticketmaster** (☎ 215-336-2000; www.ticketmaster.com). Ticket prices vary greatly, but generally range between $20 to $75, depending on demand – you'll need to book tickets well ahead of time if you want to compete with diehard Phillies and Eagles fans.

Away from the city center towards the airport, the Philadelphia Phillies Major League Baseball team take the field at **Citizens Bank Park** (off Map p286; ☎ 215-463-1000; www.phillies.com). **Lincoln Financial Field** (Map p286; ☎ 215-336-2000; www.lincoln financialfield.com; 1 Lincoln Financial Way) hosts NFL team the Philadelphia Eagles and the US professional soccer team the Philadelphia Union.

NBA stars the Philadelphia 76ers and NHL hockey team the Philadelphia Flyers play ball at the **Wachovia Center** (off Map p286; ☎ 215-336-3600; www.wachoviacenter.com; 3601 S Broad St).

SHOPPING

When some visitors consider shopping in Philadelphia, they think of grand department stores like **Macy's** (Map p286; ☎ 215-241-9000; Market & Juniper St) in the historic Wanamaker Building downtown (the 1987 sleeper hit *Mannequin* – filmed onsite – apparently influenced a generation.) It's true that there are still some classy shopping areas downtown: in an old Victorian building, you'll find the **Bourse Food Court & Specialty Shops** (Map p292; ☎ 215-625-0300; www.bourse-pa.com; 111 S Independence Mall East) and a range of high-end boutiques and stores in

the **Shops at Liberty Place** (Map p286; ☎ 215-851-9055; www.shopsatliberty.com; 1625 Chestnut St).

But many memorable shopping locales lie outside the historic center. **Historic Antique Row** (Map p286; www.antique-row.org; Pine St btw S 9th & S 12th Sts) features a string of pretty shops with American antiques from furniture to quilts and folk art. Antiques shoppers should also try the **South St Antiques Market** (Map p286; ☎ 215-592-0256; 615 S 6th St; ☑ noon-7pm Wed-Thu & Sun, noon-8pm Fri & Sat). Housed in a former synagogue, the market has a selection of vintage clothing and jewelry. Gem lovers should head back towards downtown and the oldest diamond district in the US, **Jewelers Row** (Map p286; www.philadelphiajewel ersrow.com; 8th & Sansom Sts).

Foodies won't want to miss the artisan cheeses, fresh produce and cooking supplies on colorful display at the Reading Terminal Market (see p294) and the Italian Market (see p296). The lovely **Fante's Kitchen Wares Shop** (off Map p286; ☎ 215-922-5557; www.fantes.com; 1006 S 9th St), dating from 1906, is one of the nation's oldest cookware shops.

Clothing boutiques and specialty stores can be found all over the city: some of the most appealing shopping districts include **University Square** (Map p301; www.universitysquare.biz; 3110 Walnut St) lined with outdoor cafes and green shopping galleries, and the Chestnut Hill Shopping District, filled with quaint boutiques and marked by beautiful architecture.

GETTING THERE & AWAY
Air
Philadelphia International Airport (☎ 215-937-6800, 800-745-4283; www.phl.org) is served by 25 airlines offering direct flights from Europe, the Caribbean and Canada, connections to Asia, Africa and South America and domestic flights to over 100 destinations.

Some of the major airlines:
British Airways (☎ 800-247-9297)
Continental Airlines (☎ 800-523-3273)
Delta Air Lines (☎ 800-325-1999)
US Airways (☎ 800-428-4322)
United Airlines (☎ 800-241-6522)

There's an information desk and ATMS in every terminal; some terminals also have currency-exchange desks.

Boat
The **Riverlink ferry** (Map p292; ☎ 215-925-5465; www.riverlinkferry.org) operates across the Delaware

River from Penn's Landing to the New Jersey State Aquarium in Camden.

Bus & Train

Greyhound (☎ 215-931-4075; www.greyhound.com), **Peter Pan Bus Lines** (☎ 800-343-9999; www.peterpanbus.com) and **Capitol/Bieber Trailways** (☎ 800-444-2877; www.capitoltrailways.com) buses stop at the **intercity bus terminal** (1001 Filbert St). Travel to New York ($20, two hours), Pittsburgh ($56, six to nine hours) or a number of other cities; you can find much cheaper prices if you book online – and in advance.

Trains operated by **Amtrak** (☎ 800-872-7245; www.amtrak.com) roll through the lovely 30th St Station. You can ride to New York ($35, 1½ hours), Washington DC ($35 to $48, 1½ hours) and a number of other destinations like Richmond, Boston, Harrisburg and Chicago; again, booking online is recommended.

Car & Motorcycle

Several highways lead through and around Philadelphia. From the north and south, I-95 (Delaware Expressway) follows the eastern edge of the city beside the Delaware River, with several exits for midtown.

I-276 (Pennsylvania Turnpike) runs east across the north of the city and over the river to connect with the New Jersey Turnpike. From the west, I-76 (Pennsylvania Turnpike/Schuylkill Expressway) branches off the Pennsylvania Turnpike to follow the Schuylkill River to South Philadelphia and over the Walt Whitman Bridge into New Jersey south of Camden. Just north of downtown I-676 (Vine St Expressway) heads east over the Benjamin Franklin Bridge into Camden itself. If you're coming from the east, take I-295 or the New Jersey Turnpike, which connects to I-676 over the Benjamin Franklin Bridge into downtown.

GETTING AROUND
To/From the Airport

Philadelphia International Airport is easily accessed on SEPTA's R1 airport rail line, which operates daily and takes about 20 minutes. The R1 can be boarded at Market East, Suburban, 30th St or University City stations; the one-way fare is $6. Shuttle bus and limousine services also operate between the airport and the city. The cheaper ones cost only a few dollars more than the train. One company to try is **Lady Liberty Airport Shuttle** (☎ 215-222-8888; www.

ladylibertyshuttle.com). Taxis to Center City cost a flat $28.50, and take about 20 to 25 minutes.

Bicycle

Philadelphia can be delightful on a bicycle, since it's reasonably flat, and Fairmount Park is laced with popular recreational cycling paths. Log onto the city government's **Streets of Philadelphia** (www.phila.gov/streets/bike_route_maps.html) to download an excellent bike map.

Bus

The **Southeastern Pennsylvania Transportation System** (SEPTA; ☎ 215-580-7860; www.septa.org) provides comprehensive transportation service in the city and suburbs. The one-way fare on most routes is $2, but children, senior citizens, and travelers in town for more than a few days are eligible for discounted passes – check the website for full details. Check the route maps, as well, for useful services like LUCY (Loop through University City), a bus that starts at the 30th St Station and goes through the University City area on weekdays.

Car & Motorcycle

Driving isn't recommended in central Philadelphia; parking is difficult and regulations are strictly enforced. If you need to cross downtown east–west by car, note that most streets have alternate one-way traffic. Avoid South St on weekends and every evening as the traffic jams are notorious; also avoid Christopher Columbus Blvd (Delaware Ave) north of the Benjamin Franklin Bridge on weekend evenings.

CAR RENTAL

The main rental companies have desks at the airport. Book online for better rental rates. These companies also have offices in town:

Avis (Map p286; ☎ 215-563-4477; 2000 Arch St)
Budget (☎ 215-764-5980; 30th St Station, Map p301)
Enterprise (Map p286; ☎ 215-625-6970; 123 S 12th St)
Hertz (Map p286; ☎ 215-492-2960; 31 S 19th St)

Subway & Train

SEPTA operates three subway lines, a trolley line, and regional train lines. The Market-Frankford line runs east–west along Market St from 69th St in West Philadelphia to Front St from where it heads north to Frankford. The Broad St line runs north–south from Fern Rock in North Philadelphia to Pattison Ave in South Philadelphia near the Veterans and First Union Spectrum sports stadiums. The Norristown High Speed Line cuts north from the 69th St Terminal toward Bryn Mawr and Norristown. The regional train system is vast; useful routes are R7 to Germantown and Chestnut Hill East, R8 to Chestnut Hill West and R1 to the airport. A single subway journey costs $2; train tickets run between $3.50 and $14.

Taxi

Philadelphia's cabs are carefully regulated. Downtown and in University City you can hail a cab easily enough during the day especially at 30th St Station, other train stations and around the major hotels. At night and in the suburbs you're better off phoning for one.

Fares are $2.70 for the first one-tenth of a mile, then 23¢ for each subsequent one-tenth plus 23¢ for every 37.6 seconds of waiting time. Some cabs accept credit cards.

Cab companies:

Liberty Cab (☎ 215-389-8000)
Crescent Cab (☎ 215-365-3500)
City Cab Co (☎ 215-492-6600)

AROUND PHILADELPHIA

VALLEY FORGE

Twenty miles northwest of downtown Philadelphia, the **Valley Forge National Historical Park** was the site of the Continental army's renowned winter encampment from December

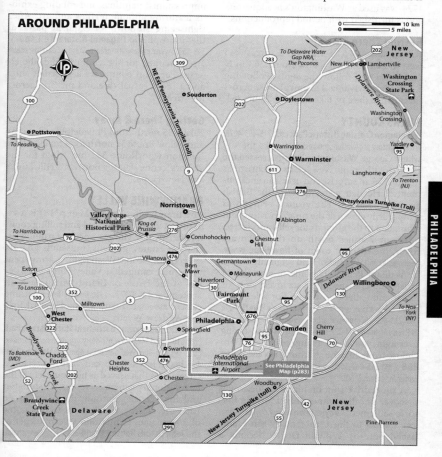

AROUND PHILADELPHIA

0   10 km
0   5 miles

19, 1777, to June 19, 1778, while the British occupied Philadelphia. Not a battlefield, the site is held as a symbol of bravery and endurance – 2000 of George Washington's 12,000 troops perished because of freezing temperatures, hunger and disease. Despite such losses, the army was reorganized and emerged to eventually defeat the British.

The park's **visitors center** (☎ 610-783-1077; www.nps.gov/vafo; ☽ 9am-5pm) contains exhibits and an information desk with maps and brochures highlighting the park's major points of interest, including the **National Memorial Arch** to the soldiers who endured that winter, and the **Monument to Patriots of African Descent**, a bronze statue honoring the 5000 African-Americans who died in the war. **Isaac Potts House**, built in 1774, was used as Washington's headquarters and is furnished with period reproductions.

Getting There & Away

By car take I-76 (Schuylkill Expressway) west to exit 25, then follow Route 363 to N Gulph Rd and follow the signs. Following I-276 (Pennsylvania Turnpike) west across the north of the city, take exit 24 to Route 363.

BUCKS COUNTY

Washington Crossing Historic Park (☎ 215-493-4076; www.ushistory.org/washingtoncrossing) marks the site where George Washington's army crossed the Delaware River into New Jersey on Christmas night, 1776, to surprise and defeat an encampment of Hessian mercenaries of the British army at Trenton. The visitors center was temporarily closed at the time of writing, but admission to the grounds for self-tours is free.

About 7 miles north on the Delaware River, the historic town of **New Hope** (www.newhopepa.com) – a tract of land originally owned by William Penn – is home to a wealth of artists and craftspeople; it's a lovely stop for lunch and gallery-browsing. For a leisurely meal with river views, try **Martine's RiverHouse** (☎ 215-862-2966; www.martinesriverhouserestaurant.com; 14 E Ferry St; mains $11-32). If you can't resist staying overnight, you'll have a range of cozy B&Bs to choose from, like the charming **Fox and Hound B&B** (☎ 215-862-5082; www.foxhoundinn.com; 246 W Bridge St; d from $160).

A short drive west on highway 202, you'll discover another impossibly adorable historic settlement. **Doylestown** (www.doylestownpa.org), thanks to the 18th-century inn established here by William Doyle, became a

well-populated village in an otherwise rural region. Today it's a gorgeous Victorian-style town filled with used-book stores, cute cafes, gourmet cheese and wine shops, the art deco **County Theater** (www.countytheater.org; 20 E State St) and a couple of important museums.

A romantic old castle-like structure contains the **Mercer Museum** (☎ 215-345-0210; www.mercermuseum.org; 84 S Pine St; adult/child $8/4; ☽ 10am-5pm Mon-Sat, to 9pm Tue, from noon Sun) and its collection of early American crafts and folk art. In another historic building is the **James A Michener Art Museum** (☎ 215-340-9800; www.michenerartmuseum.org; 138 S Pine St; adult/child $5/1.50; ☽ 10am-4:30pm Tue-Sun, to 9pm Wed), named for the town's Pulitzer Prize–winning former resident. There's a fabulous sculpture garden, impressionist paintings and rotating exhibits featuring antique textiles and art. After sightseeing, sit down for exquisite pastas at the atmospheric **Paganini Ristorante** (☎ 215-348-5922; www.paganiniristorante; State & Court Sts; mains $12-25); named for the violin legend, the elegant Paganini comprises a gourmet shop and a more casual cafe and pizzeria across the street.

Getting There & Away

Take I-95 north from Philadelphia to exit 31 and follow Route 32 north for 3 miles. At the junction with Route 532 turn right for the visitors' center, left for Bownan's Hill Tower and New Hope.

BRANDYWINE VALLEY

The Brandywine Valley (Map p318) is a vibrant patchwork of wooded and rolling countryside, historic villages, ancient farmhouses, chateau estates, gardens, museums and art collections. George Washington's army spent the winter camped at Valley Forge after defeat at the Battle of Brandywine Creek on September 11, 1777. The valley later became closely associated with artists Howard Pyle and Andrew Wyeth.

At the **Brandywine Battlefield State Historic Park** (☎ 610-459-3342; www.ushistory.org/brandywine/index.htm; ☽ 9am-4pm Wed-Sat, noon-4pm Sun Mar-Sep, 9am-4pm Thu-Sat Jan-Feb), you can visit the restored farmhouses that served as headquarters of the Revolutionary generals, George Washington and his French comrade the Marquis de Lafayette. Nearby, you'll see the former home of a ferryman, farmer and tavern keeper at the **John Chadds House** (☎ 610-388-7376; www.chadds

fordhistory.org; 1736 Creek Rd), built around 1725, and a 1714 tavern, the **Barns-Brinton House**.

In nearby Kennett Sq are the superb 1050-acre **Longwood Gardens** (☎ 610-388-1000; www.longwoodgardens.org; 1001 Longwood Rd; adult/child $16/6; ☒ daily, hours vary), established by Samuel du Pont. The gardens bloom with 11,000 different kinds of plants, roses and orchids; there's an indoor children's garden with a maze, the historic Pierce du Pont House and one of the world's mightiest pipe organs. Nighttime displays of illuminated fountains (in sum-mer), and festive lights at Christmas are breathtaking.

Famous for its collection of three generations of Wyeth family art, the **Brandywine River Museum** (☎ 610-388-2700; www.brandywinemuseum.org; US Route 1; adult/student $10/6; ☒ 9:30am-4:30pm) is housed in a 19th-century grist mill and also features other American artists like Howard Pyle and Maxfield Parrish

From Philadelphia, Route 1 heads south-west to Chadds Ford, Brandywine Battlefield Park and Longwood Gardens.

Pennsylvania

If New York is a grand, proud Rolls Royce, and New Jersey is a fun but garish apple-red Camaro, then Pennsylvania is a Honda Civic: modest but high-quality, an uncontroversial option with all of the standard features. You won't hear anyone talking about how rude and pushy Pennsylvanians are; you'd also be hard-pressed to find someone professing his undying passion for Harrisburg or proclaiming that life outside the Keystone State isn't really life at all.

Travelers passing through Pennsylvania don't have sky-high expectations of big-city excitement or jaw-dropping scenic vistas, which is exactly why they're caught by surprise when they fall in love with its lush green hills and lively urban centers. Pennsylvania is the home of two major cities, historic Philadelphia and ecofriendly Pittsburgh.

This is the state where the Battle of Gettysburg was fought, where Milton S Hershey established a candy company, where Frank Lloyd Wright built a house over a waterfall, where oil tycoons struck it rich, where Andy Warhol learned to paint and Abraham Lincoln delivered his most famous speech. It's a place where tourists line up to stare at a cracked bell, honeymooners relax in heart-shaped bathtubs at mountain retreats, and Amish boys work the fields.

Made up of equal parts green grass and polished steel, Pennsylvania is eminently likable. Admit it: you'd feel glamorous in the Rolls Royce, and you'd have a few laughs cruising around town in the Camaro, but at the end of the day, you'll be driving home in the Honda Civic.

HIGHLIGHTS:

- Taking a **horse and buggy ride** (p329) or **vintage steam-train journey** (p331) through Amish country
- Getting a fright on a candlelit ghost tour in historic **Gettysburg** (p332)
- Touring Frank Lloyd Wright's architectural masterwork, **Fallingwater** (p371)
- Staring for miles from Mt Washington at the top of the **Duquesne Incline** (p360)
- Pampering yourself with the chocolate facial at the **Hotel Hershey** (p352)
- Savoring the romance at a B&B in the mountain village of **Jim Thorpe** (p400)

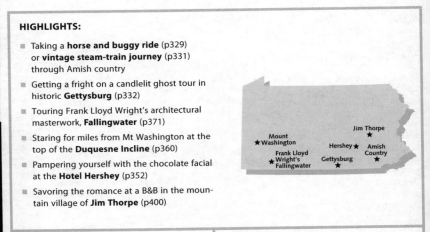

- POPULATION: 12,604,800
- AREA: 44,816 sq miles

HISTORY

The lakes, rivers and wide open green spaces now called Pennsylvania were once home to several Native American tribes: the Susquehannock, Iroquois, Eries, Shawnee and Lenape. Of course, they didn't stand a chance of survival when faced with the arrival of Dutch explorers, who sailed up the Delaware River and settled the region in 1630. The Dutch planted crops like tobacco and grain, and were followed by Swedish settlers who arrived the following year. After some political scuffles between the two nations and England, the British took control of much of the land: the Duke of York 'owned' the area where New Jersey now stands, and Charles II possessed nearby stretches of land. Since he owed a long-standing debt to the father of William Penn, he decided to grant a tract of land (today's Pennsylvania) to the younger Penn in 1681. Penn immediately established a Quaker colony there, declaring his land a place of religious freedom – and as all Pennsylvania schoolchildren know, he named his land after the region's beautiful forests (*sylvania* is Latin for 'woods'). Thanks to Penn's devotion to religious freedom, his new colony drew outsiders like a magnet, and the Welsh, German, Scottish and Irish immigrants that settled here had a profound effect on the state's future.

But it wasn't all smooth sailing for the peace-loving Quaker people. The lands of Pennsylvania were fought over during the French and Indian War, and its citizens were further challenged during the American Revolution, as Philadelphia's moderates and radicals battled it out over the state's connection with Britain. After pivotal elections took place in 1776, Benjamin Franklin became the chairman of a newly established committee whose purpose was to write a state constitution. But nation-building was about to take precedence, as Pennsylvania delegates took an active role in promoting (among other mid-Atlantic provinces) the establishment of an independent nation. Pennsylvania's game-changing role during this period is the reason we now call it 'the Keystone State.'

Of course, the summer of 1776 changed the nation forever. After June's Provincial Conference, the Continental Congress declared independence on July 2 in Philadelphia. As the newspaper headlines read that night, this day the Continental Congress declared the United Colonies Free and Independent States.' Pennsylvania developed rapidly in the years that followed, but a century later the state became the bloody battleground for several events in the Civil War. The Confederate States Army ravaged Chambersburg before the historic Battle of Gettysburg took place, capped by the hopeful and eloquent Gettysburg Address delivered by President Abraham Lincoln.

The state's later history is marked by industrial events, the Great Depression and the wars that followed. In the later 19th century, the Pennsylvania oil rush brought ambitious men from all over the country to the state's northwest, while steel and coal remained major industries in the southwest. European immigrants arrived to claim some of the plentiful jobs in factories and mines, and conflict broke out between workers and the state over conditions and payment, especially when the eventual decline of the manufacturing industry left many blue-collar workers jobless. In recent years, those grubby industrial cities have revitalized as fields like healthcare, education and tourism have taken precedence – as you'll read later, today's Pittsburgh is downright green, not to mention economically thriving.

LAND & CLIMATE

In comparison to other US states, Pennsylvania is the 33rd largest, spanning 44,820 sq miles, with more than 1000 sq miles covered by water. Major bodies of water include the Allegheny, Susquehanna, Delaware and Ohio rivers; the state's northwest also borders Lake Erie. The state is bisected diagonally from the southwest to the northeast by the Appalachian Mountains, with coastal plains in the southeast and the Allegheny plateau in the north giving way to the lowlands around Erie. The highest elevation is Mt Davis, measuring 3213ft, while the lowest point is at sea level, on the banks of the Delaware River.

Most of Pennsylvania is considered to fall within the humid continental climate zone, with lowlands (including Philadelphia) seeing cold, wet winters and hot and humid summers. The climate varies somewhat in the highlands, where snowy winters and more moderate summers are the norm. Overall, however, the state experiences four distinct seasons, with a monthly average temperature ranging from a high of 86°F to a low of 18°F.

NATIONAL & STATE PARKS

Most of Philadelphia's major sights are part of the Independence National Historic Park, and Gettysburg is home to the Gettysburg National Military Park (p338) – also a compound containing most of the region's battlefields and historic houses. Similarly, in Pittsburgh you'll find Point State Park (p358) at the downtown spot where rivers come together.

Outside of Pittsburgh, the forested areas and whitewater-rafting destinations are organized into several state parks: Ohiopyle (p374), Raccoon Creek (p373), McConnell's Mill (p375), Laurel Ridge (p375) and Moraine State Park (p375). In Pennsylvania Dutch country, you can camp at French Creek State Park (p336).

In northern Pennsylvania, in and around Erie and the Allegheny Forest, the state boasts its highest concentration of parks, many of which are managed by the **National Park Service** (www.nps.gov). In the northwest, look for including Presque Isle State Park (p381), Pymatuning State Park (p386), Oil Creek State Park (p388). In Pennsylvania's north central region, state parks include Cook Forest (p392), Chapman (p393), Kinzua Bridge (p394), Denton Hill (p395), Colton Point, Mt Pisgah (p396), Mauch Chunk Lake (p398), Beltzville (p397), Hickory Run (p398), Promised Land (p398), Lehigh Gorge (p398), Tobyhanna (p399) and Big Pocono State Park.

For more information on Pennsylvania state parks, visit the website of the state's **Department of Conservation and Natural Resources** (DCNR; www.dcnr.state.pa.us/stateparks).

GETTING THERE & AROUND

With the exception of large cities like Pittsburgh and Philadelphia, Pennsylvania is a region where you really need to have your own set of wheels to get the most out of your travel time. To give you an idea of the state's size, you could drive across the state – from Philadelphia in the southeast to Erie in the far northwest, in about 7½ hours (not including traffic or pit stops.) If you're road-tripping in a rental car, book online in advance to secure a better rate.

If you're going it alone, you'll find easily available public transportation between cities and some larger towns on the comfortable modern trains run by **Amtrak** (☎ 814-744-8407; www.amtrak.com). More frequent connections, including stops in smaller towns, are operated by intercity bus lines such as **Greyhound** (☎ 800-231-2222; www.greyhound.com), **Capitol/Bieber Trailways** (www.capitoltrailways.com) and **Fullington Trailways** (☎ 800-252-3893; www.fullingtontours.com)

PENNSYLVANIA DUTCH COUNTRY

Taking a country drive through the rolling green hills of Amish country is like being transported to gentler days: you'll see boys in straw hats and overalls riding horse-drawn plows through the fields, white cotton dresses hanging on long clotheslines, bearded men with pitchforks emerging from towering silos and children playing outside wooden farmhouses. Heading into towns, the pastoral quickly turns commercial: camera-snapping tourists swarm the old general stores and country-style buffet restaurants while Amish ladies sell sausages and shoofly pie in traditional marketplaces. But the clip-clop of horse-drawn buggies passing by outside – and the solemn expressions and old-fashioned attire of the passengers – remind you that you're not in a theme park. This is Pennsylvania Dutch Country, home to a living and breathing community of Amish, Mennonites and Brethren collectively known as 'plain people.'

Thanks in part to pop-culture representations of the Amish, like that in the 1985 Harrison Ford vehicle *Witness*, the plain people have become the object of intense curiosity by outsiders, and this region is now one of the most visited in Pennsylvania. An ironic fact, indeed, considering that their forebears emigrated from Europe to the New World to escape the attention (and persecution) of others.

LANCASTER
pop 55,350

Digging into pork tacos at a traditional Mexican eatery or catching an acoustic-music set in an indie cafe, you might forget completely that you're in the capital of Amish country. That's because the small city of Lancaster is poised on the cusp between old and new: here you'll find a country-style farmers' market, historic architecture, and handmade quilts sold in numerous boutiques, but you'll also find contemporary art galleries, chic cocktail bars and a population of

PENNSYLVANIA

PENNSYLVANIA DUTCH COUNTRY

PENNSYLVANIA

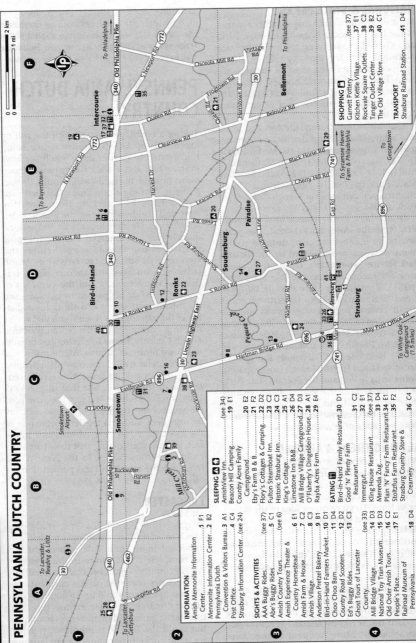

INFORMATION
Amish Mennonite Information
  Center...1 F1
Mennonite Information Center.....2 B2
Pennsylvania Dutch
  Convention & Visitors Bureau...3 A1
Post Office...4 C4
Strasburg Information Center....(see 24)

SIGHTS & ACTIVITIES
AAA Buggy Rides..........................(see 37)
Abe's Buggy Rides..............................5 C1
Amish Country Tours.....................(see 6)
Amish Experience Theater &
  Country Homestead..........................6 E1
Amish Farm & House............................7 C2
Amish Village..8 C3
Anderson Pretzel Bakery....................9 B1
Bird-in-Hand Farmers Market.......10 D1
Choo Choo Barn...............................11 D4
Country Road Scooters....................12 D2
Ed's Buggy Rides...............................13 C3
Ghost Tours of Lancaster
  County..(see 33)
Mill Bridge Village............................14 D3
National Toy Train Museum...........15 D3
Old Order Amish Tours....................16 C2
People's Place....................................17 E1
Railroad Museum of
  Pennsylvania...................................18 D4

SLEEPING
AmishView Inn..............................(see 34)
Beacon Hill Camping.........................19 E1
Country Acres Family
  Campground.....................................20 E2
Eby's Farm B & B.............................21 F2
Flory's Cottages & Camping...........22 D2
Fulton Steamboat Inn......................23 C3
Historic Strasburg Inn.....................24 C3
King's Cottage....................................25 A1
Limestone Inn B&B...........................26 D4
Mill Bridge Village Campground....27 D3
O'Flaherty's Dingeldein House......28 A1
Rayba Acres Farm.............................29 E4

EATING
Bird-in-Hand Family Restaurant...30 D1
Good 'N' Plenty Farm
  Restaurant.......................................31 C2
Immergut...32 E1
King House Restaurant..................(see 37)
Merenda Zug.....................................33 D4
Plain 'N' Fancy Farm Restaurant....34 E1
Stoltzfus Farm Restaurant...............35 F2
Strasburg Country Store &
  Creamery...36 C4

SHOPPING
Garnett Pottery............................(see 37)
Kitchen Kettle Village.......................37 E1
Rockvale Square Outlets....................38 C2
Tanger Outlet Center.........................39 B2
The Old Village Store.........................40 C1

TRANSPORT
Strasburg Railroad Station..............41 D4

artistic youth who attend the city's art and music colleges.

History

Lancaster, 57 miles west of Philadelphia, was first settled by Swiss Mennonites around 1700 and was originally called Gibson's Pasture. In the mid–18th century, it was renamed after the birthplace (in Lancashire, England) of Lancaster County's first commissioner, John Wright. Lancaster is noted for having been the capital of the US for a day (September 27, 1777) when Congress fled Philadelphia following George Washington's defeat at the Battle of Brandywine. They stopped here overnight before continuing to York, PA. Prior to the Civil War, Lancaster was a staging post on the Underground Railroad, and Thaddeus Stevens (1792–1868), a Republican politician and opponent of slavery, is buried here. James Buchanan (1791–1868), following his term as the 15th president of the US (1857–61), made his home in Lancaster.

The Old Order Amish are the most distinctive of the 'plain people' of Lancaster County, but the Amish are just one of three major groups – the Amish, the Mennonites and the Brethren – that are themselves further divided into various smaller churches and groups with differing beliefs.

The Amish, Mennonites and Brethren all trace their origins to 16th-century Switzerland. A religious sect calling itself the Brethren began in Zurich in 1525. They believed that a church should be made up of a group of individuals baptized as adults, because only adults can repent from sin and confess their faith in Christ before they are baptized. The name 'Anabaptist,' which means 'baptized again,' was applied to them by their opponents, and they were persecuted. Some Anabaptists became known as Mennonites after Menno Simons, a Dutchman who was formerly a Roman Catholic priest before becoming an early leader of the group. In 1693 a Swiss Mennonite bishop named Jacob Ammann split from the Anabaptists, and his followers eventually became known as the Amish. The first colony of Mennonites settled in 1683 in Germantown, now a suburb of Philadelphia, and the first large groups of Amish arrived in Pennsylvania in the early decades of the 18th century.

The Amish, Mennonites and Brethren are unified on the issues of separation of church and state, a Bible-centered life, voluntary adult membership and a 'forgiving love' that translates into conscientious objection to military service or even lawsuits. Where they differ is in dress, use of technology, some Biblical interpretation and language (the Amish speak Pennsylvania Dutch at home, and the others speak English).

Most of Lancaster's Brethren and Mennonites are indistinguishable from the rest of the county's worldly folk in dress, although their clothing emphasizes modesty. The distinctive Old Order Amish and Old Order Mennonites dress similarly (but not quite the same) and have certain prohibitions on the use of technology. Then there are other groups of Mennonites, Brethren and even Amish – the Amish Mennonites or 'Beachy Amish' – who wear distinctive clothing but use 'worldly' items.

The Old Order Amish, who make up the bulk of the local community, are farmers who generally travel by horse and buggy, wear distinctive clothing and prohibit certain technology. Decisions about technology are made by Amish bishops based on whether the item in question is too 'worldly' and whether its use may result in the disintegration of the closely knit community. Any prohibitions are constantly under reinterpretation.

Men wear unlapeled dark suits, suspenders, solid-colored shirts, black socks and shoes and broad-brimmed straw hats. Women wear dresses of solid-colored fabric that cover their arms and go past their knees. These dresses are covered by a cape and apron. Women wear their hair in a bun on the back of the head. Single women wear black prayer coverings for church services and white after marriage. Single men wait to grow beards (but never mustaches) until after they are married.

While many Amish won't drive a car, they'll ride with friends or hire vehicles to take them somewhere, and bus travel is acceptable. This brings us to the wheel. Bicycles, which encourage young people to go far from their homes, aren't used. Rubber wheels are permitted on wagons, tricycles and scooters, but not on large farm equipment. The most obvious example is the tractor, which must have steel wheels. Tractors are permitted around the barn and to power machinery, but not in the fields. The tractor speeds up farming and eliminates the need for labor, which is considered beneficial.

Power is acceptable if it comes from batteries or some fuel generators; gas lanterns are fine. Phones are allowed outside homes but not inside.

Until the eighth grade, children attend one-room Amish schoolhouses, where they are given the basics in reading, writing and arithmetic. They're exempt from the usual compulsory US school attendance to age 16. Any other education they receive is in the form of on-the-job training. The community is divided into church districts of 150 to 200 people. They have no central church – the district members gather at a different home every second Sunday for a three-hour service of hymn singing (without music) and scripture reading.

Lancaster County has around 15,000 Amish, most of whom live east of the city of Lancaster. Owing to the shortage of farms, some move to other parts of Pennsylvania or interstate, and there are large communities of Amish in Ohio and Indiana.

Orientation

The fertile Pennsylvania Dutch region is a network of towns and farms spread out over an area of perhaps 20 miles by 15 miles. These lie to the east of Lancaster – the area's main city and more or less its western boundary. Lancaster has a popular farmers' market, a pretzel bakery and some historic sights, including the home of President Buchanan.

Penn Sq, with its Soldiers & Sailors monument, is the town's central point. King St

---

A LANGUAGE GUIDE FOR FERNHOODLED ENGLISHERS

Here are some fun facts: the Pennsylvania Dutch aren't really Dutch at all. And though most speak a version of English, the Amish refer to anyone outside their community as 'Englisher' or 'Yankee.' Confused yet? It's understandable.

First things first. The term 'Pennsylvania Dutch' is a misnomer. The population could more correctly be called 'Pennsylvania German,' since the use of the word 'Dutch' is simply a corruption of the word 'Deutsch' (meaning 'German'). To escape persecution and scrutiny, the plain people – both Mennonites and Amish, a sect that broke away from the Mennonite church – fled German-speaking parts of Europe in the 1700s. William Penn welcomed these religious refugees to their current home in central Pennsylvania as part of his so-called 'Holy Experiment.'

As any linguist can tell you, the English language derives from the Germanic language group – believe it or not, the words you're reading right now have more in common with Afrikaans, Flemish and modern 'low German' than they do with French, Spanish or Portuguese. So it's fitting, given their history, that the Pennsylvania Dutch don't speak either English or German, but rather a mix of the two, a sort of German dialect influenced by English. And that's not all. In addition to speaking Pennsylvania Dutch at home and sending their children to receive English-language education in school, most plain people also read 'High German,' a more pure form of the language that's used in religious services and texts.

If you could be a fly on the wall at an Old Amish breakfast table, you might have trouble understanding some words, or even what the topic of conversation is. That's because, as Germans do, the Pennsylvania Dutch pronounce the letter 'w' like the letter 'v,' and vice versa, the hard 'g' is pronounced like our letter 'k,' and on and on. In addition to that, there are many common phrases and words that could leave you scratching your head, including *fernhoodle* (to confuse), *erector* (to destroy) and *doppick* (stupid).

Getting warmed up? Try translating an Amish proverb: 'Ve get too soon oldt, und too late schmart.' (Substitute a 'w' for the 'v,' and you're in business.) The plain people love proverbs and use them as frequent teaching tools for children; as windows into their culture, such sayings are also fascinating from a Yankee's perspective. A few classics include 'he who has a secret dare not tell it to his wife' and 'the man who claims to be the boss in his own home will lie about other things as well.' But enough with these (admittedly rather depressing) comments on marriage and the patriarchal household: as a favorite proverb goes, 'the most beautiful attire is a smile.'

For a daily taste of the simple life, and a little linguistic challenge on the side, log onto the **Pennsylvania Dutch Country Blog** (www.padutchcountryblog.com) and read its *Amish Proverb of the Day* feature.

(between Water and Duke Sts) and Queen St (between Orange and Vine Sts) mark the main downtown commercial area. Queen St divides the city into east and west; Orange St divides it into north and south. A one-way system operates downtown: Rte 222 runs north along Lime St and south along Prince St; Rte 462 runs east along King St and west along Orange St; Rte 23 runs east along Chestnut St and west along Walnut St.

East of Lancaster, the road most traveled by tourists is Rte 340 (Old Philadelphia Pike), along which are the towns of Bird-in-Hand and Intercourse. South of this, and also running east and west, is Rte 30 (Lincoln Hwy), which has many dairy farms and farmhouses with rooms for rent. Rte 896 (Hartman Bridge Rd) runs north and south between Rtes 30 and 340, meeting Strasburg to the south at the junction with Rte 741. To get off the beaten track, take any one of the side roads between Rtes 30 and 340.

To the north of this core is the town of Lititz, home of the country's first commercial pretzel bakery, and to its northeast is Ephrata, where the Ephrata Cloister was the site of an 18th-century ascetic religious community called the Pietists.

Though really separate, Reading, to the northeast of the true Pennsylvania Dutch region, is usually discussed as part of it. Most visitors to Reading go there to shop for factory-outlet bargains, but the Daniel Boone Homestead to the east and the Hawk Mountain Sanctuary to the north are well worth visiting. The towns of Palmyra and Lebanon, west of Reading, are also included in the region.

Information

Chestnut St Books (☎ 717-393-3773; www.abebooks.com; 11 W Chestnut St; 🕒 10am-5pm Wed-Sat) An atmospheric shop with old and rare books, maps and prints.

Lancaster County Library (☎ 717-394-2651; www.lancaster.lib.pa.us; 125 N Duke St; 🕒 10am-8pm Mon-Thu, to 5pm Fri & Sat)

Main post office (W Chestnut & N Prince Sts; 🕒 9am-4:30pm Mon-Fri, 9am-noon Sat)

Mellon Bank (28 Penn Sq) One of many banks and ATMs in Lancaster.

Mennonite Information Center (☎ 717-299-0954; www.mennoniteinfoctr.com; 2209 Millstream Rd; 🕒 8am-5pm Mon-Sat) Has general tourist advice and is also a center for information about the Mennonites; it has a wide selection of books. It shows a 20-minute film, *Postcards from a Heritage of Faith*, which explains the beliefs of the Mennonites and the Amish, as well as the differences between them. The information center is east of Lancaster, off Rte 30.

Pennsylvania Dutch Convention & Visitors Bureau (☎ 717-299-8901; www.padutchcountry.com; 501 Greenfield Rd; 🕒 9am-6pm Mon-Sat, to 4pm Sun May-Oct & 10am-4pm Nov-Apr) Conveniently located in downtown Lancaster in the Heritage Center Building in front of the Central Market, this bureau is the region's primary tourist office; it's located off Rte 30 west. It has a 15-minute audiovisual display that gives a basic overview of the region's attractions and distributes maps and visitors' guides, as well as discount coupons for attractions, accommodations and restaurants.

Visitor's Center at Penn's Square (☎ 717-735-0823; 1 W King St; 🕒 9am-6pm Mon-Sat, 10am-3pm Sun May-Oct & 9am-4:30pm Mon-Sat, 10am-3pm Sun Nov-Apr). It's an essential stop for any first-time visitor, though you might come away with more brochures than you know what to do with.

> **BEST OF**
>
> - Best shopping spree for foodies: the Bird-in-Hand Farmers' Market (p329)
> - Best reminder of a romantic past: the vintage train cars of the Strasburg Railroad (p331)
> - Best place to make a bid on a pot-bellied pig: Root's Country Market & Auction (p332)
> - Best ice-cream cone: Strasburg Country Store & Creamery (p332)

Sights & Activities

Though most out-of-towners pass through Lancaster to see the historic sites listed below, the city also has a vibrant modern arts scene centered around activities at the Pennsylvania Academy of Music and the Pennsylvania College of Art & Design. Head to Prince Street to browse through the artworks along Gallery Row; inquire at the Visitor's Center at Penn's Square for more details and information.

CENTRAL MARKET

The country's oldest **farmers' market** (☎ 717-291-4723; www.centralmarketlancaster.com; 125 N Duke St; 🕒 6am-4pm Tue & Fri, to 2pm Sat) is housed in a 120-year-old red-brick building that sits on the northwest corner of Penn Sq. In operation since the early 18th century, the marketplace has long sold fresh fruits, meat and baked goods; today you'll also find regional cuisine like Pennsylvania Dutch–style sausage, organic produce, gourmet food products and Amish crafts.

HERITAGE CENTER MUSEUM
Just in front of Central Market on Penn Sq, this charming **history museum** (☎ 717-299-6440; www.heritagecentermuseum.com; 5 W King St; admission free; 9am-5pm Mon-Sat, 10am-3pm Sun) contains 18th- and 19th-century paintings, pewter items, period furniture and other craft work and fine art done by local artisans and artists. It also has a series of changing exhibitions on the ground floor and live demonstrators, like an expert printer who shows visitors how to use an antique printing press. Check the website for schedules.

LANCASTER QUILT & TEXTILE MUSEUM
Operated in conjunction with the Heritage Center, this appealing, newly renovated **museum** (☎ 717-397-2970; www.quiltandtextilemuseum.com; 37 Market St; adult/child $6/free; 10am-5pm Mon-Sat) displays intricate quilts sewn by Lancaster County's Amish in a 1912 Beaux Art–style space. It's a must for anyone interested in textile traditions and women's crafts.

FULTON OPERA HOUSE
This gorgeous old Victorian-style **theater** (☎ 717-397-7425; www.thefulton.org; 12 N Prince St; show times vary), one of the oldest in the country and a National Historic Landmark, has hosted vaudeville, classic films and Broadway shows throughout its storied history – and the landmark was nearly torn down several times. Famous names that performed here include Sarah Bernhardt, WC Fields, Helen Hayes and Marcel Marceau.

WHEATLAND
This historic **house** (☎ 717-392-8721; www.lancasterhistory.org; 1120 Marietta Ave, Rte 23; adult/child $8/3; 10am-3pm Tue-Sat Apr-Oct, 10am-3pm Fri & Sat Nov-Dec) is an 1828 Federal mansion located about a mile northwest of downtown Lancaster. It was once home to James Buchanan – America's only bachelor president. Surrounded by 4 acres of gardens, the restored mansion also features Buchanan's furnishings, many of these gifts were from foreign heads of state.

LANDIS VALLEY MUSEUM
This 16-acre outdoor **museum** (☎ 717-569-0401; www.landisvalleymuseum.org; 2451 Kissel Hill Rd; adult/child $12/8; 9am-5pm Mon-Sat, from noon Sun), about 2½ miles northeast of town, consists of homes, workshops and stores dating from 1760 to the early 20th century. The buildings have been assembled in one place to re-create a setting of the Pennsylvanian Dutch rural life and work of the period. You can see presentations of craft making, including blacksmithing, leather working, spinning, basket weaving, tin smithing, lace making and chair caning.

From downtown, take Lime St (Rte 222) north to the exit for Rte 272, turn right and follow Rte 272 to the traffic lights just past the Quality Inn, turn left at the traffic light onto Kissel Hill Rd. The entrance to the museum is about 300 yards away, on the right.

Also recommended:
Anderson Pretzel Bakery (☎ 717-299-2321; 2060 Old Philadelphia Pike) Used to offer tours of the pretzel-making process along an overhead catwalk. Unfortunately, at the time of writing, the bakery was closed for public tours; check back for updates.
Demuth Museum (☎ 717-299-9940; www.demuth.org; 120 E King St; admission free; 10am-4pm Tue-Sat, from 1pm Sun) Displays the work of American modernist painter Charles Demuth.
Hands-on House Children's Museum (☎ 717-569-5437; www.handsonhouse.org; 721 Landis Valley Rd; admission $7; 10am-5pm Mon-Sat Memorial Day to Labor Day, 11am-4pm Tue-Sun Labor Day to Memorial Day) Next to the Landis Valley Museum, this interactive children's museum is fun for families.

Tours
Tour guides dressed in period costume lead visitors on the **Historic Lancaster Walking Tour** (☎ 717-392-1776; www.historiclancasterwalkingtour.com; 5 W King St; 1pm Apr-Oct). Stop in to the Visitor's Center at Penn's Square before lunch to secure a space.

In the spring months, **Lancaster County Tours** (☎ 888-999-4479; www.lancastercountytours.com; adult $150) runs the Lancaster County Cheese and Wine Tour, leading foodies and wine enthusiasts into small family-run shops and wineries to taste sheep's milk and gourmet treats. The day ends with a multicourse dinner with relevant wine pairings. The same company runs beer and pretzel tours in June and August and a well-known wine camp in autumn; check the website for details.

Personal guides are a good (and discreet) way to see the region, because your hired guide will sit in your car and direct you to communities and homes away from the commercial areas. Tours run year-round, weather conditions permitting.

The friendly **Old Order Amish Tours** (☎ 717-299-6535; www.oldorderamishtours.com; 63 Eastbrook Rd, Ronks), on Rte 896, takes individuals or small groups on private, culturally respectful tours of Amish farms and homes. You're not allowed to take photographs. Rates, hours and options – including stopping for a home-cooked meal in an Amish home – vary. Contact the headquarters for more information.

The **Mennonite Information Center** (☎ 717-299-0954; www.mennoniteinfoctr.com; 2209 Millstream Rd, Lancaster; 2hr guided tour per vehicle $44) provides visitors with a personal guide of Amish or Mennonite heritage. Stop into the center in Lancaster for more information: usually, the center can get you on the road with a guide within 30 minutes. It also provides useful tourist information (see p323).

Sleeping

Lancaster has some lovely B&Bs. If you're in the market for something more basic, drive southeast on Rte 462/30 to a commercial strip with plenty of hotels and motels. Further out into Pennsylvania Dutch Country, there are campgrounds and farmhouses (See Sleeping under Intercourse, Bird-in-Hand and Strasburg later in this chapter.)

O'Flaherty's Dingeldein House (☎ 717-293-1723; www.dingeldeinhouse.com; 1105 E King St; d/ste from $100/135) This tranquil Dutch Colonial–style B&B has several frilly rooms and suites – some with fireplaces – and laid-back common areas filled with dark wood antiques. On Rte 462, it's 2 miles east of town before the intersection with Rte 30.

Lovelace Manor B&B (☎ 866-713-6384; www.lovelacemanor.com; 2236 Marietta Ave; d from $135-175; ▓) Dating from 1882, this picture-perfect B&B is named after the English 17th-century poet Richard Lovelace and has a grand wraparound porch, etched glass doors and a pretty Victorian parlor. Guest rooms have romantic four-poster beds and DVD players with video libraries; guests also have round-the-clock access to a butler's pantry stocked with coffee, tea and sweet treats.

our pick **Lancaster Arts Hotel** (☎ 717-299-3000; www.lancasterartshotel.com; 300 Harrisburg Ave; d/ste from

$149/279; ▓ 🛜 ♿) This stylish boutique hotel, situated in a restored tobacco factory, features an impressive collection of locally produced artwork and cozy lamp-lit guest rooms with exposed brick walls and sleek polished wood and soft leather furnishings. A sophisticated onsite eatery serves organic cuisine and international wines.

Fulton Steamboat Inn (☎ 717-299-9999; www.fultonsteamboatinn.com; Rtes 30 & 896; d from $160; ▓ ▣ ♿) It's a short drive from town, but this boat-shaped hotel is a real hit with families thanks to an excellent onsite restaurant, clean and spacious rooms, an outdoor pool and children's recreation area, nautical decor and friendly service. You can't miss it from the roadside: just look for the big out-of-place boat.

King's Cottage (☎ 800-747-8717; www.kingscottagebb.com; 1049 E King St; d/carriage house from $160/295; ▓ 🛜) A large, airy B&B with a library, fireplace and afternoon tea. Guest rooms have DVD players, hardwood floors and antique furniture; the lavish Carriage House has a king-sized sleigh bed, a fireplace, a Jacuzzi for two and an antique dining table where the staff will deliver breakfast.

Eating

Lancaster is crawling with adorable cafes, good ethnic restaurants, good-looking pubs and fine-dining establishments. Take a stroll around the historic center for the best overview of what's on offer; keep your eyes open for the incredibly quaint Italian bakery across the street from the old courthouse. If you need to pick up picnic fixings or a quick lunch, hit the Central Market.

our pick **La Cocina Mexicana** (☎ 717-393-9193; 47 N Prince St; mains $5-8; ☯ closed Sun) This delightfully authentic and budget-friendly Mexican joint serves delicious tacos, overstuffed burritos and spicy soups – try the juicy *carnitas* (pork) taco alongside a fresh juice like *jamaica* or *horchata*.

Prince Street Cafe (☎ 717-397-1505; www.princestreetcafe.com; 15 N Prince St; mains $5-12) A happening coffeehouse and eatery across from the Fulton Opera House, the rustic-chic Prince Street Cafe serves organic teas, several coffee blends, and fresh wraps, salads and pastries. There are plenty of outdoor tables and a lounge space; the cafe also hosts acoustic music performances.

Annie Bailey's Irish Pub (☎ 717-393-4000; www.anniebaileysirishpub.com; 30 E King St; mains $7-20) A classy brewpub serving upscale comfort food such as bacon cheeseburgers, shepherd's pie and crab cakes, Annie Bailey's has a good selection of draft beers and wines by the glass.

Getting There & Away

Note: the Amish use their horses and buggies as a means of transportation, so if you're driving, at times you'll need to slow down considerably and travel at their pace for a while.

AIR

Lancaster municipal airport (☎ 717-569-1221; www.lancasterairport.com; 500 Airport Rd) is 6 miles north of town on Rte 501. **Cape Air** (☎ 800-352-0714) flies to Baltimore (BWI) several times a day. The 30-minute flight only costs $50.

BUS & TRAIN

Capitol/Bieber Trailways (☎ 800-444-2877; www.capitoltrailways.com) operates from the Amtrak station on McGovern Ave. Check the website for current information on daily buses to Philadelphia and Pittsburgh. The **Amtrak station** (☎ 717-291-5080; www.amtrak.com; 53 McGovern Ave) is about a mile north of downtown. There are three one-way trains daily to both Philadelphia ($15, one hour) and Pittsburgh ($72, six hours).

CAR & MOTORCYCLE

The quickest way to Lancaster from Philadelphia is via the Pennsylvania Turnpike (I-76); at exit 21 take Rte 222 south into town. Northward, Rte 222 leads to Reading; southeast of town it leads to Maryland. Another option from Philadelphia is to take Rte 30 west, which passes through the heart of Pennsylvania Dutch Country. From Lancaster, Rte 30 continues southwest to York and Gettysburg. Rte 283 leads northwest from Lancaster to Harrisburg, and Rte 501 heads north to I-78.

Getting Around

Red Rose Transit Authority (RRTA; ☎ 717-397-4246; www.redrosetransit.com; 47 N Queen St) is Lancaster County's bus service; one-way fares range from $1.50 to $2.70.

INTERCOURSE & AROUND

Yeah, we hear you – we'd also like to know why this small town is called Intercourse. The truth is that no one knows for sure. Founded in 1754, it was originally called Cross Keys. It's something of a mystery how it came to obtain its current name: one reason usually given is that the town stands at the intersection of the old King's Hwy (Rte 340) and the old Newport Rd (Rte 772). Another possible explanation is that the name evolved from a sign, which read 'Enter Course,' at the entrance to an old racing track on King's Hwy. Whatever the reason, Intercourse became the town's official name in 1814.

Orientation

The town is located along Rte 340 (Old Philadelphia Pike), 8 miles east of Lancaster. Almost everything worth seeing in Intercourse is situated along this route.

Information

The **Amish Mennonite Information Center** (☎ 717-768-0807; Old Philadelphia Pike; ☯ 11am-4pm Mon-Sat, shorter hrs Nov-Apr), near the Kitchen Kettle Village shopping center, has tourist information as well as information on the Amish and Mennonites.

Sights & Activities

PEOPLE'S PLACE

This **cultural center** (☎ 800-390-8436; www.thepeoplesplace.com; 3513 Old Philadelphia Pike; ☯ 9:30am-5pm Mon-Sat Sep-Jun, to 8pm Jul & Aug; ⚹) gives visitors a sensitive introduction to Amish and Mennonite life; it's very informative and has sections geared toward children. It shows *Who Are the Amish?*, a 30-minute film about Amish life from birth to death. It also has **20 Questions**, a hands-on exhibit about Amish and Mennonite life; it has one floor for children and another for adults. You'll also find plain-people clothing, buggies and religious objects. The bookstore here has a wide selection of related titles.

AMISH EXPERIENCE THEATER & COUNTRY HOMESTEAD

This large tourist center – complete with a five-screen theater, an Amish homestead open for tours, shopping areas and a restaurant – is located at the **Plain 'N' Fancy Farm** (☎ 717-768-3600; www.amishexperience.com; 3121 Old Philadelphia Pike; prices vary for various attractions; ☯ Mar-Dec; ⚹) on Rte 340 between Intercourse and Bird-in-Hand. The theater (adult/child $9.95/6.95) screens the film *Jacob's Choice*, dealing with a young Amish man's dilemma over whether to stay and follow the traditional way of life or to enter the world of the 'English.'

There are 40-minute tours of the nearby **Amish Country Homestead** (adult/child $9.95/6.95), a replica of an Old Order Amish home. The SuperSaver package (adult/child $16.95/11.95) allows entry into the homestead and theater and includes a bus tour with Amish Country Tours.

Tours

AAA Buggy Rides (☎ 717-989-2829; www.aaabuggyrides.com; 3529 Old Philadelphia Pike, Intercourse; covered bridge tour adult/child $16/8; 🕑 9am-5pm Mon-Sat) takes passengers through an antique covered bridge on a scenic back road.

HARRISON FORD'S PAY PHONE & THE WITNESS CONTROVERSY

In two scenes of the movie *Witness* (1986), Harrison Ford uses the pay phone on the porch in front of WL Zimmerman & Sons grocery store, near the junction of Rtes 772 and 340. It's since become a tourist attraction, but it's not the only setting in the movie that you might recognize if you're traveling through Pennsylvania. The ill-fated love story of John Book (Ford) and Rachel Lapp (Kelly McGillis) took place across many locations in the region:

- **The pay phone** When Harrison Ford's character, a police officer who's hiding in an Amish household, asks where to find the nearest phone, he is told Strasburg – it was thought to sound too strange to say that he was in Intercourse. Nearby on Queen St is the filming location for the scene where Book gets into a fist fight with a group of local (English) guys.
- **The barn-raising** This memorable scene, in which the community comes out in full force to build a barn together in one day, was shot in a remote field in Christiana, Pennsylvania. All of the extras were actual Mennonite actors working for Paramount.
- **The Lapp house** The film's primary setting, the Lapp family farmhouse where John Book is sent to stay, is an actual homestead near Strasburg. The home was temporarily vacated by the Mennonite family who lived there as filming occurred; the producers added a water wheel to the front pond and changed the decor before letting the cameras roll.
- **The silo** The bloody final scenes of the film weren't filmed on the farm itself, but in the former Posey Iron Works building in Lancaster. The early murder scene, which supposedly took place in a public restroom at Philadelphia's 30th Street Station was also filmed here.
- **Philadelphia** The train station murder itself may not have been filmed here, but it's clear that many shots of the station were, in fact, filmed on location. Big city locations also include the parking garage where Book is shot and a section of Chinatown where Book meets a murder suspect at a bar.

Unsurprisingly, Lancaster County's Amish community didn't want to have anything to do with the making of a big-budget Hollywood movie: the producers couldn't convince a single Amish person to advise them, though a few Mennonites pitched in to help the movie-makers choose interior decorations and edit dialogue. Still, location scouts had a hard time finding places to film. Jim Zimmerman, then general manager of the WL Zimmerman & Sons, felt the backlash from his neighbors when they feared the store owner was accepting money from producers to use his store as a film location. He declined payment and the community acknowledged it: local business actually improved at his historic hardware store afterwards. The Lancaster County Chamber of Commerce also reported significant earnings: the filming brought more than $6 million into the county's economy. Unfortunately, the National Committee for Amish Religious Freedom (composed of non-Amish lawyers and scholars) protested the film after its premiere, saying that the movie depicted Amish as practicing 'immoral and unlikely behavior.' They pleaded to the governor to prohibit its release; the government refused to do so, as such an action would be unconstitutional, but the state did agree to formally discourage further filmmaking in the region. Harrison Ford himself spoke for the film crew when he went on record saying, 'It is the very moral nature of the Amish that makes them useful to our story. We would never violate that because it would diminish our story.'

- source: *Harrison Ford: The Films, by Brad Duke*

Festivals & Events

The Kitchen Kettle Village (p329) hosts an annual weeklong **Rhubarb Festival** in May; trust us, it's great to be around during the 'Best Rhubarb Dessert in Lancaster County' baking contest. Log onto the website for a schedule of similar summer festivals at the Kitchen Kettle, including the **Annual Berry Jam Festival** in June. Also in June, the **Intercourse Community Park** (☎ 717-768-8585; 3721 Old Philadelphia Pike) hosts **Intercourse Heritage Days**, a free festival with food stands and family activities.

Sleeping

There are ample campsites, motels, hotels and B&Bs in the area. An alternative to the usual accommodations is to stay on one of the many farmhouses in the area; they welcome kids, and guests are generally welcome to milk the cows (although it's usually done by machine) and sometimes to feed the calves if they want to get close to nature. Some of these places are listed here, and the names of more are available from the visitors' centers.

Beacon Hill Camping (☎ 717-768-8775; www.beacon hillcamping.com; Rte 772 West; campsite/cabin/cottage $34/52/103; ☼ Apr-Oct; ☒ ☎) Billed as 'quiet camping for adults,' this peaceful spot doesn't allow children under the age of 16. The campground has all of the contemporary amenities (including wi-fi inside your tent if you have your own laptop or phone to access it); basic two-person cabins and more modernized cottages, with a kitchenette, bathroom, TV and coffeemaker, are also for rent.

Country Haven Campground (☎ 717-354-7926; www.countryhaven.com; 354 Springville Rd, New Holland; campsites from $41; ☼ Apr-Nov; ☎ ☝) These shady campsites, also boasting all of the modern amenities, are set on a tranquil hillside overlooking miles of farmland. Take Rte 340 east about 5 miles to White Horse and then Rte 897 (Springville Rd) north 1½ miles to the campground.

Eby Farm B&B (☎ 717-768-3615; www.ebyfarm.com; 345 Belmont Rd, Gordonville; d $85-100; ☒) This B&B comprises two houses: a brick farmhouse dating from 1814 and a more up-to-date Cape Cod–style bungalow. Rooms are clean and simply furnished and the farm is open and available for tours. To get there from town, follow Queen Rd south off of Rte 772.

AmishView Inn (☎ 866-735-1600; www.amish viewinn.com; 3125 Old Philadelphia Pike; d/ste from $174/194; ☒ ☎ ☒ ☝) At the Plain 'N' Fancy Farm

(p326), this plush new hotel is a cross between a B&B and a family lodging. It offers a complimentary hot breakfast involving made-to-order omelets, an indoor pool and a hot tub, a 24-hour fitness center, a laundry area, and a range of comfortable guest rooms, studios and one- and two-bedroom suites with private hot tubs and fireplaces.

Eating

The region is famous for its large meals. It's more correct to call the cuisine 'Pennsylvania Dutch food' rather than 'Amish food,' and it's served in a number of restaurants 'family style,' with diners often sitting together at long tables and eating as much as they please. Meals are standard, but huge and hearty, and they generally include three meats (usually chicken, beef and ham or sausage), apple sauce, pepper cabbage (a variety of cabbage), candied sweet potatoes, corn, string beans, noodles and shoofly pie (the lack of a top crust on this gooey molasses concoction attracts flies, hence its name).

On the main street, Immergut (the name means 'always good' in German) sells soft and hand-rolled pretzels for around a dollar.

Lunch Basket (☎ 717-768-3462; 3551 Old Philadelphia Pike; sandwiches & pizza $3-4.50; ☝) Next to the Amish Mennonite Information Center, the Lunch Basket is a simple but popular sandwich and pizza shop that also makes good ice cream.

Kling House Restaurant (☎ 717-768-2746; www.klingkettle.com; mains $5-12; ☼ closed Sun; ☝) In the Kitchen Kettle Village shopping area, the restaurant in this restored farmhouse serves hearty breakfasts, lunches and desserts – the house special is coconut cream pie. Try for a table on the breezy front porch.

Stoltzfus Farm Restaurant (☎ 717-768-8156; www.stoltzfusfarmrestaurant.com; Rte 772; dinner adult/child $16.95/7.95; ☼ closed Dec-Mar; ☝) In a large, barnlike building behind the Stoltzfus meat factory, this family-style place serves all-you-can-eat dinners and a la carte lunches featuring Lancaster Country staples like homemade sausage, deep-fried chicken, potato stuffing, sweet potatoes and freshly baked pies.

Plain 'N' Fancy Farm Restaurant (☎ 800-669-3568; www.plainandfancyfarm.com; 3121 Old Philadelphia Pike; dinner adult/child $18.95/9.95; ☝) Farm-to-table cooking is the proud tradition here: the 'Amish Farm Feast' is a family-style smorgasbord of classic dishes like roast beef, chicken pot pie, mashed potatoes and green beans. There's also an a la carte menu for lunch and dinner.

Shopping

Intercourse is the epicenter of shopping for Pennsylvania Dutch goods. There are stores in town and along Rtes 30 and 340 selling quilts, handmade wooden furniture, decoys, dolls, pewter, fudge, brass, clothing, hex signs (found on barns and quilts, they were originally used to ward off bad luck and evil; today they're merely decorative), tools, candles and more. It's hard to choose one over another – look around.

Kitchen Kettle Village is a collection of shops at the west end of town; offerings include **Garnett Pottery** (☎ 717-768-7199; www. garnettpottery.com), which sells locally produced pottery and ceramic gifts. Nearby, look for small shops selling well-crafted wooden furniture, including an array of differently styled chairs, and Amish-style scooters like those the plain people ride along the roadsides. You can watch candle making downstairs at the **Old Candle Barn** (☎ 717-768-8926; www.oldcandlebarn. com; 3551 Old Philadelphia Pike).

On Rte 772, for several miles northwest of Intercourse, there are a number of places selling wooden furniture, quilts and secondhand wares.

Getting There & Away

RRTA bus No 13 from Duke St in Lancaster stops up to nine times daily Monday to Saturday on Rte 772 (N Newport Rd) in Intercourse. By car from Lancaster, follow King St (Rte 462) east out of the city, then take the left fork onto Rte 340. If you're coming from Philadelphia, Rte 772 connects Rte 222 and Rte 30 with Intercourse.

BIRD-IN-HAND & AROUND

Bird-in-Hand, a few miles east of Lancaster on Rte 340, was named in 1734. The name may have been taken from the sign at the town's then–main hotel. Today, the small town has many stores and restaurants. You'll find an ATM in the lobby of the Bird-in-Hand Family Restaurant (see p330).

Sights & Activities

BIRD-IN-HAND FARMERS' MARKET

This bustling **farmers' market** (☎ 717-393-9674; www.birdinhandfarmersmarket.com; 2710 Old Philadelphia Pike; ☒ 8:30am-5:30pm Fri, Sat & selected Wed Apr-Nov

& Thu Jul-Oct) is fun for foodies: in addition to the homemade pastries, sausages, pretzels and fudge, you'll discover a fabulous array of spices, jams, sauces, all-natural sweets, farm-fresh vegetables and the ingredients to make your own funnel cake or root beer. Come hungry, there are lots of free food samples on offer. And trust us: unless you're vegetarian, you'll want to try a pretzel dog.

AMISH FARM & HOUSE

This historic farmhouse (dating from 1805) and 15-acre farm were once occupied by an Amish family, but now operate as a **museum** (☎ 717-394-6185; www.amishfarmandhouse.com; 2395 Lincoln Hwy; adult/child $8.25/5.25; ☒ 8:30am-6pm Jun-Aug, from 10am in low season) 5 miles east of Lancaster. Tours take visitors through the old blacksmith shop, a one-room schoolhouse and a covered bridge built in 1855, and past various animals and buildings spread out over 25 acres. The ticket gets you a guided tour of the house, with a description of Amish culture and way of life. After the tour, you can wander around the farm by yourself. Available add-ons include a countryside bus tour. To get there from Bird-in-Hand, take Rte 340 west to Rte 896, then turn south to Rte 30 and head west for just under a mile.

Tours

BUS

Operating out of the large Amish Experience tourist complex (p326), **Amish Country Tours** (☎ 717-768-3600; www.amishexperience.com; 3121 Old Philadelphia Pike, Rte 340; adult/child $29.95/14.95; ☒ Mar-Oct) runs several narrated bus tours from the Plain 'N' Fancy Farm (p326), located midway between Bird-in-Hand and Intercourse. The 2¼-hour tour takes the back roads past farmlands and homes, visits an Amish dairy farm to sample ice cream and stops at Amish shops and at the Mt Hope Wine Gallery for a tasting. From April to October, it leaves twice daily Monday to Saturday and once on Sunday; in November, it leaves once daily; from December to March, there are tours on weekends only. Similar tours are run by the Pennsylvania Dutch Convention & Visitors Bureau (p323).

HORSE & BUGGY RIDES

Several outfits offer countryside tours in Amish-style horse-drawn buggies. Try **Abe's Buggy Rides** (☎ 717-392-1794; www.abesbuggyrides.com;

2596 Old Philadelphia Pike, Bird-in-Hand; adult/child from
$10/5; 🕑 9am-5pm Mon-Sat).

MOTORCYCLE & SCOOTER
Country Road Scooters (☎ 717-598-3191; www.country
roadscooters.com; 220 N Ronks Rd; 2hr rental $30; 🕑 Tue
for tours and Wed-Sat for rentals, Sun-Tue rentals by appt)
Cruise past farmlands and feel the wind in
your hair atop a Yamaha scooter from this
outfit. Guided tours are offered on Tuesdays;
helmets and self-guided tours are available
everyday.

Sleeping & Eating
Country Acres Family Campground (☎ 866-675-4745;
www.bird-in-hand.com; 20 Leven Rd, Gordonville; campsite/
cabin from $28/54; 🐾 ♿) This friendly camp-
ground has tent and RV sites as well as rustic
one-room cabins (air-conditioned, but with
shared bathrooms). From Bird-in-Hand, take
N Ronks Rd south to Rte 30, then go east to
Leven Rd.

　　Flory's Cottages & Camping (☎ 717-687-6670; www.
floryscamping.com; 99 N Ronks Rd; campsite/d/cottage from
$34/64/159; 🛜 ♿) Between Rtes 30 and 340, a
mile south of Bird-in-Hand, Flory's has well-
equipped campsites, a pleasant guesthouse
and fully equipped cottages with kitchens,
porches, TVs and up to three bedrooms. It
has a cookout area and a playground.

　　Bird-in-Hand Family Restaurant (☎ 717-768-1550;
www.bird-in-hand.com; 2760 Old Philadelphia Pike; breakfast/
lunch/dinner $9/13/17; 🕑 closed Sun) Waffles, French
toast, scrambled eggs and bacon, homemade
sticky buns – the breakfast smorgasbord is a
treat at this family-run restaurant. The lunch
and dinner are bingeworthy as well.

　　Good 'N' Plenty Farm Restaurant (☎ 717-394-7111;
www.goodnplenty.com; 150 Eastbrook Rd, Rte 896; dinner $18;
🕑 closed Dec & Jan) A large family-style restaurant
that's popular with locals, Good 'N' Plenty
cooks up set-price meals of PA Dutch staples
such as baked ham, roast beef, homemade
bread and shoofly pie. To get there, take Rte
340 west to Rte 896, then head south to the
restaurant.

Shopping
Old Village Store (☎ 717-397-1291; www.ovstore.com;
Rte 340; 🕑 closed Sun in low season), established in
1890, is one of the country's oldest hardware
stores. Now it's more of a general store selling regional products and crafts; a tongue-in-
cheek sign reads 'If you see it and like it, buy
it: we may never have it again.'

The farmers' market in Bird-in-Hand
(p329) is popular for an appetizing selection
of pies, jams, meat, preserved vegetables and
fresh fruit and vegetables.

　　Two discount factory-outlet malls are
south of town on Rte 30. **Rockvale Square Outlets**
(☎ 717-293-9595; www.rockvalesquareoutlets.com; 35 S
Willowdale Dr) is at the intersection with Rte 896.
Tanger Outlet Center (☎ 717-392-7260; www.tanger
outlet.com; 311 Stanley K Tanger Blvd) is on the corner
of Millstream Rd, opposite the Mennonite
Information Center.

Getting There & Away
RRTA bus No 13 from Duke St in Lancaster
stops up to nine times a day Monday to
Saturday in Bird-in-Hand. By car from
Lancaster, follow King St (Rte 462) east out
of the city, then take the left fork onto Rte
340. If you're coming from Philadelphia, Rte
772 connects Rte 222 and Rte 30 with Rte 340.

STRASBURG & AROUND
Perhaps the most picturesque stop in Amish
country, the pretty town of Strasburg is
known for rich homemade ice cream and a
vintage railroad. Compared to some of the
region's other towns, Strasburg is wonderfully
charming and free of gaudy tourist shops and
attractions. It's located at the southern end
of Pennsylvania Dutch Country on Rte 741.

　　The **Strasburg Information Center** (☎ 717-687-
7922; www.strasburgpa.com) is at the reception desk
in the Historic Strasburg Inn, north of town,
off Rte 896. There's a **post office** (🕑 8am-4:30pm
Mon-Fri, 9am-1pm Sat) near the intersection of Rtes
896 and 741.

Sights & Activities
MILL BRIDGE VILLAGE
The most elaborate of the replicas, **Mill Bridge
Village** (☎ 717-687-8181; www.millbridge.com; 101 S
Ronks Rd; admission varies), 2 miles south of Ronks,
is a re-created colonial 'village' that includes
an Amish house, a school, a covered bridge, a
blacksmith shop, a log cabin, a broom maker,
a mill, a barnyard and a zoo. If you camp
here (p332), you get free admission to the
village.

AMISH VILLAGE
This re-created **Amish village** (☎ 717-687-8511;
www.theamishvillage.net; Rte 896 north of Strasburg; adult/
child $8/4; 🕑 9am-5pm, to 6pm Jun-Aug) consists of
several major buildings, including an Old

Order Amish house, a blacksmith shop and a schoolhouse. The admission price includes a tour of an Amish home. It's located 2 miles north of Strasburg.

STRASBURG RAILROAD

This wonderful old-fashioned **railroad** (☎ 717-687-7522; www.strasburgrailroad.com; 301 Gap Rd, Rte 741; prices vary; ☒ closed Jan), the oldest short-line in the country, runs vintage-steam-train tours on a 9-mile, scenic roundtrip tour through the countryside to the village of Paradise. The train runs several times daily, April through November. Choose from a standard coach ticket (adult/child $14/7), the open-air car (weather permitting; adult/child $16/9), the Victorian-style First-Class Parlor ($20) or the Wine & Cheese Train (evenings; $35). There are also lunch and dinner trains ($16 to $42) centered on the elegant old Lee E Brenner Dining Car. Look for thematic train journeys such as the kid-friendly Thomas the Tank Engine ride, the Great Train Robbery trip and Santa's Paradise Express.

RAILROAD MUSEUM OF PENNSYLVANIA

Opposite the Strasburg Railroad station is this large contemporary **museum** (☎ 717-687-8628; www.rrmuseumpa.org; Rte 741; adult/child $10/8;

☒ 9am-5pm Mon-Sat, from noon Sun Apr-Oct, closed Mon Jan-Mar & Nov-Dec; ⚹). Spanning 150 years of Pennsylvania railroads since 1825, it features a collection of more than 100 steam locomotives and railcars and related artifacts such as uniforms and engineers' tools. You can view a 62-ton locomotive from underneath and step onto an old caboose car; there are also hands-on activities for kids.

Can't get enough trains? In town you'll also find a huge collection of antique toy trains at the **National Toy Train Museum** (☎ 717-687-8976; www.nttmuseum.org; 300 Paradise Lane; adult/child $6/3; ☒ 10am-4:30pm Fri-Mon May-Oct). Younger kids go crazy for the **Choo Choo Barn** (☎ 717-687-7911; www.choochoobarn.com; 226 Gap Rd, Rte 741; adult/child $6/4; ☒ 10am-5pm; ⚹), an ever-changing interactive display complete with 22 operating toy trains and hundreds of hand-crafted animated figures acting out barn-raisings and circus performances.

TOURS

Ed's Buggy Rides (☎ 717-687-0360; www.edsbuggyrides.com; 253 Hartman Bridge Rd; rides from adult/child $8/4), a mile north of Strasburg, provides leisurely rides through the country on little-known back roads. You can choose between a closed or open car, weather permitting.

TEEN DREAM

There are facts of family life that even plain people acknowledge: marital passion often fades (as the proverb goes, 'kissing wears out, cooking don't'), babies grow into willful children, and kids become teenagers. Just because the Amish adolescents you see are wearing straw hats and tilling the field doesn't mean they're fundamentally different than 'Englisher' teens. Most teenagers struggle to form their own identities and gain independence from their parents, and Amish 16-year-olds have a particular tough row to hoe (no pun intended).

Rumspringa (translates to 'runaround') is the Amish teen's rite of passage. When Amish adolescents turn 16, their parents allow them certain freedoms. They may experiment with consumerism, worldly pleasures and conveniences that are strictly forbidden in the Old Order Amish – stylish 'conventional' clothes, cell phones, shopping malls, relations with the opposite sex. Some repressed Amish teens go overboard, moving away from the farm, binging on alcohol, getting body piercings, going to house parties or even getting involved with drugs. Amish parents know that this can happen, and they permit it: that's because they want their children to make their own choices. If teens go through *rumspringa* but then return to their parents' home and state their intentions to remain in the faith, they may be baptized in the church and devote themselves to the plain people's traditional way of life.

The staggering majority of teens do just this. But there's a small percentage of teens that break away permanently, never to return to the family or the simple life. The ritual has inspired curiosity among locals, especially for the Lancaster residents who have spotted Amish teens smoking outside shopping malls or picking up jeans and tube tops at Abercrombie & Fitch; a host of documentaries and books address the subject. A good title covering the coming-of-age tradition is Tom Shachtman's fascinating *To Be or Not Be Amish*, published in 2007.

PENNSYLVANIA

TO MARKET, TO MARKET

There are farmers' markets. And then there are *farmers' markets*. If you want to buy some fresh vegetables, spices and pastries, by all means, head straight to the Central Market (p323) in Lancaster or the Bird-in-Hand marketplace (p329). But if you're the type who wouldn't mind spending half a day perusing farm-fresh goods and quirky crafts, you can't miss the following country markets.

With humble beginnings – it started in 1925 as a poultry market – **Root's Country Market & Auction** (☎ 717-898-7811; www.rootsmarket.com; 705 Graystone Rd, Manheim; ☷ 9am-9pm Tue Apr-Oct, 9am-8pm Tue Nov-Mar) features a produce auction, butcher counters, flower shops, a huge bakery area and antiques. All in all, there are more than 200 vendor stands to browse. If you're in the market for a new pig or goat, animal auctions get rolling at 5pm, while the flowers go up for grabs at 4pm, and for travelers with a green thumb, shrubs go on auction at 6pm. Also look for gourmet teas, roasted peanuts, garlic knots and hand-tossed pizza and homemade beef jerky. Down the road at 720 Graystone, you'll find **Root's Old Mill Flea Market**, also open on Tuesdays.

Nearly double the size of Root's is the **Green Dragon Farmer's Market & Auction** (☎ 717-738-1117; www.greendragonmarket.com; 955 N State St, Ephrata; ☷ 9am-9pm Fri, to 8pm Jan & Feb). This sprawling marketplace is one of the largest farmers' markets on the East Coast, boasting seven large buildings and over 400 farm stands and craft merchants. Auctions include household products at 2pm, small animals at 6:30pm, and (if you're really settling into country life) a hay and straw auction at 10am. Hungry? You'll find Italian ice, empanadas, coffee, sausage sandwiches, cheese steaks, hot wings, funnel cake and soft pretzels, to name a few. Kids and adults alike enjoy poking around the sweets on offer at the vintage-style Beulahs Candyland; the market is also overflowing with baby clothes, sunglasses, sewing machines, homemade quilts, candles, art supplies and everything in between. As the locals say, 'If you can't buy it at the Green Dragon, it ain't for sale.'

For a taste of the supernatural, take the 75-minute candlelit **Ghost Tours of Lancaster County** (☎ 717-687-6687; www.ghosttour.com/lancaster; tours depart from 11 E Main St; adult/child $14/8; ☷ Apr-Nov) walking tour of the 'haunted' mansions and old graveyards of Strasburg's historic district.

Sleeping & Eating

White Oak Campground (☎ 717-687-6207; www.white oakcampground.com; 3156 White Oak Rd; campsites from $26; ☷ ☷) Has 180 year-round sites in the woods or on the grass for two adults and two children; each extra person costs $3. Take May Post Office Rd south for about 1¼ miles, then turn east on White Oak Rd and go a quarter mile.

Mill Bridge Village Campground (☎ 717-687-8181; campsite/tipi/cabin from $37/51/125; ☷ ☷ ☷) Has streamside campsites, rustic tipis and well-equipped Amish-made log cabins for rent; amenities include free admission to Mill Bridge Village (p330), daily kids' activities, large swimming pools. (A note to free spirits: Lancaster County's traditional roots are showing, unmarried couples aren't welcome here.)

Rayba Acres Farm (☎ 717-687-6729; www.rayba acres.com; 183 Black Horse Rd; d from $85; ☷ ☷) About 3 miles east of Strasburg, off Rte 741, this dairy farm has been in the family for over 100 years. Rooms are available in the old and new houses. The old farmhouse has six large carpeted rooms with shared bathroom; the new house has motel-style units.

Limestone Inn B&B (☎ 717-687-8392; www.the limestoneinn.com; 33 E Main St; d from $95; ☷ ☷) This beautiful stone house, located right in the center of the action in Strasburg, has four common areas stocked with coffee, tea and pastries and atmospheric guest rooms with individual details; one has an antique sleigh bed and fireplace, another has a Singer sewing machine sink and a claw-foot tub.

Historic Strasburg Inn (☎ 717-687-7691; www. historicinnofstrasburg.com; 1400 Historic Dr; d from $120; ☷ ☷ ☷ ☷) Dating back to 1793, this inn is set in 16 peaceful acres off Rte 896, north of town. It has a heated outdoor pool and Jacuzzi, bike rentals, pet-friendly accommodations and a cozy restaurant and pub, the Fireside Tavern.

our pick **Strasburg Country Store & Creamery** (☎ 717-687-0766; 1 W Main St; cones/sandwiches $4/7; Positioned prominently on Strasburg's main square, this landmark general store is famous for impossibly rich ice cream scooped into buttery homemade waffle cones. The deli counter also serves delicious overstuffed sandwiches and grilled hot dogs. Look around for reminders of days gone by: the marble front stoop, a vintage clock and an 1890s marble soda fountain with silver dispensers.

Merenda Zug (☎ 717-687-8027; 11 E Main St; mains $5-10) Strong coffee, a laid-back atmosphere and delicious Lebanon bologna sandwiches make this contemporary cafe a hit with locals (and tourists who need a break from Lancaster County's down-home vibe.) This is also the place to come for Ghost Tours tickets (see p332).

Getting There & Away

Strasburg is at the intersection of Rtes 741 and 896, about 3 miles south of Rte 30. There's no public transportation from Lancaster, although RRTA bus No 14 stops several times daily at Rockvale Sq, about 3 miles to the north, at the intersection of Rtes 896 and 30.

LITITZ
pop 9000

A pretty town with many 18th- and 19th-century red-brick buildings, Lititz was founded in 1756 by Moravians who had fled religious persecution in Europe. In 1861, Julius Sturgis established the first commercial pretzel bakery in the US here: the **Julius Sturgis Pretzel Bakery** (☎ 717-626-4354; www.juliussturgis.com; 219 E Main St; adult/child $3/2; 9am-5pm Mon-Sat Apr-Dec, from 10am Jan-Mar). You can take a short tour of the bakery, viewing the antique ovens built by Sturgis and learning how to twist your own pretzels.

West along Main St and around the corner is the **Wilbur Candy Americana Museum** (☎ 717-626-3249; www.wilburbuds.com; 48 N Broad St; admission free; 10am-5pm Mon-Sat). A two-room display of old chocolate-making equipment, including molds for Easter eggs, is at the rear of the chocolate shop. Once you're craving dark chocolate and caramel, head over to the fantastic **Café Chocolate** (☎ 717-626-0123; www.chocolatelititz.com; 40 E Main St; mains $5-12; 10am-5pm Sun-Thu, 9am-9pm Fri & Sat), a stylish coffeehouse and eatery specializing in all-natural chocolate treats, gourmet cocoa drinks and fresh lunch and dinner plates made from organic produce.

Lititz is located about 10 miles north of Lancaster on Rte 501.

EPHRATA
pop 13,000

Though not particularly remarkable, Ephrata – located on Rte 322, approximately midway between Lancaster and Reading – has some historic flair and an important landmark that makes it a worthwhile sightseeing stop. Stop at the **Chamber of Commerce Visitor Center** (☎ 717-738-9010; www.ephrata-area.org; 16 E Main St; 9am-2pm Mon-Fri), located in an old train station. Dating from 1889, it was a stop on the Reading & Columbia freight and passenger line.

Ephrata is home to the **Ephrata Cloister** (☎ 717-733-6600; www.ephratacloister.org; 632 W Main St; adult/child $9/6; 9am-5pm Mon-Sat, noon-5pm Sun). The town was founded in 1732 by Conrad Beissel, a Pietist (Pietism was a reform movement in the German Lutheran church in the 18th and 19th centuries). It was a communal society made up of religious celibates and ascetics of both sexes, as well as affiliated married householders; at its peak, it had about 300 people, and its last celibate member died in 1813. The word Ephrata means 'fruitful' or 'plentiful' in old Hebrew.

The striking collection of medieval-style buildings – tall, steep-roofed, wood-and-shingle structures – are in their original locations. The doors were made low to force most people to bend 'in humility.' Members of the community lived and worked under a rigorous schedule and only ate enough food to maintain their strength. Note the bed made of a 15in-wide plank, with a wooden block for a pillow.

Many books were printed at the cloister, including a translation of the Mennonites' *Martyrs Mirror*. Ephrata is also known for its Frakturschriften (broken writing), a script in which each letter is a combination of strokes, as well as for its beautiful a cappella singing. To arrive by car, take Rte 222 north from Lancaster or south from Reading to Rte 322 west.

On an unrelated note, there's a popular summer festival in the area. Outside of Ephrata in nearby Adamstown, beer enthusiasts will find the **Annual Microfest** (☎ 717-484-4386, ext 204; tickets $30) in August. More than a dozen microbreweries are represented and guests can partake in unlimited tastings, a gourmet buffet and live music. To get there from Ephrata, take PA-272 N towards Reading; it's about a 15-minute drive.

READING
pop 80,560

Reading itself doesn't have the attractions of the rest of Pennsylvania Dutch Country, but there are a few sights outside town, including

---

ALL'S FAIR

As any local Shakespeare nut will tell you, Pennsylvania's **Renaissance Faire** (☎ 717-665-7021 www.parenfaire.com; 2775 Lebanon Rd Manheim) is a cut above most others in the region. But the lovely, tree-shaded fairgrounds, which double as the home of the Mount Hope Winery, don't open only for jousters and jesters. Elaborate festivals take place here in all seasons. Tickets for all festivals cost between $20 to $50 per person, unless noted below; visit www.parenfaire.com for full listings, pricing information and opening hours. New events are added from time to time, so keep an eye out.

- **Flavor Fest** (late May) A gourmet food, wine and beer festival. Free admission.
- **Celtic Fling & Highland Games** (June) As the name suggests, this jolly event features dance, food and music traditional among the Irish, Welsh, Scots Welsh and Cornish.
- **Blues & Brews** (July) Indulge in hardshell crabs, Maryland vegetable crab and steamed shrimp washed down with icy cold microbrews and sangria.
- **Amerigreen Freedom** (July) Ring in the Fourth of July with this huge music and food festival; it used to be held in downtown Lancaster, but now it's out here in the country where you can camp overnight. Consult the website for details.
- **Renaissance Faire** (August to October) This extravagant event is a full-blown blast from the past – 1589, to be exact. Look for Bacchus serving wine, divine roasted turkey legs, elephant rides, elegantly dressed lords and ladies, fire-eaters and jugglers and… well, it's an impressive experience that you have to see for yourself.

Daniel Boone's birthplace. Reading is more noted for its huge collection of factory-outlet stores, and it modestly promotes itself as 'the outlet capital of the world.' The town gets busy starting in mid-September – when visitors combine a trip to see Pennsylvania's fall colors with some early Christmas shopping – and it stays busy until after Christmas.

History

Straddling the Schuylkill River about 45 miles northwest of Philadelphia, the Reading region was originally settled by the fishermen of the Lenape Native American tribe. The Dutch set up a trading post there in 1663, and European settlers began arriving toward the end of that century. The town was laid out in the 1740s by the sons of William Penn (Thomas and Richard), and it was named after Penn's county seat in Berkshire, England. During the 19th century, it became an important manufacturing and industrial center – a position it maintains today.

Orientation

Downtown Reading is on the east bank of the Schuylkill River. Business Rte 422 east becomes Penn St, the main street in town, which leads west over the river to the suburbs of West Reading and Wyomissing, and to the factory outlets as well. Penn St divides the

town into north and south. The north-south Business Rte 222 becomes 5th St in town.

Information

Greater Reading Visitors Center (☎ 610-375-4085; www.readingberkspa.com; 201 Washington St; ⊙ 9-11am Mon, 11am-5pm Thu, 1-5pm Fri, 11am-4pm Sat) Has lots of information about the area's attractions, including the factory outlets.

Post office (N 5th St; ⊙ 8am-5pm Mon-Fri, to 2pm Sat) Between Court and Washington Sts.

Sights

No, it's not a mirage: there really is a red-and-gold neon Japanese pagoda in the middle of the Pennsylvania woods. Sitting several stories high on a hill in Mt Penn Forest Reservation east of the town's center and with good views across Reading, the **Reading Pagoda** (☎ 610-372-0553; www.pagodaskyline.org; admission free; ⊙ 11am-4:50pm) is an offbeat photo op. To get there take Duryea Drive up through the reserve.

Sleeping

Reading is busiest from mid-September til after Christmas, so it's best to book ahead. During that time, room rates at the hotels and motels go up by as much as 40% to 50%. You can get a list of B&Bs from the visitors' center.

French Creek State Park (☎ 610-582-9680; www. dcnr.state.pa.us/stateparks/parks/frenchcreek.aspx; 843 Par

Rd; campsites from $25; 🚹) Fourteen miles southeast of Reading, this park (p336) has forested campsites as well as yurts, 'camping cottages' and cabins. Contact the park for up-to-date rates; reservations are recommended for all, but are absolutely necessary for the yurts, cottages and cabins..

Sill's Family Campground (🕿 610-484-4806; www.sillscampgrounds.com; 1906 Bowmansville Rd; campsite/cabin from $32/65; 🕑 Apr-Oct; 🚹) The nearest private campground, Sill's has 125 sites, most with water and electricity hookups. There are also cabin accommodations that range from rustic to modern. Take Rte 222 south until you get to Rte 272, then go southwest for a quarter of a mile, until you see the signs, and then go southeast on Bowmansville Rd to the campground.

Overlook Mansion B&B (🕿 610-371-9173; www.overlookmansionbedandbreakfast.com; 620 Centre Ave; s/d from $90/95; 🔀) This stately Victorian-style mansion was built in 1873; today's B&B has flowery antique wallpaper, heavy brocade and dark polished wood throughout. It's known for wonderful breakfast spreads served in your room or, on summer mornings, on the front porch or in the garden.

In West Reading and Wyomissing, west of the river, most of the places are chain motels with standard, clean rooms and no surprises.

Eating

If you're in town to shop, the factory outlets have food courts inside and are surrounded by chain restaurants. And if you're self-catering on a Sunday, don't miss a stop at the **West Reading Farmers' Market** (www.westreadingmainstreet.org/farmersmarket.htm; Penn Ave, 500 block; 🕑 9am-1pm Sun May-Nov), a good place to stock up.

Speckled Hen (🕿 610-685-8511; www.speckledhenpub.com; 30 S 4th St; mains $9-18; 🕑 from 4:30pm Wed-Sat Sep-Apr) Reading's oldest pub is a classy joint with exposed brick walls, gourmet comfort food and a dynamic schedule of live music performances. Though the main pub closes in summer, its outdoor cafe section, Plein Air, is open in warm weather for lunch Wednesday to Friday and dinner Wednesday to Saturday.

Viva Good Life Bistro & Lounge (🕿 610-685-5299; www.vivagoodlife.com; 901 Hill Ave; 5 tapas for $18) This slick tapas lounge has a generic, commercialized exterior, but it wins points for savory seafood dishes and a 'mix and match' menu of small Spanish- and Mediterranean-inspired plates. The inventive cocktails alone make

the stop worth it; in summer, don't miss the drinks infused with fresh blueberries.

our pick **Judy's on Cherry** (🕿 610-374-8511; www.judysoncherry.com; 332 Cherry St; prix fixe $19.95) This sophisticated European-style eatery, a huge hit with locals since it opened, serves Mediterranean small plates like spicy mussels and roasted beets with blue cheese ($5 each), hearth-fired pizzas, classic martinis and a three-course prix fixe menu with wine on weekday evenings.

Shopping

The major factory outlets are in Wyomissing, west of town. They sell clothes (including designer labels and sportswear), crockery, cosmetics and other items. Call or check the websites for full store listings.

VF Factory Outlet (🕿 610-378-0408; www.vfoutletcenter.com; Park Rd & Hill Ave) in the VF Outlet Village is the largest:

Reading Outlet Center (🕿 610-373-5495; www.shoptheroc.com; 801 N 9th St)

Outlets on Hiesters Lane (🕿 610-921-8130; 755 Hiesters Lane)

Reading Station Outlets (🕿 610-478-7000; 951 N 6th St)

Getting There & Away

BUS

The **Reading Intercity Bus Terminal** (🕿 610-374-3182; cnr 3rd & Penn Sts) is served by **Greyhound** (🕿 800-231-2222; www.greyhound.com) and **Capitol/Bieber Trailways** (🕿 800-333-8444; www.capitoltrailways.com). Call ahead for discounted fares on tickets to Philadelphia or New York City.

CAR & MOTORCYCLE

From Philadelphia, take I-76 (Schuylkill Expressway) north to the Pennsylvania Turnpike, then head west to exit 22; take I-176 north to Rte 422, and follow it west into downtown. From Harrisburg, you can either take I-76 (Pennsylvania Turnpike) east to exit 21, then Rte 222 northeast, or you can take Rte 322, then Rte 422 east into Reading.

Getting Around

The **Berks Area Reading Transportation Authority** (BARTA; 🕿 610-921-0601; www.bartabus.com; 1700 N 11th St) is the county bus line. The base fare is $1.60.

AROUND READING

DANIEL BOONE HOMESTEAD

The famous outdoorsman was born and raised till the age of 15 in a log house on

---

DANIEL BOONE

Daniel Boone (1734–1820) is one of America's most famous 'frontiersmen.' Boone owes much of his fame to John Filson, who added an appendix concerning 'The Adventures of Col Daniel Boone' to his book *The Discovery, Settlement, and Present State of Kentucke* (sic). He was also the model for James Fenimore Cooper's Leatherstocking character and is even mentioned in Byron's 'Don Juan.'

Boone was born east of Reading, the sixth of 11 children, to a Quaker family. He had little schooling, although he did have some early experience as a farmer, weaver and blacksmith. When Daniel was 15, his family moved to northwestern North Carolina.

The Boone family home in North Carolina was on the American frontier, and although Daniel married Rebecca Bryan and had 10 children, he spent much of his life on expeditions around the country. One of his earliest (a year before his marriage to Rebecca) was with British General Braddock in his expedition to Fort Duquesne (today's Pittsburgh) in 1755.

Boone is famous for his travels in Kentucky and for fighting against Native Americans there, beginning in 1767. He built a wagon road through the Cumberland Mountains to Kentucky, which became known as the Cumberland Gap and was a major route west for settlers. He loved the 'dark and bloody ground' so much that he decided to build Boonesboro in Kentucky in 1774. From 1775 to 1783, Boone was a major force in expanding settlement in Kentucky and defending settlements from Native Americans. Boone himself was captured several times, but he always escaped.

He was a good fighter and wilderness guide but a lousy businessman. In 1799, after losing his Kentucky lands, he went to Missouri and stayed there until his death, 21 years later.

---

the site of the present **homestead** (☎ 610-582-4900; www.danielboonehomestead.org; 400 Daniel Boone Rd, Birdsboro; adult/child $6/4; ⏱ grounds open 9am-5pm Tue-Sun, tours on Sat & Sun), located 9 miles east of Reading. The reconstructed house includes the original foundation, portions of the 18th- and 19th-century building material, period German and English furnishings and a spring in the basement. Inside the visitors' center is a video of a fellow in old garb talking as though he knew Boone. Around the homestead are 600 acres of land with hiking and biking trails.

The price of admission includes a guided tour; unfortunately, due to cuts in state funding, the hours and tour availability have been scaled back for the time being. Check ahead of time for updated hours.

To reach the homestead, take Rte 422 east to the intersection with Rte 82; continue straight through the traffic lights, and after the sign for the homestead, turn left onto Daniel Boone Rd. The entrance to the property is about a mile from the turn.

HAWK MOUNTAIN SANCTUARY
This 2400-acre **sanctuary** (☎ 610-756-6961; www.hawkmountain.org; 1700 Hawk Mountain Rd, Kempton; adult/child $7/3; ⏱ visitor center 9am-5pm, trails open dawn-dusk) 25 miles north of Reading was established in 1934 to protect migrating hawks from hunters. Today, it's a preserve for bald

eagles, ospreys, peregrine falcons, hawks and other migrating birds, such as the swift and the swallow. Spring and fall bring thousands of birds to the sanctuary, and the best spot for viewing them is the 1521ft-high North Lookout. A 4-mile walking trail connects the sanctuary with the Appalachian Trail. You can rent binoculars at the visitors' center. Bear in mind that the sanctuary gets busy on weekends. Take Rte 61 north, then Rural Rte 2 east.

FRENCH CREEK STATE PARK
The 11½-sq-mile **French Creek State Park** (☎ 610-582-9680; www.dcnr.state.pa.us/stateparks/parks/frenchcreek.aspx; 843 Park Rd, Elverson), about 14 miles southeast of Reading, off Rte 422, has over 32 miles of hiking trails. Fishing and canoeing are possible on Scotts Run and Hopewell Lakes. From Memorial Day to Labor Day, there's swimming daily 11am to 7pm in a pool beside Hopewell Lake. Wildlife in the park includes deer, squirrels and, in the spring and fall, many migratory birds. The park also has camping facilities (see p334). From Rte 422 take Rte 82 south, Rte 724 east, then Rte 345 south into the park.

Surrounded on three sides by the park is **Hopewell Furnace National Historic Site** (☎ 610-582-8773; www.nps.gov/hofu/index.htm; 2 Mark Bird Lane; admission free; ⏱ 9am-5pm), which is administered by the National Park Service (NPS). Restoration work continues on this early-19th-century village, which has a cold-blast iron-making furnace. There's an audiovisual presentation, and in summer, guides dressed in period costume demonstrate different village crafts.

LEBANON & AROUND
pop 24,100

On the east side of Lebanon, **Weaver's** (☎ 717-274-6100; 1415 Weavertown Rd) is known for its production of Lebanon bologna. There's no tour, but you can take a look at the smokehouses Monday to Saturday from 9am to 4pm.

If you head east on Rte 422, you'll come to **Willow Springs Park** (☎ 717-866-5801; www.willowspringspark.com; 199 Millardsville Rd, Richland), which has a small lake that's open for swimming from Memorial Day to Labor Day. During the same period, there's also daily scuba-diving excursions for qualified participants; during the rest of the year, diving is only possible on weekends and appointments are necessary. Scuba divers and their families can also camp here. Check the website for more information and details on equipment rental in the area. To get there from Lebanon, head along Rte 422 to the traffic lights 2 miles east of the junction with Rte 501; turn right at the lights onto Millardsville Rd, and the park is a quarter of a mile down, on the left.

Getting There & Away
Lebanon is on Rte 422, 8 miles east of Palmyra and 87 miles west of Reading.

Getting Around
County of Lebanon Transit (COLT; ☎ 717-273-3058; www.coltbus.org), about to change its name to LT Lebanon Transit, has its main bus stop at Willow and N 7th Sts. At the time of writing, the service was starting a new direct commuter service to Harrisburg for $1.80 each way; check the website for details.

SOUTH CENTRAL PENNSYLVANIA

It's not just anywhere in the world where you can find burly Harley-Davidson riders, dead-serious Civil War re-enactors and grown men dressed up as Reese's Peanut Butter Cups all within a 50-mile radius. Central Pennsylvania is just that place. A patchwork of towns, mid-sized universities and picturesque dairy farms

(yes, the ones that provide the milk to make Hershey's chocolate) threaded by the wide Susquehanna River, this region is home to the recently rejuvenated state capital, Harrisburg, and the battlefields of Gettysburg – one of the nation's most impressive historic sites. Quirkier special-interest attractions include the Harley-Davidson factory in York and the Three Mile Island nuclear plant, the site of a serious meltdown in 1979 that's considered the worst in US commercial history.

Legendary confectioner and philanthropist Milton S Hershey chose this region for his famous factory because he was born here, and because he realized that central Pennsylvania was close to port cities, where he would need to receive cocoa beans and sugar, as well as a lush green landscape where dairy cows could grow fat and healthy. Since he was from the area, he knew it to be populated with humble, hard-working people who would make fine workers in his new company. He built his factory in 1903 and started to develop a 'model town,' complete with an amusement park, swimming pool, a beautiful theater and several schools, to meet the needs of his workers and their families. Later, of course, he established homes and a school for orphan boys.

GETTYSBURG
pop 8100

Gettysburg hosted the bloodiest battle in US history, so perhaps it's fitting that visiting the grounds today – especially on weekend afternoons in high season – feels like something of a battle as well. That's because the impressive Gettysburg National Military Park, complete with museums and thematic tours, regularly floods with international tourists, large groups of students on field trips, curious road-trippers and serious Civil War buffs who stride through the historic fields wearing stiff coats and wistful expressions.

Thanks to its proximity to the Mason–Dixon Line and its position at the junction of several important roads, Gettysburg was the site of the Union and Confederate confrontation. As any kid in the Pennsylvania school system knows, the battle was a turning point in the Civil War and helped inspire Abraham Lincoln's Gettysburg Address (p342).

Orientation
The approximately 1.5 sq miles of Gettysburg are laid out around Lincoln Sq. Several large

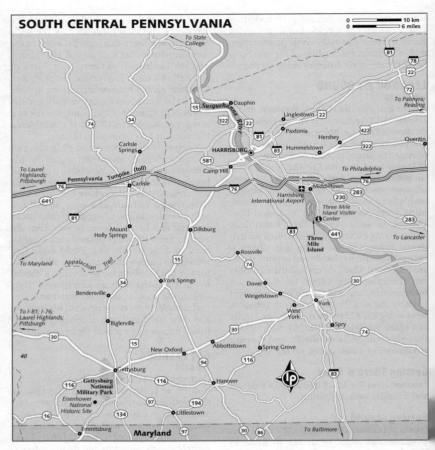

SOUTH CENTRAL PENNSYLVANIA

roads converge in the town. Rte 30 (York and Chambersburg Sts in town) and Rte 116 (Hanover, York and W Middle Sts) cross east to west. Rte 97 enters from the south (Baltimore St) and leaves from the north as Rte 34 (Carlisle St). Business Rte 15 enters town as Steinwehr Ave from the southwest and exits in the northeast as Harrisburg St. Finally, Rte 134 enters from the south as Taneytown Rd and ends in town as Washington St. Gettysburg National Military Park surrounds the town and still has homes and stores in it, as the area did at the time of the battle.

Gettysburg is around 55 miles southwest of Lancaster and 30 miles southwest of Harrisburg.

Information

Gettysburg Convention & Visitors Bureau

(☎ 800-337-5015; www.gettysburg.travel; 8 Lincoln Sq; ⏰ 8:30am-5pm Mon-Fri & 10am-3pm Sun) Friendly staff, well-equipped tourist office with maps and information.

Main post office (155 Buford Ave; ⏰ 8am-4:30pm Mon-Fri, 9am-noon Sat)

PNC Bank (6 York St) One of many ATMs in the area.

Sights & Activities

GETTYSBURG NATIONAL MILITARY PARK

Established February 11, 1895, this 8-sq-mile **park** (☎ 717-334-1124; www.nps.gov/gett/; ⏰ 6am-7pm Nov-Mar, to 10pm Apr-Oct) encompasses almost the entire area of the three-day battle. The battlefield contains more than 1600 monuments, statues, cannons and plaques set up in dedication to the brave souls who fought at Gettysburg.

The Battle of Gettysburg is the most famous battle of the Civil War. Some war buffs spend their lives studying the battle or only one day of it, and each year there are regular re-enactments of events relating to this pivotal event in US history. At Gettysburg, from July 1 to 3, 1863, the 75,000 men of Robert E Lee's Confederate army met the 97,000 men of George G Meade's Union army. The battle was the result of a chance sighting of some of Meade's troops by a group of Confederate troops who were sent to get supplies.

The battle began on July 1, with Confederate troops attacking Union troops on McPherson Ridge, west of Gettysburg. The Union troops held their position until the afternoon, when they were beaten back in a rout through town. Thousands were captured before they could regroup south of town on Cemetery Hill. The first day of battle ended with the Union troops, who had retreated, fortifying their positions while the bulk of Meade's army arrived to reinforce them.

By dawn of the second day the Confederate troops were laid out along an arc running through the middle of Gettysburg and along Seminary Hill. Facing them, a mile away to the east, was a smaller arc of Union troops on Cemetery Ridge. Lee ordered attacks against both flanks of the Union line. Confederate James Longstreet's attack smashed through the Union left flank at a peach orchard south of town and overran the Union position on Little Round Top. On the other flank, though, RS Ewell's attack didn't succeed in dislodging the Union troops and, ultimately, Longstreet's success couldn't be exploited successfully by the Confederates.

On the third day, Lee's artillery bombarded Union positions on Cemetery Ridge and Cemetery Hill; the Union artillery responded. The sickening high point came when Confederate General George Pickett led a massive charge of 12,000 men across an open field toward the Union line at Cemetery Ridge. In less than an hour, 10,000 of Pickett's men were dead or wounded, and the expression 'Pickett's Charge' entered the lexicon as a brave but futile attempt to defeat an enemy.

After the battle, there were 51,000 dead, wounded and missing troops, and 5000 dead horses. Lee's invasion of the North had been stymied, and his army was exhausted. Union General Meade 'won' the battle, but was too cautious (or too afraid) to pursue the Confederate army. Although the war continued for two more years, the Confederacy never recovered from its losses at Gettysburg.

The dead were buried all over the battlefield in hastily dug graves, and some weren't buried at all until Pennsylvania Governor Andrew Curtin ordered that land be purchased for a cemetery. This became the Soldiers National Cemetery at Gettysburg, and on November 19, 1863, the cemetery was dedicated. Near the end of the dedication ceremony, Abraham Lincoln gave a two-minute speech that became known as the Gettysburg Address (see p342).

The **National Park Service** (www.nps.gov) and the **Gettysburg Foundation** (www.gettysburgfoundation.org), a private nonprofit organization, work in partnership to manage and preserve the sights of historic Gettysburg. Many of the sites below are considered part of the park.

VISITOR CENTER

The **National Military Park Museum and Visitor Center** (☎ 877-874-2478; www.gettysburgfoundation. org/visit-museum.org; 1195 Baltimore Pike; ⊙ 8am-5pm Nov-Mar, to 6pm Apr-Oct) is a great resource; here you can pick up maps, guides and directions for a self-guided driving tour (allow two to three hours) that follows a route showing the battle action at important points. Licensed guides also offer two-hour car tours with rates starting at $55 per vehicle. Also inquire about free guided walks with park rangers of the National Cemetery and High Water Mark Trail.

The visitor center also sells a large selection of books about the battle and the Civil War, and houses the interesting **Gettysburg Museum of the Civil War** (adult/child $10.50/6.50), which exhibits uniforms, guns, implements and other historical artifacts, and screens an informational film narrated by Morgan Freeman.

Admission to the museum also gets you into a section of the museum and visitors' center that's a must-see for every visitor: the recently restored **Gettysburg Cyclorama** (www. gettysburgfoundation.org/cyclorama.htm; ⊙ 8:15am-5pm Mar-Nov, 8:30am-4pm Dec-Feb). In the late 1800s, before the age of television, Americans and Europeans alike used to line up to view 'cycloramas,' huge oil-on-canvas paintings with realistic landscapes and life-sized figures. When

PENNSYLVANIA

the viewers stood on a central platform, the murals created a 3D effect and visitors felt like they were in the middle of a historic scene. So it is at the Gettysburg version, finished in 1884 by Paul Philippoteaux, a French artist already known for his cycloramas on the Battle of Waterloo and the Crucifixion of Jesus. The massive 360-degree mural of Pickett's Charge, displayed around an auditorium and enhanced with a dynamic sound and light show, gives visitors a vivid description of the battle (kind of like a primitive IMAX movie!).

Follow the signs to the visitor center's main entrance off Rte 97/Baltimore Pike.

SOLDIERS NATIONAL CEMETERY
Across from the visitor center is the Soldiers National Cemetery at Gettysburg. It contains the graves of more than 7000 US servicemen, including 3582 Union soldiers killed in the Civil War (the remains of Confederate soldiers killed at Gettysburg were removed to the South). Nearly half of the Civil War burials here were of unknown soldiers. It was at the dedication of the cemetery that Lincoln gave his celebrated address.

THE BATTLEFIELD
The most famous part of the battlefield is probably the portion of **Cemetery Ridge** against which Confederate General Pickett hurled his cavalry – known as Pickett's Charge – resulting in 80% casualties. The spot is less than half a mile south of the visitor center, and you can walk to it on the **High Water Mark Trail**. There are other longer hikes. The 1-mile **Big Round Top Loop Trail** goes through a forest and past breastworks built by both troops. The 9-mile **Billy Yank Trail** and the 3½-mile **Johnny Reb Trail** are other options. Another interesting part of the battlefield, popular with kids as well as adults, is the **Devil's Den**, a mass of boulders used as a hideout by Confederate snipers. For these and other hikes, stop at the visitor's center first for maps, directions and personalized recommendations.

GENERAL LEE'S HEADQUARTERS MUSEUM
One of the few old homes open to the public, this pretty stone **house** (☎ 717-334-3141; www.civilwarheadquarters.com; 401 Buford Ave, Rte 30; adult/child $3/1; ◯ 9am-5pm Mar-Nov and Feb weekends, closed Dec-Jan) was built in 1834 and served as Lee's headquarters during the battle on July 1, 1863. Today it houses a small but interesting collec-

tion of artwork, clothing and memorabilia from the period.

DAVID WILLS HOUSE
The National Park Service turned this historic house – the place where President Abraham Lincoln stayed prior to giving his Gettysburg Address – into an excellent **museum** (☎ 866-486-5735; 8 Lincoln Sq; adult/child $6.50/4; ◯ 9am-5pm, closed Tue Mar-Apr & Sep-Nov, closed Tue & Wed Dec-Feb). Contrary to popular belief, Lincoln didn't write his most famous speech on the back of an envelope while on the way to Gettysburg. He actually wrote a draft in Washington, then revised it here (in the home of David Wills, a prominent attorney who invited Lincoln and also organized the construction of Soldiers National Cemetery) before delivering his speech on November 19, 1863. This museum pays tribute to him and to the town's recovery after the war with five galleries and two re-created rooms, Lincoln's bedroom and the David Wills Law Office.

JENNIE WADE HOUSE
Twenty-year-old Jennie Wade, shot by a stray bullet while making bread in her house, was the only Gettysburg civilian killed in the battle. The house was hit by more than 200 bullets. Although many Gettysburg residents prefer not to discuss it, the **Wade house** (☎ 717-334-4100; 548 Baltimore St; adult/child $7.25/3.50; ◯ 9am-7pm Mar-Nov) is believed by locals to be haunted. Allegedly, there have been incidents of 'positive movement' of items in the cellar, including a swinging chain.

LINCOLN TRAIN MUSEUM
In a historic area that's generally a snore for young children, this fun little **museum** (☎ 717-334-5678; www.gettysburgbattlefieldtours.com; 425 Steinwehr Ave; adult/child $7.25/3.50; ◯ 9am-5pm Mar-May & Sep-Nov, to 7pm Jun-Aug) stands out as a kid-friendly attraction. The Lincoln toy-train collection boasts a large system of toy trains (some dating from the 1800s) and dioramas that explain the importance of the railroad during the Civil War. There's also a simulated 'Lincoln Train Ride' in which passengers feel like they're riding with the president as he traveled to Gettysburg to deliver his famous address.

EISENHOWER NATIONAL HISTORIC SITE
The **farm** (☎ 717-338-9114; www.nps.gov/eise; adult child $7.50/5) that was the home of President

Dwight D Eisenhower (Ike) and his wife, Mamie, adjoins the southwestern corner of the national park and is administered by the National Parks Service (NPS) as a historic site. You purchase tickets at the visitor center in Gettysburg National Military Park, from where a shuttle bus takes you to the farmhouse. Frequent shuttle buses run to and from the site between 9am and 4pm.

Walking Tour

Start at the Gettysburg Travel Council (35 Carlisle St), one block north of Lincoln Sq, and walk south toward the square. On the first day of battle, Union soldiers streamed into town from the north and west and crossed **Lincoln Square** as they retreated south toward

Cemetery Hill. As they retreated, they stopped periodically to fire cannons north along the streets toward the pursuing Confederate troops.

Continue west (right) on Chambersburg St to **Christ Evangelical Lutheran Church** on your left. Here, a Union chaplain who was tending to the wounded inside was killed by advancing Confederate troops because he didn't identify himself as a man of the cloth when challenged by the Confederates.

Continue west, then go left (south) for one block on S Washington St to W Middle St, which, during the second and third days of the battle, was part of the Confederate line. Continue south for one block and turn left (east) onto W High St. Here, on the site of

LINCOLN'S GETTYSBURG ADDRESS

Four score and seven years ago our fathers brought forth on this continent, a new nation, conceived in Liberty, and dedicated to the proposition that all men are created equal. Now we are engaged in a great civil war, testing whether that nation, or any nation so conceived and so dedicated, can long endure. We are met on a great battlefield of war. We have come to dedicate a portion of that field, as a final resting place for those who here gave their lives that that nation might live. It is altogether fitting and proper that we should do this. But, in a larger sense, we can not dedicate – we can not consecrate – we can not hallow – this ground. The brave men, living and dead, who struggled here, have consecrated it, far above our poor power to add or detract. The world will little note, nor long remember what we say here, but it can never forget what they did here. It is for us the living, rather, to be dedicated here to the unfinished work which they who fought here have thus far so nobly advanced. It is rather for us to be here dedicated to the great task remaining before us – that from these honored dead we take increased devotion – that we here highly resolve that these dead shall not have died in vain – that this nation, under God, shall have a new birth of freedom – and that government of the people, by the people, for the people, shall not perish from the earth.

Abraham Lincoln, November 19, 1863, at the dedication of Soldiers National Cemetery at Gettysburg

the **United Methodist Church** (built after the war), was an earlier church in which the wounded were treated. In front of the earlier church two trenches were dug in which the dead, wrapped in blankets and packed next to each other, were buried.

Nearby, Abraham Lincoln sat in a pew in the **United Presbyterian Church**, on the corner of Baltimore St, and the retired President Eisenhower worshipped here as well. President Lincoln paraded south along Baltimore St on his way to give his famous address at the dedication of the Soldiers National Cemetery.

Turn north (left) on S Stratton St and go two blocks to the intersection with York St. Before turning west (left) on York St, look at the northeastern corner (at N Stratton St). There, after the battle, a dead, unidentified Union soldier was found holding a photo of his three children. The photo was reproduced in newspapers all over the country until his wife in upstate New York identified the man as Sergeant Amos Humiston.

Continue west on York St to Lincoln Sq; note the **David Wills House** (with the Lincoln Statue in front), where Lincoln completed the final draft of the Gettysburg Address.

Tours

Gettysburg has a vast range of tour options. You can see the historic sector from atop a horse, on a Segway, by tour bus, or in your car; there are haunted tours and church tours and battlefield tours and – if you're really in the

mood for something different – tours with a psychic medium.

For a standard bus tour, try **Gettysburg Battlefield Bus Tours** (☎ 717-334-6296; www.gettys burgbattlefieldtours.com; 778 Baltimore St; adult/child from $24.95/14), which offers dramatized audio tours on double-decker buses as well as coach buses with licensed guides onboard. Both tours run about two hours. More in-depth packages (adult/child from $41.50/24) allow visitors to choose their own stops at historic attractions like the Jennie Wade House (p340) and the Lincoln Train Museum (p340).

From April through November, tours on horseback are offered through the **National Riding Stables** (☎ 717-334-1288; www.artilleryride.com; 610 Taneytown Rd; 1/2hr ride $40/70) and the **Hickory Hollow Horse Farm** (☎ 717-334-0349; www.hickory hollowfarm.com; 301 Crooked Creek Rd; trail/guided ride per hr $45/55). Both offer basic trail rides and longer narrated journeys through Gettysburg National Military Park. If you're no equestrian, you can go on a Segway instead with **Segway Tours of Gettysburg** (☎ 717-253-7987; www. segtours.com; 380 Steinwehr Ave; tours from $45; ♿). Choose from the popular Western Battlefield tour or the shorter tour to the lesser-known Eastern Battlefield; all are handicap accessible.

Those with a taste for the paranormal have no shortage of tour options in Gettysburg: eerie events, ghost sightings and unsolved mysteries have long been tied to the battlefield and town. The original operator, **Ghosts of Gettysburg Candlelight Walking Tours** (☎ 717-337-0445; www.ghostsofgettysburg.com; 271 Baltimore St tours from $9.50; ☺ 8pm) is still one of the best. **Sleepy Hollow of Gettysburg** (☎ 717-337-9322; www. sleepyhollowofgettysburg.com; 89 Steinwehr Ave; tours $7-12; ☺ nightly) runs similar outings to ghostly sites, as well as a 'Psychic Medium Tour.' For a truly creepy night, head over to **Farnsworth House Ghost Walks & Mourning Theater** (☎ 717-334-8838; www.gettysburghauntedaddress.com; 401 Baltimore St; tours $11-20; ☺ 8pm & 9:30pm), where tours can be paired with 'ghost hunts,' a visit to a Victorian-style seance room, even a Murder Mystery Dinner.

Festivals & Events

Gettysburg Bluegrass Festival (www.gettysburgblue grass.com) Several days of rollicking concerts – Allison Krauss performed in 2010 – in May.

Gettysburg Festival (www.gettysburgfestival.org) Live jazz, farm-to-table culinary events, art exhibitions and experimental theater bring summertime crowds to venues all over town in June.

Gettysburg Civil War Battle Re-enactment (www. gettysburgreenactment.com) Exactly what the name suggests, plus food and a historic village; takes place in early July.

Gettysburg Fall Bluegrass Festival (☎ 717-642-8749) The festival is four days of concerts held over the third weekend of August.

Sleeping

Gettysburg is crammed with family-friendly hotels and wonderful B&Bs, but most are in-

credibly crowded on summer weekends. To save a few bucks, check out the cheaper hotels a few miles out of town on Rte 15 heading south or Rte 34 heading north.

BUDGET

Gettysburg has a number of large camp-grounds within 3 or 4 miles of town that are generally open March through November; log onto the www.gettysburg.travel for full listings. All have major facilities such as swimming pools, laundries, stores, propane gas and anything else you might need.

Artillery Ridge Campground (☎ 717-334-1288; www.artilleryridge.com; 610 Taneytown Rd; unpowered/powered site/cabin for 4 people $34/44/60; ☺ ☻) Three miles south of Gettysburg on Rte 134, it has bike rentals, paddleboats and a fishing pond; in addition to tent and RV sites, there are cute log cabins with bunk beds and front porches. Also organizes horseback rides to the battlefield.

Granite Hill Camping Resort and B&B (☎ 717-642-8749; www.granitehillcampingresort.com; 3340 Fairfield Rd; campsite/cabin/B&B room from $35/75/125; ☺ year-round; ☻ ☻) This spiffy mega-campground has it all: 300 shaded sites, daily hayrides, tennis courts, four playgrounds, kayak rentals, a trout-fishing pond and a minigolf course overlooking a lake. The B&B portion is brand new and housed in a restored brick farmhouse.

GETTYSBURG WITH KIDS

While a visit to Gettysburg is delightful for history buffs, younger kids can get lost in the shuffle. If you have little ones in tow, avoid possible temper tantrums by taking a break from the battlefields and heading to one of these child-friendly attractions.

Billed as 'part theatre, part adventure, part mystery,' **Lincoln's Lost Treasure** (☎ 800-838-3006; www.lincolnslosttreasure.com; 53 E Middle St; admission $38.95; ☺ 11am Sat & Sun) is an innovative scavenger hunt across historic Gettysburg. The clues and the itinerary are top secret: they won't even tell you the location of the starting point until a day before your tour, when you receive a last-minute call to your cell phone. Tickets are only available by booking online or over the phone – no walk-ins. More conventional kids' activities are on offer at the **Explore & More Hands-On Children's Museum** (☎ 717-337-9151; www.exploreandmore.com; 20 E High St; adult/child $4/6; ☺ 10am-5pm Mon-Sat Apr-Sep, closed Wed Oct-Mar), an 1860s house that was transformed into a center for children with rooms devoted to art, nature, history and exploration. It's best for children ages three to eight.

Just outside of town, children delight in the whimsical **Land of Little Horses** (☎ 717-334-7259; www.landoflittlehorses.com; 125 Glenwood Dr; adult/child $13.95/11.95; ☺ 10am-5pm Mon-Sat, from noon Sun, check website for hrs in fall, winter & spring). The place is exactly what it sounds like: a herd of miniature horses run free (well, sort of) and compete in short races. Other adorable farm animals are around for hands-on activities like milking and grooming. You'll also find a cafe and a family-focused guesthouse in case you can't tear yourself – ahem, your kids – away from the goats and ponies.

MIDRANGE & TOP END

Brickhouse Inn B&B (☎ 717-338-9337; www.brick houseinn.com; 452 Baltimore St; d $115-164; 🛜) In a three-story Victorian mansion dating from 1898, this B&B still has its original family heirlooms and hardwood floors. Well-appointed guest rooms are also filled with antiques and have private baths and bay windows. Larger suites have private porches and charming clawfoot bathtubs too.

Lightner Farmhouse B&B (☎ 717-337-9508; www. lightnerfarmhouse.com; 2350 Baltimore Pike; d/ste/cottage $139/165/189; 🛜) With nature trails and a huge wraparound porch, this lovely B&B is just a five-minute drive from the historic sights but feels like a country retreat. In addition to cozy guest rooms, there's a free-standing cottage for rent. The innkeepers arrange paranormal packages and romantic getaway weekends.

James Gettys Hotel (☎ 717-337-1334; www.james gettyshotel.com; 27 Chambersburg St; ste $140-250; 🖳 🛜) This elegant historic inn was a glamorous hot spot in the 1920s; it's listed on the National Register of Historic Places and underwent a major restoration in 1996. Now it offers sleek but traditionally decorated suites (some sleeping four) with sitting areas and kitchenettes; B&B-style amenities include freshly baked cookies and imported teas.

Inn at Herr Ridge (☎ 717-334-4332; www.innatherr ridge.com; 900 Chambersburg Rd; d $199-259; 🖳 🛜) This classy country inn, around since 1815, was once a Confederate hospital during the Battle of Gettysburg. Now the place is known as much for its first-rate restaurant (see p344) as for its quaint Victorian-style lodgings, some with fireplaces and clawfoot or Jacuzzi tubs. The refined service makes it feel special.

Eating & Drinking

On Steinwehr Ave, opposite the entrance to the park, there's a string of fast-food places.

our pick Ragged Edge Coffee House (☎ 717-334-4464; www.raggededgecoffeehs.com; 110 Chambersburg St; snacks $4-7; 🛜) This cool cafe specializes in piping-hot breakfast sandwiches, mochas and freshly squeezed juices, chicken salads and hummus wraps. Everything is fresh and family-friendly, so it's a hit with locals and visitors alike.

Lincoln Diner (☎ 717-334-3900; 32 Carlisle St; mains $5-10; 🕑 24hr) A fun, no-frills diner next to the railroad tracks, this is a popular lunch spot

serving up predictable fare like burgers, coffee, sandwiches and blueberry pie.

Dobbin House Tavern (☎ 717-334-2100; www. dobbinhouse.com; 89 Steinwehr Ave; mains $8-18; 🛠) Gettysburg's oldest colonial house contains two appealing eateries. The first, Springhouse Tavern, is a cozy alehouse with two fireplaces that serves soups and sandwiches. The more formal Alexander Dobbin Dining Rooms offer candlelit dinners in the old library, parlor, spinning room and study.

Tommy's Pizza (☎ 717-334-4721; www.tommys pizzainc.com; 105 Steinwehr Ave; pizzas $10-17; 🛠) This casual family-run pizzeria, right around the corner from the battlefield, makes for a quick lunch and a great bargain for families. Delicious specialty pies include the 'Greek' (with chopped spinach and feta cheese) and the meat-lovers' Supreme pizza.

our pick Blue Parrot Bistro (☎ 717-337-3739; www. blueparrotbistro.com; 35 Chambersburg St; mains $10-29) Situated in a historic building that was known as 'Mrs Schwartz's Oyster Parlor' in 1850, this stylish spot serves up Californian wines by the glass paired with sophisticated plates like crab dip with roasted sweet peppers and baked brie in puff pastry with fruit. Simpler burgers, beers and billiards are also on the menu.

Herr Tavern & Publick House (☎ 717-334-4332; www. innatherrridge.com/rest; 900 Chambersburg Rd; mains $13-34; 🕑 lunch Wed-Sat only) An antique tavern that's transformed into a fine dining institution, this is a place fit for a special occasion. Sample small plates, such as crab-stuffed portabella, or opt for filet mignon; all produce is fresh and organic. Also good for after-dinner desserts and drinks such as bananas foster and 'chocolate' wine.

Shopping

Gettysburg is full of shops selling Civil War trinkets, most of which appear comparable in quality and price, but you'll have to wade through a lot to find anything of quality. Innumerable items are emblazoned with the word 'Gettysburg' or some Blue (Union) or Gray (Confederate) icon. The **Gettysburg Gift Center** (☎ 717-334-6245; www.gettysburgmuseum.com; 297 Steinwehr Ave), part of the Civil War Wax Museum, is as good a place as any for trinkets. Other shops advertise antiques and you might find them worth a look.

Getting Around

Not long ago, Gettysburg opened the **Freedom Transit trolley system** (☎ 717-337-1345; http://rabbit

---

ELEPHANTS IN THE ROOM

If it's kitschy Americana you're after, you might find that the region's Civil War regalia and contemporary chocolate capital just aren't kooky enough to cut it. Not to fear: there's at least one genuinely quirky roadside attraction here that's worth a quick detour.

Discover one of the world's largest collections of elephant figures and images at **Mister Ed's Elephant Museum** (☎ 717-352-3792; www.mistereds.com; 6019 Chambersburg Rd, Orrtanna; admission free; ✆ 10am-5pm). The eccentric collector, who goes simply by 'Mister Ed,' received his first elephant on his wedding day in 1967; it was meant as a good-luck charm. Apparently the charm worked, because Mister Ed's wife is clearly a patient and understanding woman (but a practical one, too – she told her husband he needed to open the museum to house his collection because her own home was overloaded with clutter.) Since then, Mister Ed been traveling the world and picking up elephant figurines to fill the rooms: highlights include an elephant hair dryer and a tiny elephant carting a circus car made of 24-karat gold. Mister Ed's favorite elephant came from Brazil, and he's eager to share his stories with anyone who stops by. The museum also includes a vintage-style candy shop – where you can pick up sugary sweets for the road – proving beyond any doubt that Mister Ed really is a kid at heart.

To get there from Gettysburg, take US 30 W about 12 miles to the Chambersburg St roundabout.

---

transit.org/freedom/index.html; 257 N 4th St; adult $1; ✆ 10am-8pm Apr-Nov). The system encompasses several lines, but the most useful for tourists is the Lincoln Line, which goes from downtown Steinwehr Ave to the Baltimore Pike, with convenient stops at historical sites and tourist shops. If you want to leave your car somewhere and just enjoy sightseeing, consider using this new service.

Getting There & Away

Incredibly, for a major tourist destination, there's no public transportation to Gettysburg. By car, it's accessible on Rte 30 from Philadelphia, Lancaster or York; on Rte 15 from Harrisburg; and on Rtes 15 and 97 from Maryland. From Philadelphia you can also take I-76 (Pennsylvania Turnpike) west to exit 17 and follow Rte 15 south.

HARRISBURG

pop 48,300

Pennsylvania's capital is a small, picturesque city on the shores of the Susquehanna River. A decade or two ago, there wasn't much here for visitors, but the city began to revitalize in the '90s with the opening of the Whitaker Center and several new restaurants and bars. These days, it's an appealing place where joggers run along river paths, cafe tables spill onto sidewalks filled with happy-hour revelers, businessmen scurry around Strawberry Sq talking into cell phones while standing in the sandwich line, kids pedal their bikes across the walking bridge and a riverboat takes tourists on sunset cruises. It's nothing exciting compared to Pennsylvania's larger cities, but it's pretty in it's own right, with a noteworthy capitol building and a vibrant art-gallery scene adding to its charm.

Originally a ferryboat station known as Harris's Ferry, it was renamed Harrisburg in 1785 when John Harris, the son of one of the first European settlers here, refused a state-government order to name it Louisburg in honor of France's Louis XVI. It became the state capital in 1812 and was incorporated as a city later in 1860. It still retains a small-town feel, though, and it has managed to preserve many of its 18th- and 19th-century buildings, especially in the residential area near the town center and along Front St. It's not a heavily touristed place, and the nearby town of Hershey and the Three Mile Island nuclear power plant somewhat overshadow it.

Orientation & Information

Market St divides the city from north to south. Between State and Market Sts, 2nd St is a lively thoroughfare lined with cafes, bars, restaurants and shops: locals call it 'Restaurant Row.'

Harrisburg Hospital (☎ 717-782-3131; www.pinnacle health.org; 111 S Front St)

Hershey Harrisburg Regional Visitors Bureau (☎ 717-231-7788; www.hersheyharrisburg.org; 17 S 2nd St; ✆ 9am-5pm Mon-Fri)

Post office (813 Market St; ✆ 7am-6pm Mon-Fri, 8am-2pm Sat)

Sights

STATE CAPITOL

The impressive Italian Renaissance–style **State Capitol** (☎ tours 800-868-7672; N 3rd St; ⏰ 8:30am-4:30pm Mon-Fri) has 651 rooms and a 27ft-high bronze dome that's modeled on St Peter's Basilica in Rome, as well as bronze doors, paintings, murals depicting Pennsylvania's history, sculptures and stained glass. The marble staircase and surrounding balconies are modeled on the Opera House in Paris. On the 4th floor there's a viewing area from which visitors can watch the action in the senate chamber. There are free guided tours on weekdays; each lasts about 40 minutes. Inquire at the welcome center in the building's east wing or call ahead to reserve a tour.

STATE MUSEUM OF PENNSYLVANIA

Beside the State Capitol, this well-curated **museum** (☎ 717-787-4980; www.statemuseumpa.org; 300 North St; adult/child $3/2; ⏰ 9am-5pm Wed-Sat, noon-5pm Sun) houses four million objects, including Civil War artifacts, the huge Battle of Gettysburg painting by Rothermel, paintings and exhibits on archaeology, geology and political history. On the ground floor, look for the original 1681 charter granting Pennsylvania to William Penn.

WHITAKER CENTER FOR SCIENCE & THE ARTS

The wonderful **Whitaker Center** (☎ 717-214-2787; www.whitakercenter.org; 222 Market St; ⏰ 9:30am-5pm Tue-Sat, from 11:30am Sun) is a sleek, high-tech multipurpose venue containing several smaller theaters, children's attractions and event space.

The **Harsco Science Center** (adult/child $13.75/11.75; ♿) is a cool hands-on science museum that's designed for kids but equally stimulating for adults; interactive exhibits cover geology, language, weather and physics. There's also a great section for children under five. The **Select Medical IMAX Theater** (adult/child $9.50/8) shows science-themed documentaries and some feature films. The plush **Sunoco Performance Theater** (adult $17-45) stages acoustic music performances, opera, ballet and jazz. Past concert performers have included Dar Williams, G Love, George Winston and Jakob Dylan.

SUSQUEHANNA ART MUSEUM

This small but dynamic **museum** (☎ 717-233-8668; www.sqart.org; 301 Market St; adult/child $5/3; ⏰ 10am-4pm Tue, Wed, Fri & Sat, Thu 4-8pm, Sun 1-4pm) frequently puts on high-quality exhibits. Past shows include *Down the Rabbit Hole: the Bizarre Worlds of Salvador Dali* and *Jean-Michel Basquiat: An Intimate Portrait*.

HARRIS-CAMERON MANSION

Built in 1766, this elegant stone **mansion** (☎ 717-233-3462; www.dauphincountyhistory.org; 219 S Front St; adult/child $8/6; ⏰ 1-4pm Mon-Fri Apr-Dec) was the home that John Harris Jr built after the French and Indian War. (His father, John Harris Sr, was the first European immigrant to the area, sent by William Penn to settle the region and establish good relations with the natives). The house was constructed from locally quarried limestone and has been occupied by different local families in its history; at one point it operated as the Pennsylvania Female College. Today, knowledgeable guides lead visitors on historical tours through the mansion and its chandelier-lit parlors and grand solarium.

NATIONAL CIVIL WAR MUSEUM

A relatively new addition to the Harrisburg scene, this spacious, well-organized **museum** (☎ 717-260-1861; www.nationalcivilwarmuseum.org; 1 Lincoln Circle at Reservoir Park; adult/child $9/7; ⏰ 10am-5pm Mon-Tue & Thu-Sat, 10am-8pm Wed, noon-5pm Sun) promotes itself as 'the only museum in the US that portrays the entire story of the American Civil War.' The curators pride themselves on equally balanced presentations and exhibits that don't favor either the Union or Confederate sides. You'll find a great collection of artifacts in rooms devoted to themes like the Costs of War, Women in War, the Making of Armies, and Why Men Fought (to name a few). The latest permanent exhibit is an interactive display called Meet Mr Lincoln, put on in partnership with the Smithsonian.

CITY ISLAND

A peaceful green space across the Susquehanna River, City Island is connected to downtown Harrisburg by the Walnut St footbridge (and by car via the Market St Bridge). You'll find a river beach with an old-fashioned bathhouse, ice-cream stands, batting cages, nature trails, a toy train and playground for kids, a minigolf course, football fields, and a minor league baseball stadium – home to the Harrisburg Senators. From the island, a paddle steamer called the **Pride of the Susquehanna**

GALLERY HOP

On the third Friday of every month (known as *3rd in the Burg*), Harrisburg's art galleries open their doors for special exhibitions and events. There's complimentary transportation as well as cocktail and tapas specials at many eateries along the circuit – all in all, a thoroughly pleasant way to spend a summer evening. In addition to participating venues such as Mangia Qui (p347), the Midtown Scholar Bookstore (p348), Midtown Cinema (p348) and the Broad Street Market (p348), pop into the following establishments (or just swing by to support the arts during regular business hours) and also, log onto http://3rdintheburg.com/ for full gallery listings.

■ **Arthouse Lounge** (www.arthouselounge.com; 217 N 2nd St)

■ **Arts at 510** (☎ 717-724-0364; www.artsat510.com; 510 N 3rd St)

■ **Gallery at Second** (http://galleryatsecond.com; 608 N 2nd St)

■ **Gallery Blu** (☎ 717-234-3009; www.galleryblu.org; 1633 N 3rd St)

(☎ 717-234-6500; www.harrisburgriverboat.com; adult/child $9/4; ☥ noon & 1:30pm; ☥) offers 45-minute public cruises on the river with views of the Harrisburg skyline. On Thursday evenings in summer, the boat parks on the shore and opens its cocktail bar to passersby. Check the website for details on dinner cruises and other themed outings.

Tours
Step-on guides (ie the kind who will sit in the front seat of your car and direct you to the sights) are available through **Harrisburg Tours** (☎ 717-770-0235; www.harrisburgtours.com; 1483 Maplewood Dr; prices vary). Stops include the Harris-Cameron Mansion (p346), the National Civil War Museum (p346) and the State Capitol Building (p346).

Festivals & Events
The state capital hosts lively festivals throughout the year. Major events happening along the waterfront – featuring everything from artisans and live music to margarita tastings, chili cook-offs, carnival rides and film screenings – include the **Kipona Festival** (www.harrisburgarts.org/kipona; ☥ Labor Day weekend) and the springtime **ArtsFest** (www.harrisburgarts.org/artsfest; Memorial Day weekend). The fabulous lineup of food at these annual events is worthwhile in itself: think funnel cakes, vegetable fritters, pulled-pork sandwiches, cheese fries, fresh fruit smoothies... need we continue?

Sleeping & Eating
There aren't many inspiring accommodations in the center of town, just a few high-rise chain hotels like the Hilton and the Crowne Plaza. For a more memorable night's stay,

you're better off hanging your hat in nearby Hershey (see p349); Harrisburg, however, has no shortage of places for dinner and cocktails or to catch a show.

For a quick sandwich or an ice-cream cone, head to the **Strawberry Square Shopping Center** (N 3rd & Walnut Sts), which has a food court on the upper level.

Passage to India (☎ 717-233-1202; www.passagetoindiaharrisburgpa.com; 525 S Front St; lunch buffet $6.95) This Indian institution's unassuming entrance and location – it's tucked away beside a nondescript motel – means that few tourists drop by. But step inside to see the ornate interior, huge picture windows overlooking the Susquehanna River, and aromatic lunch buffet, and you'll understand why it's a local favorite year after year.

our pick Cafe Fresco (☎ 717-236-2599; http://frescocentercity.com; 215 N 2nd St; mains $8-25; ☥ closed Sun) This smart cafe-eatery features a coffee bar and breakfast menu, well-priced sandwiches and fresh salads at lunch, and Asian-inspired entrees in the evening. The colorful, mellow cocktail bar is a lovely spot for a beer or a refreshing cucumber-infused cocktail.

Zia's at Red Door (☎ 717-920-0330; www.ziasatreddoor.com; 110 N 2nd St; mains $10-32; ☥ closed Sun) This contemporary Italian eatery and wine bar is warm and stylish, turning out fine pastas and steaks to a crowd of couples and businessmen. During the weekday happy hour, martinis are $5 and a range of gourmet finger foods – like fried artichokes, olive tapenade, and ahi tuna – cost only $6.

Mangia Qui (☎ 717-233-7358; www.mangiaqui.com; 272 North St; mains $10-32; ☥ lunch Tue-Fri, dinner Tue-Sat, Sun brunch 10am-2pm) 'Mangia qui' is Italian for 'eat here' – and we're happy to follow directions.

PENNSYLVANIA

This eatery is cozy and elegant, right around the corner from the capitol; it houses two venues, a Spanish-style tapas bar with a potent house sangria and a restaurant specializing in Italian regional cooking.

Shopping & Entertainment

Apart from the specialty shops and boutiques in and around **Strawberry Square** (N 3rd & Walnut Sts) the capital city has a few noteworthy stops. The **Broad Street Market** (☎ 717-236-7923; www.broadstreetmarket.org; N 3rd & Verbeke Sts; ⏰ 7am-2pm Wed, to 5pm Thu & Fri, to 4pm Sat) is a lively organic marketplace where you can check out farm-fresh produce and pick up homemade pastries. It's the oldest continuously operated market house in the country, founded in 1860.

Across the street, there's a great indie bookstore, the **Midtown Scholar Bookstore** (☎ 717-236-1680; www.midtownscholar.com; 1302 N 3rd St; ⏰ 9am-5pm Mon-Wed, to 9pm Thu-Sat, noon-7pm Sun). Featuring an art gallery, used books, fair-trade coffee and acoustic concerts in the evenings, it's housed in a restored theater from the 1920s. You'll find a similar atmosphere at the arthouse-style **Midtown Cinema** (☎ 717-909-6566; www.midtowncinema.com; 250 Reily St), which screens classic and independent films and has an art gallery and cafe.

Getting There & Away

AIR

The slick, newly renovated **Harrisburg International Airport** (MDT; ☎ 717-948-3900; www.flyhia.com) is in Middletown, north of the Susquehanna River, about 8 miles southeast of Harrisburg.

Airlines operating out of MDT include the following:

AirTran (☎ 800-247-8726) Flies to Orlando and Atlanta.

Delta (☎ 800-221-1212) Flies to Atlanta, Cincinnati and Detroit.

United Airlines (☎ 800-241-6522) Flies to Chicago and Washington-Dulles.

US Airways (☎ 800-428-4322) Flies to Boston, Charlotte and Philadelphia.

BUS & TRAIN

The bus and train stations are in the **Harrisburg Transportation Center** (411 Market St at S 4th St), the old Pennsylvania Railroad station with a cobbled forecourt, and an elegant wood-paneled interior in the train terminal.

Catch the train with **Amtrak** (☎ 800-872-7245; www.amtrak.com) to Philadelphia ($23 to $28, 1½ hours) to Pittsburgh ($37, 5¾ hours) and New York ($47, three hours). Log onto the website for schedules on these and other routes. The less beautiful **Greyhound bus station** (☎ 717-255-6970; www.greyhound.com) is below the train station; buses operated by **Capitol/Beiber Trailways** (☎ 717-233-7673; www.capitoltrailways.com) and **Fullington Trailways** (☎ 717-232-4251; www.fullingtontours.com) also stop here. Standard fares to Philadelphia start around $24. Log onto their websites for cheaper fares and more information on destinations and routes.

CAR & MOTORCYCLE

Harrisburg is at the intersection of a number of major highways. The east–west Pennsylvania Turnpike (I-76) passes through the Harrisburg area (the I-76 runs between Philadelphia and Pittsburgh). I-81 and I-83 pass through town and connect it with Maryland to the south; I-83 also connects with York, 25 miles to the south. Rte 230 joins Harrisburg with Lancaster, which is about 43 miles to the southeast.

Getting Around

Capitol Area Transit (CAT; ☎ 717-238-8304; www.cattransit.com; 901 N Cameron St) operates the city's buses. The **CAT Transfer Center** (Market Sq cnr Market & S 2nd Sts) is the main downtown bus stop and has a customer-service kiosk where you can obtain route maps, schedules and bus passes. The one-way fare to any destination in town is $1.65; you must provide exact change if paying in cash, otherwise consider purchasing a multiride pass. CAT also runs a free motorized trolley service between the State Capitol, Strawberry Square Shopping Center and the Midtown Market District.

THREE MILE ISLAND

Three Mile Island, in the Susquehanna River, off Rte 441, about 10 miles south of Harrisburg, is America's most famous nuclear plant as a result of its partial meltdown in 1979. The plant consists of two units, named Unit 1 and Unit 2 (also known as TMI-1 and TMI-2). It cost about $1.1 billion to build, but today it would cost five times that much, making nuclear power (surprise!) vastly unprofitable. Unit 2, in which the accident occurred, is permanently shut down, but Unit 1, which was shut down after Unit 2's accident, was reactivated in 1985 and is expected to run until about 2014. The steam coming out

---

NUCLEAR ACCIDENT AT THREE MILE ISLAND

On March 28, 1979, the core of the Unit 2 nuclear reactor, which had only been operating for about three months, overheated and partially melted. In the process the plant released significant amounts of radioactive gases.

The essential problem was that a valve became stuck open and allowed water that normally cooled the core to flow out. Reactor operators failed to notice the stuck valve for over two hours (due to inadequate training). When the valve finally closed, operators noticed that water had been lost, and they added water to cool the reactor. This colder water caused many of the very hot fuel rods to shatter.

Pennsylvania's governor ordered pregnant women in the Harrisburg area to be evacuated, and many others left as well. Subsequent reports found that there were no 'significant' health effects caused by the meltdown.

The cleanup, which cost about $1 billion, included evaporating 2.3 million gallons of 'slightly radioactive' water into the atmosphere. During the 1980s, around 10,000 people were involved in the cleanup, and the last shipment of damaged fuel left Unit 2 on April 15, 1990.

It can be argued that the Three Mile Island accident was profoundly helpful to the US anti-nuclear movement. Afterwards, opponents had a clear-cut example of a near-disaster, and massive demonstrations against nuclear power followed in the 1980s. The industry has been under intense scrutiny since the accident, and construction of new nuclear plants has been at a virtual standstill until recently.

The accident also provided a salutary lesson to the nuclear industry, which thereafter sought to improve training and safety procedures and to design more user-friendly operating equipment.

---

of the tower is warm water vapor from the cooling process.

TMI (www.tmiinfo.com) used to run a visitors' center, but for the time being, the public is only invited in for scheduled open houses and community events – check the website for upcoming activities. Science geeks and road-trippers still find it an interesting stop for a photo op. To arrive by car from Harrisburg, take I-83 north, then I-283 south, Rte 230 east and Rte 441 south.

HERSHEY
pop 12,960

The self-proclaimed 'Sweetest Place on Earth,' Hershey is the headquarters of an international chocolate empire. Strategically positioned at the heart of a bucolic region where dairy cows grow plump and healthy (someone's got to make the milk that makes those famous Hershey's Kisses creamy), the town is a family-friendly destination with a large amusement park, old-fashioned hotels and B&Bs, a chocolate spa, street names like 'Cocoa Avenue' and vintage streetlamps topped with gleaming silver Kiss-shaped statues. On cloudy afternoons after a rainstorm, the aroma of chocolate actually fills the air; on summer weekends, however, the town becomes unpleasantly congested with tour

buses and families on vacation. The Hershey Outlets shopping center and several large concert and sporting venues, including the new Giant Center, also bring in regular crowds.

Most people who sink their teeth into a Reese's Peanut Butter Cup don't have a clue about the company's refreshingly noble history. Milton S Hershey, a Mennonite, didn't receive a proper education, but with the support of his wife, Catherine, he founded a successful chocolate company, established a school and home for orphan boys, and planned what he considered to be the perfect town – now known as Hershey. He donated much of his hard-won personal wealth to improve the lives of underprivileged children, a legacy that continues today in the Milton S Hershey school system.

Orientation & Information

In town, Rte 422 becomes Chocolate Ave, the main thoroughfare (you know you've arrived when you see the Hershey Kiss street lamps). Most attractions are located north of this avenue. **Visitor information** (☎ 800-437-7439; www.hersheypa.com; 251 Park Blvd; ⏰ hours vary seasonally, 9am-10pm in summer) is located inside the main entrance to Hershey's Chocolate World. There are several banks with ATMs lining Chocolate Ave.

Sights & Activities

HERSHEYPARK

Kids squeal with anticipation at the mention of this popular **amusement park** (☎ 717-534-4900; www.hersheypark.com; 100 W Hersheypark Dr; adult/child $52.95/31.95; ⏰ hours vary seasonally, 10am-10pm in summer, to 11pm weekends; ♿). The wooded 90-acre playground, originally established in 1905 by Milton Hershey as a recreation area for his workers, contains more than 65 rides and attractions, including several old-fashioned wooden roller coasters, nine water rides, carnival-style games and several stages for live entertainment. Park admission also gets you into ZooAmerica (p350). It's more economical to purchase a two- or three-day 'flex plan' or a Sunset Plan that lets you into the park only for evening hours; consult the website for pricing details. Although the park is only in full swing between Memorial Day and Labor Day, it opens at limited capacity during the holidays for Christmas Candylane, at Halloween for Hersheypark in the Dark, and in April or May for Springtime in the Park.

Chocolate lovers may be sad to learn that health regulations prohibit visitors from entering the actual chocolate factory. The consolation prize is **Hershey's Chocolate World** (☎ 717-534-4900; www.hersheyschocolateworld.com; admission free; ⏰ hours vary seasonally, 10am-10pm in summer; ♿), an ever-expanding cocoa-themed complex that houses a mock factory and tour ride where visitors learn about the chocolate-making process. After exiting the ride, there's a warehouse-sized chocolate shop, small stores selling Hershey T-shirts and toys, a 3D theater showing kid-oriented movies, a make-your-own-candy-bar center, a chocolate tasting minicourse for all ages, and myriad other temptations for your sweet tooth. The chocolate food court is famous for freshly baked cookies, gourmet hot chocolate and peanut-butter milkshakes. The tour ride is free but some activities cost a fee.

ZOOAMERICA

This 11-acre **zoo** (☎ 717-534-3900; www.zooamerica.com; 100 W Hersheypark Dr; adult/child $9.50/8; ⏰ hours vary seasonally, 10am-8pm in summer; ♿), just beside Hersheypark, features more than 200 native North American animals. The kid-friendly After Hours Tour ($35) allows an up close and personal look at the wildlife park and chances to feed the animals with the zoo's naturalists.

HERSHEY STORY

The charming Hershey Museum closed to make way for this slick new **museum** (☎ 717-534-3439; www.hersheystory.org; 63 W Chocolate Ave; adult/child $10/7.50; ♿), which teaches visitors about Hershey's origins, the science of chocolate-making, and the cross-cultural history of chocolate through interactive exhibits. In the Chocolate Lab ($10), learn to make chocolate from scratch; in the Countries of Origin ($9.95), guests sample chocolates from Africa, Indonesia and other far-flung cocoa capitals. Though it's not far from the park, there's free a shuttle service between here and Hershey's Chocolate World.

HERSHEY GARDENS

The 23-acre botanical **gardens** (☎ 717-534-3492; www.hersheygardens.org; 170 Hotel Rd; adult/child $10/7; ⏰ 9am-6pm mid-Apr–Oct; ♿) began life in 1937 as a rose garden and grew to include various other flowers, shrubs and specimen trees such as European beech and Japanese maple. There are also a Children's Garden and a butterfly house containing over 25 North American species. It's located north off Hershey Park Drive in front of the Hotel Hershey.

HERSHEY THEATRE

One of Milton S Hershey's most memorable contributions to the town is this glamorous old-fashioned **theater** (☎ 717-534-3405; www.hersheytheatre.com; 15 E Caracas Ave; ticket prices vary; ⏰ check website), which stages Broadway shows and screens classic films. Its impressive interior features shimmering walls that resemble those of a Byzantine castle, polished floors inlaid with Italian lava rock and an overhead proscenium arch inspired by the design of a Venetian bridge.

HERSHEY TROLLEYWORKS

Departing from Chocolate World's main entrance, vintage-style **trolley buses** (☎ 717-533-3000; www.hersheytrolleyworks.com; tours adult/child $12.85/5.95; ♿) take visitors on hour-long tours of Hershey with narration sung by the conductors. It's a little corny, true, but the performance is well-done, and the ride is fun for kids – it's also a real hit with senior citizens.

INDIAN ECHO CAVERNS

Beat the heat (and the Hersheypark crowds) on a scorching-hot summer day by descend-

MILTON S HERSHEY

In an age where corporate sharks and shady inside traders rule the business world, it's refreshing to remember a man who was not only a shrewd entrepreneur but also a gentleman and humanitarian. Milton S Hershey, the man behind the nation's most famous chocolate bars, left a legacy that most Americans only consider when they're opening the silver wrapping of a Hershey's Kiss. What many visitors to his 'model town' don't realize is just how inspirational the back story really is.

Hershey was born in 1857 in a rural Pennsylvania community not far from where he eventually established his chocolate company. He received no formal education, but for four years as a teenager, he served as an apprentice to a candymaker in Lancaster. His first attempts to start his own candy company were fruitless: he tried and failed in both Philadelphia and New York City. When he returned to Lancaster for a second time, he was finally able to get a caramel business off the ground. Before long, the Lancaster Caramel Company was exporting to Europe, and Hershey finally earned recognition as a prominent businessman.

In 1893, at the World's Columbian Exposition in Chicago, Hershey took a new interest in chocolate-making – and, as any good businessman would, he noticed a growing market demand for chocolate. He strove for years to perfect a recipe for milk chocolate that would be inexpensive enough to produce for the American public; up until that point, chocolate was considered a decadence reserved only for the rich, but Hershey, as he would later prove, was always more interested in the tastes and predilections of the common man.

The Hershey Chocolate Company started to take off after Hershey sold his caramel business for a nifty sum. Naturally, Hershey needed a home base for his rapidly expanding company, so he returned to the region of his birth: the abundant dairy farms and conveniently located area where the town of Hershey now stands. But he didn't just build a factory. Hershey, both smart in business and sensitive (before his time) to the topic of workers' conditions, decided to build an entire town around his company. His plans for the ideal community included several schools, churches, parks, a trolley system, swimming pools, a theatre, a zoo, public gardens, a classic department store and amusement park – now known as Hersheypark.

And he didn't stop there. Hershey and his wife, Catherine, were childless, but they always loved children, and in 1909, they founded the Hershey Industrial School for orphan boys. In doing so, Hershey started a tradition of providing first-class education and living quarters for underprivileged youth. He donated most of his personal wealth to the Hershey Trust in 1918 with the intention of supporting the Hershey Industrial School for years to come.

Hershey passed away in 1945, but the Milton Hershey School is alive and kicking: if you drive over to the main campus, you'll see the slick educational facilities and huge mansions where nearly 2000 underprivileged students (including girls) study and live free of cost. Log onto www.mhs-pa.org for more information. And next time you sink your teeth into a Hershey bar, remember the company's founder and his remarkably charitable spirit – it's enough to justify buying another, and maybe a bag of Kisses too.

ing into the depths of these limestone **caves** (☎ 717-566-8131; www.indianechocaverns.com; 368 Middletown Rd; tours adult/child $13/7; ⏰ 9am-6pm Memorial Day-Labor Day, 10am-4pm rest of year; ♿). Guides lead visitors of all ages on 45-minute tours of this beautiful natural formation, teaching kids about the formation of stalactites and stalagmites and discussing geology and Native American history. The cave temperature hovers around 52°F year-round, so be sure to bring a long-sleeved shirt. Outside, children can 'pan for gold' at the Gem Mill Junction exhibit (summer only).

Sleeping

Room rates skyrocket in the summer months; the prices quoted below are for that period. During the low season, you'll find the same lodgings much more affordable. You'll find several midrange places along Chocolate Ave.

BUDGET & MIDRANGE

Hershey Highmeadow Campground (☎ 717-566-0902; www.hersheycamping.com; campsites $41-51, cabins from $90; ♿ ♿) Fully equipped with showers, laundry, a grocery store and two swimming pools. New deluxe cabins ($135) have private bathrooms and sleep up to four; there's a three-night minimum stay in high season. To get there, follow Chocolate Ave west to the junction with Hershey Park Drive (Rte 39), turn right for about 500 yards, then left onto Matlack Rd.

White Rose Motel (☎ 717-533-9876; www.whiterose motel.com; 1060 E Chocolate Ave; d $65-139; 🅿 🛜 🅿 ♿) With basic but sparkling-clean rooms stocked with refrigerators and DVD players, helpful hosts and an outdoor pool that's great for kids, the White Rose is a real steal. It's located a mile away from Hersheypark.

Gibson House (☎ 717-534-1305; www.gibsonhouse bandb.com; 141 W Caracas Ave; d $129; 🅿) This small but lovely B&B is located in an ordinary home – though dating from 1925, it could be considered historic – but who cares when you're getting spectacular service and hearty blueberry pancakes for breakfast? Guest rooms are spacious and filled with antiques and the airy front porch is a peaceful place to recover from a day in the park.

our pick Inn at Westwynd Farm (☎ 877-937-8996; www.westwyndfarminn.com; 1620 Sand Beach Rd, Hummelstown; d $134-189, cottage $259; 🅿) A gorgeous refuge about 3 miles away from downtown Hershey, this inn and 32-acre horse farm is ideal if you'd rather not spend all day *and*

night with the Hersheypark crowds. Elegant guest rooms are spacious and light-filled, some with fireplaces, all with private bathrooms and fine linens; the lovely freestanding cottage is great for families.

TOP END

Hershey Lodge (☎ 717-533-3311; www.hersheylodge. com; 325 University Dr; d $299; 🅿 🛜 🅿 ♿) This upscale, family-friendly lodge has 665 rooms outfitted with chocolate-themed decor, huge flat-screen TVs and welcome kits for children; the grounds include a minigolf course, outdoor pools and a picturesque duck pond. Since it's officially operated by the Hershey corporation, guests have easy access to all of the town attractions – many guests stay here as part of a vacation package.

Hotel Hershey (☎ 717-533-2171; www.thehotelhershey. com; 100 Hotel Rd; d/cottage from $409/534; 🅿 🛜 🅿 ♿) Set on a 90-acre hilltop, the luxurious, Mediterranean-style hotel is the premiere place to stay in town. Facilities include a chocolate spa, an infinity swimming pool, tennis courts, a children's activity center, a golf course, an ice-skating rink and several boutiques, restaurants and cafes. Tree-shaded cottages are a cozy alternative to standard hotel rooms and suites.

DETOUR: MOUNT GRETNA

It's summertime in Pennsylvania – and even though you knew Hersheypark was going to be crowded and that historic Gettysburg was going to be blazing hot, you just don't have the fortitude of the men standing around in heavy Civil War gear in 95°F heat. What to do? We have just the thing.

Flee the masses and head to the lovely wooded haven of Mount Gretna. Founded by the Pennsylvania Chautauqua Society in the 1890s, this postcard-pretty village is dotted with charming Victorian-style cottages and the tranquil **Mount Gretna lake** (☎ 717-964-3130; http://mtgretnalake.com; 130 Lakeview Dr; adult/child $12/8; ⏰ 11:30am-6:30pm Jun-Aug), where families can swim, canoe, sun on the sandy beach, laze about in an inner tube or splash into the water from a suspended circus-style trapeze. There are hiking trails, an excellent shaded playground, a partly-outdoor theater staging music performances and theater productions, an appealing antique shop and frequent arts festivals. Apart from these well-known attractions, Mount Gretna is filled with charming forest trails and unexpected details that you'll only discover if you take a leisurely stroll – look for the community garden filled with fairy statues.

Don't miss a stop at the village's classic ice-cream parlor, the vintage **Jigger Shop** (☎ 717-964-9686; www.jiggershop.com; Gettysburg Ave & Rte 17; ice cream $3-6; ⏰ noon-10pm summer). Sitting on the breezy, tree-shaded wooden deck with a root-beer float or a hot fudge sundae, you'll almost forget about the crying children standing in long lines at Hersheypark.

To get to Mount Gretna from Hershey, take PA-117 to Mt Gretna Rd, turn right on Glossbrenner Ave and then right again onto Muhlenburg Ave. Alternatively, you can take US-322 to PA-241 to Old Mount Gretna Rd, turn left on State Rte 3002, then right on Butler Rd and right onto PA-117 (then follow directions above). Either drive will take you through winding hills and beautiful farmland.

Eating & Drinking

Hersheypark is filled with eating options from casual ice-cream stands and sandwich shops to nicer sit-down restaurants; Chocolate World has a food court with fresh salads, pizzas and, of course, a plethora of sweets. In town, most of the town's restaurants are situated along Chocolate Ave. There are a cluster of fast-food restaurants and a Panera bakery at the end of Hersheypark Drive, just past Hershey Highmeadow Campground.

Local coffeehouses include **Cocoa Perk** (☎ 717-298-1118; www.cocoaperkcafe.com; 1130 Cocoa Ave) and **Cocoa Beanery Cafe** (☎ 717-508-5986; 1215 Research Blvd); the latter is a bit out of the way, next to the Hershey Medical Center, but it's housed in a beautiful Victorian building and feels like a relaxing getaway from the Hersheypark madness. Coffee, delicious pastries, artisan breads and other gourmet treats are also on offer at the more centrally located **Breads 'N' Cheeses Coffee House** (☎ 717-533-4546; http://breadsandcheese.com; 243 W Chocolate Ave).

For a cozy breakfast or a leisurely lunch on an open-air porch, head to local favorite the **Hershey Pantry** (☎ 717-533-7505; www.hersheypantry. com; 801 E Chocolate Ave; mains $7-15; ☺ closed Sun). A relative newcomer on the Hershey scene is the excellent **Chocolate Avenue Grill** (☎ 717-835-0888; www.chocolateavenuegrill.com; 114 W Chocolate Ave; mains $10-22; ☺ closed Sun), which offers an eclectic lineup of fresh salads, wraps, seafood, steak and pasta, as well as quick service, a children's menu and a full bar.

Hotel Hershey (☎ 717-533-2171; www.thehotel hershey.com; 100 Hotel Rd) contains several highly recommended dining venues and cocktail bars; head up the hill and take a look around. The hotel's longest-running establishment, the lovely **Circular Dining Room** (☎ 717-534-8800; brunch adult/child $39.95/19.50) is famous for its decadent Sunday brunch; it's also a romantic spot for a special-occasion dinner. The brunch and evening dress code is somewhat formal and reservations are required. As for the dining room's unusual shape? Founder Milton S Hershey, according to the story, believed that poor tippers were always seated at restaurants' corner tables. With a grand statement, 'I do not want any corners,' he built the Circular Dining Room.

Getting There & Away

By car from Harrisburg, follow Rte 322 east, then Rte 422 into town. From Philadelphia

---

HARLEY HOGS

They say that the reason Harley-Davidsons are called 'hogs' is because years ago a young motorcycle racer used to parade around with a small pig on his gas tank after winning a race. Others followed his lead, and the 'hog' became inseparable from the motorcycle.

---

take I-76 (Pennsylvania Turnpike) to exit 20; take Rte 72 north, then Rte 322 west to Rte 422. From Pittsburgh take I-76 east to exit 19, then Rte 283 north and Rte 322 east.

YORK

pop 40,100

York is the home of the Harley-Davidson motorcycle final assembly plant (though the company is headquartered in Milwaukee, WI). In addition, the downtown area has some fine historic buildings and is undergoing a revival.

About 20 miles southeast of Harrisburg and 25 miles southwest of Lancaster, York was Pennsylvania's first settlement west of the Susquehanna River. Established in 1741, it was the capital of the US between September 30, 1777, and June 27, 1778, when Congress fled Philadelphia following the British victory at the Battle of Brandywine. During that period, Congress met at the York County Colonial Courthouse where the Articles of Confederation, later to become the country's first constitution, were drafted and adopted.

Travelers after information can find it at the **Downtown York Visitors Information Center** (☎ 717-852-9675; www.yorkpa.org; 149 W Market St; ☺ 9:30am-4pm) and the **Visitors Information Center at Harley-Davidson** (☎ 717-852-6006; Rte 30 & Eden Rd; ☺ 9am-5pm).

Many travelers visit York just to see **Harley-Davidson's York Vehicle Operations** (☎ 717-848-1177; www.harley-davidson.com; 1425 Eden Rd; ☺ 8am-4pm Mon-Fri), where America's legendary motorcycles are assembled. A guided tour starts with the **Rodney Gott Antique Motorcycle Museum**, which displays a bike from every production year from 1906 onwards. You then go into the assembly plant to see workers making parts and building the motorcycles. In the entrance area you can see a good film about the history of the company, and there's a gift shop that sells all kinds of Harley-Davidson merchandise.

Free tours of the plant and museum are given between 9:30am and 2pm on weekdays; each tour lasts about an hour.

To get there, take exit 9E off I-83 onto Rte 30 east; at the third set of traffic lights turn left onto Eden Rd.

PITTSBURGH

pop 313,000

Pittsburgh used to be called 'the Smoky City' because of the thick black smoke constantly churning out of iron and steel mills and leaving a dusty residue on buildings and houses – and that nickname wasn't bad compared to what an *Atlantic Monthly* journalist called the industrial city in 1868 ('hell with the lid taken off,' to be exact). Pittsburgh's undistinguished past makes today's city, a pretty tree-filled metropolis criss-crossed with rivers, dozens of bridges and a network of bike trails, doubly impressive. Thanks to big changes like stricter environmental codes and green building, plus the establishment of several reputable universities and a flourishing arts scene – and, all right, financial support from a couple of really, really rich guys – Pittsburgh is unexpectedly appealing and ecofriendly. So appealing, in fact, that business publications like *Forbes* and *The Economist* have chosen Pittsburgh several times over as the nation's most livable city. Immediate relocation may not in your plans, but not to worry – there's plenty here for visitors, from the must-see Andy Warhol Museum and the traditional Italian markets of the Strip District to the historic funicular railway running up Mt Washington and the lively university neighborhood of Oakland. As great for families and sports fans as it is for foodies and art enthusiasts, Pittsburgh truly is a revitalized city that may pleasantly surprise you.

History

The city's strategic location, at the point where the Monongahela and the Allegheny Rivers join the Ohio River, has made it a natural commercial and transportation center since the 18th century. During that period, the area became a flash point in French and British rivalry over the Ohio River Valley. In 1754, in the prelude to the French and Indian War (1754–63), the French captured a British fort at the fork of the three rivers and named it Fort Duquesne, as it was the ideal location

for controlling the upper Ohio River Valley. After the war began, however (see p35), the British returned in 1758, ejected the French and built Fort Pitt, which was named after Prime Minister William Pitt the Elder. From this, Pittsburgh was named.

During the 19th century, Pittsburgh became famous for iron and steel production, as it helped fulfill the needs of the country's westward expansion. The Civil War gave its industries further stimulus, and by the end of the war, Pittsburgh was producing 50% of the country's iron and steel. Scottish-born immigrant Andrew Carnegie then modernized and expanded steel production, becoming the world's richest man in the process. But the city's growth was not without conflict, and there were violent strikes at Homestead in 1892 and throughout greater Pittsburgh in 1919.

Despite a downturn during the Great Depression in the 1930s, the mass production of the automobile and the advent of WWII stimulated demand for steel once more. During the 1960s and '70s, the industry declined, but in the 1990s Pittsburgh re-emerged as a center for high-technology, finance and services. An urban-renewal program saw the downtown area transformed, but not without a price: many architecturally important buildings were razed to make way for glass skyscrapers. Fortunately, many (such as the Allegheny County Courthouse) remain, and some of Pittsburgh's traditional character can be seen in the older residential neighborhoods.

Although a strong blue-collar element remains, the shift in employment to the service and high-technology industries means there is now a large and growing white-collar workforce. The city's ethnic diversity is reflected in the different architectural flavors of its neighborhoods and is symbolized by the University of Pittsburgh Nationality Rooms. The North Side shows many touches of its German heritage, including Penn Brewery (originally called Eberhardt & Ober Brewery). On the South Side, Eastern European influences can be seen in the Ukrainian, Serbian and Lithuanian churches. Many Eastern European Jews settled in Squirrel Hill in the 1920s.

Bloomfield has a strong Italian heritage, while nearby Lawrenceville and Polish Hill have a mix of Irish, Italian and Polish communities. African-Americans have also settled in the city, but in terms of numbers, their presence isn't as evident as in Philadelphia. There are also people from the Middle East, most notably Lebanese and Syrians.

Orientation

As you'll see from the spectacular vantage point atop Mt Washington, downtown Pittsburgh occupies a strategic location on a triangle of land that's separated from the city's northern and southern parts by rivers. There's no consistent street pattern, although major thoroughfares in the city often run parallel to the rivers. To ease the confusion, there's a color-coded network of prominently displayed directional street signs called the Wayfinder System. Fifth Ave and Liberty Ave are the major downtown streets.

The approach to Pittsburgh from the south is spectacular. You enter through Fort Pitt Tunnel then cross Fort Pitt Bridge into the heart of the Golden Triangle, the westernmost portion of the city center (basically 'downtown'), bounded to the north by the Allegheny River, to the south by the Monongahela River and to the east by I-579 (Crosstown Blvd). The bus and train stations are in the northern corner of the triangle.

Slightly northeast of downtown and close to the Allegheny River is an area called The Strip, where wholesale and retail fresh-food stores, cheap restaurants and clubs line Smallman St and Penn Ave between 17th and 22nd Sts. It's also a good place to walk around and people-watch.

East of downtown is Oakland, Pittsburgh's university area, which is dominated by the University of Pittsburgh's Cathedral of Learning, Carnegie-Mellon University, the Carnegie complex and Schenley Park. It too has some good, cheap places to eat. Fifth Ave and Blvd of the Allies connect it with downtown.

The North Side, the part of town north of the Allegheny River, is home to the Andy Warhol Museum, Three Rivers Stadium, Carnegie Science Center, National Aviary in Pittsburgh and the small neighborhood of Troy Hill.

On the South Side, south of the Monongahela River, Mt Washington overlooks the Golden Triangle. You can drive up or take either of the two incline railways. At the bottom of the mountain, along the river beside Smithfield St Bridge, is Station Sq, full of shops and restaurants. To the east is a residential neighborhood where the main drag, E Carson St, has an interesting collection of cafes, bars and shops.

MAPS

You'll find maps of central Pittsburgh and Oakland inside free visitor guides like *Visit Pittsburgh*, available at tourist attractions and restaurants all over the city. The highly detailed **Pittsburgh Interactive Map System** (http://pittsburgh.micromaps.com) is great for planning your itinerary online. If you're planning to cycle around the city, don't miss the excellent downloadable map at **Bike Pittsburgh** (http://bike-pgh.org).

Information

BOOKSTORES

This isn't a city overrun with generic bookstore megachains – Pittsburghers, generally speaking, would rather poke around for hidden treasures in smaller bookstores.

Caliban Book Shop (☎ 412-681-9111; 410 S Craig St, Oakland) If you're in Oakland on a rainy afternoon, don't miss this wonderful place; it's filled with antique books and rare finds.

City Books Inc (☎ 412-481-7555; 111 E Carson St) On the South Side.

Townsend Booksellers (☎ 412-682-8030; 4612 Henry St, Oakland) Another excellent used bookstore.

EMERGENCY

In the case of fire and medical emergencies, or for police, call ☎ 911. Other important emergency telephone numbers:

Dentist (☎ 412-321-5810)

GlobalPittsburgh (☎ 412-624-7800) Support for international visitors.

Pittsburgh Action Against Rape (☎ 412-765-2731)

INTERNET RESOURCES

A good place to start is the Greater Pittsburgh Convention & Visitors Bureau's official website (www.visitpittsburgh.com). Another site with links to attractions, accommodations, dining, entertainment and transportation is www.pittsburgh.net. For information about the University of Pittsburgh, go to www.pitt.edu.

LIBRARIES

Carnegie Library (☎ 412-622-3114; www.clpgh.org; 4400 Forbes Ave, Oakland; ☯ 10am-8pm Mon-Thu, 10am-5:30pm Fri & Sat, noon-5pm Sun) Part of the

PENNSYLVANIA

DOWNTOWN PITTSBURGH

500 m
0.3 miles

INFORMATION
Airside Visitors' Center......(see 10)
Allegheny General Hospital......**1** C3
American Express......(see 27)
Carnegie Library
 (Mt Washington Branch)......**2** B7
City Books Inc.......**3** E8
Liberty Ave Visitors' Center......**4** B6
Main Post Office.......**5** D6
Mellon Bank.......**6** C6
PNC Bank.......**7** C6
Port Authority Transit (PAT)
 Information Center.......**8** C6
Post Office.......**9** B8
Smallman St Visitors' Center....**10** D5
United Airlines Office......(see 6)

SIGHTS & ACTIVITIES
Allegheny County
 Courthouse.......**11** C6
Andy Warhol Museum.......**12** C5
Carnegie Science Center.......**13** A5
Children's Museum of
 Pittsburgh.......**14** B4
Duquesne Incline.......**15** A6
Fort Pitt Block House......**16** B6

Gateway Clipper Fleet Dock...**17** B7
Golden Triangle Bike Rental...**18** D7
Just Ducky Tours......(see 49)
Kayak Pittsburgh.......**19** B5
Mattress Factory.......**20** A3
Mellon Bank Center.......**21** C6
Monongahela Incline.......**22** B8
National Aviary.......**23** B4
Point State Park Fountain......**24** A6
PPG Place.......**25** E6
St Anthony's Chapel.......**26** E2
Station Square.......**27** B7

SLEEPING 🛏
Hampton Inn & Suites.......**28** D5
Inn on the Mexican War
 Streets.......**29** B3
Parador B&B.......**30** A4
Priory Hotel.......**31** C4
Residence Inn Pittsburgh
 North Shore.......**32** B5

EATING 🍴
Big Mama's House of
 Southern Cuisine.......**33** C5
Courthouse Tavern.......**34** C6

Dish Osteria & Bar.......**35** E8
Franktuary.......**36** C6
Grand Concourse
 Restaurant.......(see 49)
Habitat.......**37** F5
Isabela on Grandview.......**38** A6
Kaya.......**39** E4
Las Velas.......**40** F5
Lidia's Pittsburgh.......**41** D5
Nicky's Thai Kitchen.......**42** A4
Original Oyster House.......**43** F5
Pennsylvania Macaroni
 Company.......**44** E4
Peppi's.......**45** A4
Piper's Pub.......**46** F8
Primanti Brothers
 Restaurant & Bar.......**47** E6
Primanti Brothers.......**48** E4
Restaurants at Station Square.**49** B7
Wholey's Market.......**50** E4

DRINKING 🍷
Fat Head's Saloon.......**51** F8
Grandview Saloon.......**52** A6
Monterey Pub.......**53** A3
Zen Social Club.......(see 49)

ENTERTAINMENT 🎭
Benedum Center for the
 Performing Arts.......**54** C6
City Theatre.......**55** E8
Firehouse Lounge.......**56** E4
Heinz Field.......**57** A5
Heinz Hall.......**58** C6
Mellon Arena.......**59** D6
Pittsburgh Public Theater....**60** C6
PNC Park.......**61** B5
Rex Theatre.......**62** E8
Z Lounge.......**63** F8

SHOPPING 🛍
Fifth Ave.......**64** C6

TRANSPORT
British Airways.......(see 21)
Delta Airlines.......(see 21)
Greyhound Bus Station......**65** D5
US Airways.......**66** C6
US Airways.......**67** E5

Herr's Island

Allegheny River

The Strip

Troy Hill

North Side

East Park

North Park

West Park

To Lawrenceville (1 mi);
Bloomfield (2 mi);
East Liberty (3 mi);
Pittsburgh
Ballet Theater

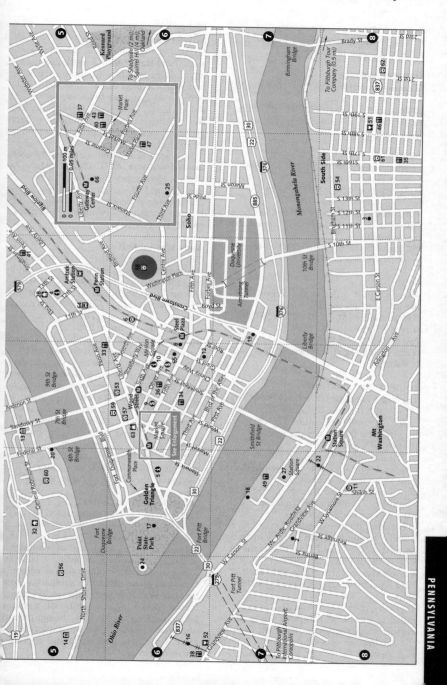

PENNSYLVANIA

Carnegie complex, this is one of the best libraries in the US. It also has branches in Allegheny Sq, on the North Side; and on Grandview Ave, in Mt Washington.

MEDICAL SERVICES

Allegheny General Hospital (☎ 412-359-3131; 320 E North Ave) On the North Side.
UPMC Montefiore (☎ 412-647-2345; 3459 Fifth Ave, Oakland) Part of the University of Pittsburgh Medical Center.

MONEY

American Express (☎ 412-471-4824; 4 E Station Square Dr; ⏰ 9am-5pm Mon-Fri)
Mellon Bank (☎ 412-234-5000; Mellon Sq) Has currency-exchange counters and ATMs.
Mutual of Omaha's Travelex Business Service Center (☎ 412-472-5151) At Pittsburgh's airport; offers currency exchange.
PNC Bank (☎ 412-762-2510; cnr Fifth Ave & Wood St) Has currency-exchange counters and ATMs.

POST

There's a post office at the airport. Other branches include the following:
Main post office (☎ 412-642-4476; cnr Seventh Ave & Grant St; ⏰ 7am-6pm Mon-Fri, 7am-2:30pm Sat)
Post office (213 Shiloh St; ⏰ 8:30am-5pm Mon-Fri, to noon Sat) At the top of the Monongahela Incline in Mt Washington.

TOURIST INFORMATION

The **Greater Pittsburgh Convention & Visitors Bureau** (☎ 412-281-7711, 800-366-0093; www.visitpittsburgh.com) operates a number of visitors' centers around the city; view full listings and information at the helpful website.

The downtown branch, on Liberty Ave in front of 4 Gateway Center, is open weekdays 9am to 5pm and weekends until 3pm; it's closed on Sunday in January and February. The visitors' center in Oakland, which is in a log cabin on Forbes Ave near the Cathedral of Learning, is open Monday 9am to 4pm and Tuesday to Sunday 10am to 4pm. In Station Sq next to the Grand Concourse, the visitors' center is open daily 9:30am to 6:30pm. There's also a center in the Strip District at 1212 Smallman St, open daily from 10am to 5pm.

Finally, the bureau has a desk in each terminal of Pittsburgh's airport: the Landside visitors' center is open daily 8am to 8pm; the Airside one is open daily from 7:30am to 6:30pm.

Sights
DOWNTOWN & NORTH SIDE

Located at the spot where the three rivers meet, **Point State Park** is a small green oasis with a huge spouting fountain. Inside the park, **Fort Pitt Block House** (☎ 412-471-1764; 101 Commonwealth Pl; admission by donation; ⏰ 10am-5pm Wed-Sun) relates Pittsburgh's early history with Native American artifacts, military artifacts and displays on the French-British conflict for control of the region.

Built around a central courtyard, **Allegheny County Courthouse** (☎ 412-350-5410; cnr Forbes Ave & Grant St; admission free; ⏰ 8:30am-4:30pm Mon-Fri), a magnificent 19th-century Romanesque-style courthouse was designed by architect Henry Hobson Richardson. Its interior resembles a medieval monastery.

Andy Warhol Museum

Offering a thoughtful retrospective of the wildly famous (and Pittsburgh-born) pop-art icon, this seminal **museum** (☎ 412-237-8300; www.warhol.org; 117 Sandusky St; adult/child $15/8; ⏰ 10am-5pm Tue-Thu & Sat-Sun, to 10pm Fri) is reason enough to visit the city. The cool seven-floor museum traces his artistic development from his childhood days, when his Eastern European parents scrimped and saved to support his drawing classes, to the later years in New York when he took celebrity portraits with a Polaroid and became famous for his white wig and his classic reproductions of Campbell's soup cans. Look for lesser-known gems like his 'time capsules' stuffed with drawings and magazine clippings, his beloved stuffed dog, the whimsical fashion-themed television programs he directed and the home video he took of a young JFK Jr playing on the beach.

Carnegie Science Center

This forward-thinking **science center** (☎ 412-237-3400; www.carnegiesciencecenter.org; 1 Allegheny Ave; adult/child $17.95/9.95; ⏰ 10am-5pm Sun-Fri, to 7pm Sat; 👶) is like a futuristic playground with hundreds of hands-on exhibits including a cutting-edge planetarium, a mini railroad village, a simulated plane ride and a submarine from the Cold War. Roboworld, the world's largest (permanent) robotics exhibition, is a unique draw. It's designed for kids, though parents often have just as much fun exploring the place. Omnimax film screenings and laser shows cost extra.

National Aviary

An unmissable stop for even the most casual bird-watcher, this impressive **aviary** (☎ 412-323-7235; www.aviary.org; 700 Arch St; adult/child $12/9.50; ☒ 10am-5pm; ♿) is home to a colorful crew of African penguins, spectacled owls, highly vocal grey and black parrots, and even a tree sloth who lazes about amid hundreds of exotic squawking birds. Visitors are welcome to wander through simulated habitats where birds fly (or peck around) freely; there are kid-friendly interactive programs nearly every hour, from penguin feedings to 'junior veterinarian' workshops.

MAMA'S BOY: ANDY WARHOL

When you're an artist, adversity is your friend. It's better – and sounds so much cooler when you become famous and biographers and journalists are clamoring to tell your story – if you can say that you came from a penniless family and had to work in the fields, or that you were creatively oppressed and your father forced you to go to law school, that no one believed in you, that you had to eat crackers and wait tables for 18 hours a day while you were waiting for a painting to sell. We're used to hearing the predictable stories of starving artists. That's exactly why Andy Warhol's childhood is so captivating. Unlike so many of his contemporaries, Andy was the child of loving and incredibly supportive parents who recognized his talent early on, made sacrifices to encourage it and figured prominently in his later career.

Born Andrew Warhola in Pittsburgh in August 1928, Andy was the youngest of three brothers born to Julia and Andrej Warhola, a Carpatho-Rusyn couple who had recently emigrated from the region now known as eastern Slovakia. Despite his family's immigrant status, his father's bouts of unemployment alternating with back-breaking shifts of hard construction work, and their truly humble two-room wooden residence – not to mention the fact that the Great Depression was in full swing in an industrial city that was already rather depressing – this is not a starving-artist story. Little Andy was shy, but he grew up in a cheerful home where family values and the practice of Byzantine Catholicism were paramount; both at home and at elementary school, he was recognized for his drawing skill. When bedridden with a rare illness, Andy was entertained by his mother, Julia, who taught him to trace pictures and encouraged him to develop his drawing talent. This was the start of a remarkable bond between mother and son that would last for the rest of his life. After his recovery, Julia signed Andy up for free classes in studio art and art appreciation.

Meanwhile, Andrej, though not as wonderfully supportive as his wife, didn't ever deter his youngest son from expanding his potential – and that's saying something, considering he himself was a somewhat gruff blue-collar worker who struggled to secure jobs during the Depression and probably didn't have much knowledge of art. Since there wasn't enough money for nonessentials, Andrej crafted some of his own tools and kitchen items; he paid for Andy's first camera and let his son fashion a basic darkroom in the basement of the house. Sadly, he died when Andy was only 13. But he left his son a valuable gift: he chose him as the son who would go to college. Andrej knew that he only had enough savings to send one of the three boys to school, and since he recognized Andy's tremendous talent and ambition, he left the funds to his youngest son.

What followed was a whirlwind: Andy studied at the Carnegie Institute of Technology (now known as Carnegie Mellon University), dropped the 'a' from the end of his name, secured illustration work from fashion magazines, entered the world of advertising design and started experimenting with Pop Art. It was only a matter of time before he established The Factory and became a member of New York's elite, painting Brigitte Bardot's portrait, dancing with Liza Minnelli at Studio 54 and playing on the beach with JFK Jr. But his own celebrity status didn't change his relationship with his mother. In 1952, Julia moved to New York to live with Andy; he often asked if he could borrow her elegant penmanship, which he remembered so fondly from his childhood. Indeed, she captioned and signed many of his artworks.

Julia died in 1972, and although Andy himself didn't talk on record much about his childhood, he always told friends that his innocent early days with his mother, when he was a sick, bedridden boy in a working-class home, were formative factors in both his career and his life.

Mattress Factory

Located in the heart of the Mexican War Streets, this revolutionary art museum (☎ 412-231-3169; www.mattress.org; 500 Sampsonia Way; adult/child $10/7; ☺ 10am-5pm Tue-Sat, from 1pm Sun; ☒) is a contemporary Pittsburgh landmark. Instead of individual works of art, the Mattress Factory features a permanent collection (and a rotating schedule) of room-sized installations created by artists who specialize in fields ranging from architecture to sound, such as the minimalist musical display by Berlin-based composer Rolf Julius and the wacky mirror and mannequin space by Japanese artist Yayoi Kusama, who lives (voluntarily!) at a psychiatric hospital in Tokyo.

Children's Museum of Pittsburgh

Another first-class children's attraction in Pittsburgh, this lively three-story museum (☎ 412-322-5058; www.pittsburghkids.org; 10 Children's Way; adult/child $11/10; ☺ 10am-5pm Mon-Sat, from noon Sun; ☒) boasts exhibits from a two-story climbing maze and a spacious art studio to a replica of Mister Rogers' Neighborhood and a garage-style workshop where kids can take apart machines to learn how they work. It also offers a packed schedule of live music performances, puppet theater and innovative storytelling.

Mexican War Streets

While many of Pittsburgh's more bohemian neighborhoods are located far from the center, the funky Mexican War Streets – filled with vibrantly painted clapboard houses and home to an eclectic community of artists and writers – are located on the North Side, an easy stroll from downtown. Many of the streets are named after battles in the Mexican War (1846–48). This section of town barely escaped the wrecking ball in the 1960s, plagued as it was with dilapidated houses, crime, drug trade and poverty. Today the neighborhood hosts a lively arts community, streets lined with Greek Revival and Victorian buildings, some which have been covered in murals, and a few classy B&Bs – harbingers, no doubt, of more widespread gentrification. Head to Taylor Ave and Monterey, Resaca and Palo Alto Sts for the most memorable views.

St Anthony's Chapel

Off the main tourist route, this church (☎ 412-323-9504; 1704 Harpster St; ☺ 1-4pm Tue, Thu & Sun, 11am-4pm Sun), above the city in Troy Hill, has over 5000 religious relics contained in elaborately carved and decorated reliquaries. The main attraction is one reliquary, in the left transept, that holds over 700 items, including (reputedly) a thorn from Jesus' crown of thorns, a splinter from his cross and a piece of stone from the Holy Sepulcher. The interior of the church is beautifully ornate, and the walls are dominated by a near-life-sized depiction of the Stations of the Cross. Viewing hours are Tuesday, Thursday and Saturday 1pm to 4pm and Sunday 11am to 4pm.

SOUTH SIDE & MOUNT WASHINGTON

Incline Railroads

The delightfully old-fashioned Monongahela Incline (☎ 412-442-2000; www.portauthority.org; each way adult/child $2/1; ☺ 5:50am-12:45am Mon-Sat, 8:45am-midnight Sun) and Duquesne Incline (☎ 412-381-1665; www.duquesneincline.org; 1197 W Carson St; each way adult/child $2/1; ☺ 5:30am-12:45am Mon-Sat, from 7am Sun) are single-car trains that run up and down the steep Mt Washington. They're all that remain of 15 incline railroads that opened up the mountain to development in the 19th century and allowed easier access to the city. These antique cars, with hand-carved cherry and maple interiors and amber-glass transoms, are surprisingly speedy – the ride takes only two or three minutes. From the top, the views of Pittsburgh are jaw-dropping. The Duquesne Incline's upper station contains a small but intriguing museum.

For an interesting trip, go to Station Sq and walk across W Carson St to the Monongahela Incline entrance. Ride up the Monongahela Incline, walk west along Grandview Ave/Mt Washington Overlook to the Duquesne Incline. Then ride down, walk over the footbridge and back east to Station Sq (the last part of the walk is less interesting, as it's mostly past parking lots).

Station Square

On the river at the base of Mt Washington, Station Square (☎ 412-261-9911; www.stationsquare.com) was once a railroad warehouse and a former terminal of the Pittsburgh & Lake Erie Railroad; now it serves as an upscale shopping and dining complex. Many of these eateries and boutiques feel a little too shiny and commercial – not exactly the romantic old-fashioned feel you might be looking for in a restored train station – but there are a few notable exceptions, like the elegant Grand Concourse Restaurant (p367), which still has its original brass fixtures and a stained-glass cathedral ceiling.

OAKLAND & AROUND
Phipps Conservatory

This wonderful **conservatory** (☎ 412-622-6914; www.phipps.conservatory.org; Curto Dr; adult/child $12/9; ⊗ 9:30am-5pm Sat-Thu, to 10pm Fri), located in Oakland's 456-acre Schenley Park, was given to the city by Andrew Carnegie's partner Andrew Phipps in 1893. The lovely property comprises 17 separate 'botanical experiences' spread out among a series of outdoor gardens and a system of quaint iron-and-glass green-houses. You'll find tropical plants, orchids, bonsai and gargoyles peeking out from behind giant topiary. The conservatory runs tours and hosts a busy calendar of events and special exhibits like a farmers' market, a temporary butterfly forest and theme nights – on certain evenings last summer, visitors (age 21 and up, of course) toasted the conservatory's succulent *Agave americana* with half-price margaritas made from blue agave.

Carnegie

The **Carnegie** (4400 Forbes Ave) is the commonly abbreviated name for the building complex containing the **Carnegie Museum of Art** (http://web.cmoa.org), the **Carnegie Museum of Natural History** (☎ 412-622-3131; www.carnegiemnh.org; adult/child $15/11; ⊗ 10am-5pm Tue-Sat, to 8pm Thu, noon-5pm Sun), the **Carnegie Library of Pittsburgh** (www.clpgh.org) and the **Carnegie Music Hall** (www.carnegiehall.org). The art museum boasts pieces by Whistler, Renoir, Monet and Cézanne in an extensive display of Impressionist, post-Impressionist and modern American and European art. The Museum of Natural History is known for its excellent dinosaur collection, including a complete tyrannosaurus rex skeleton. The 'Dinosaurs in Their Time' permanent exhibit, opened in 2007, recreates dinosaur environments from the Mesozoic Era; visitors can also explore halls dedicated to ancient Egypt, arctic life, and gems and minerals. Hands-on displays keep children entertained too. Tickets for the art museum get you into the natural history museum (and vice versa).

Cathedral of Learning

Built in 1937, the 42-story **Cathedral of Learning** (☎ 412-624-6000; cnr Bigelow Blvd & Fifth Ave) is an imposing Gothic-style structure on the University of Pittsburgh campus. Stepping into the ground-level commons area, with its vaulted ceilings supported by 50ft columns,

---

ANDREW CARNEGIE

Pittsburgh industrialist Andrew Carnegie (1835–1919) is one of the most interesting and certainly the best remembered of America's 19th-century industrial barons. He amassed a fortune by driving his steelworkers hard, often brutally, but when he retired, he gave much of his fortune away, claiming it was the duty of the wealthy to do so.

Growing up in impoverished surroundings in Dunfermline, Scotland, Carnegie emigrated to Pittsburgh at the age of 12 with his parents. While working as a telegrapher for the Pennsylvania Railroad, he caught the eye of Thomas Scott, one of the company's officials. Scott ensured that Carnegie was promoted (by the age of 24) to superintendent of the western division of the railroad. He lent Carnegie money and gave him financial advice, so that by his thirties, the young Scotsman was a wealthy investor.

Carnegie left the railroad to form the Keystone Bridge Company, and during the depression of the 1870s, he put all his assets and efforts into the emerging steel industry. He built plants, held down wages and reinvested profits in capital improvements. Soon, the Carnegie Steel Company was the dominant force in the industry. Carnegie believed firmly in 'vertical integration,' and his corporation owned everything from the raw materials to the final product. In 1901, he sold his Carnegie Steel Company to the US Steel Corporation for the then astronomical price of $250 million.

Interestingly, Carnegie had mixed feelings about the rights of labor and the duties of capitalists. His most famous ideas on the subject were published in the 1889 essay 'The Gospel of Wealth.' Carnegie wrote that it was the duty of the wealthy to return 'their surplus wealth to the mass of their fellows in the forms best calculated to do the lasting good.' In his latter years, Carnegie lived up to his words, endowing an amazing number of libraries, cultural institutions, universities and other noble causes throughout the US.

you'll notice the series of fascinating **Nationality Rooms** (www.pitt.edu/~natrooms; adult/child $3/1; ☉ 9am-2:30pm Mon-Sat, from 11am Sun). After the Cathedral opened, the university chancellor invited various ethnic communities in Allegheny County to help design classrooms that would pay homage to their respective cultural heritages. The last of these 26 classrooms was completed in 2000; now student guides lead tours through this mini-museum filled with artwork (in wood, iron, glass, fabric and other mediums) inspired by sixth-century Irish churches, Beijing's Forbidden City, Czech flower fields and African temples, to name a few. Special-interest tours are also available for kids, seniors, architecture buffs or students of religion and mythology.

Frick Art & Historical Center

The sprawling complex known simply as the **Frick** (☎ 412-371-0600; www.frickart.org; 7227 Reynolds St; admission free except at Clayton; ☉ 10am-5pm Tue-Sun) shows off the lavish Victorian-era lifestyle of one of the most affluent families in American history – that of Henry Clay Frick, the hot shot industrialist and art collector (see p365). When he died in 1919, his daughter Helen Clay Frick inherited his Pittsburgh home, **Clayton**, and the priceless paintings, carriages, decorative arts and furniture contained there and in the family's summer home in Massachusetts. An art enthusiast in her own right, she later opened his collections to the public.

Highlights include Clayton itself, the Italianate-style house that Frick and his wife, Adelaide Howard Childs, purchased in 1882. In its original form, the house was a relatively modest residence for a 19th-century multimillionaire; as the couple welcomed the birth of four children and their social status continued to skyrocket, they decided to remodel and

---

IRON & STEEL

Pittsburgh has long been one of the main centers of the American iron and steel industries. Soon after they arrived in the 17th century, colonial settlers collected iron from bogs and then from mines. By the 18th century, American iron production had increased so much that Britain passed the 1750 Iron Act, which forbade the building of mills in the colony, but allowed pig iron (crude unfinished iron) to be sent to Britain for manufacturing.

With the expansion of the US railroad industry, beginning in the 1830s, the demand for iron increased. A leading producer of iron for years, Pennsylvania also had huge deposits of anthracite coal, which, it was discovered in the mid-19th century, could be substituted for charcoal in the smelting of iron. The combination of Pennsylvania coal, Great Lakes iron ore and cheap water transportation ensured that the Midwest would be the center of the US iron industry.

The true boom came when an inexpensive way to manufacture steel – a hard metal formed by combining iron and carbon – was discovered. In 1856, Englishman Henry Bessemer created the Bessemer process for making steel, in which hot air is blasted through molten iron to burn out its impurities. By 1872, 2% of US pig iron was being converted to steel; 20 years later, it was up to 50%. By the 1920s, it was over 90%, with the US producing almost 25 million tons a year – more than any other country.

Huge new steel factories also created new labor conditions. Steel mills required thousands of workers and many more specialists than in iron production. Each worker had to be competent at an individual job, but at the same time was given less autonomy by management. Steelworkers were some of the first workers in the US to establish strong unions to battle management control of working conditions and hours.

In 1901, the US Steel Corporation, formed partly from Pittsburgh industrialist Andrew Carnegie's steel company, became the single largest industrial operation on earth. US annual steel production continued to grow until it peaked in 1969 at 141 million tons. By then, more efficient plants abroad with lower labor costs were out-competing the US steel plants. In 1975, US production was down to 89 million tons.

American steel subsequently rebounded and is now competitive. However, it is much less labor intensive these days, and the industry's relative position in the US economy has declined. The end of the Industrial Age coincided to some degree with the end of the massive US steel industry. Even the US Steel Corporation, wanting to distance itself from its origins, changed its name to USX.

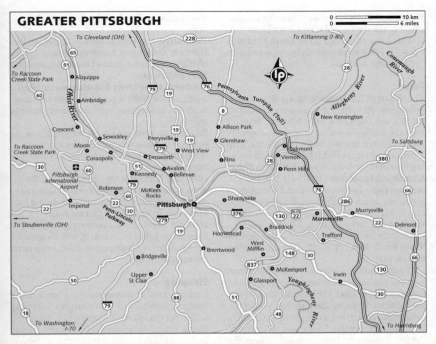

GREATER PITTSBURGH

expand the home into a chateau-like mansion almost twice the size of the original house. Frick loved to entertain – he hosted Teddy Roosevelt here in 1902. After major restorations in 1990 (with a price tag of $6 million), Clayton opened for public viewing. Ninety-three percent of the artifacts you'll see are the home's originals, including the world's only player organ. The house can only be seen by guided tour (donation required), which must be booked in advance.

Also open to visitors are the **Car and Carriage Museum**, where the family's vintage cars and carriages are on display, and the lovely **Greenhouse**, a replica of the one built for the Fricks in 1897. At the **Frick Art Museum**, Helen Clay Frick's personal collection is on display. Focusing primarily on early-Renaissance Siennese painting and 18th-century French decorative arts, the collection also contains a portrait by Peter Paul Rubens.

To get there by car, take Parkway East (I-376) to the Edgewood/Swissvale exit. At the exit ramp, follow Braddock Ave for 1.3 miles, then turn left on Penn Ave. Take a left on Lexington Ave and a right onto Reynolds St.

Pittsburgh Zoo

Pittsburgh's well-maintained **zoo and aquarium** (☎ 412-665-3640; www.pittsburghzoo.com; 7340 Butler St; adult/child $13/11; ☼ 9:30am-6pm summer, 9am-5pm fall & spring, to 4pm winter; ⚐) is home to thousands of furry and feathered (and finned?) creatures who live in re-created habitats from 'Asian Forest' to 'African Savanna.' Highlights include the Chinese Muntjac (aka the barking deer), African painted dog, Dama gazelle, pot-bellied seahorse and several penguin varieties, plus an excellent Kids' Kingdom and the large Bear Dens, built in the 1930s and therefore the oldest exhibit in the zoo.

From downtown, take Rte 28 north to exit 5 over Highland Park Bridge, then follow the signs.

Activities
BICYCLING & KAYAKING
Take advantage of the city's wonderful network of bike trails by renting a set of wheels at **Golden Triangle Bike Rentals** (☎ 412-600-0675; www.bikepittsburgh.com; 600 First Ave, downtown) – tour maps, locks and helmets are included. In summer, it opens rental kiosks at Station Sq, South Side

PENNSYLVANIA

Works and the North Side. Alternatively, you can skip the traffic and travel from point A to B with a kayak rented from **Kayak Pittsburgh** (☎ 412-255-0564; www.kayakpittsburgh.com; under Roberto Clemente Bridge, North Side).

Tours

The **Pittsburgh Tour Company** (☎ 412-381-8687; www.pghtours.com; 445 S 27th St at Southside Works; adult/child $20/10) runs the city's only hop-on, hop-off tour on a double-decker bus that originally ran in London in 1964. Stops include the Strip District and Heinz Field. For a historic walking tour of downtown, try the **Pittsburgh History & Landmarks Foundation** (☎ 877-471-5808; www.phlf.org; prices vary) – between May and October, it gives free tours on Fridays. Foodies should check out the gastronomic-themed walking tours of the Strip District, Mt Washington, Little Italy and Lawrenceville organized by **'Burgh Bits & Bites** (☎ 412-901-7150; www.burghfoodtour.com; adult $45).

If you'd rather see the city from the water, hop on one of the cruises operated by the **Gateway Clipper Fleet** (☎ 412-355-7980; www.gatewayclipper.com; Station Sq; adult/child from $12.50/8.50). Offerings range from a one-hour sightseeing trip to more involved lock and dam tours, dinner cruises and kids' voyages – check the website for full offerings.

Also great for families, **Just Ducky Tours** (☎ 412-402-3825; www.justduckytours.com; Station Sq; adult/child $19/15; 👶) offers narrated one-hour tours in a WWII amphibious vehicle that rolls around downtown before splashing into the river and cruising past the city skyline.

Festivals & Events

Following are some of the highlights of the Pittsburgh calendar:

Pittsburgh International Children's Festival (www.pghkids.org) For one week each May, children's performers from all over the world stage theater, dance, acrobatics and music performances in and around the Cathedral of Learning.

Pittsburgh Wine Festival (www.pittsburghwinefestival.com) Rated one of the nation's top 10 wine festivals, this popular May event sees winery representatives from far and wide uncorking the goods for the Grand Tasting at Heinz Field.

Venture Outdoors Festival (www.ventureoutdoors.org) Try rock climbing, yoga, kayaking and a host of other outdoor sports during this recreational festival on Washington's Landing each May.

Pittsburgh Folk Festival (www.pghfolkfest.org) In late May, the city celebrates its ethnic diversity with folk

music, dancing, cooking demonstrations – and, of course, food.

Three Rivers Arts Festival (www.artsfestival.net) This ecofriendly 10-day festival, happening downtown in June, offers a fine arts market, visual-art installations, music and family entertainment.

Pittsburgh Three Rivers Regatta (www.threeriversregatta.net) The world's largest inland regatta takes place in July; it's a family-friendly event complete with fireworks and concerts.

BikeFest (www.bike-pgh.org) Another green festival promoting outdoor activity, BikeFest offers a lineup of cycling outings and parties to raise money for a bike-friendly Pittsburgh.

Little Italy Days During this September festival, the streets of Bloomfield – Pittsburgh's very own Little Italy – come alive with accordion music, Italian folk-dancing and visitors lining up for traditional pizza and pasta.

Light Up Night (www.downtownpittsburgh.com) In November the holiday season kicks off with this downtown tree-lighting festival featuring a horse-drawn carriage parade and musical performances.

Sleeping

Unfortunately, travelers on a shoestring budget won't find Pittsburgh's sleeping scene very friendly – there's not even one youth hostel here anymore. There's plenty to choose from, however, in the midrange category, though downtown Pittsburgh's hotel rooms often fill with business travelers and Oakland area hotels are fully booked during major sporting events and graduations. Many of the more affordable places are northwest of town, near the airport – you'll need a car. For more affordable hotel options towards the airport, head down Beers School Rd toward Coraopolis, which is lined with independent and chain motels.

DOWNTOWN

Priory Hotel (☎ 412-231-3338; www.thepriory.com; 614 Pressley St; s $99-129, d $125-245; 🅿) One of the few downtown hotels with real character, the Priory comprises 25 classic rooms outfitted with oil paintings and Edwardian-style decor. Without an elevator, it's not wheelchair accessible, but it offers a complimentary shuttle service to city sights, free parking and a picturesque courtyard.

Hampton Inn & Suites (☎ 412-288-4350; www.hamptoninn.com; 1247 Smallman St; d $186-229; 🅿 📶 👶) Spacious modern rooms, complimentary breakfast and free parking make this Hampton branch a solid choice for families. It's within

HENRY CLAY FRICK

Henry Clay Frick (1849–1919), Pittsburgh's second-best-known industrialist and the son of a modest farmer, achieved his aim of becoming a millionaire by the age of 30.

Despite only a few years of schooling, Frick was always good with numbers. While still in his teens, he began working for his maternal grandfather, who owned the Overholt Distillery, and by 19 was the firm's bookkeeper. At age 20, Frick saw the value of coal for the burgeoning US steel industry and bought as much land containing coal reserves (then at low prices because of the 1870s depression) as he could. Early in his career, he obtained a $10,000 bank loan to expand his coke ovens, which converted coal to useful fuel.

While on his wedding trip in 1881, Frick fortuitously met steel magnate Andrew Carnegie in New York City. Carnegie proposed a merger between his company and the Frick Coke Company. Frick accepted and became chairman of the Carnegie Steel Company. The union joined Carnegie's steel mills with the masses of coal they needed for fuel.

Although Frick and Carnegie were business partners and industrialists, they had different views on the responsibility of the wealthy and the rights of workers. Nothing symbolized their clash more than Frick's handling of a strike at Carnegie's Homestead steel plant. Carnegie wanted the union broken, but believed that Frick went too far in calling in hundreds of armed Pinkerton strikebreakers to attack them. For his brutality in breaking the strike, Frick was stabbed three times and shot twice by New York anarchist Alexander Berkman in 1892. Frick recovered, but in 1900, he and Carnegie parted ways.

Frick became head of the new US Steel Corporation, which arose from the sale of the Carnegie Steel Company. He soon resigned, with tens of millions of dollars in assets, and moved to New York City, where he built a home at 70th St and Fifth Ave. This is now the Frick Collection Museum, which houses much of the artwork he accumulated during his lifetime. More of the family's art collection can be seen at the Frick Art & Historical Center (p362) in Pittsburgh, the legacy of his daughter Helen.

easy walking distance of the North Side and the Strip District.

NORTH SIDE

Inn on the Mexican War Streets (☎ 412-231-6544; www.innonthemexicanwarstreets.com; 604 W North Ave; d $119-189; ⬛) Located in a restored mansion that was once the home of department-store baron Russell H Boggs, this B&B offers thoughtful amenities like a DVD library and complimentary chocolate-chip cookies. The decor, with heavy drapery and dark, rich colors, is a bit dated compared to that of similar inns, but service is incredibly gracious.

Parador B&B (☎ 412-231-4800; www.theparadorinn.com; 939 Western Ave; d $150; ⬛ ☎) The concept is a little unusual – a Caribbean-style inn housed in a 19th-century Rhodes mansion? – but the Parador is a friendly, good-looking place within walking distance of the downtown sights. Each cozy guest room has a different theme and original details; you'll find a reading nook in one, an antique stove in another, clawfoot tubs in several.

Residence Inn Pittsburgh North Shore (☎ 412-321-2099; www.marriott.com/hotels/travel/pitrn-residence-inn-pittsburgh-north-shore; 574 W General Robinson St; d $179-239; ⬛ ☎ ⬛) This brand-spanking-new Marriott property is a dream come true for visitors coming into town for a Pirates game: the spacious hotel is just across the street from the entrance to PNC Park. Suites have fully equipped kitchens, first-class bedding and huge flat-screen TVs that swivel to face you.

SHADYSIDE

Shadyside, known for stylish shops and wide avenues lined with mansions, also brings in plenty of overnight guests due to its University of Pittsburgh Medical Center. The neighborhood is located about 4 miles northeast of downtown.

our pick Mansion at Maple Heights (☎ 412-586-7940; www.mansionmapleheights.com; 5516 Maple Heights Road; d $110-250; ⬛ ☎) This lovely B&B, situated in a stately English manor home dating back to 1903, charms guests with period furnishings in dark oak, a sweeping central staircase, twinkling chandeliers and a limestone fireplace where fires crackle on winter nights. Amenities (and prices) vary throughout a

PENNSYLVANIA

handful of pretty rooms and suites, but all include French toast for breakfast.

Inn on Negley (☎ 412-661-0631; www.innonneg ley.com; 703 South Negley Ave; d $180-240; 🔀) Billing itself as a B&B with the upscale amenities of a boutique hotel, the Inn on Negley in Shadyside is a Victorian-style eight-room place filled with antique furnishings, silver tea sets and wrought-iron beds. Some rooms, with Jacuzzis, private fireplaces and floor-to-ceiling windows, are ideal for a romantic getaway.

Eating & Drinking
DOWNTOWN & NORTH SIDE

For a lunchtime stop or a quick coffee downtown, head to Market Sq, which is lined with coffeeshops and delis; some of the more notable options are listed below. If you have more time, stroll across the Andy Warhol Bridge towards a better selection of eateries on the North Side.

Franktuary (☎ 412-288-0322; www.franktuary.com; 325 Oliver Ave, downtown; mains $3-7; 🕙 10am-3pm Mon-Fri) This lighthearted (and environmentally conscious) lunch spot turns out gourmet hot dogs, including the organic 'Locavore' frank, and fresh fruit smoothies.

Original Oyster House (☎ 412-566-7925; www.originaloysterhousepittsburgh.com; 20 Market Sq, downtown; mains $5-10; 🕙 10am-10pm Mon-Sat) Established in 1870, this is the city's oldest tavern. Miners and boaters used to line up at the rustic bar for raw oysters that cost just a penny each. The house special will set you back a bit more today, but thankfully – even though businessmen and lawyers now stop in for fish sandwiches and crab cakes – this atmospheric corner hasn't been gentrified.

Peppi's (☎ 412-231-9009; www.peppisubs.com; 927 Western Ave, North Side; mains $5-12) A local favorite, Peppi's is famous for jovial waitstaff and gigantic Italian-style subs made with first-rate meats and cheeses. The Cajun fries are a treat, too, at this atmospheric place with rustic wooden floors and benches and a pressed-tin ceiling.

Primanti Brothers (☎ 412-261-1599; www.primantibrothers.com; 2 S Market Sq, downtown; mains $6-10; 🕙 10am-midnight) Across the square from the Original Oyster House, this convenient location of the no-frills Primanti Bros deli serves up the sandwiches they're famous for – try the hot pastrami piled high with homemade coleslaw – alongside cold beer and heart-

stopping French fries drowning in cheese and bacon.

Monterey Pub (☎ 412-322-6535; www.montereypub. com; 1227 Monterey St, North Side; mains $8-15; 🕙 3pm-midnight Mon-Thu, to 1am Fri & Sat) This cozy Irish pub, a North Side staple, is a satisfying stop for a cold pint (or three) and rib-sticking dishes like shepherd's pie. Come on a Thursday night for Belgian beer and mussels.

Las Velas (☎ 412-281-8180; www.lasvelasmex.com; 21 Market Sq, downtown; mains $8-16; 🕙 11am-9pm Mon-Thu, to 10pm Fri & Sat) This Mexican restaurant boasts a surprisingly traditional menu – *tacos del cochinita pibil* (vinegar-marinated pork) anyone? – and a lively happy hour with $4 margaritas and $1 quesadillas.

Nicky's Thai Kitchen (☎ 412-321-8424; www.nickysthaikitchen.com; 856 Western Ave, North Side; mains $10-16) Well-prepared lunch specials, like pineapple curry and roast-duck noodle soup, are a steal at this popular Thai spot. In warmer weather, you'll have to fight for a table on the flowery patio.

Habitat (☎ 412-773-8848; www.habitatrestaurant.com; 510 Market St, downtown; mains $12-28; 🕙 6:30am-10pm) Located inside the new Fairmont Hotel, this chic international eatery offers an eclectic menu based on seasonal produce – current favorites include Tandoor chicken tacos and lobster *lo mein*. It's also a cool spot for a glass of wine – there's a great list here.

Also recommended:

Big Mama's House of Southern Cuisine (☎ 412-3 471-2910; 1603 Penn Ave, downtown; mains $4-10) Super-casual spot for BBQ chicken, ribs and pulled-pork sandwiches.

Courthouse Tavern (☎ 412-338-8608; www.courthousetavern.com; 310 Forbes Ave, downtown; mains $6-15) Great burgers and strong coffee.

PITTSBURGH PICKS

- Finest crash course in pop art: an afternoon at the Andy Warhol Museum (p358)
- Most staggeringly beautiful panoramic view: the top of the Duquesne Incline, Mt Washington (p360)
- Coldest pint in an unforgettable setting: Church Brew Works (p369)
- Best place to drool over Italian cheeses and chocolates: Pennsylvania Macaroni Company (p367)

PENNSYLVANIA

STRIP DISTRICT

Many first-time visitors to the Strip quickly find themselves in the mood for food – not only eating, but cooking too. That's because the neighborhood teems with fabulous old-fashioned bakeries and marketplaces where you can browse Italian cheeses, homemade pastas, freshly caught fish, and organic vegetables and fruits. If you're shopping for a gourmet picnic, pick up your baguettes, chocolate and provolone at the wonderful **Pennsylvania Macaroni Company** (cnr 20th St & Penn Ave). **Wholey's Market** (cnr 17th St & Penn Ave) also serves delicious takeaway fish sandwiches; for a quick bowl of pad thai or some piping hot egg rolls, look for the ethnic food stands lining either side of Penn Ave.

Primanti Brothers Restaurant & Bar (☎ 412-263-2142; www.primantibrothers.com; 46 18th St; mains $6-10; 24hr) Frequently featured on food-focused travel shows, the original Primanti Bros deli (there are six other branches in the city) is a nighttime institution for overstuffed sandwiches and frosty beer. It's nothing fancy, but the place is often packed.

Kaya (☎ 412-261-6565; www.bigburrito.com/kaya; 2000 Smallman St; mains $8-24; 11:30am-10pm Mon-Wed, to 11pm Thu-Sat, to 9pm Sun) A casual tropical-style eatery serving Caribbean and Spanish cuisine – as well as free-flowing microbrews and cocktails – to a young crowd. Vegetarian fare includes a popular black-bean dip and a tomato and cucumber gazpacho. At happy hour, come for half-priced sangria paired with chips and mango salsa.

Lidia's Pittsburgh (☎ 412-552-0150; www.lidias-pittsburgh.com; 1400 Smallman St; mains $12-24) One of a few upscale Italian eateries overseen by the star of public television's *Lidia's Italy*, this place is well-known for weekend brunch and wraparound booths where you can cozy up with a date and an order of osso bucco or gnocchi with duck sauce.

SOUTH SIDE & MOUNT WASHINGTON

For a happening bar and restaurant scene on the South Side, take a stroll along E Carson Street; families with kids in tow will find dozens of suitable dining options in the Station Sq complex near the riverside. If you're in the market for a romantic dinner with a view – or better yet, a lively happy hour with killer views at sunset – catch the Duquesne Incline to the top of Mount Washington, where a string of bars and restaurants have terraces jutting over the cliffside.

our pick **Grandview Saloon** (☎ 412-431-1400; www.thegrandviewsaloon.com; 1212 Grandview Ave, Mt Washington; mains $8-18) The open-air terrace at this casual bar-restaurant is a lively locale for salads, burgers and pastas on the clifftop; it fills with the happy-hour crowd in warmer weather, but the enclosed dining area remains quiet.

Piper's Pub (☎ 412-381-3977; www.piperspub.com; 1828 E Carson St, South Side; mains $8-22) A classic pub with a much-loved Sunday brunch – and live music, microbrews and hearty meals at night – Piper's is a longtime neighborhood favorite.

Dish Osteria & Bar (☎ 412-390-2012; www.dishosteria.com; 128 S 17th St, South Side; mains $15-31; 5pm-2am Mon-Sat) A stylish wine bar and bistro specializing in Sicilian cuisine, Dish is an appealing spot for a late-night martini or tiramisu with espresso. The kitchen stays open until midnight.

Grand Concourse Restaurant (☎ 412-261-1717; www.muer.com; 100 W Station Sq Dr; mains $22-45) Set in the magnificent main hall of the former railroad terminal (at the foot of Mt Washington in the Station Sq complex), the Grand Concourse is known for its seafood. But since half the appeal is the old-fashioned ambience, it's just as much fun to have classic cocktails in the Old Station Baggage Room.

Isabela on Grandview (☎ 412-431-5882; www.isabelaongrandview.com; 1318 Grandview Ave, Mt Washington; prix fixe per person $70) This fine-dining institution is fit for a special occasion, with a wine list and service that are nearly as impressive as the sweeping view. The prix fixe menu is on the pricey side – then again, when was the last time you had a fish course high on cliffs over a city lit with one million lights?

OAKLAND & SQUIRREL HILL

These university-centric neighborhoods, as one might imagine, are loaded with independent coffeehouses, budget-friendly pizzerias and sub shops, and a wide range of ethnic eateries. If you're looking to grab a quick bite, follow the textbook-wielding Pitt students to the outdoor food stands around Schenley Plaza. If you're driving here from downtown, take Boulevard of the Allies to Forbes Ave, passing through the Carnegie Mellon campus; it's a 15-minute drive.

Original Hot Dog Shop (☎ 412-621-7388; 3901 Forbes Ave, Oakland; mains $4-8) Derided by some but adored by many, 'The O' is an iconic hot-dog joint where students and tourists dig into franks and fries around a long U-shaped

TOP OF THE HOPS

There's something so satisfying about the idea of throwing a leg over a barstool and knocking back a pint of ice-cold pale ale in Pittsburgh. Perhaps its the city's gritty industrial past – it's so easy to imagine the hard-working steel workers and miners heading over to their local watering hole after a long day's labor – or maybe its the word on the street. As any true beer enthusiast could tell you, Pittsburgh's not about generic kegs and All-American commercial brands: this is a city with several excellent breweries, some historic, others new, where seriously good beers are being hand-crafted and poured every day.

And so, thirsty travelers, we present to you the best brews in town. This isn't a list of the coolest bars where you'd want to see and be seen – this is a round-up of the tastiest beers for the discriminating consumer. Cheers! (Or as the city's proud Italian-Americans would say, *salute*!)

- **East End Big Hop Harvest Ale** The aroma of the delicious India Pale Ale, crafted with freshly picked 'wet hops,' has been likened to the smell of just-cut grass. Find it at the **East End Brewing Company** (☎ 412-537-2337; www.eastendbrewing.com; 6923 Susquehanna St, Squirrel Hill North/Homewood).

- **Church Brew Non-Denominator Doppelbock** This bold doppelbock has a toasted nose and a creamy tan head with a chocolatey caramel aroma. Find it on tap at the ever-popular Church Brew Works (p369).

- **Voodoo Big Black Voodoo Daddy** OK, technically this isn't brewed in Pittsburgh proper – the **Voodoo Brewing Co** (☎ 412-468-0295; www.voodoobrewery.com; 215 Arch St, Meadville) is just outside the city in Meadville but participates in tastings and events in Pittsburgh. This smooth black ale, with a 12% alcohol content, has a roasted chocolate flavor – look for it in bottle-shops.

Other bars with wide selections on tap and a devotion to high-quality microbrews include **Fat Head's Saloon** (☎ 412-431-7433; www.fatheads.com; 1805 E Carson St) on the South Side and the **Sharp Edge Beer Emporium** (☎ 412-661-3537; www.sharpedgebeer.com; 302 S Clair St) in Shadyside.

counter. Fun for a cheap lunch, but skip it at night unless you want to bump (literally) into a parade of drunk college kids.

Kiva Han (☎ 412-687-6355; 420 S Craig St, Oakland; mains $5-10) Grad students and art-museum staff refuel at this indie cafe. Try the Thai tofu salad or just stop in for a cup of coffee or an Italian soda – the place has far more character than Starbucks across the street.

Rose Tea Cafe (☎ 412-421-2238; 5874 Forbes Ave, Squirrel Hill; mains $6-20) A lunchtime favorite for authentic Taiwanese food and bubble tea (and quick, if chilly, service), Rose Tea Cafe offers a huge menu of fresh-tasting dishes you're unlikely to find at your corner Chinese.

our pick **Spice Island Tea House** (☎ 412-687-8821; www.spiceislandteahouse.com; 253 Atwood St, Oakland; mains $8-18; ☺ closed Sun) Don't be fooled by the name: this often-crowded eatery serves delicious teas, yes, but also a wide range of spicy South Asian dishes as well as beer and wine. Try the wonderful coconut rice or one of several Burmese specialties.

Silk Elephant (☎ 412-421-8801; www.silkelephant. net; 1712 Murray Ave, Squirrel Hill; mains $10-20) Creative Thai-style tapas and flavorful cocktails attract plenty of dinnertime regulars to the Silk Elephant while the sleek decor, all glowing lanterns and flowing fabrics, brings in late-night dates.

BLOOMFIELD & LAWRENCEVILLE

It's a snap finding a decent bowl of pasta or a glass of good red in Bloomfield – Pittsburgh's Little Italy – but part of the fun is just wandering around the neighborhood in search of a cozy trattoria. Both Bloomfield and Lawrenceville are located to the northeast of downtown Pittsburgh. If you're driving, take Liberty Ave through the Strip District, about a 10-minute trip.

Stagioni (☎ 412-687-5775; www.stagionipgh. com; 4770 Liberty Ave, Bloomfield; mains $6-22) Small, homey, and somewhat rustic Stagioni turns out Italian-style comfort food like pistachio-crusted pork chops and fettuccini Bolognese. It's strictly BYOB, so pick up a bottle of Chianti in the neighborhood beforehand.

Coca Cafe (☎ 412-621-3171; www.cocacafe.net; 3811 Butler St, Lawrenceville; mains $8-23) This colorful eatery is famous for gourmet breakfasts – avocado omelets and challah French toast are favorites – and fresh soups, salads and sandwiches at lunchtime. Best of all for parents who don't want to sacrifice either style or substance, Coca is kid-friendly.

Tram's Kitchen (☎ 412-682-2688; 4050 Penn Ave, Bloomfield; mains $10-16) Craving pho? Locals say this is the best place in the city to get it. The no-frills Vietnamese is nothing to look at, but it's rightfully famous for rich soups, heavenly spring rolls and a uniquely delicious iced coffee.

our pick **Church Brew Works** (☎ 412-688-8200; 3525 Liberty Ave, Lawrenceville; mains $10-23) Now here's an unforgettable place to stop for a cold pint: in 1996, this abandoned church was transformed into a brewery and restaurant with copper brew vessels in the apse and pews fashioned into dinner tables. Hand-crafted pale ales and wood-fired pizzas are the house specialties.

Entertainment

The **Pittsburgh Cultural Trust** (www.pgharts.org) and the **Pittsburgh Tribune-Review** (www.pittsburgh live.com) list upcoming cultural events and performances.

THEATER & MUSIC

First-class theater performances are set on a three-quarter thrust stage at the **Pittsburgh Public Theater** (☎ 412-316-1600; www.ppt.org; 621 Penn Ave). The **Benedum Center for the Performing Arts** (☎ 412-456-6666; www.pgharts.org; 719 Liberty Ave), originally built in 1927 as the Stanley Theatre and beautifully restored by HJ Heinz II in 1984, hosts Broadway shows and performances by the Pittsburgh Ballet Theatre. For more avant-garde dramatic productions, head to the adventurous **City Theatre** (☎ 412-431-2489; www.citytheatrecompany.orgl; 1300 Bingham St). The Pittsburgh Symphony Orchestra plays at the elaborately designed **Heinz Hall** (☎ 412-392-4900; www.pittsburghsymphony.org; 600 Penn Ave) and in summer at Point State Park.

CINEMA

The **Beehive** (☎ 412-687-9428; 3807 Forbes Ave, Oakland) is an art-house movie theater showing US and foreign cult and classic films. It has an excellent coffee shop. Also in Oakland, the **Pittsburgh Playhouse** (☎ 412-471-9700; 222 Craft Ave, Oakland) puts on first-run alternative movies and hosts regular festivals. The **Rex Theatre** (☎ 412-381-2200; 1602 E Carson St, South Side) features mostly first-release movies, plus some classic and foreign films for $6.50; before 6pm, films cost only $4.

LIVE MUSIC

Mellon Arena (☎ 412-642-1800; www.ticketmaster.com; 66 Mario Lemieux Place) hosts larger contemporary musical acts. Oakland and the South Side have a number of venues for rock music, R&B and jazz, like the one-time vaudeville venue **Rex Theater** (☎ 412-381-6811; www.rextheater.com; 1602 E Carson St). Several other excellent indie venues are nearby along E Carson St. Further afield, **Brillobox** (☎ 412-621-4900; www.brillobox. net; 4104 Penn Ave, Lawrenceville) stages hipster-friendly music acts in a dive bar–like setting with strong cocktails and a decent pub-grub menu. With an excellent sound system and a large dance floor, **Shadow Lounge** (☎ 412-363-8277; www.shadowlounge.net; 5972 Baum Blvd, East Liberty) features live music by local artists and DJs, ranging from rock and jazz to African-inspired percussion.

DANCE CLUBS

As in any city, there's a quick turnover in the nightclub scene; it's always best to check local listings to see what's new in town. Filled with sultry lounge areas and vintage decor, the popular **Firehouse Lounge** (☎ 412-434-1230; www. firehouse-lounge.com; 2216 Penn Ave, the Strip) boasts a busy cocktail bar, a large deck strewn with throw pillows, and a happening dance floor. Eighties, soul and house music – and a great selection of microbrews – are the norm at funky **Z:Lounge** (☎ 412-431-1800; www.zlounge.pgh. com; 2108 E Carson St, South Side). Night owls looking for a taste of glamour like **Zen Social Club** (☎ 412-528-4847; 125 W Station Sq Dr), which comes alive with hip-hop music and R&B on weekends. This slick club stays open until 3:30am – but beware, there's a strict dress code.

SPECTATOR SPORTS

Pittsburghers are sports-crazy, and they've got world-class athletic facilities to prove it. On the North Side along the river is **PNC Park** (☎ 412-321-2827; www.piratesmlb.com; 400 Stadium Circle) home field for the Pittsburgh Pirates baseball team. A short walk downriver, the Pittsburgh Steelers play football at **Heinz Field** (☎ 412-323-1200; www.steelers.com; 100 Art Rooney Dr). The Pittsburgh Penguins ice-hockey team compete downtown at **Mellon Arena** (☎ 412-642-1800; www.mellonarena.com; 66 Mario Lemieux Place).

Shopping

Much to the delight of visiting shoppers, Pittsburgh is not a city overwhelmed by huge, generic chain stores: city residents generally prefer specialty shops, small boutiques, old-fashioned marketplaces and stores selling secondhand books. Of course, there are exceptions: you'll find plenty of familiar stores in the former railroad warehouse complex of **Station Square** (☎ 800-859-8969; www.station square.com; 125 W Station Sq Dr) and in downtown malls such as **Fifth Avenue Place** (☎ 412-456-7800; www.fifthavenueplacepa.com; 120 Fifth Ave). Otherwise, those interested in independent shops should check out **East Carson Street** (www.southsidepgh.com) in the historic South Side. Along this stretch, you'll see old-fashioned Victorian architecture, vintage shops, cigar emporiums, and stores carrying everything from antiques to musical instruments.

Design-minded shoppers and foodies should head to the Strip. The **Strip** (www.neigh borsinthestrip.com; Penn Ave) is home to a string of excellent markets where you'll find rare cheeses, spices, tea, coffee, chocolates and cured meats, as well as culinary-themed shops where you can browse futuristic cooking tools and kitchen supplies. At the far end of the Strip and into Lawrenceville, you'll find the creative neighborhood designated the **16:62 Design Zone** (www.1662designzone.com; btw 16th St Bridge & 62nd St Bridge). These blocks are packed with art galleries, studios and boutiques dedicated to forward-thinking home decor and interior design. Moving towards Oakland, the quaint **Shadyside Shops** (www.shadysideshops.com; cnr Walnut St & Ellsworth Ave, Shadyside) consist of upscale clothing boutiques and home-design stores.

Getting There & Away
AIR

Pittsburgh International Airport (☎ 412-472-3500; www.pitairport.com), 16 miles west of downtown, is the headquarters of **US Airways** (☎ 412-922-6407, 800-428-4322) and has direct connections to Europe, Canada and Japan, as well as to all major centers in the US.

Airlines with city offices:

British Airways (☎ 800-247-9297; Suite 2415, 1 Mellon Bank Center, 500 Grant St)

Delta Air Lines (☎ 412-456-2240, 800-221-1212; Suite 2420, 1 Mellon Bank Center, 500 Grant St)

United Airlines (☎ 800-241-6522; Westin William Penn Hotel, Mellon Sq)

US Airways (800-428-4322; 4 Gateway Center & 525 Grant St)

Other airlines that serve Pittsburgh include **American Airlines** (☎ 800-433-7300), **Continental Airlines** (☎ 800-525-0280) and **Northwest Airlines** (☎ 800-225-2525).

The following are some examples of standard economy fares: to New York's JFK airport, $149/258 one way/roundtrip; to Los Angeles, $918/1836. The roundtrip airfare to Philadelphia starts at $158.

BUS & TRAIN

Right next to each other, the **Greyhound bus station** (☎ 412-392-6526; www.greyhound.com; 55 11th St) and **Amtrak station** (☎ 412-471-6172; www.am trak.com; 1100 Liberty Ave) are located downtown within easy walking distance of many sights. On Greyhound, several daily buses go to New York City (from $59, 9½ to 12 hours) and Philadelphia (from $51, 6½ to 9½ hours). Two Amtrak lines serve Chicago ($113, 10 hours), Washington DC (from $56, eight to 10 hours), New York ($102, 9½ hours) and various other cities. Try booking online for cheaper fares.

CAR & MOTORCYCLE

Pittsburgh is amply served by the interstate system. I-79 passes through western Pittsburgh, connecting it with West Virginia to the south and Lake Erie to the north. From I-79, I-279 leads into town. I-76 (Pennsylvania Turnpike) passes through the north and east of Pittsburgh; from the east, take exit 6 onto I-376 into town; from the north, take I-79/279.

Getting Around
TO/FROM THE AIRPORT

Super Shuttle (☎ 800-258-3826; www.supershuttle.com; from per person $21) runs vans to and from the airport. Reserve a ride ahead of time through the website. A taxi from the airport to downtown starts at around $40.

If you're driving your own car, take I-376 W to exit 53 to arrive at the airport.

BUS & THE 'T'

The **Port Authority Transit Information Center** (☎ 412-442-2000; www.portauthority.org) operates the city's local-transport system, including the extensive Light Rail system, the 'T' between downtown and the South Side, and the Inclines running up Mount Washington. Port Authority Transit buses are free within downtown's Golden Triangle during the day;

fares to other parts of the city cost $2 to $3.50 for adults and $1 to $1.35 for children.

CAR & MOTORCYCLE

It's best to take a good look at your map or GPS before turning the key in the ignition: Pittsburgh's highways and roads can be confusing and crowded at approaches to the tunnels and on many bridges across the Allegheny and Monongahela Rivers. It's easy to find yourself suddenly on a bridge approach with no turnoff, then – without warning – you're out of downtown and on the North or South Side.

The two main thoroughfares connecting the North and South Sides via downtown are I-279 and I-579. Penn Lincoln Parkway (I-376) runs east–west beside the Monongahela River. Most downtown streets have alternate one-way traffic systems, and parking can be difficult; a tourist map of the city, available from one of the visitors' centers, indicates public parking lots.

At the airport, all major car-rental companies are represented. Of course, it's recommended that you book online in advance to secure a better rate.

TAXI

Although most taxis are carefully regulated, if you're arriving by bus or train, be aware that some taxis at the stations may be operating uninsured or are otherwise unsafe – especially if they're unmarked. Look for legitimate taxis like those from **Eagle Cab Company** (☎ 412-765-1555) or **Yellow Cab** (☎ 412-665-8100; www.pghtrans.com), which offers a useful online tool if you'd like to get an estimate on a cab ride between two destinations. As a basic guideline, a taxi between Oakland and downtown starts at around $8.50, while a ride between Lawrenceville and the South Side costs around $12.50.

SOUTHWESTERN PENNSYLVANIA

It's easy to understand the historic significance of this region: simply think of this wonderland of woods and rivers as the former getaway destination of Pittsburgh's rich and famous. Southwestern Pennsylvania is dominated by the big city originally built on iron and steel; these days, those industries have

declined and the city has successfully reinvented itself as a center of commerce, art and education. But at one time there was a strict divide between the rich businessmen who planned the city and the blue-collar workers who risked their lives working in mines and putting up skyscrapers. While those workweary Pittsburghers worked overtime, their wealthier counterparts took a breather from the city's grime by heading southeast to the Laurel Highlands, a popular outdoor playground that is especially noted for its whitewater rafting in the Youghiogheny (generally just called 'the Yock') River.

The highlands' best-known attraction, Frank Lloyd Wright's Fallingwater, proves the point: the famous architect built his masterpiece for the Kaufmann family, owners of the ritzy Pittsburg department store of the same name. On a related note, heading east from Pittsburgh and to the northeast of the highlands, you'll see the exit for Johnstown. The city isn't notable for much these days, but it's the site of the worst flood in American history – an 1889 event caused in part (surprise!) by the somewhat careless behavior of the upscale hunting and fishing club that was established upstream by a group of wealthy Pittsburghers. You'll need to visit the museum to get the story.

LAUREL HIGHLANDS & AROUND

The beautiful Laurel Highlands are a hilly, forested region comprising Ohiopyle State Park, the Youghiogheny River, Frank Lloyd Wright's Fallingwater and Kentuck Knob, Bear Run Nature Reserve, and a 30-mile scenic stretch along Rte 40. For information on the area, stop at the **Laurel Highlands Visitors Bureau** (☎ 724-238-5661; www.laurelhighlands.org; 120 E Main St, Ligonier) in the town hall in picturesque town of Ligonier (on Rte 30 about 40 miles east of Pittsburgh). Apart from the Laurel Highlands, you'll find several other noteworthy state parks in closer proximity to Pittsburgh – those closest to the city are listed first below.

Sights

FALLINGWATER

Over the river and through the woods – in a daily parade of rental cars, family minivans and tour buses – travelers from all over the world arrive at Frank Lloyd Wright's **Fallingwater** (☎ 412-329-8501; www.fallingwater.org;

PENNSYLVANIA

Rte 381, Mill Run; adult/child from $18/12; closed Wed & Jan-Feb, open weekends only Dec) to marvel at a true masterpiece of modern architecture. Named one of '50 Places of a Lifetime' by *National Geographic Traveler*, the impressive house was constructed from concrete and sandstone (quarried onsite) and consists of a series of levels cantilevered over a stream and waterfall.

The place was commissioned in 1935 by Edgar Kaufmann, the Pittsburgh department store baron, and his wife, Liliane, who wanted a weekend getaway in the woods. Wright, of course, had no interest in building a generic vacation home; instead, he took inspiration from his travels and realized his innovative visions at Fallingwater. He believed that people should live minimally and be at one with nature, and according to his philosophy, the architectural structure itself should influence the lifestyle of its inhabitants. With open spaces that encourage social gatherings, low ceilings and large windows that draw visitors' eyes toward the great outdoors, and spacious terraces that beckon guests outside over the waterfall, the design of Fallingwater did just that. Liliane Kaufmann – a highly educated and well-traveled woman, as well as a legendary hostess – was initially disappointed by the house's tiny bedrooms and lack of storage space. But as she later stated in a letter to the architect, living in Fallingwater did indeed change the way she looked at the world: 'Living in a house built by you has been my one education – and for that... I will always be grateful.'

The Kaufmanns' son, Edgar Jr, donated Fallingwater to the Western Pennsylvania Conservancy in 1963. Its furnishings and fittings are intact and displayed as Wright designed them. Reservations are required for the excellent guided tour and for the more expensive In-Depth Tour ($65), Sunset Tour ($110 including hors d'oeuvres) and Brunch Tour ($115). Family-focused tours are available for the regular tour price, but must be booked a week in advance.

Fallingwater is located 3 miles north of Ohiopyle on Rte 381.

KENTUCK KNOB

A less-frequented Frank Lloyd Wright monument, the lovely **Kentuck Knob** (724-329-1901; www.kentuckknob.com; 723 Kentuck Rd, Chalk Hill; adult/child $18/12) is a low-level house with honeycomb skylights that's built into the side of a rolling hill 2000ft above sea level.

Wright built the house in 1953 (when he was 86 years old) for the Hagan family of Uniontown. Bernadine and IN Hagan were friends of the Kaufmanns, for whom Wright had built Fallingwater many years earlier, and asked the legendary architect if he would consider designing a similarly innovative house on their 80-acre mountain property. Wright, of course, was in high demand in the later part of his career, so he had his hands in several projects at the time, including the Guggenheim Museum (see p95) in New York. But as the architect famously said of his designs for Kentuck Knob, he could 'shake it out of his sleeve at will.' That he did. He only saw the site itself one time; local builders carried out his elegant blueprints in time for the Hagans to move into Kentuck Knob on their 26th anniversary in July 1956. The couple spent three decades in their restful abode before IN, sadly, became ill; the couple sold the home in 1986 to Lord Palumbo of England. Like the Kaufmanns and the Hagans, Palumbo recognized Wright's genius. After his purchase of the house, he wrote 'I think that both I and the state of Pennsylvania owe a great debt of gratitude to Mr and Mrs IN Hagan for an inspired commission from an architect of legendary renown.'

Reservations are made through Fallingwater's offices; combination tours and special tickets (like the Brunch tour and the intimate 'Remains of the Day' tour) are also available for an extra charge.

Kentuck Knob is located southwest of Ohiopyle off Rte 2010.

BEAR RUN NATURE RESERVE

Half a mile north of the must-visit Fallingwater, on the western slope of Laurel Ridge, the 5061-acre Bear Run is administered by the **Western Pennsylvania Conservancy** (724-329-8501; www.paconserve.org). The reserve provides a habitat for white-tailed deer, bobcats and black bears. In addition, more than 130 bird species have been observed here. This reserve also has 20 miles of hiking trails through oak and hemlock forests beside the Youghiogheny River Gorge, and there's cross-country skiing in winter. Camping is allowed in six camping areas, but you must bring your own water.

RACCOON CREEK STATE PARK

The 7575-acre **state park** (☎ 412-899-2200; www.dcnr.state.ps.us/stateparks/parks/raccooncreek.aspx), 25 miles west of Pittsburgh on Rte 18, offers plenty of opportunities for outdoor recreation throughout the year. During warmer weather, **Raccoon Creek Lake** is a popular locale for swimming, fishing and canoeing; there are also miles of hiking and horseback-riding trails. In winter, activities include ice fishing, ice skating and, on designated trails and roads, cross-country skiing and snowmobiling.

Raccoon Creek is rich with bird species; in the southeast of the park is a large **wildflower reserve** with hundreds of native varieties that bloom from April to fall (but are seen at

EARTHLY INSPIRATION: FRANK LLOYD WRIGHT

These days, the word 'organic' is everywhere – in the produce section of the supermarket, at coffee shops, at restaurants and spas – and as any USDA official can tell you, the term is often misused or substituted as a synonym for 'healthy' or 'natural.' Thanks to such mass misunderstanding of the word, a casual visitor to Fallingwater or Kentuck Knob might not grasp the true spirit or principles behind what Frank Lloyd Wright called 'organic architecture.'

Wright's inspirations came straight from nature. He believed that manmade structures should relate to their physical environment and that the landscape itself should determine the design of the structure. To understand the significance of his vision, one must put his career into context. Wright was born in 1867 and came of age in the Beaux Arts era, known for highly decorative design and architecture. At a time when most architects were looking to Europe for direction and copying flowery Victorian houses and buildings, Wright was working as a draftsman under Louis Sullivan – the man credited with the famous 'form follows function' theory. Wright considered his respected mentor's words, ultimately deciding for himself that 'form and function are one.'

The young architect shook up Chicago's local design scene because he didn't care about European trends and he loathed what he considered to be the excessively ornate Victorian buildings surrounding him. Instead he preached harmony and simplicity to a startled public, pointing out the perfect beauty of nature, the importance of family space in the home, the pointlessness of embellishment and the misery caused by waste and clutter. When Wright went to work, applying the principles of organic architecture to every preliminary sketch and construction site, he produced a dazzling display of structures – more than 500 by the time of his death in 1959. He built modest prairie houses designed to bring families into one central space, a house over a waterfall with low ceilings to draw the inhabitants' gaze outdoors and tiny bedrooms to encourage socializing in the spacious common areas (Fallingwater), a house integrated into the desert landscape of Arizona (Taliesin West), structures in which beams and cantilevers were concealed to create a more calming effect, houses without storage space to discourage the accumulation of unnecessary clutter... the list goes on. As Liliane Kaufmann noted (p371), living in a Frank Lloyd Wright house was an education. His houses were fully developed works of art, not the kind of place where you change the pictures on the wall periodically or move chairs and tables around – you'll note that at Fallingwater, the furniture is indeed custom-designed and bolted to the floor, as if on a ship.

To summarize Wright's vision, it's best to quote the architect himself: 'So here I stand before you preaching organic architecture: declaring organic architecture to be the modern ideal and the teaching so much needed if we are to see the whole of life, and to now serve the whole of life, holding no 'traditions' essential to the great tradition. Nor cherishing any preconceived form fixing upon us either past, present or future, but – instead – exalting the simple laws of common sense – or of super-sense if you prefer – determining form by way of the nature of materials...' (*An Organic Architecture*, 1939).

Recognizing the innovation and fearlessness behind these design philosophies makes it possible to properly value Frank Lloyd Wright's contributions, not only to Pennsylvania, but to history. An unapologetically all-American artist with a tireless desire to build beautiful and environmentally aware structures, Wright is the grand forerunner to today's 'green' architects and a true legend before his time.

PENNSYLVANIA

their colorful best in the second week of May.) The park allows camping mid-April to mid-October. Check the website for details on campsites and rustic cabin accommodations. To get to the park, take Rte 60 north from Pittsburgh to exit 9, then follow the signs.

OHIOPYLE STATE PARK
This scenic 20,500-acre **state park** (☎ 724-329-8591; www.dcnr.state.pa.us/stateparks/parks/ohiopyle.aspx) is bisected by the 1700ft Youghiogheny River Gorge and surrounds the village of Ohiopyle (oh-HI-oh-pile), a center for whitewater rafting and outdoor activities. The park is crowded in summer, especially on weekends; the best times to visit are May and September. Located at the Bike Trail Bridge, the Ohiopyle

State Park Visitor's Center is a great place to pick up trail maps and plan your trip.

Of special note is **Meadow Run**, a system of natural waterslides. Across the river and immediately east of Ohiopyle village is **Ferncliff Peninsula**, a 4-acre teardrop of land formed by a loop in the river. The area is covered with wildflowers in season.

LAUREL HIGHLANDS TRAIL
The 70-mile **hiking trail** runs northeast from Ohiopyle State Park through Laurel Ridge, Laurel Summit and Laurel Mountain State Parks to the Conemaugh River near Seward on Rte 56, northwest of Johnstown. Some parts are rough, particularly in the south, but since most of the trail follows the ridge top,

SOUTHWESTERN PENNSYLVANIA

the going is generally easy to moderate. In winter, it's suitable for cross-country skiing and snowshoeing. There are eight camping areas with toilets and water; campsites must be booked in advance. For more information about the trail, contact **Laurel Ridge State Park** (☎ 724-455-3744; www.dcnr.state.pa.us/stateparks/parks/laurelridge.aspx).

HARMONY
pop 868

About 25 miles north of Pittsburgh on Rte 19, the village of Harmony is a National Historic Landmark. The town was the home of the Harmony Society, a communal group founded in 1804. Possessions were owned collectively, and within a few years, the Harmonists had planted thousands of acres of farms and orchards and had constructed over 100 buildings. In 1807, members made the self-extinguishing decision to adopt celibacy. In 1814, the Harmonists moved to Indiana, then Ohio, before dissolving in 1905. The village of Harmony was purchased by Abraham Zeigler, a Mennonite whose descendants still live here.

Several original buildings remain, including one that is now the **Harmony Museum** (☎ 412-452-7341; www.harmonymuseum.org; 218 Mercer St; ☼ 1-4pm Tue-Sun), where Harmonist and early Mennonite exhibits are displayed. From Pittsburgh, take I-79 north to exit 27, onto Rte 19, which leads to the town of Zelienople; Harmony is signed from there.

MORAINE STATE PARK

About 10 miles north of Harmony, **Moraine State Park** (☎ 412-368-8811; www.dcnr.state.pa.us/stateparks/parks/moraine.aspx) is named after the moraine, fragments of rock left by receding glaciers after the last Ice Age. In the more recent past, it was heavily mined and drilled for coal and oil, but the area was so well restored that little evidence of those days remains. The 3225-acre **Lake Arthur** is a 1960s re-creation of a glacial lake that existed here thousands of years ago. It was produced by damming the tributaries of Muddy Creek and has formed a series of habitats that now support a wide variety of bird species. Sailing, windsurfing, canoeing and fishing are available, and you can go swimming at a couple of beaches. Along the northern shore is a paved 7-mile bike trail and there is a 6-mile loop trail specifically for mountain bikes; rentals are available on North Shore Drive.

The only available camping is at the North Country National Scenic Trail shelter (watch for signs off Link Road), but the park office can give you information about private campgrounds just outside the park. Coming from Pittsburgh, Moraine State Park is east of I-79 and off Rtes 8 and 442.

MCCONNELL'S MILL STATE PARK

Near Moraine State Park, the **McConnell's Mill State Park** (☎ 724-368-8091; www.dcnr.state.pa.us/stateparks/parks/mcconnellsmill.aspx) got its name from the restored 19th-century grist mill that operated here beside Slippery Creek until 1928. But the main attraction is the 400ft-deep **Slippery Rock Gorge**, carved by a receding glacier some 20,000 years ago. Experienced rock climbers hone their skills on **Breakneck Ridge**, while novice climbers practice on **Rim Road**, near the mill. Slippery Creek, which runs through the gorge, is popular for kayaking and whitewater canoeing, but there are no rentals in the park. Trout fishing in the creek near Armstrong Bridge is also popular. There are several hiking trails, the longest of which is the scenic 6-mile **Slippery Rock Gorge Trail**.

Moraine State Park and McConnell's share the first-come, first-serve camping facilities at the North Country National Scenic Trail shelter off Link Road. Basic heated cabins are also available for rent and sleep up to six; contact the park for reservations. The state park is located west of I-79 off Rte 422 and Rte 19.

ALONG ROUTE 40

Rte 40, which cuts through the southwest corner of Pennsylvania, was the first federal public-works project in the nation, and it helped open the Ohio River Valley to settlement by Europeans. Begun in 1811 in Cumberland, Maryland, it pushed on to Wheeling, West Virginia, in 1818, then on to Vandalia, Illinois, in 1830. The National Road, as it was called, was the primary route from the East Coast to the western frontier until the 1850s. Today's Rte 40 follows essentially the same direction and is called the **National Road Heritage Park** (www.nationalroadpa.org). Its purpose is to preserve and promote the cultural, historic, natural and recreational resources along the road. There are a number of places to stay, but bring camping gear if you plan to sleep out.

PENNSYLVANIA

THE BATTLE OF FORT NECESSITY

In late 1753, George Washington, then in the colonial army, was sent to present-day Pittsburgh on a diplomatic mission to persuade the French to leave the Ohio River Valley, but was unsuccessful. The following year, the British built a fort where the Allegheny and Monongahela Rivers meet to form the Ohio River (in today's Point State Park), but it was captured by the French, who named it Fort Duquesne.

As the British forces (mostly Virginians) retreated, they encountered a detachment of French troops, killing a number of them in the subsequent skirmish. The British commander was also killed, and Washington, at the age of 22, was made a colonel and was placed in charge of the expedition.

Washington and his troops withdrew to Great Meadows, which he described as a 'charming field for an encounter.' Anticipating French retaliation, he built a 'fort of necessity' and surrounded it with trenches. A combined French and Algonquian force of about 700 attacked Washington's 400 men on July 3, and following a day of fighting, Washington surrendered. After negotiations, he and his men were allowed to walk home, and the French burned the fort.

The battle marked the beginning of the French and Indian War (see p35).

In 1755, Washington returned to the area as an aide to British General Edward Braddock. In a poorly planned attack, Braddock was killed near Fort Duquesne (and eventually interred next to Rte 40), as were over 900 redcoats. The British continued to lose the war until William Pitt the Elder, the British prime minister, dedicated more of Britain's resources to it. By 1760, the British had gained virtual control of North America, a fact later ratified by the 1763 Treaty of Paris.

FORT NECESSITY NATIONAL BATTLEFIELD

Eleven miles southeast of Uniontown, this **battlefield** (☎ 724-329-5512; adult/child $5/free; ◷ 8am-sunset) commemorates the battle that began the French and Indian War on July 3, 1754. It contains a replica of the original fort – actually just a one-room log building encircled by a low wooden palisade. The visitors' center has an audiovisual display on French-British rivalry in North America, George Washington and the Battle of Fort Necessity. Guides in period costume give talks on local history at scheduled times (check with the visitors' center). The battlefield also encompasses the nearby, but unrelated **Mt Washington Tavern**, built in 1828 for travelers on the National Road, and the **grave of General Braddock** (a mile west on Rte 40), whose body was moved to the roadside in 1804, though he was killed 50 years earlier.

LAUREL CAVERNS GEOLOGICAL PARK

This **park** (☎ 724-438-3003; www.laurelcaverns.com; adult/child/senior $11/9/10; ◷ closed Dec-Mar) boasts Pennsylvania's largest cave, measuring 450ft in depth. A one-hour guided tour takes visitors through parts of the cave's 2.8 miles of passageways; the temperature is a constant 52°F, so bring warm clothing (and shoes with nonslippery soles). At the time of writing, spelunking tours were suspended due to a problem with the local bat population, but adventurous visitors (ages 11 and up) can still participate in an in-cave rappelling workshop ($33 including the cost of the regular tour). Reservations are required.

Laurel Caverns Geological Park is located about 12 miles southeast of Uniontown off Rte 381.

Activities

SKIING & WHITEWATER RAFTING

The ski season in the highlands runs roughly from mid-December to early April. There's cross-country skiing in state parks and forests and in Bear Run Nature Reserve (p372), and there are several resorts that also offer downhill skiing. Ski packages that include accommodations, rentals, lift tickets and skiing lessons are available at the resorts.

Seven miles east of Rte 381, **Seven Springs Mountain Resort** (☎ 814-352-7777; www.7springs.com; 777 Waterwheel Dr; lift tickets adult/child $63/47) delights local snowboarders and skiers with a vertical drop of 750ft; snow tubing and sleigh rides are fun options for younger children. Outside of winter, the resort features golf, a full spa and plenty of family-friendly outdoor activities. Nearby, the **Hidden Valley Resort** (☎ 814-443-8000; www.hiddenvalleyresort.com; 1 Craighead Drive) has ski slopes as well as well-priced whitewater rafting packages (starting at $89 per person).

Rafting trips are run on the Youghiogheny River in Pennsylvania and Maryland, as well as on nearby rivers in West Virginia. The Youghiogheny is generally divided into the 'Middle Yough' (9 miles of easy rapids, classes I and II), 'Lower Yough' (7 miles of moderate rapids, classes III and IV) and 'Upper Yough' (11 miles of moderate-to-challenging rapids, classes IV and V). The Middle and Lower Yough are in Ohiopyle State Park, and the Upper Yough is in Maryland.

Several rafting companies are located in the village of Ohiopyle on or near the main street (Rte 381). Rates vary according to the day of the week (it's more expensive to go on a weekend), the season and whether you need a basic escort guide or a 'fully guided' trip with a professional actually steering your raft. **Laurel Highlands River Tours** (☎ 800-472-3846; www.laurelhighlands.com) does guided trips on the Middle Yough for $30 to $65 per person, the Lower Yough for $43 to $95 and the Upper Yough for $120 to $155. All trips include lunch. Other recommended companies offering guided trips and/or renting equipment are **Wilderness Voyageurs** (☎ 800-272-4141; www.wilderness-voyageurs.com), **White Water Adventurers** (☎ 800-992-7238; www.wwaraft.com) and **Ohiopyle Trading Post** (☎ 888-644-6895; www.ohiopyletradingpost.com).

KAYAKING, CYCLING & HIKING

Whitewater canoeing and kayaking, for which the aforementioned companies offer courses, are also immensely popular here, as is cycling along Ohiopyle State Park's 28-mile riverside bike trail. The park also features an off-road mountain-bike trail and more than 41 miles of hiking trails.

Bicycle rental is available around Ohiopyle village; renting a mountain bike for a day costs around $25 per person. For an organized outing, contact the Hidden Valley Resort (p376) for bike tours along the Allegheny Passage; rates start at $99 per person. An appealing alternative is Laurel Highlands River Tours' 'Pedal and Paddle Package,' which includes a 9-mile bike ride followed by rafting or canoeing on the Middle Yough. Rates are $31 to $46 per person, depending on your choice of watercraft.

The southern trailhead of the **Laurel Highlands Trail** is on King Rd just north of the village. You can hike or drive to overlooks above the river at Baughman Rock, Tharp Knob and the Kentuck Scenic Overlook.

Festivals & Events

Year-round festivals bring the Laurel Highlands to life. In January, the town of Somerset hosts the annual **Fire & Ice Festival** (www.somersetincpa.org) and Ligonier puts on the **Ligonier Ice Fest** (www.ligonier.com). Both are great excuses to spend time outdoors in winter, featuring impressive ice sculptures and live carving demonstrations; the former also puts on a fireworks show.

In March, look for **Celtic Fest** (www.cwklaywinery.com), an Irish-themed festival with lively food and music, at the Christian W Klay Winery in Chalk Hill. June brings the self-explanatory **Five Alarm Mountain Madness Sanctioned Chili Cook-off** (www.nemacolin.com/events-calendar) and August means the **Laurel Hill Bluegrass Festival** (www.friendsoflhsp.org) at Laurel Hill State Park. During weekends in October, the Seven Springs Mountain Resort (p376) is home to **Autumnfest** (www.7springs.com), centered around live music, crafts and harvest-produced cuisine.

Sleeping

The majority of accommodations are located in or around Ohiopyle State Park.

Tall Oaks Campground (☎ 724-329-4777; www.talloakscampground.com; 544 Camp Riamo Rd; campsites/cabins per person $11/16; 🅿 🛜 ♿) This secluded campground has a newly renovated swimming pool, over 100 wooded sites and simple cabins outfitted with bunk beds. You'll also find a game room and a country store where you can buy provisions. Located a mile south of Farmington on Rte 381.

Kentuck Campground (☎ 724-329-8591; campsites $21, yurts per night $40, 1-week minimum stay; ♿) More than 200 sites with access to public restrooms and hot showers, plus three 'platform tents' and four yurts with bunk beds and refrigerators. Open March to December.

Scarlett Knob Campground (☎ 724-329-5200; www.scarlettknobcampground.com; campsites $22.50; ♿) Privately run, on a hillside adjoining the north of the park, this campground has wooded sites with strictly enforced quiet hours. Caters to boaters.

Fern Cliff & Mackenzie Guesthouses (☎ 800-472-3846; www.laurelhighlands.com/lodging/guest_houses.cfm; s/d/tr $75/83/119; ♿) Laurel Highlands River Tours run this pair of cozy country-style guesthouses – you can rent just a room or the entire place – close to bike trails and the river. Most bathrooms are shared and a continental breakfast is complimentary.

PENNSYLVANIA

Lodge at Chalk Hill (☎ 724-438-8880; www.the lodgeatchalkhill.com; Rte 40 E, Box 240, Chalk Hill; d $84, d with kitchenette/ste $100/179; 🅿 🛜 ♿) This comfortable lodge, overlooking a small lake, is set on 37 forested acres. Spacious rooms with kitchenettes work well for families; guests can also enjoy a lighted running trail, a children's recreation area and complimentary catch-and-release fishing.

Nemacolin Woodlands Resort (☎ 724-329-8555; www.nemacolin.com; 1001 Lafayette Dr, Farmington; RV site/d/ste/house from $150/359/579/949; 🅿 🛜 🛎 ♿) This family-friendly luxury resort has six accommodation options ranging from an upscale RV park to the Falling Rock boutique hotel and a French-style chateau. Nemacolin features a golf course, pool and spa (plus a kids' spa), an 'adventure center' where guests of all ages can try a climbing wall or ropes course, and a variety of restaurants and bars – not to mention staff who will organize any outing in the area, from dogsledding to polo. The resort recently earned 'Pet Proud' status thanks to its canine-focused amenities, so feel free to bring the family dog.

Eating

In Chalk Hill, you'll find a few sandwich shops, pizzerias and diners. For something more memorable, try Hopwood's classy French restaurant **Chez Gerard** (☎ 724-437-9001; www.chezgerard.net; Rte 40; 3-course lunch $24; 🕑 closed Mon-Wed) or Farmington's **Historic Stone House Restaurant** (☎ 866-800-5248; www.stonehouseinn.com; 3023 National Pike; mains $13-20; 🕑 from 4pm Thu & Fri, from noon Sat & Sun, closed Jan-Mar), where hearty gourmet dishes such as chicken and dumplings are served in a quaint and cozy house that dates from 1822. The Stone House is also a B&B (double rooms from $97) with some traditional, pretty rooms and a handful of newer suites with Jacuzzis and Ralph Lauren decor.

Near the Ohiopyle Visitors Center, the friendly **Ohiopyle House Cafe & Mariettaville Tavern** (☎ 724-329-1122; www.ohiopylehousecafe.com; 144 Grant St, Ohiopyle; mains $5-13) has a little of everything: weekend breakfast buffets, a children's menu, vegetarian lunches, a terrace for al fresco meals, and a full list of cocktails, wine and beer. It'll even pack lunches for you to take on your cycling or rafting excursion.

Getting There & Around

I-76 and Rte 30 run east–west from Pittsburgh to Bedford. There's no public transportation

to Ohiopyle, though there are buses from Pittsburgh to Uniontown, 20 miles to the west. Rte 381 passes through the park, connecting with I-70/76 (Pennsylvania Turnpike) to the north and Rte 40 to the south; Rte 40 runs northwest to Uniontown and southeast into Maryland.

JOHNSTOWN
pop 21,650

The city of Johnstown, once a busy port on the Pennsylvania Main Line Canal, earned notoriety in 1889 when it became the site of one of the worst natural disasters in American history. Positioned at the fork of the Little Conemaugh and Stoneycreek Rivers, Johnstown was hit by a gigantic rolling wave of water when the South Fork Dam – about 10 miles upstream – failed one rainy spring afternoon. Low-lying buildings were swept away, fires broke out, thousands of lives were lost, and the once-prosperous city was left a smoking graveyard of tangled train carriages and human bodies. See p379 for more on this historic disaster.

Johnstown was named after Joseph Schantz, a Swiss Mennonite immigrant who changed his surname to Johns and founded the town at the start of the 19th century. Apart from the 'Great Flood,' the city has been ravaged by river waters multiple times, and it never returned to its former prosperity – in 2003, the US Census reported that Johnstown was the least likely city in the US to attract newcomers. Still, the city sees plenty of students: it's the home to the University of Pittsburgh at Johnstown.

Information & Sights

Helpful resources in town include the **Cambria County Library** (☎ 814-536-5131; www.cclib.lib.pa.us; 248 Main St) and the **Johnstown & Cambria County Convention & Visitors Bureau** (☎ 814-536-7993; www.visitjohnstownpa.com; 416 Main St, Suite 100).

JOHNSTOWN FLOOD MUSEUM

This interesting **museum** (☎ 814-539-1889; www.jaha.org/floodmuseum; 304 Washington St; adult/child/senior $7/5/6) exhibits flood debris, survivor stories and vintage photographs of the damage done by the flood. With the help of some additional funding – for a more evocative 3-D model of the series of events leading to the flood, for example – the museum would be excellent. In its current state, the place feels a bit dated, but it's a must-see nonetheless for anyone with a remote interest in natural (or man-made, as this case is often considered) disasters. In the theater on the 2nd floor, a documentary/reenactment film tells the story of the 1889 event and its aftermath. It's interesting to note that the building, originally a library, was rebuilt with money given by Andrew Carnegie after the flood – apparently he felt indebted to the Johnstown community since the flood was caused by a burst dam at the private club he helped to finance. See the boxed text for more on Carnegie's involvement.

INCLINED PLANE

Modest Johnstown is, surprisingly, a town marked by extremes: the 1889 flood was the worst (non-hurricane flood) in US history, while its **Inclined Plane** (☎ 814-536-1816; www.inclinedplane.com; 1-way adult/child $2.25/1.50) is the steepest vehicular incline in the world. It was built after the flood to improve access to higher ground and to develop the upper suburb of Westmont; the plane goes 900ft up Yoder Hill at a 71.9% gradient from Johns St (Rte 56). Steel workers used to commute via these large cable cars – each of which has room for a couple of cars or for 65 passengers – and during the floods of 1936 and 1977, Johnstown residents climbed aboard the incline to escape the water-logged downtown. At the top is a visitors' center, where you can

---

THE JOHNSTOWN FLOOD

The Johnstown flood of May 31, 1889, was the worst non-hurricane flood in US history. When the South Fork Dam (about 10 miles northeast of Johnstown up the Little Conemaugh River) broke, a wall of water roiling with debris was sent crashing into town.

The dam was originally built by the state with the intention of creating a water supply to support a canal system. However, by the time the dam was finished in 1853, the canals were obsolete. It was allowed to deteriorate for four years before being bought first by the Pennsylvania Railroad, then by a US congressman from Altoona, who removed the discharge pipes and sold them but did little maintenance. Every spring, people who lived along the river wondered if the dam would hold. The dam actually did break in 1862, but fortunately, the lake water was so low that minimal damage was caused. Then, in 1879, Benjamin Ruff bought the dam and built an exclusive club beside the 2-mile-wide lake.

Ruff enlisted wealthy Pittsburgh industrialists Andrew Carnegie, Henry Clay Frick and Andrew Mellon, among others, to finance the club. It was officially christened the South Fork Fishing & Hunting Club, but locals referred to it as the 'Bosses' Club.' Ruff recruited Edward Pearson, who wasn't an engineer, to rebuild the dam. Pearson refused engineering advice from Cambria Iron officials downstream, who were worried about the dam. He didn't replace the discharge pipes; he renovated the dam with hay, tree stumps and manure, installed only one spillway and, worst of all, lowered the height of the dam. To keep their fish from swimming downstream, club members had a screen installed over the spillway. The screen became clogged with debris.

In the week before May 31, heavy rains saturated the Johnstown area. On May 30, the lake waters rose an inch every 10 minutes. At 3:10pm on the 31st, the dam broke, and the water swept 14 miles along the floodplain toward Johnstown. It took only 45 minutes for the lake to empty. On the way, the water smashed through several small towns, tore up train tracks and obliterated a 75ft-high stone viaduct. A railroad engineer raced his train ahead of the flood with the whistle tied down to warn people.

Just under an hour after the dam broke, a 35ft-high wall of water choked with debris roared into town at 40mph. People tried to get out of the way, but parts of the town were already under 2ft to 7ft of water from the previous week's rain, and progress was difficult. The water eventually stopped at the seven-arched Pennsylvania Stone Bridge, below the junction of the Stoney Creek and Conemaugh Rivers. Tons of debris – most of the town of Johnstown, trains, logs, machinery, animals and hundreds of people – jammed up against the bridge. Many people were trapped in rolls of barbed wire from the Gautier Wire Works in town.

The debris, covered in oil spilled from railroad tank cars, caught fire (possibly lit by coals from steam engines) and burned for two days, killing 80 people trapped against the bridge in the water.

The official death toll from the flood was 2209. Typhoid killed 40 more. Many of the victims were never identified, and hundreds disappeared never to be found.

see the drum turning the cable, buy an ice-cream cone, and stand on the platform with views over the river valley. Adjacent to the visitors' center is the City View Bar & Grill.

Sleeping & Eating

About 5 miles south of town, at the junction of Rtes 56 and 219, is a commercial strip with motels and fast-food outlets. You won't find any memorable hotels here: head into the Laurel Highlands if you don't want to sleep in a chain motel.

Woodland Park (☎ 814-472-9857; 220 Campground Rd; campsites from $20; mid-Apr–Oct;) Near Ebensburg, about 18 miles north of town, this campground has shaded tent sites and standard amenities. Take Rte 56 east to Rte 219 north. Follow 219 to Rte 22 west for 3¾ miles to Campground Rd and follow it a mile north to the campground.

ourpick Coney Island Lunch (☎ 814-535-2885; www.coneyislandjohnstownpa.com; 127 Clinton St; sandwiches $2-4; closed Sun) This corner luncheonette, famous for grilled hot dogs and burgers, feels like it's out of another era. Take a load off at one of the no-frills booths and sink your teeth into the house special – the Sundowner, a cheeseburger topped with fried egg, chopped onion and chili sauce.

Szechuan Chinese Restaurant (☎ 814-535-8845; 124 Main St; mains $5-12; closed Mon) A couple of blocks from the Flood Museum, this clean and friendly Chinese eatery is a solid option for a quick and filling meal; try a heaping plate of noodles or green tea and wontons.

City View Bar & Grill (☎ 814-534-0190; www.city viewbarandgrill.com; 709 Edgehill Dr; mains $8-24; closed Mon) This clifftop bar-restaurant, next door to the upper station of the Inclined Plane, is a local favorite thanks to sweeping views over the city, classic steaks, happy-hour specials and live music on weekend nights. The casual lunch menu features salads and wraps, while the place takes on a more romantic feel at night. From the bar, you can see into the cable-car engine room, which dates from 1889.

Getting There & Away

AIR
John Murtha Johnstown-Cambria County airport (☎ 814-539-3510; www.flyjohnstownairport.com; 479 Airport Rd), outside town, is served by United Express. There are three daily flights on weekdays (and three flights on weekends)

to Washington-Dulles Airport. To get to the airport from Johnstown, take Rte 56 east to Rte 219 north, then take the first exit to the airport.

BUS
Greyhound (☎ 800-231-2222; www.greyhound.com; 130 Clinton St) has a bus stop in Johnstown, but tickets aren't sold there – travelers must purchase them through the website or by phone. There are two buses daily to Harrisburg ($49, 4½ hours), Philadelphia ($66, 7½ hours) and Pittsburgh ($20, 2½ hours).

TRAIN
From the **Amtrak** (☎ 814-535-3313; www.amtrak. com; 47 Walnut St) station there are daily trains to Harrisburg ($34, four hours), Philadelphia ($58, six hours) and Pittsburgh ($14, two hours).

Getting Around

Cambria Country Transit Authority (☎ 814-535-5526; www.camtranbus.com) provides the local bus service. Timetables and bus passes are available from the 'Bus Stop' general store in the **Transit Center** (541 Locust St), where local buses arrive and depart; alternatively, you can pay the exact fare onboard. Fares start at $1.50.

AROUND JOHNSTOWN
Johnstown Flood National Memorial

If you've been through the Flood Museum, chances are you'll also be interested in driving out to the site where the South Fork Dam used to stand. This **national memorial** (☎ 814-495-4643; www.nps.gov/jofl; adult/child $4/ free), located about 10 miles upstream from Johnstown, stands in the original location of Lake Conemaugh, where the members of the South Fork Hunting & Fishing Club would boat and swim. After the flood of 1889, the lake drained and the wealthy out-of-towners abandoned their warm-weather getaway; now the former lake is a large grassy area. A short trail leads from the visitors' center to the site of what is left of the dam. The visitors' center has exhibits similar to the Johnstown Flood Museum and a gripping dramatized 35-minute black-and-white film entitled Black Friday; if you just want to drive up to the site and look around, you don't need to pay the park fee.

From Johnstown, take Rte 56 east to Rte 219 north and follow it to the St Michael/

Sidman exit. Take Rte 869 east for 1½ miles, then make a left onto Lake Rd at the sign for the memorial. Follow Lake Rd for 1½ miles to the visitors' center.

Windber Coal Heritage Center

The **center** (☎ 814-467-6680; http://echf.windberpa.org; 501 15th St, Windber; adult/child $6/1.50) is a fascinating museum that documents the area's rich, labor-intensive coal industry and the everyday life of coal miners and their families from the late 19th to the early 20th century. Often dubbed 'underground farmers,' these miners looked for 'black gold.' The museum includes videos, interactive displays, and tools from former miners. It's located about 12 miles southeast of Johnstown off Rte 56.

Allegheny Railroad Portage

When the Allegheny Railroad Portage opened in 1834, it reduced traveling time between Pittsburgh and Philadelphia from three weeks to four days and helped open up the west. A major feat of engineering, the portage consisted of a series of inclined planes over the Allegheny Mountains. The 2.3-sq-mile national **historic site** (☎ 814-884-6150; www.nps.gov/alpo/index.htm; adult/child $4/free), about 25 miles northeast of Johnstown, off Rte 22, provides interpretive programs and guided hikes.

NORTHERN PENNSYLVANIA

Say the words 'northern Pennsylvania' and most East Coasters will think of huge, unpopulated forest areas, cheesy-romantic getaway resorts in the Poconos where the Jacuzzis are shaped like hearts or wine glasses, the windwhipped shore of Lake Erie – and, thanks to the runaway popularity of *The Office*, the seemingly ordinary town of Scranton. It's true that that the region isn't much of a cultural destination, but in terms of natural features, the northernmost part of the state is full of grace. The Allegheny National Forest is a paradise in autumn as hikers and cyclists take to the hills to delight in the leaves' changing colors; outdoorsy types also head year-round to Pine Creek Gorge, also known as Pennsylvania's Grand Canyon, and the Pocono Mountains to ski, swim and camp.

ERIE & AROUND

pop 104,000

The port town of Erie lies on the southern shore of Lake Erie, about 127 miles north of Pittsburgh. Erie enjoys vast lake views and summertime water activities; south of the city, the land is decidedly less beautiful, but it also happens to be the place where the world's commercial oil industry began in the mid-19th century, especially around Oil City, Titusville and Oil Creek.

History

Erie is named after the Eriez Indians, who were killed off by the Seneca Indians during the 17th century. The town was laid out in 1795 and played an important role in America's victory in the Battle of Lake Erie during the War of 1812 with Britain. Today, Erie is an important industrial and manufacturing center. North of town, the Presque Isle peninsula helps form a natural sheltered harbor on the lake. Erie is the shallowest of the Great Lakes and is especially vulnerable to pollution, which by the 1970s had wiped out much of the lake's marine life. A combined community effort reversed this, and the fish population recovered.

Orientation

Peach and State Sts are the main north–south streets. State St leads north to the lake's public dock at Dobbin's Landing. The area around Dobbin's Landing has been redeveloped and includes the Bicentennial Tower and Erie Maritime Museum. Rte 5 splits in two as it runs east–west through Erie – as 6th St, it heads through downtown, while as 12th St, it skirts downtown's southern edge.

Information

There are a number of banks with ATMs along State St downtown.

VisitErie (☎ 800-524-3743; www.visiteriepa.com; 208 E Bayfront Pkwy; ⊗ 9am-5pm Mon-Fri) Visit the website to download a copy of the official Visitor's Guide.

Main post office (629 State St; ⊗ 9am-4pm Mon-Fri)

Sights & Activities

PRESQUE ISLE STATE PARK

Presque Isle (the name means 'almost an island' in French) is a peninsula one mile across at its widest point and 6½ miles long; it's attached to the mainland just west of Erie. The peninsula is actually getting longer – despite

PENNSYLVANIA

continual loss of sand from the main body (breakwaters have been put in place to slow this process down), there is growth at Gull Point, at the eastern end. The peninsula forms and protects Presque Isle Bay, considered to be one of the finest natural harbors on the Great Lakes. The new **Tom Ridge Environmental Center** (TREC; ☎ 814-833-7424; http://trecpi.org; ⏰ 10am-6pm) serves as a visitors' center and the main gateway to the park; features include a children's Discovery Center, interactive nature exhibits, a Big Green Screen (something like a smaller IMAX theatre), a 75ft glass-enclosed TREC tower affording views over the lake, artist-in-residence demonstrations, a cool nature shop and the Sunset Cafe eatery. At the center, you can also arrange guided tours of the park or a pontoon trip on the lagoons.

In addition to beautiful coastline, the 3200-acre park contains six distinct ecological zones and around 600 plant species; it is also an important spot for migrating water and wading birds, as well as land birds (particularly the hawk). Over 320 bird species have been recorded here, and many can be seen at **Gull Point Sanctuary**. The **Perry Monument**, near the Gull Point Sanctuary, commemorates Commodore Perry's victory in the Battle of Lake Erie, which took place on September 10, 1813.

The park guards beaches that are great for swimming as well as 11 miles of hiking trails and the 13.5-mile **Karl Boyes National Recreational Trail**, designed for cycling, jogging and inline skating. Bikes, four-wheeled surreys, inline skates and paddle boats can be rented at **Yellow Bike Rentals** (☎ 814-835-8900; Waterworks Pumphouse; ⏰ 10am-8pm summer) near the park's Cookhouse Pavilion. On Graveyard Pond across from Misery Bay, you'll find the **Presque Isle Canoe & Boat Livery** (☎ 814-838-3938; ⏰ 10am-5pm Mon-Fri, to 8pm Sat & Sun), where you can rent canoes by the day or hour. The strong winds on Presque Isle Bay make a relaxing paddle difficult, but are ideal for windsurfing and sailing. Recreational scuba diving is also allowed (provided you can show your certification) in certain water areas in the park; inquire at TREC.

To get to the park, take I-79 or Rtes 19 or 5 to 6th St, then head west to Peninsula Drive and turn north. A water taxi ($6 round-trip) runs between Dobbin's Landing and Liberty Park to the park's Waterworks.

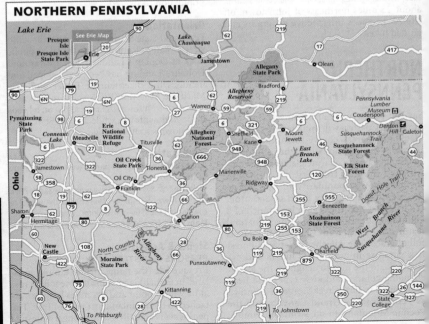

NORTHERN PENNSYLVANIA

DOBBIN'S LANDING

The large, contemporary **Erie Maritime Museum** (☎ 814-452-2744; www.eriemaritimemuseum.org; 150 East Front St; adult/child $8/5; ☺ 9am-5pm Mon-Sat, from noon Sun Apr-Oct, off-season hrs vary) hosts a number of exhibitions that informs visitors about the War of 1812, the USS *Wolverine* (the US Navy's first iron-hulled ship), life aboard a wooden warship and the maritime history of northwestern Pennsylvania. There's also a video about the US Brig *Niagara*, Pennsylvania's official flagship. The current ship is a replica of the *Niagara*, which took part in the Battle of Lake Erie. When it's not away sailing, it docks behind the museum, where visitors can view it; a free tour is included as part of the admission price (if the ship's there, that is!).

On the pier is the 187ft **Bicentennial Tower** (☎ 814-455-6055; ☺ hrs vary seasonally, 9:30am-10pm Jun-Sep), built in 1995 to commemorate Erie's 200th birthday. You can take an elevator to the top to take in great views of the bay and town, especially at sunset. At the bottom, you can buy food to feed the ducks and birds.

DISCOVERY SQUARE

Discovery Square comprises three museums. Housed in the 1839 Greek Revival–style Old Custom House, **Erie Art Museum** (☎ 814-459-5477; www.erieartmuseum.org; 411 State St; adult/child $4/2; ☺ 11am-5pm Tue-Sat, 1-5pm Sun; ♿) has temporary exhibitions, as well as permanent displays, of American, European and Asian paintings, drawings and sculptures. On permanent display is a scene depicting local people (looking rather like characters from *The Muppets*) in a former Erie diner. There are also craft days and workshops for kids.

A few doors down, the **Erie County Historical Society** (☎ 814-454-1813; www.eriecountyhistory.org; 419 State St; adult/child $5/3; ☺ 9am-5pm Tue-Sat) houses the Museum of Erie County History, which displays changing exhibitions, vintage maps and photographs and has an extensive library on local history. The historical society also manages related museums and sites nearby, like the **Watson-Curtze Mansion** (☎ 814-871-5790; 356 W 6th St), displaying the trappings of Erie's old industrial wealth and featuring an antique planetarium; the **Cashier's House** (☎ 814-454-1813; 417 State St), dating from 1839; and the **Battles**

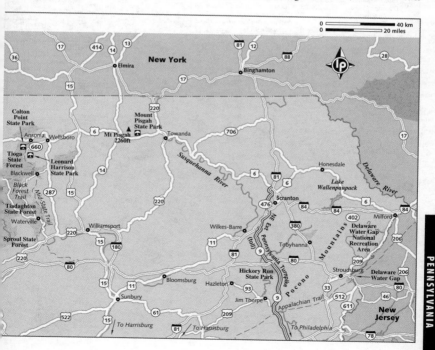

Museums of Rural Life (☎ 814-454-1813; 436 Walnut St, Girard). Visiting one of these sites gets you into the others for free or for a discounted price; all of the necessary information may be found at the historical society.

The fun and colorful **Experience Children's Museum** (☎ 814-453-3743; www.eriechildrensmuseum. org; 420 French St; admission $5; ☼ 10am-4pm Tue-Sat, 1-4pm Sun, closed Tue Sep-May; ♿) is a hands-on museum with all sorts of activities and displays designed to stimulate children. Highlights include the Aerodynamics exhibit (in which kids learn about physics with plastic tubes and balls), the Healer Within human-anatomy exhibit, a bubble machine, a recycling activity and a magnet exhibit with six interactive stations.

WINERIES

Bottoms up: this is a region known for wine-growing. The fertile Lake Erie shoreline – stretching from Pennsylvania and into New York and Ohio – is ideal for growing white wine grapes, so expect tasty chardonnay and riesling. If you're in the mood for wine, your best bet around Erie is about 12 miles east of town. Here you'll find a number of vineyards clustered around the small town of North East. For more information on good-quality wineries in the area, log onto the helpful webpages of the **Lake Erie Quality Wine Alliance** (www.lakeeriewine.com) and the **Chautauqua-Lake Erie Wine Trail** (www.chautauquawinetrail.org), which covers the 45-mile stretch (and over 20 wineries) between Pennsylvania and western New York.

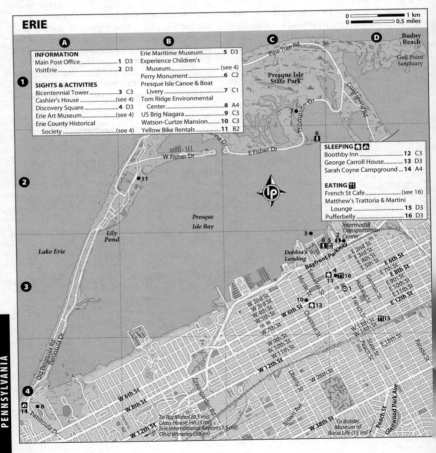

ERIE

INFORMATION		
Main Post Office	**1**	D3
VisitErie	**2**	D3

SIGHTS & ACTIVITIES		
Bicentennial Tower	**3**	C3
Cashier's House	(see 4)	
Discovery Square	**4**	D3
Erie Art Museum	(see 4)	
Erie County Historical Society	(see 4)	
Erie Maritime Museum	**5**	D3
Experience Children's Museum	(see 4)	
Perry Monument	**6**	C2
Presque Isle Canoe & Boat Livery	**7**	C1
Tom Ridge Environmental Center	**8**	A4
US Brig Niagara	**9**	C3
Watson-Curtze Mansion	**10**	C3
Yellow Bike Rentals	**11**	B2

SLEEPING ☐☐		
Boothby Inn	**12**	C3
George Carroll House	**13**	D3
Sarah Coyne Campground	**14**	A4

EATING ☐		
French St Cafe	(see 16)	
Matthew's Trattoria & Martini Lounge	**15**	D3
Pufferbelly	**16**	D3

If you're especially thirsty for gewürztraminer, you could cross the border and drive east to New York state's Finger Lakes region, about a 2½-hour drive on Rte 17. See p192 for information on wineries in the Finger Lakes region.

Tours

From Dobbin's Landing, **Victorian Princess Cruise Lines** (☎ 814-459-9696; www.victorianprincess. com; tickets $12-32.95) operates sightseeing, dinner, lunch, brunch and happy-hour cruises; and **Presque Isle Boat Tours** (☎ 814-836-0201; adult/child $15/10) sends the steamer *Lady Kate* on a short narrated cruise of Lake Erie. The ships sail four times daily in summer and on a limited schedule in fall and spring.

Festivals & Events

One of Erie's most notable festivals is called **Celebrate Erie** (www.celebrateerie.com) Taking place in August on State St between 4th and 12th Sts, this family-friendly event features arts, good food, crafts, a children's area, cultural exhibitions and music performances. A huge fireworks display over Dobbin's Landing is the grand finale. The **Taste of Erie** culinary festival runs in conjunction with Celebrate Erie; check the website for more information.

When the weather cools off in September, the **Great Lakes International Film Festival** (www. greatlakesfilmfest.com) and the **Erie Irish Festival** (www.erieirishfestival.com) come to town. Both cost a nominal fee or donation of canned goods.

Sleeping

Sara Coyne Campground (☎ 814-833-4560; www.sara scampground.com; 50 Peninsula Dr; campsite $23; 🅿 ♿) Just outside Presque Isle State Park, this neat campground has a laundry, several restaurants, clean showers, children's activities and bike rentals. The sites are close together, but the beach is close to most; it's even possible to pitch your tent on the pretty lakeshore.

Glass House Inn (☎ 800-956-7222; www.glass houseinn.com; 3202 W 26th St; d from $60; 🅿 🔲 ♿) This colonial-style 30-room inn is clean, comfortable and family-run, though the decor is a bit dated. Kids like the outdoor pool; each room comes with a microwave and mini-fridge. It's located 2 miles from the state park.

George Carroll House (☎ 814-459-2021; www. georgecarrollhouse.com; 401 Peach St; d from $75; 🔲) A Queen Anne–style B&B located in downtown Erie, this good-looking place contains spacious, spick-and-span guestrooms with private bathrooms; the look is pared-down and simple compared to the usual lace curtains and antiques found at historic inns.

our pick **Boothby Inn** (☎ 866-266-8429; www. theboothbyinn.com; 311 W 6th St; d $130-170; 🔲 🛜) A charming (and more upscale) option, also in downtown, Boothby Inn boasts crackling fireplaces, an enclosed porch and freshly baked cookies – in short, the works. There are only four guest rooms and each is decorated thematically to reflect the owners' world travels in France, Japan, Scotland and Africa.

TOP SIX WINERIES

It's not Napa or Bordeaux, but the fertile region around Erie has climate and soil that's ideal for growing white wine grapes and even pinot noir. Without further adieu, we present to you, dear wine lovers, the top of the lot:

- **Arrowhead Wine Cellars** (☎ 814-725-5509; www.arrowheadwine.com; 12073 E Main Rd; ⏱ 10am-6pm Mon-Sat, noon-5pm Sun) This winery grows grapes on a 250-acre farm and features a large winery gift shop. Next door you'll find a 'pick your own' fruit market.

- **Heritage Wine Cellars** (☎ 800-747-0083; www.heritagewine.biz; 12160 E Main Rd, North East; ⏱ 9am-5pm Mon-Sat) This family-run winery has been going strong for more than 150 years; the Concord grapes thrive here and tastings are held in a restored 18th-century barn.

- **Mazza Vineyards** (☎ 800-796-9463; www.mazzawines.com; 11815 E Lake Road, Rte 5, North East; ⏱ 9am-8pm Mon-Sat, 11am-4:30pm Sun in summer, tours by appointment) Tours and tastings are available year-round at this well-known winery. Look for the Mazza wine shop in downtown Erie as well.

- **Presque Isle Wine Cellars** (☎ 800-488-7492; www.piwine.com; 9440 W Main Rd, Rte 20; ⏱ 9am-5pm Mon-Sat) In operation since 1968, this commercial winery also sells equipment and offers instruction to amateur winemakers.

THE BATTLE OF LAKE ERIE

In the War of 1812, the British gained command of the Great Lakes. Oliver Hazard Perry, a 27-year-old lieutenant, was sent to engage them. The natural bays and inlets on the south side of Presque Isle provided Perry with the raw materials and protection needed for building six of his fleet's ships, including the brigs Lawrence and Niagara. Many of the seamen in Perry's fleet were African American. Ironically, the peninsula presented the final obstacle to the launch of the ships into Lake Erie. A sandbar at the entrance to the bay prevented them from moving through, but the problem was solved by floating the ships across the bar on empty tanks known as 'camels.'

Perry engaged the British fleet at Put-in-Bay, near present-day Sandusky, Ohio, on September 10, 1813. Both fleets had equal firepower, and two hours into the battle, Perry lost his flagship, *Lawrence*, and most of its crew. Transferring to *Niagara*, he sailed into the British fleet, and within an hour, the British flag was lowered in surrender. Perry then penned the immortal words: 'We have met the enemy and they are ours...' The victory opened US supply lines and ended the British threat to the northwest.

Breakfast is served in a grand chandelier-lit dining room.

There are also several motels west of town around Peninsula Drive (Rte 832) near the intersections of Rte 5 (West 12th St) and Alternative Rte 5 (West 8th St/West Lake Rd).

Eating & Drinking

Erie is no dining capital: you'll find mostly chain restaurants and fast-food outlets here. If that's what you're seeking, head to Peach St south of 26th St and around Peninsula Drive between the intersections of Rte 5 (West 12th St) and Alternative Rte 5 (West 8th St/West Lake Rd). If you're heading into the state park, just stop at a supermarket and pack your own picnic.

There are, however, a few places to try when you need a real meal or a cold cocktail. For a spicy Indian buffet with a family-friendly price tag, there's **Raj Mahal Restaurant** (☎ 814-838-1055; 2740 W 12th St; lunch buffet $6.99). Stylish **Matthew's Trattoria & Martini Lounge** (☎ 814-459-6458; www.matthewstrattoria.com; 153 E 13th; tapas $4-13; ☾ 5pm-midnight Mon-Sat) offers savory tapas, hand-crafted beers and wines by the glass in a relaxed setting with cozy loveseats and a sophisticated lighting scheme. Housed in a restored firehouse that dates from 1908, the **Pufferbelly** (☎ 814-454-1557; www.thepufferbelly.com; mains $8-22) is classy bar-restaurant serving gourmet sandwiches, steaks and salads as well as a lovely Sunday brunch. Next door, its new sister property the **French Street Cafe** (☎ 814-455-1558; 410 French St) is a quaint stop for pastries, desserts and specialty coffees.

Getting There & Away

Erie International Airport (☎ 814-833-4258; www.erieairport.org; 4411 W 12th St) is southwest of town. It's served by **Northwest** (☎ 814-833-3030), **US Airways** (☎ 814-838-3552) and **Continental Express** (☎ 814-835-3895).

Greyhound buses leave from the **Intermodal Transportation Center** (☎ 814-453-2171; www.greyhound.com; 208 E Bayfront Pkwy). There are two buses daily to Pittsburgh ($25 to $34, 3½ hours).

If you're driving from Pittsburgh, I-79 takes you directly to Erie. I-90 heads west to Ohio and east to New York along the lakeshore.

Getting Around

Erie Metro Transit Authority (EMTA; ☎ 814-452-3515; www.ride-the-e.com) operates the local bus service. The one-way fare is $1.10. Some routes don't operate on Sunday or holidays. For a taxi, call **Erie Yellow Cab** (☎ 814-455-4441).

PYMATUNING STATE PARK

This **state park** (☎ 412-932-3141; www.dcnr.state.pa.us/stateparks/parks/pymatuning.aspx) is the largest state park in the Commonwealth. Located about 45 miles southwest of Erie and straddling the Ohio border, it's accessible on Rtes 6 or 322 west of I-79.

The park contains the 21½-sq-mile Pymatuning Reservoir – the largest artificial lake in the state – built to control the flow of the Beaver and Shenango Rivers and to protect the waters entering the Pymatuning Swamp. The land around the reservoir provides habitat for a wide variety of bird species, and in the fall, the **Pymatuning Wildlife Management Area** is home to 20,000 Canada

PENNSYLVANIA

geese. The **visitors' center** (☎ 814-683-5545) on Ford Island, in the park's north, has exhibits on local flora and fauna and information about park activities.

There are four protected swimming beaches (open Memorial Day to Labor Day); fishing is popular on the lake, and in winter, there's cross-country skiing. The park has several camping areas, including a cluster of basic cabins that are available for guest use year-round; some areas were closed at the time of writing, so call ahead for pricing and availability. Food and other supplies can be found at the camp store or carried in from Jamestown.

ERIE NATIONAL WILDLIFE REFUGE

The name is misleading: this refuge begins about 40 miles southeast of Erie. It's made up of two parts: the 5206-acre **Sugar Lake** division lies between Titusville and Meadville, while the 3571-acre **Seneca** division is 10 miles to the north. The **visitors' center** (☎ 814-789-3585; www.fws.gov/northeast/erie; 11296 Wood Duck Lane, Guys Mills; ☒ 8am-4.30pm Mon-Fri) is in the Sugar Lake division, just off Rte 198.

The refuge provides diverse habitats for wildlife. Migratory birds, such as Canada geese and wood duck, nest here, as do raptors such as the red-tailed hawk, bald eagle, osprey and kestrel. Of the 40-odd species of mammals, the most common are beaver, muskrat, white-tailed deer and woodchuck. There are several walking trails from which you can view the wildlife, and you can fish for bass, perch or trout in the lakes and rivers.

If you're traveling to the park with children, visit the website first to download the 'Nature Explorer Program' packet that encourages kids to be flora and fauna detectives and find clues throughout the refuge.

Access to Sugar Lake is via Rtes 27, 173 and 198; access to Seneca is off Rte 408.

TITUSVILLE

pop 5800

Titusville is located about 42 miles southeast of Erie on the banks of Oil Creek (admittedly not a great name for a small river – the imagery doesn't exactly inspire a relaxing canoe ride!).

Named after Jonathan Titus, one of the early surveyors of the area, Titusville was founded in 1796. Lumber was the main industry until Edwin Drake drilled the world's first

oil well. Not surprisingly, Titusville was also the home of the first 'oil millionaire' in history, Jonathan Watson, the owner of the land where Drake started drilling. Today, Titusville is a small working town that's developing its tourism around oil history; it's worth a stop on a road trip to see the world's first commercial oil well.

Sights
DRAKE WELL MUSEUM

This memorial park and **museum** (☎ 814-827-2797; www.drakewell.org; 202 Museum Lane; adult/child $6/3; ☒ 9am-5pm Tue-Sat May, 9am-5pm Tue-Sat & noon-5pm Sun Jun-Oct) commemorates the spot where oil was first drilled by Edwin Drake of the Seneca Oil Company in August 1859. Through artifacts, documents and photographs, the museum there examines the development of the oil industry and its social and economic impact. You'll find a replica of Drake's old engine house, a walking trail leading to the 'oil pits' where Native Americans found oil before the arrival of Columbus, vintage drilling machinery, informational films, guided tours and plenty of outdoor space where kids can run and play.

To get there, take Rte 8 southeast from Titusville for 1¼ miles, then go east on Bloss St to the park just past the bridge.

Sleeping & Eating

Oil Creek Campground (☎ 800-395-2045; www.oilcreek campground.com; 340 Shreve Rd; campsite/cabin from $22/35; ☒) Just outside Oil Creek State Park, this campground offers wooded sites and basic cabin accommodations; the facilities include a llama petting pen, playground and fishing pond. The turnoff for the campground is 4 miles south of Titusville off Rte 8; it's then another 1½ miles east along Turkey Farm Rd.

Blue Canoe Brewery (☎ 814-827-7181; www.theblue canoebrewery.com; 113 S Franklin St; mains $6-18; ☒ closed Mon) This good-looking brick brewpub is well-liked by locals for its tasty pulled-pork sandwiches, good microbrew selection, and live banjo and guitar music. Try the beer sampler; you can take a growler home with you if you find something you like.

In town, there are fast-food places on Franklin St, Central Ave and W Main St.

Getting There & Away

Titusville is at the intersection of Rtes 8 and 27, about 15 miles north of Oil City. It is about

PENNSYLVANIA

CRUDE OIL

Crude oil is found under the western slopes of the Appalachian Mountains in western Pennsylvania, southwestern New York, eastern Ohio and West Virginia. It's renowned for its paraffin base (from the Latin *para finum* – little affinity – meaning it has little affinity for chemical change; that is, it is very stable). It also has high natural lubricity and viscosity and is relatively free of impurities such as sulfur, tar or asphalt.

---

a 40-minute drive east of I-79 or about 40 minutes north of I-80.

OIL CITY & AROUND
pop 10,600

The aptly named Oil City, straddling the Allegheny River and its tributary Oil Creek, was the center of the 19th-century oil industry in the region. Oil was shipped along the creek to Oil City, from where it was transported by steamboat or barge to Pittsburgh. One of its claims to fame is that oil magnate John D Rockefeller raised his first million dollars here.

The countryside is littered with remnants from that time, but the streams and much of the wilderness of the Allegheny foothills have recovered from the early industrial onslaught. Let's not mince words: Oil City is a fairly unattractive industrial town. Unlike some others, it still refines oil and manufactures related machinery; it's also the headquarters of the Quaker State Corporation – one of the first companies to produce motor oil.

Orientation

Seneca and Center Sts form the downtown core, which is bounded to the south by the Allegheny River and to the west and north by Oil Creek. South of the Allegheny River, over the State St Bridge, is another small commercial center. Rte 8 becomes Seneca St (one way, southbound) and Elm St (one way, northbound) in town. With the exception of the Venango Museum, the things to see are outside Oil City proper.

Information

Post office (Seneca St; ☼ 8:30am-1pm & 2-4pm Mon-Fri) Opposite the Venango Museum.

Oil Region Alliance (☎ 800-483-6264; www.oilregion.org/tourism; 217 Elm St; ☼ 9am-5pm Mon-Fri Jun-Oct, to 4pm Nov-May) This tourism office also has a full listing of the region's historic sites on its website.

Sights

VENANGO MUSEUM OF ART, SCIENCE & INDUSTRY

In a lovely Beaux Arts building that's recognized by the National Register of Historic Places, this **museum** (☎ 814-676-2007; www.venangomuseum.org; 270 Seneca St; adult/child $4/2; ☼ 10am-4pm Tue-Fri, 11am-4pm Sat, 2-5pm Sun) offers changing exhibits on the region's industry and culture. Look for the working 1928 Wurlitzer Theater Organ.

MCCLINTOCK WELL

The McClintock Well, the oldest continuously operating oil well in the US (it has been pumping since August 1861) is an interesting piece of history, but not much to look at.

As you head north out of town on Rte 8, turn left onto Waitz Rd at the derelict blue building marked 'bmi' just before the bridge. Walk about 80 yards west between two fences and continue across some railroad tracks; look to your right and you'll see the small well, which is quietly pumping oil into green Quaker State Corporation tanks.

OIL CREEK & TITUSVILLE RAILROAD

This restored **train** (☎ 814-676-1733; www.octrr.org; office at 7 Elm St, train departs from 409 S Perry St; adult/child $17/11; ☼ hrs vary, Sat & Sun Jun-Oct & selected weekdays), dating from 1892, takes visitors on a three-hour ride along a 13½-mile scenic rail line through Oil Creek Valley from Perry St station in Titusville to Rynd Farm station, 4 miles north of Oil City. On the way, it stops at Drake Well Museum and at Petroleum Center in Oil Creek State Park. There's an open-air car, amenities for cyclists and boaters who want to be dropped off upstream, and special excursions like the Murder Mystery Dinner & Train Ride, the Peter Cottontail Express (for kids) and the Santa Train (at Christmas). Reservations are essential in October, the busiest period because of the beautiful fall colors on display.

OIL CREEK STATE PARK

Don't be deterred by the name: this state park, located just north of Rynd Farm station and over the bridge, is green and attractive. The

park office (☎ 814-676-5915; www.dcnr.state.pa.us /stateparks/parks/oilcreek.aspx; ⏲ 8am-4pm Mon-Fri & 10am-6pm Sat & Sun) is at Petroleum Centre, an oil-industry hub during the 1860s boom – although today, with the area's restored natural beauty, you wouldn't know it.

The park has over 52 miles of hiking trails, including the 32-mile **Oil Creek Hiking Trail**, which follows the Oil Creek Valley from Drakes Well in the north to Rynd Farm in the south. There's also a 9.5-mile paved cycling trail; you can rent a set of wheels at Petroleum Centre on weekdays.

The trails provide access to remote parts of the park that are good for **bird-watching**. The creek also offers conditions for beginner-level **canoeing**, but the season only runs from March to June. In winter, there's **cross-country skiing**. If you're carrying in a picnic, you can use the pavilions, grills and restrooms at the **Blood Farm Day Use Area** (what is it with the names around here?).

PITHOLE

Speaking of dismal names... there isn't much left of Pithole, a ghost town off Rte 227 that's about 6 miles east of Oil Creek State Park. Here, you'll only find cellar holes on a hillside. The discovery of oil in January 1865 attracted many people, and the town was laid out the following May. By September, Pithole had 15,000 people, 57 hotels, a daily paper and the third-busiest post office in the state. When the oil ran out, so did the people. By the following year, the population had rapidly reduced to 2000, and in 1870, it was down to only 281. Since then, nature has reclaimed most of the land.

Sleeping

For camping in the area, try the Oil Creek Campground (p387). In town, there aren't many accommodation options, so consider yourself lucky if you're here in high season: between May and the end of October, you can stay at the delightful **Caboose Motel** (☎ 800-827-0690; www.octrr.org/caboosemotel; 407 S Perry St; d $90; 🅿 🖧). Located next door to the train station of the Oil Creek & Titusville Railroad, the motel comprises 21 caboose cars that have been turned into cozy guest rooms with TVs and bay windows. Each caboose has a story that's explained on the website. If you're looking for a bit of quirky Americana on your road trip – or if you had a fascination with trains in your childhood – this is about the most memorable budget hotel you're going to find.

THE WORLD'S FIRST OIL WELL

When we think of oil, we usually think of the Middle East, Texas or the North Sea, but today's mammoth oil industry had its humble beginnings back in the mid-19th century in Titusville, Pennsylvania.

For thousands of years, Native Americans had petroleum in medicine and paint. They collected it from springs or along the tops of creeks, where it appeared naturally. In the 19th century, European Americans used it in its natural, foul-smelling state as a medicine, to grease wagon wheels and to burn for light. By the early 1850s, whale oil was becoming scarce, and people began refining petroleum into kerosene.

In 1859, the Seneca Oil Company was leasing a natural-oil spring in the Oil Creek Valley near Titusville; wanting to increase production, it sent Edwin Drake to accomplish the task. He first dug for oil, then he decided to drill, so he recruited William 'Uncle Billy' Smith, a salt-well driller from near Pittsburgh, to build the well.

Smith built a derrick, engine house and steam engine. Drilling began in June, but was unsuccessful until Drake hit on the idea of driving a cast-iron pipe down into the rock first, then drilling inside it. On August 26, the drill bit hit a cavity; the drilling material was pulled out and work was stopped for the day. The next morning, when Uncle Billy went to check the well, he found it full of oil. After a pump was attached, the well yielded 20 barrels a day – double that of any other production method at the time.

Oil speculators soon followed Drake, and many wells were dug in the area along Oil Creek at places such as Petroleum Center and Pithole. By 1862, the region was producing thousands of barrels of oil daily, driving the price of oil so low that Drake's well proved unprofitable and had to be shut down.

Eating

You'll see several fast-food places along Seneca St.

For a good cappuccino or a light lunch, pop into the adorable **Spilling the Beans Coffee House** (☎ 814-677-1177; www.spillingthebeanscoffee.com; 2 W Front St; snacks $2-7; ☻ 6am-6pm Mon-Fri, 7:30am-3pm Sat & Sun; ♿). The outdoor patio is a great place to relax with a newspaper when the weather is warm. For pizza and pasta in a casual, family-friendly setting, try **Genova Pizza** (☎ 814-677-7283; 351 Seneca St; pizzas $12-20). For something a bit more upscale, head over to **Yellow Dog Lantern Restaurant** (☎ 814-676-1000; 218 Elm St; mains $14-26) for gourmet pastas and grilled fish.

Getting There & Away

Rte 62 heads west to I-79; Rte 8 runs south to I-80. If you're coming into Oil City from the Pittsburgh Area, take the Clarion exit off I-79 onto I-80 East. Then take the Barkeyville exit onto Rte 8 North and follow it through Franklin into Oil City.

Getting Around

Venango Bus Public Transport (☎ 814-677-0818) operates the local bus service Monday to Saturday. Schedules are available from the visitors' center. Fares within Oil City and to the nearby towns of Franklin and Cranberry are $1.50.

HERMITAGE & SHARON

pop 31,200

There's only one real reason that out-of-towners pass through Hermitage and its neighbor town of Sharon – it's because these towns near the Ohio border are home to a collection of 'world's largests.' Other than checking these places off an offbeat road-tripper's must-see list, there's little reason to stay here. Hermitage, in particular, is rather dull, with no real center other than the ugly commercial strip along Rte 62. Sharon, however, is an older town located on the Shenango River; with some fine old red-brick buildings on State St, the main street downtown, it has more aesthetic merit.

Information

The stylish **Mercer County Visitors Center** (☎ 800-637-2370; www.visitmercercountypa.com; 50 N Water Ave; ☻ 9am-5pm Mon-Fri, 9:30am-5pm Sat) is just off State St in downtown Sharon.

Sights

Lining the entry road into Hermitage's **Hillcrest Memorial Park** (2619 E State St) is the **Avenue of 444 Flags** (www.avenueofflags.com), the 'world's largest display of American flags.' There's one flag for every day that the 52 US citizens from the US Embassy in Iran were held hostage in 1979–81; there are other American flags dedicated to people who served the community or country.

Next door, **Kraynak's Santa's Christmasland** (☎ 724-347-4519; www.kraynaks.com; 2525 E State St; ☻ 9am-5pm Mon-Sat) is said to be the largest Christmas store in the world. True or not, it does have a huge collection of artificial trees, trains, stuffed animals, toys, candy and animated figures.

In Sharon, **Daffin's Candies** (☎ 724-342-2892; www.daffins.com; 496 E State St, Rte 62; ☻ 9am-9pm Mon-Sat, 11am-5pm Sun; ♿) claims to be the 'world's largest candy store.' At the back, in a small room called the Chocolate Kingdom, are some large candy animals on permanent display including a 400lb chocolate turtle, a 125lb chocolate reindeer and a 75lb chocolate frog.

Also in Sharon, **Reyers** (☎ 724-981-2200; www.reyers.com; W State St) claims to be the 'world's largest shoe store.' In other words, if you can't find the perfect suede boots, running shoes or leather sandals here, you're one picky customer.

Festivals & Events

Hermitage hosts a few modest festivals, including the **Hermitage Arts Festival** (www.hermitage.net/calendar/index.html£art) in July and the **Holiday Light Parade** (www.hermitage.net/calendar/index.html£holiday) in late November. About 30 miles south of Sharon, in Ohio, is the noteworthy **Shaker Woods Festival** (www.shakerwoods.com; 1101 Timberline Dr, Columbiana, OH). Occurring during three weekends in August, the event features over 200 artists dressed in period clothing demonstrating old-fashioned crafts or performing music and dance. Grilled meats and vegetables are cooked over an open flame, adding to the old-fashioned charm. To get there, take 80 West to OH-11 S, then follow the signs to Columbiana.

Sleeping & Eating

Rte 62 is lined with ordinary motels. In Sharon, there's one notable gem: the **Buhl Mansion Guesthouse & Spa** (☎ 724-346-3046; www.buhlmansion.com; 422 E State St; d from $350; ✖ ☎)

This castlelike mansion built by steel magnate Frank Buhl is now a luxurious B&B with an original oak staircase and hand-painted murals; guest rooms all have large Jacuzzi tubs, down comforters and fireplaces. It's meant for romantic getaways, so no kids are allowed.

In Sharon, **Quaker Steak & Lube** (☎ 724-981-7221; www.quakersteakandlube.com; 101 Chestnut St; mains $6-15) is a former gas station converted into a restaurant that sells chicken wings in a variety of sauces, ranging from mild to atomic.

Getting There & Away

To arrive from I-80, take Rte 18 north to Sharon; from I-79, Rte 62 runs west to Hermitage and Sharon.

ALLEGHENY NATIONAL FOREST & AROUND

This sprawling wooded region is a recreational destination for families, cyclists and hikers. But it's not just another bunch of trees – as you'll read below, Allegheny National Forest had to fight for its life less than a century ago after large-scale deforestation.

When the 797-sq-mile Allegheny National Forest (ANF) was first proclaimed by President Coolidge in 1923, people called it the 'Allegheny Brushpatch' because it had been stripped of most of its timber in the late 19th and early 20th century. Thousands of acres of old-growth forest had been cut down for the shipbuilding and construction industries, and much of the land was polluted by oil exploration and iron smelting. The local wildlife population, as a result, was drastically reduced.

In the Great Depression of the 1930s, thousands of men were given work planting trees and combating the effects of pollution. The timber has since grown back, and today, the ANF consists mostly of hardwoods such as hemlock, maple, white ash, yellow poplar and black cherry. Under the management of the US Forest Service (USFS), parts of the ANF continue to be harvested, and Allegheny black cherry is one of the most valuable woods in the world.

The ANF is once again full of wildlife, including black bear, elk, deer, raccoon, fox, beaver, muskrat, turkey and grouse. Black bears aren't usually harmful unless you come between a mother and her cubs; generally, they can be scared off by yelling, waving and clapping. Don't keep food in your tent; bears have a keen sense of smell – keep it in a car or out reach by hanging it from a line 10ft above the ground between two trees.

Orientation

The US Army Corps of Engineers administers a series of lakes and dams in the region as part of a system of flood-control projects in the Allegheny and Upper Ohio River Valleys. The ANF also encompasses several state parks. The ANF, running along New York's southern border, sits on the rugged northwestern section of the Allegheny Plateau; the elevation of much of the area covered by the forest is between 1000ft and 2300ft.

The major landmark, the Allegheny Reservoir to the north, crosses the state border into New York. The southern end of the reservoir forks to form two bodies of water: to the east, Kinzua Bay stretches for 8 miles into the forest; to the west, the Allegheny River flows west, then south, marking the western boundary of the ANF. The Clarion River forms much of the forest's southern border.

PUNXSUTAWNEY PHIL

Punxsutawney, a town about 90 miles northwest of Pittsburgh, on Rte 36 near Rte 119, is home to the famous 'weather forecaster' Punxsutawney Phil, a groundhog. Groundhog is another name for woodchuck, which is a type of marmot.

According to legend, if Phil casts a shadow on Groundhog Day (February 2), winter will last six more weeks. The elaborate ceremony takes place at Gobbler's Knob, a hill just outside town, but for most of the year Phil lives in the children's library in Mahoning East Civic Center in town. In June, there's also the Groundhog Festival, when Phil is given a 'magic potion' to ensure that he lives a long time. For information on the ceremony and festival, call ☎ 800-752-7445 or 814-938-7700, or visit www.punxsutawneyphil.com.

Punxsutawney Phil was immortalized, of course, in the (classic?) 1993 film *Groundhog Day*, starring Andie MacDowell and Bill Murray.

Warren, west of the reservoir, is the main town in the region and is the best place to pick up supplies. There's a large supermarket in town, and if travelers want a taste of civilization after (or before) roughing it in the forest, it also has some restaurants and motels.

Kane, southeast of Kinzua Bay, is a major town to the east. The other principal settlements are Ridgway, in the southeastern corner of the ANF; Marienville, which is south-central; and Tionesta, in the southwest. At the forest's center is the village of Sheffield.

Rte 6 crosses the ANF from Warren through Sheffield then runs southeast to Kane. Rte 62 follows the ANF's western border and the Allegheny River south of Rte 6. Rte 66 runs southwest from Kane to Marienville and onto Cook Forest State Park.

Information

In Warren, the USDA Forest Service distributes information on activities and camping in the ANF through the **Warren County Visitors Bureau** (☎ 814-726-1222; www.wcvb.net; 22045 Rte 6; ☽ 8am-4:30pm Mon-Fri); the helpful staff also sells topographical maps of the region. The Forest Service also has an office at **Kinzua Point Information Center** (☎ 814-726-1290; ☽ 9am-4pm Fri-Sun Memorial Day-Labor Day), on Rte 59 at the fork of the Allegheny Reservoir, 9 miles east of Warren.

The USFS has a few ranger stations where you can get information. The best is **Bradford Ranger Station** (☎ 814-362-4613), at the junction of Rtes 321 and 59, 12 miles southwest of Bradford. Also of interest to campers and hikers is the **Allegheny National Forest Vacation Bureau** (☎ 800-473-9370; www.visitanf.com; 80 E Corydon St, Suite 114, Bradford; ☽ 8am-4pm); the agency provides maps, information on outdoor recreation and travel planning advice. Visit the website to download and print the current official visitors' guide. Most travelers plan on camping and bring their own equipment, but the ANF is happy to help you arrange cabin, hotel or B&B accommodations. No matter where you stay, be sure to stock up on insect repellent before heading into the forest. To get to the ANF Vacation Bureau, take Rte 219 to exit Elm & Forman St.

Sights

The **Allegheny Reservoir** is an 18¾-sq-mile lake held back by the Kinzua Dam (built in 1966), which together form part of a project to control flooding in the Allegheny and Upper Ohio River Valleys. Much of the land that is now underwater was granted to Chief Cornplanter (son of a Seneca woman and a Dutchman) in 1791. His descendants were removed from the land and sent to live in New York in the 19th century.

Below the dam, look for the **Kinzua Dam Visitor Center** (☎ 814-726-0164; 1205 Kinzua Rd; ☽ 9am-5pm), operated by the US Army Corps of Engineers. There are great views from **Jake's Rock**, near the Kinzua Dam, and at **Rimrock**, across Kinzua Bay on Rte 59.

The 13½-sq-mile **Hickory Creek** area, east of Tidioute, is a designated 'wilderness' and can be reached from the **Hearts Content Recreation Area**, which itself contains stands of old-growth hemlock and white-pine forest. The only other wilderness consists of seven islands on the Allegheny River between Buckaloons Recreation Area and Tionesta; they are collectively called the **Allegheny Islands Wilderness**.

The **Tionesta Lake** area is in the southwest corner of the ANF, about 15 miles northeast of Oil City. The natural lake, fed by the Allegheny River and Tionesta Creek, is surrounded by 2000 acres of old-growth forest. The **visitors' center** (☎ 814-755-3512; 477 Spillway Rd; ☽ 10am-4pm Memorial Day-Dec) in Tionesta has information on the lake and hiking trails. At the eastern end of the lake, near the Nebraska Bridge, is a usually submerged **ghost town**. You can only see it when the water is particularly low; even the bridge itself is sometimes underwater.

To the south, in **Cook Forest State Park** (☎ 814-744-8407; www.dcnr.state.pa.us/stateparks/parks/cookforest.aspx; 113 River Rd, Cooksburg), is the Forest Cathedral Natural Area, which contains one of the largest old-growth forests of white pine and hemlock in Pennsylvania. Many trees exceed 3ft in diameter and approach 200ft in height. About 30 miles southeast of the ANF and east of the town of Benezette, off Rte 555, is **Elk State Forest** (☎ 814-834-3723; www.dcnr.state.pa.us/forestry/state forests/elk.aspx). Here roam over 300 wild wapiti (elk), which were introduced from the west (the eastern wapiti became extinct in the 19th century). The best time to see them is in the early morning or late afternoon.

Both of these parks are technically open year-round, though they all but close down in winter; visit the parks' websites for more information on current activities and camping opportunities.

Activities

HIKING

There are over 600 miles of hiking trails throughout the ANF, and you can camp along most of them. The **Warren County Visitors Bureau** (☎ 814-726-1222; www.wcvb.net; 22045 Rte 6, Warren) and the ranger stations (see Information, p392) have trail maps, topographical maps and information on conditions. For guidebooks, check out *Fifty Hikes in Western Pennsylvania*, by Tom Thwaites.

The 86.8-mile section of the **North Country National Scenic Trail** is the longest in the ANF. To the south, it connects with Baker Trail in Cook Forest, and to the north to trails in Allegheny State Park in New York. The trail enters the ANF west of Marienville and runs north to the New York border. For more information or to arrange for a trail guide, contact the **North Country Trail Association** (☎ 866-445-3628; www.northcountrytrail.org).

Other good trails include the 16.7-mile **Mill Creek Loop Trail**, just south of the Twin Lakes recreation area, near Kane; the 14.7-mile **Twin Lakes Trail**, between the Twin Lakes recreation area and the North Country National Scenic Trail; the **Beaver Meadows Trail System**, near the Beaver Meadows recreation area, which is north of Marienville (it's a 7.1-mile system of five interconnecting trails); and the 11.6-mile **Hickory Creek Trail**, which starts near Hearts Content campground and loops through the wilderness between Middle Hickory and East Hickory Creeks.

CANOEING

April through October, the reservoirs, lakes, rivers and creeks of the ANF offer opportunities for novice and experienced paddlers. There are plenty of boat-launching sites, campgrounds and outfitters renting canoes and equipment. A reliable outfitter to try is **Allegheny Recreational Rentals** (☎ 814-817-1283; http://rentrecreation.com; 217 W Washington St, Bradford; daily canoe rental $20). It also rents camping supplies, fishing equipment, GPS devices and scooters. You'll find similar outfitters in and around Warren and Tionesta; some offer two-to three-day guided trips on the Allegheny River that include camping.

The **Allegheny Reservoir** has 91 miles of shoreline, and there are free boat ramps at the Kiasutha, Willow Bay and Dewdrop campgrounds, as well as at the Elijah Run and Roper Hollow launch sites. It's a pleasant 45-mile float on the calm **Allegheny River** south from Kinzua Dam at the reservoir to Tionesta, where the river curves westward, away from the forest. **Tionesta Creek** is a calm 45-mile run through scenic wilderness from Chapman State Park (5 miles south of Warren) to Tionesta Dam, near Tionesta. The water level from Sheffield to the dam is too low to paddle after mid-May or early June. The creek partially follows Rte 6, then Rte 666.

The **Clarion River** can be paddled for 60 miles from Ridgway to its confluence with the Allegheny River. The first 19 miles of the float (from Ridgway to Hallton) are faster water and have four rapid areas that the park service classifies as 'intermediate' until mid-May. The first rapid is 6 miles south of Ridgway, near a railroad trestle – beware of the underwater pipe beneath the trestle. The other rapids are at the 15-, 15.5- and 16-mile points. These three rapids are known as 'X,' 'Y' and 'Z.'

For 12 miles, **Brokenstraw Creek**, between Spring Creek (about 15 miles west of Warren) and the Allegheny River near Buckaloons campground, has some of the best fast-water canoeing. **Beaver Meadows Lake**, a small lake in the Beaver Meadows recreation area, just 5 miles southwest of Clarendon, is good for wildlife-watching and has a campground and canoe launch.

The 805-acre **Chapman State Park** (☎ 814-723-0250; www.dcnr.state.pa.us/stateparks/parks/chapman.aspx), about 5 miles southwest of Clarendon, has a small lake where the Tionesta Creek begins and is good for flat-water paddling. Contact the park office for details.

CROSS-COUNTRY SKIING

The ANF has 54 miles of ski trails, with additional trails in nearby state parks and forests. **Laurel Mill Trail** (11.6 miles), starting about 2 miles west of Ridgway on Spring Creek Rd, is the longest within the national forest and offers easy to intermediate skiing. It's groomed when conditions allow it. Outside the ANF, the more challenging **Quehanna Trail**, southeast past Benezette in **Moshannon State Forest** (☎ 814-765-0821; www.dcnr.state.pa.us/forestry/stateforests/moshannon.aspx), is much longer at 73 miles.

BIRD-WATCHING

The ANF provides a variety of habitats for birds, from the frequently seen red-winged blackbird to the less common bald eagle. Migrating raptors and waterfowl arrive in

PENNSYLVANIA

early March, and songbirds arrive in mid-April. A comprehensive checklist indicating the seasonal presence of bird types is available from the USFS. Some good viewing spots are along the Allegheny and Clarion Rivers, the North Country National Scenic Trail, the Allegheny Reservoir and Tionesta Lake.

FISHING
The ANF has some of the best fishing in the country's northeast, combining as it does the Allegheny Reservoir, many small lakes and the Allegheny River and its tributaries. Fish vary from walleye and muskellunge in the Kinzua Dam to brook and brown trout in the mountain streams. For information, check with the **Warren County Visitors Bureau** (☎ 814-726-1222; www.wcvb.net; 22045 Rte 6, Warren) and the ranger stations; call the 24-hour **fishing hotline** (☎ 814-726-0164) for water conditions. Licenses are available from campgrounds, bait shops and gas stations.

Sleeping
Camping is allowed for a maximum of 14 continuous days on ANF land, including along hiking trails. There's no camping within 1500ft of the Allegheny Reservoir, except in developed campgrounds.

The campgrounds are rated from grade 1 (where campgrounds are walk-in only, have no water or toilets and usually involve no fee) to grade 5 (where campgrounds are accessed by paved roads, have electricity, hot showers, interpretive programs and sites for RVs). Fees at most designated camping areas vary from $14 to $22, depending on facilities. You can make reservations through the **National Recreation Reservation System** (NRRS; ☎ 877-444-6777; www.recreation.gov), which charges a reservation fee. If you're looking for a last-minute site, call **Bradford Ranger Station** (☎ 814-362-4613). Most of the higher-grade campgrounds are open mid-April to mid-December, while the lower-level ones are open all year.

Many of the designated maintained campgrounds are near the Allegheny Reservoir: Tracy Ridge and Willow Bay, close to the New York border, are accessible by car, but four others are only accessible by boat or on foot – Hooks Brook, Handsome Lake, Hopewell and Pine Grove. Near Kinzua Bay, on the southeastern fork of the reservoir that stretches toward Kane, there are developed campgrounds at Kinzua Beach, Dewdrop, Kiasutha, and

Red Bridge, but Morrison is only accessible by boat or on foot.

Close to the Allegheny River, there are campgrounds at Buckaloons and Hearts Content. Other campgrounds are at Twin Lakes, south of Kane; Beaver Meadows, 5 miles north of Marienville; Loleta, 6 miles south of Marienville; Minister Creek, in the center of the forest off Rte 666; Chapman State Park, operated by the state; and Tionesta Lake, near the town of Tionesta.

There are also many privately operated campgrounds in the region. Contact the **Northern Alleghenies Vacation Region** (☎ 800-624-7802; 315 Second Ave) tourist office in Warren.

Getting There & Away
The nearest intercity buses stop at Oil City and Erie and at Jamestown, NY. You'll need your own wheels to get around.

Rte 6 runs east of I-79 to Warren and through the ANF to Kane. From Erie, take Rte 19 south to Rte 6 east, or take I-90 north to Rte 17 east to Jamestown, NY, where it hooks up with Rte 60/62 south to Warren. Rte 62 runs northeast, from Oil City along the Allegheny River and the western perimeter of the ANF to Warren, then on to New York state.

From Pittsburgh, take Rte 28 north to I-80 at Brookville, where it meets Rte 36, which runs northwest to Tionesta. Northeast off Rte 36, Rte 949 leads to Ridgway, while Rte 899 heads north to Marienville.

ROUTE 6: ALLEGHENY NATIONAL FOREST TO SCRANTON
Rte 6, otherwise known as the Grand Army of the Republic Hwy in honor of the Civil War fallen, is a designated National Recreational Trail. It traverses more than 400 miles across the north of the state through some of Pennsylvania's most beautiful scenery. With the fall colors of the forests, mid-September through October is a particularly good time to visit.

Sights
KINZUA RAILROAD BRIDGE
Just east of the ANF, the 301ft-high Kinzua Railroad Bridge, in Kinzua Bridge State Park, stretches 2053ft across the Kinzua Creek Valley. The second-highest railroad viaduct in the US and the fourth-highest in the world, it's fairly spectacular – though not what it once was. The **Knox & Kane Railroad** used to

run steam trains from Kane and Marienville across the bridge; unfortunately, a tornado ripped through the area in 2003, damaging the viaduct and the state couldn't afford to repair it. A few years later, sadly, arsonists set fire to the sightseeing train cars. Now a private corporation owns the tracks, and unfortunately they have no interest in restarting tourist rides on this famous railroad.

To get to the bridge, follow Rte 6 northeast of Kane until just past the town of Mt Jewett, then take the first road north (left) to the park.

SUSQUEHANNOCK TRAIL SYSTEM

About 60 miles east of Kane, this 85-mile system heads south off Rte 6. It's a series of old railroad grades and logging and fire trails that loop through the 412-sq-mile Susquehannock State Forest and connects with the 42-mile **Black Forest** and 100-mile **Donut Hole** trails further south. A map and information are available from the office at the entrance (open daily 8am to 4pm) or from the state's **District Forester** (☎ 814-274-8474).

DENTON HILL SKI AREA

In the northern tip of Susquehanna State Forest is the Denton Hill State Park and **Ski Denton** (☎ 814-435-2115; www.skidenton.com; all-day lift ticket adult/child $42/29), a downhill and cross-country skiing area. It has night skiing and some of the steepest slopes in the northeast; ski rentals and lessons are available as well as snow tubing for kids. Five luxury chalets accommodate up to six people each; each costs $150 a night and guests get lift tickets on discount. Contact Ski Denton for availability.

In warmer weather, the area becomes a mountain biker's paradise, with ski lifts carrying cyclists high up the mountain. An eight-hour lift ticket for this summertime activity costs $25.

The state park is located about 7 miles east of Coudersport on Rte 6.

PENNSYLVANIA LUMBER MUSEUM

Fans of *Northern Exposure* or hipster lumberjack gear should drop by this **museum** (☎ 814-435-2652; www.lumbermuseum.org; 9am-5pm Wed-Sun). Opposite the entrance to Ski Denton, it showcases the history of logging in the region and includes a restored logging camp, a steam-powered sawmill, a nature trail and a picnic area.

PINE CREEK GORGE

Known to tourists as Pennsylvania's 'Grand Canyon,' this striking natural feature is a 47-mile-long valley that reaches a depth of 1450ft at Waterville to the south near Williamsport. Off Rte 6, you can reach the canyon south from Ansonia or by taking Rte 660 west from Wellsboro.

Pine Creek Gorge passes through **Leonard Harrison State Park** and **Colton Point State Park**, both of which offer camping from early April to mid-October. There's whitewater rafting and canoeing in spring on Pine Creek when the water is high enough, and the state parks also have short hiking and horseback-riding trails.

From Ansonia, the 30-mile **West Rim Trail** roughly follows the creek south to meet the 190-mile **Mid-State Trail** just north of Blackwell.

WELLSBORO
pop 3250

Ten miles east of Pine Creek, Wellsboro is the main town in the area and the seat of Tioga County. It's a picturesque place, with a tree-lined Main St lit at night by electric 'gaslights.' The **Tioga County Visitors Bureau** (☎ 717-724-0635; www.visittiogapa.com; 114 Main St; 9am-4:30pm Mon-Fri) offers information and maps on the area.

There are several lodging options in town. **Penn Wells Hotel & Lodge** (☎ 800-545-2446; www.pennwells.com; 62 Main St & 4 Main St; d in hotel/lodge from $130/136) is an old-world hotel with a bar and

KINZUA RAILROAD BRIDGE

From the mid-19th century, rapid industrial growth around Buffalo, NY, produced high demand for coal. The railroads carried the coal that fueled the fires of industry, heated homes and also powered the trains. But between Pennsylvania's coal and the awaiting industry to the north lay an obstacle – the Kinzua Valley.

The Kinzua Railroad Bridge was first built in 1882 to allow a branch of the Erie Railroad to ship coal north across the valley. Remarkably, it took a 40-man crew only 94 working days to complete what was at the time the world's highest viaduct and the longest rail viaduct. Completely rebuilt in 1900 to carry heavier loads, it was in service till 1959.

an elegant dining room that's open to the public; down the street is the more contemporary Penn Wells Lodge, featuring larger rooms and a fitness center with swimming pool.

The town also has appealing options for bagels, ice cream and casual meals. For two eggs and home fries, try **Wellsboro Diner** (www.wellsborodiner.com; 19 Main St; breakfast $4-10). Delicious burgers and draft beer are on offer at the **Gaslight** (☎ 570-724-1031; 35 Main St; mains $7-15).

MT PISGAH STATE PARK

This **state park** (☎ 570-297-2734; www.dcnr.state.pa.us/stateparks/mtpisgah.aspx) consists of 1302 acres along Mill Creek and at the foot of Mt Pisgah (altitude 2260ft); it features a series of short hiking trails, some of which become cross-country ski trails in winter. There's also canoeing and fishing on **Stephen Foster Lake** and swimming in a nearby pool. There are good views of the lake from a hilltop pavilion – a plum spot for a picnic.

The park is located 45 miles to the east of Wellsboro and 2 miles north of Rte 6 (the turnoff is in the village of West Burlington).

SCRANTON
pop 74,300

Steve Carell fans all over the world think they know what Scranton's like from the opening credits of *The Office*: bleak industrial parks, gray streets, a dive bar, ice-encrusted cars. But the city is a bit more than the home of the fictional Dunder Mifflin paper company (though it's worth noting that the show's creators, who adapted the British show for US television, specifically chose this city as a symbol of unpretentious middle-class America.)

First settled in 1771 and first known as Slocum Hollow, Scranton is an industrial city that was later named after Seldon Scranton, founder of the Delaware, Lackawanna & Western (DL&W) railroad in 1853. The city lies in Lackawanna Valley at the center of the anthracite coal-mining area that fueled northeastern Pennsylvania's iron and steel industries in the 19th century. Coal's heyday lasted till around 1950, when increasing road haulage and the introduction of diesel locomotives reduced demand for it. Since then, Scranton has successfully developed alternative industries, such as printing and electronics – Dunder Mifflin unbleached stationery stock, anyone?

Log onto the webpage of the **Lackawanna County Convention & Visitors Bureau** (☎ 570-963-6363; www.visitnepa.org) for visitor information and maps. There are several places to mail a postcard, including the central shopping center's **post office** (☎ 570-941-0502; Mall at Steamtown; 🕙 9am-5pm Mon-Fri, 9am-noon Sat); several ATMs can be found along Washington Ave.

Sights
STEAMTOWN NATIONAL HISTORIC SITE

The history of the railroads, both local and national, can be seen at the **Steamtown National Historic Site** (☎ 570-340-5200; www.nps.gov/stea; 150 S Washington Ave; admission $6; 🕙 9am-5pm, to 6pm July-Labor Day), in the former DL&W rail yard. The visitors' center comprises two museums covering technology and history; both display exhibits, audiotapes and films and information about the history of steam trains in Pennsylvania.

Outside is a working roundhouse (where steam trains were stored and repaired) and several operating steam locomotives. You can also take a 30-minute ride in a historic commuter car pulled by a vintage steam locomotive or a diesel-electric locomotive; the Scranton Limited runs from Wednesday to Sunday (with extra departures in July and August) and costs an additional $3 per person. It's a great activity for kids; little ones can also get involved with the Junior Ranger program. Inquire at the main office for more information on the above activities.

OTHER ATTRACTIONS

You can learn more about the fossil fuel and the life of the migrants who came to Scranton to mine it by visiting the **Pennsylvania Anthracite Heritage Museum** (☎ 570-963-4804; www.anthracitemuseum.org; Bald Mountain Rd, McDade Park; adult/child $6/4; 🕙 9am-5pm Mon-Sat, to 5pm Sun). Next door, a walking tour led by ex–coal miners is available 300ft down in the cool darkness of the former **Lackawanna Coal Mine** (☎ 800-238-7245; 🕙 10am-4:30pm Apr-Nov). Both are located in the 200-acre **McDade Park**, off Keyser Ave, west of town. To get there, take exit 57B off I-81 or exit 38 off I-476 (Pennsylvania Turnpike, Northeast Extension) and follow the signs.

Getting There & Away

Martz Trailways bus terminal (☎ 570-343-1265; www.martztrailways.com; 23 Lackawanna Ave) is opposite the Steamtown Mall; **Capitol/Bieber Trailways** (☎ 800-444-2877; www.capitoltrailways.com) and **Greyhound** (☎ 800-231-2222; www.greyhound.

buses also stop here. There are three daily buses to New York City ($48 one way, 2½ to three hours) and two to Philadelphia ($48 one way, four hours).

I-476 (Pennsylvania Turnpike, Northeast Extension) runs north directly to Scranton from Philadelphia. I-81 north and I-84 and Rte 6 east connect the city with New York State and New Jersey.

WILLIAMSPORT
pop 29,450
Once the center of a huge lumber industry that brought immense wealth to the region, Williamsport was first settled in the late 18th century. It became the main northern river port in the valleys of the Susquehanna. The industrial wealth made millionaires out of quite a few ambitious men, and toward the end of the 19th century, many built grand mansions along W 4th St near Campbell St – part of which today is known as Millionaires' Row.

Maps & Information
For information, contact the **Lycoming County Visitors Bureau** (☎ 800-358-9900; www.vacationpa.com; 210 William St) downtown.

Sights
Little League baseball began in Williamsport in 1939, and annually, in the third week of August, young baseball teams from around the world compete in the **Little League World Series** (www.littleleague.org). About 50,000 people line up annually in Williamsport for peanuts and applejacks. During the rest of the year, you can visit the **Little League Museum** (☎ 570-326-3607; www.littleleague.org/learn/museum.htm; Rte 15; adult/child $5/1.50; ⏰ 10am-5pm Mon-Sat, from noon in summer, hrs vary in low-season), about a mile south of town, which recounts the development of Little League baseball from its humble beginnings.

Getting There & Away
Susquehanna Trailways (☎ 800-692-6314; www.susquehannabus.com) has daily buses to Philadelphia and New York City.

Williamsport is located on Rte 15, about 16 miles north of I-80 along the western branch of the Susquehanna River.

THE POCONOS
A natural 'four-season' choice for nature, sports and outdoor enthusiasts, the Poconos are a touristy area, especially on weekends and in the fall, when visitors come to see the changing colors of the hardwood trees. Many people stay at the expensive resorts offering guided programs and a range of activities (as well as heart-shaped beds). However, the Poconos can be seen for a reasonably modest price if you do a little of your own research.

Orientation
Southeast of Scranton, and running northeast from Bucks County, are the Poconos, which contain 2400 sq miles of mountains, streams, waterfalls, lakes and an abundance of forest that is home to more than 100 varieties of trees and many rare species of plants and animals. The range of ecosystems found here, and the need to preserve them, led the Nature Conservancy to name the Poconos one of the world's '40 Last Great Places.' The name 'Pocono' comes from 'pocohanne,' a Lenape word meaning 'stream between the mountains.' The mountain region contains one state forest and eight state parks.

Information
The Poconos occupy the northeast corner of Pennsylvania, bordering New York and New Jersey. I-80, I-84 and Rte 6 head east and west through them, and Rte 191 runs north and south through most of the length of the region. The northeastern extension of the Pennsylvania Turnpike, I-476 (Rte 9), cuts through the southeastern corner.

Stroudsburg, at the intersection of several highways, including I-80, is the main commercial center in the Poconos. The **Pocono Mountains Vacation Bureau** (☎ 570-421-5791; www.800poconos.com; 1004 Main St, Stroudsburg; ⏰ 9am-5pm Mon-Fri) operates several information centers throughout the region and distributes travel guides tailored to special interests like skiing, camping, golf and watersports. If you're heading to the Poconos in autumn, be sure to check out the website's fall foliage reports to find out where you can view the most dazzling display of orange, red and yellow leaves.

JIM THORPE
pop 4680
The small, scenic town of Jim Thorpe – set in the hillside rising above the Lehigh River – is one of the prettiest in Pennsylvania. Originally settled in 1815 as Mauch Chunk (Bear Mountain), in 1954 it combined with

the neighboring town of East Mauch Chunk and changed its name to Jim Thorpe, in honor of the great Native American athlete (see the boxed text). Many of its early buildings are still intact.

Log onto the webpage of the **Jim Thorpe Chamber of Commerce** (☎ 570-325-5810; www.jimthorpe.org) for historical information as well as dining and shopping listings. On Race St is **Stone Row**, a collection of original row houses built in 1849 by Asa Packer (1805–79), a wealthy industrialist who founded the Lehigh Valley Railroad and Lehigh University. You can also visit his 18-room Italianate **mansion** (☎ 570-325-3229; www.asapackermansion.com; ⓥ 11am-4pm late May-Oct), built in 1861 and constructed over a cast-iron frame. To get there, head up Packer Hill off Lehigh Ave. On Rte 903, about half a mile east of town, is the **Jim Thorpe Memorial**, the athlete's final resting place.

Outdoor recreation is available at **Mauch Chunk Lake State Park** (☎ 570-325-3669; 625 Lentz Trail), 3 miles southwest of town, and **Beltzville State Park** (☎ 610-377-0045; 2950 Pohopoco Dr, Lehighton), about 7 miles east of town.

DELAWARE WATER GAP NATIONAL RECREATION AREA

Administered by the NPS, this 37-mile-long, 109-sq-mile national recreation area straddles the Delaware River. It's on the border with northwestern New Jersey (see also p247) and is full of opportunities to hike, mountain bike, ski, canoe, raft, sail, view wildlife and camp.

Orientation & Information

The **visitor center** (☎ 570-476-0167; www.delawarewatergap.com; ⓥ 9:30am-5:30pm Mon-Thu, to 6:30pm Fri, to 4:30pm Sun, weekends only Oct-Apr) at Delaware Water Gap (take exit 53 off I-80) has information on the Poconos and the National Recreation Area (NRA). There are also visitor centers in Marshalls Creek, Tannersville, White Haven, Hickory Run and Hawley.

The 'gap' itself, at the southern end of the NRA, is a 1400ft-high chasm formed by the Delaware River cutting its way through the Kittatinny Mountains. Promoted as 'Pennsylvania's Niagara Falls,' **Bushkill Falls**, north of Bushkill off Rte 209, is a series of eight waterfalls, the largest of which drop 100ft over siltstone and shale. Further north, **Dingman's Falls**, off Rte 739, is the highest in the state at 130ft.

Sights & Activities
HIKING
Ranging in difficulty from novice to expert, the Poconos have more than 116 maintained hiking trails that can be used for overnight or day excursions. These trails include about 25 miles of the **Appalachian Trail** in the New Jersey section of the Delaware Water Gap NRA, which itself has more than 60 trails. Several state parks offer hiking and camping, including **Hickory Run State Park** (☎ 570-443-0400; www.dcnr.state.pa.us/stateparks/parks/hickoryrun.aspx), near White Haven, which has 45 miles of trails. **Promised Land State Park** (☎ 570-676-3428; www.dcnr.state.pa.us/stateparks/parks/promisedland.aspx), further north near Greentown, has 29 miles of trails.

MOUNTAIN BIKING
The Poconos have a variety of mountain-biking facilities, and many Pocono resorts offer bicycle riding (check in the *Poconos Vacation Guide* at the Vacation Bureau, p397). Biking trails range from forest paths to canal towpaths and abandoned railroad beds. In **Lehigh Gorge State Park** (☎ 570-443-0400), near Jim Thorpe, bicyclists can traverse 25 miles of gentle grades along the western bank of the Lehigh River through the Lehigh Gorge. Nearby, the steep, 15-mile **Switchback Gravity Railroad Trail** is an abandoned railroad bed, which begins on Hill Rd in Jim Thorpe.

Bike rental is available in Jim Thorpe. **Blue Mountain Sports** (☎ 800-599-4421; www.bikejimthorpe.com; 34 Susquehanna St) charges $27 a day; skis, kayaks and snowshoes are also available for rent.

SKIING
The Pocono Mountains have a number of large ski areas. **Camelback** (☎ 800-233-8100; www.skicamelback.com; Tannersville) is in Big Pocono State Park, just south of I-80. It has 33 trails, a vertical drop of 800ft and snowboarding facilities. North of Stroudsburg, **Shawnee Mountain** (☎ 570-421-7231; www.shawneemt.com; Shawnee on Delaware) offers 23 trails and a vertical drop of 700ft. Close to each other on either side of I-80 northeast of White Haven are **Jack Frost & Big Boulder Ski Areas** (☎ 570-443-8425; www.jtfbb.com). The vertical drop at Big Boulder is 475ft at Jack Frost, the drop is 600ft. The resort's website and information line give details on lodging options.

Cross-country ski trails can be found in the resorts, and many hiking trails in state parks and forests become cross-country ski trails in winter.

WATERSPORTS

Mauch Chunk Lake and Lake Wallenpaupeck are two of the many lakes offering opportunities for **sailing** and **canoeing**. For the more adventurous, there's whitewater canoeing and **rafting** on the Lehigh River through the Lehigh Gorge and on the Delaware River. A number of companies provide rentals and guided trips. **Kittatinny Canoes** (☎ 800-356-2852; www.kittatinny.com), at Dingman's Ferry, has guided canoeing, kayaking and rafting trips that start around $43 per person. **Pocono Whitewater Adventures** (☎ 570-325-3655; www.whitewaterrafting.com; 1519 State Rte 903, Jim Thorpe) has guided day trips for $49. **Adventure Sports** (☎ 570-223-0505; Marshalls Creek) and **Lehigh Rafting Rentals** (☎ 800-443-7238; www.lehighrafting.com; White Haven) rent equipment and run guided trips from $46.95 per person.

Sleeping

The Poconos offer luxury resorts (including the 'couples resorts,' with their heart-shaped pools and beds for honeymooners) and family resorts offering room-and-recreational packages, but there are also many regular hotels, motels, B&Bs, housekeeping cottages, small country inns and campgrounds. The *Poconos Vacation Guide*, available from the Pocono Mountains Vacation Bureau (see p397) has a listing of accommodations, and you can reserve a room by calling ☎ 800-722-6667. Prices often rise on weekends and public holidays.

CAMPING

Several state parks offer camping. **Hickory Run State Park** (☎ 570-443-0400; www.dcnr.state.pa.us/stateparks/parks/hickoryrun.aspx), south of the junction of I-80 and I-476/Rte 9 (Pennsylvania Turnpike, Northeast Extension) and **Promised Land State Park** (☎ 570-676-3428; www.dcnr.state.pa.us/stateparks/parks/promisedland.aspx), off I-84, have lots of campgrounds with toilets and showers, as well as more primitive sites. **Tobyhanna State Park** (☎ 570-894-8336; www.dcnr.state.pa.us/stateparks/parks/tobyhanna.aspx), off Rte 423, has 140 sites; rates at the above campgrounds run from $22 to $36.

Hemlock Campground (☎ 570-894-4388; www.hemlockcampground.com; 362 Hemlock Dr, Tobyhanna), off Rte

---

JIM THORPE, HOMETOWN HERO

Born in Oklahoma in 1888 and given the name Bright Path, Jim Thorpe was a Native American who became one of America's greatest athletes. At the 1912 Olympic Games in Stockholm, he won both the decathlon and the pentathlon, breaking many records in the process. Unfortunately, soon after, despite protesting that he didn't know he had been breaking any rules, he was stripped of his medals for having played professional baseball (for $60 a month) and thereby forfeited his amateur sporting status.

Between 1913 and 1919, he played on three major-league baseball teams, including the New York Giants, and from 1915, he played professional football. In 1920, he became the first president of the American Professional Football Association (later renamed the National Football League). When he gave up professional sport in the mid-1920s, he found it difficult to adjust and went to Hollywood, lured by promises of stardom, but the Depression arrived, and he was only able to find work as a laborer. Alcohol eventually got the better of him, and by 1951, he was penniless, having spent much of his money on his fellow Native Americans or having otherwise given it away.

After his death in 1953, his wife sought to have a memorial built in his honor. When neither his home state of Oklahoma, nor the town of Carlisle, PA, where he had gone to school, would help her, she approached the Pennsylvania communities of Mauch Chunk and East Mauch Chunk. She'd heard about them in the news, because their citizens were trying to save the towns by setting up a local economic development fund. The communities agreed to combine and change their name to Jim Thorpe in an effort to promote local tourism and to honor the man and his achievements.

Eventually, Jim Thorpe's Olympic records were restored, and his medals were given to his family. Today, his daughter, Grace, is campaigning to have him named the 'Greatest Athlete of the Century.'

611, is one of the many private campgrounds in the region. It has full facilities and well-spaced sites starting at $31. The secluded, wooded **Mt Pocono Campground** (☎ 570-839-8950; www.mtpoconocampground.com; 30 Edgewood Rd, Mt Pocono) is off Rte 196. It has a grocery store, hot showers and sites from $30.

HOTELS & GUESTHOUSES

Jim Thorpe has some beautiful old B&Bs; most are designed for couples and bringing children along is discouraged. Business Rte 209 south of town has more hotels.

Lantern Lodge (☎ 570-669-9433; www.lanternlodge.com; Rte 209; d $80; 🔀 🔥) A couple of miles outside of Jim Thorpe, this Italian-owned inn is clean and efficiently run. It's not as charming as the town's inns, but it welcomes children and has a good onsite restaurant (Italian, of course).

Angel of the Morning B&B (☎ 570-325-2961; www.angelofthemorningbb.com; 504 North St; d $125-145; 🔀) In a Victorian house filled with antiques, this couples-friendly inn is cozy and romantic – and the kind innkeeper, Rosemary, is happy to suggest places to eat or hike. There are only three bedrooms, so book ahead.

our pick **Inn at Jim Thorpe** (☎ 570-325-2599; www.innjt.com; 24 Broadway; d $135-179; 🔀 🛜 🔥) This ornate Victorian inn is more family-friendly than many other accommodations in town: it's possible to book adjoining rooms here. In addition to adding ecofriendly amenities (energy-saving lights and water-saving shower heads), the inn has recently added another building across the street, 55 Broadway, that has 55 charming minisuites and apartments with whirlpools, fireplaces, and large flat-screen TVs.

Defeo Manor (☎ 570-325-8777; www.manorbedandbreakfast.com; Opera House Sq; d $140-165; 🔀) This quaint Queen Anne–style B&B, which looks like a castle in the center of Jim Thorpe, offers two options: the Blue Room, furnished with a fireplace made of Victorian cherry wood, and a huge suite with a private turret. The hosts are happy to serve breakfast to your room if you like.

Eating

If you're packing for a picnic, you can pick up supplies in Stroudsburg, Jim Thorpe, Hazleton or Lehighton.

Molly Maguires Pub & Steakhouse (☎ 570-325-4563; www.jimthorpedining.com; 6 Hazard Sq; mains $6-17; 🍸) Jim Thorpe's oldest pub is a strikingly beautiful place; the original marble furnishings and hand-carved bar bring you back to another era. The numerous draft beers, spicy wings, burgers and steaks, not to mention lively happy hours and a new deck, bring the locals and tourists back every night.

FLOW Bar + Restaurant (☎ 570-325-8284; www.thecccp.org; 268 W Broadway; mains $14-28; 🍸 closed Mon & Tue) A minimalist eatery located in an old stone factory, FLOW is part of the Carbon County Cultural Project art center. The menu of pastas and salads changes constantly according to the local produce available; some tables are set over a stream that runs under the restaurant.

our pick **Albright Mansion** (☎ 570-325-9815; www.albrightmansion.com; 66 Broadway; breakfast/prix fixe $8/39) This atmospheric Civil War–era mansion is now famous for lavish breakfasts, English tea in the afternoons and elegant prix fixe dinners. Try the crepes stuffed with brandied pears and ground almonds – truly divine.

Getting There & Away
BUS

Susquehanna Trailways (☎ 800-692-6314; www.susquehannabus.com) operates part of the Greyhound network between Philadelphia and Scranton and stops in Jim Thorpe, Lehighton and Hazleton. The journey time to Philadelphia is 2¼ hours; fares and times aren't fixed, so contact the company ahead of time for information.

CAR & MOTORCYCLE

From Philadelphia, I-476 (Pennsylvania Turnpike, Northeast Extension) leads directly into the Poconos, as does I-80 from New Jersey and I-84 from New York. I-81 south from New York state (Binghamton) skirts Scranton to join I-380, which connects with both I-84 and I-80.

Directory

CONTENTS

ACCOMMODATIONS

This guide includes recommendations for all budgets, but it emphasizes midrange accommodations. Unless otherwise noted, 'budget' is considered under $125, 'midrange' $125 to $250 and 'top end' over $250. New York City is the main exception, where midrange starts at around $200.

Accommodation rates are based on standard double-occupancy in high season. These are a guide only. Special events, summer weekends and holidays can drive prices higher; in seasonal tourist spots, like Jersey Shore, low-season rates can be much lower.

Note: prices do not include hotel taxes and fees, which add 14% to 15%. When booking, always ask for the rate with tax.

Every hotel in the region has nonsmoking rooms, and an increasing number are 100% nonsmoking, so the nonsmoking icon (🚭) is not used. Accommodations catering to families take the child-friendly icon (👶). The wi-fi icon (📶) is used where wireless internet access is available in rooms, paid or free. The internet icon (💻) indicates an internet terminal is available for guest use.

Reservations are always advised, but outside of high-season tourist hotspots – when hotels can book up months ahead – you can usually find a room; it just may not be your preferred option. Many hotels offer specials on their websites, but low-end chains sometimes give a moderately better rate over the phone. Chain hotels also increasingly have frequent-flyer deals; ask when booking.

Travel agency websites (p415) are a good way to get discounted hotel rates.

B&Bs

B&Bs in the region are typically historic homes transformed into plush romantic retreats, serving full breakfasts and run by sociable, independent innkeepers; many re-create the Victorian era extravagantly. A few promote themselves as more casual, inexpensive 'European-style' B&Bs. B&Bs are competitively priced against the area's good hotels, ranging generally from $150 to $250, though top-end B&Bs styling themselves as special-occasion destinations charge more. Meanwhile, booking a room with shared bathroom in a casual B&B can be a bargain, with rates under $100.

B&Bs often close out of season, have minimum-stay requirements and may not take young children to preserve a romantic atmosphere; always call ahead to avoid surprises. Reservations are usually necessary. In addition to listings in this guide, check these national and regional websites:

Bed & Breakfast Inns Online (www.bbonline.com)
Bedandbreakfast.com (www.bedandbreakfast.com)
BnB Finder (www.bnbfinder.com)
Pennsylvania Mid-State B&B Association (www.bedandbreakfastpa.com)
Preferred Inns of New Jersey (www.njinns.com)
Select Registry (www.selectregistry.com)

Camping

Most federal lands and state parks offer camping (see Activities, p64, for agency websites).

'Primitive' campsites offer no facilities; these include free dispersed backcountry camping and hike-in sites (under $10 per site). In campgrounds, sites almost always provide toilets (flush or pit), drinking water, fire pits and picnic benches; some 'developed' campgrounds add hot showers, BBQs and RV sites, and have nicer facilities overall. Camping rates have risen recently: expect to pay $20 per site per night; most can be reserved in advance. Public campgrounds often have seven- or 14-night limits.

In New York and Pennsylvania, camping on most federal lands can be reserved through **Recreation.gov** (☎ in US 877-444-6777, international 518-885-3639; www.recreation.gov; no reservation fee). For New York state park campgrounds, make reservations with **ReserveAmerica** (www.reserve america.com); Pennsylvania state parks also have a separate **reservation service** (☎ 888-727-2757; www.pa.reserveworld.com). In New Jersey, make reservations directly with each state park; see the **New Jersey Division of Parks and Forestry** (www. njparksandforests.org).

Private campgrounds tend to cater to RVs and families (tent sites may be few and lack character); facilities may include playgrounds, convenience stores, swimming pools and other activities and supplies. Many have camping cabins, ranging from canvas-sided wooden platforms to log-frame structures with real beds, heating and private bathrooms.

In New York and Pennsylvania, **Kampgrounds of America** (KOA; ☎ 406-248-7444; www.koa.com; PO Box 30558, Billings, MT 59114-0558) has a range of private campgrounds. Each state also has a campground owners' association that lists its members:

New Jersey (www.newjerseycampgrounds.com)
New York (www.nycampgrounds.com)
Pennsylvania (www.pacamping.com)

Hostels
Hostels are not big in the Northeast. Upstate New York and Pennsylvania have a decent number, and there are choices in Manhattan and Philadelphia, but New Jersey has almost none. They are inexpensive, communal places to stay, with kitchens and the bonhomie of fellow travelers; rooms include sex-segregated dorms and private accommodations. These days, hostels often provide linens and forego 'chores,' though you are expected to clean up after yourself. Rates outside of cities run $10 to $25; city hostels can be $25 to $40.

A handful of hostels in New York and Pennsylvania are affiliated with **Hostelling International USA** (HI-USA; www.hiusa.org). For independent hostels, check listings with **Hostels.com** (www.hostels.com) and the **Hostel Handbook** (www. hostelhandbook.com).

Lodges
Lodges and mountain resorts are found throughout the Poconos, Adirondacks and Catskills. They exude a rustic upscale ambience, and typically offer restaurants, recreation centers (with pools, golf, tennis and so on) and facilities to help you access local activities. They tend to center around skiing in winter and lake swimming and golf in summer. Several are mentioned in this guide.

In addition, these regions offers tons of condominiums, either booked through resorts or independently. For the latter, see **Vacation Rentals by Owner** (www.vrbo.com). Condos are fully furnished houses or apartments; they are ideal for groups or extended stays.

An entirely different experience can be had by staying at a rural Pennsylvania farm; see **PA Farm Vacations** (www.pafarmstays.com) for more information.

Motels & Hotels
Motels were originally inexpensive 'drive-up rooms' along the highway, where you parked your car outside your door. Today, this remains their calling-card: motels tend to be cheaper, plainer accommodations, with exterior room doors opening onto a parking lot. Hotel rooms, meanwhile, open onto secured interior hallways, and they tend to be better furnished and well-kept.

That said, distinctions get blurred in all kinds of ways. The advent of national chains has meant that motels are often the equivalent of hotels in terms of upkeep and style. That's the appeal of a chain, after all; you know what to expect from the sign. In this book, we focus on independently owned properties, but all cities and most towns have a range of chain properties. As a rule the least expensive places are those just of highway exits.

The most notable trend today is fashionable 'boutique' properties: motels are being remade into funky, retro digs, and hotels reimagined as hip 'designer lifestyle' palaces. As you might expect, rates for these places range near the top.

BOOK YOUR STAY ONLINE

For more accommodations reviews and recommendations by Lonely Planet authors, check out the online booking service at www.lonelyplanet.com/hotels. You'll find the true, insider low-down on the best places to stay. Reviews are thorough and independent. Best of all, you can book online.

Advertised prices – 'rack rates' – can be lowered in all sorts of ways: first, check websites for internet-only deals; ask about discounts for age, student or military status, auto club membership, credit card or frequent-flyer programs; and inquire about extended-stay rates. Sometimes persistence alone wins the day.

Here is the contact information for some of the major chains:

BUDGET
Days Inn (☎ 800-329-7466; www.daysinn.com)
Motel 6 (☎ 800-466-8356; www.motel6.com)
Super 8 (☎ 800-800-8000; www.super8.com)
Travelodge (☎ 800-578-7878; www.travelodge.com)

MIDRANGE
Best Western (☎ 800-780-7234; www.bestwestern.com)
Choice Hotels (☎ 877-424-6423; www.choicehotels.com)
Hampton Inn (☎ 800-445-8667; www.hamptoninn.com)
Holiday Inn (☎ 800-465-4329; www.holidayinn.com)
Howard Johnson (☎ 800-446-4656; www.hojo.com)
Ramada (☎ 800-272-6232; www.ramada.com)

TOP END
Hilton (☎ 800-445-8667; www.hilton.com)
Hyatt (☎ 888-591-1234; www.hyatt.com)
Marriott (☎ 888-236-2427; www.marriott.com)
Radisson (☎ 888-201-1718; www.radisson.com)
Sheraton (☎ 800-598-1753; www.starwoodhotels.com/sheraton)
Westin (☎ 800-937-8461; www.starwoodhotels.com/westin)

ACTIVITIES

For a proper introduction to all of the outdoor activities in this region, see the Outdoor Activities chapter (p66). This section provides agencies, organizations, outfitters and web resources where you can learn more. For a list of state park and national land-

management agencies, see National & State Parks (p62).

Hiking & Backpacking
The Bicycling & Mountain Biking section has contact information for canalways and rails-to-trails.
Adirondack Mountain Club (☎ 518-668-4447, 800-395-8080; www.adk.org) The authority on New York's Adirondacks; books, topo maps and lots of online advice. Maintains trails and leads excursions.
Appalachian Mountain Club (☎ 800-372-1758; www.outdoors.org) America's oldest conservation and recreation organization; maintains Appalachian Trail in New York, New Jersey and Pennsylvania.
Appalachian Trail Conservancy (☎ 304-535-6331; www.appalachiantrail.org) Umbrella organization coordinates trail management with the NPS (www.nps.gov/appa); get through-hike advice and links to over 30 trail clubs.
Explore PA Trails (www.explorepatrails.com) State-run website lets you find info and maps on all kinds of trails – hiking, biking, skiing, canoeing and more.
Finger Lakes Trail Conference (☎ 585-658-9320; www.fltconference.org) Maintains extensive trail network in New York's Finger Lakes region, with maps and trail descriptions.
Keystone Trails Association (☎ 717-238-7017; www.kta-hike.org) Advocacy group for Pennsylvania trails, with trail descriptions and links to local and regional trail clubs.
Local Hikes (www.localhikes.com) Emphasizes hikes near cities and hiker reviews of trails, with photos and topo and driving maps. Wide-ranging coverage in this three-state region.
New York–New Jersey Trail Conference (☎ 201-512-9348; www.nynjtc.org) Advocacy group for New York metro region trails; get great trail descriptions and maps for Hudson River Valley, the Catskills and northern New Jersey; links to local clubs.
North Country Trail Association (☎ 866-445-3628; www.northcountrytrail.org) Maintains North Country National Scenic Trail, which includes a range of New York and Pennsylvania trails.
Urban Escapes (☎ 212-609-2547; www.urbanescapesnyc.com) Outdoor adventures for urban denizens in Manhattan and Philly, mixing Harriman hikes and Delaware and Lehigh River trips with brewery and winery tours.

Bicycling & Mountain Biking
Bike Adirondacks (www.bikeadirondacks.org) Touring and mountain bike routes in the Adirondacks; lists bike shops and events.
Bicycle Coalition of Greater Philadelphia (☎ 215-242-9253; www.bicyclecoalition.org) Advocacy group that

covers counties surrounding Philadelphia and southern Jersey. Essential for city cyclists.

Bicycle Touring Club of North Jersey (☎ 973-284-0404; www.btcnj.org) The largest cycling club in New Jersey; weekly rides.

Erie Canalway National Heritage Corridor (☎ 518-237-7000; www.eriecanalway.org) Complete recreation information.

Five Borough Bicycling Club (☎ 347-688-2925; www.5bbc.org) NYC-based club sponsors free day trips to all boroughs, plus weekend trips. Lots of links and general advice.

Henry Hudson Trail (www.monmouthcountyparks.com) Full info on this 22-mile multi-use trail running west from Highlands, New Jersey.

Lake Champlain Bikeways (☎ 802-652-2453; www.champlainbikeways.org) Mile-by-mile route info for the bike network surrounding Lake Champlain; lists shops and accommodations.

League of American Bicyclists (☎ 202-822-1333; www.bikeleague.org) National advocacy group publishes *American Bicyclist* magazine; touring advice and a database of local bike clubs and repair shops.

New York Bicycling Coalition (☎ 518-436-0889; www.nybc.net) Nonprofit advocacy group for New York cyclists; links to statewide clubs, shops and events.

Parks & Trails New York (☎ 518-434-1583; www.ptny.org) A nonprofit advocacy group with info on over 100 multi-use trails in New York. Links to many state and national groups.

Pedal PA Bicycle Touring (☎ 215-250-5758; www.pedalpa.com) Pennsylvania-based touring company with extensive links to bike clubs throughout the state.

Rafting, Kayaking & Canoeing

American Canoe Association (ACA; ☎ 540-907-4460; www.americancanoe.org) National nonprofit conservation organization, with great water trails and instructor database.

American Whitewater (☎ 866-262-8429; www.americanwhitewater.org) National nonprofit with flow reports and links to local paddle clubs in all three states.

Appalachian Mountain Club, Delaware Valley Chapter (www.paddlenow.com) Information and trips along and near the Delaware River.

Kayak Online (www.kayakonline.com) Good resource for kayak gear and outfitters in the region.

Northern Forest Canoe Trail (☎ 802-496-2285; www.northernforestcanoetrail.org) Great trip planner for Adirondack canoe trips, with lodging, outfitters and maps.

Philadelphia Canoe Club (www.philacanoe.org) Links to paddling clubs in the three-state region and organizes trips.

Susquehanna River Trail Association (www.susquehannarivertrail.org) Advocacy organization, with river descriptions and links to recommended outfitters.

Skiing

See destination chapters for information on ski resorts.

Cross-Country Ski Areas Association (www.xcski.org) Membership organization, with links to member resorts across the region.

Cross Country Skier (www.crosscountryskier.com) Magazine has ski center lists and trail reports.

Cross Country Ski Areas of New York (☎ 800-225-5697; www.crosscountryskinewyork.com) Statewide resource for ski centers.

Olympic Sports Complex at Mt Van Hoevenberg (www.whiteface.com) Lake Placid's Olympic Complex is active year-round.

High Point XC Ski Center (www.xcskihighpoint.com) High Point State Park has New Jersey's best ski center.

Pennsylvania Cross Country Skier's Association (www.paccsa.org) Statewide resource for ski centers.

Ski Resorts Guide (www.skiresortsguide.com) Comprehensive guide to resorts, with downloadable slope maps, lodging info, ticket prices and more.

SnoCountry Mountain Reports (www.snocountry.com) Snow reports and summer recreation by resort, with links.

Fishing

Nearly all fishing requires an appropriate license, but each state has dozens of different kinds. Regulations over what you can catch are even more complex and change regularly. As such, anglers need to spend a few minutes with the websites of the appropriate state agency, listed below. Licenses are available online. Note that a Delaware River fishing license is valid from any of the three states, and recreational anglers using licensed charter boats don't need their own license.

New in 2010, most saltwater and tidal fishing requires registration if you fish in federal waters, or catch anadromous species (saltwater fish that spawn in freshwater) such as river herring, shad and striped bass. See the national registry program for details.

National Saltwater Angler Registry Program (☎ 888-674-7411; www.countmyfish.noaa.gov)

NJ Division of Fish & Wildlife (☎ 908-637-4125; www.njfishandwildlife.com) For fishing permits.

NY Department of Environmental Conservation (☎ 518-402-8845; www.dec.ny.gov)

PA Fish & Boat Commission (☎ 717-705-7930; www.fish.state.pa.us)

Recreational Boating & Fishing Foundation (www.takemefishing.org) This national nonprofit is an all-in-one resource: get fishing guides, comprehensive advice and links to all fishing and boating regulations and permits by state.

Sailing

Rentals and training can be found in many centers. Many sailing schools also do rentals for properly certified sailors.

American Sailing Association (☎ 310-822-7171; www.asa.com) Promotes safe recreational sailing and lists sailing schools by state.

Sail NY (☎ 646-360-0048; www.sailny.org) The nonprofit New York City Community Sailing Association provides affordable sailing lessons and recreational sails.

Surfing & Windsurfing

Duke Storm (www.dukestorm.com) A coupla Jersey surfers report on the local scene.

NJ Surfing Club (www.njsurfingclub.com) Covers the Jersey coast, with swell reports, surf cams and lists of shops and lessons.

NY NJ Surf.com (www.nynjsurf.com) The surf community, with forecasts and lists of local shapers.

Surfrider Foundation (www.surfrider.org) Nonprofit advocacy and environmental group protecting beaches, with five chapters in NJ and NY.

For other boards sports – like windsurfing and kiteboarding – see these:

Adirondack Boardsailing Club (www.abcsail.org) Adirondack lake windsurfing, with great links to sights and groups throughout NY and NJ.

NJ Windsurfing & Watersports Association (www. windsurfnj.org) Covers all types of watersports on the Jersey shore.

US Kitesurfing Association (www.uskite.org) Links to local organizations.

US Windsurfing Association (ww.uswindsurfing.org) Links to local members.

Wildlife- & Bird-Watching

In addition to the state-run resources below, check state-park websites (see p62).

Audubon Society (☎ 212-979-3000; www.audubon. org) Links to local chapters in all three states.

Birding & Wildlife Trails (www.njwildlifetrails.org) Brochures on wildlife trails for bird-watching, sponsored by the NJ Audubon Society.

NJ Division of Fish & Wildlife (www.njfishandwildlife. com/wildlife.htm) Info on Jersey species.

NY Department of Environmental Conservation (www.dec.ny.gov) Click through to its New York's Watchable Wildlife program

Pennsylvania Wilds (www.pawilds.com) State-run website for wildlife viewing.

Rock Climbing

ADK Mountains (www.adkmountains.com) News and links to climbing guides and schools in the Adirondacks.

Gunks.com (www.gunks.com) A blog and community website all about the Catskill's Shawangunk Mountains.

PA Climbing (www.paclimbing.com) Blog and reviews of PA climbing sights, with guides.

Rock & Snow (☎ 845-255-1311; www.rockandsnow.com; 257 Main St; ⏰ 10am-4:30pm Mon-Fri) This store in New Paltz is a prime destination for Gunks climbers and guides.

BUSINESS HOURS

Unless there are variations of a half hour in either direction, the following are the opening hours for the listings in this book.

Banks 9am to 4:30pm or 5pm Monday to Friday, some also 9am to noon Saturday.

Bars and clubs Bars usually 5pm to midnight, to 2am on Friday and Saturday; clubs usually 9pm to 2am Wednesday to Saturday; hours may be longer in major cities.

Businesses 9am to 5pm Monday to Friday; some post offices also 9am to noon Saturday.

Restaurants Breakfast 6am to noon, lunch noon to 3pm or 4pm, dinner 5pm to 11pm or midnight.

Shops 10am to 7pm Monday to Friday, 11am to 8pm Saturday and Sunday; some close on Sunday; shopping areas and malls keep extended hours.

CHILDREN

Traveling with kids is easy in the region. Indeed, locals are often eager to help and connect with traveling families. In this book, hotels that cater to families are marked with the child-friendly icon (👶).

Practicalities

Restaurants of all stripes have high chairs; if they don't have a separate kid-tailored menu, they usually are happy to make something to order. Many diners and family restaurants break out paper placemats and crayons for drawing. Most public toilets have a baby changing table (sometimes in men's toilets too), and gender-neutral 'family' facilities are becoming more frequent in public buildings.

Motels and hotels typically have rooms with two beds, which are ideal for families. They also have 'roll-away beds' or 'cots' for an extra charge. Most chains and tourist hotels allow children to stay free; the age cutoff varies, ranging from 12 to 18. Some B&Bs, to preserve a romantic atmosphere, don't allow children; ask when reserving.

Car-rental agencies are required by law to provide an appropriate child seat or restraint, but you must request one when booking.

In addition, most tourist bureaus list local resources for children's programs, childcare facilities and so on.

Sights & Activities

This guide's full of kid-friendly museums, parks and amusements; see individual destinations and also New York with Children (p102).

For more outdoor advice, read *Kids in the Wild: A Family Guide to Outdoor Recreation* by Cindy Ross and Todd Gladfelter and *Parents' Guide to Hiking & Camping* by Alice Cary. For all-around information and advice, check out Lonely Planet's *Travel with Children*. Other useful resources:

Kids.gov (www.kids.gov) Eclectic, huge national resource; download songs and activities, and scan links to much more.

Parents Connect (http://gocitykids.parentsconnect.com) A Nickelodeon-sponsored website with excellent city-focused coverage of kid-centric play and resources; covers NYC, Philadelphia and Pittsburgh.

CLIMATE CHARTS

For general information on when to travel to the region, see When to Go (p18). Each state

chapter also has a Land & Climate section with more specific information. The **National Weather Service** (www.nws.noaa.gov) has an addictive array of radar and satellite maps. Our climate charts provide a snapshot of regional weather patterns.

DANGERS & ANNOYANCES

Ah, Gotham. You've heard of Babylon, and now you're here – and if you're standing in Times Square reading this, you'll wonder what all the fuss is about. Sure, there's lots of traffic, and annoying, jostling crowds blocking all the places you want to visit – but guns, violent crime, riots? Nah.

Crime

For the traveler, petty theft is the biggest concern, not violent crime. Pack your street smarts and you'll be fine. When possible, withdraw money from ATMs during the day

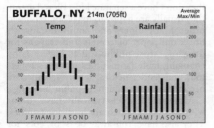
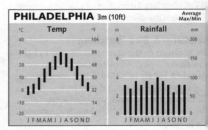
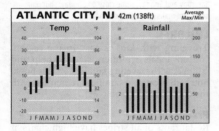
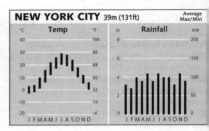
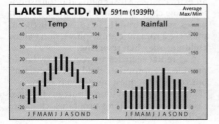
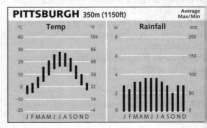

or at night in well-lit, busy areas; use a money belt and don't flash wads of cash around. When driving, don't pick up hitchhikers, and lock valuables in the trunk of your car (*before* arriving at your destination).

In hotels, locking valuables in your room safe or hotel safe is prudent, and don't open your hotel door to a stranger (if suspicious, call the front desk to verify who they are).

Guns, so prominent in the news, would seem to be everywhere, but you'll rarely see them outside of fall hunting season. Then again, if it *is* hunting season, check with park rangers and wear bright colors when hiking in the woods.

Scams

Spoiler alert! Those three-card-monte card games along Houston St are rigged, and the expensive electronics, watches and designer items sold on the cheap from sidewalk tables are either fakes or stolen. Those truly fascinated by all the myriad ways small-time American hucksters make a living (usually with credit card, real estate and investment frauds) should visit 'Consumer Guides' on the government's website, www.usa.gov.

Panhandlers

Unfortunately, all the East Coast's big cities, and even smaller ones like Atlantic City, have resident homeless populations. Seeing panhandlers on sidewalks asking for change can be upsetting and sometimes annoying, but they are almost never dangerous.

How you respond is a matter of conscience. To do more than give change and a smile, consider a donation to a charity that cares for the urban poor. For help finding a charity, visit **Charity Navigator** (www.charitynavigator.org).

DISCOUNTS

Travelers will find a plethora of ways to shave costs on hotel rooms, meals, rental cars, museum admissions and just about anything else that can be had for a price. Persistence and ingenuity go a long way when it comes to finding deals in America.

Students and seniors (generally age 60 and up) are not issued separate discount cards, but they benefit from savings of all kinds; typically savings are 10% to 15% off, but occasionally it can be 40% to 50%. Simply carry proof of age or student status; international students should consider getting

an **International Student Identity Card** (ISIC; www.isiccard.com), which provides its own discounts and should convince any dubious merchants of your student status. US students can buy the **Student Advantage Card** (www.studentadvantage.com). For US citizens 50 years and older, the **American Association of Retired Persons** (AARP; www.aarp.org) is another source of travel discounts. American seniors should seriously consider getting an **America the Beautiful Senior Pass** (www.nps.gov/fee_passes.htm), which allows free access to all federal lands and 50% off usage fees like camping. Buy online at http://store.usgs.gov/pass.

Auto-club membership (p419) comes with a raft of discounts; AAA also has reciprocal agreements with several international auto associations. Other people whose status might lead to discounts are war veterans, the disabled, children, business travelers and foreign visitors. These discounts may not be advertised – it always pays to ask.

Discount coupons paper every tourist locale. Read the fine print, as they always have conditions and restrictions. For hotels, browse **Roomsaver.com** (www.roomsaver.com).

FOOD

Reviews in Eating sections are typically broken down into three price categories: budget (for meals costing $12 or less), midrange (where most main dishes cost $12 to $25) and top end (where most main dishes cost more than $25). These price estimates do not include tax, tip or beverages. See the Tipping section, p410, for tipping advice.

For more on regional cuisine, see the Food & Drink chapter (p54).

GAY & LESBIAN TRAVELERS

New York City is out and proud, with one of the largest gay populations in the country, and throughout the region, tolerance is the rule and the level of openness tends to be high. Philadelphia and Pittsburgh also have visible gay communities. For highlights, see Gay & Lesbian New York (p109) and the Village People itinerary (p30).

Of course, generalizations are difficult, and bigotry exists. For instance, New York and New Jersey both recognize same-sex civil unions, but have failed to pass gay-marriage laws; more conservative Pennsylvania doesn't recognize civil unions and has never brought a gay marriage bill to a vote. In more socially conservative areas, like rural Pennsylvania and upstate New York, it can be best to follow a 'don't ask, don't tell' policy.

Damron (☎ 415-255-0404, 800-462-6654; www.damron.com) publishes several excellent travel guides, including accommodation and city guides. Other useful national resources:

Advocate (www.advocate.com)

Gay & Lesbian National Hotline (☎ 888-843-4564; www.glnh.org) A national hotline for help, counseling, information and referrals; see website for hours.

Gay Yellow Network (www.gayyellow.com) Yellow page listings for dozens of US cities.

Gay.com (www.gay.com) Comprehensive resource; lots of travel information.

National Gay and Lesbian Task Force (☎ 202-393-5177; www.thetaskforce.org) A national advocacy group; website has current news and lists of referrals.

Out Traveler (www.outtraveler.com)

Purple Roofs (www.purpleroofs.com) Lists queer accommodations, travel agencies and tours worldwide.

HOLIDAYS

See also the Events Calendar (p23)

On national public holidays, banks, schools and government offices (including post offices) are closed, and transportation, museums and other services are on a Sunday schedule. Holidays falling on weekends are usually observed the following Monday.

New Year's Day January 1
Martin Luther King Jr Day Third Monday of January
Presidents' Day Third Monday of February
Easter March or April
Memorial Day Last Monday of May
Independence Day July 4
Labor Day First Monday of September
Columbus Day Second Monday of October
Election Day Second Tuesday of November
Veterans' Day November 11
Thanksgiving Fourth Thursday of November
Christmas December 25

INSURANCE

It's expensive to get sick, crash a car or have things stolen from you in the USA. For more information on car-rental insurance, see p420. For health insurance, see p423.

If you have a home-owner's policy, check to see if, and to what extent, it covers items stolen from a rental car. If you have prepaid a large portion of your trip, cancellation insurance is a worthwhile expense. For information about types of coverage and rate comparisons, visit **Insure.com** (www.insure.com). Worldwide travel insurance is available at www.lonelyplanet.com/travel_services. You can buy, extend and claim online anytime – even if you're already on the road.

INTERNATIONAL VISITORS
Entering the Region

A passport is required for all foreign citizens. Unless eligible under the Visa Waiver Program (see p408), foreign travelers must also have a tourist visa. To rent or drive a car, travelers from non-English-speaking countries should obtain an International Drivers Permit before arriving.

Travelers entering under the Visa Waiver Program must register with the US government online (https://esta.cbp.dhs.gov) at least three days before arriving; earlier is better, since if denied, travelers must get a visa. Registration is valid for two years.

Upon arriving in the US, all foreign visitors must register in the US-Visit program, which entails having two index fingers scanned and a digital photo taken. For information on US-Visit, see the **Department of Homeland Security** (www.dhs.gov/us-visit).

VISAS

All visitors should reconfirm entry requirements and visa guidelines before arriving. You can get visa information through www.usa.gov, but the **US State Department** (www.travel.state.gov) maintains the most comprehensive visa information, with lists of consulates, and has downloadable application forms. **US Citizenship & Immigration Services** (www.uscis.gov) mainly serves immigrants, not temporary visitors.

The Visa Waiver Program allows citizens of certain countries to enter the USA for stays of 90 days or less without first obtaining a US visa. Currently, 36 countries participate: Andorra, Australia, Austria, Belgium, Brunei, Czech Republic, Denmark, Estonia, Finland, France, Germany, Greece, Hungary, Iceland, Ireland, Italy, Japan, Latvia, Liechtenstein, Lithuania, Luxembourg, Malta, Monaco, the Netherlands, New Zealand, Norway, Portugal, San Marino, Singapore, Slovakia, Slovenia, South Korea, Spain, Sweden, Switzerland and the UK. Under this program you must have a return ticket (or onward ticket to any foreign destination) that is nonrefundable in the USA. If your passport was issued or renewed after October 26, 2006, you need an 'e-passport' with a digital chip; otherwise, you need a machine-readable passport.

Visitors who don't qualify for the Visa Waiver Program need a visa. Basic requirements are a valid passport, recent photo, travel details and often proof of financial stability. Students and adult males also must fill out supplemental travel documents. Those planning to travel through other countries before arriving in the USA are better off applying for their US visa in their home country rather than while on the road.

The validity period for a US visitor visa depends on your home country. The actual length of time you'll be allowed to stay in the USA is determined by US officials at the port of entry. If you want to stay in the USA longer than the date stamped on your passport, visit a local **USCIS** (☎ 800-375-5283; www.uscis.gov) office well before the stamped date to apply for an extension.

CUSTOMS
Each adult visitor is allowed to bring 1L of liquor and 200 cigarettes duty-free into the USA. In addition, each traveler is permitted to bring up to $100 worth of gift merchandise into the USA without incurring any duty.

Embassies & Consulates
The **US Department of State** (www.usembassy.gov) website has links for all US embassies abroad.

Because the UN is in New York City, most countries maintain consulates in Manhattan.

Australia (Map p92; ☎ 212-351-6500; www.australian nyc.org; 150 E 42nd St)
Canada (Map p92; ☎ 212-596-1628; www.newyork. gc.ca; 1251 Ave of the Americas)
Denmark (Map p92; ☎ 212-223-4545; www.dknewyork .um.dk; 885 Second Ave, 18th fl)
Finland (Map p92; ☎ 212-750-4400; www.finland.org; 866 United Nations Plaza, Suite 250)
France (Map p96; ☎ 212-472-8110; www.consulfrance -newyork.org; 934 Fifth Ave)
Germany (Map p92; ☎ 212-610-9700; www.germany. info; 871 United Nations Plaza)
Ireland (Map p92; ☎ 212-319-2555; www.consulate ofirelandnewyork.org; 345 Park Ave, 17th fl)
Israel (Map p92; ☎ 212-499-5000; www.israelfm.org; 800 Second Ave)
Italy (Map p96; ☎ 212-737-7930; www.consnewyork. esteri.it; 690 Park Ave)
Japan (Map p92; ☎ 212-371-8222; www.ny.us.emb -japan.go.jp; 299 Park Ave, 18th fl)
Mexico (Map p92; ☎ 212-217-6400; 27 E 38th St)

Netherlands (Map p92; ☎ 212-246-1429; http:// ny.the-netherlands.org; 1 Rockefeller Plaza, 11th fl)
New Zealand (Map p92; ☎ 212-832-4038; www. nzembassy.org; 780 Third Ave)
Norway (Map p92; ☎ 212-421-7333; www.norway.org; 825 Third Ave, 38th fl)
Sweden (Map p92; ☎ 212-888-3000; www.sweden abroad.com; 445 Park Ave, 21st fl)
UK (Map p92; ☎ 212-745-0200; http://ukinusa.fco.gov. uk; 845 Third Ave)

INTERNET ACCESS
Few places are as plugged in as New York and the Northeast. Nearly every hotel and many restaurants and businesses offer high-speed internet access. In listings, icons indicate when hotels offer internet terminals (🖳) and in-room wi-fi (🛜); with few exceptions, hotels offer in-room plug-in and wi-fi in the lobby. Always ask about rates.

Most cafés offer inexpensive internet access, and most transportation stations and city parks are wi-fi hotspots. Public libraries also provide free internet terminals, though sometimes you must get a temporary non-resident library card ($10).

For a list of wi-fi hotspots (plus tech and access info), visit **Wi-Fi Alliance** (www.wi-fi.org) and **Wi-Fi Free Spot** (www.wififreespot.com). If you bring a laptop from outside the USA, invest in a universal AC and plug adapter. Also, confirm that your modem card will work.

LEGAL MATTERS
If you're stopped by the police for any reason, bear in mind that there's no system of paying fines on-the-spot. For traffic offenses, the police officer will explain your options to you. Attempting to pay the fine to the officer is frowned upon at best and may result in a charge of bribery. There is usually a 30-day period to pay a fine, and most matters can be handled by mail.

If you're arrested, you have the legal right to remain silent as well as to have access to an attorney; the legal system presumes you're innocent until proven guilty. There's no legal reason to speak to a police officer if you don't wish to, but never walk away from an officer. Any arrested person is legally allowed (and given) the right to make one phone call. If you don't have a lawyer or family member to help you, call your embassy or consulate. The police will give you the number on request.

Drinking & Driving

The minimum age for drinking alcohol is 21. You'll need a government-issued photo ID (such as a passport or US driver's license) to prove your age. Stiff fines, jail time and other penalties may be incurred if you're caught driving under the influence (DUI) of alcohol or providing alcohol to minors. The blood alcohol limit is 0.08%. During festive holidays and special events, road blocks with breathalyzer tests are sometimes set up to deter drunk drivers. Refusing a breathalyzer, urine or blood test is treated as if you'd taken the test and failed.

MAPS

For a good road atlas, try **Rand McNally** (www. randmcnally.com) and its Thomas Brothers city guides, as well as the state gazeteers by **DeLorme** (www.delorme.com); both can be found in most bookstores. If you are a member of **AAA** (www. aaa.com) or one of its international affiliates, you can get AAA's high-quality free maps from any regional office. Another online resource for driving directions and free downloadable maps is **Google Maps** (http://maps.google.com).

Map geeks and backcountry hikers wanting topo maps can find them at good bookstores and at national parks and many state parks. Or order them from **Trails.com** (www.trails.com) or the **US Geological Survey** (USGS; ☎ 888-275-8747; www.usgs.gov). Meanwhile, **Jimapco** (www.jimapco. com) specializes in the Northeast and publishes excellent Adirondacks recreation maps.

Online, **National Geographic** (www.nationalgeo graphic.com) sells all the mapping products you'd ever want. GPS gear and software can also be purchased from **Magellan** (www.magellangps.com) and **Garmin** (www.garmin.com).

MONEY

Prices quoted in this book are in US dollars ($). See Quick Reference inside the front cover for exchange rates.

The ease and availability of ATMs have largely negated the need for traveler's checks. However, traveler's checks in US dollars are accepted like cash at most midrange and top-end businesses (but rarely at budget places). Personal checks not drawn on US banks are generally not accepted. Exchange foreign currency at international airports and most large banks in New York, Philadelphia and Pittsburgh.

Major credit cards are widely accepted, and they are required for car rentals. Most ATM withdrawals using out-of-state cards incur surcharges of $2 or so.

Tipping

Tipping is standard practice across America. In restaurants, for satisfactory to excellent service, tipping 15% to 20% of the bill is expected; less is OK at informal diners. Bartenders expect $1 per drink; café baristas a little change in the jar. Taxi drivers and hairdressers expect 10% to 15%. Skycaps at airports and porters at nice hotels expect $1 a bag or so. If you spend several nights in a hotel, it's polite to leave a few dollars for the cleaning staff.

PHOTOGRAPHY

All camera supplies (print and slide film, digital memory, camera batteries) are readily available in local drugstores, which usually provide inexpensive film developing (including one-hour service) and burn photo CDs and DVDs.

Don't pack unprocessed film (including the roll in your camera) into checked luggage because exposure to high-powered X-ray equipment will cause it to fog. As an added precaution, 'hand check' film separately from carry-on bags at airport security checkpoints.

When photographing people, politeness is usually all you need (though street performers appreciate a tip). However, in Pennsylvania, the Amish do not like having photographs taken of them; the most respectful approach is to put your camera away and not even ask.

For a primer on taking good shots, consult Lonely Planet's *Travel Photography*.

POST

The **US Postal Service** (USPS; ☎ 800-275-8777; www.usps. gov) is reliable and inexpensive. For 1st-class mail sent and delivered within the USA, postage rates are 44¢ for letters up to 1oz (17¢ for each additional ounce) and 28¢ for standard-sized postcards. International airmail rates for postcards and letters up to 1oz are 75¢ to Canada, 79¢ to Mexico and 98¢ to other countries.

You can have mail sent to you c/o General Delivery at most big post offices (it's usually held for 30 days). Most hotels will also hold mail for incoming guests.

PRACTICALITIES

For phone, dialing and electrical advice, a good online resource is www.kropla.com.
- Voltage is 110/120V, 60 cycles (the US standard).

- The *New York Times* is the national newspaper of record; see p78 for more NY magazines.
- The region is saturated with radio stations and all the major TV and cable networks.
- Video systems use the NTSC standard (not compatible with the PAL system).
- Distances are measured in feet, yards and miles; weights in ounces, pounds and tons.
- All three states are on US Eastern Time. Noon in New York equals 9am in San Francisco and 5pm in London. During daylight-savings time, from April through October, clocks go forward one hour.

SHOPPING

When the going gets tough, the tough go shopping – or at least, that seems to be the basic approach around here.

You know about New York City: it's as close as there is to an epicenter of US consumerism. You can, quite literally, get anything and everything; the New York City chapter describes neighborhoods and has specific recommendations (p110). Or just walk.

Mostly because the state has no sales tax on clothing, discount factory outlet malls are very big in New Jersey. Two of the biggest are in Secaucus (p243), a short drive from Manhattan, and in Atlantic City (p269). Atlantic City casinos also hold a notable collection of high-fashion boutiques.

Philadelphia is no slouch, with some atmospheric and lively markets, antiques and food (p311). Art and antiques are specialties of New Hope and Lambertville (p259), sister towns on either side of the Delaware River. If you're looking for the next Warhol, Pittsburgh's art galleries are hopping with possibilities. In Pennsylvania Dutch Country (p319), you can buy lovely handmade Amish crafts, notably quilts, wooden furniture and food products. Pennsylvania also has no tax on clothing and has more discount factory outlets.

TELEPHONE

Always dial '1' before toll-free (☎ 800, 888 etc) and domestic long-distance numbers. Some toll-free numbers only work within the US. For local directory assistance, dial ☎ 411.

To make international calls from the US, dial ☎ 011 + country code + area code + number. For international operator assistance, dial ☎ 0. To call the US from abroad, the international country code for the USA is ☎ 1.

Pay phones are readily found in major cities, but are becoming rarer. Local calls cost 50¢. Private prepaid phone cards are available from convenience stores, supermarkets and pharmacies.

Most of the USA's mobile-phone systems are incompatible with the GSM 900/1800 standard used throughout Europe and Asia. Check with your service provider about using your phone in the US. In terms of coverage, Verizon has the most extensive network, but AT&T, Sprint and T-Mobile are decent. Cellular coverage is generally excellent, except in the Alleghany and Adirondack mountains.

TOURIST INFORMATION

Each state has regional tourism departments, and nearly every town has a chamber of commerce or Convention and Visitors Bureau (CVB) promoting tourism. These are listed under towns throughout this guide; in addition to providing information, local offices occasionally help travelers book hotel rooms. Also, each state maintains highway 'welcome centers' and rest stops stocked with tourist brochures and flyers.

To order materials ahead of time, and for links to regional tourist agencies, contact the state tourist bureaus:

New Jersey Division of Tourism (☎ 800-847-4865; www.visitnj.org)

New York Division of Tourism (☎ 800-225-5697; www.iloveny.com)

Pennsylvania Division of Tourism (☎ 800-847-4872; www.visitpa.com)

TRAVELERS WITH DISABILITIES

The USA is a leader in providing facilities for people with disabilities. The Americans with Disabilities Act (ADA) requires that all public buildings – including hotels, restaurants, theaters and museums – and public transit be wheelchair accessible. However, always call ahead to confirm what is available.

The downtown areas of cities have audible crossing signals and curbs with wheelchair ramps. Telephone companies are required to provide relay operators – available via teletypewriter (TTY) numbers – for the hearing impaired. Most banks provide ATM instructions in Braille. All major airlines, Greyhound buses and Amtrak trains assist disabled travelers; describe your needs when making reservations, and they will help make the necessary arrangements.

Some car-rental agencies offer hand-controlled vehicles and vans with wheelchair lifts at no extra charge, but you must reserve them well in advance.

A number of organizations specialize in serving disabled travelers:

Access-Able Travel Source (☎ 303-232-2979; www.access-able.com) A comprehensive website with many links.

Disabled Sports USA (☎ 301-217-0960; www.dsusa.org) Offers sports and recreation programs for the disabled, with chapters in New York, New Jersey and Pennsylvania.

Flying Wheels Travel (☎ 507-451-5005; www.flyingwheelstravel.com) A full-service travel agency specializing in disabled travel.

Mobility International USA (☎ 541-343-1284; www.miusa.org) Advocacy and educational programs for people with disabilities.

Moss Rehabilitation Hospital's Travel Information Service (www.mossresourcenet.org/travel.htm) This hospital's website provides a concise list of useful contacts.

Society for Accessible Travel & Hospitality (SATH; ☎ 212-447-7284; www.sath.org) New York–based advocacy group; publishes *Open World* magazine.

Travelin' Talk Network (www.travelintalk.net) Social site run by Access-Able.

VOLUNTEERING

Whether you wish to practice sustainable tourism or simply to interact more closely with the local people, volunteer opportunities abound. An afternoon or day spent volunteering can be a nice way to break up a longer trip, and it is guaranteed to provide a memorable experience you would never get just passing through.

National and state parks always need volunteers to help maintain trails, control weeds and so on. See the agencies listed in the Environment chapter (p403) and under Activities (p64) and also contact the **Sierra Club** (www.sierraclub.org).

Several regional agencies match volunteers with nonprofit groups; activities range from tutoring to park clean up, to assisting with events, to serving meals to the hungry. Many one-day opportunities are possible.

New York Cares (☎ 212-228-5000; www.newyorkcares.org) A Hands On Network affiliate.

New York City Service (www.nycservice.org) The city-sponsored volunteer portal.

Philadelphia Cares (☎ 215-564-4544; www.philacares.org) A Hands On Network affiliate.

Volunteer New Jersey (www.volunteernewjersey.org)

WOMEN TRAVELERS

Women traveling by themselves or in a group should not encounter any particular problems in the Northeast. The community website www.journeywoman.com facilitates women exchanging travel tips, with links to resources. The **Canadian government** (www.voyage.gc.ca) also publishes the useful, free, downloadable booklet *Her Own Way*; online, look under 'Publications.'

These two national advocacy groups might also be helpful:

National Organization for Women (NOW; ☎ 202-628-8669; www.now.org)

Planned Parenthood (☎ 800-230-7526; www.plannedparenthood.org) Offers referrals to medical clinics throughout the country.

In terms of safety issues, single women need to exhibit the same street smarts as any solo traveler, but they are more often the target of unwanted attention or harassment. Some women like to carry a whistle, mace or cayenne-pepper spray in case of assault. Pepper spray is legal (with restrictions) in New York, New Jersey and Pennsylvania; federal law prohibits it being carried on planes.

If you are assaulted, it may be better to call a rape-crisis hotline before calling the **police** (☎ 911); telephone books have listings of local organizations, or contact the 24-hour **National Sexual Assault Hotline** (☎ 800-656-4673; www.rainn.org). Or go straight to a hospital. Police can sometimes be insensitive with assault victims, while a rape-crisis center or hospital will advocate on behalf of survivors and act as a link to other services, including the police.

WORK

Seasonal work is common in summer at resorts, camps and on the Jersey Shore, and in the winter at the ski areas. For information contact local chambers of commerce or the resorts themselves.

If you are a foreigner in the USA with a standard nonimmigrant visitor's visa, you are expressly forbidden to take paid work in the USA and will be deported if you're caught working illegally. In addition, employers are required to establish the bona fides of their employees or face fines, making it much tougher for a foreigner to get work than it once was.

To work legally, foreigners need to apply for a work visa before leaving home. Student exchange visitors need a J1 visa, which the following organizations will help arrange:

American Institute for Foreign Study (AIFS; ☎ 866-906-2437; www.aifs.com)
BUNAC (☎ 020-7251-3472; www.bunac.org)

Camp America (☎ 020-7581-7373; www.campamerica.co.uk)
Council on International Educational Exchange (CIEE; ☎ 800-407-8839; www.ciee.org)
InterExchange (☎ 212-924-0446; www.interexchange.org) Camp and au pair programs.

For nonstudent jobs, temporary or permanent, you need to be sponsored by a US employer (who will arrange an H-category visa). These are not easy to obtain.

Transportation

CONTENTS

GETTING THERE & AWAY

AIR
Airports & Airlines

New York, New Jersey and Pennsylvania have five primary international airports. New York's Kennedy and New Jersey's Newark are international gateways for the country, and between them they receive flights (or connections) from just about every nation; they are equally convenient if your first destination is NYC. LaGuardia has the fewest international flights.

John F Kennedy International (JFK; ☎ 718-244-4444; www.panynj.gov)

LaGuardia (LGA; ☎ 718-533-3400; www.panynj.gov)

Newark Liberty International (EWR; ☎ 973-961-6000; www.panynj.gov)

Philadelphia International (PHL; ☎ 215-937-6800, 800-745-4283; www.phl.org)

Pittsburgh International (PIT; ☎ 412-472-3500; www.pitairport.com)

AIRLINES FLYING TO/FROM NEW YORK, NEW JERSEY & PENNSYLVANIA

The national airlines of most countries have flights to New York, and the region's international airports are hubs for US carriers serving the world. Note that Continental and United merged in 2010, creating the world's largest airline (called United). Newark was Continental's hub, and it's anticipated that this will lead to reduced services on main routes.

Online, www.smilinjack.com has links to international airlines, and www.seatguru.com has extensive airline information, including seat-by-seat reviews for each aircraft.

Airlines flying to/from the USA:

Aer Lingus (airline code EI; ☎ 800-474-7424; www.aerlingus.com)

Aerolíneas Argentinas (airline code AR; ☎ 800-333-0276; www.aerolineas.com.ar)

Air Canada (airline code AC; ☎ 888-247-2262; www.aircanada.com)

Air France (airline code AF; ☎ 800-237-2747; www.airfrance.com)

Air India (airline code AI; ☎ 800-223-7776; http://home.airindia.in)

Air New Zealand (airline code NZ; ☎ 800-262-1234; www.airnewzealand.com)

Alitalia (airline code AZ; ☎ 800-223-5730; www.alitalia.com)

American Airlines (airline code AA; ☎ 800-433-7300; www.aa.com)

British Airways (airline code BA; ☎ 800-247-9297; www.britishairways.com)

Cathay Pacific (airline code CX; ☎ 800-233-2742; www.cathaypacific.com)

Delta Air Lines (airline code DL; ☎ 800-221-1212; www.delta.com)

El Al (airline code LY; ☎ 800-223-6700; www.elal.com)

Iberia (airline code IB; ☎ 800-772-4642; www.iberia.com)

Icelandair (airline code FI; ☎ 800-223-5500; www.icelandair.com)

Japan Airlines (airline code JL; ☎ 800-525-3663; www.jal.com)

KLM (airline code KL; ☎ 800-225-2525; www.klm.com)

Korean Air (airline code KE; ☎ 800-438-5000; www.koreanair.com)

Lufthansa (airline code LH; ☎ 800-399-5838; www.lufthansa.com)

Northwest Airlines (airline code NW; ☎ 800-225-2525; www.nwa.com)

Qantas (airline code QF; ☎ 800-227-4500; www.qantas.com.au)

Scandinavian Airlines (airline code SK; ☎ 800-221-2350; www.flysas.com)

Singapore Airlines (airline code SQ; ☎ 800-742-3333; www.singaporeair.com)

South African Airways (airline code SA; ☎ 800-722-9675; www.flysaa.com)

Thai Airways (airline code TG; ☎ 800-426-5204; www.thaiair.com)

United Airlines (airline code UA; ☎ 800-864-8331; www.united.com)

US Airways (airline code US; ☎ 800-428-4322; www.usairways.com)

Virgin Atlantic (airline code VS; ☎ 800-821-5438; www.virgin-atlantic.com)

Tickets

There are no ticket-buying strategies that are particular to this region. However, since the New York, Newark and Philadelphia airports are relatively close to one another, it's worth comparing flights among them to see if one destination is a better deal or has more convenient arrivals. Getting a cheap airline ticket is a matter of research, reserving early – at least three to four weeks in advance – and timing. Flying midweek and in the off-season (normally, fall to spring, excluding holidays) is always less expensive, but fare wars crop up anytime.

For a good overview of online ticket agencies, visit **Airinfo** (www.airinfo.aero), which also lists travel agents worldwide.

The big three agency websites are **Travelocity** (www.travelocity.com), **Orbitz** (www.orbitz.com) and **Expedia** (www.expedia.com). Similar and worth trying are **Cheap Tickets** (www.cheaptickets.com) and **Lowest Fare** (www.lowestfare.com). Typically, these sites don't include budget airlines like Southwest.

Meta sites are good for price comparisons, as they gather information from many sources (but don't provide direct booking): try **Kayak** (www.kayak.com), **Mobissimo** (www.mobissimo.com) and **Sidestep** (www.sidestep.com).

Bidding for travel can be very successful if you're careful. Try **Hotwire** (www.hotwire.com), **Skyauction** (www.skyauction.com) and **Priceline** (www.priceline.com). See www.biddingfortravel.com for advice about Priceline, which can be great for car rentals.

INTERCONTINENTAL (RTW) TICKETS

Round-the-world (RTW) tickets are great if you want to visit other regions besides the USA; otherwise, a simple round-trip ticket is usually cheaper. They're of most value for trips that combine New York with Europe, Asia and/or Australasia.

RTW tickets use the routes of an airline alliance, such as **Star Alliance** (www.staralliance.com) and **One World** (www.oneworld.com); and they are valid for a fixed period, usually a year. Most RTW fares restrict the number of stops within the USA and Canada. Some airlines 'black out' a few heavily traveled routes. In most cases a 14-day advance purchase is required.

For RTW tickets, try **Air Brokers** (www.airbrokers.com), **Air Treks** (www.airtreks.com), **Circle the Planet** (www.circletheplanet.com) or **Just Fares** (www.justfares.com).

INTERNATIONAL AGENCIES

Two international booking agencies serving the most countries worldwide – including Africa, Asia, Australia, Europe and the UK – are **STA Travel** (☎ 800-781-4040; www.statravel.com) and **Flight Centre** (☎ 877-992-4732; www.flightcentre.com).

From Canada, flights to New York can be relatively expensive (compared to driving or

TRANSPORTATION

CLIMATE CHANGE & TRAVEL

Every form of transport that relies on carbon-based fuel generates CO_2, the main cause of human-induced climate change. Modern travel is dependent on aeroplanes and while they might use less fuel per kilometre per person than most cars, they travel much greater distances. It's not just CO_2 emissions from aircraft that are the problem. The altitude at which aircraft emit gases (including CO_2) and particles contributes significantly to their total climate change impact. The Intergovernmental Panel on Climate Change believes aviation is responsible for 4.9% of climate change – double the effect of its CO_2 emissions alone.

Lonely Planet regards travel as a global benefit. We encourage the use of more climate-friendly travel modes where possible and, together with other concerned partners across many industries, we support the carbon offset scheme run by ClimateCare. Websites such as climatecare.org use 'carbon calculators' that allow people to offset the greenhouse gases they are responsible for with contributions to portfolios of climate-friendly initiatives throughout the developing world. Lonely Planet offsets the carbon footprint of all staff and author travel.

the train), unless you are coming from the West Coast. Two online agencies are **Travel Cuts** (☎ 866-246-9762; www.travelcuts.com) and **Travelocity** (☎ 800-457-8010; www.travelocity.ca).

From Latin America, there are fewer direct flights to New York. Two agencies serving a wide range of Central and South American countries are **OTEC Viajes** (www.otecviajes.com) and **Viajo.com** (www.viajo.com).

LAND

For bus, car and train travel from neighboring states within the USA, see Getting Around. Most of the same transportation companies service the entire Northeast US.

The region's only international land border is shared between New York and Canada in the north. It is relatively easy crossing from the USA into Canada; it's crossing from Canada into the USA that can pose problems if you haven't brought all your documents. See International Visitors, p408. The **US Customs & Border Protection Agency** (http://apps.cbp.gov/bwt/) tracks current wait times at every border crossing. Some borders are open 24 hours, but most are not.

The busiest entry points are at Buffalo and Niagara Falls. For border wait times returning to Canada, visit www.cbsa-asfc.gc.ca/general/times/menu-e.html.

BUS

Greyhound has direct connections between main cities in Canada and northern USA, but you may have to transfer to a different bus at the border. Book through either **Greyhound US** (☎ 800-231-2222, international customer service 214-849-8100; www.greyhound.com) or **Greyhound Canada** (☎ 800-661-8747; www.greyhound.ca). Greyhound's Discovery Pass (p418) allows unrestricted travel in both America and Canada.

THINGS CHANGE...

The information in this chapter is particularly vulnerable to change. Check directly with the airline or a travel agent to make sure you understand how a fare (and ticket you may buy) works and be aware of the security requirements for international travel. Shop carefully. The details given in this chapter should be regarded as pointers and are not a substitute for your own careful, up-to-date research.

CAR & MOTORCYCLE

If you're driving into the USA from Canada, don't forget the vehicle's registration papers, liability insurance and your home driver's license. Canadian auto insurance is valid in the USA. Canadian driver's licenses are valid and an international driver's permit is a good supplement.

If your papers are in order, taking your own car across the US–Canadian border is usually quick and easy, but occasionally the authorities of either country decide to search a car *thoroughly*. On weekends and holidays, especially in summer, traffic at the main border crossings can be heavy and waits long.

TRAIN

Amtrak (☎ 800-872-7245; www.amtrak.com) and Canada's **VIA Rail** (☎ 888-842-7245; www.viarail.ca) run daily services from Montreal to New York, and from Toronto to New York via Niagara Falls. Customs inspections happen at the border, not on boarding.

SEA

Cruise ships stop at New York, Philadelphia and New Jersey, typically as part of longer journeys. A good specialized cruise ship travel agency is **Cruise Web** (☎ 800-377-9383; www.cruiseweb.com).

You can travel to and from New York on a freighter. Freighters are slower and take longer, but they aren't Spartan (some advertise cruise ship–level amenities), and they are much cheaper (sometimes by half). Excellent sources of information are the **Cruise & Freighter Travel Association** (☎ 800-872-8584; www.travltips.com) and **Freighter World Cruises** (☎ 800-531-7774; www.freighterworld.com).

GETTING AROUND

When time is tight, flying between cities can be worth the extra expense, particularly if, say, your agenda is NYC and Pittsburgh or Buffalo, and nothing in between. Otherwise, the major cities are well-served by trains, but driving is the easiest, most flexible option; renting a car is necessary for exploring rural and wilderness areas. A number of commuter bus lines serve the region's large and medium towns, and these are the cheapest option. It can often be a convenient, cost-effective strategy to use public transportation from the airports and within major cities, and then rent a car for travels beyond and in between the metropolises.

AIR

Domestic, regional flights are common and frequent, though they can be expensive; avoid peak commuter times.

If you're arriving from abroad or another major US airport, it's usually much cheaper to buy a through ticket to small airports as part of your fare rather than buying them separately.

Another alternative is an air pass, available from the major airlines flying between the USA and Europe, Asia and Australia.

Domestic Airports

This busy region maintains a relatively large number of smaller city and municipal airports, though most are too small to be useful for travelers. While some are 'international' airports, most of these flights are to Canada.

Albany International Airport (☎ 518-242-2200; www.albanyairport.com) New York.

Atlantic City International Airport (☎ 609-645-7895; www.acairport.com) New Jersey.

Buffalo-Niagara International Airport (☎ 716-630-6000; www.buffaloairport.com) New York.

Erie International Airport (☎ 814-833-4258; www.erieairport.org) Pennsylvania.

Harrisburg International Airport (MDT; ☎ 717-948-3900; www.flyhia.com) Pennsylvania.

Lancaster Municipal Airport (☎ 717-569-1221; www.lancasterairport.com) Pennsylvania.

Syracuse Hancock International Airport (☎ 315-454-4330; www.syairport.org) New York.

Airlines in New York, New Jersey & Pennsylvania

The main domestic carriers serving the region:

AirTran (☎ 800-247-8726; www.airtran.com)

Alaska Airlines (☎ 800-252-7522; www.alaskaair.com)

American Airlines (☎ 800-433-7300; www.aa.com)

Delta Air Lines (☎ 800-221-1212; www.delta.com)

Frontier Airlines (☎ 800-432-1359; www.frontierairlines.com)

JetBlue (☎ 800-538-2583; www.jetblue.com)

Midwest Express (☎ 800-452-2022; www.midwestexpress.com)

Northwest Airlines (☎ 800-225-2525; www.nwa.com)

Southwest Airlines (☎ 800-435-9792; www.southwest.com)

Spirit Airlines (☎ 800-772-7117; www.spiritair.com)

United Airlines (☎ 800-864-8331; www.united.com)

US Airways (☎ 800-428-4322; www.usairways.com)

Virgin America (☎ 877-359-8474; www.virginamerica.com)

Air Passes

International travelers who plan on doing a lot of flying, both in and out of the region, might consider buying an air pass. Air passes are available only to non-US citizens, and they must be purchased in conjunction with an international ticket. Conditions and cost structures can be complicated, but all include a certain number of domestic flights (from three to 10) that must be used within 60 days. Sometimes you must plan your itinerary in advance, but sometimes dates (and even destinations) can be left open. Talk with a travel agent to determine if an air pass would save you money based on your plans.

Two of the biggest airline networks offering air passes are **Star Alliance** (www.staralliance.com) and **One World** (www.oneworld.com).

BICYCLE

Regional bicycle touring is very popular; it means coasting winding backroads (since bicycles are not permitted on freeways), and calculating progress in miles per day, not miles per hour. Cyclists must follow the same rules of the road as automobiles, but don't expect drivers to respect the right of way of cyclists. **Better World Club** (☎ 866-238-1137; www.betterworldclub.com) offers a bicycle roadside assistance program.

For a list of bicycling associations, tour groups and magazines, see p403. Turn to the Outdoors chapter (p68) for cycling and mountain biking highlights. Many of the canalways and routes here can make for epic one- and two-week journeys.

For advice, and lists of local bike clubs and repair shops, check the website of the **League of American Bicyclists** (www.bikeleague.org). If you're bringing your own bike, visit the **International Bicycle Fund** (www.ibike.org), which lists bike regulations by airline and has lots of advice. In the past, most international and domestic airlines have carried bikes as checked baggage without charge when they're in a box. However, many have changed their regulations and have imposed or increased fees (typically $50 to $100, but sometimes higher). Amtrak trains and Greyhound buses will transport bikes, sometimes charging extra.

Also, it's not hard to buy a bike once you're here and resell it before you leave. Every city and town has bike shops; if you prefer a cheaper, used bicycle, try flea markets, garage sales and the notice boards at hostels and colleges. These are also the best places to sell your bike, though stores selling used bikes may also buy from you. Long-term bike rentals are also easy to find; recommended rental places are listed throughout this guide.

BOAT

There is no long-distance river or canal public transportation system in the region. However, it's possible to rent boats for canal or coastal touring on your own; see destination chapters under 'Boating' for possibilities.

New York and Philadelphia run local commuter ferry services in and around their metropolitan areas. See Local Transportation p421.

BUS

To save money, travel by bus, particularly between major towns and cities. Gotta-go middle class Americans prefer to drive, but buses let you see the countryside and meet folks along the way. As a rule, buses are reliable, relatively clean and comfortable, with air-conditioning, sort-of reclining seats, onboard lavatories and no smoking permitted.

For all bus lines, seating is first-come, first-served, and (with the exception of Greyhound) there is no discount for advance ticket sales; simply buy your ticket immediately before boarding.

Many bus stations are clean and safe, but some are in dodgy areas; if you arrive in the evening, spend the money on a taxi. Other towns have just a flag stop. If you are boarding at one of these, pay the driver with exact change.

Greyhound

The national long-distance carrier **Greyhound** (☎ 800-231-2222; www.greyhound.com) is one of the main bus lines in the region. It traditionally has maintained the most extensive route system and usually has its own terminal. To improve efficiency and profitability, Greyhound has now stopped service to many small towns; routes generally trace major highways and stop at larger population centers. To reach country towns on rural roads, you may need to transfer to local or county bus systems; Greyhound usually has their contact information.

BUS PASSES

Greyhound's **North American Discovery Pass** (www.discoverypass.com; $285-645, $4 purchase fee), which is available to both domestic and international travelers, allows unlimited, unrestricted travel for periods from seven to 60 consecutive days in both the USA and Canada. Besides the length of the pass, the only real decision to make is which country you want to start your travels in.

International travelers can buy the pass before arriving in the US on the internet at least two weeks in advance. Or, purchase one in person at select Greyhound terminals up to two hours before departure.

COSTS

Substantial ticket discounts can be had if you purchase seven days in advance, and special promotional fares are regularly offered. If you're traveling with a friend, ask about Greyhound's companion fares, where the second traveler gets 50% off with a three-day advance purchase.

As for other discounts: tickets for children ages two to 11 are 40% off. People over 62 can get a 5% discount. Students who purchase the Student Advantage Discount Card ($20) will get 10% off most routes.

Samples of standard (non-seven-day-advance) Greyhound fares: New York City–Pittsburgh ($60, 9½ to 12 hours), New York City–Philadelphia ($20, two hours), New York City–Buffalo ($70, 7½ to eight hours) and Philadelphia–Pittsburgh ($55, six to nine hours).

RESERVATIONS

Greyhound bus tickets can be bought over the phone or on the internet. If you purchase 10 days in advance with a major US credit card, tickets will be mailed to you. International credit cards are accepted when buying in person at the terminal, or online in advance for Will Call tickets, where you pick the tickets up at the terminal (bring ID). Greyhound terminals also accept traveler's checks and cash.

On Greyhound, a prepurchased ticket does not reserve or guarantee a seat on a bus. Seating is primarily first-come, first-served, but you can pay extra for 'priority seating' (add $5), which reserves a seat and lets you board first.

Other Carriers

There are a number of other regional carriers some of which coordinate their service with

Greyhound. See the destination chapters for more specific city and town bus information.

Adirondack Trailways (☎ 800-776-7548; www. trailwaysny.com) New York State.

Capitol/Bieber Trailways (www.capitoltrailways.com) NYC, Philly, Harrisburg, Syracuse and smaller towns.

DeCamp Bus Lines (☎ 800-631-1281; www.decamp. com) Northern NJ–NYC commuter service.

Fullington Trailways (☎ 800-252-3893; www.fulling tontours.com) NY and PA towns.

New Jersey Transit (☎ 800-772-2222; www.njtransit. com) All NJ and NYC.

Peter Pan Trailways (☎ 800-343-9999: www.peter panbus.com) NYC, Philly, Newark & Albany.

Susquehanna Trailways (☎ 800-692-6314; www. susquehannabus.com) NYC–Philly–Williamsport.

CAR & MOTORCYCLE

Driving a car is flexible and convenient, except in Manhattan, where it is expensive, stressful, and often inconvenient; avoid having one in New York City. Philadelphia can also be negotiated successfully without a car. Beyond that, an automobile gives you the independence to set your own schedule, and it's essential for getting to sights outside of major towns. That said, renting a car can be expensive, and the best strategy is usually a combination of public transportation and car rental.

Automobile Associations

The **American Automobile Association** (AAA; ☎ 800-874-7532; www.aaa.com) has reciprocal membership agreements with several international auto clubs (check with AAA and bring your membership card). For members, AAA offers travel insurance, tour books, diagnostic centers for used car buyers and a greater number of regional offices, and it advocates politically for the auto industry.

An ecofriendly alternative is the **Better World Club** (☎ 866-238-1137; www.betterworldclub. com), which donates 1% of earnings to assist environmental cleanup, offers ecologically sensitive choices for services and advocates politically for environmental causes. Better World also has a roadside assistance program for bicycles.

In both organizations, the central member benefit is 24-hour emergency roadside assistance anywhere in the USA. Both clubs also offer trip planning and free maps, travel agency services, car insurance and a range of discounts (car rentals, hotels etc).

Bring Your Own Vehicle

For details on driving your own car over the border, see p416. Otherwise, international travelers shouldn't even think about freighting their car unless they're moving to the USA.

Driver's License

Foreign visitors can legally drive in the USA for up to 12 months with their home driver's license. However, it is recommended that you also get an International Driving Permit (IDP); this will have more credibility with US traffic police, especially if your home license doesn't have a photo or is in a foreign language. Your automobile association at home can issue an IDP, valid for one year, for a small fee. You must carry your home license together with the IDP. To drive a motorcycle, you need either a valid US state motorcycle license or an IDP specially endorsed for motorcycles.

Rental

Car rental is a very competitive business. Most rental companies require that you have a major credit card, that you be at least 25 years old and that you have a valid driver's license (your home license will do). Some national companies may rent to drivers between the ages of 21 and 24 for an additional charge. Those under 21 are usually not permitted to rent at all.

Good independent agencies are listed in this guide, in the local Yellow Pages and by **Car Rental Express** (www.carrentalexpress.com), which rates and compares independent agencies in US cities; it's particularly useful for searching out cheaper long-term rentals.

Major national companies:

Alamo (☎ 877-222-9075; www.alamo.com)
Avis (☎ 800-331-1212; www.avis.com)
Budget (☎ 800-527-0700; www.budget.com)
Dollar (☎ 800-800-3665; www.dollar.com)
Enterprise (☎ 800-261-7331; www.enterprise.com)
Hertz (☎ 800-654-3131; www.hertz.com)
National (☎ 877-222-9058; www.nationalcar.com)
Rent-a-Wreck (☎ 877-877-0877; www.rentawreck.com)
Thrifty (☎ 800-847-4389; www.thrifty.com)

Companies specializing in RV or camper rentals include:

Adventures on Wheels (☎ 800-943-3579; www. wheels9.com)
Cruise America (☎ 800-671-8042; www.cruise america.com)
Happy Travel Camper Rental & Sales (☎ 800-370-1262; www.camperusa.com)

Car rental prices can vary wildly; as when buying plane tickets, shop around, checking every angle and several websites. Airport locations may have cheaper rates but higher fees; city center offices may do pick-ups and drop-offs; and adjusting the days of your rental can completely change the rate. Weekend and weekly rates are usually cheaper. On average, the daily rate for a small car ranges from $35 to $75, while weekly rates are $200 to $400. If you belong to an auto club or a frequent-flier program, you may get a discount (or earn frequent-flier miles), so ask. Or, see about arranging a cheaper fly-drive package before you travel. No matter what, advance reservations are always recommended.

Some other things to keep in mind: most national agencies make 'unlimited mileage' standard on all cars, but independents might charge a few dollars extra for this; limited mileage plans rarely work out unless you aren't going far. Some rental companies let you pay for your last tank of gas upfront; this is almost never a good deal. Tax on car rentals varies by state and agency location; always ask for the total cost *with tax*. Most agencies often charge more if you pick the car up in one place and drop it off in another (they add a 'drop off' charge). Be careful about adding extra days or turning in a car early; extra days may be charged at a premium rate, and an early return may jeopardize the low weekly or monthly deal you originally arranged.

Some major national companies, including Avis, Budget and Hertz, offer 'green' fleets of hybrid rental cars, although these can cost significantly more. For car-sharing in New York City (including the boroughs), Philadelphia and Pittsburgh, **Zipcar** (☎ 866-494-7227; www.zipcar.com) charges hourly/daily rental fees with free gas, insurance and limited mileage included; prepayment is required. Check the website for locations; no one-way rentals allowed.

Insurance

Don't put the key into the ignition if you don't have insurance, which is legally required, or else you risk financial ruin if there's an accident. If you already have auto insurance (even overseas), or if you buy travel insurance, make sure that the policy has adequate liability coverage for a rental car where you will be driving; it probably does, but most states specify a minimum level of coverage.

Rental car companies will provide liability insurance, but most charge extra. Always ask. Rental companies almost never include collision damage insurance for the vehicle. Instead, they offer an optional Collision Damage Waiver (CDW) or Loss Damage Waiver (LDW), usually with an initial deductible of $100 to $500. For an extra premium, you can usually get this deductible covered as well. However, most credit cards now offer collision damage coverage for rental cars if you rent for 15 days or less and charge the total rental to your card. This is a good way to avoid paying extra fees to the rental company, but note that if there's an accident, you sometimes must pay the rental car company first and then seek reimbursement from the credit card company. Check your credit card policy. Paying extra for some or all of this insurance increases the cost of a rental car by as much as $10 to $30 a day.

Road Conditions & Hazards

Residents track traffic conditions more closely than the weather, which changes less often and with less serious consequences to one's day. Roads and highways are generally in good shape, but there are so many that traffic jams and road repairs are a constant fact of life. For traffic updates in all three states, call ☎ 511 or visit these websites: in New York (www.511ny.org), New Jersey (www.511nj.org) and Pennsylvania (www.511pa.com).

Otherwise, the main hazard involves wildlife on the roads. This is not confined to rural areas. Deer are ubiquitous in suburbs and small towns throughout the region, and you should stay alert and take deer warning signs seriously, particularly at night.

Road Rules

In the USA, cars drive on the right side of the road. The use of seat belts and child safety seats is required in all three states. Motorcyclists and their passengers must wear helmets.

The speed limit is generally 55mph or 65mph on highways, 25mph to 35mph in cities and towns and as low as 15mph in school zones (strictly enforced during school hours). It's forbidden to pass a school bus when its lights are flashing. Residents are notorious for speeding on the highways; joining them doesn't lessen the risk of getting a ticket.

Most states have laws against (and high fines for) littering along the highway. Sure, few get caught, but don't do it anyway. Also, it is illegal in New York and New Jersey to talk on a handheld cell phone while driving; use a hands-free device instead.

Penalties are very severe for 'DUI' – driving under the influence of alcohol and/or drugs. Police can give roadside sobriety checks to assess if you've been drinking or using drugs. If you fail, they'll require you take a breath test, urine test or blood test to determine the level of alcohol or drugs in your body. Refusing to be tested is treated as if you'd taken the test and failed. The maximum legal blood alcohol concentration is 0.08%.

It is illegal to carry 'open containers' of alcohol in a vehicle, even if they are empty. Containers that are full and sealed may be carried, but if they have ever been opened, they must be carried in the trunk.

HITCHHIKING

Hitchhiking in the USA is potentially dangerous and definitely not recommended. Indeed, drivers have heard so many lurid reports they tend to be just as afraid of those with their thumbs out. Hitchhiking on freeways is prohibited. You may see people hitchhiking (and stopping) in rural areas, but these places aren't any safer than anywhere else, and with sparse traffic, you may well get stranded.

Even hitching to and from a hiking trailhead should be avoided – try to arrange something at a ranger station or with other hikers.

LOCAL TRANSPORTATION

Metropolitan areas – such as New York City, Philadelphia, Pittsburgh and northern New Jersey – support a range of public transit options: buses, commuter trains, subways and ferries. In summer, several Jersey shore communities maintain local shuttle services, as in Atlantic City and Long Beach Island. For specific details, see the Getting Around sections for the relevant cities and towns.

Bicycle

Manhattan, Philadelphia and Pittsburgh all make efforts to support cyclists with dedicated bike lanes, downtown bike racks, and so on. Bikes can usually be carried on public transportation. It would be hard to rely solely on bicycles for sightseeing, but they can make an

excellent option for a day or limited trips. For more on regional and urban cycling, see p68.

Boat

New York City has commuter ferry services (and water taxis) that encircle Manhattan Island and connect to Brooklyn, Staten Island, and New Jersey's Hoboken and Jersey City; in summer, NY ferry service also connects to Sandy Hook. Philadelphia operates ferries to Camden's waterfront.

Bus

Most cities and larger towns have dependable local bus systems. They are designed for commuters and may have more limited service in the evening and on weekends. Fares typically cost $2 to $2.50 per trip.

Subway

New York's subway is the largest in the nation, and it is the preferred way to negotiate the city; the PATH extension connects to Hoboken, Jersey City and Newark Airport. Philadelphia and Pittsburgh have more limited subway/light rail systems, but these are still recommended and useful for sightseeing. Buffalo also has a light rail system. For more on regional commuter trains, see p421.

Taxi

Taxis are metered, with flagfall charges from $2.50 to start, plus up to $2 per mile; in New York City, prices are higher, include idling, and there are surcharges for peak times. Rates to/from airports are usually set or standard fees; ask to verify. Cabbies charge extra for handling baggage, and drivers expect a 10% to 15% tip. Taxis cruise the busiest areas in the downtowns of the major cities; otherwise, it's easiest to call and order one.

TRAIN

Similar to regional buses, Amtrak is the national railroad with the most extensive routes between major cities, and there are several regional commuter rail lines that serve smaller towns and suburbs.

Amtrak

The major cities in the region are connected by **Amtrak** (☎ 800-872-7245; www.amtrak.com), with stops at smaller towns along the routes. The main Amtrak routes radiate from New York City: north to the New York cities of Albany,

TRANSPORTATION

TRANSPORTATION

Saratoga Springs and Montreal, Quebec; northwest to the New York cities of Albany, Syracuse, Buffalo and Niagara Falls; and southwest to the New Jersey cities of Newark, Princeton and Trenton and to the Pennsylvania cities of Philadelphia, Harrisburg and Pittsburgh. There's also high-speed Acela trains between New York City and Philadelphia (and to Boston and Washington DC).

For service beyond this region, see Amtrak's website.

CLASSES & COSTS

Fares vary according to the type of train and seating; on long-distance lines, you can travel in coach seats, business class, or 1st class, which includes all sleeping compartments. Sleeping cars include simple bunks (called 'roomettes'), bedrooms with private facilities and suites sleeping four with two bathrooms. Sleeping car rates include meals in the dining car, which offers everyone sit-down meal service (pricey if not included). Food service on commuter lines, when it exists, consists of sandwich and snack bars. Bringing your own food is recommended on all trains.

Various one-way, round-trip and touring fares are available, with discounts of 15% for seniors age 62 and over and for students (with a 'Student Advantage' card, $20, or with an ISIC), and 50% discounts for children ages two to 15. Web-only 'Weekly Specials' offer deep discounts on certain undersold routes. To get many standard discounts, you need to reserve three days ahead.

Generally, the earlier you book, the lower the price. If you want to take an Acela or Metroliner train, avoid peak commuter times and aim for weekends.

Amtrak Vacations (☎ 800-268-7252; www.amtrak vacations.com) offers packages that include rental cars, hotels, tours and attractions. Air-rail packages offer train travel in one direction and then return by plane.

Examples of Amtrak's long-distance services include New York to Philadelphia ($67, 1½ hours), New York to Pittsburgh ($100, nine hours), New York to Buffalo ($80, 8½ hours) and New York to Montreal ($62, 11 hours).

RESERVATIONS

Reservations can be made any time from 11 months in advance to the day of departure. Space on most trains is limited, and certain routes can be crowded, so it's best to reserve as far in advance as you can. This also gives you the chance to get fare discounts.

TRAIN PASSES

A USA Rail Pass is available only to international travelers (not to US or Canadian residents). The pass offers unlimited coach-class travel within a specific region for either 15 or 45 days, with the price depending on region, number of days and season traveled (fares range from $390 to $750).

Present your pass at an Amtrak office to buy a ticket for each trip. Reservations should be made as well, as far in advance as possible. You can get on and off the train as often as you like, but each sector of the journey must be booked. At some rural stations, trains will only stop if there's a reservation. Tickets are not for specific seats, but a conductor on board may allocate you a seat. First-class or sleeper accommodations cost extra and must be reserved separately.

Other Services

Regional commuter rail service covers much of the New York City, northern New Jersey and Philadelphia metro regions. Train lines connect at hubs in New York Penn Station, Newark Penn Station, and Philadelphia, allowing travelers to move easily between these cities. For specifics on services and fares, check the Getting There & Away sections in the destination chapters.

Long Island Rail Road (LIRR; ☎ 718-217-5477; www.mta.nyc.ny.us/lirr) Connects New York City with Brooklyn, Queens and Long Island.

Metro North Railroad (☎ 212-532-4900; www.mnr.org) Runs from Manhattan's Grand Central Station north to Westchester, the Hudson Valley and Connecticut.

New Jersey Transit (☎ 800-772-2222; www.njtransit.com) Connects through Newark and Hoboken to New York's Penn Station, Philadelphia, down the shore to Bay Head, and throughout northern and central Jersey.

PATH (PATH; ☎ 800-234-7284; www.panyny.gov/path) Connects Manhattan to northern New Jersey at Hoboken, Jersey City and Newark Airport.

Port Authority Transit Corporation (PATCO; ☎ in NJ 856-772-6900, in PA 215-922-4600; www.ridepatco.org) Connects Philadelphia with Camden and connects to NJ Transit's Atlantic City line.

Southeastern Pennsylvania Transportation Authority (SEPTA; ☎ 215-580-7800; www.septa.org) Covers Philadelphia and its suburbs extensively, and connects with New Jersey at West Trenton, Trenton, with connections to further points.

Health

CONTENTS

BEFORE YOU GO

Generally speaking, the USA is a healthy place to visit. There are no prevalent diseases, and the country is well served by hospitals and clinics. However, due to the high cost of health care, international visitors should consider taking out comprehensive travel insurance.

Hospitals, medical centers, walk-in clinics and referral services are found easily. Ask the staff of your hotel to recommend a local doctor or clinic. In an emergency, call ☎ 911 for an ambulance to take you to the nearest hospital emergency room (ER), but note that both the ambulance and the ER will be incredibly expensive. Many city hospitals have 'urgent care clinics,' which are designed to deal with less-than-catastrophic injuries.

Make sure you're healthy before traveling. If you're embarking on a long trip, make sure your teeth are in good condition. If you wear glasses, take a spare pair and your prescription. You can get new spectacles made up quickly and competently for around $100. If you require a particular medication, take an adequate supply and bring the prescription with you. Pharmaceuticals are expensive in the USA.

INSURANCE

Travel health insurance is essential – some hospitals refuse care without evidence that the patient is covered. If you have a choice between lower or higher medical expenses options, take the higher one for visiting the USA.

Some policies specifically exclude 'dangerous activities' such as scuba diving, motorcycling and even hiking. If these activities are on your agenda, avoid this sort of policy.

You may prefer a policy that pays doctors or hospitals directly, rather than requiring you to pay first and file a claim with the insurance company later. If you have to file a claim later, keep all documentation. Some policies ask you to call collect ('reverse charge') to a center in your home country for an immediate assessment of your problem.

Check whether the policy covers ambulance fees or an emergency flight home. If you have to stretch out, you'll need two seats and somebody has to pay for them!

See also Insurance, p408.

RECOMMENDED VACCINATIONS

Generally, no immunizations are required for entry, though cholera and yellow fever vaccinations may be necessary for those coming from infected areas.

MEDICAL CHECKLIST

Following is a list of items you should consider including in your medical kit – consult your pharmacist for brands available in your country.
- Antibiotics if you're traveling well off the beaten track; see your doctor, as they must be prescribed, and carry the prescription with you.
- Antifungal cream or powder for fungal skin infections and thrush.
- Antihistamine for allergies, eg hay fever; to ease the itch from insect bites or stings; and to prevent motion sickness.
- Antiseptic (such as Betadine) for cuts and grazes.
- Aspirin or paracetamol (acetaminophen in the USA) for pain or fever.
- Bandages, Band-Aids (plasters) and other wound dressings.
- Calamine lotion, sting relief spray or aloe vera to ease irritation from sunburn and insect bites or stings.
- Cold and flu tablets, throat lozenges and nasal decongestant.

HEALTH

- Insect repellent, sunscreen, lip balm and eye drops.
- Scissors, tweezers and a thermometer – note that mercury thermometers are prohibited by airlines.
- Sunblock.
- Water purification tablets or iodine.

INTERNET RESOURCES

For comprehensive health information and advice for travelers, browse the website of the **US Centers for Disease Control & Prevention** (www.cdc.gov/travel). The World Health Organization publishes a superb book, called *International Travel and Health,* which is revised annually and is available online at no cost at www.who.int/ith/en. Another general interest website is **MD Travel Health** (www.mdtravelhealth.com), which provides complete travel health recommendations for every country, updated daily, also at no cost. **Lonely Planet** (www.lonelyplanet.com/health) has lots of good travel health advice, and many other travel health sites are listed.

IN NEW YORK, NEW JERSEY & PENNSYLVANIA

AVAILABILITY & COST OF HEALTH CARE

In general, if you have a medical emergency, the best bet is to find the nearest hospital and go to its emergency room. If the problem isn't urgent, you can call a nearby hospital and ask for a referral to a local physician, which is usually cheaper than a trip to the emergency room. You should avoid stand-alone, for-profit urgent-care centers, which may perform a large number of expensive tests, even for minor illnesses.

Pharmacies are abundantly supplied, but you may find that some medications that are available over-the-counter in your home country require a prescription in the USA, and as always, if you don't have insurance to cover the cost of prescriptions, they can be shockingly expensive.

INFECTIOUS DISEASES

In addition to more common ailments, there are several infectious diseases that are unknown or uncommon outside North America. Most are acquired by mosquito or tick bites.

Giardiasis

This parasitic infection of the small intestine occurs throughout the world. Symptoms may include nausea, bloating, cramps and diarrhea, and may last for weeks. To protect yourself from Giardia, avoid drinking directly from lakes, ponds, streams and rivers, which may be contaminated by animal or human feces. The infection can also be transmitted from person-to-person if proper hand washing is not performed. Giardiasis is easily diagnosed by a stool test and readily treated with antibiotics.

HIV/AIDS

As with most parts of the world, HIV infection occurs throughout the USA. You should never assume, on the basis of someone's background or appearance, that they're free of this or any other sexually transmitted disease. Be sure to use a condom or other prophylactic device for all sexual encounters. A good resource for help and information is the **US Centers for Disease Control** (www.cdc.gov).

Lyme Disease

This disease has been reported in many states, but most documented cases occur in the northeastern part of the country, especially New York, New Jersey, Connecticut and Massachusetts. Lyme disease is transmitted by deer ticks, which are only 1mm to 2mm long. Most cases occur in the late spring and summer. The Center for Disease Control (CDC) has an informative, if slightly scary, web page on **Lyme disease** (www.cdc.gov/ncidod/dvbid/lyme).

The first symptom is usually an expanding red rash that is often pale in the center, known as a bull's-eye rash. However, in many cases, no rash is observed. Flu-like symptoms are common, including fever, headache, joint pains, body aches and malaise. When the infection is treated promptly with an appropriate antibiotic, usually doxycycline or amoxicillin, the cure rate is high. Luckily, since the tick must be attached for 36 hours or more to transmit Lyme disease, most cases can be prevented by performing a thorough tick check after you've been outdoors. For information, see Tick Bites (p426).

Rabies

Rabies is a viral infection of the brain and spinal cord that is almost always fatal. The rabies virus is carried in the saliva of infected animals and is typically transmitted through an animal bite, though contamination of any break in the skin with infected saliva may result in rabies. In the USA, most cases of human rabies are related to exposure to bats. Rabies may also be contracted from raccoons, skunks, foxes, and unvaccinated cats and dogs.

If there is any possibility, however small, that you have been exposed to rabies, you should seek preventative treatment, which consists of rabies immune globulin and rabies vaccine, and is quite safe. In particular, any contact with a bat should be discussed with health authorities, because bats have small teeth and may not leave obvious bite marks. If you wake up to find a bat in your room, or discover a bat in a room with small children, rabies prophylaxis may be necessary.

West Nile Virus

These infections were unknown in the USA until a few years ago. No recent cases have been reported in New York, New Jersey or Pennsylvania, but they have been reported in a number of other states. The virus is transmitted by culex mosquitoes, which are active in late summer and early fall, and generally bite after dusk. Most infections are mild or asymptomatic, but the virus may infect the central nervous system, leading to fever, headache, confusion, lethargy, coma and sometimes death. There is no treatment for West Nile virus. For the latest update on the areas affected by West Nile, go to the website of the **US Geological Survey** (http://diseasemaps.usgs.gov).

ENVIRONMENTAL HAZARDS
Heat Exhaustion

Dehydration or salt deficiency can cause heat exhaustion, which is characterized by fatigue, lethargy, headaches, giddiness and muscle cramps. Always carry – and use – a water bottle on long trips.

Heat Stroke

Long, continuous periods of exposure to high temperatures can leave you vulnerable to this serious, sometimes fatal, condition. It occurs when the body's heat-regulating mechanism breaks down and the body temperature rises to dangerous levels. Avoid excessive alcohol intake or strenuous activity.

Symptoms include feeling unwell, lack of perspiration and a high body temperature of 102° to 105°F (39° to 41°C). Hospitalization is essential for extreme cases, but meanwhile get out of the sun, remove clothing, cover with a wet sheet or towel, and fan continuously to bring down body temperature.

Hypothermia

Skiers and winter hikers will find that temperatures in the mountains can drop quickly to below freezing, or a sudden soaking and high winds can lower your body temperature rapidly. Travel with a partner whenever possible, or if you're alone, be sure someone knows your route and when you expect to return.

Seek shelter when bad weather is unavoidable. Woolen clothing and synthetics that retain warmth even when wet are superior to cotton clothing. Carry a good-quality sleeping bag and high-energy, easily digestible snacks such as chocolate or dried fruit.

Get hypothermia victims out of bad weather as quickly as possible and make sure they're in dry, warm clothing. Give hot liquids (not alcohol) and high-calorie, easily digestible food. In advanced stages, place victims in warm sleeping bags and get in with them. Don't rub victims – place them near a fire or, if possible, in a warm (not hot) bath.

Bites & Stings

Common-sense approaches to these concerns are the most effective: wear boots when hiking to protect from snakes, wear long sleeves and pants to protect from ticks and mosquitoes. If you're bitten, don't overreact. Stay calm and follow the recommended treatment.

ANIMAL BITES

Do not attempt to pet, handle or feed any animal, with the exception of domestic animals known to be free of any infectious disease. Most animal injuries are directly related to a person's attempt to touch or feed the animal.

Any bite or scratch by a mammal, including bats, should be promptly and thoroughly cleansed with large amounts of soap and water, followed by application of an antiseptic, such as iodine or alcohol. The local health authorities should be contacted immediately for possible post-exposure rabies treatment, whether or not you've been immunized

HEALTH

against rabies. It may also be advisable to start an antibiotic, since wounds caused by animal bites and scratches frequently become infected.

MOSQUITO BITES

When traveling in areas where West Nile or other mosquito-borne illnesses have been reported, keep yourself covered (wear long sleeves, long pants, hats and shoes rather than sandals) and apply a good insect repellent, preferably one containing DEET, to exposed skin and clothing. In general, adults and children over 12 should use preparations containing 25% to 35% DEET, which usually lasts about six hours. Children between two and 12 years of age should use preparations containing no more than 10% DEET, applied sparingly, which will usually last about three hours. Neurologic toxicity has been reported from DEET, especially in children, but appears to be extremely uncommon and generally related to overuse. DEET-containing compounds should not be used on children under age two.

Insect repellents containing certain botanical products, including oil of eucalyptus and soybean oil, are effective but last only 1½ to two hours. Products based on citronella are not effective.

Visit the **Center for Disease Control** (CDC; www.cdc.gov/ncidod/dvbid/westnile/prevention_info.htm) website for prevention information.

SNAKE BITES

There are three types of venomous snakes in the New York, New Jersey and Pennsylvania region: the northern copperhead, timber rattlesnake and massasauga rattlesnake. They do not cause instantaneous death, and antivenins are available. First aid is to place a light constricting bandage over the bite, keep the wounded part below the level of the heart and move it as little as possible. Stay calm and get to a medical facility as soon as possible. Bring the dead snake for identification if you can, but don't risk being bitten again. Do not use the mythic 'cut an X and suck out the venom' trick; this causes more damage to snakebite victims than the bites themselves.

SPIDER BITES

In this region the only spider that causes significant human illness is the black widow. The black widow is black or brown in color, measuring about 15mm in body length, with a shiny top, fat body, and distinctive red or orange hourglass figure on its underside. It's found throughout the Northeast and usually hides in barns, woodpiles, sheds, harvested crops and the bowls of outdoor toilets.

If bitten by a black widow, you should apply ice or cold packs and go immediately to the nearest emergency room. Complications of a black widow bite may include muscle spasms, breathing difficulties and high blood pressure.

TICK BITES

Ticks are parasitic arachnids that may be present in brush, forest and grasslands, where hikers often get them on their legs or in their boots. Adult ticks suck blood from hosts by burrowing into the skin and can carry infections such as Lyme disease.

Always check your body for ticks after walking through high grass or thickly forested areas. If ticks are found unattached, they can simply be brushed off. If a tick is found attached, press down around the tick's head with tweezers, grab the head and gently pull upwards – do not twist it. (If no tweezers are available, use your fingers, but protect them from contamination with a piece of tissue or paper.) Do not rub oil, alcohol or petroleum jelly on it. If you get sick in the next couple of weeks, consult a doctor.

The Authors

JEFF CAMPBELL
Coordinating Author, New Jersey

Jeff grew up in central Jersey (exit 8A), moved to San Francisco, married a Jersey girl and now finds himself once again a resident of the Garden State – raising his own Jersey girl and boy! For Lonely Planet, he's been the coordinating author of the award-winning *USA* three times, plus *New York, Washington DC & the Mid-Atlantic Trips, Hawaii, Florida, Southwest USA* and others.

SARAH CHANDLER
New York State

Sarah hails from Minneapolis, known to New Yorkers as 'the flyover.' Raised on a steady diet of Woody Allen films and Blondie, she long dreamed of punk shows at CBGB. Since moving to Jersey and then NYC after college, she has waited tables in a trattoria, summered in Saratoga Springs, chased a thief in Washington Square Park, hiked the High Peaks, tubed the Catskills, gotten lost in the Shawangunks at twilight, temped in the Rockefeller Center, spent all her money on theater tickets, and woken up to mist rising off the Hudson at dawn. She secretly dreams about accidentally inheriting a brownstone in the West Village with good light, a garden and a jazz club nearby.

BRIDGET GLEESON
Philadelphia, Pennsylvania

Though Bridget grew up just 2 miles from the chocolate factory in Hershey, Pennsylvania, she's been off in South America for years writing about snorkeling in Brazil and whale-watching off the coast of Argentinian Patagonia. Returning to the US to cover her home state, she saw everything from a fresh perspective: suddenly, the Amish market was a gourmet paradise, Pittsburgh was a culture capital, and even the milk chocolate tasted sweeter than ever. Bridget was the author and a contributing photographer of Lonely Planet's *Buenos Aires Encounter* before contributing to *Argentina* and *Brazil*; she also writes for Delta Sky, AOL Travel, Tablet Hotels, and Mr & Mrs Smith.

THE AUTHORS

LONELY PLANET AUTHORS

Why is our travel information the best in the world? It's simple: our authors are passionate, dedicated travelers. They don't take freebies in exchange for positive coverage so you can be sure the advice you're given is impartial. They travel widely to all the popular spots, and off the beaten track. They don't research using just the internet or phone. They discover new places not included in any other guidebook. They personally visit thousands of hotels, restaurants, palaces, trails, galleries, temples and more. They speak with dozens of locals every day to make sure you get the kind of insider knowledge only a local could tell you. They take pride in getting all the details right, and in telling it how it is. Think you can do it? Find out how at **lonelyplanet.com**.

DAVID OZANICH New York City, Long Island, The Culture, Food & Drink
David left the wilds of LA for New York when he was 18 and enrolled in NYU film school. Having fallen in love with NYC, he never left and still lives in Greenwich Village lo these many years later. When not writing for Lonely Planet (he worked on *New York, Washington DC & the Mid-Atlantic Trips*), he pens teen novels (*Likely Story* for Knopf), plays *(The Lightning Field)*, and screenplays. He also spent a year blogging about *One Life to Live* and *The Bold and the Beautiful* for Soapnet.com. Yes, that's true and he's not ashamed.

Behind the Scenes

THIS BOOK

This 3rd edition of New York, New Jersey & Pennsylvania was written by a team of authors coordinated by Jeff Campbell who also wrote several chapters including History, Environment, and New Jersey. David Ozanich wrote the New York City, Culture, and Food & Drink chapters, and the Long Island section. Sarah Chandler wrote New York State and Bridget Gleeson the Philadelphia and Pennsylvania chapters. Previous editions were written by Tom Smallman, Michael Clark, David Ellis and Eric Wakin. This guidebook was commissioned in Lonely Planet's Oakland office, and produced by the following:

Commissioning Editor Jennye Garibaldi
Coordinating Editors Jocelyn Harewood, Simon Williamson
Coordinating Cartographer Jacqueline Nguyen
Coordinating Layout Designer Yvonne Bischofberger
Senior Editor Katie Lynch
Managing Editors Sasha Baskett, Melanie Dankel
Managing Cartographers Alison Lyall, Adrian Persoglia
Managing Layout Designer Indra Kilfoyle
Assisting Editors Jessica Crouch, Carly Hall
Assisting Cartographers Anita Banh, Valeska Canas, Owen Eszeki, Andy Rojas, Andrew Smith
Assisting Layout Designer Wibowo Rusli, Jacqui Saunders
Cover Research Naomi Parker, lonelyplanetimages.com
Internal Image Research Sabrina Dalbesio, lonelyplanet images.com
Indexer Joanne Newell

Thanks to Carolyn Boicos, David Connolly, Ryan Evans, Martin Heng, Yvonne Kirk, Gerard Walker, Celia Wood

THANKS
JEFF CAMPBELL

In Jersey, you're nothing without family, and I'd be nothing without mine. Thanks to Cookie, Kim, Lisa and Bruce, Eric and Caroline, Andy and Val, and last but not least my wife, Deanna, who went the extra mile. I'm also indebted to friends Kip and Sheri, Mary Lu, Christina, Janice, David, Alex, Paul, and Scott, as well as to Patrick Barth, my canoe expert, and Katie and Michael, who showed me a great time in Asbury Park. Thanks also to Kathy Kelly for her Jersey Devil lore. Finally, we had a great LP crew: thanks to Jennye, David, Bridget and Sarah.

SARAH CHANDLER

Thanks to Jennye Garibaldi for letting me dive into this adventure. Thanks to Dirk and Lanny van Allen

---

THE LONELY PLANET STORY

Fresh from an epic journey across Europe, Asia and Australia in 1972, Tony and Maureen Wheeler sat at their kitchen table stapling together notes. The first Lonely Planet guidebook, *Across Asia on the Cheap,* was born.

Travelers snapped up the guides. Inspired by their success, the Wheelers began publishing books to Southeast Asia, India and beyond. Demand was prodigious, and the Wheelers expanded the business rapidly to keep up. Over the years, Lonely Planet extended its coverage to every country and into the virtual world via lonelyplanet.com and the Thorn Tree message board.

As Lonely Planet became a globally loved brand, Tony and Maureen received several offers for the company. But it wasn't until 2007 that they found a partner whom they trusted to remain true to the company's principles of traveling widely, treading lightly and giving sustainably. In October of that year, BBC Worldwide acquired a 75% share in the company, pledging to uphold Lonely Planet's commitment to independent travel, trustworthy advice and editorial independence.

Today, Lonely Planet has offices in Melbourne, London and Oakland, with over 500 staff members and 300 authors. Tony and Maureen are still actively involved with Lonely Planet. They're traveling more often than ever, and they're devoting their spare time to charitable projects. And the company is still driven by the philosophy of *Across Asia on the Cheap*: 'All you've got to do is decide to go and the hardest part is over. So go!'

BEHIND THE SCENES

for your 1000 Islands suggestions. Molly Regan, thanks for the home-away-from-home in Buffalo. Thanks to everyone in Rhinebeck and Rhinecliff: you make me want to live there. Thanks to Chrissa Pullicino and the NYC crew. To Peggy Trezona, you can't imagine how grateful I am for the lovely meals

and support. Dorothy Hoffman and Mark Wanvig, thanks for your gorgeous house and the 4am coffee. Finally, to Jennifer Christensen: thanks for braving the Adirondacks with me.

BRIDGET GLEESON
Thanks to my parents for raising me in such an idyllic setting as central Pennsylvania. I'm also grateful to my brother Patrick (my resident expert in Philadelphia) and to my mother Margaret, for accompanying me to see Fallingwater. As always, I'm thankful to Rodolfo Diaz for accommodating my crazy travel schedule. It was a pleasure to work for the first time with Jennye Garibaldi and Jeff Campbell at Lonely Planet, and thank you, especially, to the Lonely Planet readers I always meet on the road – you inspire me to improve my work and renew my passion for travel.

DAVID OZANICH
David Ozanich would like the thank the following scholars of New York and Long Island for their wit, company, and insight: Daniel Lubrano, Rob Coburn, Averitt Buttry, Karen Schmidt, Jenny Weitsen, Celeste Orangers, John Haven, Nate Harris, Randy Barone, Brandon Presser, Mike Echo Sullo, Walker Vreeland, Scott Eason, Tim Herzog, Charles McGarvey, Joanne, John Jenkinson, Nicole and Zach Dean, Scott Lauer, and Gray Coleman.

ACKNOWLEDGMENTS
Many thanks to the following for the use of their content:
Globe on title page ©Mountain High Maps 1993 Digital Wisdom, Inc.

Index

444

MAP LEGEND
ROUTES

Tollway	Mall/Steps
Freeway	Tunnel
Primary	Pedestrian Overpass
Secondary	Walking Tour
Tertiary	Walking Tour Detour
Lane	Walking Trail
Under Construction	Walking Path
Unsealed Road	Track
One-Way Street	

TRANSPORT

Ferry	Rail
Metro	Rail (Underground)

HYDROGRAPHY

River, Creek	Canal
Intermittent River	Water
Swamp	Lake (Dry)

BOUNDARIES

International	Regional, Suburb
State, Provincial	

AREA FEATURES

Airport	Land
Area of Interest	Mall
Beach, Desert	Market
Building	Park
Campus	Reservation
Cemetery, Christian	Sports
Forest	Urban

POPULATION

CAPITAL (NATIONAL)	CAPITAL (STATE)
Large City	Medium City
Small City	Town, Village

SYMBOLS

Sights/Activities
- Beach
- Castle, Fortress
- Christian
- Jewish
- Monument
- Museum, Gallery
- Point of Interest
- Pool
- Ruin
- Skiing
- Surfing, Surf Beach
- Trail Head
- Winery, Vineyard
- Zoo, Bird Sanctuary

Eating
- Eating

Drinking
- Drinking
- Café

Entertainment
- Entertainment

Shopping
- Shopping

Sleeping
- Sleeping
- Camping

Transport
- Airport, Airfield
- Border Crossing
- Bus Station
- Cycling, Bicycle Path
- General Transport
- Parking Area
- Petrol Station
- Taxi Rank

Information
- Bank, ATM
- Embassy/Consulate
- Hospital, Medical
- Information
- Internet Facilities
- Police Station
- Post Office, GPO
- Toilets
- Wheelchair Access

Geographic
- Lighthouse
- Lookout
- Mountain, Volcano
- National Park
- Pass, Canyon
- Picnic Area
- River Flow
- Shelter, Hut
- Waterfall

LONELY PLANET OFFICES

Australia (Head Office)
Locked Bag 1, Footscray, Victoria 3011
☎ 03 8379 8000, fax 03 8379 8111

USA
150 Linden St, Oakland, CA 94607
☎ 510 250 6400, toll free 800 275 8555
fax 510 893 8572

UK
2nd fl, 186 City Rd,
London EC1V 2NT
☎ 020 7106 2100, fax 020 7106 2101

Contact
talk2us@lonelyplanet.com
lonelyplanet.com/contact

Published by Lonely Planet Publications Pty Ltd
ABN 36 005 607 983

© Lonely Planet 2011

© photographers as indicated 2011

Cover photograph: Mt Jo, Adirondack State Park, New York Stat SIME/Ripani Massimo. Many of the images in this guide are availab for licensing from Lonely Planet Images: lonelyplanetimages.com.

Printed by Hang Tai Printing Company Ltd, Hong Kong
Printed in China

MIX
Paper from responsible sources
FSC™ C021741
www.fsc.org